To Neill

FROM Bea - Christmas 1998

Into the Far, Wild Country

~

True Tales of the Old Southwest

BY GEORGE WYTHE BAYLOR

Into the Far, Wild Country

~

True Tales of the Old Southwest

BY GEORGE WYTHE BAYLOR

EDITED WITH AN INTRODUCTION BY JERRY D. THOMPSON

TEXAS WESTERN PRESS
THE UNIVERSITY OF TEXAS AT EL PASO
1996

© 1996
Texas Western Press
The University of Texas at El Paso
El Paso, Texas 79968-0633

First Edition
Library of Congress Catalog No. 96-60102
ISBN 0-87404-237-2

All Texas Western Press books are printed on acid-free paper, meeting the guidelines for permanence and durability of the Committee on Production Guidelines for Book Longevity of the Council on Library Resources.

Cover art: The Shining Plain by Tom Lea
Section divider page illustrations by José Cisneros

Contents

Around our camp-fires at night Lieutenant Baylor entertained us with accounts of early days on the frontier. He was born August 24, 1832, at old Fort Gibson in the Cherokee Nation, now the state of Oklahoma. His father, John Walker Baylor, was a surgeon in the United States Army. Lieutenant Baylor was a soldier by training and by inheritance. In 1879 he was in his forty-seventh year and stood six feet two inches tall, a perfect specimen of a hardy frontiersman. He was highly educated, wrote much for papers and magazines, was a fluent speaker, and a very interesting talker and story-teller. He was less reserved than any other captain under whom I ever served. He had taken part in many Indian fights on the frontier of Texas, and his descriptions of some of his experiences were thrilling. Lieutenant Baylor was a high-minded Christian gentleman and had been a member of the Episcopal Church from childhood. In all the months I served with him I never heard him utter an oath or tell a smutty yarn. He neither drank whiskey nor used tobacco. Had he written a history of his operations on the frontier and a biography of himself it would have been one of the strangest and most interesting books every written.

James B. Gillett, Six Years with the Texas Rangers

Introduction

EARLY ON THE MORNING OF 3 AUGUST 1879, a tall and slender lieutenant in the Texas Rangers departed San Antonio for the arduous 638-mile trek to Ysleta in far West Texas. Accompanying the six-feet-two-inch, forty-six-year-old Ranger was his wife, Sallie Garland Sydnor, and their two daughters, fourteen-year-old Helen and four-year-old Mary. A sister-in-law, Kate Sydnor, and six Ranger recruits were also making the trip. The women and children rode in a large hack drawn by a pair of sturdy mules, followed by a wagon carrying a carefully packed old fashioned piano, household furnishings, the lieutenant's prized violin, and a coop of fighting chickens—three hens and a rooster. Foodstuffs and forage for the animals came in a two-mule wagon. Bringing up the rear of the small caravan was a two-wheeled cart with two men who were bound for New Mexico and afraid of traveling alone.[1]

Earlier, the bearded, straight-backed George Wythe Baylor had written Gov. Oran M. Roberts asking for a commission in the Rangers, saying that he had been in Texas, off and on, for thirty-three years, was familiar with the frontier, and had been a colonel in the Confederate Army.[2] Receiving his commission in July 1879, Baylor hurried to Austin to meet with Governor Roberts and Adj. Gen. John B. Jones, both stung by the violence of the recent El Paso Salt War and determined to bring peace to the El Paso area. Years later, Baylor recalled Roberts' last words as he left the governor's office: "Lieutenant Baylor, I want you to remember out in that far, wild country, you represent the honor and dignity of the great state of Texas." Tall and erect, Baylor replied, "Governor, as far as an army of ten men can do it, you may rest assured I will."[3]

Across the Medina and Frio rivers Lieutenant Baylor led his small party in that hot and bone dry summer of 1879. They pressed ever westward, past Uvalde and across the crystal-clear waters of the Nueces River to San Felipe Springs, then along the Old Military Road up the Devils River and by Howard's Well to the Pecos River and west to Fort Stockton. Always on the lookout for hostile Indians, they hurried on through a vast greasewood desert and over cactus-studded Wild Rose Pass into the brown-tinted canyons of the Davis Mountains and up Limpia Creek to Fort Davis. West into the desert again at Barrel Springs, they continued on to El Muerto, Van Horn Wells, and Eagle Springs, all overland stage stations dotted with the wooden crosses and rock tombstones of less fortunate travelers. After passing through a foreboding and rocky Quitman Canyon, they reached the Rio Grande and turned upriver to the weathered and sun-beaten remains of Fort Quitman. On 12 September 1879, after forty-one fatiguing days on the road, the party pulled into the cottonwood-shaded plaza of Ysleta, county seat of El Paso County. Baylor was about to enter one of the most exciting periods in an already long and eventful life.

George Wythe Baylor was born at Fort Gibson in the Indian Territory 24 August 1832, the eighth and youngest child of Dr. John Walker Baylor and Sophie Weidner.[4] Since his father was an assistant surgeon in the 7th United States Infantry, George Wythe grew up, he recalled, with the sound of drum and bugle reverberating in his ears. George was only four when his physician father left the army and moved the family to Second Creek near Natchez, Mississippi, where he died in 1836. After his father's death, his mother took the family back to Fort Gibson and eventually to Pine Bluff, Arkansas, where James L. Dawson, who was married to George's sister, Sophie Elizabeth, had acquired a plantation. The family later moved to Little Rock and then back to Fort Gibson where George entered grammar school and learned to read and write.[5]

From an early age, George Wythe Baylor's destiny seemed to loom on the broad and ever-widening southwestern frontier. The year his father passed away, an older brother and physician, John Walker, died of wounds received at the Battle of San Jacinto. A decade later, another physician brother, Henry Weidner, fought with Gen. Zachary Taylor in the Mexican-American War.[6] Yet it was another older brother, John Robert, to whom George was the closest, and whose volatile and controversial career he would choose to follow.

When George Baylor's brother-in-law, John Dawson, killed a Creek trader named Seaborn Hill near Fort Gibson in 1844, John Baylor was charged as an accomplice. To escape arrest, George remembered, both his brother and Dawson rode south into the vast expanses of the infant Republic of Texas.[7] Although authorities offered a sizeable reward for their capture, John Baylor was able to eventually settle with a new wife, a Marshall belle named Emily Jane Hanna, at Ross Prairie near La Grange, Fayette County. When lawmen were rumored to be on his trail, he defiantly told an uncle he was prepared to "resist the law at all hazards." The uncle, Robert Emmett Bledsoe Baylor, prominent jurist, clergyman, and one of the founders of Baylor University, offered to use his influence with Sen. Thomas Jefferson Rusk and Pres. Franklin Pierce to obtain a pardon, but was afraid that if law officers arrived at Ross Prairie, John would "kill the marshall or one of his deputies," an act, Judge Baylor warned his nephew, would "complete your final ruin."[8]

In December 1845, at the age of thirteen, George Wythe crossed Red River to live with his brother at Ross Prairie. He would later remember his early years in Texas as among the happiest of his young life. On the frontier at the time, Fayette County provided an abundance of game, fertile soil, and fruitful crops.

In Texas, George was able to obtain a good education, first at Rutersville College, only seven miles from La Grange, and later, largely through the influence of his uncle, R.E.B. Baylor, at Baylor University at Independence.[9] After completing school, George made his way to San Antonio where his mother had settled. For a time he worked at the Alamo as a clerk for the Commissary Department of the United States Army, sleeping in a room next to the chapel, and in his spare time, guiding visitors around the grounds, always pointing out the spot where Davy Crockett had died.[10] Here, in the shadow of the Alamo along the San Antonio River, rumors and exaggerated stories of the California Gold Rush were common. He would later say that he was lured west by the "golden dreams of the new El Dorado."[11] Always the adventurer and dreamer, a characteristic he would carry throughout his life, George, in March 1854, struck out on muleback for California. With an unbinding optimism, another trait he would carry into old age, he had no doubt that he would strike it rich in California.

A few surviving family letters provide glimpses into his six-year California sojourn. Family members were understandably anxious for the safety of the twenty-year-old gone west; older brother John had even complained earlier that George, who was nicknamed Pat by the family, was "careless about writing as . . . such a boy he is." Wanting to see George follow a more conventional career, John was hoping he would take up the law or some other profession.[12]

With a small party of men, George made his way west from San Antonio, across the Medina and Frio rivers, past a Lipan Apache village in a grove of oak trees at what was soon to be the community of Uvalde, and across the

Nueces River to the Rio Grande at San Felipe Springs. He would remember later that not a house could be seen after leaving Castroville, except for the newly erected military posts that were being built along the San Antonio–El Paso Road, until the party reached the village of San Elizario, twenty-three miles downriver from Franklin, or what the Americans were beginning to call El Paso. Through the heart of Apache country to the Mexican settlement of Santa Cruz, and then north to the desolate adobe village of Tucson and along the Gila River to Fort Yuma on the Colorado River the adventurers pushed ever westward.[13] Safely in California, George became part of the noisy, eager, polyglot horde of prospectors anxious to locate the next million-dollar bonanza. But like so many others, before and after, George never struck it rich in California. Instead he spent time trekking, camping, and hunting grizzly bears. Perhaps his most hair-raising escapade came when, as a self-appointed vigilante, he killed a local desperado in a gun battle north of Santa Rosa in Anderson's Valley. Severely wounded himself, he was charged with attempted murder and held in jail for a month, but after acquittal by a sympathetic jury, he became somewhat of a local hero in Santa Rosa and back in San Francisco, where it was feared that his injuries might be permanent.[14] As was the custom at the time, a benefit was held in San Francisco for the gallant young man who had attempted to arrest "a dangerous character who was a fugitive from justice." The benefit was advertised as a "compliment to his gallant and public spirit."[15]

In 1856, George joined the San Francisco Vigilance Committee and did service at "Fort Gunny Bags." It was at this time that he met Judge David S. Terry who was being held by the vigilantes for stabbing a vigilante agent. Although Terry was a member of the California Supreme Court, he belonged to the Law and Order Party which Baylor and other vigilantes claimed included all the lawless elements in the city.[16]

One of his greatest thrills in California came when he met an older sister, Mary Jane West, widow of Lt. James West of the 7th Infantry, by accident in a San Francisco church. Mary, whom the family called Molly, wrote home to Texas that George had been forced to borrow $100 and was "careless" as ever. Despite George's inability to find employment or strike it rich, both were happy in California where there was "no heat, musquitoes [sic], and fevers . . . nothing to remind us of the past . . . always something to amuse and interest."[17] Mary wrote of listening as George "sang some of our Velasco songs." She even sent their mother a daguerreotype of George "just as he was ready to start in his miner's dress."[18]

George wrote from Stockton saying that California had the "finest climate and soil in the world" and that he was returning to the mines since he could not find employment in San Francisco. He was sure to "do well on Kern River," where in the southwestern foothills of the Sierra Nevada he and several partners had staked out a quartz vein.[19] George had entered into an agreement with Volney E. Howard, well-known Mississippi newspaper editor, southern duelist, and Texas congressman, for the processing of the ore from the vein.

On a cold, rainy, disagreeable day in December 1858, with the mountains "a solid bank of snow," George wrote from near Kern River with his usual optimism to say that he and his partners were grinding eight tons of quartz a day. George was hoping to make an "immense fortune," but was nevertheless "impatient for spring to be homeward bound."[20]

In early spring 1859, with a violin he had bought in California that would remain with him for the rest of his life, George made his way back to San Francisco, where with money borrowed from his older brother John, he booked passage on a steamer for Panama. From the squalor of Panama City, he caught the recently completed narrow-gauge railroad that sped passengers across the isthmus rain forest to Colón on the Caribbean in less than seven hours, there purchasing a ticket on a steamer bound for New Orleans. From the Crescent City he then took passage on another steamer that took him down the Texas coast to Indianola where stages ran regularly to San Antonio. The only trouble on the trip was the "musquitoes . . . blood thirsty set of winged cannibals," but the sea air, he wrote, "did me great good." By late spring he was back in San Antonio to be joyously welcomed by his aging and grey-haired mother and two older sisters, Sophie and Fan. "I have been busy," he wrote, "kissing & hugging them all."[21] While he was in California, San Antonio had "wonderfully improved" and he became almost lost in making his way through the town until "a familiar landmark in the form of some old Mexican casa" had come in view.

In the fall of 1859, George rode north to join his brother John at Weatherford on the northwestern frontier of Texas. In 1855, while George was prospecting for gold in California, John had secured an appointment as special agent to the Southern Comanches, some of whom were confined on a reservation on the Clear Fork of the Brazos River. Initially, John Baylor found the Indians to be "wild, restless, and discontented, and it was with difficulty they could be induced to remain on the reservation."[22] Although the Comanche, who were raiders and hunters by nature, had little knowledge of agriculture, Baylor hoped to turn them into good farmers.

From the very beginning, Robert S. Neighbors, supervising agent for the Reservation Indians in Texas, and Baylor clashed. When Baylor returned to Fayette County to move his family to the agency, Neighbors accused him of

George Baylor's older and controversial brother,
Colonel John Robert Baylor. (Virginia Sturges)

leaving his post and blamed him for a small party of Comanches, leaving the reservation. According to Neighbors, Baylor had "shown a want of both tact and energy in the management of the affairs of his Agency" and had "failed to gain the confidence of the Indians."[23] In May 1857, George learned that his brother had been dismissed by Neighbors.

For several years the Northern Comanche and other hostiles had raided fiercelessly across the Red River. With many of the settlers, who lived near the reservation, unable to distinguish one tribe from another, much less different bands of Comanches, the Reserve Indians were frequently blamed for crimes committed by their northern brethren.[24] Frontiersman John S. Ford, who was sent to the area with a detachment of Rangers, wrote that he could not "detect the Reserve Indians in the commission of a single depredation or to trace one to their doors."[25] Sensing an impending confrontation, John Baylor nevertheless orchestrated a campaign of blaming the Reserve Comanches for committing depredations off the reservation.

Stung by his dismissal, John Baylor turned on Neighbors with a burning hatred bound on revenge. Traveling to and fro, his fiery temper ablaze, he addressed mass meetings, instigating suspicion and hatred of all Indians. A man of considerable charm, magnetism, and charisma, and with his finger on the pulse of public opinion, Baylor attracted many settlers to his cause. Lengthy petitions were soon on their way to Austin and Washington and settlers began attacking any Indians, including women and children, who were caught off the reservation.[26] Along with H.A. Hamner, Baylor established a newspaper at Jacksboro and later at Weatherford. The *White Man* was "the strong advocate of the Frontier, the white man, and the advancement of civilization."[27] There is even evidence that Baylor set out to frame the reservation Indians by leaving arrows and bows, which he had accumulated while he was agent, at the scene of depredations.[28] Before George could join his brother in North Texas, a war between the Reserve Indians and the settlers was on the verge of erupting.

In June 1859, an Indian named Fox, who was carrying official dispatches, was caught off the reservation by angry whites and brutally murdered. When a party of Indians accompanied by an army officer went to Jacksboro in search of the murderers, Baylor made plans to attack the reservation and insisted the Indians be removed to a location north of Red River.[29] Baylor even went as far as to intercept supplies furnished by the United States government bound for the reservation. Hoping to starve the Indians and drive them out of Texas, he threatened to kill anyone cooperating with the Indian Bureau. John Baylor also talked of hanging S.P. Ross, Comanche agent, as well as Neighbors.

Several months before George arrived at Weatherford, some 250 men and boys from several frontier counties joined John Baylor at Jacksboro on the morning of 23 May 1859 as he marched on the Comanche reserve. A short distance from the Indian agency, Baylor was met by a detachment of United States troops and angry Indians. When Baylor demanded that the troops stand aside, Capt. J.B. Plummer refused, saying that he had orders to protect the Indians and that he was determined to do so. Retreating from the reservation, Baylor's small army killed and scalped an aged Waco man, said to be between eighty-five and ninety years old, deaf and nearly blind. Farther on, Baylor's small army also shot an elderly Indian woman who was said to be working peacefully in her garden.[30]

Hearing of the two murders, José María, Comanche war chief, charged off the Brazos reserve with fifty warriors and attacked Baylor. In the running fight, Baylor was said to have lost three men while one Comanche fell dead. Jim Pock Mark, an Anadarko chief, allegedly rode up to the ranch house where the whites had taken refuge and called for Baylor to come out and give him single combat, a challenge that went unanswered. Nevertheless, for several weeks, Baylor lurked near the reserve, threatening another attack. To incite his followers, he was said to have carried twelve scalps of white women he had taken from a band of Delaware.[31]

With the northwestern frontier of Texas on the verge of exploding into uncontrolled violence and bloodshed, Washington at last ordered the Reserve Indians removed. The exodus out of Texas began on 1 August 1859. With Maj. George Thomas commanding a military escort and accompanied by Neighbors and the other agents, the Indians were escorted across Red River into Indian Territory. But even on the trek north, Neighbors remained fearful that Baylor would attack the column. On 8 August 1859, Neighbors wrote his wife: "I have this day crossed all the Indians out of the heathen land of 'Texas' and am now 'out of the land of the Philistines.' If you want to hear a full description of our Exodus out of Texas, read the *Bible* where the children of Israel crossed the Red Sea."[32] Five weeks later on 14 September 1859, as Neighbors returned to Fort Belknap on business, he was shot in the back with a double-barrelled shotgun and killed. Years later, John Baylor's son and George's namesake, George W. Baylor, would say that it was his father who drove the Indians out of Texas.[33]

With the reservation Indians gone from Texas and George arriving at Weatherford, John Baylor turned his attention to the hostile Comanches who had remained off the reservation and were continuing to raid the frontier settlements. In June 1860, following a raid on the Clear Fork of the Brazos in which one of George's young friends, Josephus Browning, was killed, he joined "six cowboys," including brother John, in pursuing the raiders. During a five-day scout, twelve Comanches were killed and fifty-five head of horses recovered. One of the Comanches who was killed was a chief who had in his possession a shield with a woman's scalp attached, neatly painted and beaded. Also recovered from the Comanches was the scalp of George's young friend, Josephus Browning[34]

Back in the settlements, the six Indian fighters were greeted as conquering crusaders. George was singled out for praise by the *Galveston Tri-Weekly News*, which said the "quiet, amiable, determined young man, killed five Indians."[35] In Young, Palo Pinto, and Parker counties, crowds at jubilant barbecues came forth to cheer the men. For his efforts, George was even given a new shotgun by the excited citizens.[36] At Weatherford, Comanche scalps, gruesome trophies of war, were hung on a rope that was stretched across a large room in the Parker County courthouse for what George called a "scalp dance."[37] But not everyone saw the men as heroes. Anti-Baylor men, George remembered years later, gave the men "Hail Columbia" and said they "were as bad as the Indians." George, in particular, was criticized for saying "that he killed and scalped six Indians one morning before breakfast."[38] Caught up in his success at fighting Comanche, George listed his occupation with the 1860 census enumerator for Parker County as "Indian Killer."[39]

In January 1861, George was elected captain of a group of men from Palo Pinto and Young counties for a "Buffalo Hunt" to be led by his older brother. In reality, however, the expedition was a campaign against the Comanches and was so named to disguise its real purpose. With 250 men, the expedition proceeded as far west as the Salt Fork of the Brazos River near present-day Post, Texas. Spotting only a few hostile Comanches, who easily fled, and finding what was left of an abandoned Indian village, the campaign, which traversed several hundred miles in the midst of winter, was largely a failure. Well into the campaign, John Baylor wrote the Weatherford *White Man* that a large number of his men were sick, many horses were jaded, and most of the men would be returning home. Then with eighty-nine men who remained in "fine spirits and full of fight," Baylor pressed on toward the southwest with little success.[40] Still the Comanches remained elusive.

In early March 1861, the "Buffalo Hunters" were back in the settlements. Although clearly a failure, the "Buffalo Hunt" had done much to prepare George Baylor for a larger conflict that lay ahead. The men had departed with only ten days' rations and had remained in the field for six weeks, during which time they had faced fierce Texas northers, sickness, and one hardship after another.

By the time of the "Buffalo Hunt," George Baylor had begun to devote more attention to the secession crisis sweeping Texas. With Virginia roots planted deeply into the soil of the Lone Star State, there was little doubt as to where the Baylor brothers stood on the crucial issue. As the crisis built in strength, the Baylor brothers traveled south to San Antonio to visit their aging mother and sisters. Caught in the excitement of the time, the sisters made a Lone Star flag which the brothers attached to a captured Comanche lance. While passing through Austin on their return to Weatherford, George hoisted the flag in front of the old Capitol Hotel; he would later boast that it was the "first 'secesh' flag raised in Texas." In fact, the flag raising almost caused a riot when several Austin Unionists strongly objected.[41]

This image of John Robert Baylor was painted by Carl G. Iwonski in San Antonio in 1861.
(Daughters of the Republic of Texas)

On 17 March 1861, George, who was twenty-seven, was elected first lieutenant of a company raised in Parker County. The company, commanded by H.A. Hamner of the *White Man,* was officially enrolled at Weatherford on 17 April 1861, three days after the fall of Fort Sumter.[42] George had hopes of serving on the northwestern frontier of Texas but was ordered three hundred miles to San Antonio where the company rendezvoused and was mustered on 8 May 1861. Two weeks later Hamner's company officially became part of the 2d Texas Mounted Rifles of the Confederate States of America. Moreover, he was sent with his brother, who was appointed lieutenant colonel of the regiment, to garrison the forts along the 658-mile San Antonio-El Paso Road.[43]

After a brief stay at Fort Clark, Lieutenant Baylor, who assumed the duties of regimental adjutant, arrived at Fort Bliss near El Paso in July 1861. Within weeks he was with his brother in the occupation of the Mesilla Valley, where a rowdy group of secessionists welcomed the small Texas army to Mesilla. After occupying the town, the largest settlement on the overland trail between San Antonio and San Diego, California, Federals from nearby Fort Fillmore under the inept leadership of an infirm Maj. Isaac Lynde half-heartedly tried to drive the Texans out.[44] In the skirmish at Mesilla, Lt. Col. John Baylor not only refused to give up the town but drove the advancing Federals off. George hastily wrote home to Texas of being in a "real battle." The "minie balls, grape shot, & bomb shells kicked up a great dust & scared some of the boys at first who have never heard a cannon," he continued.[45] When the Federal garrison from Fort Fillmore, led by Major Lynde, attempted to flee eastward through St. Agustín Pass in the Organ Mountains, the Texans, with only 190 men, were able to pursue and capture eight companies of the 7th Infantry and three companies of Mounted Rifles.[46] Ironically, it was in the 7th Infantry that George's father had served as an assistant surgeon. The Baylor brothers' success at St. Agustín Pass was hailed throughout Texas and would long remain one of the crowning achievements of their lives.

Not long after the surrender at San Agustín Springs, news arrived that Forts Buchanan and Breckenridge to the west of Mesilla had been abandoned and that two companies of dragoons and two companies of infantry were on their way to the Rio Grande. About the same time, a tired group of men came riding out of the desert from the west. As it turned out, the small party of weary travelers was led by Albert Sidney Johnston who had resigned his commission and command of the Department of the Pacific to offer his services to the Confederacy. Johnston, one of the most respected men in Texas, had left his family behind in Los Angeles to cross the eight hundred miles of desert in six weeks.[47] Arriving at Mesilla, Johnston took temporary command of the small Rebel force in an attempt to capture the Federals, who

Colonel George Wythe Baylor in his Civil War uniform.
(Hill Memorial Library, Louisiana State University)

were headed for the Rio Grande. From Mesilla on 14 August 1861, George wrote a nephew in Texas: "Gen. Sidney Johns[t]on from Calif. is here and will no doubt assist us in capturing all the Federal troops in this department—he will be of great assistance to us as all the soldiers know him. I hope the Yankees will soon be satisfied that they cannot whip us, and that peace will be declared."[48] Receiving word of Major Lynde's humiliating surrender, however, the Federals burned most of their commissary supplies and spiked their cannon near Cooke's Springs west of Mesilla and slipped through the mountains to the safety of the Federal bastion of Fort Craig.

Although Lieutenant Baylor was sick for several days, he evidently had made a big impression on Johnston. As Johnston departed for Richmond on 8 August 1861, George remembered him saying, "I don't know if I will be given a command, but if I am, I want you to serve on my staff."[49] In late August 1861, after obtaining a leave of absence from his brother, George caught the stage and headed east to join Johnston and the fury of a war, the carnage and suffering of which he could not have imagined at Mesilla.

From Bowling Green, Kentucky, two days before Christmas 1861, the optimistic and cocky lieutenant wrote home to Texas: "There is a bright, beautiful world beyond this where we will meet some day but Providence did not intend the Yankees should kill me."[50] On Christmas Day, he wrote again to say that a "desperate battle" was expected before New Year's.[51]

Initially, George expressed some reservations about leaving his brother in the West. Lt. Col. John Baylor, who had proclaimed himself governor of the Confederate Territory of Arizona, had written suggesting that George might want to return to Texas and raise a company of his own.[52] By early January 1862, however, George wrote to say that had become better acquainted with his duties and that he had decided to stay with General Johnston. The young lieutenant had become excited while listening to Col. Nathan B. Forrest relate how he had led a daring dash through central and northern Kentucky.[53] Moreover, George was reluctant to leave General Johnston's staff with a big battle appearing eminent.

The "desperate battle" that the young lieutenant had anticipated finally came on 6 and 7 April 1862 on the banks of the Tennessee River in southwestern Tennessee. The Battle of Shiloh, bigger than Waterloo and resulting in more casualties than all American wars to that point in history, changed forever Baylor's perception of war. While participating in the charge of the 2d Texas Infantry, he had been slightly nipped on the nose by a minie ball and, as he would later admit, was badly frightened.[54] With some 24,000 casualties, Union and Confederate, the battle would remain, until his death, a pivotal and sobering event in his life. At twenty-eight, the brash young officer had become a veteran. Yet his most lasting recollection of the battle came on the afternoon of the first day when he held the mortally wounded Johnston in his arms as the general's life ebbed away. Baylor would remain convinced for the remainder of his life that had Johnston not been killed at Shiloh, the Rebels would have routed Gen. Ulysses S. Grant's Federals on the second day of the battle.

In the days and weeks following the Confederate defeat, Baylor remained uncertain about his future. He contemplated joining his brother, but Colonel Baylor was back in Texas and the Confederate Army in New Mexico Territory under Brig. Gen. Henry Hopkins Sibley had been turned back at Glorieta Pass high in the mountains near Santa Fe and was badly demoralized and in retreat. While preparing to accompany General Johnston's body to New Orleans for burial, George applied for orders to rejoin his regiment in Texas. Although temporarily relieved from duty with the Army of Mississippi, he received orders from Richmond directing him to report to Gen. Pierre Gustave Toutant de Beauregard, if he had not already been assigned to the 2d Texas Mounted Rifles.[55] After temporarily joining Beauregard at Jackson, Mississippi, he learned that his brother was recruiting what was to become the Arizona Brigade back in Texas. Writing the Secretary of War, George W. Randolph, from Jackson in July 1862, George asked for a commission as lieutenant colonel in the brigade. General Johnston, he wrote, had "promised me his influence to secure a position in the army."[56]

Learning that his mother had died in San Antonio at the age of seventy-eight, he hurried home to Texas. After dividing $500 in gold, money his mother had saved for him while he was in California, with his two sisters, Fan and Molly, he rushed off to Eagle Lake near Columbus on the lower Brazos River where the Arizona Brigade was being drilled and equipped.[57] Although suffering from temporary blindness in his left eye, he was appointed a major and placed in command of the 2d Regiment of the brigade. With hopes of recapturing New Mexico and Arizona, he worked hard to train and organize the brigade.[58]

In the meantime, Pres. Jefferson Davis had learned from one of General Sibley's staff that Col. John Baylor, while in New Mexico, had ordered the poisoning of a band of Apache Indians who had attacked the gold mining camp of Pinos Altos and killed one of Baylor's company commanders. Embarrassed by the publicity surrounding the revelation, while at the same time the Confederacy was recruiting Cherokee Indians, Davis stripped Baylor of his commission in the Confederate Army, although Baylor technically remained as governor of Arizona Territory.[59]

In Texas, George Baylor, now promoted to colonel, spent some time in Houston where he met Sallie Garland Sydnor, daughter of John S. Sydnor, one of the wealthiest businessmen in Galveston and a man who had once run the largest slave market west of New Orleans.[60] Following the Battle of Galveston on 1 January 1863, in which Union forces were soundly defeated, it was Sallie Sydnor who had the honor of presenting Gen. John B. Magruder with a sword on behalf of the women of Texas.[61]

Sallie Sydnor and George Baylor were married on the morning of 22 April 1863 by the Episcopal minister at Christ Church in Houston.[62] She was twenty-one; he was thirty. Sallie was described as a "highly educated and refined woman . . . a skillful performer on the piano" and someone with a "bright, sunny disposition and kind heart."[63] In the years to come, she was to become not only a faithful and loving wife but a devoted and dedicated mother, capable of enduring primitive frontier conditions far from her accustomed luxuries, all of which she could not have envisioned in April 1863.

Colonel Baylor arrived in Louisiana in early 1863, just as Federal forces pushed into the Bayou Teche region in the south-central part of the state. At New Iberia, one soldier in the Arizona Brigade recorded that the ladies of the town "strewed our way with roses," sang the "Bonny Blue Flag," and shouted "hor[r]ay for the Texas boys."[64] At Brashear City, the fulcrum for Union operations in the southern part of the state, Maj. Sherod Hunter of Baylor's regiment staged a daring raid. Using a strange flotilla of skiffs, sugar coolers, and rafts, 325 men paddled down Bayou Teche and the Atchafalaya for eight hours to strike the rear of Brashear City at sunrise. In the attack, forty-six Federals were killed, 1,200 captured (many of them convalescents), and 2,500 rifles, 200 wagons, and eleven artillery pieces seized.[65] The Arizona Brigade went on to fight at Thibodaux, LaFourche, and at Donaldsonville on the Mississippi River where Col. Joseph Phillips, at the head of the brigade's 3d Regiment, was killed.[66] Tired of war, one soldier recorded that there was a "general dissatisfaction" in the brigade caused by "short rations and strict discipline" and that many of the Texas boys were threatening to go home.[67]

With a Federal invasion of the Texas coast expected, the regiment was ordered back to the Lone Star State. In November 1863, however, the brigade was again sent to the Bayou Teche region. At Carrion Crow Bayou, Baylor's regiment helped to outflank Federal forces and, as part of Gen. James P. Major's Brigade, fought on Vermillion Bayou. Then by December 1863, the regiment was again back in Texas. Federal forces, although repulsed at Sabine Pass in September, had occupied a large part of the Texas coast as well as Brownsville and the Lower Rio Grande Valley. The 2d Arizona was sent to Sandy Point, south of Houston, to halt any invasion of the upper coast.[68]

It was in the larger 1864 Red River Campaign that George Baylor was to achieve his greatest success as a regimental and brigade commander. Maj.

Gen. Nathaniel P. Banks, commanding the Union Department of the Gulf, launched an invasion up Red River as part of a coordinated assault on the Confederacy. With another Union Army moving south from Little Rock, Arkansas, the two armies hoped to converge at Shreveport before pushing into the rich heartland of East Texas. Twenty-two armed Union vessels, mostly ironclads under Rear Adm. David Dixon Porter, accompanied General Banks' army. To halt the Federal invasion, Maj. Gen. Richard "Dick" Taylor, Yale graduate and son of Zachary Taylor, amassed all the troops available and once again Baylor was back in Louisiana. On the eve of battle, 6 April 1864, Baylor, who was outraged at the devastation wrought by Federal troops in Louisiana, wrote his sister: "We hate them more than we have done before . . . nothing is too brutal or mean for them to do . . . stealing everything from everybody . . . I cannot believe God will make us the slaves of such a set of heathens."[69]

On 7 April 1864, Baylor's regiment, attached to Gen. Walter P. Lane's brigade, was on the left wing of General Taylor's army when the fighting began at Wilson's Farm, three miles north of Pleasant Hill. Strongly posted on the crest of a hill, Baylor's bold and aggressive Texans waited until the Federals had advanced to within fifty yards and then laid down a devastating fire, driving the bluecoat advance back in considerable disorder.[70] With the famous Rebel yell, Baylor, ordering his men to attack, drove the hated Yankees back through the tall pines for nearly a mile. The advancing Texans halted only when they ran out of ammunition. Retreating to their original positions, the regiment was ordered to sleep on their weapons.[71]

The next day, 8 April 1864, at Sabine Crossroads, the regiment was placed on the Confederate left and ordered forward. Finding Union forces in strength behind a wooden fence, the Rebels were forced to cross an open field for half a mile in the face of intense enemy artillery and rifle fire. Nevertheless, the Confederate advance successfully drove the Federals from one position and then another, prisoners were taken and one piece of artillery was seized. Although his men had won a "glorious victory," Baylor was forced to admit, however, that his loss was "quite severe in killed and wounded."[72] Only darkness ended the fighting as the Texans again lay on their arms in the Louisiana darkness. Moreover, in the last Rebel charge that won the day, brigade commander Col. Walter P. Lane was severely wounded. Consequently, as senior colonel, Baylor was forced to take command of the brigade. He would remain in command for the rest of the campaign.

Advancing early the next morning, 9 April 1863, Baylor reported seeing the results of the previous day's battle. All along the road to Pleasant Hill the aftermath of battle—burned wagons and the Federal dead and wounded—

were grim testimony to the previous day's ferociousness. As the Rebels advanced, many Union stragglers threw down their weapons and surrendered.[73] Baylor had not seen such carnage since Shiloh. About three miles from Pleasant Hill, the brigade found Banks' Army in strength and Baylor prepared his men for battle. Lane's brigade was dismounted and sent to the Rebel left in a flanking movement. Again the enemy was driven back to their breastworks in what Baylor said was a very "strong position." Here the fighting became "close and hot." Repulsed, Baylor claimed his force simply was "not strong enough."[74] As darkness fell on northwest Louisiana, the Texans were unable to tell friend from foe and Baylor reported being fired at by one Rebel regiment and then another.

Although Taylor was thrown back at Pleasant Hill, Banks continued his retreat the next day and the Rebel army hastened to follow. From Prothro's Bridge, four miles above Grand Ecore on Red River on 19 April 1864, Baylor led the brigade to Monett's Ferry where they arrived two days later. Here Baylor's Confederates tried unsuccessfully to prevent Banks from crossing Cane River.[75] On 3 May, Baylor's men were able to capture the *City Belle* on Red River with a portion of the 120th Ohio on board. Two days later the Union gunboat *Covington* was set on fire as her crew fled to the east bank of the river. *Signal No. 8* was captured, as was the steamboat *Warren*, which was loaded with supplies.[76] Baylor was thankful that none of his men were killed or wounded in the duel with the Union gunboats.[77]

At Mansura, on 16 May 1864, Banks turned on his pursuers and Baylor was again forced to temporarily fall back. Then at Yellow Bayou near Norwood's Plantation two days later, Taylor moved to prevent Banks from crossing Atchafalaya River and Baylor, with Gen. John A. Wharton as overall cavalry commander, attacked the Federals at daylight. Dismounted, the brigade was forced into a ditch and were forced to hastily erect breastworks. Later, during an advance across an open field, the action became "very hot" as the Texans drove the enemy back.[78] Although his ranks were decimated by the Union artillery, Baylor's men fought bravely, he reported, but the losses were "quite severe." In fact, Baylor was almost killed when his horse was shot from under him.[79] Years later he would recall the Red River campaign and write that it was his pleasure to have been involved in escorting Banks "out of Louisiana."[80]

Although Baylor's success as a brigade commander during the campaign was the crowning accomplishment of his Civil War career, it also contained the seeds of what came close to being his complete undoing. The source of his near-destruction was thirty-five-year-old Gen. John Austin Wharton, a wealthy and arrogant orator and jurist who arrived in Louisiana shortly after the battles of Sabine Crossroads to assume command of the Rebel cavalry. From a distinguished Texas family and related to the Baylors through marriage, Wharton fought with the 8th Texas Cavalry (Terry's Texas Rangers) early in the war in Tennessee, and after Terry's death led the regiment at Shiloh. Later as a brigade commander, he fought well at Stones River and Chickamauga and was promoted to major general.

The trouble between Baylor and Wharton began on Marksville Prairie when Wharton criticized Baylor for not attacking the Union line, despite the fact, Baylor asserted, his forces were outnumbered two to one. The next day, Baylor and the other colonels in the brigade were summoned to Wharton's headquarters and given a tongue lashing. Certain his brigade had performed well, the "reprimand was not appreciated," Baylor wrote.[81] At the same time, Baylor received a telegram from his mother-in-law in Houston saying that his wife was gravely ill. Although both Gen. Edmund Kirby Smith, commanding the Trans-Mississippi Department, and Gen. John B. Magruder, in charge of the District of Texas, New Mexico, and Arizona, approved a thirty-day leave, Wharton wrote on the application: "I know nothing of Mrs. Baylor's health. Colonel Baylor is needed with his regiment." Egotistical, proud, and often defiant, traits he shared with his older brother, John Robert, Baylor took Wharton's statement as insinuating that he was lying about his wife's health.[82]

Baylor was also resentful that he had not been promoted to brigadier general, especially since he had commanded a brigade during most of the campaign. Determined to be promoted, Baylor decided to go to Richmond in person to put his case before Pres. Jefferson Davis. But first, back in Texas and prior to traveling to Richmond, he met General Wharton at General Smith's headquarters, at which time Wharton agreed that Baylor would be promoted and urged Baylor to return to his brigade. Within days, however, Baylor learned—much to his disgust—that his regiment was being dismounted, the ultimate insult to any Texan. Moreover, he was being placed under Col. David S. Terry, a junior colonel who was to be promoted to brigadier general. Baylor had despised Terry ever since his vigilante days in San Francisco when Terry was almost hanged. His fiery temper ablaze, Baylor defiantly sent word that he would see Wharton in hell before he would serve under Terry. These actions were clearly an act of insubordination, he would later admit, but angry and insulted, Baylor was determined to press the matter and headed to Houston to see General Magruder.[83] Unable to find Magruder, Baylor struck out for the Fannin Hotel where his wife and in-laws were staying. On the way there, while crossing the bridge over Buffalo Bayou, he coincidentally came across General Wharton, who was riding in a carriage with

Gen. James E. Harrison, and an angry confrontation quickly developed. At first Wharton demanded to know what Baylor was doing in Houston. "Where is your command?" he shouted at Baylor.[84]

"In Hempstead," Baylor replied.

"You had better be with it," Wharton responded, claiming he was concerned about possible desertions.

There had been no desertions, Baylor retorted, but there certainly would be if he was ordered to report to Terry. "Justice has not been done me," Baylor loudly proclaimed.

"Who has done you injustice?" Wharton shot back angrily.

"You, sir," Baylor replied, recalling his previous complaints against Wharton.

As the discussion became even more heated, Wharton ordered Baylor arrested. Yelling that he would see General Magruder and have justice, Baylor accused Wharton of being a demagogue. Wharton replied by referring to Baylor as a "damned liar," at which point Baylor took a swing at Wharton, just as General Harrison urged the carriage forward and down the road.

As Wharton rode off, Baylor rushed to see Magruder. Baylor, who was so agitated that he was crying, found Magruder eating breakfast at the Fannin Hotel. As the two retired to Magruder's private room upstairs, Baylor continued to weep. Finding the room locked, the two retired to an adjacent room where Magruder asked Baylor to remain calm and left for a few minutes. Only moments after Magruder left, Wharton, who was unarmed and smoking a cigar, entered the room with General Harrison by his side. Insults and angry assertions were again exchanged and the highly agitated Wharton struck Baylor on the cheek. In retaliation, Baylor drew his Navy Colt revolver, and although General Harrison tried to intervene, Baylor fired a single shot into Wharton's left side. Moaning "Oh, oh," Wharton fell dead.[85]

Hearing of the shooting, Sallie Baylor raced to her husband's side just as he was being marched through the streets by a squad of soldiers with bayonets fixed. Still clutching her husband's arm, she was allowed to remain with Baylor as he was taken to jail. As night fell, rumors circulated through the streets that a mob of General Wharton's friends was determined to lynch Baylor. Consequently, Baylor's followers swore to defend him to the death and even break him out of jail, if necessary.[86]

News of Gen. Robert E. Lee's surrender at Appomattox Court House, Virginia, reached Texas before Baylor could be tried by court-martial. Subsequently the case was transferred to civilian court. A Houston grand jury originally charged Baylor with manslaughter but the charge was later changed to murder. In particular, Wharton's heart-broken mother, Eliza, did everything in her power to have Baylor prosecuted as vigorously as possible.[87] Baylor was released on bail and the legal proceedings dragged on for three years. In May 1868, a jury was unable to decide the case and a second jury six months later found Baylor not guilty.[88] Still, despite his acquittal, Baylor would always be known throughout Texas as the man who killed General Wharton. The incident also left traumatic scars on Baylor. Even as an old man, relatives recalled, he could not talk of the incident without tears in his eyes.[89] Then and later the death of General Wharton would be viewed as a great tragedy. In reference to the shooting, a contemporary writer perhaps put it best when he wrote: "At such a time when a nation was falling and armies were disbanding and hopes were perishing, and sorrow filled every soul, the minds of men were not normal."[90]

In the wake of Wharton's death and the Confederacy in ruin, George Baylor, now thirty-six, faced a most uncertain future. With legal proceedings still active against him, he remained with his wife's family in Houston and Galveston for several years. In 1872, he found a job with the Life Association of America and moved his family to Dallas where he remained for the next three years, dabbling in county and state Democratic Party politics. Despite the fact that John Baylor tried and failed to secure the party nomination for governor the same year George moved to Dallas, George cheered the election of Richard Coke and what generations of Texans would call the "Southern Redeemers."[91] As a die-hard ex-Confederate, he despised the Texas Scalawags and the Radical Republican rule of Gov. E.J. Davis as much as anyone in the state. In 1874, he also worked to secure the election of ex-governor Throckmorton to the United States House of Representatives.

During the three years spent in Dallas, Baylor took every opportunity to hunt and fish, often camping in the outdoors for weeks at a time. It is uncertain whether the insurance company fell on hard times or George simply grew tired of Dallas and urban life. Regardless, once again he decided to return to the Texas frontier. In January 1875, claiming that his health was delicate, he moved his family to "western Texas . . . to establish a sheep ranch" on the Leona River, west of San Antonio.[92] Five weeks after arriving on the Leona River near Uvalde, he told friends that his health had "been fully restored by the change of climate."[93] George eventually wound up at Chalk Bluff, a picturesque location in the Nueces Canyon, northwest of Uvalde.[94] His brother John had settled at the hamlet of Montell a few miles upriver and a number of nephews were assuming positions of political prominence in Uvalde County. At Chalk Bluff George tried some farming in the rocky bottomland and raised game chickens. The richness of the country afforded abundant hunting and the Nueces River was full of fish.

Although he remained at Chalk Bluff for several years, his restless nature again got the best of him. He would later say that "being in bad health, I found I was no match for the big-fisted, broad-backed Germans gardening."[95] In February 1879, he wrote Gov. Oran M. Roberts asking for a commission in the Texas Rangers. After "two years on scant rations and no pay," he said, a salary of seventy-five dollars with quarters and rations sounded good. Baylor's application was accompanied by the endorsement of seventeen prominent Texans, mostly men he had known during the Civil War.[96] Governor Roberts passed the application on to Adj. Gen. John B. Jones who wrote Baylor saying that no vacancies were presently available. Five months later, however, Baylor learned that in far-off El Paso County a dispute over access to the salt deposits near the Guadalupe Mountains had erupted in violence. Moreover, Ranger Lt. John B. Tays, commanding a detachment of ten Rangers at Ysleta, had been forced to surrender to an angry mob of men at San Elizario. Three men Tays had been protecting were then taken out and executed. Disgraced, Tays resigned from the Rangers and Baylor was soon on the long road to El Paso. Arriving in Ysleta on 12 September 1879, after six hard weeks on the road, Baylor faced what appeared to be an almost impossible task—he had to calm the violence and racial tensions that had led to the Salt War, stop the banditry that was epidemic in the area, and somehow halt the Indian raids in the Trans-Pecos. Governor Roberts perhaps put it best when he told Baylor to restore "the honor and dignity of the great state of Texas."[97]

In time Baylor purchased some forty-eight acres of land and became comfortably settled at Ysleta. Sallie, who had withstood the long trip west amazingly well, was able to open a small school. Always the horticulturist, Baylor planted melons, a peach orchard, and a small vineyard. His fruits and vegetables, especially peanuts, were frequently the talk and envy of Ysleta as well as El Paso.[98] With his knowledge of Spanish and his friendship with many of the leading Spanish-speaking citizens of El Paso, San Elizario, and Ysleta, dating from his days in the Civil War, Baylor did much in the weeks that followed to calm the lingering and bitter hatreds of the Salt War. Only three weeks after arriving in Ysleta, however, another problem came to occupy his total attention. Apaches attacked a hay camp near Fabens, downriver from Ysleta. With Sgt. James B. Gillett, his second in command, and nine Rangers, Baylor left Ysleta at midnight, halted briefly at San Elizario, where he was joined by Gregorio García as guide, and reached the scene of the attack at sunup. Finding the trail of eighteen Apache raiders opposite the Mexican village of Guadalupe, the Rangers splashed across the Rio Grande. Joined by twenty-three Mexicans, Baylor followed the Apaches westward

George W. Baylor at the time he was serving in the Texas Rangers.
(University of Oklahoma Library)

into the rugged Sierra Ventana where the Indians turned and a vicious fire-fight ensued in which Baylor was nearly killed. Unable to dislodge the Apaches in the rugged terrain and fearful their horses would be stampeded, the Rangers and the Mexicans retreated back to Guadalupe and the Rio Grande where they were lavishly entertained.[99] Although the pursuit had been unsuccessful, Baylor had taken a giant step toward calming the ethnic tensions along the border. In so doing, he became one of the few Texas Rangers to ever be befriended and welcomed on the right bank of the Rio Grande.

Five weeks after the fight in the Sierra Ventana, Baylor learned that Victorio, indisputably one of the greatest of all Apache warriors, had ambushed a party of Mexicans in the Candelaria Mountains just west of the old Camino Real that stretched across the desert from El Paso del Norte to Chihuahua. Moreover, Victorio skillfully pulled the same death trap on a second band of Mexicans who had gone in search of the first party. In all twenty-nine Mexicans lay dead. When a plea for help reached the river villages, Baylor readily volunteered the services of his Ranger squad. Ironically, many of the Mexicans Baylor rode with in pursuit of the wily Victorio were individuals indicted in the violence at San Elizario during the Salt War and for whom he held arrest warrants. Eventually, 179 men reached the scene of the two massacres. After burying the bodies of the Mexicans in a mountain crevasse, Baylor, unable to find Victorio's Apaches, again retreated to the Rio Grande.

In early August 1880, Baylor received news that Col. Benjamin H. Grierson and a squad of cavalrymen had fought off Victorio on a rocky spur of Devil's Ridge above Tinaja de las Palmas, east of Quitman Canyon and west of the Eagle Mountains. With thirteen men and five Tigua scouts, Baylor left Ysleta for the scene of the fight. Reaching Tinaja de las Palmas, he found dead horses bloating in the summer heat, bullet marks on rocks, and the dried blood of a soldier, all evidence that Colonel Grierson had made a gallant stand.[100] The scene brought back memories of Shiloh, Sabine Crossroads, Pleasant Hill, and other battlefields he had seen during the Civil War.

Continuing east to Eagle Spring on the northeast side of the Eagle Mountains, the Rangers found a wrecked and stripped stagecoach and the bodies of the driver and passenger, their bodies mutilated, mail sacks opened, and letters stuffed in the men's fatal wounds. Farther east near Bass Canyon in the Carrizo Mountains, the telegraph line had been torn down, all the insulators broken, and several hundred yards of wire carried away. Riding north along the towering escarpment that formed the eastern edge of the Sierra Diablo, Baylor at last found Colonel Grierson and two hundred of his men, mostly Buffalo Soldiers, camped at Rattlesnake Springs, north of present-day Van

Horn.[101] The Buffalo Soldiers had reached the water first, and in a running fight across several miles of barren desert had prevented Victorio from reaching the rugged canyons of the Guadalupe Mountains to the northeast. Baylor briefly discussed with Grierson the idea of going into the Sierra Diablo after Victorio, but both agreed that such an endeavor would have to be on foot and tactically quite risky.[102] Retracing their route instead, the Rangers found where the Apaches had struck out for Mexico and where they had attacked the stage at Quitman Canyon, killing the only passenger, an old Union general, James J. Byrne. By late August, Victorio and the Apaches were safely camped at Lake Guzmán in northern Chihuahua, Baylor reported.[103]

Undoubtedly, Baylor's greatest success came in January 1881 when he pursued a small band of Victorio's Apaches into the Sierra Diablo. Surprising the Apaches high in the arid mountains on a cold dawn, 29 January 1881, Baylor and his men killed six Indians, including women and children, and captured an Indian woman and two children. Because of the blankets they were wearing, Baylor claimed the Apache women and children who were killed could not be distinguished from the men. Furthermore, the regulations of the frontier battalion did not require such distinctions, he told Austin.[104] However, while in reality the attack he was so proud of was little more than a massacre, it nevertheless was widely heralded by the Texas press at the time and by Ranger historians well into the next century.

Back at Ysleta, he watched as much of the good will he had worked to establish with the Spanish-speaking citizens on both sides of the Rio Grande was partly undone by his young and hot-headed sergeant, James B. Gillett. In September 1880, Gillett had ridden downriver from Ysleta to Fort Quitman where he trailed two murderers across the river into Mexico. Prevented from making any arrests by the Mexican authorities, Gillett vowed to take a different approach in the future.[105] Less than a year later in Ysleta during February 1881, he arrested two men, one of whom was innocent, for the brutal murder of a newspaper editor in Socorro, New Mexico. For his endeavors, he collected $500, a sizeable reward for the time. Yet a brother of one of the men arrested, Enofrio Baca, who was also charged in the murder, remained at large. To complicate matters, Enofrio Baca's uncle, José Baca, was county judge of El Paso County.

Learning that Baca was working as a clerk at a store in Zaragoza, across the river from Ysleta, the undaunted Gillett persuaded another Ranger, George Lloyd, to accompany him in a daring but illegal kidnapping of Baca. Splashing across the river, the two rode up to the small store in Zaragoza where Gillett rushed inside, grabbed Baca, placed a pistol to his head, and spirited the man away to Texas, as Mexican law enforcement officials followed in close pursuit, firing at the Rangers as they crossed into Texas.[106] Upon learning what had happened, Baylor, who was usually calm and collected, was furious, accusing Gillett of a "most imprudent act" and a "flagrant violation of law."[107] Nevertheless, Baylor allowed Gillett to take Baca upriver by train to Socorro, where he was turned over to local authorities. Gillett, who refused a sizeable bribe from the county judge to release Baca, collected $250 for his efforts and watched as Baca was lynched by an angry mob from a crossbeam of a corral gate.[108] The incident caused such a stir along the border that Secretary of State James G. Blaine wrote Governor Roberts inquiring into the incident. Roberts, in turn, demanded to know what had happened. Baylor, trying somehow to rationalize Gillett's imprudence, defended his sergeant the best he could and the incident soon faded into history.[109]

Baylor did much more than fight Apaches while serving with the Rangers in the Trans-Pecos. In January 1881, he informed Austin that El Paso was "infested with lawless characters," and something had to be done.[110] Even the mayor of El Paso admitted that the town was "overrun with vagabonds, thieves, gamblers, burglars, and murderers" and that it was "impossible for civil authorities to protect life and property."[111] As a result of all these troubles, the mayor and aldermen pleaded with Baylor to station the Rangers in town. Within days of receiving authority to do so, Baylor had his Rangers in camp at El Paso. So popular were the Rangers that the town's leading citizens signed a petition asking the adjutant general to keep the men in El Paso permanently.

Not long after arriving in El Paso, Baylor was able to seize ten horses and twelve mules stolen from Tombstone, Arizona, although four rustlers escaped.[112] Apprehending horse and cattle rustlers in the El Paso area was particularly difficult, he quickly learned, since the thieves frequently slipped across the Rio Grande to Mexico, only a stone's throw away.

While his Rangers were in El Paso, Baylor continued to reside at Ysleta. It was there that Baylor's pampered oldest daughter, Helen, married Ranger sergeant James Buchanan Gillett on 10 February 1881. On 5 September 1884, a son, James Harper Gillett was born. Later, when Gillett left the Rangers to work as a guard for the Santa Fe Railroad and then as deputy marshal in El Paso, Helen accused him of intimacy with one of the town's soiled doves and sued for divorce on grounds of adultery.[113]

Putting more pressing problems aside, Baylor would often lead his men out of the summer heat of the desert into the conifer-crowned and cooling heights of the Sacramento Mountains in southern New Mexico, allegedly to scout for Apaches raiding off the Mescalero Reservation. He was forced to admit, however, that such forays were really an excuse to give himself and his men some rest and relaxation and an opportunity to hunt and fish. The mountains, Baylor wrote, do more to "restore my health than anything else I know of."[114] On one hunting trip, Baylor and his Rangers killed fifty turkeys, fifteen deer, and two antelope.[115] In time, Baylor became so fond of the Sacramentos that he built a small hunting cabin on the Sacramento River on the southern edge of the mountains. "This wild country is the Indian paradise," he wrote, "we found Elk, Bear, Deer (both white and black tail) and turkeys abundant. The grass and water are fine and wild fruit abundant. Raspberries, strawberries, cherries, gooseberries, currants and plums grow wild and in great profusion. Whil'st acorns and pinnon nuts afford plenty of food for the bear as well as other game . . . I don't blame them for not wanting to leave, for with its great shady pines and oaks, beautiful glades filled with grass and brooks, it is a land worth fighting for."[116]

Back in El Paso in March 1883, Baylor assisted Albert J. Fountain, head of the militia in Doña Ana and Lincoln counties, New Mexico, in breaking up the John Kinney rustling ring operating out of Rincon near present-day Hatch. Baylor also captured Doroteo Sains, a cattle rustler who worked for Kinney and who was part of the Doña Ana County "gang of thieves."[117] Kinney, a "braggart," known to "talk loud, drink hard, [and] lack prudence, [had] killed two men, [and] brags of killing others." Kinney was selling meat to John Krater, a butcher in El Paso whom Baylor arrested but was not able to convict. By November 1883, Baylor had the El Paso County jail so full of lawbreakers that several accused criminals had to be kept under guard in the Ranger camp.

In April 1883, Baylor took the train south to Chihuahua to meet with the acting governor, Dr. Mariano Samaniego, a "personal friend" from the Civil War, to arrange for the arrest and extradition of a number of criminals who had fled south along the line of the recently-completed Mexican National Railroad.[118] By June, he was back at El Paso and wrote the adjutant general in Austin that he was heading for the Sacramento Mountains.

In January 1884, Baylor left Ysleta with the deputy sheriff of Doña Ana County, Dennis Finley, in pursuit of Ignacio Bazan, who had stolen three wagons, eleven mules, and six horses from Lake Valley, New Mexico.[119] With extradition papers from Gov. Luis Terrazas, Baylor and Finley followed Bazan's trail deep into the mountains of Chihuahua. In fact, Baylor was gone for so long that it was feared in El Paso that he had been killed.[120] He eventually wrote from the mountains southwest of Chihuahua to say that Bazan was still on the run but the wagons had been found and some of the stock recovered. In all, Baylor was gone for over six weeks while crossing numerous mountain ranges and traveling over 1,800 miles.[121]

With the completion of the Texas and Pacific Railroad to El Paso in 1881, Baylor was forced to devote more time to enforcing the law in the small towns that sprang up along the tracks to the east. Squads of Rangers had to be stationed not only at Ysleta and El Paso but at Toyah, Carrizo Pass, Murphyville (Alpine), and Pecos City. Although he was able to recruit more men, those he enlisted often turned out to be no better than the thieves and bandits he was trying to arrest. On more than one occasion, newly recruited Rangers fled into the night carrying weapons badly needed by the Rangers.

In the hot summer of 1883, Baylor received a telegram regarding a deadly gun battle at Toyah. "Cowboys tried to take the town of Toyah. One killed three wounded and five prisoners. None of rangers hurt," he wired Austin.[122] The cowboys, led by a young man named Kelley, had threatened to "clean up the town" and had fired several shots into railroad cars and were also firing their pistols and rifles in town, intimidating and frightening the small population. A squad of Rangers in the town quickly formed a posse and ordered the cowboys to give up their weapons. When the cowboys refused and took refuge in a caboose, the Rangers attacked, mortally wounding Kelley and killing two others.[123] That winter another band of rowdy cowboys shot up several railroad cars in Pecos City and Baylor was forced to send in the Rangers. When the Rangers, under Sgt. L.S. Turnbo, finally arrived to restore order, local citizens, fearing for their lives, refused to allow them to leave. Baylor admitted that Pecos had one of the "worst populations to look after" in all of West Texas.[124]

In the spring of 1884, Baylor received an urgent telegram from Austin saying that he was being given the rank of major and being placed in charge of seven Ranger companies operating against fence cutters in central Texas, northwest of Austin.[125] Fence cutting had become so epidemic in the region that the state legislature had recently made the practice a felony. Fearing that the Rangers' withdrawal from El Paso would result in a new crime wave, local citizens became greatly alarmed. Claiming that "local officers are not able to hold in check the criminals and law breaking characters which infest our county," 150 citizens of the town petitioned Austin to keep the Rangers in El Paso. Baylor, too, told Adj. Gen. W.H. King that local citizens were "very much opposed to our leaving."[126]

Austin, however, was more concerned with fence cutting than with crime in El Paso, and Baylor and his men were soon on the train to San Antonio and Austin. After being delayed by bad roads near the capital, Baylor finally arrived in Brownwood on 14 March 1884.[127] The Brown County sheriff, in hopes of gaining reelection, was clearly in sympathy with the fence cutters, Baylor reported. In Blanco, Llano, and McCullough counties, however, he found everything quiet. Riding on to Coleman County, east of San Angelo, the problem was worse, but he still predicted that the action by the state legislature in making fence cutting a felony was certain to end the practice within sixty days.[128] Riding north to Baird in Callahan County and then southwest into Runnels County, there was little doubt, he thought, that "fence cutting will be quite too dangerous a past[t]ime to engage in."[129] He did go as far as to lead a night raid near Ballinger in Runnels County that captured eight fence cutters, some of them "hard looking characters."[130] From Ballinger he rode on to Fort Chadbourne in hopes of catching other fence cutters and arresting some stage robbers operating in the area.[131] By April, he was back in Austin to be congratulated and applauded for his efforts, before going on to San Antonio and west by train through the night to Ysleta.

With the fence cutting largely over, Baylor took Sallie and Mary to Galveston where Confederate veterans were gathering for their annual reunion. In the seaside city, while Sallie visited old friends, he took Mary to the beach and fishing in the warm gulf waters. On his way back to Houston and San Antonio, he wrote Austin asking permission to stop at Montell in Uvalde County to assist his brother in apprehending a gang of cattle and sheep rustlers operating in the oak-shrouded canyons of the upper Nueces.[132] John had written to say that the only thing thieves had not stolen from his ranch at Montell was a prospect hole he had dug in a nearby mountain.

At Ysleta in the summer of 1882, at the urging of several friends and with the endorsement of the El Paso *Lone Star*, Baylor had jumped into the rough-and-tumble web of El Paso County politics when he announced his candidacy for sheriff on the Democratic ticket. But the incumbent, Benito Gonzales, proved to be a formidable opponent.[133] At the county convention in Ysleta in September, Baylor was certain he had enough votes for the party nomination, since he had lined up considerable support from Ysleta, where he was well known, as well as from Concordia and El Paso. Although the delegation from Ysleta came through as promised, Gonzales received such a large vote from San Elizario and Socorro that Baylor's supporters asked that his name be withdrawn before the delegations from Concordia and El Paso could even vote.[134] Stung by his defeat and claiming that Gonzales was a "rascal & thief," the stubborn and defiant Baylor immediately announced he would run for sheriff on an Independent or People's ticket.[135] Baylor went as far as to claim that if he "caught 100 Mexicans stealing and turned them over to Sheriff Benito Gonzales, they would be free in a week."[136] Although his Ranger duties did not permit as vigorous a campaign as he would have liked, he did stage several noisy political rallies, especially at San Elizario, where Gonzales had considerable support but where Baylor was enthusiastically endorsed by his old friend, Gregorio García.[137] On Election Day in early November 1882, Baylor carried El Paso by a vote of 307 to 106 but lost the county, 452 to 628.[138]

By February 1885, Baylor's company of Rangers was the only unit continuing to operate in West Texas. Two months later he received orders that he had anticipated and dreaded. Company A of the Frontier Battalion was to be disbanded effective 15 April 1885.[139] Nevertheless, Baylor could take great pride in looking back over the six years he had served with the Rangers, knowing that he had done much to bring law and order to a vast and untamed region of the Lone Star State.

No longer with the Rangers, Baylor remained active in the social and political life of the region. As he relaxed at Ysleta, his new lifestyle provided a break from the long, fatiguing and often dangerous Ranger patrols he had come to know. Missing the excitement and prestige of life in the Rangers, however, he entered into negotiations with the citizens of Silver City to undertake a campaign against renegade Apaches who were continuing to raid the southwestern part of New Mexico. When an agreement failed to materialize, Baylor again turned his attention to politics.[140] Elected to the Texas House of Representatives in 1886, he hurried to Austin to present petitions and memorials to the 20th Legislature and introduce numerous bills affecting West Texas. One bill created Brewster County, soon to become the largest in Texas. Another carved six new counties out of the vast expanses of Tom Green County. Four counties, including Jeff Davis, were formed from an equally large Presidio County.[141] Baylor also introduced legislation creating the 41st Judicial District for far West Texas.

When his reelection bid failed in 1888, he was appointed clerk of the United States District Court in El Paso. One year later he also became clerk of the United States Circuit Court.[142] In 1892, he resigned to run for El Paso County tax assessor-collector, but was unsuccessful. A year later, he sought the office of United States consul in Ciudad Juárez. Although fluent in Spanish and endorsed by seven ex-governors of Texas and the *El Paso Herald*, he did not have enough political clout in Washington and was rejected by Pres. Grover Cleveland.[143]

Unable to keep out of local politics, Baylor became involved in a feud with the mayor of Ysleta, I.G. Gaal. Gaal, a Hungarian immigrant who had come to El Paso to supervise the construction of the railroad shops, had settled at Ysleta where he ran for mayor in 1889. Although a Republican, Gaal was able to convince enough Democrats to vote for him to win the election.[144] But just one year later Gaal was narrowly defeated by Benigno Alderete, who had previously served as county commissioner and mayor. By accident one day in June 1890, Baylor met Gaal on the steps of the El Paso County Courthouse and according to the *El Paso Times*, Gaal insulted Baylor, not a person to smart off to. Baylor slapped Gaal across the face and would have done much more, the local press reported, had not County Attorney G.F. Neill intervened. When Gaal preferred charges against Baylor in El Paso, Baylor responded by bringing charges against the ex-mayor in Ysleta. Nevertheless, Baylor was hauled into the justice of the peace court where after several months of wrangling, the court ruled in Gaal's favor and ordered Baylor to pay $5.45.[145]

At Ysleta, Baylor's daughters consumed much of his time. In 1893, Helen, after her divorce from James Gillett, married Frank Jones, a captain in the Rangers who had been sent to El Paso. Less than a year later Jones rode downriver with five Rangers to Pirate's Island on the United States side of the Rio Grande where the "Bosque Gang" of horse and cattle thieves were known to hang out. The Rangers found the gang, led by Jesús María Olguín and his son, Severio, on the Mexican side of the river and a gun battle erupted in which the Rangers were pinned down and fired on from an adobe house and from behind a wall. Jones was hit first in the thigh and then in the heart, the latter shot killing him instantly.[146] With the Rangers driven off, it was two days before Baylor could recover his son-in-law's body. In the weeks following the deadly gun battle, a grief-stricken Helen, Baylor recorded, could not bear to live in the house she had shared with her husband. In Baylor's words, the gun battle had not only killed "a good, true & noble man," but broke the heart of "a loving young wife."[147]

Another psychological blow came in February 1894 when word reached El Paso that John Robert Baylor was dead at Montell at the age of seventy-one.[148] The two brothers had fought Comanche in North Texas, Federals during the Civil War, and rustlers in the hills around Uvalde. "General Baylor," as George would always refer to his older brother, had been the one man he admired the most and whose valor he had always tried to emulate.

At El Paso after Helen's second husband's death, Baylor watched as she gave birth to a second grandson, Frank Baylor Jones. In 1895, Helen remarried, this time to Samuel M. Lee, manager of El Paso's Grand Hotel. Lee took the family to live in Guadalajara, Mexico, where he was employed as a construction superintendent for a railroad company.[149] With a lingering hate for her first husband and a disavowal of her second, Helen changed her two sons' last names to Lee.

In 1898, at the age of sixty-six, Baylor moved briefly to Uvalde. Three years later he went to Guadalajara, where Mary had decided to open a school. Except for a brief stay in Cuernavaca, he would spend the next fifteen years

George W. Baylor at the time he was writing articles for the El Paso Herald.
(Texas Collection, Baylor University)

of his life in Guadalajara. The inability to find steady employment in Mexico and help Mary with the expenses of her school, played heavily on his mind. In November 1902, he wrote over 132 post cards and several letters to politicians and influential friends in Texas in hopes of becoming the sergeant-at-arms at the capitol in Austin. Although supported by ex-governor James S. Hogg, he was nevertheless unable to muster enough political support to obtain the position.[150] Finding a temporary job with an American silver mining company, he rode seventy miles on horseback through the mountains to the village of Ayutla where he supervised the Mexican miners and helped build *acequias*, and stone walls, and worked as a carpenter.[151] At the picturesque village, Baylor took time to play his violin for the local children and in quieter moments, read passages from his *Bible*.[152]

Back in Guadalajara, he tried to secure a contract with the Mexican Central Railroad to supply cedar telegraph poles, but the agreement failed to materialize.[153] He did find a part-time job with the *Guadalajara News*, which he labeled the "cheapest and meanest paper in the West."[154] Now seventy years of age, he rose every morning before sunrise to walk the streets of the city until noon, soliciting subscriptions and ads, for which he was paid twenty dollars a month, or roughly a dollar a day. Hoping to "victimize at least one Mexican per month," he worked briefly for the New York Life Insurance Company.[155] "I despise the business and therefore can't make a successful agent," he confessed.[156] Because of Baylor's fluencey in Spanish, William Hunter, an old Confederate, wrote offering him a job at Brownsville, Texas, selling real estate and insurance, but this also fell through. For a time he sold plants and fruit trees for American nursery companies but he received little compensation. What little money he was able to make went to pay the family servants as well as rent, electricity, and food.

Baylor's Mexican sojourn brought years of deepening sadness and sorrow. On 25 May 1903, Helen died unexpectedly in a Monterrey hospital after a short illness. She was only thirty-nine and her death dealt a severe blow to the old soldier. "I can see her when a child running to meet me and throwing her arms around my neck with a glad cry of joy," he wrote.[157] "I dread waking up at night for I can see her face & hear her sweet voice," he continued.[158] He wanted desperately to go to Monterrey to visit his daughter's grave but did not have the money for the train ticket.[159]

Less than a year later, before sunrise on Easter Sunday, 3 April 1904, his wife of forty-one years, Sallie Sydnor Baylor, died of pneumonia at their home at No. 15 Alhondiga.[160] "Sad and lonely," with all his "brothers gone and now my wife & child," he felt as if he had been "shot through the heart."[161] Although an Episcopalian, he found solace in playing his violin at

George W. Baylor with the violin he obtained in California during the Gold Rush.
This image was taken shortly before his death in San Antonio at the age of eighty-three in 1916.
(Texas Collection, Baylor University)

the Methodist Church and in his growing correspondence with relatives back in Texas.

With Helen and Sallie gone, he did everything he could to help Mary with her school. He pitied Mary, who rose every morning at 4:30 and worked until long after dark. Often in the evenings, however, after the day students had left and the boarding students were preparing for bed, he would play his violin as Mary accompanied him on the piano or the guitar. These brief moments were some of his fondest memories of life in Mexico. Growing old and with his eyesight failing, he worried about Mary, "the dearest child in the world" and a "jewel if there ever was one."[162] What if Mary "should die or give up from bad health . . . what would we do?" he asked. [163] But there was security in having "a nice home, a piano, guitar, my violin [and] four book cases filled with [the] best books."[164]

Baylor was also happy that Mary's school had proven successful. At one time there was as many as thirty-one students enrolled, including several German youngsters as well as Americans and Mexicans. He was especially attracted to a small, seven-year-old Mexican boy named Felipe Salcedo. When Felipe's mother died, his father, a liberal and wealthy businessman from Torreón, brought the boy to the Baylors to educate.[165] An "amiable, good boy," Felipe remained with them for seven years, and when his father came to take him to a Jesuit school in Saltillo, Baylor confessed that he would "miss the little fellow."[166] Baylor did have a laugh, however, when Felipe wrote to say that he did not like the Jesuits and if his father did not send him back to Guadalajara, he would "manage it" himself.[167] The family also took in another child, three-year-old Arthur Baylor Bridges, whose mother had died of yellow fever in Monterrey. When the boy's father abandoned him, the Baylors adopted him. When another student, Margarita Velasco, became an orphan, she too was adopted.[168]

Baylor took the greatest pride in his two grandchildren. By 1909, James Harper Lee had given up his job as a timekeeper and gang boss for a railroad construction company and was fighting bulls all over Mexico, even demanding a thousand dollars a fight, an unheard of sum of money at the time. Harper even dreamed of going to Spain to make a million dollars.[169] In time, he became relatively famous as the "first Yankee matador" and the subject of a book, *Knight in the Sun*. Frank, or Francisco Baylor Lee, suffered from a congenital heart ailment and was said to have been almost a midget in size. Nevertheless, Panchito served as his older brother's valet and was regarded in Guadalajara as somewhat of a genius. He was an accomplished pianist, composer of *zarzuelitas* or short musical comedies, and at the age of fourteen, he founded a weekly review, *Casos y Cosas*.[170] "Panchito is going to make a success

George W. Baylor's famous grandson, James Harper Lee, the first "Yankee matador." (Virginia Sturges)

of his little paper, getting new ads each issue," Baylor proudly proclaimed in 1908. "He is a great pet among the Mexicans as well as the Americans."[171] But on Christmas Eve, 1908, as neighbors joyously celebrated the holiday season, Frank died suddenly at the age of fifteen. "All night I prayed to God to take me [and] spare my little boy," the grandfather wrote in tears.[172] With Mary unconsolable, Baylor was left "alone to carry his dead, frail little boy to the grave." His heart was "bleeding at every pore," he wrote.[173]

In Guadalajara, Baylor began to write articles for the *El Paso Daily Herald* that in seven years would number fifty-two.[174] In 1905 and 1906, he also wrote for the *Galveston Daily* and *Semi-Weekly News*.[175] He also took pleasure in corresponding with and composing articles for the *Confederate Veteran*.[176] As a result he received letters from old veterans he had known during the Civil War, as well as men he had commanded during the campaigns against Victorio.

During his stay in Mexico, Baylor was so pressed for money that he could not attend the annual Confederate reunion which he had always enjoyed. In 1906, he wrote the Mexican Central and Mexican National railroads hoping to obtain passes since, he said, he had risked his life in crossing "into Mexico in four campaigns against Victorio . . . but there are no Apaches now to worry the Mex. Cent. or train robbers so the old Texas Ranger is not needed."[177] Although he continued to struggle financially, Baylor did manage to rent a larger home and move Mary and her school to Colonia Reforma, a fashionable suburb. He also contracted to build a home of his own—his legacy to Mary and something he had dreamed of for years. Before the house could be completed, however, he began to quarrel with the contractor and with his "old Rebel blood" on fire, told the builder "to go to hell."[178] When a storm blew away the newly-completed roof of the house, Baylor gave up the project entirely. Deciding to exchange his house and property in Ysleta, despite the fact that vandals and burglars had carried off all the doors, windows, and furniture, for property in Guadalajara, he was able, with money from the sale of a piece of land in Galveston, to begin construction on another house.

In 1910, just as the family was moving into their new home, the Mexican Revolution struck Mexico and Guadalajara. "A bigger lot of asses & cowards never got together than attacked the Methodist Girl's School where there were nothing but women and children," he angrily wrote in December 1910.[179] Although revolutionaries were roaming the streets of the city chanting "*Mueran a los Gringos*," and destroying property, he was certain Pres. Porfirio Díaz and his cabinet could restore order. Fearful nevertheless that the Baylor home and school would be attacked, the old warrior "prepared for a real battle." Armed with a shotgun and a machete, as Mary stood by with a rifle and pistol, he was determined to go down fighting. "We could hear the mob howling & an occasional shot fired & it sounded ugly enough," he wrote, "but I am too old a Johnny Reb to run just because the skirmishers begin firing."[180]

In August 1913, as the revolution continued to rage across Mexico, the American consul arrived at the Baylor home at 1190 San Diego with orders from Pres. Woodrow Wilson and the State Department directing all Ameri-

cans to leave Mexico.[181] Reluctantly, Baylor agreed, and leaving the large
house in charge of a servant, the aging and grey-haired old Rebel colonel, his
idealistic daughter, and their adopted children, left Guadalajara for Mexico
City, where they caught the train to Vera Cruz. After traveling by boat to
New Orleans and then overland to Houston, Baylor told the local press he
wanted to go back to Chalk Bluff on the Nueces River for the last few years
that he could expect to live.[182] Instead, he settled in San Antonio where he
died on the morning of 27 March 1916. He was buried in an unmarked grave
in the Confederate Cemetery with the Albert Sidney Johnston Camp of Confederate veterans in charge of arrangements; the old warrior was eighty-
three. Only newspapers in El Paso and San Antonio bothered to note his
passing.[183] Twenty years later, the State of Texas placed a centennial marker
at the grave.[184]

It was said in Texas that there were two kinds of Baylors—fiddlers and
fighters. Although George Baylor could certainly play the violin, he was
clearly destined to be remembered among the latter.

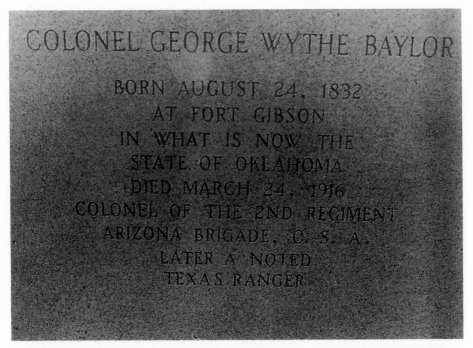

Grave marker erected by the State of Texas at the Confederate Cemetery in San Antonio,
twenty years after Baylor's death. Baylor actually died on the morning of 27 March 1916.
(Author's photo)

NOTES

1   James B. Gillett, *Six Years with the Texas Rangers* (New Haven: Yale University Press, 1963), 141-42.

2   George W. Baylor to O.M. Roberts, 3 February 1879, in James M. Day and Dorman Winfrey, eds. *Texas Indian Papers: 1860-1916* (Austin: Texas State Library, 1961), 4:412-14. Also, Kenneth A. Goldblatt, "George Wythe Baylor, Frontier Hero" (M.A. thesis, University of Texas at El Paso, 1969), 80.

3   *El Paso Herald*, 13 January 1900; John L. Waller, "Colonel George Wythe Baylor," *Southwestern Social Science Quarterly* 24 (1943): 29.

4   Edward R. Baylor, *A Baylor Genealogy: The Tedious Family History of Some of the Baylors who Lived in the United States in 1989* (Woods Hole, Mass.: 1989), 16, 25.

5   Ibid., 15. Also, Orval Walker Baylor and Henry Walker Baylor, *Baylor's History of the Baylors: A Collection of Records and Important Family Data* (Le Roy, Ind.: Le Roy Journal Publishing Co., 1914), 31-32.

6   *A Baylor Genealogy*, 15.

7   James Henry Gardner, "The Lost Captain: J.L. Dawson of Old Fort Gibson," *Chronicles of Oklahoma* 21 (1943): 227-29. Also, Houston *Telegraph and Texas Register*, 23 October 1844.

8   R.E.B. Baylor to John R. Baylor, 13 October 1854, Sturges Papers.

9   L.E. Daniell, *Personnel of the Texas State Government* (Austin: City Printing Co., 1887), 104-5.

10   George W. Baylor to Susie [Hamer], 6 March 1906, Baylor-Carrington Papers, Texas Collection, Baylor University, Waco, Texas. Susan Hamer was the daughter of Henry Weidner Baylor, sheriff of Uvalde County and the son of John Robert Baylor.

11   Ibid.

12   John R. Baylor to My Dear Mother, 19 December, no year, Sturges Papers.

13   Baylor to John, 21 September 1904, Baylor-Carrington Papers.

14   *El Paso Herald*, 8 November 1902.

15   Miscellaneous Newspaper Clipping, Edward Clifton Wharton and Family Papers, Special Collections, Hill Memorial Library, Louisiana State University, Baton Rouge, La. See also Ch. 11, Sec. I.

16   Waller, "Colonel George Wythe Baylor," 24; Goldblatt, "George Wythe Baylor," 10; *El Paso Herald,* 8 November 1902.

17   Mary Baylor to My Dear Mother, 15 September [1857], Sturges Papers.

18   Ibid.

19   Pat to My Dear Mother, 14 August 1855, Sturges Papers.

20   Pat to My Dear Mother, 5 December 1858, Sturges Papers.

21   George W. Baylor to Ned, 18 July 1859, Edward Clifton Wharton Papers.

22   *Report of the Commissioner of Indian Affairs for the Year 1856* (Washington: A.O.P. Nicholson, 1857), 177. Also, J.R. Baylor to R.S. Neighbors, 7 October 1855, Letters Received, Office of Indian Affairs, Texas Agency, 1855-1857, Record Group 75, National Archives.

23   Robt. S. Neighbors to Geo. W. Manypenny, 20 February 1856, LR, OIA, Texas Agency, RG 75. Also, John R. Baylor to Neighbors, 17 January 1856 and Baylor to Neighbors, 10 March 1856, both in LR, OIA, Texas Agency, RG 75.

24   Kenneth F. Neighbours, *Indian Exodus: Texas Indian Affairs, 1835-1859* (Nortex, 1973), 126-27.

25 John S. Ford to J.A. Wilcox, 12 April 1859, LR, OIA, Texas Agency, RG 75. Also see George Klos, "Our People Could Not Distinguish One Tribe from Another: The 1859 Expulsion of the Reserve Indians from Texas," *Southwestern Historical Quarterly* 97 (April 1994): 605.

26 Klos, "Our People Could Not Distinguish One Tribe from Another," 609.

27 Jacksboro *White Man*, 8 March 1860; Weatherford *White Man*, 13 September 1860.

28 Neighbours, *Indian Exodus*, 126.

29 J.R. Baylor to Editor, 1 April, 1858; Baylor to Editor, 15 April, 1858; Baylor to Editor, 17 May 1858; Baylor to Editor, 30 August 1858; miscellaneous newspaper clippings in LR, OIA, Texas Agency, RG 75.

30 Neighbours, *Indian Exodus*, 135. Also, Klos, "Our People Could Not Distinguish One Tribe from Another," 612-13; and San Antonio *Daily Herald*, 14, 19 May, 2, 7 June 1859.

31 Neighbours, *Indian Exodus*, 135.

32 Quoted in Ibid., 137.

33 Ibid., 118. For Neighbors' death, see Kenneth Franklin Neighbours, *Robert Simpson Neighbors and the Texas Frontier, 1836-1859* (Waco: Texian Press, 1975), 283-84.

34 *El Paso Herald*, 3 August 1901.

35 *Galveston Tri-Weekly News*, 14 August 1860.

36 George Wythe Baylor to E.C. Wharton, 21 August 1886, Albert Sidney Johnston Papers, Jenkins Garrett Library, University of Texas at Arlington.

37 *El Paso Herald*, 10 August 1901.

38 Ibid.

39 8th Census (1860), Parker County, Texas, NA.

40 Weatherford *White Man* quoted in *Galveston Weekly News*, 16 March 1861. See Ch. 15, Sec. I.

41 *El Paso Herald*, 9 November 1901; El Paso *Evening Tribune*, 16 November 1892.

42 Muster Roll (No. 1463) of Capt. H.A. Hamner's Company of Mounted Volunteers, Texas State Archives, Austin, Texas; Daniell, *Personnel of the Texas State Government*, 104-5; Compiled Service Record, George W. Baylor, Confederate Adjutant General's Office, RG 109, NA.

43 George W. Baylor to Wm. Bird, 19 June 1861, Letters Received, Adjutant General's Records, Record Group 401, Texas State Archives, Austin, Texas.

44 Martin H. Hall, "The Skirmish at Mesilla," *Arizona and the West* 1(Winter 1958): 343-51; John R. Baylor to T.A. Washington, 21 September 1861, *The War of the Rebellion: A Compilation of the Official Records of the Union and Confederate Armies* (Washington, 1889), Ser. I, Vol. 4:17-20. Hereafter referred to as *OR*, by series, volume, and page.

45 Pat to Dear Pet, 14 August 1861, Sturges Papers.

46 John R. Baylor to Sir, 1 August 1861, typescript in George Wythe Baylor IV, Papers, Tucson, Ariz. Also, John R. Baylor to T.A. Washington, 21 September 1861, *OR*, 1, 4:17-20; Terms of Surrender of U.S. Troops to C.S. Troops, 27 July 1861, *OR*, 1, 4:7; *Mesilla Times*, 27 July 1861.

47 Martin H. Hall, "Albert Sidney Johnston's First Confederate Command," *McNeese Review* 13 (1862): 3-12; A.S. Johnston to Jno. R. Baylor, 27 August 1861, letter in private collection. Also, William Preston Johnston, *Life of Albert Sidney Johnston* (New York: D. Appleton & Co., 1878), 287-89; Charles P. Roland, *Albert Sidney Johnston: Soldier of Three Republics* (Austin: University of Texas Press, 1964), 255-58.

48 Pat to Dear Pet, 14 August 1861, Sturges Papers.

49 Ibid.

50 Pat to My Darling Pet, 23 December 1861, Sturges Papers.

51 Pat to Dear Brother, 25 December 1861, Sturges Papers.

52 Fan to My Dear Brother, 5 January 1862, Sturges Papers.

53 Pat to Sister Mollie, 2 January 1862, Edward Clifton Wharton Papers. Also, Pat to Dear Brother, 16 January 1862, Sturges Papers.

54 Baylor to E.C. Wharton, 21 August 1866, Johnston Papers, Jenkins Garrett Library, University of Texas at Arlington.

55 S. Cooper to Geo. Wythe Baylor, 24 April 1862, George W. Baylor CSR, AGO, RG 109, NA.

56 Geo. Wythe Baylor to George W. Randolph, 15 July 1862, George W. Baylor CSR, AGO. RG 109, NA.

57 Baylor to Susie, 21 June 1906, Baylor-Carrington Papers. "My son, take this money and buy you a home. I have felt the need of one all my life," his mother wrote.

58 Col. Peter Hardeman commanded the 1st Regiment of the brigade, Col. Joseph Phillips the 3d Regiment, and Col. Spruce M. Baird the 4th Regiment.

59 Jerry Thompson, *Colonel John Robert Baylor: Texas Indian Fighter and Confederate Soldier* (Hillsboro: Hill College Press, 1971), 77-79; Martin H. Hall, "Planter vs. Frontiersman: Conflict in Confederate Indian Policy," *Essays on the American Civil War* (Austin: University of Texas Press, 1968), 45-72; Bruce S. Allardice, *More Generals in Gray* (Baton Rouge: Louisiana State University Press, 1995), 32-33.

60 Claude W. Hayes, *Galveston: History of the Island and the City* (Austin: Jenkins Garrett Press, 1974), 1:364, 406, 500, and 2:930-33; Gary Cartwright, *Galveston: A History of the Island* (New York: Atheneum, 1991), 79. Sydnor had arrived in Galveston in 1838, and had become alderman and mayor of the city in 1846. In 1861, he was elected a colonel of militia and went to Richmond in hopes of securing artillery for the defense of the city. He later resigned to engage in the auction and commissary business in Houston.

61 Hayes, *Galveston: History of the Island and the City*, 2:586.

62 Goldblatt, "George Wythe Baylor," 44.

63 Gillett, *Six Years with the Texas Rangers*, 205.

64 Diary of William N. Carothers, 6 May 1861, Duncan C. Carothers Papers, Texas State Archives.

65 L Boyd Finch, "Surprise at Brashear City: Sherod Hunter's Sugar Cooler Cavalry," *Louisiana History* 25 (Fall 1984). Also see n. 2, Ch. 4, Sec. II. Also, William N. Carothers Diary, 23 June 1863, Texas State Archives. See n. 2, Ch. 3, Sec. III.

66 Goldblatt, "George Wythe Baylor," 47-48. Also, n. 35, Ch. 2, Sec. II.

67 William N. Carothers Diary, 22 August 1863, Texas State Archives.

68 Special Order no. 21, *OR*, 1, 34, 2:903-4.

69 Pat to Dear Sister, 6 April 1864, Edward Clifton Wharton Papers. Still considered the best sources for the Red River Campaign are: Ludwell H. Johnson, *Red River Campaign: Politics and Cotton in the Civil War* (Kent, Ohio: Kent State University Press, 1993); and John D. Winters, *The Civil War in Louisiana* (Baton Rouge: Louisiana State University Press, 1963).

70 Geo. Wythe Baylor to Ogden, 18 April 1864, *OR*, 1, 34, 1:616-17; Johnson, *Red River Campaign*, 125.

71 Baylor to Ogden, 18 April 1864, *OR*, 1, 34, 1:616-17. Also see n. 9, Ch. 4, Sec. II.

72 Geo. Wythe Baylor to Ogden, 18 April 1864, *OR*, 1, 34, 1:617.

73 Ibid., 618.

74 Ibid., 623.

75 Ibid. In the margin on page thirty-three of George Baylor's *Bull Run to Bull Run* (Richmond: B.F. Johnson Publishing Co., 1900), George W. Baylor scribbled, "Banks was the best a.g.m. & a.c.s. we ever had in Taylor's C.S. A. and from Mansfield to Yellow Bayou, La. supplied all our wants. It was [the] first time I had plenty of grub."

76 Ibid., 624.

77 Ibid.

78 George W. Baylor, "With My Regiment in the Campaigns of Louisiana and Texas and events that led up to my trouble with General John A. Wharton," copy courtesy of George W. Baylor IV. Also, George W. Baylor IV to Jerry Thompson, 5 September 1971, Editor's files.

79 Mamie Yeary, ed., *Reminiscences of the Boys in Gray, 1861-1865* (Dayton: Morningside, 1986), 45.

80 Ibid.

81 Baylor, "With My Regiment."

82 Ibid.

83 Ibid.

84 The testimony of Gen. James E. Harrison, who was with General Wharton, and that of Capt. R.H.D. Sorrell, who was with Baylor, agree as to the confrontation and the language exchange. Houston *Tri-Weekly Telegraph*, 19 April 1865; *State of Texas vs. George W. Baylor*, Cause no. 4271, Harris County District Court, Houston, Texas. See also: Houston *Tri-Weekly Telegraph*, 7, 10, 12, 15, 16, 19 April 1865; *Galveston Weekly News*, 12, 16 April 1865; *Galveston News*, 7, 8 April 1865; 8 December 1895; *Dallas Herald*, 13 April 1865; William P. Ballinger Diary, 9 April 1865, William P. Ballinger Papers, Center for American History, University of Texas at Austin.

85 *Galveston Weekly News*, 12 April 1865.

86 Baylor, "With My Regiment."

87 E[liza] P. Wharton to [William P.] Ballinger, 13 May 1865, Ballinger Papers.

88 Dallas *Weekly Herald*, 30 May, 12 December 1868.

89 *A Baylor Genealogy*, 25. Wharton came "into Gen. Magruder's private room after we had had a difficulty on the street, and struck me in the face and called me a liar," Baylor wrote in 1898. "He ought to have known I would resent it at once, for he had seen me in battle. The whole thing has been a lifelong sorrow to me." Baylor, "Of a Noted Military Family," *Confederate Veteran* 6 (April 1898): 164-65. Also, Anne J. Bailey, *Between the Enemy and Texas: Parson's Texas Cavalry in the Civil War* (Fort Worth: Texas Christian University Press, 1989), 201.

90 Norman G. Kittrell, "Governors Who Have Been and Other Public Men of Texas," 56. Typescript, Center for American History, University of Texas at Austin.

91 *Dallas Weekly Herald*, 30 March 1872; 25 July, 1 August, and 10 October 1874.

92 *Dallas Weekly Herald*, 14 December 1872.

93 *Dallas Weekly Herald,* 16 January 1875.

94 Baylor's property consisted of thirteen acres, one hundred feet on each side of the river, one mile downriver from the north end of Chalk Bluff.

95 *El Paso Herald*, 13 January 1900.

96 George W. Baylor to O.M. Roberts, 3 February 1879, *Texas Indian Papers*, 4:412-14.

97 *El Paso Daily Herald*, 13 January 1900.

98 El Paso *Lone Star*, 11 March 1882; 19 September, 17 November 1883; 5 March 1884; 17 June 1885.

99 San Antonio *Daily Express*, 24 October 1879.

100 Baylor to Jno. B. Jones, 3 December 1879, Adjutant General's Office, RG 401, Texas State Archives.

101 Baylor to Jones, 26 August 1880, AGO, RG 401, TSA.

102 Ibid. Also see Ch. 1, Sec. III.

103 Baylor to Neal Coldwell, 31 August 1880, AGO, RG 401, TSA. Also, Ch. 1, Sec. III.

104 Baylor to Jones, 9 February 1881, AGO, RG 401, TSA; *Galveston Weekly News*, 10 February 1881. Also, Ch. 8, Sec. III.

105 Gillett, *Six Years with the Texas Rangers*, 211-14, 217.

106 Ibid., 214-16. Also, Keith Milton, "Whistlin' Extradition," *True West* 39 (May 1992): 14-19.

107 Gillett, *Six Years with the Texas Rangers*, 217. Also, Monthly Returns, Company A, Frontier Battalion, AGO, RG 401, TSA.

108 Gillett, *Six Years with the Texas Rangers*, 219-20.

109 Ibid., 221-22.

110 *Galveston Weekly News*, 13 January 1881.

111 Ibid.

112 El Paso *Lone Star*, 19 October 1881.

113 Marshall Hail, *Knight in the Sun: Harper B. Lee, First Yankee Matador* (Boston: Little, Brown and Co., 1962), 4, 23, 27, 36.

114 Baylor to King, 25 May 1883, AGO, RG 401, TSA.

115 El Paso *Lone Star*, 23 August 1882.

116 Baylor to King, 9 July 1882, AGO, RG 401, TSA; Waller, "Colonel George Wythe Baylor," 34.

117 A.F. Fountain to Baylor, 15 March 1883; Baylor to King, 18 March 1883; Miscellaneous newspaper clippings; all in AGO, RG 401, TSA.

118 Baylor to King 18 March 1883, AGO, RG 401, TSA. See n. 3, Ch. 5, Sec. III.

119 El Paso *Lone Star*, 9 February 1884.

120 El Paso *Lone Star*, 13 February 1884; *San Antonio Daily Express*, 12 February 1884.

121 Outline of Pursuit of Ignacio Bazan, n.d., AGO, RG 401, TSA.

122 Baylor to W.H. King, 18 July 1883, AGO, RG 401, TSA.

123 Baylor to King, 21 July, AGO, RG 401, TSA.

124 Baylor to King, 30 December 1883, AGO, RG 401, TSA.

125 Special Orders No. 53, 7 March 1884, AGO, RG 401, TSA.

126 Petition of the Citizens of El Paso County, 13 March 1884, AGO, RG 401, TSA.

127 Baylor to King, 2 March 1884, AGO, RG 401, TSA.

128 Baylor to King, 16 March 1884, AGO, RG 401, TSA.

129 Ibid.

130 Baylor to King, 4 May 1884, AGO, RG 401, TSA.

131 Baylor to King, 7 May 1884, AGO, RG 401, TSA.

132 Baylor to King, 10 July 1884, AGO, RG 401, TSA.

133 El Paso *Lone Star*, 26 July 1883.

134 El Paso *Lone Star*, 6 September 1882.

[135] El Paso *Lone Star*, 9, 13 September 1882.

[136] Quoted in Waller, "Colonel George Wythe Baylor," 34.

[137] El Paso *Lone Star*, 1 November 1882.

[138] El Paso *Lone Star*, 14 November 1882.

[139] King to Baylor, 30 September 1884, AGO, RG 401, TSA; Goldblatt, "George Wythe Baylor," 98.

[140] El Paso *Lone Star,* 2 January 1886.

[141] Goldblatt, "George Wythe Baylor," 100; *Journal of the House of Representatives of the Twentieth Legislature, State of Texas* (Austin: Triplett and Hutchins, 1887), 214, 460, 673, 804.

[142] *El Paso Herald*, 25 June 1888; Goldblatt, "George Wythe Baylor," 100.

[143] *El Paso Herald*, 7 October 1892, 28 March 1893.

[144] Nancy Hamilton, "The Ysleta Riot of 1890," *Password* 24 (Summer 1979): 103-4.

[145] *El Paso Heral*d, 10 June 1890; El Paso *Times*, 11 June 1890. Also, *G.W. Baylor vs. I.G. Gaal*, Cause no. 408, El Paso County Precinct 2, Justice of the Peace Records.

[146] Baylor to W.H. Mabry, 9 July 1893, AGO, RG 401, TSA; El Paso *Times*, 1 March 1953. Jones was accompanied by Cpl. Karl Kircher and Pvts. F.E. Tucker, S.W. Saunders, Edwin Aten, and R.E. Bryant. Baylor's letter was published in its entirety in Tom Bailey and Ralph J. Weaver, "The Nine Lives of Captain Frank Jones," *Frontier Times* 34 (Spring 1960): 6-9, 36-40. This article was reprinted in *Old West* 60 (Summer 1979): 6-9, 31, 34-37.

[147] Baylor to Mabry, 9 July 1893, AGO, RG 401, TSA.

[148] Austin *Daily Statesman*, 9 February 1894; *San Antonio Express*, 9 February 1894; Dallas *Morning News*, 9 February 1894; Thompson, *John Robert Baylor*, 97.

[149] Hail, *Knight in the Sun*, 23.

[150] Baylor to Susie, 20 December 1902, Baylor-Carrington Papers.

[151] Baylor to Susie, 29 April 1903, Baylor-Carrington Papers. Also, Bayor to Susie, 12 February 1903; Baylor to John, 12 February 1903; Baylor to Susie, 16 April 1903; all in Baylor-Carrington Papers.

[152] Baylor to Susie, 16 April 1903, Baylor-Carrington Papers.

[153] Baylor to Hal, 15 June 1903, Baylor-Carrington Papers.

[154] Baylor to Susan, 9 September 1903, Baylor-Carrington Papers.

[155] Ibid.

[156] Ibid.

[157] Baylor to Hal, 15 June 1903, Baylor-Carrington Papers.

[158] Ibid.

[159] In January 1904, Samuel Lee, a man with a "heart as big as a pumpkin," wrote to say that he had placed a black marble stone on Helen's grave that was inscribed "Sacred to the memory of Helen Baylor, beloved wife of S.M. Lee—born Decem[b]er 10, 1865, died M[a]y 15, 1903." Baylor to Susan, 31 January 1904, Baylor-Carrington Papers.

[160] Funeral Notice, Mrs. Geo. W. Baylor, AGO, RG 401, TSA. Also, Baylor to Florence and Hal, 23 April 1904.

[161] Baylor to Florence and Hal, 23 April 1904, Baylor-Carrington Papers.

[162] Baylor to Susan, 31 January 1904, Baylor-Carrington Papers.

[163] Baylor to John, 21 September 1904, Baylor-Carrington Papers.

[164] Ibid.

[165] Baylor to Florence, 27 July 1904, Baylor-Carrington Papers.

[166] Baylor to Susie, 8 October 1909, Baylor-Carrington Papers.

[167] Ibid.

[168] Houston *Chronicle*, 3 October 1913.

[169] Baylor to Susie, 2 September 1910, Baylor-Carrington Papers.

[170] Hail, *Knight in the Sun*, 23.

[171] Baylor to My Dear Old Friend, 11 September 1908, Baylor-Carrington Papers.

[172] Baylor to My Darling, 26 December 1908, Baylor-Carrington Papers.

[173] Ibid.

[174] *El Paso Herald*, 9, 18, 23 December 1899; 13, 20, 27 January, 3, 10, 17, February, 10, 11, 13, 14, 15, August, 9 October, 15, 22, December 1900; 23 February, 23, 30 March, 6, 13, 20, 27 April, 4, 25 May, 29 June, 27 July, 21 September, 9, 16, 23 November 1901; 15, 22 February, 7 June, 1, 8, November 1902; 24 June 1905; 6, 10 January 1906.

[175] Galveston *Daily News*, 19 February 1898; 29 November 1905; 14 January 1906.

[176] *Confederate Veteran*, 5 (December 1897), 609-13; 6 (April 1898), 164-65; 6 (November 1898), 526; 7 (July 1899), 306; 13 (April 1905), 176; 14 (October 1906), 17 (May 1909), 219; 21 (February 1913), 72-73.

[177] Uncle Pat to My Dear Nini, 26 May 1906, Edward Clifton Wharton Papers.

[178] Baylor to My Dear Old Friend, 11 September 1908, Baylor-Carrington Papers.

[179] Baylor to Susie, 2 December 1910, Baylor-Carrington Papers.

[180] Ibid.

[181] Houston *Chronicle*, 3 October 1913; Goldblatt, "George Wythe Baylor," 114.

[182] Houston *Chronicle*, 3 October 1913. Baylor's letters written while he was in Mexico contain numerous passages praising the tranquility of Chalk Bluff and his desire to return there.

[183] *San Antonio Express*, 28 March 1916; *El Paso Herald*, 1 April 1916. The cause of death was officially listed as exhaustion and senility. Warner D. Farr, *Resting Rebels: A Historical and Medical Study of the San Antonio Confederate Cemetery* (San Antonio: privately published, 1990), 66. Mary died in poverty at La Vernia, Texas, near San Antonio, early in 1942.

[184] The marker erroneously gave the date of his death as 24 March 1916. A more recent military marker gives the date as 17 March 1916.

Early Years

~

You want me to write my life, do you.

Well . . . it would be quite a history

as I came to Texas in '45

and have seen much pathos

and tragedy in my day.

George W. Baylor, December 1904

I

*BESIDES HIS PERSONAL RECOLLECTIONS, Baylor also recorded the
experiences of other men he met who had also experienced life on
the vast and bloody frontiers of Texas. Baylor's nephew, Joseph
Addison Hatch, recalled his involvement in 1850 with the ill-fated
Parker H. French Expedition. Another nephew, Joseph Dawson,
remembered the fight in 1851 between two factions of the disbanded French Expedition at Corralitos, Chihuahua. Another
man, James Wiley Magoffin, a Matamoros, Santa Fe, and Chihuahua trader who settled at El Paso del Norte in 1849, sketched
for Baylor his arrival on the coast of Texas, as well as a later brush
with Apaches on the Rio Grande. Charles Ferguson, another
Santa Fe and Chihuahua trader who also settled at El Paso del
Norte, told Baylor of a confrontation he had with Apaches near
Corralitos, Chihuahua, in 1849. Of equal importance is Luz Villanueva's various fights and hair-raising confrontations with hostile Comanches.*

*Baylor's vivid reminiscences of the six years he spent in gold-
rush California depict more the environmental transformation of
the area than they do the day-to-day activities of the miners. His
tales of hunting grizzly bears are valuable in understanding what
eventually happened to these animals in not only California, but
the rest of the Trans-Mississippi.*

*Today, Baylor's account of his violent and deadly clashes with
Comanches in North Texas in 1859-1861 and his use of such
words as "savage" may seem repugnant. It must be remembered,
however, that such views were typical and even applauded on the
Texas frontier at the time. Baylor, who was described by contem-
poraries as a righteous and refined Christian gentleman who never
used profanity, tobacco, or alcohol, was also an uncompromising
Indian fighter who gave no quarter.*

*Overall, Baylor's writings indicate a liberal knowledge of litera-
ture and the classics. For the era in which he wrote, Baylor was
well educated. Consequently, only a slight editing of his articles
was necessary.*

~

CHAPTER ONE

My First Deer

ALONG IN THE WINTER OF 1846 my cousins, Howard, Ralph, and Wythe Bledsoe came over from Gay Hill, Washington County, where their father had settled near our uncle, Judge R.E.B. Baylor, to join me in a camp hunt.[1] There were thousands of deer and turkeys every where on Ross Prairie, near La Grange, where my brother, John R. Baylor, had settled.[2] At that time there were only two settlers besides him living there, Monroe Hill and George Kerr, and any morning you could look out on the beautiful prairie south of our home and see herds of deer grazing much like cattle or flocks of turkeys, and perhaps a coyote trotting along unconcernedly, and in the spring the boom of the prairie chickens could be heard from every direction.[3] Oh how lively was Texas in her early days, decked out in thousands of flowers, many of them unknown today, as cattle and other domestic stock have destroyed them. I can recall often in my boyhood days, seeing a herd of deer, and when I would ride towards them they would pay but little attention to me until I was quite close to them, for they seemed to know the range of my old muzzle loading "human rifle," and would start off with great bounds, their white tails in the air, and they seemed to know exactly where the nearest herd of deer would be found, and would run to them and stop. I would follow, and in a short time, when many herds had joined each other, it was a grand sight to see them—the row of white flags as they scampered off. But deer now don't know the range of modern guns and keep running.

Of course we could kill all the game we wanted at home, but boy-like, we wanted to camp out and go to a better place. So we went down to our Uncle William Baylor's, near the Colorado River twelve miles below La Grange, and were joined by our cousins, William, John, and Wythe Baylor, who was one of the brave Terry Rangers during our family quarrel.[4]

We crossed the river at old Charlie Mullin's, one of the Texas pioneers—at that time having a bunch of horses and a few cattle, and a field of the rich, red sandy land, that had only to be tickled to fill a barn with corn.[5] It was also close to William Creek bottom, some miles in width and very thick with undergrowth, and here were bear that had regular roads to Uncle Charlie's corn field, and they managed to get nearly as much corn in roasting ear time as he did, and a lot of bucks just stayed in the field, and turkeys "world without end."

Uncle Charlie was the soul of hospitality, and entertained us royally, as was the custom in those days. He was also a great wag. On one occasion a tenderfoot stopped with him, who was looking at the country with a view of settling. One evening in walking down the river bank, he discovered an old she bear and three bear cubs up a mulberry tree getting their supper. It was not over a quarter of a mile from the house so he ran back, arriving out of breath, and asked for a gun. "Well, then, how am I to get the bear?" he asked. "Why, just go back, get as close as you can to the tree, then climb the tree and the old bear will fall out and kill herself and you can easily catch the cubs." He then furnished his guest a knife to stick the bear with and a sack to bring back the cubs in. He obeyed the instructions and made the rush and climbed the tree to the first limbs, and was astounded to see the old bear tumble out of the tree, (all the cubs following suit) and make off at a 2:40 gait.

We then took the road that went through Williams Creek bottom and camped for the night. Wolves howled, owls hooted, and many queer noises of night birds and beasts made us feel a little nervous, but we built up big fires, having laid in plenty of wood, and whistled to keep our courage up. We could also hear the bark of a dog at the only house between there and Halletsville, except old Tom Shadowen's on the Navidad [River].

By daylight we were up; old bucks had whistled at our camp fire and the woods resounded with the gobbling and yelping of turkeys. After a hearty breakfast we were off, although, for howling of grey wolves during the night and knowledge that bears and panthers were near, made us feel like staying close together. But of course such a mob could never get near enough to kill anything, as each one was bragging of what he could or would do in case he met a bear, panther, or even a lion.

After a regular fusillade we returned to camp with a turkey and a few cat squirrels. After dinner we tried single line formation, started up the creek bottom. We had an old hound named Mungo Park that had a voice like a fog horn, and was good after coons, possums, and varmints, but two hundred yards was his limit after a deer, unless he could smell blood, and that appealed so strongly to his stomach that he never quit the trail unless he found wolves ahead of him, and as he had been interviewed by them several times he always called a halt until reinforcements came—the change in his cry giving notice of danger ahead.

I was on the right flank and the others scattered along at intervals, Old Mungo skirmished along the center, managing to run all of the deer out of shooting distance. All of the boys had shotguns except myself, and I had one of those Old Kentucky rifles stocked out to the end, and that meant as long as a fence rail, double triggers, and calibre that took just 120 bullets to the pound, and when I had a small yellow gourd of powder, a pound of buckshot and a box of c.c. caps, my cup of happiness was full. I put a buckshot in the palm of my hand and how carefully I pulled the stopper from my gourd with my teeth and poured just enough powder to cover it—that was a charge. Those old rifles would be a curiosity now, but I have heard Gen. Albert Sidney Johnston say when the minie was first used, "We have gained the range, but at the expense of accuracy."[6] The old Tennessean or Kentuckian that could not take a squirrel's eye out or bark him, as it was called—that is to hit the bark just behind his foreleg, so the bark striking next to his heart would kill him— was no shot at all, but to my deer.

I skirted along the east edge of the bottom, in the tall sedge grass, where the beds where deer would lie down, almost touched each other on acres of ground. But one old buck's head and horns were all that could be seen above the grass, and my old gun was too heavy for me to draw a bead on anything but the side of a house, so I got into the timber again, for I needed a rest for my rifle to do my "suction." I usually after finding a herd of deer, got me a chunk, leaned it up against a tree, and took a deliberate pop at the deer that happened to stand broadside, they gazing at me as unconcernedly as though they were not in the least danger; and often they were not, for "buck ager" was a disease I was very subject to.[7] But if I happened to pull the trigger at the right time and drew blood, I had an ol' half hound named Sam Houston that was quite as skillful a general as the old warrior himself, and he would stand quietly until I told him to "go for him," when he would be off, and if he smelled blood the deer was my meat; but if I missed the deer, he would sneak back, his tail between his legs, and looking as mean as if he had missed the deer himself instead of me.

I heard Old Mungo open and come towards me, and I happened to be by the side of a fallen cottonwood tree. I could just see over the tree, and hearing the brush crack, I peeped out and not twenty yards off stood an old doe broadside, looking back towards Mungo. He had just finished his limit.

I had received minute instructions from an old hunter, Hugh White, the best reel player that ever drew horse hair across cat guts, who was a 'near neighbor' in those days, living on Cummings Creek, some ten or twelve miles away. "George, when you get so that you can see a deer's eyes plain he is about seventy-five yards off, draw a bead on his knee and raise your gun until half way up his 'fore shoulder' and pull the trigger.[8] You will knock him down in his track every time. Don't breathe while you are drawing a bead or you will wobble off and miss."

I slipped my old rifle over the top of the cottonwood log as easily as possible until half of the six feet was on the deer's side and cocked it. But slight as the noise was, the doe heard it, or may have heard my heart thump against my ribs, but turned her big black eyes on my head. I could recall White's instructions, but in order to begin at the doe's knee, I had to tiptoe and by the time I had got to the "fore shoulder," I was seized with such severe "buck ager" that I shook all over. My gun wobbled, the log seemed to move and the doe did too. I held my breath until I felt like I was going to break a blood vessel and in desperation pointed at the bulk and blazed away. The doe sprang in the air, with her flag at half mast and whipping her hams, tore through the woods.

I raised a warhoop, as White told me that the way my deer acted was a sure sign that she was hit, and kept yelling at the boys so until they did not know whether I had caught a bear or one had caught me, but they came on the run, and as soon as Mungo smelt the blood he sat down, and pointing his nose in the air, gave a squall like the old Negro cook had caught him in the gourd of soap grease and made a lick at him with a clapboard and missed him, set out on the trail and all of us joined in the chorus. It was a short race, and soon we heard the deer bawling in a way to make our hair stand on end. When we got to them, Mungo had her by the throat and we made a finish of her with our knives. Of course they had to bloody me as it was my first deer. We were all happy enough, and though I have killed thousands of deer since, that one gave me more genuine pleasure than all the others put together.

We sent one of the boys for a horse and took our deer to camp, and then had no trouble killing a number of turkeys, and started home. Old Uncle Charlie complimented us on our kill and entertained us royally.

To give an example of what could be done in those early days, old Charlie settled on his farm and had one or two horses and a small mare colt. In the course of time he raised from her and her increase, 300 head of horses. There were no wire fences then, not even to keep off the mustangs that abounded all over the prairies to [the] Lavaca River and beyond, but in an evil hour he decided to move his family and stock to the frontier, and went to Erath County. My brother, John R. Baylor, wrote to him and advised him not to move for the Comanches would be sure to get his horses, and sure enough he had not been on his ranch a week until the Indians made a raid and took every head of horse that he had and left him afoot to commence the struggle of life over again, and Ike, the eldest son, afterwards became a member of the legislature. To such sudden changes were old Texans subjected, but they were a glorious race of heroes.

NOTES

1   Gay Hill, Washington County, not to be confused with the community of Gay Hill in Fayette County, was settled in the early 1830s and named for Thomas Gay, an early settler. Walter Prescott Webb and H. Bailey Carroll, eds., *The Handbook of Texas* (Austin: Texas State Historical Association, 1952), 1:677.

    Robert Emmett Bledsoe Baylor, uncle of John and George Wythe Baylor and one of the founders of Baylor University, was born in Kentucky on 10 May 1793. Baylor came to Texas at the age of forty-eight in 1840 and served on the Supreme Court of the Republic of Texas. For twenty years he traveled on horseback throughout the area, the *Bible* in one saddlebag and law books in the other, organizing churches and courts, administering the law by day, and preaching the gospel at night. In 1853, Judge Baylor assisted John R. Baylor in being admitted to the state bar and getting elected to represent Fayette County in the Texas House of Representatives. Austin *Texas State Gazette*, 7 May, 13, 20 August, 29 November 1853; J.R. Baylor to Dear Loo, 29 January 1852, John R. Baylor Papers, Texas State Archives; Webb and Carroll, *Handbook of Texas*, 1:124. Also, Jerry D. Thompson, *Colonel John Robert Baylor: Texas Indian Fighter and Confederate Soldier* (Hillsboro: Hill College Press, 1971), 6-7.

2   Ross Prairie is eighteen miles east of La Grange, just south of Fayetteville. John R. Baylor, twenty-four, is listed on the 1850 census as a farmer with real estate of $5,500. Emily, twenty-one, his Louisiana-born wife, and their three children, John, Keith, and Henry are also enumerated. 7th Census (1850), Fayette County, Texas, National Archives, Washington, D.C. Also, Austin *Texas State Gazette*, 6 July 1850.

3   George Kerr is not listed on the 1850 Fayette County, Texas, census. J.M. Hill, age thirty-one, a Georgia-born farmer with real estate of $3,500 is listed. 7th Census, Fayette County, Texas.

4   William Baylor, fifty-nine, a farmer with real estate of $3,000, is listed on the 1850 Fayette County census along with his wife and six children. A Jas. A. Baylor, fifty-two and insane, is enumerated in the same household. Ibid.

5   Virginia-born Charles Mullins, age fifty-eight, and a farmer with real estate of $2,300, is listed on the Fayette County census with seven children and no wife. Ibid.

6   The minie ball, a conical bullet with a hollow base, expanding when fired to fit the rifling, was named after C.E. Minie, the French inventor.

7   Buck ager is buck fever, a nervous agitation experienced by a beginning hunter when first sighting game.

8   Rising in southern Lee County, Cummins Creek flows south-eastward some thirty-seven miles through Lee, Fayette, and Colorado counties to the Colorado River just north of Columbus.

CHAPTER TWO

Parker H. French
Expedition of 1850~1851

~

THE FOLLOWING ACCOUNT OF THIS REMARKABLE EXPEDITION was given the writer by Joseph Addison Hatch, at present a citizen of Uvalde, Texas, who accompanied the party as far as El Paso.[1]

Hatch's life has been one of such stirring events that a brief sketch of him will no doubt be pleasant reading to such a cosmopolitan city as El Paso, where the descendants of John Alden, of Puritan stock—the Cavaliers, Huguenots, and Roundheads—are to be found mixing in the social swirl.

Hatch was born in Woods Hole, a suburb of Falmouth, Massachusetts, February 8, 1829. His father was a sea captain in East Indian service, commanding a vessel called the *India*, Caleb Bastow, owner. Hatch went to school in Nantucket, and then learned the carpenter's trade in New Bedford. His mother's maidens name was Phoebe Cartwright Starbuck; through her he is related to the celebrated woman minister of the Gospel, Phoebe A. Hanaford, in charge of the church of the Holy Spirit in New Haven, Connecticut, and well known in the literary world as the author of the Daughters of America and other delightful works, both in prose and verse.[2] Hatch is also related to Lucretia Mott, Maria Mitchell, the great linguist; and those who choose to trace him back, will find the great American statesman and scientist Benjamin Franklin, and even the doughty warrior William the Conqueror on his family tree.

But enough is given to interest your readers in the wild scenes he has passed through and I will give his narrative in his own quaint language:

My father, mother, sister, and myself came to Texas in the year 1849. A paternal uncle, Sylvanus Hatch, had come to Texas with Austin's first 300 families in the year 1825, and returning, brought out his family in 1829.[3] He gave such a glowing description of the new unsettled country, its wide, flower-covered prairies, beautiful rolling hills and valleys, the grassy savannahs, the immense herds of buffalo, deer, turkeys, and the streams full of fish, hollow trees full of honey—that my father finally decided to join him. Owning his own vessel, he put in everything that would be necessary in a new country, and with his family sailed for Texas, landing at Port Lavaca.

An uncle R[ufus] Hatch, an officer in the U.S.A., had also been in Texas, being after the War of 1812, stationed on the Sabine River.[4] Both of the brothers were in the Battle of New Orleans. Sylvanus was aide to Gen. Andrew Jackson, being adjutant of the Seventh Louisiana Volunteers.[5]

He had first left the parental nest enticed by glowing accounts of eternal spring and flowers, so fascinating to people born where half the year is winter, and settled in Plaquemine Parish, Louisiana, purchased a plantation and married a southern girl—that being (at that early period we had no North, no South) all that was necessary to make him a southern man. He remained with General Jackson until the close of the war, when the American volunteers defeated the best disciplined troops of England, under [Gen. Edward] Packenham. It would seem that England ought to be able to get a lesson from that battle but they had to learn it all over again in the Transvaal.

My father, after looking around, decided to locate at Chocolate Bayou, seven miles from Port Lavaca, now Calhoun County. He owned two leagues of land and Austin gave him a league of the reserved lands, where the town of Edna now stands, so he had ample domain. He resided there for years, being totally blind for fourteen years before his death—his blindness caused by taking calomel for yellows. A patient that was not bled to death then was salivated.

Being of a roving, restless disposition, as soon as the nuggets of gold were found in Sutter's Mill race, I determined to get me a good, stout canvas sack and go to the new El Dorado, fill it with hunks of gold, return, marry, settle down on a princely estate, and be happy forever—as all heroes do in novels.

About this time there appeared on the horizon a brilliant comet, of earthly mold, however, known to several sad men as Parker Hood French—I believe a relative of our brave Confederate general who made classic the name of Hood's Brigade.[6]

French had the manners of Lord Chesterfield, the genius of Richelieu, and about the luck of Napoleon—verifying the old adage, "A good beginning makes a bad ending."

He landed at Port Lavaca with as much style as Cortez did in Mexico. He had bought out old Dan Rice's busted circus outfit of chariots and gaudy animal cages, gewgaws, and his entry into Texas was calculated to captivate the youth and awe the general public. After French landed and took possession of the country he proceeded to San Antonio and began levying tribute on his subjects.

Among the first was [Bvt.] Maj. [Edwin B.] Babbitt, U.S.A. ordnance department, stationed at San Antonio—a prudent, conscientious, Christian gentleman whom the writer well knew in early days at Fort Townsend, in the Choctaw Nation.[7] French had produced some quasi-authority from the secretary of war, instructing Major Babbitt to give him any assistance in his power in fitting out his expedition to cross the Great American Desert, and assist in developing the resources of Uncle Sam's dominions on the Pacific Coast.

French had taken advantage of the great gold excitement to advertise his scheme, and his order from the secretary of war enabled him to drive up to the old Alamo of sacred memory and load up his wagons with supplies. He got about 125 muskets, buck and ball cartridges in abundance to be used by his teamsters against Indians or any other marauding bands. He had agreed to carry passengers across the plains to the gold fields of California and was to furnish transportation and bear all expenses, and each passenger was to pay him $250 gold (invariably in advance). He had converted the circus outfit into wagons, carriages, buggies, and any nondescript species of the go all that would haul (not transport) a passenger. He had bought everything that sight drafts of Burbank & Fisher of New Orleans or Howland [&] Aspinwall of New York would purchase, got 130 good mules from Burns & Taylor who lived near Victoria, giving them a sight draft on Burbank & Fisher.[8] This came back protested but French had calculated that he would be far on his way to California before Burns & Taylor could hear from the check and it would be worth a man's life to start out through this country, at that time filled with hostile Indians.

There was about four hundred men in our procession and old Dan Rice himself would have been deceived if he had seen us when the order to move forward from the military plaza was given. Only a brass band and handsomely equipped drum major would have been necessary to complete the delusion. Among the motley assembly about 200 had paid $250 gold apiece, the others were wagon makers, blacksmiths, carpenters, cooks, and teamsters, who were to work their way over if their services were needed in their various vocations.

We had gotten as far as old Fort Inge on the beautiful blue waters of the Leona [River], and camped in one of the lovely live-oak groves on its banks.[9] The men scattered about, bathing, fishing, telling camp yarns, and having a good time generally.

French had his large headquarters tent stretched, with the dining room and cook's tents near by, and was taking in with pride his circus. A dusty travel stained man rode up to his tent and though French may have his doubts as to the object of the new arrival, whom he recognized as Burns, from who he had bought his mules, his Chesterfield manners at once were brought into play.

He rushed forward and grasped Burns by the hand before he could dismount, and with the sweetest smile and most cordial manner exclaimed: "Why, Burns, my dear fellow, I am so delighted to see you, and know you have decided to go to California with me. Here, cook, get Mr. Burns a nice dinner. I know he must be tired and hungry. Here, Pedro! take this gentleman's horse, unsaddle and water him—stake him in good grass. I declare, Burns, this is an unexpected pleasure."

No doubt it was, for French had calculated with the old tubs that used to run between Port Lavaca and New Orleans and slow methods then prevailing, he would be out of reach of any of his creditors before they could hear from "his bankers."

If Burns had any idea of balancing his account with French by filling him with lead, he was completely disarmed by this cordial greeting. After dinner he then broached the subject of his drafts, saying: "Mr French, I sent your draft to Messrs. Burbank & Fisher and it came back protested, stating that you had no funds there."

"Why, Mr. Burns, that is incomprehensible. I will show you their letter to me, authorizing me to draw on them for any amount needed to equip my expedition."

Going to his trunk, sure enough he produced a letter confirming his statement and properly signed by Burbank & Fisher (or someone else). "Now, Mr. Burns, I am very much hurt and mortified by the conduct of these gentlemen, but you shall not lose anything. Here is another letter from Howland Aspinwall, the wealthiest banker in New York, and his check is just as good as you see, to draw from any amount. You will get your money by paying a small discount in San Antonio, or wait and get your gold from New York."

Burns got his draft and was as sure of his money as though he already had it in a sack at home and left camp next morning for San Antonio, and we pulled out for El Paso, or rather Ponce's ranch, Coon's, Franklin, Magoffinsville, or El Paso, which ever name pleases the reader best.

We had the usual trials and tribulations of such a mixed crowd, and for water, grass, and the thieving Indians always ready to stampede and steal our stock. On one occasion when we were camped on Devil's River, the Indians made an attempt to stampede and steal our stock, quite brilliant in conception but not carried out.

Among our men was one of Col. Jack Hays's old rangers, and once when he was to go on guard, we were sitting at the mouth of the corral, formed by our wagons always where we camped, to be ready to fight from, and also to run our mules into in case a stampede was attempted.[10] He was talking about old times in Jack Hays's service, and suddenly pointed out what he said was a single smoke of Indians, and later we saw their signal fires. He said we might look out that night for they were up to some devilment.

When time for us to turn out the mules to graze awhile came, he asked me if I wanted to go on guard with him. Of course I did—anything that promised a little excitement—so we started out to get beyond where our herd would be going down a path made by bear and other game.

He being ahead, suddenly motioned to me to lie down and began to crawl forward. We were about two hundred yards from camp. In a few moments I heard him fire and ran to him. In a moment the whole camp was in a turmoil of excitement.

The *cavallado* ran back into the corral and the men in arms. The old ranger said: "I think I've killed an Indian. I got to see him first and kept perfectly still until he crawled up close to me and I shot. But they are a mighty onsartin kind of animal and will possum until you get close to 'em and stave a dogwood switch through you. So we will approach cautiously, ready to shoot."

We found the Indian not more than thirty or forty feet from where we stood—dead. He had his bow and quiver and an infernal machine made of rawhide with gravel in a bladder attached to it to stampede the mules and was evidently waiting for them to get a little ways from the wagons and dash in between them and our camp and start them and his *compadres* would complete the job.

As soon as the stock was secured we made a search to see if he had any horse or other Indians with him. We soon found his horse tied to a tree, and he was caparisoned with a beautiful silver mounted Mexican saddle and silver mounted bridle, no doubt taken from some Mexican *caballero* they had murdered. He had a beautiful quiver full of arrows and a fine bow, an arrow strung on it ready for use. He was evidently an old stager. His body was covered with scars. On his neck was a necklace of fish bones, some of them dyed black. The old ranger said he was a Comanche and his necklace was intended to keep tally of the scalps he took, the dark ones for Mexicans and the white ones for his pale faced brothers. His band must have taken his death very seriously as they followed us up Devil's River and beyond towards Escondido Springs, trying every way to stampede our stock, but there were too many who knew all their tricks for them to succeed, except a few animals that would straggle off from the herd.[11]

We were on the old emigrant route and Nat[haniel C.] Lewis, father of the sheriff of Bexar County, and [Benjamin Franklin] Coons, were ahead of us hauling supplies for the government at El Paso.[12] We got along very well until we crossed the Pecos River and here we had quite a sad accident. One of my men, a fine young fellow named Robert Chamberlain, was killed accidently.[13] One of the sentinels came in off guard and started to set his gun against the wagon wheel when it fell, the hammer struck the tire, and it fired. A ball and three buckshot struck Chamberlain in the breast, killing him instantly. The load just passed over my head as I was sitting down.

His father, an old man, knelt over him, and his grief was pitiable. "I left a good home with plenty of everything in Vermont," he cried, "and could have been happy enough. But now in a search of gold I have lost my dear boy, my only son."

We buried the young man—a sorrowful group around the lone grave in the desert—and after placing heavy rocks on it to keep the coyotes from digging up the body, resumed our march. The old father could not be comforted and constantly upbraided himself for being avaricious, and the cause of his son's early death. He was only twenty-one, and a great favorite with every one.

The old man was heard moaning during the night but finally the sound ceased and when we went to see what was the matter his bed was empty. At daylight twelve men took his trail and after following some ten or twelve miles found him lying on his son's grave. He never recovered his mind and had to be kept under guard all the time. We left him in El Paso.

Our hardest trip was from El Muerto on the northwestern slope of the Davis Mountains to Eagle Springs.[14] It must be 60 or seventy miles, and there was no Van Horn Wells half way, or if there was, French knew nothing about it. Now opposite to it is Torbert Station on the Southern Pacific. A traveler gliding along now in a palace car can not realize what we endured on this hot, long, dusty tramp in August.

We had filled all of our barrels and canteens, but they had given out before we got over half way; for a man can get drier on those elevated plains than any place on earth. Our teams gave out entirely and we staggered into the canyon where Eagle Springs is, one at a time. Had the Apaches been there no doubt they would have killed the entire party.

Those ahead had formed around the spring with drawn pistols and the men marched by in line. The water came in the hole in the bank just about as fast as a man could dip it up with a tin cup, and each one got a cup full and passed on until all had a drink and began again in the same order. This was a good thing, for if there had been an abundance of water some of the men would have killed themselves.

Our human anaconda kept marching around in a circle drinking a cup full at a time until all were satisfied and then our poor mules and horses came in for their share. But all we could do for them was to fill some buckets and wet a big sponge and with this rinse their mouths and nostrils—a tedious job—and with their natural gifts for finding out what you want to do and not doing it, they kept us hard at work for some time.

We could not remain here long and as soon as we got everything filled with water we put out again for the Rio Grande forty more long weary miles. I had gone the day before to the peak west of the springs and left my mule at the foot of the hill. I had heard that if you wanted to get up where you would see antelope in the middle of the day you could find out where they went to water. There were immense herds in the valley and I was intensely watching them, for as we were holding the Ojo de Aguila, I thought they would be compelled to go to some other spring. But they were certainly very indifferent about water.

Casting my eyes to the northwest, however, I saw an old Indian trail that came from around the mountain and sure enough the Apaches were on the war path.

A party of them had discovered me first and were trying to cut me off from the springs. I ran down the mountain as hard as I could and mounted my mule and lit out for camp. They raised a yell and put after me and on fresh animals were gaining on me rapidly.

I made for a low scrubby tree and jumped down on the ground and kneeling, took aim with my Colt pistol at the party not more than sixty or seventy yards distance, where they stopped when I dismounted. As luck would have it I killed a horse. The Apache pulled off his rigging and started at a trot up the mountain side.

Taking advantage of the lull I put out like an old buck for a thicket on foot, my mule right at my heels and as badly scared as I was, at the yelling and clatter made behind us. When I got to the thicket of cat claw I kept down the arroyo that leads to Eagle Springs, and when the Apaches would crowd too near I would turn and fire a shot at them. I kept yelling as loud as I could and making the best time I could towards camp, and the men hearing me began yelling too and came meeting me and as soon as the Apaches heard them they wheeled and were soon out of sight. They evidently had not discovered us before and were on a scout of observation.

We left Eagle Springs for the Rio Grande and when we got nearly half way at a small sharp mountain near the road the Apaches charged from behind the hill on our train. We had a howitzer, such as the United States Army had at one time used, that they could carry on a saddle and called a "Mountain Howitzer."

French had arranged it some way on the blacksmith's forge, and it was in front and a very innocent looking instrument of death. Lieutenant Darby has rendered it famous by his ludicrous description of its being examined by army experts, and a mule that was under suspicion something was wrong when the fuse began to hum and began to kick up to the dismay of the inspectors.

Our gun answered a good purpose and turned loose at the charging Apaches, knocking over a number of horses and badly demoralizing the party. We saw no dead left on the plain—they all managed to get away some how and we were too tired and thirsty to make any effort towards following them.

Those of your readers who have followed these sketches will realize this place as 18 mile water hole, where old Victorio and his band had Gen. [Benjamin H.] Grierson and his staff hived and where that old Confederate Eli Terry, contractor in El Paso, carried Will Lambert when wounded by the Apaches, to the top of this hill on his back and the Indians shooting at him all the time.[15]

Lt. Charles Nevill of the Rangers, was also nooning here, when a carrier from me brought him with his company back to Eagle Springs when we followed the Apaches that killed old Morgan, the stage driver, and a passenger from San Antonio.[16]

The way seemed long and weary; we had very little water to start with and it soon gave out. Before we reached the mouth of Quitman Canyon our mules gave out entirely and we had to unhitch them from the wagons and drive them on the road.[17] Had our Indians stayed with us to this point they would have had a picnic. The poor mules would frequently fall down, and we would after a little rest, help them up again and they would stagger along.

If it was hot on the mesa it was hotter down in the canyon. After we passed the Apache post office, big rocks with Indian tracings, our mules must have had a smell of the river or seen the welcomed sight of the green topped cottonwoods for they broke away at such a lively gait we could not keep anywhere near them. A real Indian stampede could not have put more mettle in their heels and a cloud of dust was all we saw as they rushed toward the river.

The government had cut down a place where the road first strikes the Rio Grande so that animals could get down to water. It was, however, to the left of where the road turns to the river bank. The frantic famished animals did not look for anything but water and went over the cliff like a herd of buffalo and quite a number broke their legs or necks and we had a time of it getting them down to where they could be brought up the bank of the river. Our men were nearly as bad as the mules, and many were made deathly sick by drinking too much water. I contented myself by frequently bathing my face and head and taking a mouthful now and then.

Among my messmates was a young man named William Pepper, of South Carolina. His father was quite a prominent and wealthy man. Another was [J.] Evans and the two Chamberlains, the young one who had been killed accidentally, and his father, that we had to take care of and feed like a child.[18] There were three others in my mess, but I can't recall their names.

When we got to Eagle Springs four men on the best horses were sent on ahead by French to procure assistance from the United States government and probably the famous order of the secretary of war that had proven the talisman at San Antonio was again used. We were out of nearly all kinds of supplies, especially bread, which a person craves almost as much as the old tobacco fiend does the Virginia weed. One of the four men, who was a noted gambler, came back and brought a sack of biscuits from Ysleta with him. As soon as we heard of this rich pay streak we hurried over to his mess and tried to buy some. Young Pepper and myself went and he offered the sport a dollar a piece for half the sack, but got no bread. He finally offered $5.00 a piece for half a dozen but the sport flatly refused to give or sell a taste of them—which we put down as a mean selfish trick to be remembered.

A beef had been killed and our mess got the head and proceeded to cook it in the most approved style. Moving our fire we dug a hole, put the head in, and covered it with hot ashes and coals again. This is the sweetest way meat was ever cooked, and a dainty morsel is a fat bear's paw cooked in this way, provided a person can overcome the squeamishness it occasions from its resemblance to a darky's foot.

Along towards midnight when we thought our beef head was ripe, I went over to visit the gambler and maybe to invite him for supper. When I got there he was fast asleep and had his saddle for a pillow. The coveted sack of biscuits was under it and his head lying on one end of the saddle had tilted it up and the mouth of the sack was conveniently gaping open. I thought it a pity to disturb his slumbers, so I put my hat down carefully and filled it with biscuits and slipped back to our mess. It was one of those delicate occasions where no questions were asked about where the man came from and we feasted until the head and biscuits were gone and afterwards slept the sleep of the just and innocent until daylight.

The next morning about meal time, though aurora was smiling over the top of the mountains and the sky blue and clear, we heard thunder and lightning in the shape of "cuss words" from the gambler's mess; he was offering all we had offered him, to any who would point out the blankety blank blank that stole his biscuits promising to make a hole through them that a calf could jump through—the size of the hole and calf being represented by x, the unknown number. No one seemed to care enough about algebra to help him solve the problem, so he came straight for our camp and asked me if I knew anything about who took his bread. I was like George Washington, and couldn't bear to tell a lie, so did not answer the question, but said: "It's a pity you did not sell those biscuits to Pepper, for now you would have had the gold in your pocket." He looked at me, but seeing that I was a kid, a long ways from my guardian and armed as well, all my mess and ready for squalls, he turned and walked away. The incident was closed.

After resting a day or so we went for our wagons left at the head of Quitman Canyon and brought them all to the Rio Grande, but having to make several trips it took four or five days.

We had now lost so many animals by Indians, accidents, and starvation for water, that we had to send to El Paso and borrow enough mules to take us to that place. As the road was very heavy sand in many places we were pretty well fagged out when we arrived at El Paso. The men in the party who had become uneasy about French seeing his management was not the best, and from whom he had borrowed every dollar he could, held a caucus and decided to take possession of the train, and as they had already paid him for their passage to California they concluded they had the best claim to the transportation, and decided if they were ever to see El Dorado they must take the matter in their own hands. They elected a man named Maguire to take command, I can't recall his Christian name, and the outfit was moved up to White's Ranch, some six miles above El Paso.[19]

French had employed me at San Antonio as a carpenter and wagon maker and it was whil'st performing this duty that I had the closest call for my life on the whole expedition. When we reached San Elizario, French sent me to repair some wagons that had broken down at a little Mexican town where there was a church.[20] They were ahead of the main body of men. When I reached the lower side of the town, it was dark, and as I was alone, I stopped at a Mexican house, and asked to stay all night—just a place to sleep, did not want to eat—so they put me in a room to myself. There were no men on the place, and two or three women and a lot of children in the room adjoining. But after dark two or three Mexicans rode up and dismounted. They did not come in my room to speak to me, but I could hear them talking to the women without being able to catch what was said as I understood very little Spanish. I naturally felt a little suspicious of them. The Mexican War had not been over long enough for them to feel at all kindly to Americans.

I had a good Colt pistol and a good horse, so was prepared for any emergency. The horse I unsaddled and staked close to the door, leaving it open. In case a stranger tried to approach him I knew he would snort and wake me up.

I spread down my saddle blanket for a bed and used my saddle for a pillow, covering with another blanket. It was, fortunately for me, a bright, moonlight night.

About ten o'clock I saw the head of one of the Mexicans who peeped in as if not certain that I slept, reappear. This he repeated several times. So I put my Colt revolver by my side under the blanket, and cocked it, for I didn't fancy his movements a bit. After a while he came and stepped in softly and went close to the door and pulled a big butcher knife from a crack in the adobe wall, and slipped out again. This was some relief to me, as I thought he only wanted the knife for some purpose, and did not want to harm or disturb me. However, my nerves were too highly wrought up for me to sleep and I lay wide awake.

About midnight his bushy head again darkened the door and he stepped towards my pallet. I saw him plainly with the big knife. I was lying with my feet towards the door, and as soon as he came towards me I suddenly covered him with my pistol and he sprang for the door and tried to slam it, when I fired.

I then ran to the door and saw another Mexican trying to untie my horse. I fired one shot at him and two more as he ran. The women had come out and were yelling and screaming at the top of their voices. It did not take me long to saddle up and pull out from there, and went on until I found the wagons and drivers camped.

I never knew what a narrow escape I had made until some time afterwards when Maj. [William H.] Emory, who made the boundary survey between Mexico and the United States, camped below this same ranch. A young man of his party named [Edward C.] Clark[e], a son of Senator Clark[e], of Rhode Island, and another young man whose name has escaped me were both murdered at this same ranch and their bodies concealed.[21] Some time afterwards one of the boundary commission saw a Mexican mounted on young Clark[e]'s horse, still using his saddle and bridle, and arrested and took him to the camp. He was questioned about his ownership, and after trying to lie out of it, finally gave in and told where the arms, clothing and outfit of the murdered men were concealed, and gave the names of their murderers. They were arrested and hanged to the cottonwood trees in the *acequia*, and one of them had a bullet hole through his arm. He said it was done by an American who stayed at his ranch one night.

Whil'st at White's Ranch, Maguire sent me to repair some wagons that had broken down between El Paso and our camp, where the road was awfully rough and rocky, and I had several men under me. I made several trips to El Paso for such articles as I needed in making the repairs, and

learned that Capt. [Henry S.] Skillman, an old frontiersman, who was afterwards killed by Capt. [Albert H.] French, of the U.S.A., during the Confederate War, had come in and brought an order to Maj. [Jefferson] Van Horn[e]
to take possession of the train and arrest French.[22]

Some of the other men heard the same report and one overheard an officer say he was very, very sorry to have to execute such an order as the men of
the expedition would be left in El Paso without transportation of any kind
and many of them without any money.

As soon as I reported to Maguire what I had heard, he told me to take all
the nuts off the wagon wheels and conceal them, and as soon as the other
men confirmed my account he called all the expedition together, and getting
up on a wagon stated the case to them saying: "Whatever we are going to do
must be done at once, or we will be left afoot, and lose our money paid
French also. We give up the train to Major Van Horn[e], or cross into Mexico
and trust to the officials there."

On a vote it was decided to cross the river as that would put an end to
Van Horn[e]'s authority, and we might make some better conditions with the
jefe of El Paso del Norte. So all was bustle in camp. The nuts were replaced
and we started back down the river, keeping on the east bank close to the
river.

When we got to the upper end of the settlement we passed noiselessly
down below some three miles to a crossing and stopped on an island in the
middle of the stream. The Mexicans had heard us, though it was after midnight when we passed El Paso, and a body of cavalry had gone down the
river keeping parallel to our train, and were now drawn up in battle array on
the west bank. Some 200 were opposite us, so we were so to speak, between
the "devil and the deep sea."

Our newly elected leader, however, proved himself equal to the occasion,
and after a consultation with the Mexican commander, and the *jefe político*,
and some solid arguments, in gold, no doubt, we were permitted to cross to
the land of God and liberty, and encamped on the bank of the Rio Bravo del
Norte, where the Santa Fe Expedition had such a tough time, but for the
kind-hearted old Mexican priest, Padre [Ramón] Ortiz, would have fared
worse.[23]

There was sympathy for our commander too. Maguire was an Irishman
and a strict and devout member of the Catholic Church, and at that time the
priest had as much power as either the civil or military power in Mexico. I
was ahead of the procession as we crossed into Mexico, driving one of Dan
Rice's haughty chariots that we had dubbed the "Jack Hays" in honor of the
leading star among the old Texas Rangers.

I expect Major Van Horn[e] was glad to be rid of a very disagreeable duty.

Our being allowed to cross was quite a windfall to the Mexicans for at that time nearly all the merchandise used in Chihuahua and even further south, was hauled across the plains from St. Joseph, Missouri, and wagons were almost worth their weight in silver.

All the wagons were sold to the Mexicans for cash, and all the mules and horses were appraised and their price marked on their shoulders with a piece of chalk. Each man give his account and it was scaled to suit what he was entitled to in pro rata division. So a man with twenty dollars took a mule marked twenty dollars, a very simple method of bookkeeping and balancing accounts.

Everything that belonged to French was sold, and he had a general assortment—tents, harness, blacksmith's and carpenter's tools, gutta-percha, pontoons for crossing steams, etc.[24]

I got for my share a mule valued at $40 and worth about $20 and I sold him for that before some one could steal him. The amount we got was about twenty percent of what French owed us. I stayed in Paso del Norte until my cash amounted to $50, not knowing exactly what Uncle Sam might consider my status to be, but as I had trusted to the mercy of the Mexicans in crossing into Mexico I determined to go back to Texas soil again.

I had got to be pretty ragged, barefooted and bareheaded. A kind hearted Mexican I got acquainted with gave me a hat and a pair of shoes, second hand and not a good fit, but improved my looks and feelings. I went to the post, where as I stated Major Van Horn[e] was commanding and Capt. [Andrew W.] Bowman, assistant quartermaster.[25] There were two companies of dragoons and two companies of infantry.

It has been a long time and I can only remember now among the officers stationed there Lt. [John Darragh] Wilkins, of an infantry company, and Lt. [William H.] Woods of the cavalry.[26] Lt. Jerome [Napoleon] Bonaparte was also there in 1851.[27] I had remained in Paso del Norte hoping to find a way to get to California. The members had split up into small parties, some going on, and some remaining with French.

I went straight to Captain Bowman's office, and not finding him went to his quarters and found him engaged in a sociable game of cards with some of the officers, and knocked at the door; he came out and asked what I wanted. I stated my condition and told him I was a carpenter and wanted work. He asked me where I had learned my trade. I answered in Bedford, Massachusetts, and he looked me over and seeing I was quite a kid, said: "I don't know if I need another man, but come to my office in the morning and I'll let you know."

I was on time and my heart in my mouth, 25¢ being my cash balance. He wrote on a slip and said: "Report to Quartermaster Sergeant Billy Williams and tell him to take you to Mr. Cary, the foreman of the shops, and tell him to put you to work." No one but a tramp in the same condition can tell how relieved I felt.

After I had been working in the shops for some time Lieut. Wilkins' little girl, a sweet child about nine years old, died and he came into the shop to see Cary about making a coffin. Cary was from a good Maryland family, well educated and very gentlemanly, but unfortunately a drunkard. He was an unusually handsome man and great favorite on account of his pleasant manners, but when he got a taste of whisky he went on a regular toot for weeks at a time.

Lieutenant Wilkins, seeing Gary was drinking, came to my bench and asked me if I could make a coffin. "I think so, sir, if you wish I will try." All right, you can go ahead.

So I hunted up some plank that had been sawed with a whip saw out of a large pear tree, and made a handsome coffin, polishing it with wax. He went to Paso del Norte and got silver mountings, and it was greatly admired by the officers. The lieutenant, and his wife especially so, and ever after took a kindly interest in me, and eventually got me promoted.

I had received $45 per month and rations. One pay day I was quite astonished, when in addition to my pay, I got a sealed envelope. I was afraid it was an order firing me, but was agreeably surprised to find it an order to take charge of the shops as foreman in Cary's place, and my new pay would be $75 per month, rations and quarters.

Not long after that I was ordered by Major Van Horn[e] to inspect quite a number of government wagons that were to be condemned, and he charged me not to give up a single one that could possibly be repaired. There were some 300 of them. Lieutenant Woods, on the contrary, told me to condemn as many of them as possible. I learned afterwards to go "snooks" in the business, and organize a train to haul government supplies.

Captain Bowman had gone to Chihuahua on business, and Woods was acting quartermaster until his return. I went through the lot and only found three beyond repair and so reported to Major Van Horn[e]. Lieutenant Woods was perfectly furious, for I had gained his ill will any how. He ordered me to make a handsome bird cage for his *señorita* in Paso del Norte, and Major Van Horn[e], who frequently came into the shops, saw it, and asked who it was for, and when I told him, he said: "did you make it during work hours of public material?" I answered, "Yes, sir." "Then you make out a bill for your time and material and the lieutenant will have to pay for it." So when this new matter came up, he threatened to make me pack a thirty pound log around a ring. This aroused my fighting blood at once, and I said, "If you try it you'll never make another man pack a log." He would have liked no doubt, to have discharged me, but Captain Bowman returned and on inquiring into the matter, reported Lieutenant Woods and he was court martialed in Santa Fe and suspended for a year without pay. At that time it was not very healthy for an officer to try the same punishment on a citizen that soldiers were subject to and several tragedies were the results of harsh treatment.

Once on the trip from Santa Fe to El Paso a heavy rain came up and one of the wagons got bogged down in a mud hole and the mules could not get it out. An officer came up, began cursing the teamster, and finally unhitched his sabre and struck him over the head with the flat side of the scabbard. The man stepped back to the front of his wagon, got his musket since all of the teamsters carried guns on account of the Indians—and shot him dead, and skipped for Mexico as he had a horse tied behind his wagon.

NOTES

1 In 1900, Hatch was living with his son and daughter-in-law in the Nueces Canyon, north-west of Uvalde. Hatch was a close neighbor of Sidney Baylor, son of John R. Baylor and George W. Baylor's nephew. The Massachusetts—born sixty-seven-year-old Hatch is listed as a carpenter in the 12th census, Uvalde County, Texas.

2 Phoebe Ann Coffin Hanaford, Universalist minister, abolitionist, and temperance advocate, was author of popular books on Abraham Lincoln and George Peabody. Frank Monaghan, "Phoebe Ann Coffin Hanaford," *Dictionary of American Biography* (New York: Charles Scribners' Sons, 1960), 4:216-17.

3 A Sylvanus Hatch is not listed among the "Old Three Hundred." Lester G. Bugbee, "The Old Three Hundred," *The Quarterly* of the Texas State Historical Association 1 (October 1897): 108-17.

4 Rufus Hatch served as a first lieutenant in the 11th Infantry during the War of 1812. Records indicated that he resigned on 10 August 1813. Francis B. Heitman, *Historical Register and Dictionary of the United States Army from Its Organization, September 19, 1789, to March 2, 1903* (Urbana: University of Illinois Press, 1965), 1:511.

5 Heitman, *Historical Register,* does not list a Sylvanus Hatch.

6 Sketches of French can be found in Kenneth M. Johnson's introduction to Edward McGowan, *The Strange Eventful History of Parker H. French* (Los Angeles: Glen Dawson, 1958), iii-v, and in M. Baldridge, *A Reminiscence of the Parker H. French Expedition through Texas & Mexico to California in the Spring of 1850,* ed. John B. Goodman III (Los Angeles: Privately printed, 1959). Also, William Miles, *Journal of Sufferings and Hardships of Capt. Parker H. French's Overland Expedition to California in 1850* (Fairfield, Wash.: Ye Galleon Press, 1970); Ben E. Pingenot, "The Great Wagon Train Expedition of 1850," *Southwestern Historical Quarterly* 98 (October 1994): 183-225. After the failure of his "California Expedition," French

practiced law at San Luis Obispo and at San Jose where he served as district attorney of Santa Clara County. In 1854 he was elected to the California State Assembly. A year later he became involved in William Walker's Nicaraguan venture; although distrustful of French, Walker appointed him minister to the United States. The State Department refused, however, to receive him or examine his credentials. Proclaiming himself the "Honorable Parker H. French, Minister Plenipotentiary and Envoy Extraordinary from the Republic of Nicaragua to the United States," he retired to New York where he resided in luxury for some time. Returning to Nicaragua, he was summarily dismissed by Walker, whereupon French returned to the United States to lecture on Central America before returning to California where he published a newspaper, first at Sacramento and then at San Francisco. In November 1861, the one-armed French was arrested in Connecticut and charged with fitting out a privateer for Confederate service. Released without trial in February 1862, he served as a sutler in the Union Army. French later appears in Philadelphia and St. Louis. The place and date of his death have yet to be ascertained. Another sketch, partly based on Baylor's articles, can be found in Rex W. Strickland, *Six Who Came to El Paso: Pioneers of the 1840's* (El Paso: Texas Western Press, 1963), 19-26.

7 The Connecticut-born Babbitt was a quartermaster in the 3d Infantry. Babbitt was breveted a brigadier general in the Union Army in March 1865 for faithful and meritorious service. He died on 10 December 1881. Heitman, *Historical Register*, 1:177-78.

8 William H. Aspinwall and Gardiner Greene Howland headed a shipping empire that stretched into Latin America and Europe. Using clipper ships and, by 1850, steamers, the firm held several mail contracts, including those from New York to New Orleans and Panama to California and Oregon. Aspinwall also financed the building of the Panama Railroad in the years between 1851 and 1855. Duncan S. Somervell, *The Aspinwall Empire* (Mystic, Connecticut: Mystic Seaport Museum, 1983), 46.

9 Established on 13 March 1849 on the left bank of the Leona River near Uvalde, Fort Inge helped to guard the San Antonio-El Paso Road, also known as the Lower Military Road. J.K.F. Mansfield to Lorenzo Thomas, 8 October 1860, Letters Received, Adjutant General's Office, Record Group 94, National Archives. Hereafter referred to as LR, AGO, RG 94, NA. Also, Thomas Tyres Smith, *Fort Inge: Sharps, Spurs, and Sabers on the Texas Frontier, 1849-1869* (Austin: Eakin Press, 1993) and Robert Wooster, *Soldiers, Sutlers, and Settlers: Garrison Life on the Texas Frontier* (College Station: Texas A&M University Press, 1987), 8-10.

10 According to Michael Baldridge, French hired four Texas Rangers as interpreters and guides. "These Rangers were a peculiar people and led a wild life," Baldridge wrote. "It seemed as if pistols and Bowie knives had been their toys and playthings in childhood, and they knew how to use them." Baldridge, *A Reminiscence*, 11-13.

11 Nineteen miles east of Fort Stockton, Escondido consisted of an upper (Tunas), middle, and lower springs, each about ten feet across. The lower spring was the first water travelers found west of the Pecos River. All three springs were favorite Comanche and Apache camping sites. Wayne R. Austerman, *Sharps Rifles and Spanish Mules: The San Antonio-El Paso Mail, 1851-1881* (College Station: Texas A&M University Press, 1985), 40.

12 Bald-headed Nathaniel C. Lewis was born at Falmouth, Massachusetts, on 11 June 1806. According to family legend, Lewis ran away from home and went to sea at an early age then came in 1830 to Texas where he became a merchant at Indianola. He was in the army of the Republic of Texas in 1839-1840, and represented Bexar County in the Texas House of Representatives. Lewis came to work for Ben Coons as a wagon master and eventually

opened a store on San Antonio's Main Plaza. At the same time he acquired a large cattle herd and by the 1850s was carrying on an extensive freighting business between San Antonio and El Paso. Nathaniel Lewis, Jr., sheriff of Bexar County, was Lewis's son by his second wife, Mary Fannie Liffering. Ben E. Pingenot, "Journal of a Wagon Train Expedition from Fort Inge to El Paso del Norte in 1850," *Military History of the West*, 25 (Spring 1995): 82; Roy L. Swift, *Three Roads to Chihuahua: The Great Wagon Roads that Opened the Southwest, 1823-1883* (Austin: Eakin Press, 1988), 110; and Frederick C. Chabot, *With the Makers of San Antonio* (San Antonio: Artes Graficas, 1987), 327-30.

In June 1849, the St. Louis-born Coons, a Santa Fe trader, built a store on land at El Paso purchased from Juan María Ponce de León. He later constructed a tavern and ran a ferry on the Rio Grande. Coons became involved in the San Antonio-El Paso trade and in 1852 drove some 11,000 head of sheep from Chihuahua to California. Strickland, *Six Who Came to El Paso*, 15-19. Also, Pingenot, "The Great Wagon Train Expedition," 186-225.

13 In recalling this incident, Baldridge identifies the guard as Caleb Thurston. Baldridge, *A Reminiscence,* 12-13. William Miles wrote of Chamberlain's death: "But alas! in an unlucky moment he received the charge of a gun in his stomach. He fell, and all he uttered was *Oh! Oh!* In ten minutes he was a corpse." Miles, *Sufferings and Hardships*, 15.

14 Dead Man's Hole, or El Muerto, was a spring at the base of foreboding El Muerto Mountain, about thirty-two miles west of Fort Davis and about thirteen miles northeast of Valentine. A stop on the San Antonio-El Paso stage and mail route, it was raided a number of times by Mescalero Apaches in the 1850s.

Twenty miles west of Van Horn's Wells, thirty-one miles from the Rio Grande, and eighteen miles southeast of Sierra Blanca, Eagle Springs or Ojos del Aguila, was another watering hole and stage stop on the route from San Antonio to El Paso. Roscoe P. and Margaret B. Conkling, *The Butterfield Overland Mail, 1857-1869* (Glendale: Arthur H. Clark Co., 1947), 2:36-37, 311-33. For a description of Eagle Springs in 1854, see William H. Emory, *Report on the United States and Mexican Boundary Survey, Made Under the Direction of the Secretary of the Interior* (Washington: Cornelius Wendell, 1857), 1, pt. 2:5.

15 See Ch. 1, Sec. III.

16 See Ch. 8, Sec. III.

17 Quitman Canyon or Cañon de los Lementos, is a passage through the rugged and arid 6,000-foot Quitman Mountains, eight miles southwest of modern Sierra Blanca and six miles southeast of Fort Quitman on the Rio Grande.

18 Besides Robert Chamberlain, who was killed accidentally, four other Chamberlains, Cromwell, H.H., Griffin, and T.B., are listed in the French party. Miles, *Sufferings and Hardships,* 12-13.

19 In 1848, T. Frank White established a trading post at Frontera, some six miles upriver from El Paso del Norte. Here White built a customhouse and collected duties on merchandise and livestock coming from Mexico. W.H. Timmons, *El Paso: A Borderlands History* (El Paso: Texas Western Press, 1990), 105-8; and Leon C. Metz, *Desert Army: Fort Bliss on the Texas Border* (El Paso: Mangan Books, 1988), 21.

20 At the time, San Elizario, the largest community on the United States side of the river, was the county seat of newly created El Paso County. C.L. Sonnichsen, *Pass of the North: Four Centuries on the Rio Grande* (El Paso: Texas Western Press, 1968), 94-97.

21 Hatch has the boundary survey under John Russell Bartlett confused with that of William H. Emory. Edward C. Clarke was stabbed to death at a San Elizario fandango. A jury of six Americans and six Mexicans convicted William Craig, Marcus Butler, and John Wade

of the crime and all three were hanged in the town plaza. A fourth man, Alexander Young, escaped but was caught and also hanged. John Russell Bartlett, *Personal Narrative of Explorations and Incidents in Texas, Mexico, California, Sonora, and Chihuahua Connected with the United States and Mexican Boundary Commissions during the Years 1850-1853* (New York: D. Appleton Co., 1854), 1:160-61. Also, Sonnichsen, *Pass of the North,* 137-38.

22 With 257 soldiers of the 3d Infantry, a train of 275 wagons, and 2,500 head of livestock, Major Van Horne arrived to establish "The Post Opposite El Paso del Norte," the first week of September 1849. Van Horne commanded the post until he was relieved by Maj. Electus Backus on 24 June 1851. Backus was replaced by Maj. Gouveneur Morris on 14 August 1851. Post Returns, El Paso, Texas, AGO, RG 393, NA; Metz, *Desert Army,* 26. Skillman and two of his men were killed by Captain French and twenty-five men of Company A, 1st California Cavalry, at Spencer's Ranch near Presidio del Norte shortly after midnight, 14 April 1864. Jerry Thompson, "Drama in the Desert: The Hunt for Henry Skillman in the Trans-Pecos, 1862-1864," *Password* 38 (Fall 1992): 107-26.

23 Padre Ortiz is best remembered for his kind treatment of the Texan Santa Fe prisoners in 1841. Ortiz had shirts and underwear made, meals cooked, and water heated for baths for the men. During the Mexican-American War, however, Col. Alexander Doniphan took Ortiz hostage and forced the priest to accompany his army in the invasion of Chihuahua. "Until his death in 1896, Ortiz commanded the love and respect of everyone on both sides of the International Boundary," C.L. Sonnichsen wrote. Sonnichsen, *Pass of the North*, 108-9, 118.

24 The breakup of the French Expedition is described in some detail in Baldridge, *A Reminiscence,* 24-25.

25 Brevet Captain Bowman, an 1841 West Point graduate from Pennsylvania, was regimental quartermaster of the 3d Infantry. He served as an infantry colonel during the Civil War and died in 1869. Heitman, *Historical Register*, 1:234; Post Returns, El Paso, Texas, October 1849 to August 1851, AGO, RG 393, NA. For Bowman's account of his trek to El Paso, see: "Report of Regimental Quartermaster, Capt. A.W. Bowman, 3rd Infantry," House Exec. Doc. 2, 32d Cong., 1st Sess., 1851 (Serial 634), 250.

26 Brevet First Lieutenant Wilkins, Company C, 3d Infantry, was stationed at San Elizario from December 1849 to September 1850. Wilkins was an 1846 graduate of West Point. Second Lieutenant Woods, an 1852 West Point graduate, was post adjutant at Fort Bliss. Wilkins served as a major in the infantry in the Union Army during the Civil War and died in 1900. Woods rose to the rank of brigadier general of volunteers in the Union Army during the war and died in 1885. Post Returns, El Paso, Texas, October 1849 to August 1851, AGO, RG 393, NA; and Heitman, *Historical Register*, 1:1036, 1058.

27 Bonaparte, a great-nephew of Napoleon I and an 1852 West Point graduate, was a lieutenant in the Mounted Rifles. Lieutenant Bonaparte's grandfather, King Jerome of Spain, had moved to Baltimore, Maryland, where the grandson was born. In 1854, Lieutenant Bonaparte went to France where he was commissioned a colonel in the army of Napoleon III. He fought in Algeria, Italy, the Crimean War, and in the Franco-Prussian War before returning to the United States. He died in Massachusetts in 1893. Smith, *Fort Inge*, 62-63.

CHAPTER THREE

El Paso Del Norte

in 1850

~

ANOTHER INCIDENT OF THE TIMES, showing how wild and woolly El Paso and her twin sister, Paso del Norte was, was a characteristic fandango given in the latter town by some of the citizens.[1] It was on the arrival of a train from St. Joseph, Missouri, via Santa Fe, with merchandise for Chihuahua and even for towns far west of that ancient and historic city, though Chihuahua was generally the distributing point for all the vast region beyond, now thrown open to the world, by the Mexican Central Railroad under the wise and progressive administration of President [Porforio] Díaz who brought order out of chaos, and placed Mexico in the front ranks of the nations of the world. The coming of these trains was always looked forward to eagerly by all classes in Paso del Norte, for they carried generally a conglomeration of humanity, from the reckless gambler to the restless Yankee in search of wealth, saint and sinner alike, and money was turned loose with a lavish hand, gathered and kept by the prudent, and thrown into the air by the thoughtless again, but to return to Hatch.

Among those [in El Paso] at that early day I can recall Don Santiago Magoffin; Nichols, one of Jack Hays's old Texas rangers, who remained with French until they got to Mazatlán and then joined Walker's filibusters and went to Nicaragua and died there; two Texans also, Fred and William Pierpont, from Port Lavaca, Texas.[2] Fred was a clerk in the quartermaster's department and married a Mexican lady in Doña Ana. He was bitten by a little pet dog and died from hydrophobia. Will Pierpont went on to California, [while] Fred kept an overland stage stand below San Elizario. Their father was an old Texan and owned a ranch at the mouth of the Lavaca River.

After I was put in charge of the carpenters, I had a cook named Martin, a good cook and good man, but like so many of the men who drifted out to that wild country, addicted to drinking and gambling, utterly useless and unreliable after they got one drink. I missed Martin one evening and heard that he had been staggering down towards the ferry boat between the two towns.

A good cook was an item, so knowing that the big Santa Fe train had arrived in Paso del Norte, and my cook had a splendid chance to get a knife stuck in his ribs before dawn, I hastened after him with the hopes of overhauling him before he got to the ferry.

Martin had already crossed and I made straight for the place where the fandango was to be held, to try and find Martin and get him across the river again before dark. There were about one hundred wagons in the train and probably one hundred and fifty men—teamsters, guards, cooks, gamblers, speculators, and all the riff raff gathered on such occasions. I passed through the hall where dancing had commenced and noticed a number of the government employees and a good sprinkling of Uncle Sam's boys in blue, bent on having a good time, which, of course, meant dancing and drinking with the class of women generally found—good, bad, and indifferent—(the good leaving early) and winding up with a general row.

Martin had wobbled through the dance room and gotten to the court yard, and I found his heels sticking out of a Mexican adobe oven, such as they used for cooking bread, roasting meat and fowls, and baking fruits. I doubt if any better way was ever invented. Martin was peacefully sawing gourds, and beyond locomotion, and in a bomb proof of the best kind, so I began to think of myself, as I had not brought my revolver, not expecting to cross the Rio Bravo.

Going back into where the dancing was going on it was apparent that a storm was brewing. The trainmen and soldiers and government employees were monopolizing the pretty señoritas, and the Dons were glowering at them, their black eyes emitting sparks like summer sheet lightning, dim and noiseless at first, but it soon broke forth with a vivid flash of lighting and a roar.

The women ran to one end of the room (where I happened to be), cowering down to escape the bullets now flying fast and faster. The sharp crack of the revolvers and yells of angry combatants must have been miniature pandemonium with a Pandora's box thrown in. It was impossible to get to the only door leading to the street, there the fight being hottest, and I was compelled to be a spectator.

I saw one great tall American knock down a Mexican policeman with his revolver that he had emptied, and then seize the policeman's sabre and begin slashing right and left.

It was getting too warm for me, so I grabbed the wooden sticks in the window and with a frantic strength soon tore out enough to crawl through and drop out on the street, just as the cry of "*gendarmes*" was raised. I was on my feet in an instant, and sprinting away like a jack rabbit. Three of the lancers seeing the speed I was developing concluded I must have murdered some one and was the principal culprit, and came clattering after me, and no doubt would have spitted me, but a friendly adobe wall around a vineyard offered a barrier to them. I just flew on top and tumbled over inside and ran down towards the river, they keeping parallel with me, but could only see me when I stood up straight and made such a break for liberty that they pushed ahead, I stooped down and dodged into the vineyard hiding under a large grape vine, and curling up into the smallest space possible. They ran to the lower side of the vineyard to cut me off from the ferry.

The fight in the fandango room was raging, but gradually grew quiet as the "*gendarmes*" arrested all parties that had not given "leg bail" as I did, and I again started back to the wall to make for the ferry. The three lancers, however, were on the watch, two coming back to look for me, and one remaining at the ferry. As bad luck would have it these two saw me and a foot race was on.

Knowing pretty well from hearsay that board in the Mexican jail was no picnic, I had no idea of surrendering until knock down arguments were used. I put on a speed that made their Mexican ponies hustle, went over the eastern wall of the vineyard like a deer and broke for the ferry. But I heard them yell to their *compadre* and I made for the willows and small cottonwood trees on the bank of the river, and although the river was pretty full and decidedly cold, I followed the example of the bull frog from Yank-a-tank, and plunged into the turbid stream, dived as far as I could, and struck out boldly for Texas soil. I reached the bank pretty well tired out, dirty and chilled to the bone, cursing Martin and cooks in general and fandangos in particular. I arrived at the quarters of the post and there I met a new danger.

The sentinel, a German, hearing all the shooting and yelling, concluded that war was declared and the battle on, and I was the advance of the enemy. He halted me and demanded the countersign, which I didn't have, or he would shoot, cocking his musket with an ominous click to suit action to words. I told him who I was and his greeting was: "Vas dot you, Joe?" "Yes call the sergeant of de guard," soon brought that officer, no doubt also anxious to get some tidings from the battle. I explained to him the condition of affairs and told him to let Captain Bowman know, that there were quite a number of United States soldiers over there drinking and the row was a very serious one.

The captain came to my room and asked for particulars, and as soon as I gave him my report he took a file of soldiers at once and started for Paso del

Norte. There was no such ceremonious program then as now about crossing the line, and the captain made a quick march for the fandango room, and on parley with the Mexican officers nothing redder than "*vino dulce*" was shed, and all the soldiers and government employees were turned over to him and marched back under guard to sober off in the guard house. After the smoke of battle had cleared away it was found that two Americans and seven Mexicans were killed and quite a large number wounded. This was a fair sample of what was considered as having a glorious time.

Among the officers at the post Lt. Jerome Bonaparte was the favorite with soldiers and citizens. Shortly after this, Capt. [Samuel Gibbs] French of the U.S. Army left El Paso for San Antonio with quite a train, and I decided to return to my home.[3] We left El Paso in March 1852, and everything went along smoothly until we had passed the El Muerto Spring, and were encamped in a pretty valley where there are a good many liveoak trees, at the foot of the Davis Mountains.[4]

There were about one hundred wagons in the train all belonging to the U.S. Government and a company of dragoons as escort. There were four carpenters along and each one had twenty-five wagons to keep in repair. Among the teamsters of my twenty-five, was an old man of some fifty years of age named Davis, who belonged to my mess. When we drove into camp our cook, a young man about twenty-one years old, named Rowland Sawyer, spoke to Davis and said, "Davis, if I'll help you unhitch your mules won't you help me cook supper?" "Why of course," said Davis, and they began to unharness and then the trouble began. The lead mule didn't know Sawyer and began to cut up, and Sawyer began kicking him in the ribs. Old Davis who was very fond of his team, and kept them in order, said, "Look here, Sawyer, I don't kick and abuse my mules and don't intend that you or anybody else shall." Sawyer stood and never said a word but whipped out a big Bowie knife and ran at Davis and stabbed him through the heart.

I had heard the row and was sitting up on the front of the wagon and jumped and grabbed a stretcher to try and stop Sawyer, but was too late. Sawyer stood a moment as if dazed, looking at his victim as the blood spurted from his breast and said, "Boys, I've killed my best friend, and ought to be hung for it."

I said, "I think so too, boys, and if you'll help me, we'll hang him right now before he changes his mind."

Sawyer, although a kid, was quite a desperado, and had killed three white men, and boasted that he had never counted the Mexicans.

Our mess all being of one mind, we got a rope and the question was asked who could tie a hangman's knot. I answered, "I can," and got a piece of stout new rope and fixed it all right, but it did not work smoothly and one of the men went to the wagon to get a bar of soap to put on it.

When we got ready and were about to gratify Sawyer's desire, up rode Captain French with several officers and his escort who had been hunting for deer and antelope on the roadside, and on learning our business put a stop to it, and put Sawyer under arrest. It was a pity for we would have saved Judge Lynch from having hung him afterwards. But the ways of providence are mysterious. Among those who came up with Captain French was—[William A.] Meacham, a West Pointer, but not in the service at that time.[5] He is living on the Leona [River] near Uvalde now.

Captain French sent Sawyer back to San Elizario or Ysleta, where a company of soldiers was stationed. Sawyer who had $500 in gold with him, managed to bribe a sentinel, and speaking Spanish fluently and being a first class monte dealer, he had no trouble once outside in getting assistance from the Mexicans.

He got a good outfit and passed us on the road and drove into San Antonio ahead of us. Here in violent passion he killed his grandfather, an old man named Weeks.

The state offered $500 and the citizens $1,000 for him dead or alive, with strong preference for him dead. Some time afterwards I was in a saloon in Lavaca playing billiards with Joseph Sanders, when a man came in, passing by me, and going to a stove in a back room. Although I had only a hasty view of his face (he had his hat pulled down as far as he could get it) I recognized my old mess mate, Sawyer, and whispered to my partner, "There is a fellow that has $1,500 offered for him dead or alive."

Going into the back room Sawyer sat down by the stove and I got a good look at him so that no mistake could be made. It was raining and a cold norther was blowing, so I felt pretty sure he would remain by the stove as it was late at night and pitch dark.

It so happened that the owner of the saloon, a Mr. Pendleton, was also sheriff, so we stepped up to the bar and told him what was up. He said, "Why we will just take him in out of the wet." He handed each of us a revolver and took a double-barreled shotgun that was always behind the counter, loaded with blue whistlers in case of need, and went out a side door to the back of the room where Sawyer was and the only door except the one we were to go in.

I told my companion that Sawyer was quick and gritty. My friend was made of good stuff, too. He joined the U.S. Army afterwards and was killed at Chickamauga. We gave the sheriff time to get around and then both stepped to the door, our pistols drawn and cocked. The minute Sawyer flashed his eye on me he sprang to his feet and in a second went crash[ing] through a window on the end of the room and around the corner out of the sheriff's reach. "It won't do to go through that door, if someone ain't outside guarding it, I would get it in the back," [I thought]. The sheriff ran around when he heard the crash and turned loose at the noise of his retreating footsteps as [Sawyer] tore off through the mud and water.

The whole town was aroused when they learned who he was, and he made for a large Chihuahua train of Mexicans that had come to the post for goods, and although the train was surrounded he managed to escape. The next we heard of him he had committed some outrage on Little River, near where Cameron now stands, and a neck tie party was organized by Judge Lynch and Sawyer was the principal performer. So he died with his boots on.

NOTES

1   The recollections of Joseph Addison Hatch as told to Baylor.
2   Kentucky-born James Wiley Magoffin was a successful Santa Fe-Chihuahua trader who was appointed special agent to Gen. Stephen W. Kearny during the Mexican-American War. After the war, Magoffin established a settlement, Magoffinsville, on the north bank of the river. Besides Magoffin's home, the village included warehouses, stores, and other buildings, all protected by a substantial adobe wall. Strickland, *Six Who Came to El Paso,* 12-14; W.H. Timmons, "American El Paso: The Formative Years, 1848-1854," *Southwestern Historical Quarterly* 87 (July 1983), 1-36. Magoffin's wife, Susan Shelby Magoffin, kept a journal of the trek from Missouri to El Paso del Norte: *Down the Santa Fe Trail and into Mexico,* ed. Stella M. Drumm (Lincoln: University of Nebraska Books, 1982). For Magoffin's arrival in Texas, see Chapter 12, this section.
    Fred and William Pierpont are probably the sons of William Pierpont, a Connecticut Yankee who settled in southern DeWitt County at the time of the Texas Revolution. His home, post office, and stables became known as Pierpont Place. Carroll and Webb, *Handbook of Texas,* 2:376.
3   With eighty men of the 1st Infantry, French led 150 wagons from San Antonio to El Paso in the summer of 1851. An 1843 West Point graduate, French resigned his commission in May 1856 and retired to Mississippi to oversee a plantation he had acquired by marriage. During the Civil War, he became a brigadier general in the Confederate Army of Tennessee. He died at the age of ninety-two in 1910. Pingenot, "Great Wagon Train Expedition," 185. Also, Ezra J. Warner, *Generals in Gray* (Baton Rouge: Louisiana State University Press, 1959), 93-94.
4   Groves of live oaks can be found in a few of the canyons along State Highway 166, which roughly follows the San Antonio-El Paso Road for eighteen miles west of Fort Davis. Hatch is probably referring to Skillman's Grove, named after Henry Skillman and now the site of the annual Bloys Camp Meeting.
5   Meacham was born in December 1826 in North Carolina. The 1880 and 1900 Uvalde County censuses list him as a stockraiser. Heitman, however, does not list him as a West Point graduate. 10th and 12th Census, Uvalde County, Texas.

CHAPTER FOUR

Fight at Corralitos

THE FOLLOWING INTERESTING ACCOUNT of the Parker H. French expedition, was given to me by my nephew Maj. Jos[eph] Dawson, who was only about twenty years old at the time.[1] The major is well known on the western frontier, especially by the old antebellum army officers, and owners of the trains on the old emigrant route from San Antonio to El Paso. The major was acting quartermaster for Gen. [William J.] Hardee's division, C.A.S., at Shiloh and has seen much service in the frontier at the time that Skillman, Big Foot Wallace, and others made themselves famous. The major is hale and hearty at over seventy, and engaged in shipping timbers for mines in Mexico, from Uvalde.

After the men took possession of French's train he crossed over into Paso del Norte, no doubt taking the same view that the main body of men did, that Mexico was a safer place for him than Uncle Sam's dominion—and the Mexico of that day was a very different thing from the orderly well governed republic under Porfirio Díaz. A few of French's men still remained with him and believed he had been very badly treated. They were strengthened in this belief by a statement made by a Spaniard named Philipe, who was with Benjamin Franklin Coons, and had formerly been clerk in the bank of Howland [and] Aspinwall in New York City. He said the signature to the letter of credit French had from Aspinwall was genuine, and it was customary for the secretary of war to give orders to citizens to enable them to purchase supplies from government commissaries. This was what French had done at San Antonio giving sight drafts on Howland [and] Aspinwall. French contended he had been made a cat's paw of, and badly treated, by his bankers.

El Paso was at that time the property of Benjamin Franklin Coons, who purchased [the property] from [Juan María] Ponce [de León], paying him fifteen hundred dollars. Hence the name of Franklin given the town, by the Mexicans called Frank-a-leen. The city dropped his name but the mountains overlooking will be ever known as the Franklin Mountains.

There were seven of us who stayed by French in his time of trouble, namely Robert [M.] Trimm, who had served with French on board an East Indian; North West, probably an assumed name; Harry Britt; Chris Steiner, a German; Bob Lockridge, a sporting man from Mississippi, a bold, daring fearless fellow and splendid shot; and a man we nicknamed Ramrod Harris; he was the man who brought through the order to arrest French and was paid $1,000 by Joe Devine of San Antonio to make the trip, a very hazardous one at that time on account of the Apache and Comanche Indians, who roamed over the entire country from San Antonio to California, and a good sprinkling of American roughs and Mexican brigands.[2] He had wonderful nerve and was a dead shot. I also remained.

French determined to push on to California, and left by the old route via Samalayuca, Sand Hills and Santa Maria Lake, and reached Corralitos safely.[3] This was a beautiful hacienda owned by Don José María Zuloaga, a wealthy Mexican, who owned a large number of cattle, horses and sheep, and the mines near there.[4] The land was rich and well watered by the Casas Grandes River and supplied the ranch with corn, wheat, beans, melons and other crops in abundance.

Here we were joined by three half-breed Creek Indians, Pink and Sam Hawkins and George Brenton, a cousin of theirs. They were relatives of Boney Hawkins, a well-known and wealthy Creek Indian, and nephews of Rol[ey] McIntosh, the chief of the Creek Nation.[5] I had gone to school with them in the Nation (so had the writer) and they were glad to meet me and we were glad to have reinforcements to our little band of such good material in case of a fight with Indians or any one else, as the sequel proved.

We found encamped at Corralitos two companies of French's expedition, that had gone ahead of us, and were resting for a few days. One of the parties numbered fifteen men, all afoot, having two pack mules. These came to our camp, and complained that the others had taken advantage of them in the division of the stock at El Paso del Norte and got more than their share of the mules. They wanted French to use his influence to make them divide.

The other party, thirty-five in number, had every one riding an extra animal, besides the pack animals and a surplus of them. They had elected a man named [David] Cooper as captain and he had refused to divide or aid the other party in any way. Lockridge and myself went to the camp and talked to the company and to Cooper, but he refused to divide or assist the smaller party in any way, and was pretty rough in his language. We went to our camp and reported to French and he decided to go down in person and give Cooper a talk, but the fifteen men did not join and we had no thought of trouble but expected French would out talk Cooper and get some of the mules.

Cooper met us with a surly look and cold greeting. French then said: "Mr. Cooper, I don't think you are treating those men afoot fairly. They have paid $350 apiece for their passage from New York and are entitled to a fair divide of the transportation, and your party by some means have twice as many as you need. Now I think you should give them a mule apiece and some of your extra pack mules."

Cooper refused point blank, and a hot discussion was on at once. We were all well armed; each man had a pair of Colt revolvers and rifle except Harris who had a double-barrelled shot gun loaded with buckshot. Cooper's men were also well armed but not accustomed to the frontier methods. About twenty were gathered around us, and fifteen were behind logs, trees, and lying down with their saddles as rests to shoot from in case of a fight.

After a few hot words Cooper drew his pistol and fired at French, breaking his right arm, but he immediately drew a revolver with his left. Before French could shoot, Harris had drawn and shot Cooper through the heart killing him instantly.[6] I had a pair of revolvers and a fine rifle made for me by old man [Charles] Hummel of San Antonio and in the fight emptied them all.[7] It was short and sharp but we had the best shots and experience on our side. A man named [John] Holmes was killed at the first round and three others in rapid succession.[8] This completely demoralized the twenty men around us and they broke away as fast as their legs would take them. The other part of their company had been blazing away indiscriminately at all of us, but their men fled in confusion and Lockridge and the three Creeks charged them and they followed suit. French, though suffering greatly, emptied a pair of revolvers with his left hand. We took possession of their camp but did not follow them though we could easily have killed a lot of them, after they broke to run. Five of them were killed when the fight began and two wounded. French had his arm broken and Lockridge had a slight wound in his thigh. That was all the damage to our side.[9]

We did not take anything except their mules and drove them to the corral and sent for the foot men and turned over a riding animal to each one and enough pack mules to carry their grub and blankets. We received their heartfelt thanks and the hearty curses of the Cooper gang which evened things nicely.

We sent the balance of the animals to the Cooper party with our compliments and also a message to the effect, that if they had not been such hogs, there would have been no dead men, or trouble. They were willing enough to get a mount and transportation again and gladly accepted French's offer, and being on foot in a strange land for a brief period even reminded them "that fellow feeling makes us wondrous kind."

Don José María Zuloaga took their wounded men to the hacienda and kindly treated them, as he did French, so after the dead were buried, everything grew quiet and peace reigned in Corralitos once more.

We were camping in the house of a Mexican señora. I cannot recall her name—probably ex-Mayor Joseph Magoffin or Capt. Juan Hart will know (Jim Lucas afterwards married her daughter).[10] She told us we had better leave for the *alcalde* had sent a courier to Janos for a company of Mexican cavalry, and we all would be arrested, disarmed, and marched to Chihuahua afoot in irons.[11]

The fate of George Wilkins Kendall and the Santa Fe Expedition were too recent not to be remembered, and we were just where Benjamin Franklin was after our ancestors had signed a declaration of independence. He said, "Gentlemen, we have got to hang together now, or we will hang separately." Our warring elements were drawn together as quickly as the North and South after war with Spain was declared and the Cooper party, foot men and the French party, were soon within the señora's adobe walls and all our animals safety corralled. This made us, armed as we were at that time, a formidable body, that it would not be to trifle with. The manner of constructing those old Mexican houses made them strongholds that unless artillery was used could not be taken except by siege or overwhelming numbers (they were built to keep out the Apaches and Comanches) as was proven at the Alamo. The tops of the houses had walls carried three or four feet above the roof and the holes cut in them for the gutters to carry off the rain, made perfect port holes. A council of war was held and determined we would never surrender or give up our arms and we made all preparations for a fight.

A cloud of dust in the direction of Janos gave us timely notice that the Mexican cavalry were coming and our men, some fifty strong, were on the roof of the señora's house and those adjoining, and anxiously awaited to see what we had to meet. The Mexican commander came on with some seventy men, badly armed with *[e]scopet[a]s* with *musales* like a trombone, tingling sabers and spurs, ragged and dusty; they had a cannon mounted on wooden wheels drawn by two mules and just about as big as a good sized sausage stuffer.

They filed into Corralitos and formed in front of our men and right under the cover of our guns, expecting to impress us with their war-like appearance, but it had the contrary effect and caused more merriment than a little. The Mexican officer demanded our unconditional surrender.

French made me spokesman and interpreter, as I had been in San Antonio many years and spoke Spanish, and when this demand was made known we gave him an unconditional "No, never," and the men gave him the grand ha-ha. Yet these ragged, dusty, ill armed, ill paid men, were all that stood between the well-dressed rich people of the interior, and the blood thirsty Apaches and Comanches that roamed often having so terrorized the small towns as to exact tribute from them. They bore little resemblance to the well armed, well fed, and handsomely equipped *rurales* under President Díaz, but they managed to hold their own in many a desperate encounter with these bands of marauding Indians.

The Mexican commander was highly incensed at our treatment of his demand, and answered angrily: "I will show you, you can't come here and violate our laws, and insult Mexico with impunity; if you don't surrender, I'll move my soldiers back and open on you with my cannon." I interpreted what he said to the men and told them to be ready, and then said to the *comandante*: "Don't you dare move your men or cannon or we will open fire on you." Our men brought down their guns and the ominous clicking of hammers was heard along the line, and it looked like after whipping each other, we must whip the Mexicans before we could get out of the country.

After this stage of the game, Don José María Zuloaga rode up to the Mexican commander and said: "Señor you are wrong, these men have come to Mexico by permission of the authorities at Paso del Norte, and have violated no law of Mexico, but have had a quarrel among themselves, and settled it in American style, and are now good friends again. You will likely lose your life and many of your men if you do not withdraw." This seemed to strike the *comandante* as good common sense so he said: "Well, Don José, it is your *hacienda*. If you are satisfied, we will withdraw," and his men withdrew and camped under the big *alamos* on the river.

That night we had a grand *baile*, and mingled as friends and danced until Lucero arose in the east to proclaim day. Our former enemy got gloriously full and happy and hugged us and patted us on the back and we parted the best of friends. No one would ever have imagined that only a few hours before we had been drawn up in battle array ready to destroy each other.

The peaceful settlement of our Mexican international trouble seemed to have a soothing effect on all parties. The señora whose house we had taken possession of when we thought we were in a tight place, had besought us with tears, weeping and wailing, not to fight from the house, and said she was quite sure, no matter how the battle terminated, her property would be confiscated by the government for giving shelter to a foreign enemy.

The foot party were greatly rejoiced to be able to ride instead of "hoofing it" to California. The three Creek Indians joined them and they pulled out at once, not caring to risk a trip across the hot plains with the Cooper outfit, for fear of another battle for the ownership of the mules.

French did not, of course, take stock in the *baile*, his arm giving him a great deal of pain. So the second day after the fight, José M. Zuloaga gave us letters to all Mexican authorities and also to Gov. [José] Cordero at Chihuahua, then governor of the state, giving an account of the trouble at Corralitos, and asking kind treatment for the party.[12] At that time Zuloaga was a power in Chihuahua, and French's condition demanded medical attention.

We left Corralitos and started for Chihuahua, having to keep a sharp look out for old Mangas Colorad[as], the Apache chief, who claimed the whole country belonged to him, and was on the lookout to collect tribute from all who traveled through his domain.[13] We luckily never saw any of his toll-gate keepers and reached Chihuahua, after five or six days' travel. French's arm, on account of the constant motion of travel, had become terribly inflamed and swollen; nothing but the pure dry air of that section prevented mortification from setting in.

Arriving in the city we camped at Señora Campulade's near the old bull ring, and after presenting our letter to the governor, started out to hunt for a physician. The governor received us cordially and showed us every attention, and recommended a Dr. Dubois, a Frenchmen, to us as a proper person to treat French. We found him and after he examined the broken arm he said that the only way to save the patient's life was to amputate the arm, which was done.[14] This, of course, necessitated a halt for five weeks, when we again took up the line of march for Mazatlán.

Governor Cordero gave us letters to the governor of Durango, asking that our party should be well received and given every assistance in completing the journey to the Pacific Ocean.

We left Chihuahua with regret, as we had received nothing but the kindest treatment from the citizens of the town, and there were many ways of enjoying life; the city with its beautiful cathedral, plaza, music, flowers and beautiful women, had made our stay a pleasant one. We had no trouble at all on the route until we reached the immense hacienda of La Garca, situated on the Nasas River and bordering on the state of Durango.[15]

The owner of the ranch, whose name I cannot recall, found among our mules one that had the Hacienda La Garca brand, that had not been vented (contrabanded) and he came into the corral where we had our stock and had one of his peons rope the animal to take it out, but we told him Lockridge had bought the mule from Coons at El Paso, a man well known and had paid him for it, and offered to pay the claimant twenty dollars for the animal, but as the mule was an unusually fine one the *dueño* refused to sell, and said, "the mule is mine and I intend to take him." There was nothing for us to do but to appeal to the God of Battles, and seizing our arms, we told him he would have to kill us all before he could get the mule. This he did not care to do, as an exaggerated account of our fight at Corralitos had preceded us. We were glad of a peaceful settlement and packed up and took up the line of march for Durango.

We were well received by the governor of Durango, and after a short rest, left for Mazatlán, but had not gone far until we had a courier sent after us to ask us to join in a campaign after some Comanches that had come into the edge of Durango and robbed a *pasado*, taking a large amount of money and plunder, and a number of horses and riding off triumphantly. We returned at once and were joined by a troop of Mexican cavalry and followed the trail of the Comanches who numbered a hundred warriors, and overtook them at the Hacienda Chorro, about six leagues from Durango. The Comanches were going along leisurely right by the *hacienda*, but the Mexicans had corralled their horses and mules.

As soon as we got near enough we raised a yell and charged the Indians, who, as soon as they discovered there were [Americans] after them, raised the cry, "Los Americanos," and fled, leaving their immense herd behind. Our horses were so badly blown that we could overtake only a few, but we killed three and wounded quite a number that escaped by clean running. These Comanches were only armed with bows, arrows and lances, and lorded it over the Mexicans, at that time, poorly armed. We found at Durango the following Texans that joined us in the fight, or rather race, after the Comanches: John Dusenberry, afterwards in the C.S.A. and after the war a well known citizen of Harris County, Ab. Cage, a nephew of Col. Jack Hays, the noted Texas Ranger, Harry Britt, Bob Lockridge, and Dick Clark. These Texans had come via Matamoros and were heading for the gold fields of California. After the fight the governor of Durango and the citizens vied with given the freedom of the city, and had bull fights and *bailes* galore.

And French particularly, being one armed and having led the charge on the Comanches, won the plaudits of the men and the hearts of the women. The reputation for bravery was of inestimable value to him subsequently as will appear later on.

The governor wanted us to remain and offered us one hundred dollars per month with our rations and $350 cash for every Indian scalp taken. Some of the Americans stayed, but our little band took the road for Mazatlán again. We followed the old trails made by the Spaniards in early days, and passable only for footmen or pack trains and those horse back. The trail led through the only pass in the Sierra Madre known at that time. We had our first view of the grant Pacific Ocean from the divide. It looked very much like a great blue prairie, but called forth none of the enthusiasm of Balboa and the

Spaniards, because we knew it was thereabout. But it was a sense of relief to know that we would soon be on a vessel and bound for a gunnysack of gold in the new El Dorado. But some of us were still to be tried in the fiery furnaces before seeing the promised land.

Gradually we went our way from the western slope of the Sierra Madre amid'st tropical fruits, flowers and the brilliant feathered birds, until at last we reached the city of Mazatlán, and glad to rest after our long and tedious journey.

We found in Mazatlán about 140 Americans, all eager to reach the gold fields, and anxiously awaiting means of transportation. A meeting was held and it was agreed that we should contribute, each according to his ability, money enough to charter a sailing vessel then lying in the harbor, to take us to San Francisco. Some could give only a very little, and others, being quite well off, made up the amount and the vessel was chartered and the day set to sail.

It was agreed by the captain of the vessel that he was to take every American in Mazatlán, whether they had contributed any money or not. This was a God send to many of the poor devils, who in their eagerness to reach California, had barely been able to reach Mazatlán and were trapped.

French had persuaded our men not to go, and said to me, "Don't go, Jim; I've got a good thing on hand that will pay you better than mining. I have some money and will pay you up all I owe you, (I had loaned him every cent I had) and if you will wait a little while we will go to San Francisco together."

I had sold my arms and mules and put $150 into the vessel charter, and did not fancy seeing the vessel sail without me and I had a mind of presentiment that I had better take passage on her, but French with his smooth tongue and winning manner, fooled me just as easily as he had others. He never even hinted to me what his plan was to beat the California gold miners, and did not ask me to join him.

He had noticed as we came down the western slope of the mountains a cut on the divide of a spur of the mountains where after you entered the cut only one animal could travel the trail for a mile, and here were posted at each end of the cut a guard of Mexican soldiers and customhouse officers to prevent smuggling into the interior. French conceived the idea of capturing a *conducta* of silver amounting to $200,000 and getting away with it.[16] He had managed to pick up twelve or thirteen toughs, such as can be found in any seaport, and though they were only partially armed, he started back to meet a *conducta* of silver he learned was coming and timed it so as to get possession of the cut just before the *conducta* was due.

He surprised the guard at the west end, and after a sharp fight in which several of the guard were killed, he took their arms and leaving a guard over them, hurried to the east end of the cut and soon had the guard prisoners without any bloodshed. When the *conducta* arrived they simply walked into a trap and were taken prisoners by French, who immediately left the trail and started for the coast about Mazatlán where he had arranged for a vessel to meet him and get the silver aboard the ship. Some of the guard had managed to escape, and as soon as they reached Mazatlán a strong force of cavalry was started out after French, but as it was some sixty miles to where he had held up the *conducta*, he had a pretty fair start. But he never calculated how slow a Mexican pack mule can be, especially when taken off of his regular trail, nor how rough the country was over which he had to travel, and the Mexican *[m]ozos* who were with the train and always chosen for their honesty and fidelity, probably did all in their power to delay the party so the Mexican soldiers by making a forced march overtook him before he could reach the sea and surrounded him. He showed fight, but seeing the hopelessness of a struggle with such odds against him, after a few volleys which killed one of his men and wounded several, he hoisted the white flag and surrendered and was taken back to Durango.

I never saw any of his men before nor after the robbery, and was in blissful ignorance of the scheme until a *gendarme* came to my room and arrested me as an accessory before the fact, and then for the first time I learned what French had done.[17] I had given him to understand that any legitimate business to make money I could join him in, but not otherwise, so he had left me to my fate.

I was put in prison and although I protested my innocence and wrote to the American consul, he never came near me nor paid the least attention to me, nor to investigate the matter. To say I was blue, was, to put it very mildly, deeply, darkly, beautifully blue and hardly in it. I had no money and knew no one and was a long way from Texas and my family.

After I had been confined sometime and prison fare and prison life had made my life a burden to me, a happy thought occurred to me, and I sent for the British consul (whom I had met casually) named Charles Sylvester, and told him I was a British subject. As a matter of fact, my great-great-great-grandfather, John Baylor, was born at Riverton, in Devonshire, England, and just at that particular time my heart warmed towards our mother country, and I felt that such a slight breach as the revolution ought not to stand in the way and "blood was thicker than water." I yearned with an exceeding, great sincere yearn to repair any damage done during the American fratricidal strife by my Virginia ancestors, and wanted to be a loyal British subject.

Sylvester never questioned me closely as to what part of England I was born in, when I expected to return, nor put any hard questions to answer. I think he thoroughly understood the situation, and seeing I was only a youth, felt the sympathy born of being of the same race and speaking the same language. I told him if he wanted to write to French, I felt sure that he would testify that I knew nothing whatever of his plan to rob the *conducta*. He said, "I am perfectly satisfied of that fact or you would not be here now," and bidding me good cheer he left me and went straight to the *jefe político's* office and in a marvelously short time my prison door was opened, and thanks to her gracious majesty, Queen Victoria (God bless her memory), I was a free man once more.

During the short time of my stay in Mazatlán I had formed the acquaintance of a kind-hearted old Mexican named Bernardo Gonzales, who was the proprietor of a Mexican *pasado,* and he was very kind to me.

The English consul told me to remain in Mazatlán awhile as it would look much better than trying to get away as soon as I was released, and would satisfy the Mexican authorities that he had acted in good faith (which he undoubtedly did). I promised him faithfully that I would not leave and could safely have sworn to it on the *Holy Bible*, but I did not tell him that I did not have a cent and therefore could not leave.

I stayed in Mazatlán about a month and my old friend Gonzales saw to it that I did not go hungry. It began to be quite a serious question with me about my future; how I was to either get to California or back to San Antonio, Texas.

One day a vessel touched at Mazatlán and a passenger got off and came to the Gonzales *pasado*, and who in the world should it be but my old friend, Benjamin Franklin Coons, on his way from San Francisco to El Paso, Texas. To say that I was rejoiced would not be justice to my real feeling. Here was a good friend dropped down from the skies, when everything seemed darkness.

Coons told me that he had gotten the contract from the government to haul the supplies for the troops at El Paso, from San Antonio, and had employed about a hundred men in San Antonio to drive his ox-teams to El Paso, and after they reached there and were paid off they intended to go on to California. The train followed the old immigrant route from San Antonio to California until they reached the Pecos River, and then turned up that turbid stream on to Stockton and Fort Davis, where the men could occasionally get a drink of pure water. All would have been well, but I don't think if Coons had driven six yoke of oxen from Fort Lancaster to the Guadalupe Mountains, drinking the Pecos water, being stifled with the alkali dust in the valley, his friends would have had no trouble in getting him to mount upon his wagon and curse all creatures. In addition to the government supplies, Coons had a generous supply of old Bourbon and Robertson County whiskey for the hospital.

If all of the one hundred teamsters had been from a local option district, carried by a unanimous vote, I don't see how they could have kept from drinking. But after all, the meanest part of the road had been passed over, and they had reached the beautiful Pine Springs, just beyond Delaware Creek and almost under the shadow of Guadalupe Peak. The shape, and sweet pure cold water, the abundant nutritious gramma grass, all seemed to say, let's take a drink. The vast caravan had been so strained that it sprung a leak, to use a nautical phrase, and the leak was found to be class Bourbon, and soon there was a drunken crowd and pandemonium turned loose. Instead of thanking Coons for being as thoughtful and bringing such good stuff into such a country, they threatened to kill him, and he barely escaped with his life, and had a lone ride to El Paso, and reported the matter to Major Van Horn[e] of the Third United States Infantry. The major knew of course, that these supplies being destroyed by a lot of drunken man, meant that his men might go hungry, and at once started two troops of cavalry to the rescue.[18]

As soon as Coons left, the mob had taken possession of the train, and were having all the good whiskey they wanted and their choice of the government rations, and enjoying themselves largely, but when they saw the long line of cavalry winding up the side of the mesa, it put a serious side to the matter, and when a demand was made for unconditional surrender, not one had the hardihood to refuse Uncle Sam's demand, especially when backed by boys in blue.

Of course they had to give some excuse for getting drunk—many a man besides Tom O'Shanter had been—and they must be novel and knew even before a confiding wife will believe them. So the teamsters said that when they got on the mesa overlooking the valley between Guadalupe Peak and Crow Springs, and saw another expanse of white alkali and sand dunes, and had heard rumors of a desert 130 miles long without water, it was the last straw that broke the camel's back, and they were compelled to brace it up again with whiskey. Probably this was as good a reason as any tippler ever gave, but the real reason we have hinted at. Driving oxen two or three hundred miles over alkali plains, even where the pretty little town of Pecos City now stands, drinking Pecos River water, would have justified them before a jury of west Texas cowboys. The United States commissary took charge of the army supplies and the U.S. officers of the men, and they collected their oxen and strung out across Crow Flat and made the trip to Crow Springs safely. I can't recall now what arrangement Coon's agent made with the teamsters, but they were settled with and drifted to California.

After Coons had reported the mutiny of his teamsters to Major Van Horn[e] he started across the plains to California via Tucson, Yuma and Warner's Ranch, and thence to San Francisco to pay a visit to that inimitable wag and humorist, Lieutenant Darby, U.S.A., well known as Squibob, John Phoenix, or as editor-in-chief of Judge Ames's paper, the *San Diego Herald*.

Lieutenant Darby was his brother-in-law having married his sister. After a visit and rest Coons was anxious to return to El Paso to attend to his business there, but was not anxious to make the trip across the Yuma Desert from Warner's Ranch to Fort Yuma again. (The writer made that trip in August, 1854, and can safely swear that no one but his Satanic Majesty would care to make a second trip, even with plenty of good, cool drinking water.) Coons did not care to, and finally believed no worse route could be found, so decided to return via Mazatlán, Durango and Chihuahua.

Our delight and surprise was mutual. I, because I had found an old friend and saw my way to return to Texas, and Coons was glad to have my company, as I had been over the route and spoke Spanish fluently. It was very gratifying to me to be able to settle up my board bill with my kind-hearted old *amigo*, Don Bernardo Gonzales. He had acted from pure kindness of heart, and never expected any return. I will never forget this good Samaritan, who cared for me, a stranger, and did not cross to the other side as the American consul had done.

Coons had plenty of money and got good rigs and the best horses he could find in Mazatlán, and we started by ourselves on the long overland trail again. When we arrived at Durango, French was still in prison. Coons begged me to go with him to see French, but I said, "No he has robbed me and deceived me and I will have nothing to do with him."

Coons went along and said French received him in grand style. Such was the wonderful charm of this talented man's manner, that he had become a lion among the pretty *señoritas*, who sent him flowers and the nicest food and delicacies. Mexico was then a suckling infant in her swaddling clothes, and ideas of good government were very crude.

French had fought the Comanches, their ancient enemies, for them, and they did not consider he had committed such a great moral wrong in trying to capture $200,000, and as to smuggling, that was a fascinating and a quite legitimate profession. He not only had the females on his side but I learned afterwards that he had so charmed the governor that he not only released him, but gave him $10,000 in gold and authorized him to organize a company of Americans and return to Durango to fight the Comanches, who had become so bold that they would rob and run to the mountain vastness and leisurely camp until necessary to make another raid on the *haciendas*.

Very different from the young giant Mexico of today, with her well armed *rurales*, her railroads, manufactories, and all the improvements of the age, and keeping step with the foremost nations of the earth.

We did not tarry on the road. At every city or *hacienda* Coons bought fresh horses and we covered the many leagues in quick time and without ever having seen a Comanche or Apache warrior, traveling mostly at night, and safely reached El Paso. Though then only a little "adobe" dirt-dauber looking place, it was happiness enough to see the American flag and be again on American soil.

We learned that French, after being released, went to California and struck the country at the time the grey-eyed man of destiny, [William] Walker, was organizing his filibustering expedition to Nicaragua and became minister plenipotentiary to that short lived, ill-fated government. It is needless to say that the governor of Durango never saw his *dinero* again and when French went on to represent the Walker government he claimed his person as ambassador was sacred and neither Uncle Sam nor Aspinwall could reach him for alleged crookedness.

On arriving at El Paso I found that Capt. A[ndrew W.] Bowman, who was A[djutant] Q[uarter] M[aster], U.S.A., was trying to find some one who would risk his life and go down on the old emigrant route from San Antonio to California and take dispatches to a government train loaded with supplies for the troops at El Paso. At that time there had been no mail established between El Paso and San Antonio and the only means of communication was by these trains, or moving columns of soldiers, Captain Bowman was very uneasy about this train as it was overdue and the Mescalero Apaches, under old Espejo, their chief, had a strong band of warriors and was always ready to take advantage of any chance to rob immigrant trains and others, and always remained near Wild Rose Pass in the Limpia Canyon near where Fort Davis was established afterwards.

I met the train and escort near Van Horn's Wells. They were under command, or the commissary department was, of Capt. Samuel French, who was afterwards in the Confederate States Army and served in Virginia, and not to be confounded with Cap. [Albert H.] French who killed or rather massacred Capt. James [Henry] Skil[l]man, who was in the C.S.A. and on picket duty in the Davis Mountains.[19] They had been personal friends, and through treachery French had located Skil[l]man and killed him. It has been said that the matter so preyed on French's mind that it became unbalanced before his death.

Captain Bowman paid me $300 for making the trip and that put me on my feet again. Long afterwards I was sutler at Fort Davis and a bright young Englishman named John Woodland, clerked for me. Woodland was a quiet, sober, brave, reliable young man and afterwards met a tragic death as he was one of the party who joined Capt. [James] Walker's company of the second regiment, C.S.A., acting volunteers, when Lt. [Reuben] Mays and twelve members of the company were massacred by the Mescalero Apaches under Nicolás, their war chief Espejo being old and infirm.[20]

NOTES

1 The Kentucky-born Dawson is listed on the 1900 Colfax County, New Mexico Territory, census as sixty-nine and a farmer living at Cimilorio (Vermejo Park). Dawson, who was George Baylor's nephew, was born in Grayson County, Kentucky, on 10 November 1830. After the failure of the French Expedition, Dawson, with his mother and father, drove a team of oxen to California. Two years later, he moved 1,000 head of cattle from Arkansas to California and in 1859 became a partner of Charles Goodnight. Acting as a guide, he led one of the first cattle drives from Texas to Colorado. During a cattle drive to Colorado in 1861, Dawson was attacked by hostile Indians and wounded in the hand with an arrow. After the war, Dawson served as a Ranger but was attracted to the tall grasses of northeastern New Mexico where he purchased a tract of land some thirty-six miles southwest of Raton from Lucien Maxwell. Here he ran several hundred head of cattle and one hundred horses. Instead of wood, Dawson began to burn coal scraped from a nearby mesa. By 1899 coal was being mined at a town called Dawson; the town would eventually boast a population of 6,000. With profits from coal, Dawson retired to southern California where he died on 27 December 1918 at the age of eighty-eight. He was buried in Los Angeles. 12th Census, Colfax County, New Mexico Territory; and Toby Smith, *Coal Town: The Life and Times of Dawson, New Mexico* (Santa Fe: Ancient City Press, 1994), 1-5, 13. Also, J. Evetts Haley, *Charles Goodnight: Cowman and Plainsman* (Norman: University of Oklahoma Press, 1949), 20, 207, 227. For Dawson-Baylor genealogy, see James Henry Gardner, "The Lost Captain: J.L. Dawson of Old Fort Gibson," *Chronicles of Oklahoma* 21 (1943): 217-49.

2 Strickland identifies the courier who carried the arrest warrant, along with a letter from Howland & Aspinwall dishonoring French's drafts and a letter of protest from individuals French had defrauded in San Antonio, as Henry Skillman. Skillman had reached El Paso from San Antonio in six days. Strickland, *Six Who Came to El Paso*, 6. Only a C. Lockwood, not Lockridge, is listed in the French party. Miles, *Sufferings and Hardships*, 11-12, 20.

3 Corralitos is about 160 miles southwest of El Paso on the Rio Casas Grandes between the villages of Janos and Casas Grandes.

4 Zuloaga was the *jefe políticio* of Galeana. He temporarily supported the Imperialists during the period of French intervention but finding little support in Galeana for the Conservative cause, he declared his loyalty to the liberals and Benito Juárez. Zuloaga died in Galeana in 1868. *Diccionario Porrua de Historia, Biografía y Geografía de Mexico* (Mexico City: Editorial Porrua, 1970), 2:2352.

5 According to Baldridge, French had formed an alliance with ten or twelve desperadoes and six or seven half-breeds from the Cherokee Nation. Roley McIntosh, half brother of William McIntosh, signed the 1825 Treaty of Indian Springs which allowed the United States to gain possession of most of what remained of Creek land in what is today Georgia and Alabama. William McIntosh was subsequently killed on 29 April 1826, while Roley McIntosh led many Creeks to the Indian Territory. Baldridge, *A Reminiscence,* 31; and J. Leitch Wright, Jr., *Creeks and Seminoles: The Destruction and Regeneration of the Muscogulge People* (Lincoln: University of Nebraska Press, 1986), 242-43, 304-7.

6 Quoting a man named Spofford Rounds who was in the Cooper party, Baldridge said that Cooper was shot through both thighs. However, William Miles recorded that Cooper was shot in the hip and in the stomach. McGowan asserts that the Corralitos gunbattle resulted

when the French loyalists "started after the train with the determination of capturing it from its owners, plundering them, and dividing the spoils." Baldridge, *A Reminiscence*, 31; Miles, *Sufferings and Hardships*, 20; and McGowan, *Parker H. French*, 7.

[7] Hummel was born at Diershelm bei Kehl, Baden, in 1819. He settled in San Antonio with his family in 1846. At the outbreak of the Civil War he fled to Mexico but later returned to San Antonio where he operated a stationery business. Chabot, *With the Makers of San Antonio*, 383-84.

[8] Holmes was badly wounded in both arms. Baldridge, *A Reminiscence*, 32; and Miles, *Hardships and Sufferings*, 20.

[9] McGowan reported that five of the French party were also killed. McGowan, *Parker H. French*, 8.

[10] Joseph Magoffin, full-bearded son of pioneer businessman James W. Magoffin and Susan Shelby Magoffin, was justice of the peace, collector of customs, and twice mayor of El Paso (1881-1885, 1897-1901). Juan Hart, son of Simeon Hart and Jesusita Siqueiros, was an engineer and long-time editor of the *El Paso Times*. John Middagh, *Frontier Newspaper: The El Paso Times* (El Paso: Texas Western Press, 1958); John Judy Middagh, "Frontier Journalism in El Paso, 1872-1900," M.A. thesis, Texas Western College, 1952; Sonnichsen, *Pass of the North*, 72-73, 123, 176, 211-16, 353-56, 362-63; and Timmons, *El Paso*, 170-72.

[11] The old presidio village of Janos, on the Rio Casas Grandes, is about thirty miles south of the United States-Mexico border.

[12] As the governor of Chihuahua from 1852 to 1857, Cordero fought Apaches, Comanches, and in 1847, the Americans. A supporter of the Plan de Ayutla, he died in Ciudad Chihuahua in 1867. *Diccionario Porrua*, 1:516.

[13] See Ch. 10, this section.

[14] According to McGowan, part of French's arm was amputated at Corralitos "under the most primitive conditions." McGowan, *Parker H. French*, 9.

[15] About one hundred miles south of the Chihuahua-Durango border, the Nazas River drains a large part of north-central Durango.

[16] *Conducta* (management, director, or conduct) is used here to mean "shipment."

[17] McGowan wrote that French was arrested for robbing a mail coach. McGowan, *Parker H. French*, 11.

[18] Newly appointed boundary commissioner John Russell Bartlett, on his way to El Paso to assume his duties, came across part of Coons's stranded wagon train at the Salt Lakes near the Guadalupe Mountains. Bartlett, *Personal Narrative*, 1:48. For an excellent account of the circumstances that led to the stranding of the wagon train, see Pingenot, "Great Wagon Train Expedition," 212-15.

[19] See n. 22, Ch. 2, this section. W.W. Mills, in his *Forty Years at El Paso*, is critical of Baylor for saying that Skillman was "massacred." As Mills indicates, there is no evidence that French and Skillman were ever friends. Moreover, Skillman's death had nothing to do with French's later mental illness. Mills, *Forty Years at El Paso*, 85.

[20] The English-born Woodland, thirty-three, is listed on the 1860 El Paso County census as a "trader" at Fort Quitman. 8th Census, El Paso County, Texas. Baylor describes Woodland, who was killed in the Mays' Massacre, further in Ch. 2, Sec. II.

CHAPTER FIVE

California in 1854

ON MY ARRIVAL IN SAN ANTONIO I found that I had saved, after leaving
Parker H. French, the sum of eight hundred dollars, Mexican silver dollars,
"dobies" as we called them then.[1] Silver was not so rotten then as politicians
make it out now, and I went to old Nat Lewis, or Don Luis, as the Mexicans
called him, who had an adobe store on the south side of the main plaza, and
he gave me a premium of five percent for the "dobie" dollars, paying me in
gold doubl[o]ons—French, German, and principally Mexican.[2]

As before stated, I went on to Port Lavaca, and helped give the bloody
handed young murderer, Rowland Sawyer, a stampede that eventually caused
him to have his neck broken near where Cameron now stands, by a vigilance
committee. After a short visit, I went to New York on the *Hazard*, and narrowly escaped being run down—once off Pensacola and once off Sandy
Hook. After a pleasant visit to a sister, I took passage on the *Crescent City* for
Cuba, intending to join [William L.] Crittenden's men who went to aid the
Cubans.[3] We went to Key West, expecting to be transferred to the *Pampero*,
but a high sea and stiff wind delayed her until her coal gave out and she went
to Tampa to coal. This saved my life. We continued (there was quite a party)
on the *Crescent City* to Havana; just before arriving there we were fired on by
a Spanish man of war. They fired first a blank cartridge, and the captain
ordered all below the water line, and we steamed ahead. There then followed
solid shot over our deck, but the vessel ran under the guns of Morro Castle
and the Spanish men of war ceased firing.

We were right close under the walls, in speaking distance, and the Span-
ish *comandante* hailed us with, "What vessel is that?" Our captain answered,
"The United States steamer *Crescent City* bound from New York to New
Orleans." The *comandante* asked, "Is Purser Smith aboard?" Our captain

replied, "Yes, he is aboard." "I have orders from the commander of the port," said the *comandante*, "not to allow you to come in," to which our captain replied, "I am going in anyhow, and you can turn your guns loose if you want to."

There was on board a young American who had a brother with Crittenden. He shook his fist at the Spanish flag and uttered these prophetic words, "I know not how many of my countrymen lie within your dungeons, but the day will come when the hated Spanish flag will be pulled down, and the star spangled banner will wave above the walls of Morro Castle."

When we stopped the Spanish authorities put a guard ship near us, and the war vessels sent armed boats and surrounded us with a strong cordon that prevented anyone from landing. There were on board some two hundred citizens of Cuba. None of them were allowed to land, nor would they (the Spaniards) receive the mail, or allow communications with the shore. We got to Havana in the evening and remained until morning. At daylight I was up and climbing up on one of the masts, I had the pleasure of beholding a stirring beautiful sight—the marines of the war vessels of all the different nations in the harbor, beating to quarters with bands playing, flags flying, etc.

We left very soon, and after we entered the Mississippi River we met a vessel of the same line and turned over our mail matter and also the Cuban passengers, greatly to their joy.

After we left Havana, Crittenden and his men were led out of Morro Castle and shot. The British consul took his stand outside the castle gate, hoisted the English flag, and said, as the prisoners marched by in irons under a strong guard, "If there are any Englishmen here or any who claim British protection, let them walk under the folds of the British flag." Out of 160, there were only seventeen Englishmen. One hundred and forty-three Americans were shot down, but they did as bravely as the heroes of the old Alamo.

I considered myself lucky that I did not get to join the "filibusters" and after a short stay in New Orleans, went home to Lavaca again.

Although I had made such a failure in getting to California by land, I had not given up my golden dreams and felt quite sure that all I had to do was to get there and the gold nuggets and *chispas* would find their way to my pockets. So I determined to try the sea, and went to Port Lavaca and took the steamer for New Orleans, on the first of March, 1854, being delayed by bad weather and sailing qualities of the old tubs that used to run between Texas and Louisiana. I missed the *Pampero* and had to remain in that beautiful city for two weeks. It was no hardship, with its operas, theaters, flowers, beautiful women, and courteous citizens, a young man in the spring of early manhood could easily pass two weeks without regret for loss of time.

The *Daniel Webster*, afterwards so conspicuous in the Civil War, was the next vessel, and I got my ticket for San Francisco and we sailed from the Crescent City on March 15th '54, for San Juan, Nicaragua.[4] The vessel was crowded with passengers, as everybody that could raise the money to pay their fare was beating toward the Golden Gate of the golden state, expecting to find the golden sands full of gold nuggets. My own expectations had not abated one bit since I had started "der plains across" with Parker H. French, and no thought of the fate of the milk maid's fortune crossed my mind. My heart was full of hope.

As may be supposed there were all kinds of people from nearly all parts of the world on the *Daniel Webster*, but probably quite as rough a crowd as went across the plains, for it required a pretty full purse to pay passage, and only those who were pretty well fixed at home could stand the expense. The accommodations were decidedly primitive, especially for sleeping, berths being double, one back to the other. All well enough for friends or married people, but not so nice for strangers if of opposite sexes. I saw there was quite a stir among the lady passengers, and soon found that they were looking for the parties who had beds in the same rooms. There was on the streamer a pretty young woman named Carrie and she had looked me up as her berth was back of mine. She was from Illinois and introduced herself and asked me if I had any objection to changing berths, as she wished to find another lady to take mine. I said certainly, with pleasure, if it will accommodate you. She then told me something of herself, that she had no kindred in the world except her brother, who had gone to California and had been quite lucky, and sent her money to come out to San Francisco. She anticipated great joy at meeting him again and keeping house for him. He was to come down from the mines and meet her in 'Frisco and had prepared a nice home for her.

Miss Carrie started out to find some lady who would exchange berths with me, but after a diligent search she returned to say, with much embarrassment and dismay, that she could find no lady to take the front berth, and was the odd lady on the vessel. Often our whole lives are changed by just such a simple occurrence as this. Had she made the exchange, I would never have had more than a casual acquaintance, but as it was we became quite well acquainted.

Her being alone without a protector and being a modest, pretty woman, and well educated, she appealed strongly to me and I told her that she could rely upon me as a brother until her brother claimed her in 'Frisco. Any one who would have said anything to wound her feelings and show her any rudeness would have soon found that she had a "big brother" to right her wrongs.

My little sister then began to make arrangements, such as would suggest themselves to a modest girl, and pinned up a large shawl between the berths and chose the back one for herself. All went smoothly whil'st going down the grand old father waters. There was much to interest us as we passed the lovely old mansions, orange groves, with broad-leafed bananas, neat white-washed Negro quarters, and the broad, level fields of sugar cane, corn, cotton, and gangs of Negroes at work. But as soon as we passed Belize and the *Daniel Webster* began to nod and heave to the blue sea, there was one of the sickest little sisters in the back berth that ever crossed the "*Gulfo de México*." Sea sickness had taken possession of her, and the great leveler of social boundaries had produced that "O, Lordy let me die and sink to the bottom of the ocean or be eaten by the sharks" kind of sensation, and I had to take care of her like she was a little child or real sister.

"Sorrow may endure for a night, but job cometh in the morning," and so my sister after her sorrowful night, was glad to come back on deck and breathe the sweet, bracing sea breeze, and felt no more sickness.

We arrived safely at San Juan del Norte or Greytown, and took the steamer for the Lake of Nicaragua and at its western shore disembarked and struck out across the divide between the Gulf of Mexico and the Pacific Ocean.[5] It was a ludicrous sight to see the passengers, some four hundred, all strangers, out on the trail on diminutive donkeys and mules, the ladies riding on men's saddles and man fashion. Often some large, fat female would completely hide the donkey except his ears and feet. Many who had never ridden had to take a tumble and it afforded a constant source of amusement to all except the principals. Shouts of laughter borne on the gale kept everyone in a good humor until the twelve miles was passed, and we were ready to again go on board the steamer.

We arrived safely at the Golden Gate and landed at the wharf and [I] bid my little sister an affectionate farewell. She said, "Good bye, Tex. I can't tell how much I appreciate your kindness, and I hope I may see you again." Neither of us expected to ever meet again. I left for the mines at once to bag that hunk of gold and she remained in joyful anticipation of a happy meeting with her brother, a hope never realized, as will appear later on.

I went first to Grass Valley, and after a short stay there went to Nevada.[6] I had decided before I made any investment to try and learn something of the business by experience, just as now often the sons of wealthy men come to West Texas, dressed in the height of fashion. They soon shed their fine clothes, get a woolen shirt, leggings, Texas saddle, spurs, Mexican hat, and mount a bronco. The sun and chaparral soon make them genuine cowboys. I determined to work for wages until I found I could tell a good claim from a salted one and went to "Lord's Diggins'" and hunted up the boss and asked for a job. He asked, "Do you know how to mine?" "Oh, yes," I answered.

"Well, come here to this shaft in the morning." I didn't ask about wages. I was anxious to become an expert miner.

Next morning bright and early I was on hand and he gave me a hat, stuck a candle in the front and handed me a pick, a short handled shovel, and I got into a tub with an old miner who was dressed for the occasion, and the boss said, "Your pard will show you where to begin work." We soon lost sight of the blue dome of Heaven and after we got down, I thought some where near Pekin[g], I said, "See here, pard; don't you think the bottom has dropped out of this hole?" "Oh, no, it is only four hundred feet deep and we are not half way down," he answered. Finally arriving at bed rock we stopped and went into a drift and my pard told the foreman of the shaft that I had come down to work in the drift, so he showed me where to begin. I saw a lot of men picking away at a kind of cement gravel that was as hard as flint rock, but they said it would melt when put in water. Some of the men were on their knees picking in the side of the drift; others were lying on their backs and picking overhead. I set to work, determined to drift for a month anyway, but the first lick I hit jarred me all over and when the perspiration began to ooze out and filled my eyes so that I couldn't see good my intentions to drift a month oozed out with it, and I drifted back to the main shaft and went up in the second bucket. As soon as I topped the shaft the boss explained, "Why, hello, my young man, are you done already? Yes, if that's what you call drifting, I'll just drift away from here," I answered. "Where did you come from?" said he. "Texas," I answered. "Well, you had better drift over to Hangtown; they are nearly all Texans and [they] hang a fellow now and then just to see him kick."

So I put out for Hangtown, or Placerville, as it is called now, willing to take my chance among Texans.[7] I found that there was great excitement in the camp. Some monumental liar had come in from Gold River and reported that nuggets of gold could be scooped up by the frying pan as big as walnuts in the crevices of the river bed, and the richest placer digging found in California, had been discovered there. So there was a stampede, and having nothing to detain me, I, too, was seized with the fever, the very name suggesting untold wealth. I got on a boat called the *Reindeer*, and got off at Benicia and bought me a good chunk of a mule and some grub and pulled out for Gold River, hoping to get all I could carry back to Texas before the rush was made.[8]

I got to the diggings and being alone made but little noise and the woods being pretty thick, I got up quite close to a fellow who had been working for a long time. For several days I was panning out of rifle boxes. I knew that some miners would not let anyone know how much they were making unless it was some chum. So I concluded to play Paul Pry, and stopped to see him finish and hear what he had to say. I did not have to wait long, for when he got to the "skin down" he raised up suddenly and after a twirl over his head sent his gold pan as far skimming out into the river as he could with the exclamation: "Gold River, I left diggings paying twenty to thirty dollars a day to come to this blankety-blank river and can hardly raise the color." Looking up and seeing me, he said, "and here comes another damn fool. Well, stranger, come on up to camp anyhow and we will wait until the other boys come in from prospecting up the river, and in the meantime have our regular beans." After the partners returned they gave the same experience and said it was a fraud and they intended to leave, so I concluded to drift away again.

I went to Humboldt Bay, and took the steamer *Fremont* for San Francisco, Gen. [John Charles] Fremont himself was on board the boat named in honor of him, having been looking after some mining claims. I had learned on the stage between Grass Valley and Nevada from the passengers that my uncle, Capt. George Starbuck, was living in Happy Valley, a suburban village of San Francisco, and they told me if I would go to a little green store they could point out his house to me. They said he was well off, having made quite a little fortune in a novel speculation. He had been living in Sidney, Australia, for some years, and hearing that horses were in great demand in California on account of the gold diggings and rush of people, and also that house servants were in very great demand, he determined to take advantage of it and sent four hundred head of horses and three hundred women (this was before the discovery of gold in Australia in 1852). The women agreed that after they got to San Francisco they would work for him for a year to pay for their passage from Sidney to 'Frisco.

On his arrival at San Francisco there was such a demand to hire these girls that he auctioned them off to the highest bidder, and so spirited was the bidding that they brought fabulous sums, and his horses also sold at big prices so the speck was very satisfactory. My uncle had been city gauger in Sidney and he was appointed wharfinger at the Long Wharf in San Francisco.

As soon as I landed I went to look for my uncle, and when I got to the house I learned that one of the Sidney women, a widow named Clegg, was keeping house for him. She had a remarkably pretty daughter who came to the door when I knocked and said Mr. Starbuck was not in, and would I come in and wait; he would be back soon. I saw him coming and said, "Why, here he comes now. I have never seen him, but know him from his resemblance to my mother." I did not tell him whose son I was but said, "I am your nephew," and he began to guess whose son I was, and finally after guessing all the others, got me down as Joe Hatch, his sister's son. The old man was glad to see me, as he had not kept up with his family's history or movements, and I gave him all the family news and my own experience as a miner. That amused him very much.

The next day, I went to 'Frisco to take in the sights and was walking slowly when I heard a female voice call out, "Oh, Texas," and looking across the street I saw a young lady beckoning with a parasol, and crossing over who should it be but my little sister. We were mutually glad to again meet, and on my asking about the brother her eyes filled with tears, and she told me that after we separated she learned that the steamboat on which he was coming to meet her, had her boiler explode and sank, and he was either killed or drowned, and all her bright anticipations of going to the mines and keeping house for him had ended in grief and sorrow. She was staying with a lady friend, but was greatly distressed as the money her brother sent her was about gone and she had not been able to get a place as governess and she must find some employment, or get a situation as a house servant. I told her I did not think it would come to that, and that I had an uncle in the city who was well known and had influence and I did not doubt but that he could aid her in finding a situation. I escorted her home and bid her be of good cheer, that she still had a brother, and as soon as I saw my uncle I would let him know about her, and then let her know the result of my inquiries.

I told my uncle what I knew about her and the sorrow she had gone through, and asked him if he could not get her a place as governess among some of his friends. "Yes, certainly I can," he answered, "and I am glad you spoke to me. A friend of mine who lost his wife a few weeks ago, wants a governess and housekeeper, as he has two little children, and I will speak to him at once." The result was that I had the pleasure of telling my little sister that I had gone with my uncle to see the widower, and he would like to have her come and take charge of his home and would give her fifty dollars a month. He was a nice gentlemen, in a good paying business, and had a pretty home. She was a very pretty girl—light complexion, blue eyes and very dark hair—and so well was he pleased with her, that he fell in love with her, and after a proper length of time they were married. I don't know whether she is alive today or her husband, but if this would meet her eye, I hope she will have a kindly remembrance of her Texas brother, now an old crippled Confederate soldier.

As I came down from Humboldt, one beautiful moonlight night, I was standing on the prow of the steamer watching the phosphorescent light made as she cut through the waves and thinking of home. A miner was standing near me and his whole attitude betrayed the disappointed man. We began talking and he told me he had been quite successful at first in mining, but in a moment he decided to return to Feather River and it had taken his last dollar to get to San Francisco, where he hoped to get a job and earn money to get back to his wife and children, content to spend the rest of his days working for them at home. They lived in Illinois, near Chicago.

I told him of my uncle, and that he had better go out to Happy Valley, as it would be much more economical than in the city and maybe my uncle could put him in a way of finding employment. He put up at a house nearby and after supper I went over to see him and proposed going into the city to see the sights. After wandering around awhile we heard a brass band playing with might and main and went to see what it meant and found that it was in a large gambling house that ran clean through from one street to another. It was lighted up most brilliantly and had resplendent mirrors, and the bar with elaborate fixtures, and in addition to the large brass band, there were two good string bands so that the music never ceased. Pretty girls were waiting at the tables, and some were even dealing monte or some of the various games, and above all could be heard the cry "Keno," or drawling tone of some dealer at his table as he raked in the stakes of gold dust or eagles or often fifty dollar octagonal slugs—as they were called—no silver was in sight; the rich silver mines were unknown; it was the golden age of the Golden Gate City.

There were forty-two gambling tables, and they were attended by two gaudily dressed women who either dealt the cards or with "peels" hauled in money won or pushed out money lost. The establishment was run by a Texan named Johnson, who came to 'Frisco from Galveston, and prided himself on conducting a perfectly square game. The dealer at the faro table was a man and at his table, a fellow evidently a thorough sport acquainted with all the tricks of the trade, was betting heavily and losing steadily. He had a good big sack of coined gold, and I noticed he often put down the fifty dollar eight sided gold slugs, common in California at that time. He finally set his sack down on a card and fixed his eyes on the dealer and detected him drawing two cards at once. He put his hand behind him, drew a revolver, and shot the dealer square in the forehead, and raked the pile of gold in his sack, remarking, "I won the money, I guess he won't wax the cards any more," and lighting a cigar, he coolly walked out of the saloon. Johnson made no kick because the waxed cards showed for themselves.

My companion after looking around for some time, said: "Tex, I haven't got but two dollars in the world, and you know that's no money in California. I am going to try my luck." There were only two tables where they would allow a bet less than a dollar, so he changed his two dollars into halves and began betting. His luck varied, but at last his fickle jade of fortune turned entirely in his favor until his winnings amounted to $13,000. He then began to lose and I gave him a punch in the back and when he saw my face he realized what I meant and took off his old slough hat and raked his pile into it, saying, "Well, Tex, this will do me for tonight."

We went straight to the Wells-Fargo Express office and bought a ticket which the company sold at that time to accommodate miners who had gold dust instead of coin. He then kept out fifty dollars and got exchange on New York for the balance of the money.

The next morning, rigged out in a new suit of clothes, for "fine feathers make fine birds," no one would ever have recognized the disconsolate, broken down miner of the evening before. We decided to come back together as far as Greytown. He was supremely happy, and said: "Tex, I am going home and buy me a little farm. My folks will never know how I got the money for I will never tell, for I never gambled before and they will never guess how I made a raise."

When we got on board the *Cortez* I walked back towards the stern of the vessel and hearing a familiar voice on the vessel next to us—the *El Dorado*—who should I see but my old commander, Parker H. French, surrounded by a bevy of admiring ladies and gentlemen and relating his adventures. William H. Walker, "the grey eyed man of destiny," was in a vessel then off the Golden Gate—getting ready to carry men to invade Nicaragua and French was promised the position of minister plenipotentiary. It is needless to follow Walker. He failed and was shot by the Nicaraguans.[9]

The old *Cortez* was crowded—about 1,200 passengers and I was among the steerage or second-class, and among them were two ladies who were well able to go in the cabin, but could not get tickets and were compelled to go home. The fare was miserable and one of them said: "Tex, if you will get me a bottle of pickles I will give you ten dollars. I believe I will die with the miserable fare we have." "I will," I said. "Never mind about the money; I'll get the pickles." So I saw the steward and cook and offered five and finally ten dollars for a bottle, but they said it would cost them their places if it were known that they had given even a bottle of pickles, as orders were strictly enforced. Passengers in steerage could only have what was set before them. There was a long hatch way and along it were shelves filled with pickles, jellies and delicacies for cabin passengers, so I got me a piece of marlin (small rope) and a piece of scrubbing brush handle and made a noose at the end of the marlin, and putting a small piece of wire at the end of the handle, was ready for business.

There was always a man on watch below, but at about 12 o'clock, midnight, I saw him nodding, and with my handle dropped the noose over a bottle and yanked it up. He was awakened by the slight noise and jumped up and made a grab at the bottle, but I was too quick with my lasso and got it safely up and dropped it in a pile of rope and walked quickly back towards the wheel house, gazing intently into the ocean. The watchman had only to run up the hatchway and come to me. He said, "Say, did you see anyone with a bottle of pickles?" "Why, no, have you lost any?" I asked. "Yes, some thief managed to get one," he replied. "Well, that must have been the fellow I saw running back towards the stern of the vessel," I said. So he struck out on a trot for the imaginary thief and I picked up the bottle and struck at a trot for my little friends. As soon as I got down to them, they said, "Oh, there's Tex," "Mum's the word," I answered as I slipped the bottle to them. I repeated the trick every now and then and finally got into the good graces of the carpenter by helping him do some work and told him these lady friends of mine could not eat hard tack and asked him for some biscuits. So he gave me a few each day. When I parted from the ladies they said, "If it had not been for you, Tex, we would have been buried in the Pacific."

When I got to the place opposite the mountains that rise out of the Nicaragua Lake, where the steamer takes on passengers, I got a job repairing the steamers and stayed about six weeks and then took passage on the *Omete-pec* for Greytown. It is eighty miles across the lake and we took the boat to the head of the San Juan River. There we took the *Castilla Rapids*, a smaller boat, to the rapids of that name and there we walked, and a short railroad of about half a mile around the rapids carried our baggage to the steamer *Ruth* that took us down the San Juan to the steamer at Greytown.

NOTES

1   Recollections of Joseph Addison Hatch as told to Baylor.

2   See n. 12, Ch. 2, this section.

3   As part of the Narcisco López Expedition, Crittenden, with fifty other Southern volunteers, was captured, tried, and executed at Havana on 13 August 1851.

4   During the Civil War, the Union had two steamers named *Daniel Webster*. Baylor is probably referring to the one that transported Federal troops from Brazos Santiago to the North following the Twiggs surrender in San Antonio in February 1861.

5   See David I. Folkman, Jr., *The Nicaragua Route* (Salt Lake City: University of Utah Press, 1972), 23-42.

6   Deep in the Sierras northeast of Sacramento, Grass Valley, unlike other California boom towns that were dependent on placer gold which soon ran out, prospered on rich veins of gold-bearing quartz. Such deposits sustained the community for several decades. At this time, Grass Valley was the home of the voluptuous actress and dancer Lola Móntez.

7   East of Sacramento in the foothills of the Sierra Nevadas, Placerville, first called Old Dry Diggings, was a jumble of log and frame buildings sprawled along the winding course of an old pack-mule trail. Because the settlement had such a reputation for wicked deeds, it

was also called Hangtown. Out of pride, however, town fathers renamed the community Placerville. Donald Dale Jackson, *Gold Dust: The Saga of the Forty-Niners* (New York: Alfred A. Knopf, 1980), 44-45, 241-42.

8 Benica, at Carquinez Strait separating San Pedro Bay from Suison Bay, was a major jumping-off place for the gold fields and the headquarters and supply depot for the United States Army.

9 William Walker was executed at the age of thirty-six by the Honduran military on 12 September 1860. The "Grey-Eyed Man of Destiny," the most successful of filibusters, left a legacy of anti-Americanism throughout Central America and Mexico. Albert Z. Carr, *The World and William Walker* (New York: Harper & Row, 1963), 270-72.

CHAPTER SIX

Squire Brown of Texas and the Grizzly Bear

~

ON A LOVELY EVENING IN THE FALL OF 1855, the writer and his companions were eating their regular meal of beans on Mismo Gulch, Kern River, California, when a quartet of dusty looking miners, driving a couple of burros loaded down with the usual picks, pans, blankets and grub, crossed La Mismo near us, went a short distance below and camped. They did not give the usual hearty greeting among "honest miners" in those days, or anything denoting a friendly disposition. We spotted them at once as a party that had said that we had more ground than we were entitled to, and they intended to jump one of our claims.

There were four of us. First there was Capt. Theo[dore] D. Maltby, of Hartford, Connecticut, one of the Texas Mier prisoners, who was as brave as a lion.[1] He had received a dangerous wound in the head at the Battle of Mier, and was too near death's door to draw beans at the decimation of the prisoners—which was, I expect, about the only time a soldier was glad not to draw his rations. Next came Moses Kirkpatrick, a Kentuckian, who was my chum and bunk fellow crossing the plains from Texas, and who afterward became a senator in California. E.C. Calhoun, also from Kentucky, who afterward became a judge at Fresno, and the writer of these lines, completed the party.

Our neighbors unpacked and went to cooking at once. After dinner they seemed to make themselves very much at home. They rested awhile and finally one of them whose name was Brown got his pick, pan and shovel, came up within a hundred yards of our camp and commenced digging where he had dug a prospect hole. As the others remained in their camp, we held a hurried consultation and decided it would not be very knightly to double team on him, so I volunteered to go down and interview him. I put on an overcoat that had a deep capacious pocket, and put a five-shooter Colt's in the right hand pocket. I then belted my Navy Colt's and knife around me and went to where he was. He did not see me until I was right over him, and I hailed him with: "Hello, my friend, what are you doing?"

"Going to work this claim," was his reply.

"Yes, but this claim belongs to my company."

"So I heard, but they say you all got twice as much as you are entitled to."

I answered that we had discovered the gold in La Mismo, and were therefore entitled to double claims of 300 feet each, but we had only taken 200 foot claims, as it was not a very long gulch, so as to give others a chance.

"Well," he drawled, "we'll work this claim."

"All right, but as soon as you begin, I'll begin to work on you." He straightened up and looked at me.

"I believe you are in earnest."

"Yes," I answered, "I mean just what I say."

"Whar you from?" said he.

"Texas," was my answer.

He gathered up his pick, pan and shovel, and without another word went back to his camp. He and his companions were soon packed up and on the trail to Keyville.

Afterwards I met Brown and he said to me: "I thought you were a lot of d—d tenderfeet and we could bluff you out of a claim, but I knowed that was no go when you said you was from Texas. What's your name?"

I told him.

"What! Any kin to old Bob Baylor?"[2]

"Yes, he is my uncle."

"Well, well, well. I know him better than bread. He held court many a time in my neighborhood. He would hear lawyers all day and preach a good Baptist sermon at night; marry all the young folks in his deestrict and never charge any fee; come from Alabama; never could be beat for judge. Tom Harrison of Waco run aginst him once and the first house he stopped at they told him he needn't light, no use to argue 'ginst the judge.[3] And when night come, and he wanted to stop at supper, the women folks told him he couldn't stay all night if he had anything to say agin' brother Baylor. So Tom went to Waco next day, and said it warn't no use to run for judge agin' a man that was a good lawyer, preacher, fiddler, and tied the marriage knot for all the young folks in the deestrict without any fee."

Naturally we drifted to talk of good old times in Texas, and I soon made it quite clear to him that I would rather hunt and fish than to eat, and I found that was his forte also. I had a beautiful lemon and white setter of the Carlton breed which some of the officers gave me in San Antonio, and he proved the best slow track deer dog I ever saw. But one grizzly bear hunt satisfied him. I could always tell which way the bear went from the direction Callo went. Brown, when we got to bragging about dogs, whistled and a yellow looking cur that had been snappping at real and imaginary flies trotted up to him.

"Now," said Brown, "thar is the best bar dog that ever was pupped. He is part hound, part cur, and half wolf, and when he smells blood a deer can't get away from him. And as for turkeys, he just nachely seems to know exactly how fur a fat old gobbler ken fly; he circles around and if he don't find the trail he knows he's up a tree and never stops till he finds him. And he got as keen a nose as a durn coyote that never misses any thing you leave on the ground about camp. And as for bar, e-um-um, I never knowed a bar to git away from Bose after he jumped him, and I've killed a steamboat load of black bar round bout Little River, Brazos and the Yegua and Navasote. I'm just dying to set Bose on a big old grizzly bar."[4]

"But, Mr. Brown," said I, "that was black bear, and a grizzly or cinnamon, or even the black ones here, are quite a different animal, and are in the habit of hunting the hunter. I have had some experience with them and would advise you if you come across a big one, and he don't see you, whistle softly to Bose and take the back track.

"No, siree, Bose and me ain't afeered of the biggest bar in the mountains and all I want is to get to see one and set Bose on him."

"Well," said I, "if you will go down here, cross the river near Erskine's Hill, and take the trail to Fort Tejon and then turn to the left where you get out about two miles, you will likely find one as big as an ordinary Texas steer.[5] But before you shoot pick out a pine tree near by that you can climb."

"Oh, never fear. When 'Old Betsy' speaks there'l be bar meat for breakfast."

Brown was a great, tall, lanky fellow, about six feet two, dark-skinned, bald-headed, and looked as he walked along like he had at least four joints between his hips and feet. He was hump-shouldered, and his back bone worked like a caterpillar as he shambled along. I could not help but laugh in anticipation of what a figure he would cut at top speed, with a grizzly bear close to him popping his teeth together and giving a snort that nothing but an enraged grizzly can get up.

Brown left camp one morning before daylight, and following my directions by sunrise was out where an old grizzly could be seen almost any time. Taking a station where he commanded a fair view of the mountain side, he waited anxiously for a "bar" to appear. He was finally gratified, for an immense grizzly put in his appearance, feeding along leisurely on choke cherries, sumach berries and such bugs or acorns as came handy. Brown was in a fever of excitement for fear the bear might wind or see him, and Bose would not have a fair start. But the bear came on down towards him, and as soon as he got within a hundred yards, Brown jumped up and broke out with "Sick 'im, Bose! Sick 'im! Sick 'im! Take him in, old boy."

The old boy did move off at a lively rate, and as soon as he got sight of the bear he gave a yelp of joyful anticipation at the prospect of a scrap. The grizzly did not see or hear Bose or Brown, as they were too windward, but when Bose got within twenty steps of the grizzly the latter saw some animal was coming for a fight. That was just to his hand, and he came on to meet the dog. He snapped his teeth and gave a snort, chasing Bose around, every now and then making a swipe at him with his great paw, and knocking down enough chaparral to make a clearing for a turnip patch. Bose soon discovered this was not hunting black bear in the Yapaun thicket in Texas, and became thoroughly demoralized. He did what every dog will do as soon as he gets badly scared, he started back for his master. All old hunters are familiar with this peculiarity of dogs, and Brown knew, as soon as he saw Bose tuck his tail between his legs and start back, that it was going to be a serious matter for Brown. So he changed his tune to, "You Bose! You son of a seacook! Be gone. Don't you hear me? Be gone!"

But Bose heeded him not, and Brown bethought him of my advice and looked around for a tree. He found to his horror there was only one tree any where near, and that was at least two hundred yards off. What was worse was that it was off in an obtuse angle that would bring him in full view of the bear. But he lit out for it, his long legs working like carriage spokes, his elbows working like the piston rod of a switch engine, and the caterpillar movement of his back getting in the work. As Bose ran towards where he left his master, and Brown made Lexington time away from there, the grizzly caught sight of Brown, and giving up the small game, took after him. Brown, who had cast back a hasty glance, took in the situation at once and had to change his tune.

"Sick 'im Bose! Take him, fellow! Wool 'im!"

Bose, hearing his master's voice and seeing the bear was not after him, and possibly being ashamed of his disgraceful retreat, or likely understanding the danger to his master, for dogs get to be almost human in their reasoning, took after the bear and his coyote speed came in just right. The bear was doing his best to overtake Brown and Brown was getting right down to his work to get to the tree. Bose ran and nipped the grizzly on his hams which made him change his direction in double quick time, for that is one of the things a bear can't stand. So he wheeled with a roar, partly of rage and partly of surprise, and took after Bose who was intelligent enough to run in the opposite direction from his master. As soon as Brown got to the pine he dropped "Betsy" and scaled up it like a gray squirrel. As soon as he got to a limb he could rest on, although he was panting like a hen laying in August, he had again to change his orders.

"Sick 'im, Bose! Wool him, old boy! Stay with him." This last advice he piously hoped Bose would understand, as the pine tree was not so very tall and his long legs hung down a good deal farther than he though was safe. Bose carried out instructions to the letter. He found the big animal was a sure enough bear, and could not catch him. So he circled around him, giving him a nip now and then, and always running farther away from his master, until the grizzly got back to the starting place. Bose then dodged and suddenly disappeared in the thick brush, when making quite a circuit, he took Brown's trail and soon came back to where his master was treed.

Brown watched the old grizzly as he walked off, his head high in the air, with a jerky kind of step and giving a snort of defiance. As soon as he disappeared, going toward the rough mountains to the west, Brown slipped down out of the tree. Picking up "Old Betsy," he patted Bose on the head and made quite a detour himself, hitting the trail for camp.

I saw him a few days afterwards and he said: "I tell you, George, I sholy don't intent to set Bose onto no more grizzly bar."

NOTES

[1] Maltby, a native of Connecticut, was wounded in the head at Mier. In November 1845, one year after being released from prison, he married Mary Jane West, widow of Lt. James West and George Baylor's favorite sister. Maltby died in New Orleans of yellow fever at the age of fifty-eight on 27 October 1871, after an illness of six days. Joseph Milton Nance, *Attack and Counter-Attack: The Texas-Mexican Frontier, 1842* (Austin: University of Texas Press, 1964), 646; Joseph Milton Nance, ed., *Mier Expedition Diary: A Texan Prisoners' Account* (Austin: University of Texas Press, 1978), 75.

[2] See n. 1, Ch. 1, Sec. I.

[3] Thomas Harrison, a Mexican-American War veteran, became a brigadier general in the Confederate Army and distinguished himself at Shiloh and Stones River. He became a district judge in 1866 and died in Waco on 14 July 1891.

[4] For an excellent study of grizzly bears in California, see Tracy I. Storer and Lloyd P. Tevis, Jr., *California Grizzly* (Lincoln: University of Nebraska Press, 1955).

[5] Fort Tejon, in the Canada de las Uvas fifteen miles southwest of the Tejon Indian Reservation, near the present town of Lebec, was established by the 1st Dragoons on 10 August 1854. In 1858, the fort became a station on the Butterfield Overland route. It was abandoned in 1864. Robert Frazer, *Forts of the West* (Lincoln: University of Nebraska Press, 1965), 32-33.

CHAPTER SEVEN

California in 1857

ABOUT THE YEAR 1857 A PARTY OF SAN FRANCISCANS left the city for a camp hunt. Among them the writer can recall Col. James Tobin, of the law firm of Tobin & Landers, Judge Hydenfeldt, Gallagher, an attorney, Charlie Le Gay, Clements and the writer. Whether the Clements was "Mark Twain" or not, deponent saith not; he certainly was full of life and fun.[1]

Colonel Tobin was very musical and a quartette was organized, the writer having his violin. Judge Hydenfeldt was sedate and learned; Gallagher a glorious, big-hearted fellow; Charlie Le Gay quite green—in fact a tenderfoot; Clements out for all the fun that could be gotten out of a camp hunt in which the writer heartily joined.

Having arranged about grub and camp utensils, blankets, arms, and ammunition, we took the steamer for Petaluma, where arrangements had been made for horses and a pack-mule and a Mexican to handle them.[2] Everybody took a hand in cooking to suit his taste, and after the first day we found small game, and later on deer in abundance, and very fat, as it was in September.

We passed the pleasant little village of Santa Rosa, and our legal brethren having friends there, made our stay very pleasant.[3] The writer was a stranger at the time but had the melancholy pleasure of stopping at the county jail afterwards for a month, as will appear later on. We made a stop also at Russian River at the house of Mr. Fitch.

One of the young men of the family played the guitar and sang sweetly, and our quartette and my violin made an evening pass pleasantly and rapidly. Next we went to the creek east of the house where there was a natural soda fountain. Taking along plenty of syrup we drank to our fill. The spring boiled up in the center of the creek bed and certainly gave a most delicious drink.

The next halt was in Anderson's Valley, where a Mr. Coleman had an ideal country home. It was a lovely little vale surrounded by high mountains, a clear stream running through it. Coleman had planted an orchard and vineyard and had a spring that afforded plenty of water to irrigate his garden and orchard, a comfortable frame house, and being a Kentuckian, had a good spring-house and plenty of buttermilk, poultry, and the many good things that come in a new county—fat hogs and cattle, game swarming in the woods, and the stream full of mountain trout. One would suppose a man could have been happy and the words of the past come to mind:
And here in the lone little vale I exclaimed,

> With a maid that was lovely to soul as to eye,
> Who would blush if I praised and weep if I blamed,
> "How calm could I live and how blest could I die?"

The quotation may be wrong, but a matron was there, and first-class, blue grass cooking, with no cause for blushing, hams such as you would find only in the mountains of Kentucky, Tennessee or Virginia.

But this modern Eden was as open to the attack of the devil as the home of Adam and Eve. As soon as we struck camp a middle aged typical Kentucky farmer came to call on us and offered eggs, chickens, milk, butter and forage, so we were in clover. As soon as he heard my name he came to me and shook my hand and said, "Young man, I am glad to see you. Your name is a very familiar one to me. A sister of mine, Leticia, married a Wm. Miller Baylor, who moved to Texas and you are perhaps his son George." "No," I said, "but he is my uncle and I know all his family."

Noticing he carried his arm in a sling and looked rather pale and peaked, I asked him what was the matter. He said that he had been waylaid and shot from the brush near his home by a man named Barnes and some of his friends; that the bullet, evidently from a rifle, had broken his right arm, struck a rib and followed it around, and lodged against the back bone, and he had barely pulled through with his life. I asked the cause of the trouble and he said that he was the agent for a small band of Indians living in the valley and that Barnes had abused one of the young girls and cut her with a knife, and he denounced him as a low-down contemptible brute and coward, and a few days afterwards had been shot from the brush. Menefee, the sheriff of the county, had come up with warrants for his arrest, but Barnes, who had some property and friends, managed to keep out of his way, and afterwards sent Coleman word he intended to stay in the valley until he killed him and then leave.

Coleman was an uncle of William Tell Coleman, a prominent merchant of San Francisco, and prominent just at that time as No. 33, secretary of the vigilance committee of that city. The writer had stood guard at "Ft. Gunny Bags" and after James King of William, an editor, had been shot, we had done some judicious hanging.[4] Judge David S. Terry had stabbed a man and was under arrest. Had the man died Terry would have been hanged, as certainly as others had been.[5] A plug ugly bruiser named "Yankee Sullivan" was so sure he would be hung that he committed suicide. There was, in opposition to the vigilantes, a "Law and Order Party" that sided with the Gamblers, strange to say.

Our little party was divided on the question, so at our first camp the vote was that the question should not be brought up at all during the hunt, so it was taboo and never mentioned, but this last act revived it and our vigilantes were pretty pronounced in their opinions as to what should be done with such a man as Barnes.

You may be sure, as a kinsman, Coleman's quarrel was mine, as soon as I heard it, and I told him as Barnes was there with the avowed object of finishing him we would show him, it was a game two could play at. I said: "I don't want to quit my party now, but when they return to San Francisco I will remain with you and give you such protection as I can until the fellow leaves. He told me then that he had it pretty straight that Barnes, a younger brother, and an old German named Peter Sala, had waylaid him and that it was old Sala's rifle ball that struck him.

Our party went down the valley and camped near the narrow canyon leading to the Pacific Ocean. One of the Indians came to me and offered to go with me and butcher and pack in any deer I might kill. We had not gone half a mile when his quick eye caught sight of a fine doe about 100 yards off, and at the crack of my rifle she dropped in her tracks, shot square through the shoulders. I can see him now, a great tall fellow of six feet, as he raised his hand up and covered his mouth, staring at me and the deer in astonishment. He would have been a good model for a sculptor. His tribe, he told me, were called the Sha-bel-de-nah pomah, which being translated in his linage meant "the near by people." They were a splendid looking set of people, having plenty of game and the ocean near by with clams and fish without stint, and the woods filled with berries of various kinds. A woman who violated the laws of chastity was killed, hence they were greatly stirred up over the attempt of Barnes. Mine was the first venison in camp, and enjoyed accordingly, in steak and roast ribs.

The brook was full of speckled trout but no one had been able to get a mess. They said the trout usually "hid out" as soon as they showed up, and though they could see them plain enough they would not bite but would back off or hide under the banks or rocks. I had read old Sir Isaac Walton and knew pretty well what the trouble was, and in such clear water as we had there we must observe the old English rule to fish "Fine and far off." So I concluded their lines were too large.

In my boyhood I had learned from the Seminoles how to make a line out of horse hair, so I pulled out some hairs from a horse's tail and rolled up my pants on one leg, wet the palm of my hand, and soon had a nice line of four strands of hair rolled or twisted together. Then I went into my violin case and got some of the wire off of a G string and made a small hook, and after an animated chase after frogs and grasshoppers was ready for business. We were camped close to the creek and I noticed when I went for water a lot of trout disappeared like a flash under a bank overhung with brush, so I went just above it and stirred up the mud, waited until it ran down, and creeping around with a nice dogwood pole dropped in a frog. I soon had a jerk and after a brief fight got a trout and kept on until I had a mess. That evening I killed a fine buck below the camp and that night we had music galore. Our quartette sang "Roy's Wife" and I played "Old Zip Coon" while Clements "cut the pigeon wing."

Our party went to the coast and up it. At one camp we enjoyed a clam roast, our digger Indian bringing a basket full of fresh clams from the rocks. It was a bitterly cold night and I suggested giving all our saddle blankets to the Indian, but Colonel Tobin said nay, we would lose his services, as he would be sure to catch cold. He wrapped up in one not very heavy saddle blanket and snored all night.

The next day I went out after elk, and a shower coming on, I got into a hollow sugar-pine tree, and a fine herd of old bucks and does came into the little valley I was watching, but the wind gave me away before I could get a shot. They went tearing off through the brush like a herd of Texas steers.

Our party returned to the city, but I remained with Coleman. He told me he had kept posted as to Barnes' movement and he was harbored by a man about three miles below on the creek, and still said he intended to kill Coleman before leaving the country. Coleman did not leave his home, not being able to use either pistol or rifle.

Among Coleman's neighbors was an old Kentucky farmhand named Tom something, and another from the mountains of Tennessee named Ingram. He had a hooked nose and eyes like a hawk. His nephew was with him, a young fellow with keen black eyes and firm strong jaw, that denoted grit. They hailed from Texas, having crossed the plains, and of course were skilled in the use of firearms.

We held a council of war and concluded instead of sitting around until picked off or waylaid we would carry the war into Africa. "A little learning is a dangerous thing," was demonstrated here. I was sure that Barnes having waylaid and shot my uncle, and the sheriff having attempted to arrest him, I had a perfect right to either kill or capture him without being deputized or having a warrant for his arrest. At any rate, we decided it was better to hunt them than to sit around the house and have them pick us off at leisure. Having looked to our arms to be sure there would be no snapping or hang fire in case of a scrap, we went to bed and Mrs. Coleman promised to "call us early," not to be queen of the May, but to get us a strong cup of coffee.

I took an old Kentucky rifle and a five-shooter. There was a shot gun in the house but we left it with Mrs. Coleman in case our enemies had taken the same notion as we had. It saved young Barnes from being killed, as the sequel will show.

We were called about 3 a.m. and by the time we saddled up, our breakfast of hot coffee and biscuit, and a slice of ham with eggs was ready and we took up the line of march for the camp where we were told the men were being harbored. It was quite cold and I confess I was shivering, whether from cold or fear I cannot say, but when I was a boy we had a half bull[dog] and half hound that always stood shivering and his teeth rattling when I was trying to chuck a cat or coon out of a tree, but the moment the varmint struck the ground old Sam Houston, as we called him, sailed in, and when he got a good hold shut both eyes and it was all up with Mr. Coon. So we must not think a boy is scared because he turns pale or even cries.

All the chivalry in my nature was aroused. This man Barnes had bulldozed a weak-kneed fellow and run him off and took his wife, a very pretty little black-eyed woman; had abused the young Indian maid and then waylaid my uncle like a cold-blooded assassin and tried to murder him, and was still around the brush on the dodge, vowing blood should flow.

We rode along the main road down the valley, and when beyond the camp turned to the right to the foothills and dismounted a quarter of a mile from it and tied our horses and stole along Indian file until we came to a small branch that the camp was on. The place was well chosen, as the canyon was quite narrow and rough and a dense thicket where the branch left the hills. We crossed this branch and saw a beaten trail going into the canyon. Though it was not daylight, we took our stand on the brow of the hills overlooking the camp and, lying down, patiently waited for daylight. The horned owls began their mournful hooting, while a screech owl complained in a quavering tone at being disturbed. I never did like them, and our old darkies used to make my hair stand on end by their grave yard stories, and always said "when de screech owl come hollerin' 'round de house, sure sign some-body gwine to die." Very few people ever got over the impressions made on them in childhood. So the cold chills ran up and down my backbone in response to the bass and treble of our serenaders.

Other birds began to sing. The thrush tuned up, and red birds joined in the chorus. The owl quit and the east began to show its lovely hues. I would have preferred then to have been in dear old Frisco with Lon Townsend, Louis Pardee, or my dear old sister, practicing some of De Berriot's pieces for violin and piano.

Our campers soon began to stir and the axe gave notice that a man was about. Soon a bright light lit up the front of his tent and we saw his wife come out, and saw all the preparations for a breakfast. Luckily for us the wind was in our favor, and two or three curs nosing about did not detect us, or our game would have been spoiled.

The camper came out and putting his hand to the side of his mouth gave a yell, and that was, in Texas Ranger parlance, "a dead give away." We knew our men were close by as well as if we had seen them, and sure enough they soon made their appearance, coming out of the brush canyon following the trail we had seen. There were only the two brothers, and as they went we slipped down to the trail and followed. The camper had fixed up a rough table in front of his tent with rude benches around it.

Both men and the camper and wife were seated at the table and busy eat-ing, and never even looked up, so intense were they in storing away their rations. The dogs first discovered us, as we approached, and at the first bark of the canine sentinel, I said, "Let's charge them, boys," so we went at full speed and as we were within twenty steps when they saw us we got to the table almost by the time they got on their feet. They sent plates and benches in every direction. The older brother ran down the bed of the creek, and three of the boys followed him, all doing first-class panting. I took after the other one, who crossed the creek at a bound, and started up the west side for the brush canyon. I yelled at him to "halt" and "surrender," but I might as well have called on a jack rabbit to halt, so I raised my gun, and ran back as quick as possible, and took aim at his back, and just as I was ready to pull the trigger he stumbled, and I brought down my gun as I fired and tore up the ground just beyond his head. I again yelled "surrender, or I'll kill you," but he had bounced up off the ground like an India rubber ball and seemed to be flying, so I opened fire with my five-shooter, and it had the effect of getting all the speed in him out, and he soon distanced me.

Hearing several shots, I ran back to see what the other boys were doing. I found them about a hundred yards below the camp, looking up in the trees, into brush heaps, and as badly puzzled a lot as I ever saw. They said they had followed, feeling pretty sure they would catch Barnes, as the ground became more open below, and had fired a shot out of a six-shooter to stop him, but it was like touching a match to a sky-rocket, he just sailed out of sight and disappeared as suddenly as if the earth had swallowed him up, which it did, in fact. He had gotten the camper to dig a hole in the bank of the creek under the roots of an old oak tree that hung down nearly to the bed of the creek. He just could squeeze in at the mouth, but it had been coyoted inside, giving room to lie down, and all the dirt had been carefully carried away or scattered. This we learned long afterwards.

We went back to the camp and told the man he was liable to a heavy fine and imprisonment for harboring a fugitive from justice, and moreover, told him it wouldn't be healthy for him if we heard of Barnes or his gang being at his camp again. We then went to our horses, for with two fellows loose in the brush, we thought it best to look out for them and rode home.

Coleman was disappointed that we had not bagged our game, but hoped, in which his wife heartily joined, that the men would take the hint that it was not quite such an easy game as they had expected and would leave the country. But it only seemed to have made them fighting mad. A friend of Coleman's told us the elder Barnes was over at a house not a mile away, up on the side of the mountain, and had sworn he would kill all of the party that had tried to arrest him, kill Coleman and burn down his house.

So we were in for it, and had to fight it out in true Kentucky mountain style. Barnes had a name of being a desperado, and certainly had grit and gall. We learned that old Peter Sala was with him, but his brother was either wounded or had enough of it. So we determined to try them once more. There were two houses, or single rooms, about 15 steps apart. The houses were pretty well on the side of the mountain. A man and his wife were in the eastern room and Barnes and the woman had the western room. There was a good deal of timber on the mountain, and we started out early and got up on the side of the mountain east of the houses and hid our horses, and came down to the houses. We knew in reason that Barnes and his friends would be looking and watching towards Coleman's home, which was in plain view.

We had left old Ingram with Mrs. Coleman, and I took the double-barrelled shotgun instead of the rifle, for we argued, that unless the man where Barnes was stopping took a hand we would have the advantage in numbers, and the law on our side as a reward had been offered for Barnes. We were again lucky enough to surprise them and were right between the two rooms before they saw us, and the man living there was doing some kind of work and the two women were in the east room.

We ran right to the door of the house we were told Barnes was in, I being in the lead. As I reached the door old Peter Sala stepped out with a cocked rifle in his hand and stood on the right hand side facing me. He was left-handed and as we stood the muzzles of our guns nearly touched. His old rifle was nearly as long as a fence rail and looked awful big to me. He said in a rough way, "What do you want?" I answered, "We have come to arrest Mr. Barnes; there is a warrant out for him and the sheriff has tried to arrest him. I don't want any difficulty with him, but we are determined to take him."

"You can't do it," was the curt reply, and there was a flash and report of a pistol almost in my face. I felt a sharp pain in my left thumb and stomach, and three other shots followed in rapid succession, all in a direct line with my body, and I could feel the sting like a hot iron after every shot in my left hand.

Barnes had gotten behind the door on the right hand side. As it was half open it left a crack between the door and facing, where he could see me but I could not see him, thought I could see the flash and smoke of the pistol each time.

Old Peter looked me right in the eye, as much as to say, "I think you have got your dose," and started to throw up his gun to shoot one of the boys.

Under such circumstances the mind works fast. I knew if I shot him while his rifle covered my body, a convulsive clutch of his finger might touch the double trigger and send the big rifle ball through me. But the instant his rifle moved, I did not take time to throw my gun to the shoulder, but as a boy I had hunted with Jerry Dent of the United States Army at Fort Towson, and threw my gun on his breast and fired. The whole load of buckshot went square through him and he sank down. Tom had fired at the same time and then sprang with his rifle clubbed to brain him, but saw he was done for.

Barnes had fired two shots through the weather-boarding in the direction of the boys, hoping to hit them, and had stepped to the bed on the right as you entered the room and picked up another revolver. I threw my gun on him and he tried to jump back, but he was too late, and got part of the load of shot in his side. Seeing there was a window at the end of the room and think-ing he might get out and give leg bail, I drew my five-shooter and ran around to guard against it. By the time I got around I heard four shots in rapid suc-cession, too quick for one person, and ran back as quick as possible and found Barnes lying on the ground in the agonies of death and Ingram standing near him.

Barnes was good grit, and the minute I ran around to the back of the house and he heard me, he came boldly out of the door and fired at Ingram, cutting a lock of hair from his temple. Before Barnes could fire again, Ingram put two bullets through his heart and another in his side as he fell. His mistress, when she saw him fall, raised a real panther yell and made a dash at me with a long, glittering dagger, but I told her if she put herself in a man's place she would get a man's fare and not to come any nearer to me, and I spoke to the man and told him he had better take charge of her, which he did.

Barnes's first bullet was a dead line shot, but a miracle, almost, preserved my life. The belt that I wore had an iron ring sewed on it in front and the strap that it buckled with was sewed onto this ring. The first shot, as I have said, struck the thumb nail of my left hand, which was over the top of the gun, and burst the ball of my thumb open, and then struck the iron ring that was welded one-half on one side and one-half on the other; the force of the bullet raised a great knot on my stomach and broke the skin, so that the blood ran pretty freely and I made pretty sure I was shot through. The other shots cut the ramrod in several places and ran down between the barrels each time, shivering off a piece of stock, but the bullets passing through the thimbles of the gun were split up in fine pieces, which lodged in the stock, though several of them struck my hand, cutting one of my fingers nearly in two and cutting deep holes in the palm of my hand.

If I had shown the white feather and turned my back I would have had a bullet between my shoulder blades, and if the first or other shots had been to the right or left of my gun barrel he would have killed me. The insignificant, apparently useless iron ring saved my life, or Providence did not intend I should die at that time. A man is much like an animal, and when he gets to fighting does not mind cuts or bullets.

We went back to our horses and rode home. Our friends were in a great state of excitement, as they heard the shooting and did not know the result until we came back, and seeing my arm in a sling knew I was shot. The boys said the first word when we got to our horses and looked at my hand: "There goes all the music." I had no idea I could ever use it again.

Coleman and his wife were very grateful, as they should have been, as we had risked our lives in their defense. My wound was dressed, but my thumb began to swell and turn black.

The second day we received a genuine surprise when eight or ten men rode up near the house and one came up and said they had come to arrest us for murder. The spokesman intimated that he belonged to the "law and order party" of San Francisco and learned I was one of the vigilantes that hung men without law, and they had come to arrest us and take us to Santa Rosa and put us in jail. I told him I thought he had a strange idea about law and order, as he was taking the part of a cold-blooded assassin and brutal coward, and as to surrendering to him and his crowd we had no idea of doing anything of the kind, and we intended to go into Santa Rosa and surrender to the sheriff, but if any of Barnes' or Sala's friends interfered with us they would get as good a fight as we could put up. This ended the matter and they went off.

My hand was paining me so that I was afraid I would lose it, so we determined to start before day and maybe miss our friends and get a doctor. After about four or five miles we heard the sound of galloping horses behind us, and looking around saw six or eight men coming at full speed. We took it for granted it meant war again, so agreed hurriedly to give them the best lick in the shop.

Coleman only had one hand and myself the same; Tom had his rifle and Ingram his six-shooter. As soon as the foremost fellow reined up by my side, who proved to be a German, I had him covered with my revolver, and although I believed that "thrice armed is he whose cause is just," yet I believed with Josh Billings, "better he who gets in his lick first." The least move meant death on his part, and I would have pulled the trigger, but his look of astonishment satisfied me he did not intend war. "What do you mean?" said he. "What do you mean?" said I, "a crowd of you all armed, galloping up to us this way." "We meant no harm, only wanted to see what sort of looking fellow you were. You are the fighting Texan, I suppose?" "Yes, I am a Texan, and will fight if necessary." He then said they were friends of Sala, but were satisfied if we went in and surrendered. So they turned off and went galloping through the woods like a lot of Comanches. We were not so dead sure about their good intentions, and kept a sharp lookout for an ambuscade.

We reached Santa Rosa safely and after my hand was dressed we were given a preliminary hearing and bound over to appear before the grand jury. The women, God bless them, had heard of the fight and its cause, and took our part enthusiastically, and we gave bond without any trouble. Mac-Menifee, the sheriff, said he was glad we had saved him the job; that he did not fancy a bit arresting Barnes.

At that time Sherwood Coan, or Sherry Campbell, his stage name, a cousin of my brother-in-law, Capt. Theo. D. Maltby, was staying with us, and as I frequently saw the minstrel troupe he was with, they all took an interest in me and agreed to give me a benefit at Maguire's Opera House. I can recall now with gratitude, after nearly half a century, the names of E. Horn, Jerry Bryant, Sherry Campbell, Barker, Billy Burch, the funny bones—all have passed to the other side of the River Styx, peace to their ashes.

Judge John Love, a relative of Captain Maltby, and the Hon. H.S. Foote of Mississippi, somewhat of a fighter himself, who had been principal in several duels, volunteered to defend me, [so I] surrendered and stayed in jail a month before court met. He said it was to gain the sympathy of the people, but that was mine already. The ladies sent me flowers every day, and all my meals came from the same source. My special friend and champion was Mrs. Ross, wife of Judge Ross, for whom I have had a warm attachment ever since.

We were all tried before Judge McKinstry, charged with assault to commit murder in the first degree, but after a jury, mostly from Missouri and Kentucky, heard the evidence, instructions of the court and the speech of Colonel Love, and a fiery argument from Governor Foote, it did not take them long to bring in a verdict in substance, "served 'em right."

NOTES

1 Mark Twain (Samuel Langhorne Clemens) did not arrive in California until 1864. Clemens had gone west to Nevada Territory in 1861 as confidential secretary to his brother, Orion, who was the newly appointed secretary to the territorial governor. Goldblatt, "George Wythe Baylor," 15.

2 Petaluma is about forty miles north of San Francisco.

3 Santa Rosa is north of Petaluma and about sixty miles north of San Francisco.

4 James King of William added "of William" (his father's given name) to his name so he could be distinguished from several other James Kings. King was a former banker who became a crusading editor of the San Francisco *Evening Bulletin* and an opponent of vice and corruption in the bay city. Said to have been the richest man in San Francisco, he was mortally wounded by a member of the San Francisco Board of Supervisors, whom King had exposed as a New York criminal elected through fraud. Coleman, a veteran of a previous vigilante committee, recruited some 2,600 members into a new vigilante committee that set up headquarters in a converted liquor warehouse ringed with sandbags called Fort Gunnybags. The vigilantes hanged Casey, who had murdered James King of William, and another accused murderer, Charles Cora, from the roof of Fort Gunnybags. Robert M. Senkewicz, *Vigilantes in Gold Rush California* (Palo Alto: Stanford University Press, 1985), 176-77, 199-200; and George R. Stewart, *Committee of Vigilance: Revolution in San Francisco, 1851* (Boston: Houghton Mifflin, 1964), 128.

5 Terry, judge of the California Supreme Court, stabbed a law-and-order stalwart named Hopkins. Terry was arrested, charged with a series of crimes, but quietly released. On 13 September 1859, Terry killed David C. Broderick, United States senator from California and a Free Soil Democrat, in a duel near Lake Merced. Terry then rode east to Virginia City, Nevada Territory, where he practiced law. During the Civil War, Terry commanded the 8th Texas Cavalry (Terry's Texas Cavalry). He returned to California after the war and was killed in 1889 by a deputy marshal during another feud. Terry's Texas Cavalry should not be confused with Terry's Texas Rangers, which was originally commanded by Col. D.S. Terry, a brother of David S. Terry. Senkewicz, *Vigilantes in Gold Rush California*, 166-71; A. Russell Buchanan, *David S. Terry of California: Duelling Judge* (San Marino: Huntington Library, 1956), 20-71; and Marcus J. Wright, *Texas in the War, 1861-1865*, ed. Harold B. Simpson (Hillsboro: Hill College Press, 1965), 30, 124.

CHAPTER EIGHT

Adventures with Wild Animals

~

In the year 1857, when the writer was "an honest miner" on Kern River, California, a man by the name of Linn was appointed agent for a small band of Digger Indians that were located on Posey Creek.[1]

Linn was an old miner and frontiersman, and after many ups and downs, had concluded to try farming in a small way—raising fruits and vegetables to supply the miners of Kern River and adjacent camps. At the time the Mammoth Lead Mining Company had a large quartz mill. Major Erskine also had one and the Keys Brothers another, and a great many people were coming into that country prospecting.

Linn settled in the beautiful little valley that probably now bears his name, and intended to use the rich valley that already was covered with a heavy growth of wild clover, itself a good paying crop. This clover the Indians are fond of, and from that may have originated the saying "he's in clover." Grizzly bears were as fond of this clover as the Diggers and were about as plentiful in that region at that time.[2]

One evening Linn went out hunting near his camp, taking with him one of the Digger warriors that he had great confidence in and who was much attached to him. The Indian had nothing in the way of arms but his bow and a quiver of arrows and a small cur that could easily trace his ancestors to the coyotes. But though insignificant in appearance, he had more in him than appeared in a cursory glance. He took an important part in the story I am relating.

Linn took a well beaten path along the edge of the valley where the clover was very high and as it was getting late an old she grizzly and her cubs had come down from the mountain side to drink and eat clover. They were just in the edge of the high clover, and Linn and his Indian were within fifty yards of them before he saw them. An old she grizzly with cubs is probably the most dangerous creature in the world. I doubt if the king of beasts, the lion, or man-eating tiger, are any more savage or dangerous. The hunters realize their danger, for when the old bear reared to take a look at them, and then dropped down and started towards them, they knew the sooner they took to the trees the better, and made all haste to some post oaks that grew all around the edge of the valley. The Indian ran up one like a monkey, but Linn was not so fortunate. He, however, climbed high enough to get hold of a stout limb. He had a dragoon Colt revolver. The bear made for him, and being a large one reared up and caught him by one of his feet. He had on a pair of heavy mining boots and swung on to his limb with both hands for dear life, the bear striking at him with her immense claws.

The Digger warrior, seeing his friend's peril, slid down and running up quite close, sent an arrow into the grizzly's ribs, and set the dog on her. The little cur at once ran up and grabbed the bear by the hind leg, and that is something a bear can't stand. So turning Linn loose, she made for the dog. The cur, as all dogs will, ran for his master with the bear close behind. The Indian had no chance to climb a tree so ran to a large one and began to dodge around it. For some time he was so quick that the bear could not touch him but he could not use his bow in such close quarters except to thrust with an arrow in his hand. The dog was doing his best and attacked the bear, nipping him at every opportunity; but I have always noticed that any wild animal will quit dogs to attack a man.

Linn could not aid his Indian but began to hope that the noise they made would bring them help from the Indian village. The bear seemed at last to have reasoned out an attack. She made a grab at the Indian on one side and as quick as lightning sprang on him. The brave little cur flew at the grizzly but the enraged beast paid no attention to him. Linn said that he then determined as the Indian had risked his life to save him, he would save the Indian or die in the attempt. He sprang down on the ground, got his rifle and shot the bear through the body. The grizzly quit the Indian and started for Linn, the little cur still holding on to him. Linn was too badly bitten in the foot to run so he grabbed his revolver and began firing. He had already shot twice from the tree and had three loads left. The first two shots did not check the grizzly, but his last was fired at close quarters. As the bear reared up on its hind legs to strike, he shot her square in the mouth and broke her neck. She fell over, her big carcass still, that a moment before was so full of life and fury. Great is Colt, say I.

I met Linn a few days afterwards and he gave me an account of the affair. He went to the Indian at once but he was dead—the grizzly had crushed his skull like an egg shell. Noticing that Linn's dove colored overcoat had innumerable rents in the back and shoulders in parallel lines, I asked him how it had been done. He answered that it was the work of a California lynx. He then told me that one evening late, he took his rifle, leaving his revolver at home, and went out to try for some deer that browsed in and near his field. Crawling to get near enough for a shot, while he was under a live oak tree on all fours he encountered the lynx. The lynx was probably watching the deer, (a doe and two fawns), hoping they would pass under the tree, and afford him a supper and breakfast; but pounced down on Linn and tried to grip his throat. Fortunately for him, it was very cold and he had his coat collar turned up around the neck, and the beast only got hold of the collar and other clothing, or the man would not have come out winner in the desperate fight that ensued.

The lynx, an unusually large one, and likely enough very hungry, kept his hold on him, and began fiddling on his back with his hind feet in a way that promised to soon get through his clothes and reach the meat. Linn was so astonished that for a moment he hardly knew what to do, but he had struggled to his feet, and being unable to use his rifle, drew a butcher knife he had, and tried to stab the lynx. The knife was one he had used a long while in the northern part of the state in crevicing for gold, that is picking it out of the seams of the rocks, at Feather River, and it was as dull as the traditional meat axe. It did no more than glance off the ribs of the lynx, and only angered him. The lynx was on Linn's right shoulder so Linn could not strike him a fair blow or get hold of him anyway. The cat had the best of it every time, clawing the man, lacerating his hands, spitting and growling. Linn found it nearly impossible to keep his feet, with this weight on his back, and he dreaded the cat changing its hold for if he should get him by the neck, with his strong jaws and long teeth, he could have broken his neck. Then Linn tried falling on the lynx with all his weight and lying on top of him. This did not stop the fiddling with the hind feet, but started the forepaws to work, and they were armed with the sharpest and longest claws and soon made the "fur-fly" for Linn's scalp.

Linn tells that he was now getting out of wind, not having been in training for such a scrap, and it began to look as though this animal of thirty-five or forty pounds was to come off victor. But finally Linn managed to get the cat under his right side, and placing the butcher knife's point against the beast's side, threw his weight on the handle and drove it through the lynx's side. The cat hung on savagely until the blood from his lungs filled his mouth and he gasped in the last throes of death. Man armed with only a dull knife is still quite a dangerous customer. This is the only instance that I ever knew of a lynx, or a catamount or wild cat attacking man, though I have heard they do sometimes in the northern states during cold spells driven by starvation.

At the risk of being tedious I must tell of a desperate encounter your worthy mayor, Judge Joseph Magoffin, had with two full grown jaguars or leopards as they are called in West Texas.[3]

At the time I speak of they were quite common, and very few saddle shops but what displayed one or more skins which were commonly used to ornament saddles. They are very rare now, one was seen in the Nueces Canyon a few years ago, but they have drifted west and nothing short of hunt, especially in the worst chaparral, would repay the hunter. I hope our vice-president, Teddy, will honor us with a visit and he may have a beautiful leopard skin to add to his mountain lions.

Sometime after the war, Judge Magoffin was with a train going from San Antonio to El Paso and stopping to camp at Turkey Creek or the Nueces River, concluded to go out and kill a mess of quail for supper. He had not gone far until he walked within twenty-five yards of two immense jaguars, or leopards, lying down under a tree, evidently asleep. He only had a shot gun loaded with number eight shot and was not out for leopards or lions, and therefore was quite as much astonished as the animals were at this "unexpected pleasure." The judge says he remembered that it was currently reported that a man could strike terror into the heart of a wild, ferocious animal, by looking them in the eye and out of countenance so to speak.

Here was an opportunity to demonstrate this fact in the interest of science. So he posed as a Roman gladiator might, and began to try and strike terror into them so as to beat a hasty retreat himself. The leopards had raised their heads and were examining him critically, but showed no signs of fear or bashfulness. If there had been but one he might have "buffaloed" him or had he been like Tom Conklin, and been able to cross fire on them, it might have been a successful ruse. But he said they didn't dismay worth a cent, but on the contrary, struck terror into his soul, when they began to switch their tails back and forth in a way that he knew boded no good for him. So he began to back slowly at first, but like a locomotive gaining from momentum. When he got what he thought was a good start he faced about and fled ingloriously for camp. I have no doubt but what he can be induced to give Teddy Roosevelt details in case the vice-president would like to try the experiment.

Another encounter with a mountain lion occurred near Van Horn. Lt. Kirk Turnbo of my company and a squad of Rangers was stationed there, and Dr. Buck was appointed surgeon of the department. The doctor built a box house of cedar and the floor was some three feet from the ground. He had a big, lubberly half grown cur at the house, and one day the dog gave a yell of pain and thumping was heard under the floor, and the doctor concluded as everything grew quiet that Dick, the pet of Company A, had come over to keep his hand, or teeth in, and had given his dog the shake. Next morning, however, when the doctor called the dog to feed him, he did not show up, and looking under the house he was very much astonished to see only the hind quarters of his dog. The head and half the body were gone and the back bone and ribs cut as straight as though a butcher's cleaver had been used. Examining the ground he found the tracks of an immense panther, and swore by the great horn spoon he would get even with him. As doctors generally manage to kill plenty of people without resorting to strychnine, he had none with him, but at night he tied a small rope to the dog's hind leg and blew out the lights and waited for a bite. This was a novel kind of fishing, but he had a good double barreled shotgun well loaded with blue whistlers.

The doctor sat up until midnight and then went to bed, setting his gun handy and tied the rope to his left arm. Just before daybreak he was awakened by a vigorous pull at his bait and found himself on the floor. Moving pretty steadily towards the window he managed to grab his gun and when he got to the window he sat back like an old tongue steer and aimed at a dark object outside and fired, and fell backwards as the rope was turned loose. Not caring to risk a wounded panther in the dark he waited for daylight and soon found the trail and plenty of blood. Within 150 yards of his house he found the dead panther and an immense one too.

NOTES

[1] Kern River drains a large part of the southern Sierra Nevadas, including the western slopes of Mount Whitney and what is today Sequoia National Park, before emptying into Kern Lake in the upper San Joaquin Valley.

[2] California miners had a tendency to refer to any lowly group of Indians as Diggers. The Diggers were primarily gatherers and foragers who dug for anything edible such as seeds, nuts, berries, roots, snakes, lizards, and rodents. The name today is generally used to refer to natives of the Great Basin.

[3] See n. 2, Ch. 3, this section.

CHAPTER NINE

Buster the Grizzly

NOT A GREAT WHILE AFTER OLD BUSTER, THE TERROR OF KERN RIVER, gave me such an awful scare, old Ham, who lived in a little valley on the lower trail between Kern River and White River, came by our mill and sang out: "George you ought to go down to my camp and stay a few days, there are more quail, deer and bear, than you ever saw. The ground is covered with post oak acorns and the game has collected in there thick, and they are big and fat; the clover is up nicely, and the grizzlies are in there every night, and have regular roads all over the valley and sides of the mountains, where they come in to feed. You needn't take any grub. I left plenty in camp and you will find a frying pan, coffee pot, oven and everything you need. I am going over to Keysville with a load of goods for Kenedy, and won't be back for several days. Better take all your shooting irons. They's the biggest grizzlies over there I ever saw, and you may run into them."

I thanked him for the invitation but promised myself not to have any truck with another grizzly, specially old Buster, unless I had all the advantage on my side. After my narrow escape from my last grizzly, I determined never to go into the woods unless I was well heeled, so I got me a big two-edged hack knife and make it as keen as I could. I had a good navy Colt and I got a light stub twist German "doppelbixie," a one-barrel rifle, a shotgun, and I had my Hawkins. I loaded the German shot-barrel with a big load of No. 5 shot, intending to shoot the bear's eyes out if he crowded me, and then trust to my heels for safety.

The knife and pistol I hoped would never have to be used. My speed was my main dependence. I went back about two weeks after old Buster scared me so badly, to look at the sign, and the shortest step I found was about nine feet, and the longest about twenty—the last where I was going down the mountain at the angle of 45 degrees under full head of steam before I had time to "whistle down brakes."

I took my blankets and armaments and started down full of life and hope of a glorious time all to myself and reached Ham's hay camp about noon. Found everything to my taste, and went to get some fresh meat; wounded a fine doe, but did not get her; and then went around the little valley to look at the signs.

I saw there were several bears, from the different sized tracks. One track about the size of an ordinary frying pan satisfied me my ancient enemy was among the number, and I had no idea of trying him a quarter race again, unless I could get the advantage—and that I knew I could do, though it was hardly sportsmanlike.

Bears nearly always enter their feeding grounds at one point and leave at another. I saw where they went out on the south side of the valley and took an axe and went up and set my rifle across the trail—that is to command it.

Every bear that leaves on the trail will stop exactly in the same track, and when the ground is wet, will wear down a hole four or five inches deep, so there was no trouble about where to set the rifle.

And it is not every hunter that knows how to set a gun. I'll give a brief account of it just as I set mine. I cut two small saplings, size of my wrist, leaving forks on them about three feet from the bottom which is sharpened, and cut off just above the forks—you drive them in the ground at a right angle from the path, about six inches deep and so that when you lay your gun on the forks the muzzle will be four or five feet from the trail. Tie the gun firmly on the forks. Cut a stick about a foot long and drive down a stake opposite and close to the trigger, and tie your short stick to it, letting it rest against the trigger—then tie a stout string to the end of this stick and pass under the barrel of the gun at the front fork—across the trail—and tie to a stout stake driven in the ground. Let your string be two and a half feet from the ground. You are apt to shoot too low unless the barrel is two and a half to three feet above the ground. A big grizzly stands pretty high off the ground.

With your gun fixed in this way you "ketch 'em coming or going," for as soon as the bear runs against your string it pulls the end of your lever and bang goes the gun.

On my way into camp I fired into a flock of quail and got half a dozen, about as many as I could "chamber" for supper and breakfast; and after dressing them nicely, but skinning, lazy miner style, I built me a kind of fort out of some bales of clover Ham had put up, having the entrance close up against a big hay stack put up old style with a pole in the center.

My idea was if a grizzly tried to make me get up I would scale up the stack and get hold of the pole and with my revolver make a good stand-off fight.

Having put on coffee and bread I was frying my quail, when I heard a splashing in the branch of the stream just in front of me, and lifting my frying pan off the fire and listening, I made out it was a bear walking up the bed of the branch, which was grown up thick in willows. Setting down my pan "one time and two motions," I scaled on top of the hay stack before you could say scat. But Mr. Bear kept on up the branch, and I slid down and was soon enjoying quail fried brown, hot strong coffee, and a good old greasy camp bread.

I crawled into room No. 1, Sprawl's Hotel, and was soon sound asleep and knew little until I heard the California quail in the morning chattering to each other. I had slept in my clothes and kept my moccasins on, knowing that a grizzly would never wait for a fellow to dress if he called on him, so I was soon out.

I heard my rifle first; loud and clear it rang out on the mountain, and roar of rage and anger followed it, so I knew my rifle had got in its work.

I did not care about interviewing that bear until he had time to make his will, for fear he might connect me in his mind with the infernal machine and I knew a grizzly only had one way of settling any doubt he might have on the subject and that was by tearing the suspected party into tatters. So I cooked my breakfast and then went up to the bear trail to see what had been done. I found the brush knocked down around my rifle, grass torn up, trees bit, and blood and hair over the brush and leaves, and finally I got the trail off. On the bear road there was so much blood on the trail I was sure I would find him dead in a short distance and followed the trail at a pretty good gait but had my German gun slung by a strap over my shoulder and my rifle ready for use, also my legs.

I saw from the size of the tracks made, it was not the big grizzly, and therefore was not so much afraid of him. I knew from experience that they were as different in their dispositions as the human race, for I had met some that took to their heels as soon as they saw me. Others stood and looked as much as to say, "you let me alone and I'll let you alone," and one, my friend Buster, that just took after me, when I had not said an impertinent word to him.

The trail led up the side of the mountain southeast of the valley and finally got into thick, scrubby brush, and oak sapling. The bear still bled freely, but there were no good trees to climb and I began to feel sort of shaky about following the trail when it entered a very thick place, especially as many a hunter had been killed or crippled for life by following a wounded grizzly into a thicket; for they are very cunning and "lay for you" and make a rush for you when you least expect it. But I relied on being able to hear him first and get in a shot. I got up near the head of a canyon that came up from the valley, where the brush became so thick I had to get down on all fours and crawl—stopping to listen every forty yards.

All at once I heard a snort and teeth pop not over fifty feet from me and the brush crack. I had been crawling with great difficulty a moment before but I straightened up suddenly and sent over the top of that brush like a flying squirrel and have no recollection of having hit the ground except in a few places until I reached the valley. My clothes were a sight and my face and hands scratched more than if I had been dragged down the mountain by the heels.

As soon as I could pull myself together, I started for camp and not having anyone else to unburden my bosom to, I began to talk to myself and among other things said, "Well, you darned fool, if you ever follow another wounded grizzly into a thicket, I hope he'll ketch you and eat you up."

After getting back to camp and killing another set of quail and getting a good square meal and rest, I felt much braver than I had in the morning, and besides my face and my feelings were considerably lacerated by the way the grizzly had treated me.

I formed a new campaign in my mind and proceeded at once to carry it out. I got a dead stick and trimmed it down to fit the shot-barrel of my German gun and then made a bullet mold by sticking it down into the damp ground and working a hole. Then melting some lead I poured it in. As it was damp it sputtered at a great rate. But finally it cooled down, and when I dug it up I don't think I ever saw an uglier looking bullet—beat any dum dum. I put a kicking load of powder down the gun, rammed hard, and patched my chunk of lead and rammed it home, putting a good wad on top. I opened a brief conversation with myself and said, "What do you think old Buster will think when that hunk of lead hits him about the bulge of the ribs?" and I chuckled to myself with glee, in anticipation of the fun.

I set my gun in the same place and drove two stakes down by the side of the stock to keep it from turning as my rifle had done. At bed time I heard some very heavy animal coming up the creek and had a presentiment from the amount of noise made that it was my old enemy. I scaled up on the hay stack and drew my revolver ready for anything that might happen, but a feeling of relief and grim satisfaction came over me as he passed on up the creek and I thought of the load in the set gun.

I knew he would fill up on acorns and then take a mess of young clover and leave the valley about daylight, so I turned in for the night, feeling just a little nervous about having such an ugly customer running around loose without muzzle or bell on, and with the possibility of his coming into camp. But I was tired and enjoyed the sleep of youth and health.

Daylight came, and I hardly had time to get up when I heard my set gun go off with the sound of a Fourth of July anvil, and a roar of rage, that seemed equal, and chased the echo of the gun around among the hills and canyons.

As I had been interviewed by the old grizzly only a short time before when there had been nothing to "rile" him, I did not care to see him just then, so I got a good substantial breakfast, examined my arms, putting on a fresh cap on my rifle and revolving the pistol to see if it worked all right, and went up to the set gun. Sure enough there was the track of the monster old grizzly going straight for the gun and all around looked like two old range bulls had been fighting—brush and saplings mashed down, bark bitten off the trees, and blood scattered all over the grass and leaves.

I examined the signs very carefully and scanned the brush all around very thoroughly, and discovered he had followed the old beaten bear walk, and took up the trail, walking very slowly and ready to run on the very slightest noise. But I argued to myself, "That chunk of lead, as heavy and rough as it was, was enough to kill an elephant so I will follow the trail a little ways anyhow." So I poked along and almost before I knew it I was way up on the side of the mountain nearly to where I had stampeded the morning before.

Before the trail got to the canyon mentioned the bear walk separated, and my big bear took the left hand trail, and did not enter the thick brush where the other had laid for me. I began to think it would be best to give up the chase, but I found a piece of fat about a yard long hanging on a bush the trail crossed, and then knew the grizzly was shot too far back and low down to strike a vital part—but knew he would be awfully sick, and I would be almost sure to discover him before getting close to him.

He went down the canyon bank, and as it was very brushy and thick down in the bed of the canyon I could not follow, but walked down the canyon bank and listened carefully. I soon heard splashing in the water. I got the direction, but was sometime in locating the spring in some willows, right across the canyon in front of me, and noticed a movement in the willows, and a monster grizzly stepped out in full view and started towards the head of the brushy canyon.

I was in a clump of pine trees and leaning my rifle against one I took a deliberate shot. He was about one hundred yards away. He gave a jump and a growl, snapping around at his side, but again moved on. I fired again and put another ball into him, and was loading hastily again, and keeping my eye on the grizzly, when I heard a stick break behind me and it came near stampeding me again, for I was thinking of the other wounded grizzly, and was greatly relieved to see that it was one of the men we had hired at the mill taking out quartz.

Some miners had stopped at the camp the evening before, and I told them of the wounded grizzly, and it being Sunday [a miner] had come down to help me look for him. We both then began to shell him in good style, and as he kept moving up the canyon we kept opposite, but no sooner did he spy us than he quit the beaten trail and started for us, but we kept shooting and when he got about half way up our side, I put a ball right in the sticking place.

That passed through his heart, and he rolled down the hill to the bottom. Such human like groans I never heard as he gave. It almost made my hair stand on end. But all grew still and we went down to the monster, and after I cut his throat to let him bleed freely I took a look at his old broad head and teeth, powerful arm, and long strong claws. I thanked Providence he had not got hold of me when he first gave me such a scare.

We butchered him and he looked larger than a Texas steer, and weighed twice as much. Taking a piece of liver, the heart, and some of the fat, we went to camp, and as we got dinner ready, Ham came in with his burro train and we enjoyed the dinner hugely.

Ham went with his entire pack train and we brought in the grizzly. I remember his hide and head was all one burro could pack and I think there were six or seven burros well loaded. Those who saw the carcass estimated that he would weigh at least 1,600 pounds. I gave Ham a quarter, we had one for our camp, and Ham sold the hind quarters in Keysville at 25 cents per pound, so I was well paid for my trip, not counting the fun and satisfaction of getting square with old Buster.

We found that he had been shot square through the ribs at some former period, and one rib broken by the ball on each side, but too high up to prove fatal. A very slight scar still showed in the upper portion of his lung; a few inches lower down and he would never have given me the scare he did. I always had a suspicion that Ham set me on that grizzly because he considered him a bad and dangerous neighbor.

CHAPTER TEN

How Mangas Coloradas Died

~

THE FOLLOWING ACCOUNT OF THE DEATH OF THIS BLOOD-THIRSTY APACHE
was given the writer by [Charles] Ferguson, an old frontiersman and Indian
fighter, and the owner of one of the large trains that before the days of railroads and Pullman palace cars, were used to haul goods from St. Louis and
Santa Fe down into Chihuahua, Mexico. Ferguson had left Santa Fe with ten
large wagons, each wagon having ten mules to haul it. Besides these he had
some extra mules and a few saddle ponies, while Ferguson himself rode an
unusually fine saddle mule.

The writer will give the account in the words of Ferguson, as taken at the
store of [Charlie] Lawrence, in El Paso, Texas, some years ago. I am sorry I
cannot recall his Christian name. He was a small, wiry Irishman, with a
sharp nose and keen grey eyes that reminded one of a hawk, and every line of
his face showed he knew no such word as fear.

Ferguson said: "I was on my way to Chihuahua in 1849, and had arrived
nearly at Bernardo Springs, in Old Mexico, when I saw a cloud of dust rising
west of the springs, and made out that it was quite a formidable van of Indians heading for the same water. I ordered my men to whip up, and we made
as quick time as possible, and beat the Indians to the water. As soon as they
got near they saw we had driven our wagons so as to form a corral around the
spring. This was the only water nearer than Corralitos, where there was quite
a large hacienda, and the ore from the silver mines was smelted.

"The Indians proved to be a hundred warriors, under the noted Apache
chief Mangas Colorad[as], Red Sleeve or Bloody Sleeve.[1] They formed in line

of battle and Mangas rode towards my train, making signs for me to come out and talk. So I went out to meet him looking well to my arms first. He was very insolent in his bearing, and demanded that I should pay him, as tribute for permission to pass through his country, my riding mule, five sacks of corn, and cigars enough for all the warriors. This would have been an easy way out of the trouble, provided any faith could have been put in his word. I had only five Americans besides myself, and five Mexicans. My wagon master, Bradford Daily, was a brave man and a good shot, and all my men were armed with the favorite rifle of that day, made by Hawkins of St. Louis. All had dragoon Colt revolvers-five shooters, and I knew my Mexicans would stand by me. In fact, we had to fight or all be killed.

"Old Mangas kept us surrounded for four days, during which time we never unhitched our mules, feeding and watering them where they stood. Each day we had a talk, each one going unarmed in front of his men, and in perfectly open ground. Mangas said he intended to stay until he starved our mules, killed us and took all our goods, which he could have done, as he could have sent part of his warriors off to water at the Corralitos River and still have men enough left to prevent us from sending a courier to the hacienda of Corralitos or moving our train.[2]

"The fourth morning I concealed my Bowie knife and went out to test Mangas. I told Daily that unless Mangas would agree to leave with his men, I intended to kill him or be killed, and if a fight came off not to come to my assistance but stay with the wagons, as the Indians would be sure to charge and leave Mangas to do me up. Mangas was a big six-footer, and nearly three times as large as I was. When we met, Mangas was very haughty and insolent and reiterated his demand, and he evidently considered that he as good as had all our scalps and *efectos*. We were standing close together, and he saw I was fighting mad, when with a sudden motion he drew a long, keen knife that he had concealed in his hair. Mine was out in an instant and I stabbed him. In return he slashed me on the head with his knife. Strangely enough he did not attempt to stab me, but kept slashing me, while I stabbed him lick for lick. He first slashed my right hand so badly that I had to change my knife to the left hand. He then cut my left wrist so badly that I had to again change to the right, and seeing that he was more than a match for me in strength, I managed to get hold of his right hand with my teeth and bit it so savagely that in the struggle he dropped his knife, when I gave it a kick that sent it clear out of his reach. He then beat and kicked me until I was black and blue for days afterwards, but I hung on with my teeth like a bull-terrier, and never let up stabbing him until he fell dead. I had literally cut his heart out. I was covered with my blood and his, and weak from my wounds, and thought I had been fighting for an hour or more. But my men said it was over in a minute and a half. I reached the wagons and a volley from my men kept off the Indians, who, seeing their chief killed, after charging by the wagons and sending in a flight of arrows, rode off and left us. On examination of my wounds by my men found none likely to prove fatal, but there are fifty-four of them on my body today to show for themselves."

Ferguson then rolled up his sleeves, and from the scars one might easily suppose he had been through a Gullett gin or a sausage machine. His men killed nine of the Indians in the charge on the train, so the pluck and superior arms of the men saved their lives. "The Mexican government," continued Ferguson, "gave me $159 for killing Mangas Colorad[as]. He was the father of the Managas who so long kept the frontier of Mexico, Arizona and Texas in terror with his raids and murders, and who was finally captured by Colonel Newby, of the United States Army, and sent to Florida."[3]

Continuing further, he said: "I was shot in the jaw by an Indian in 1845, between the pueblos of Fresnillo and Durango. I had six men with pack mules and $5,000 in silver. My men stopped at a spring to take a drink of whiskey, and I rode a little way ahead of them. The Indian was concealed behind a tree and shot me, and then stuck his head out from behind the tree to see if he had killed me. At that moment I killed him.

"I also fought a duel with Milt Faver, who afterwards settled in Texas near Presidio del Norte. We were with the [Henry] Con[ne]l[l]y and [Edward James and William Henry] Glas[g]ow train on the plains in 1847, and fell out about who was to stand guard.[4] We concluded to 'shoot it out,' according to the custom of those days. We stood back-to-back, walked ten steps, then wheeled and fired. Milt missed me, but I broke his arm, which settled the matter in my favor about who stood guard."

I could fill a book with Ferguson's adventures. I agreed to see him another day, but never did, and do not know where he is or whether he is dead or alive. Precious few of those old fellows are alive today.

NOTES

1 Mangas Coloradas was probably the greatest of Apache chiefs.

2 Ferguson's account seems credible since Mangas Coloradas was known to be in Northern Mexico for the first six months of 1849. Ferguson's characterization of Mangas as "insolent" and "haughty" also matches other accounts of the Apache warrior, as does Mangas' demand for five sacks of corn, a tactic he used with some success at the Butterfield Overland stage stations in New Mexico and Arizona in the late 1850s. Ed Sweeny to Jerry Thompson, 6 December 1995, editor's files.

3 Ferguson's account appears to lose credibility with the knife fight. Well past seventy, Mangas came into Pinos Altos in 1862 to parley. He was seized, tormented, and executed by soldiers in the California Column under Gen. Joseph R. West (not Newby), allegedly while attempting to escape. The only Newby in the United States Army at the time was in the east. The Mangas Coloradas who was sent to Florida was the son of Chief Mangas Coloradas. Mangas, the son, broke out with Geronimo in May 1885 and was the last Chiricahua captured in October 1886. Edwin R. Sweeny, *Cochise: Chiricahua Apache Chief* (Norman: University of Oklahoma Press, 1991), 204-5; Dan Thrapp, "Mangas Coloradas," *Encyclopedia of Frontier Biography*, 2:935-36; Edwin R. Sweeny to Jerry Thompson, 6 December 1994; and Heitman, *Historical Register*, 1:744.

4 Mark L. Gardner, ed., *Brothers on the Santa Fe Trails: Edward James Glasgow and William Henry Glasgow, 1846-1848* (Niwot: University of Colorado Press, 1993). For Ferguson, see 81, 141-42.

CHAPTER ELEVEN

Apaches Defeated
By Circus Tricks

~

SOME TIME DURING THE YEAR 1855, when the Old Butterfield route was established to carry the mail from California to connect with the mail line in Texas, a devilish young madcap named C.W. Garner was one of the men employed by the Overland Stage Company to guard the stage from the attacks of the murderous, thieving Apache Indians that infested the dreary road between La Mesilla and Tucson, Arizona.[1] Old Mangas Colorad[as], meaning Red Sleeves, or a more liberal translation, Bloody Sleeves—and the blood of many a good American stained his bloody hand and sleeve—was always on the watch and never failed to take advantage of the least careless-ness of the emigrant trains that were crossing the plains from the states to the golden land of promise. Although the Apaches knew that the most they could get from the Overland Stage would be the four mules and the curtains and leather boots and always a hard fight, yet on several occasions when they had massacred the entire guard they had secured the great prize coveted— the arms and ammunition of the guard, for the Indians as a general thing had few guns.

Garner was born in the staid, quiet city of Philadelphia and being of a very frolicsome cast of mind did not find among the peaceful Quakers enough suitable soil to sow the very large crop of wild oats he had on hand. He came west to grow up with the country even before Horace Greely discovered it was a fine place to expand in. Our boundless plains gave him plenty of room and the danger was the spice that he found lacking in Quakerdom.

At this time there were two rival hotels in La Mesilla, and the one that had a very large bell seemed about to win most of the transient customs, with the big bell as its best drawing card. So the other hotel ordered an immense Chinese gong brought from California. Garner, whose sympathies evidently were with the first named hotel, in order to help his landlord, took a dinner with the gong man, stole the gong and stowed it in the Overland coach. It was done in a spirit of mischief but later, in the hands of Garner, the gong proved to be equal to the ram's horn that brought down the walls of Jericho.

The Overland Stage started from Cook[e]'s Springs and was going down through Apache Pass near Cook[e]'s Peak.[2] From this mountain the Indians could see the stage or emigrant train ten or twelve hours before it reached the pass, and make all arrangements to ambuscade them in case there was any carelessness on the part of the stage guards.

On the day of our story, about midway of the pass the Apaches were discovered, and the guard prepared for what might be a death struggle. It was here the fertile genius of Garner shone out—*Ut luna inter ignes minores* [As the moon among lesser stars].[3] He bethought him of the Chinese gong and, knowing how superstitious the Indians were, soon conceived the idea of carrying out the tactics of the Chinese in their battles with the English, but with better success. The Chinese, dressed as harlequins, hobgoblins and devils advanced, turning somersaults, and the Johnny Bulls took them on the wing. Garner was well connected in Philadelphia, and had spent quite a large fortune left him. Afterwards he joined a circus and, being quite an athlete, could turn somersaults and do contortions to the queen's delight. Hastily shedding his clothes but his drawers and shoes, he covered his head and face with some flour they luckily had along. Then he seized the gong and stick and advanced on the astonished Apaches, informing them that he could fly and that his war medicine was so powerful that no bullet could injure him, and that arrows would glance from his shield before they even got to it.

He also informed them [he would] kill and scalp every last rascal and leave their worthless carcasses for the coyotes to eat, and the buzzards to pick their eyes out. Having thus harrowed up their feelings all he could, he advanced in grotesque manner and before getting in range of their arrows he ran towards them swiftly turning a somersault. He struck the gong a blow that in the deep canyon, roared like thunder and was handed back and forth by the echoes from cliff to cliff. This broke the center of the Apache line of battle. The right and left were treated to the same tactics and the Indians fled in wild terror. The gong kept up its terrible clamor, Garner aiding the confusion by a fresh vault in the air and wildest war hoopings to accompany the gong. The stage quietly drove on and soon was on the plains and comparatively safe. Garner afterwards drifted down into old Mexico, and reports brought back to El Paso said he was killed in some difficulty with the Mexicans. Chances are his family never knew what became of him. I did not "know him well," but he certainly was "a fellow of infinite jest."

NOTES

1 For a sketch of "Clown" Garner, see Morgan Wolfe Merrick, *From Desert to Bayou*, ed. Jerry D. Thompson (El Paso: Texas Western Press, 1991), 74.

2 Knifing between the Dos Cabezas and Chiricahua mountains in southeastern Arizona, Apache Pass is 120 miles to the west of Cooke's Springs. Cooke's Peak, an 8,408-foot sentinel, fifty-six miles west of Mesilla and just north of the Mesilla-Tucson Road, has been called the Matterhorn of the Southwest. Fort Cummings was built at Cooke's Springs near the base of the mountain in 1863. While Lt. George Baylor was in Mesilla at the beginning of the Civil War, a stagecoach was attacked in the canyon west of the springs and the entire party massacred, including Freeman Thomas, a conductor on the route, and Emmett Mills, younger brother of El Paso Unionist, W.W. Mills. Mills, *Forty Years at El Paso*, 195-96; Anson Mills, *My Story* (Washington: Byron S. Adams, 1921), 67-69, 74-75. See Ch. 1, Sec. III.

3 A fragment from *Juvenal,* 13: 226: *micat inter omnes Julius sidus, velut inter ignes luna minores* [he, a star, sparkles, Julius among all, as does the moon among lesser stars.]

CHAPTER TWELVE

Tales of
Don Santiago Magoffin

~

AMONG THE PIONEERS OF EL PASO, none should be held in more affectionate remembrance than Judge James [Wiley] Magoffin, being of good old blue grass Kentucky stock, a brother of Gov. Beriah Magoffin of that state, and a warm-hearted and courtly gentleman of the old school.[1] His house was the scene of many a pleasant social event. The judge left Kentucky when a mere youth and started out like the knights of old to find either the El Dorado or the fountain of youth and came as near as any one the writer ever saw in locating both.

In 1861, as a young lieutenant and adjutant of the battalion of the Second Regiment of Mounted Rifles, C.S.A., commanded by Lt. Col. John R. Baylor, the writer recalls with pleasure the many happy hours spent under Don Santiago's hospitable roof. Instead of the dismal place now occupied by a few Mexican milk-men, the old place was in good condition. A fine grove of alamos surrounded the houses occupied by the judge's family. A sward under the grateful shade of the alamos of green alfalfa, made it like an oasis in the desert surrounding it. Within the patio of the family home grew lovely flowers, and during the grape season every morning a peon brought from across the Rio Grande a great basket of the luscious El Paso grapes, cold from the night air, and sweet as honey. These and all other fruits were placed on a large table in the patio, and everybody helped himself the first thing in the morning. We surely did enjoy it, for all the El Paso grapes before that time we ever tasted were brought in wagons to San Antonio and were wilted.

In the main plaza north of the building was our parade ground, where dress parade was held every evening. To the sweet music of a Mexican band we marched out, in all our pride and pomp of glorious war. Those were the halcyon days of the Confederacy, and we had no thought of its sad end or of the desolation and sorrow it was to bring to our country.

The judge's family consisted of himself, his wife, two boys, Sam and Joseph, and a very charming young daughter.[2] These, with the young Confederate officers, made it a gay fort.

Don Santiago, as we called the judge, with a keen sense of the ludicrous often recounted his adventures as a young man. He sailed from New Orleans with a miscellaneous crowd, all bent on wild adventures. Among the lot was one of Artemus Ward's profession, an exhibitor of wax works, who had Napoleon, Julius Caesar, Wellington, Nelson and many others in life size. At Matagorda Bay they were wrecked and at that time the Cauraucahuas [Karankawas], a hostile band of cannibal Indians, held the coast country in strong force. The vessel made the bay inside of Decrow's Point and was beached. Luckily all hands and the miscellaneous cargo of groceries, dry goods, and wax works were all landed. A fort was hastily constructed of boxes and bales, for the captain of the vessel told them that they might expect to be boiled, fried, fricasseed or roasted if they fell into the hands of the cannibals. At first a strict guard was kept, and sentinels paced their weary rounds. There were worlds of game, fish, and oysters, and the commissary held out well. But after a while, as no Indians appeared, guard duty became exceedingly irksome, and young Magoffin on mischief bent, called a convention to consider the situation, having previously arranged all the details in pure democratic style. He got up and stated the object of the meeting. That so far, the burden of the campaign had fallen on the raw troops and he saw no reason why Julius Caesar, Napoleon, Washington, and the array of great military geniuses should not be made to guard duty. The wax work owner opposed the matter and argued that his living when he reached Mexico depended on these valuable works of art, and that the exposure to the sun would ruin them. After a heated debate by young Magoffin, and a tearful rejoinder by the owner of George Washington, they compromised. It was decided that the generals and admiral were to stand guard at night, with one sentinel of the raw militia to receive their report. So Caesar and Napoleon watched the land side, and Nelson guarded attack from the sea.

In due course of time a vessel was sighted which took them off and carried them on to Matamoros. Don Santiago worked his way on through the republic of Mexico, and finally married a most estimable Spanish lady, Señorita Valdez, and settled in El Paso.

Among the many events of his life in the early days of El Paso, he went up to Las Cruces in all the style and grandeur then in vogue, having an ambulance, four fine mules, outriders, etc. When they reached the usual place to noon, which was chosen because it was open to the Rio Grande and afforded no chance for the Apaches to ambuscade them when they went down the bank to water their stock, they never looked in the low scrubby chaparral brush back from the camping grounds. All went down with the stock to guard it from possible stampede and after filling their canteens, washing their faces, and letting their animals drink their fill, they started up the bank with Don Santiago ahead. But as soon as his head got on a level with the bank a sight met his astonished optics that made him drop out of sight quickly. About 25 Apaches had taken possession of his ambulance and were helping themselves to everything portable—harness, blankets, grub, and among other things, a stove-pipe beaver hat which the judge carried to impress the natives. There was nothing to do but watch them, as they were too numerous to be attacked. So they stood ready to repel any attack and trusted the Apaches would leave as soon as they looted the camp. The Indians soon had out the judge's brown jug and emptied it. On further search they brought out a basket of the best brand of champagne from under the seat. This discovery brought from them a whoop of joy, the brown jug having already made them hilarious. They had out several bottles and went to work industriously to get out the corks. As it was hot, and the champagne well shaken up, it was naturally in a very highly explosive condition. The first one who got the wire cut and the cork nearly out must have had it pointed at the face of the chief, for it went off with the report of a pocket pistol, taking that worthy in the eye. One of the Indians had on the beaver and another had on the old-fashioned leather box in which it was kept, such as you never see nowadays. That one shot settled the fight. The Apaches tumbled over each other in their terror and dropped everything, stampeding like a herd of mustangs. The judge and his men then rushed to the ambulance and recovered all their property, the Indians never making a halt as far as they could see them on their way to the Organ Mountains.

NOTES

[1] Born at Harrodsburg, Kentucky, in 1799, of Irish stock, Magoffin was trading into Mexico as early as 1825. He served as United States consul at Saltillo and later in the same position at Ciudad Chihuahua for fifteen years. A man of substance and position, he married María Gertrudia de los Santos Valdez de Veramendi, a native of San Antonio, Texas, at Saltillo in

1834. Five years after his first wife's death in 1845, he married her sister, Dolores Valdez. In 1846, Magoffin accompanied Gen. Stephen W. Kearny to Santa Fe where he persuaded Gov. Manuel Armijo to retire without a fight. Hoping to repeat his success in Chihuahua, he was arrested at El Paso del Norte as a spy and taken to Ciudad Chihuahua where he was almost executed. After the war in 1849, he settled at what is today El Paso. During the Civil War he supported the Baylors and Gen. Henry H. Sibley and even served briefly in the Confederate Army. After the war his El Paso property was confiscated although most of it was later recovered. Magoffin died at San Antonio on 27 September 1868. Dan Thrapp, "James Wiley Magoffin," *Encyclopedia of Frontier Biography* (Spokane: Arthur H. Clark Co., 1990), 2:930; Rex W. Strickland, *Six Who Came to El Paso: Pioneers of the 1840's* (El Paso: Texas Western Press, 1963), 26-34.

2   Besides Samuel and Joseph, Magoffin was the father of five daughters, Josephine, Ursula, Annita, Angela, and Gertrudis, who died very young. Strickland, *Six Who Came to El Paso*, 28. The nineteen-room territorial-style adobe home of Joseph Magoffin, which was built in 1875, and located near the El Paso central business district, is a state historic site today.

CHAPTER THIRTEEN

Luz Villanueva:
Comanche Fighter

~

THIS THRILLING NARRATIVE THE WRITER HAS FROM THE BRAVE MEXICAN, [Luz Villanueva,] who has probably killed more Indians in personal combat than any one on the frontier.[1]

Luz was born in the state of Coahuila and will be 82 years old next February, 1901. Having lived where Indian raids were frequently made, he was well versed in the use of fire arms and knowledge of woodcraft that gives the frontier men of Mexico as well as the United States confidence in themselves and keeps them ready for any emergency, ready to face any kind of danger at short notice, and enabled them to win the battle after a desperate struggle of half a century.

Luz came to Uvalde fifty-three years ago, having crossed the Rio Grande at Brownsville and gradually drifted up towards this place. He first worked as a vaquero for Joseph R. Black. There were few people in this part of the state at that time, only a few hardy and bold old frontiersmen having the courage to settle when all the country north of them for over a thousand miles was filled with warlike, blood-thirsty Indians, and only a few posts far apart in the way of protection. But the woods were full of deer, bear, turkeys, buffalo and other game and trees and cliffs were filled with bees and their sweet stores. It was literally a land flowing with milk and honey.

Luz had his "baptism of fire" before he came here. His first fight was at the little pueblo of Candela in the State of Coahuila, on the Saltillo Camino

Real.[2] At that time he was *pastor* in charge of the herd of sheep and cattle of Don Flugenio Robledo, a short distance from the pueblo.

The Comanches and Lipans acting in concert attempted to take the herd, Luz was only armed with a flint lock musket—obsolete now, but it gained American independence and many a great battle in Europe, and with the right kind of man behind it, it was not to be despised. The Indians had only lances and bows and a few arrows and *escopetas*.

Felipe Robledo, a son of Don Flugenio, happened to be with the herd also. But for that the Indians would not only have taken the herd, but Luz's scalp also, to grace their shields after a return to Texas. Don Felipe being well armed and brave, with Luz kept the Indians at bay, and saved the herd, but Felipe was struck in the breast by a "*corta lanca*," a short handled lance, something like the *assagai* of the Zulus, and killed. The Indians had attacked the pueblo at the same time, but were beaten off and the citizens rallied to the rescue of Luz and Don Felipe, and prevented the robbing of the herd. The Indians would charge by close to Felipe and his brave "*pastor*," send a flight of arrows and scamper always on their fleet ponies. Luz was wounded eight times slightly with arrows, and a bullet grazed his skull.

Luz's first fight on Texas soil was at the "Charco Ocho Miles" near the town of Uvalde, known as "Eight Mile Water Hole," and now on the ranch of Mr. Vanham. It is a pond on the Leona northeast of the town of Uvalde, that always has water, is full of fish, and was a favorite camping ground of the Comanches and Lipans, in their raids on the frontiersmen. Luz at the time (1861) was employed as a vaquero by Capt. Bill Adams, and was out cow-hunting.[3] He had camped for the night at the "*Charco*" keeping his horse saddled near him. At daybreak, being aroused by the trampling of horses' feet, he saw thirty-two Comanches ride down opposite to him to water their horses and themselves.

He had taken the precaution to camp on the west side near some large rocks and as soon as he discovered them, he mounted his horse and rode off, knowing they were after his scalp. For one man well armed on horse back is safer than ten men with a herd of horses. The Indians did not care to risk losing a warrior for one horse but would risk a good deal for a bunch.

The Indians raised a yell and ran after him but after he fired three shots at them from one of the old time brass mounted pistols (that caused the death of "Jeemes Hambrick" according to Derby's account), the Comanches quit following him.

He had also a good Sharp's rifle, and was in better fix to fight than in Old Mexico. The Indians had bows and lances and one or two had old muskets but Luz escaped without a wound. The next time Luz had a scrap with the

Comanches was on Sycamore Creek in the Nueces Canyon. The creek emp-
ties into the Nueces River, and at the time Chappey Moore had a ranch at its
mouth. At present Wm F. Hardeman has charge of the ranch for the Francis
Smith Company of San Antonio.

Luz with Mark Bannion was cow-hunting, and quite a large herd had
gathered and were being held by Mark Adams and twelve Mexican vaqueros,
at Walnut Springs, about four miles east of the ranch. Luz, seeing a bunch of
cattle near the spring, on a hill went to drive them to the herd. Five
Comanches were hid in the rocks near the spring, and evidently had arrived
in the night and were asleep not knowing the herd and guard were so near.
They were first awakened by Luz galloping near them and seeing how much
they were outnumbered they took to their heels at once, running up the side
of the mountain. Luz soon began throwing lead at them from his old reliable
Sharps, sending eight bullets after them. This soon brought the other men,
and the trail was followed by the blood of one of the Indians to the top of the
mountain where they found him dead. The Indians being afoot, their trail
could not be followed in the rocks.

So completely surprised were the Indians that they stampeded, leaving all
their bows, arrows and lances in their camp. Among the trophies captured
were four horses belonging to citizens in and near Uvalde, and a mule
belonging to Mr. Griner, about two dozen *teguas* [moccasins] and a Mexican
saddle.

Luz's next meeting with the Comanches was when Henry Adams, a
brother of Capt. Bill Adams, and Frank Robinson, father of our present
county judge, were killed.[4] Luz and his brother were horse hunting at the
mouth of the Nueces Canyon and discovered fresh Indian signs on both sides
of the river. They went at once to Captain Adams and told him, but he told
them they must be mistaken, and hinted pretty strongly that he thought they
were afraid. Luz answered, "The horses are yours, Captain, and we lose
nothing; if you do not believe us, you may lose your horses." These same
Indians had that morning killed his brother, Henry, and Frank Robinson, as
stated, and were on their way down the Nueces on a raid among the settlers
and committed many outrages.

Luz's next experience was on the west prong of the Nueces River [while]
cow hunting. He was *mayordomo* for Captain Adams, and had 60 Mexicans
building a fence of rocks and poles. The Comanches attacked their camp. There
were only a few men there at the time, all the others being at work on the fence,
and the Indians made a clean sweep of everything they could carry off. Those
men in camp escaped and ran to the working party near by, who came and took
the trail of the Indians. Only a few of Luz's men were armed, but they made the

best display they could of their guns and numbers, so the Indians made no attempt to fight, but were anxious to get off with their plunder.

Luz was out after the oxen they used to haul poles and water for the men. He saw the Indians coming and was lucky enough to be above them and hid behind a cedar tree until they got opposite him. Then he opened fire on them and kept it up until the men from the camp joined him. The Indians made no halt, but as their trail showed blood, Luz and his men followed them, as they had a few horses, and found one dead Comanche. He was evidently a chief, as he had a leather strap fastened to the top of his head, that reached to the ground, and was covered with silver plates hammered out of Mexican dollars and smaller coins towards the bottom of the strap; he also had silver earrings. Luz got his shield, bow and quiver of arrows.

Another time on the west prong of the Nueces, Luz was cow hunting and came on four mounted Indians. One of them had a horse the same color as Mark Adams's and wore a beard, so Luz thought it was Adams, hunting a beef to kill for the men. He had plenty of time to have shot before they saw him. As soon as he discovered they were Indians he began firing. Two of the Indians stopped to fight and two ran, probably their squaws. Luz's brother, Pedro, who was riding the fence, hearing so much firing, came to him, but not until Luz had fired some thirty or forty shots.

That evening they followed the trail and found a red American blanket at a water hole. It had fourteen bullet holes in it and the water was quite red from the blood of a wounded Indian. The Indian probably died and they hid or buried his body. They left the blanket. Luz hoped he had gone where he would not need one.

Luz's next round with the Comanches was at Kickapoo Springs, where Bill Adams had a ranch. Luz was corporal or *mayordomo*, and had nine Mexicans with him on a cow hunt. Luz told his men to stop and rest and he rode up on a hill near by to look around for cattle or maybe Indians—for they were always in evidence, especially when one did not want them. Indians had been watching them and hid in some cedars on the opposite side of the hill and knowing they would be discovered, opened fire on him as soon as he topped the hill. Luz was not hit and he returned their fire and exchanged three or four shots before his men got to him. They were not long for they knew at once what the racket meant. The vaqueros at once began an attack and the Indians considered discretion the better part of valor and left. The Mexicans followed and found one dead Comanche hid under a bank. They were going south to raid the settlement on the Nueces, Frio, and Sabinal.

After this Luz had charge of the beeves for the Confederates at Fort Clark, in the early part of the war between the North and South. The detail was under Captain Hamner of Company "A," Second Regiment, Mounted Rifles, of which Colonel John S. Ford, (Old "Rip") was colonel, John R. Baylor, lieutenant colonel, and [Edwin] Waller, major.

The Indians attempted to steal their horses (he had eleven mounted men), but failed. The next day they tried to stampede the herd of beeves. The herd had been carried out to graze. Luz rode to a hill to see if all was clear of danger, and the Indians tried to cut him off from his men, but having a good horse he out ran them, got into a canyon and stood them off until part of his men came to his relief and the Indians beat a retreat.

Luz next went to El Paso with Sam Lytle and John Adams, who were furnishing beef to the Confederate troops. Luz kept the beeves on the plains about where Fort Bliss is, but they were never molested, having a good guard and the open country not being favorable for such raids. Luz returned to San Lucas Springs where Adams had a ranch, sixteen miles west of San Antonio. From there he again returned to his old stomping ground, the old Bill Adams Ranch at the mouth of the Nueces Canyon, a lovely location among grand old live oaks and pecan trees. This did not suit the thieving Comanches, who usually passed down there when making a raid on the settlements on the Nueces and Leona rivers, so they took great pains to make it as unsafe and disagreeable as possible for those who settled there.

On one occasion Luz was up three or four miles above the ranch and came suddenly on a band of about twenty Comanches in the grove in front of Chalk Bluff—*barranca piedras* or relief, as it was called by the Mexicans and old Spaniards, who settled where Montel[l] now is, and founded the old mission of San Bruno [Nuestra Señora de la Candelaria del Cañon] where Jno. R. Baylor built his home.[5]

The Indians had a herd of about 100 head of horses stolen during an extensive raid, having captured a Mexican boy near the coast at San Diego. Luz, being mounted at the time on a burro instead of his horse, at once knew his life depended on making a bluff for he could not run, nor hope to make a fight to win against so many Indians.

He was lucky enough to have discovered them first and opened fire on them with a Winchester. He began shouting commands to an imaginary company of men, and waving his hat to the right and left as if to bring them up in line. The Comanches were badly rattled by this unexpected attack when they thought all danger was past and they had their horses safe from further pursuit, so their first move was to hurry off the drove of horses, and get out of reach of the Winchester balls that were flying as fast as Lucas could pump them.

In the confusion the Mexican captive took advantage of the broil and being mounted on a fine bay horse, broke ranks and joined Luz, hearing his own tongue spoken. Luz had raised his voice to the highest pitch and ordered his "men in buckram" to come up on each side, surround the Indians and take their horses.

Panic stricken, the Indians were seen tearing off through a cloud of dust and Luz and his reinforcements were making good headway in the other direction. Luz told the boy to take the lead, for he knew the burro would keep up or die and he was pretty badly scared up by the unusual noise, and the little beast took Luz to the Adams Ranch in Paul Revere time.

The captive's name was Trinidad. Luz took him to [Col. Ranald S.] M[a]ckenzie who was at Fort Clark, and the colonel wrote a letter to the boy's father at San Diego, but it was years before the father came to the town of Uvalde to reclaim his son.[6]

Luz's last fight was between San Pedro Creek and the Rio Diablo or Devil's River.[7] He was out camp hunting by himself, having that perfect confidence in himself that comes to every one raised as he had been on the frontier, and who had been so lucky in his encounters. At daylight one morning he went to look for his horses, intending to cook his breakfast and move camp to a new hunting ground. This was in 1880, his other fights were from 1861 up to the close of the Confederate War, some of them during the '70s.

Luz took the trail of his horses—he had seven—and soon found a party of nine Comanches out on the same business. They had killed two of the horses, broken the leg of another, and had two ponies and a mare and two-year-old colt in their possession.

The Indians were doubtless[ly] enjoying a feast of roast horse ribs and other dainty tidbits, but also keeping an eye open for the owner, but Luz was too old a *ranchero* to be caught in a trap and dropped down in a little sway as soon as he discovered them. It was open all around but he had no time to choose a fighting ground. Only two Comanches showed themselves at first, and began a pow-wow to try and get Luz's Winchester first and scalp afterwards. They first spoke in broken English, saying, "If you give us your Winchester, we won't kill you."

Luz made no answer to this kind invitation. They then spoke in Spanish making the same proposition. Luz answered boldly, knowing any sign of fear would seal his fate: "Here is my Winchester, you can come and take it if you want it, but I won't give it up."

The Comanche spokesman then said: "You give up your gun and we will go off and won't hurt you. You can bring it to us or leave it and go off yourself, if you don't we will never leave until we kill you."

Luz answered, "Bueno, if you kill me you get my gun but I will kill as many of you as I can." Saying this, he fell down on his back, and crossing his feet to give him a rest, fired at the same time as the Comanches. They exchanged a number of shots and seven more Indians showed up, who were hid in a dry ravine, waiting, no doubt in hopes he would bring his gun up and surrender it, when they could kill him.

The fight now being on, the Indians got all around him, but he had the advantage of being in the lowest place and when they showed up he let drive at them—their bullets all passed over him. He kept in his low place, and revolved around to answer their shots.

But this running around was made to cover a move of one of the warriors who was trying stratagem, as lying did not succeed. Hardly any of your readers but have noticed, during the spring months a round plant that becomes broken off at the ground, and during a high wind goes bounding along the road to the alarm of your horse. One of the warriors had put several of these together and pushed them slowly ahead of him reserving his fire until pretty close, and the first notice Luz had of his trick was the sharp crack of his rifle and a bullet went through his left leg just above the ankle.

Good God, where was the shot from, was his thought. The next shot struck his leg just above the knee. The next shot went through the fleshy part of his thigh and did not strike the bone. This time he was getting near the vitals.

He probably thought his first shot was near the head, but Luz changed his position and by turning around had saved his life. He located the Indian by the smoke of his gun this time and taking rest on his feet, put a bullet through the bunch of weeds. The Indian fired also and grazed Luz's ribs. The warrior sprang to his feet and gave a yell to his men, staggered forward a few steps, and fell on his face, and as he rose, Luz saw the blood spurting from his breast, and as he turned he saw a great red splotch on his back and knew he was rid of him. This put quite a damper on the Indians who now drew off. They had been fighting on foot and evidently were well armed. From the rapid firing, Luz thought they had Winchesters or United States breech loading rifles.

After the firing ceased the chief determined to have one more shot and rode back thinking doubtless[ly] he would have a better chance from horseback, but forgetting him as the sound of the horse's feet had put him on his guard—they had been fighting two hours or more and Luz's belt that had 150 cartridges when he began, now was empty, and only one remained in his gun.

He saw the horses' ears appear and then the Indian's head. Taking good aim he fired his last shot and heard the Indian fall and heard the horse run back to the other Indians. The bullet had struck him square in the forehead. The seven Indians then left thinking they had paid pretty dearly for trying to get a gun.

Luz was now in a pitiable condition—he had left his camp without any breakfast and had bled so much that he was too weak to walk, even if his wounds had not been so severe; he had on a coat and managed to tear it up and bandage his wounds so as to partly check the flow of blood. He lay there from the 10th of March 1880 to the 13th, without food or water. I asked Luz if he did not suffer from hunger and thirst and feel afraid the lobos or coyotes would attack him. He said he seemed in a dream, and suffered so much pain that he never thought of either food or water or wolves.

The third day a detachment of United States cavalry under Lieutenant Johnson and some Mexicans following the trail from San Felipe Spring (now Del Rio) found him and the two dead Indians. Luz begged the lieutenant to shoot him through the head and put him out of his pain but the lieutenant said, "You are crazy Luz, we will take you to San Felipe, and put you in the hospital and cure you." The soldiers were white men and had a surgeon with them. Luz could not tell his name, but said it sounded like Shan.

The scouts returned taking Luz and he was placed in the hospital, his wounds dressed, and it was six months before he was able to leave. Then he came to Uvalde where he has resided ever since, no doubt willing to play quits with the Indians.

Luz seemed doomed to get more than his share of wounds and mishaps. Hauling water one day on a cart it upset and fell on him, breaking his crippled leg and his trusted Winchester rifle. He seemed to grieve as much over the broken gun that stood by him so faithfully in his fights, as he did over the broken leg. Drs. Harrison and Watts cut off his leg and the gallant old warrior now hobbles around on his crutches.

In conclusion, when I told Luz I wanted to publish an account of his fights, he said, "Please send Senor Weenchaistray (Winchester) one paper; maybe so, he send me another gun." I think the company ought to get his old brass mounted rim-fire for the good it has done and send him another rifle.

NOTES

1 Luz Bianueva, thirty-eight, with no real estate or personal property, is listed on the 1870 Uvalde County census as a "cattle hunter." Luz was living with Rafael and Pedro Bianueva, probably his brothers, and two other "cattle hunters." 9th Census, Uvalde County, Texas.

2 Nestled at the north end of the Sierra Moreno on the Rio Candela, the village of Candela, Coahuila, was on the Laredo to Monterrey Road, at least one hundred miles east of the Camino Real that linked San Antonio de Bexar with Monclova and Saltillo. Several sharp peaks, Cerro Boludo, Cerro Chiche, El Chucharazo, and the spectacular and picturesque Pico Candela rise just behind the village.

3 At the beginning of the Civil War, William C. Adams organized a company of mounted volunteers (Company C) from unionist Uvalde County. As part of Lt. Col. John R. Baylor's 2d Texas Mounted Rifles, he assumed command of Forts Lancaster and Stockton, and, by 7 September 1861, Fort Davis. During Sibley's New Mexico Campaign, Adams and Company C remained in the Trans-Pecos guarding the San Antonio-El Paso Road. Clayton W. Williams, *Texas' Last Frontier: Fort Stockton and the Trans-Pecos, 1861-1865* (College Station: Texas A&M University Press, 1982), 6, 15, 21-23; and John R. Baylor to Adams, 12 August 1861, Adams Papers, Fort Davis National Historical Site, Fort Davis, Texas.

4 On 29 May 1861, Adams and Robinson were ambushed and killed at the Nineteen Mile Waterhole Crossing near Chalk Bluff on the Nueces River. Robinson, who was tall and red-headed, was so feared by Indians of the area that they had painted his picture on a rock on the Llano River. Both men were scalped and Robinson had his beard cut off. In the raid, the Comanches also killed Julius Sanders and scalped Mary Kelsey and left her for dead.

5 Today, Chalk Bluff can be seen at a point where State Highway 55 enters the Nueces Canyon, about fourteen miles downstream from Montell. It was at Montell that John R. Baylor settled after the war. Baylor's home can be seen today on the east side of State Highway 55 on the west bank of the Nueces River, near a historical marker commemorating his life. It was at Chalk Bluff that George Baylor settled temporarily after the war. Founded in 1762 for the Lipan Apache by Felipe Rábago y Terán, captain of the San Sabá Presidio, and Fray Diego Jimínez, in charge of the missions along the Rio Grande, Nuestra Señora de la Candelaria was abandoned about four years later because of its precarious location. Webb and Carroll, *Handbook of Texas*, 2:292.

6 Colonel Mackenzie, commanding the 4th United States Cavalry, was at Fort Clark from 1873 to 1874 and from 1877 to 1879. Mackenzie is best remembered for his forays into Mexico after hostile Indians and his defeat of Comanches and Kiowas at Palo Duro Canyon in September 1874. Michael D. Pierce, *The Most Promising Young Officer: A Life of Ranald Slidell Mackenzie* (Norman: University of Oklahoma Press, 1993), 57, 123; and Charles M. Robinson III, *Bad Hand: A Biography of General Ranald S. Mackenzie* (Austin: State House Press, 1993), 132-33, 251-54.

7 San Pedro Creek rises in southwestern Val Verde County and flows generally west sixteen miles into what is today Amistad Reservoir. The fight would have been in the vicinity of San Felipe Springs at present-day Del Rio.

CHAPTER FOURTEEN

Fighting Comanches in North Texas

~

ABOUT THE 11TH OF JUNE 1860, Frank Browning and Josephus, a younger brother, rode off from the home of their father, Uncle Billy Browning, who lived on Hubbard's Creek, near where it enters the Clear Fork of the Brazos River in Young County.[1]

The family consisted of father, mother, two girls as well as I recall, and the two sons, Frank, about twenty-five years of age, and Josephus, the youngest of the flock, about twenty-one years old—the pride of his old father and the idol of his mother and sister. Uncle Billy owned quite a nice stock of cattle and the boys took care of them, whil'st the women folks looked out for the household matters, raised chickens, milked the cows, and cooked the best of meals. Uncle Billy was the old guard to keep the Comanches from the hearthstone, and the boys to keep the run of the stock, branding calves, etc. So the family machinery ran very smoothly and they lived in comfort in a fresh, rich country, where the woods were full of bee trees and game of every kind abounded—turkeys by the millions, with the streams alive with fish and near by buffalo beyond computation. Such a country as will never be seen again to live in.

There was, however, one dark cloud that hung over this entire country, and often cast over its bright firesides its gloom and stained with blood the lintel of a once happy home. The Comanches had been run out of this country on account of the many bloody murders committed by them on innocent women and children, and the United States troops had taken the part of the Indians. Maj. [George H.] Thomas (afterwards quite a celebrated Federal general) was in command of the troops near the agency, and the frontiersmen engaged in the fight at the Comanche reservation were under the command of Gen. John R. Baylor, afterwards a member of the Confederate Congress, and brigadier general, C.S.A.

General Baylor had been their agent, but [he] did not suit the government for the following reasons: He frequently had the Comanches come in after a hunting trip bringing horses and sometimes scalps, and they invariably gave the same account as to how they came into possession of them—[they] had a fight with the Kiowas, had whipped them and taken their stock. He noticed however, that none of the Comanches were ever wounded or killed, for if there had there would have been howling in camp.

These battles were something on the style of the Spanish victories in Cuba. His superstitions were aroused that all was not right, and when a party came in bringing some horses that he knew belonged to [Fred] Gentry near Georgetown, Williamson County, he felt pretty sure that they were lying about it. They had taken a young squaw with them. So General Baylor got his *alcalde*, an old Lipan Indian, appointed to keep order on the reservation, and sent for the young squaw. The old Lipan strung his bow and put an arrow on the string, while General Baylor drew his pistol and cocked it. He then told the squaw that she must tell the truth about these horses or they would kill her. So she let the whole thing out. So he wrote Gentry and the story of the squaw and that of the Indian raid, which he heard from Gentry, corresponded exactly. He then wrote to Washington City stating that he had positive proof that the Indians under his charge were murdering and robbing our own people and asked for instructions.[2]

In a brief time, he received a curt notice that his services were no longer required as Indian agent. This, of course, aroused his anger. There were at this time two parties on the frontier known as "Indian" men and "Baylor" men. The Indian men were making lots of money by contracts to supply the reservation, and the frontiersmen were being murdered and robbed almost daily. As soon as General Baylor got notice from Washington that he was dismissed, he got some of the neighbors together and began watching the Indians and sent runners to the surrounding counties and in a remarkably short time they were on the ground ready to drive the Indians from Texas soil or kill them. Among those who came were Col. [Allison] Nelson, Judge Motherill, Capt. Pete Garland, Capt. [James] Buck[ner] Barry, Judge Everett, Judge Joe Bledsoe, and Gen. R[ichard] M[ontgomery] Gano, and quite a host of others, and the campaign ended after one fight in which only a portion of the frontiersmen were engaged and where quite a number of Indians and a few of the Texans were killed.[3]

Maj. [George H.] Thomas agreed that if the Texans, who numbered about twelve hundred men, would withdraw he would take the Indians out of the state, which he did.[4] And they were located at Fort Sill, across Red River, and ever afterwards they thought it perfectly in order to murder and rob Texans at any and all times. General Baylor, who was my brother, and his immediate neighbors were especially marked for their vengeance, and scarce a light moon passed that stock were not killed, horses stolen, or someone murdered. Appeals to the governor seemed utterly useless, so we had to depend on our good arms and the *lex talionis* to keep anywhere near even.

When we met the Comanches we neither gave nor asked quarter and it was war to the knife and knife to the hilt. General Baylor had quite a large stock of cattle, but the fine range (at that time almost unoccupied) caused the cattle to stray off from home and the northers sent them on a trot to the south. So we had plenty to do looking after them. Often we went for a several days' scout together with some of our neighbors to be better prepared for Mr. Lo, for we never knew at what moment we might run together.

On one of these trips my brother (General Baylor), Tom S. Stockton, Elias Hale, Jack Baylor, Jr., myself, and a Negro boy named Allen, had gone on a drive up Hubbard's Creek and we were camped for the night near the creek, it being a rule always to move camp after dark. Having cooked and eaten we would then slip off and hide for fear Indians were watching us. Next morning bright and early we saw a horseman coming at a gallop on our trail, and our hearts were in our mouths for we knew it meant bad news for some of us. It proved to be John Maulding, who had been sent out by Joe Matthews to tell us the sad news that the Indians were making a raid on our settlements and had killed and scalped Josephus Browning and had shot Frank Browning full of arrows. We were some ten miles above Browning, and we started home immediately with heavy hearts, for the brothers were universal favorites in the settlements.

I felt a sincere affection for Josephus, as we had fished and hunted together and often visited each other. He was an amiable, brave, manly, handsome young fellow, full of life and fun, but especially did I feel sympathy for the old father, the loving mother, and the gentle sisters. On arriving at the Browning home, a heartrending sight met our gaze. As we entered the hall between the two log rooms we found Frank sitting up leaning against the wall as pale as death and evidently in death agonies. He could not breathe when lying down. Beside him the girls and old father with loving hands were doing all they could to ease his pain. On a table in one of the rooms lay stretched in death my young friend, a large piece of his scalp having been cut from his temple. His throat was cut, his breast was full of stabs from the scalping knife, and his hands were cut to pieces showing that he had used them to ward off the knife that they had used in cutting his throat and scalping him with, during his death agony. Near him in an agony of grief sat the old mother, looking on the pale rigid face of her baby boy. No torn stained coat like that of Joseph of old to leave a hope that the child lived, but cold and mutilated lay the form that a few hours before had ridden from her sight full of life. Stopping only long enough to give such consolation as words could only give, we hurried on home, some five miles above the Browning place, and began making our preparations to follow the Indians trail. I took a last look at my young friend and by his dead body made a solemn vow that if I overtook his murderers I would avenge his death. You will see how I keep my vow.

We learned afterwards from Frank, who recovered from his wounds and lived many years, and may yet be alive, that he and Josephus, who were both armed with guns and revolvers, were about three miles from home on the south side of Hubbard's Creek, looking among their cattle, when they discovered seven Indians, all mounted, only a short distance off, who raised a war-whoop and started towards them.[5] They quickly decided to try and outrun the Indians and make it home, about three miles, which was an unfortunate decision, for we learned that the Indians had stolen blooded race stock, whose mettle we tested afterwards. Had the boys taken to a thicket they might have lost their horses, but the Indians, seeing them armed, would have been afraid to have risked losing some of their warriors, and would not have followed them.

The distance between them and the Indians was reduced rapidly and the brothers fired first with their guns, and, putting them in their gun-holders (we had no scabbards then), they drew their revolvers and began firing when the Indians got in close quarters. But as bad luck would have it, without hitting either the Indians or their horses. And to make matters worse, Josephus, who was on the slowest horse and whose pistol was rendered useless by a cap falling under the hammer, received three arrows in his back. The Indians had discovered in a moment that something was wrong with his pistol, and closed in on him. As soon as Josephus felt that he was mortally wounded, he called to Frank saying: "Brother, I'm dying, don't stop for me. Try and get back to father and mother; the Indians may murder them all." Brave hearted boy, willing to die to save the loved ones at home, Frank immediately dropped back saying: "Joe, I'll never leave you as long as I am alive." So he then began firing at the Indians and kept them at bay for a while. But they, with their usual cunning, had counted his shots, and knew that he could have only one or two more left and began to close in on him. Soon they shot three arrows into his back. Josephus began to reel in his saddle and soon fell to the ground from loss of blood. Frank then gave the reins to his horse, a fleet one, and outstripped his bloodthirsty pursuers and carried the news of death to the sad household.

As soon as the news got out, kind neighbors went to search for the dead body. They found his body by seeing the buzzards soaring in circles over the spot. The Indians had scalped him while still alive, as his fingers were cut to pieces and full of his own hair, showing that he had tried to pull the keen, cruel knife from his throat and head.

My brother decided not to try to follow the Indians at once. He had been their agent, been on buffalo hunts with them, always using the bow, which he contended was better than a six-shooter in killing buffalo, as he could carry thirty or forty arrows in his quiver and there was no report to frighten the game or his horse, and often one arrow would bring down a buffalo. He said he knew they would keep a spy out to see if they were followed and once satisfied that they were not, they were as careless as any people in the world. Two days were spent in cleaning our arms thoroughly, molding bullets, cutting and greasing "patching," sharpening our knives, baking bread and grinding coffee, etc.

I ran a lot of bullets into the old bullet molds we used for five-shooter Colts for close quarters, and six-shooter navy balls to use in my shotgun, a splendid stub-twist, long, double-barreled gun that would bring down a deer at a hundred yards—such a gun as the southern planter used before the war to shoot deer before the hounds. I had tried mine in many a chase with my dear old friend, Dr. John J. Inge, when he lived at Weatherford, and I knew what she could do, and that means a lot at close quarters. I had put up a number of loads of shot in strong wrapping paper to just fit my gun—fifteen of the sixshooter and twenty of the five-shooter balls to the load—so as to load quickly. My brother had a Colt's six-shooting rifle carrying a navy ball—the first, I expect, ever seen or used in an Indian fight—and I never saw a better offhand shot with a rifle, shotgun or pistol than he was.

Our party consisted of six cowboys, namely John R. Baylor, being the eldest, thirty-nine years old, was acknowledged captain; John Barclay Dawson, Tom Stockton, Elias Hale, A[r]menius (or as we called him" "Min") Wright, and the writer, George Wythe Baylor, all except J.R. Baylor being unmarried.

Dawson, Stockton, and Hale were armed with good rifles and navy revolvers. Wright and myself as end men had double barreled shotguns. Wright's was of number ten gauge and the longest gun I ever saw. We were mounted on good Texas bred horses, mine my favorite gray hunting mare, well bred and perfectly trained so that she was not afraid of a gun. One could get up or off on either side (that trait save my life), and you could dismount and she would stand or go to grazing and not leave you. Old Nance, here's to your memory—but for your good qualities and behavior I would not be scribbling here today. I was "the man on the white horse" that always called for an extra number of shots from one side or the other during the War Between the States. Brother Jack rode a splendid well trained animal, a very bright sorrel, swift as an antelope. He had been stolen by the Comanches in Bell County and we dubbed him "Belton." They rode him down, lanced him through the lungs and left him for dead, but he lived and got even with them, as will be seen further on.

Everything being ready, we struck out from my brother's ranch to "cut for sign," as we cowboys called it. As the Indians had left going northwest, we started after them and striking the trail, we soon discovered that there were seven mounted men and one loose animal—Josephus's horse not caring to leave the range had given them some trouble, but they finally caught and probably rode him. The trail led up through the post oaks north for six or seven miles, and then came in to the river, it being quite low and standing in deep holes. Here the trail was lost and we dismounted to work it out. A good many range horses and cattle had been watering there and had put out the trail. I was keen sighted and my heart was set on the work and I soon found the trail that went towards a deep hole with shelving rocks above it. They had eaten and rested, it being in the night and their familiarity with the place satisfied us that they were Comanches, whose agency had been near there or they could not have found such an obscure place in the dark.

Looking around to see which way they had left, I found a sad reminder of being on the right track—the bloody scalp of my young friend. I could only grit my teeth and work the harder to find the trail, and after following a certain horse track that I had noticed before the trail, I came to a deep path leading up to the west bank of the river and found a well defined trail leading off to the west. I took the scalp back to the boys, and after we had eaten a snack and filled out canteens with water we struck out on the trail, and after going ten or fifteen miles up the beautiful valley it turned sharp to the right, going up a steep ravine to the high ground. Here we found my brother's prediction of a spy being left behind, verified. A small round pile of ashes, the grass mashed down, and a point that commanded a view of the trail back to the river, showed where their vedette had been left. If we had followed them the next day after the murder he would have seen us and then good-bye Comanches. We followed on at a good walk and camped at dusk.

All slept, feeling no uneasiness and were off at daybreak. We followed the trail until dinner and nooned on the Clear Fork below Phantom Hill, an old deserted United States military post.[6] We had passed a government train during the day and they had quickly corralled their wagons and got out their guns [thinking] we were Indians, but were glad to find themselves mistaken. We told them our mission, and the wagon master (I wish I could remember his name or that of any of his men) gave us some hard tack and also gave us quite an addition to our ammunition. It was a lucky thing for us, as the sequel will show. I got a pound or more of buck shot and a few old buck and ball cartridges, a lot of powder and some good caps. The other boys were treated to like reinforcements. The train wished us good luck and moved on.

At our camp I got out my fishing line (I don't think I was ever without one). My mother used to say if I were ever drowned it would be easy to identify my body, for in one pocket they would find a fishing line and hooks and in the other fiddle strings and a piece of resin. I was soon fishing and my only hook snapped by a big catfish; but I tied my line to a big chunk, put a piece of meat on one end of the stick and sharpened the other short end, attaching the line near the sharpened end and threw the chunk and line into the water. A fish soon swallowed the bait and the chunk went floating off cutting all kinds of shines, disappearing for a while, then popping up again. The sharp end of the stick was in his gills and the end with the bait down deep in his gullet so that he could not get rid of it. After the fish had worried himself out I swam in and brought him to the bank, about a thirty pound fat, head, cat. We had broiled fish for dinner.

Taking the trail again we pushed on at a good swift walk until night, and after supper we laid down tired and slept sound enough. Brother Jack gave notice that we must be off bright and early for we were getting a good long way from the settlements and liable to run into an Indian village and get more on our hands than we bargained for. Before daylight we were up, had cooked our breakfast, got a pint of good strong coffee aboard, with Uncle Sam's hard tack and a jerky, and I took the lead trailing. Old Nance moved at a good long trot. I could see the trail often two hundred yards ahead of me by the mesquite grass being pressed down.

We struck the camp where the Indians had been the night before, and old Nance pricked up her ears as we came to a little creek with its dogwood and liveoak thickets. Old Belton gave us to understand that it was fresh Indian sign as he began to snort, his eyes nearly popping out of his head, trembling and the sweat running down his face. They had lolled around the shade and probably rested there a day and night, thinking they were safe. Getting the trail off north, we kept up our lick and at about 12 o'clock right ahead of me about a half mile in the valley I saw three horses and what I took to be an Indian lying down. I halted brother and he rode to my side. I pointed out the stock and the object on the ground.

After a good look at the surroundings he said there was nothing for us to do but to ride straight toward them in Indian file, ready for a charge if they were asleep or discovered us. On reaching the camp we found a beautiful stream of clear water, but our horses took a sniff of it only, which was enough as it was almost pure alkali. We found the Indian horses tied and hobbled and our Indian was a pile of beef thrown on the ground on a hide and partly covered by the same. It was green and putrid, but brother said they would come back for it as it was just ripe enough for their taste. He knew the country and they had gone to a fresh stream of water about seven miles off and would soon return for the horses and meat. We rode back to the creek and took the bridles off our horses to let them graze a little, and I lay down to await results.

It seemed not over fifteen minutes, until lying with my ear on the ground, I heard the sound of horses' feet, and peeping over the bank bareheaded, I saw two Indians riding towards their horses. They were not over seventy-five yards off. Our horses at the same time raised their heads to look at the newcomers. I said in an excited stage whisper, "Here they are boys," and brother said, "Bridle and mount." The Indians had seen the ears and tops of our horses' heads and knew what it meant and whirling, were off, whipping like jockeys. It was an exciting moment. I grabbed old Nance's forelock, jammed the bit in her mouth and it seemed as though I never would bridle her and that she was seven feet high, and so I happened to be the last man off.

I had not gone a hundred yards until the buckskin string that I had tied to the end of my pistol scabbard owing to the vigorous use of my spurs broke and away went my revolver. We did not then have gunscabbards and broad belts and pistol scabbards such as my Texas Rangers had in after years. I pinned my faith to my old shotgun and had seen but two Indians, so made a halt for my pistol; Nance had speed and I was soon up with the crowd, but for the life of me I could not say which was Indian and which was cowboy. John Dawson, who was very dark skinned, had lost his hat and his long black hair was streaming back. He held his gun up in his hand as they did and gave them an "Indian" look. I soon saw, however, that brother Jack and old Belton had shot ahead of one of the Indians, leaving him on his left some fifty feet. Brother said he knew the Indian could not well shoot him unless he was left handed and he was carrying his bow in his left hand. He had left this fellow for us and was after the other, who he saw was mounted on a beautiful strawberry roan animal, and leaving the other Indian to his fate.

Having located the two Indians and getting ahead of the boys, I noticed the hindmost one began reining in his horse to the right so as to drop in behind brother. Keeping an eye on him I steered old Nance to the right and cut loose at him. The entire charge was over his head and the mesquite leaves came down in a shower about him. This did what I intended it should— drew his attention to me instead of brother. He immediately wheeled to the left through some liveoak brush and I went tearing after him. The brush knocked the cap off of my gun as it was on the half cock. I did not know it at the time, but soon had a painful reminder of it. He went at a swift pace and I just could see brother and his Indian to my right ahead of me. Being in open ground, as we continually passed little thickets it made a moving panorama of Indian and cowboy. My especial pet was making good time working his moccasins and quirt, and we soon got near an open prairie dog town that looked two or three miles wide.

To our left we had just passed a liveoak thicket and I noticed the Indian take a hurried glance back and I expect he decided that the open prairie dog town with no Texan ahead of him and five behind him was no good place for a lone Indian on a rather slow pony. I had closed the distance between us to about seventy yards and the others were that distance behind me and to my right. The Indian sprang from his horse to the ground with the agility of a cat and turned facing me. At once it flashed over me that this was a favorite trick of theirs, as old Indian hunters had told me. His idea was to shoot me in the back as I passed him and then get my horse. So I made up my mind he would have to shoot me in front. I began to pull on old Nance's bit, but rode straight at him, intending to ride him down if I could. He sprang to the left just as I reached him and my mare swerved a little to the right but halted just as he let drive with an arrow.

The suddenness with which my mare stopped threw me against the pommel of my saddle and the spike of the arrow cut a piece out of my belt and the pommel of my saddle. Ordinarily the left side, according to cavalry tactics, is the right side to mount and dismount from, but when a Comanche is standing with bow and arrow in hand ready to spit me, I decided to disregard army regulations and slid off the right hand side as easily as a mud turtle slides off a log, and none too quick as another arrow just grazed my back. I sprang forward and leveled my gun between his eyes. I have an idea it looked as big to him as two camp kettles.

He could see himself lying on his back and the buzzards picking out his eyes, and the happy hunting grounds fading in the distance. He seemed dazed for a moment and chanted a kind of death song, "Uha-ha-ha, Uha-ha-ha," swaying back and forth like a clock pendulum. I followed his movements until sure of my aim between his eyes and pulled the trigger but the gun failed to fire. I quickly cocked it without taking it down from my shoulder and pulled again and saw with horror that the cap had dropped off the tube of my gun. So did the Indian discover that the gun would not fire and threw his hand back as quick as a lightning flash and drew an arrow from his quiver. Old Nance (bless her) stood stock still or I would have been a dead man. In an instant I sprang back to her shoulder and grabbed a cap from my vest pocket. The boys coming up and dismounting, the Indian started for the thicket behind us. He made the bound of an old buck, zig-zagging at each jump, but I had shot snipe on a windy day and woodcock in the brush and would as soon have had him flying as running. At the crack of my gun he fell and rolled over like a rabbit shot at full speed. But he whirled on his back and kept the air full of arrows, shooting first at one and then the other of us, until the boys riddled him with bullets.

I then began loading my gun and asked John Dawson to follow brother Jack. He was in plain view and I saw the smoke of his gun once or twice and finally saw him dismount and fire. His Indian had begun to leave him and show his contempt by gestures, but at the crack of brother's rifle (who after dismounting took a rest off his knee) the Indian fell forward, clasping his horse's neck and another Indian (not noticed before) rode up to his side and held him on his horse. Brother gave these two a parting shot and hearing a horse coming at full speed behind him, whirled around, and as he said, saw an Indian plainly, his bow held up in his hand and paint on his face. He took deliberate aim at his heart and pulled the trigger. His rifle failed to fire and before he could cock the hammer again the Indian was nearly on him and yelled out, "What do you mean Jack?" Then he came near fainting when he saw who it was. What a thread our lives sometimes hang on. In the chase brother had fired his repeating rifle and cocked to shoot again and let down the hammer, thinking to out run the Indian. He repeated this maneuver twice so when he came to shoot at John Dawson he had come on an empty barrel in the cylinder. It seemed like providence was on our side. Brother and John came back and we examined our Indian. I noticed four buckshot in the bottom of his moccasin and he was sprinkled with them up to the small of his back.

According to the custom prevailing, we took his scalp and equipment. And here our eastern friends are entitled to an explanation (especially those who get their ideas of the noble red man from Cooper's novels) as to why we scalped our enemies. The Indians believe that if they can carry off their dead and hide or bury them (and they will take all desperate chances to do so) with a whole scalp they will go to paradise. Their idea of that blissful spot is a beautiful land with groves of shade trees, beautiful springs of sweet clear waters, where plum thickets, acorn trees, and loaded grapevines are found, and where buffalo, deer, fish, honey, and all game abound—gentle, fat, and easy to kill—the best of grass and splendid war horses, and last but not least, where the women are all young and beautiful.

Their idea of hell is a place where the water is alkali or salty, game poor and wild, the grass is scant, horses, buffalo and deer scarce, and the women old, ugly, skinny squaws. And all Indians who lose their scalps go to this place. And as we were not in the missionary business we sent everyone to hell we could by scalping them. We had seen so much of their brutality to our women and children that we had no qualms of conscience about serving them in such a way as would make them give our settlements a wide berth in the future, which they did afterwards.

But to go back, brother always carried a very heavy hunting knife that the Indians knew, as he always used it in killing panthers when hunting with them, and to leave his mark he struck the Indian across the head, spitting his skull wide open. This looked like very summary proceedings but we were in a hurry administering and wanted to give him a receipt for all the men, women, and children he had murdered and horses stolen, as well as give notice to his friends and kinfolks to keep off of our grass. Gathering up the ponies the Indians left, we struck out for home and knowing that we would not get any water to drink until we got back to our old camp at least thirty miles distant, we took our trail back. It was fearfully hot, being the 20th of June 1860, and the sun came down with a glare and fierceness seen and felt only on the western plains.

By dark we had reached our old camp and though the water was as red as blood and the rays of light could not penetrate it, by putting my tin cup with the mouth down, to the bottom of the hole and turning it over, I got a cool drink of the sweetest water I thought I had ever tasted. Our horses too enjoyed it and after being unsaddled and taking a roll they went to eating the rich grass at once. We soon had our coffee on and filling up with Uncle Sam's hard tack and "Old Ned." We laid down to rest awhile, one keeping guard. Knowing the Indians, if any were below us, would probably follow our trail, we saddled up and moved out from the creek about half a mile to a good flat with mesquite trees and good grass, and slept sound until the birds sang reveille. Before day we made a hasty breakfast and took our trail back, hoping to meet some straggling band of Comanches.

About sunup I was riding behind, and I heard brother Jack say, "Look boys, yonder's some Indians." I asked how many, as the Indians had immediately disappeared on discovering us. We galloped to the spot where we had seen them and to our left in a beautiful valley with here and there a mesquite and liveoak tree, we saw seven Indians riding down it at a full gallop towards Paint Creek.[7] They were driving about eight loose horses. We at once raised the yell, afterwards heard on many a battlefield, and now remembered as the "Rebel Yell," and went clattering after them, using whip and spur. They had about four hundred yards start on us, but we were soon gaining on them so fast that they dropped their loose horses and it was every Indian for himself and the devil take the hindmost, which I hope his Satanic majesty did.

I had tied the gunny sack of hard tack behind my saddle, having sewed it all up except a hole in one corner big enough to pull out the bread, and tied it with a stout string. After about a mile race the corner came untied and the hard tack whole, half and small pieces, began to stream out behind me. The boys said I looked like a comet.

Brother and I kept well together for a mile, but as he was very heavy and I very light and our horses about the same rate of speed, Old Nance soon forged ahead and in running the two or three miles race, I got some two hundred yards ahead of the other boys, and evidently nearer than the Comanches liked, so one of them rode zig-zag behind his party and shot two or three arrows at me, but I could see them and well to the right or left to avoid them. When the Indians got near a large creek we thought to be Paint Creek, they entered a bend in it in the shape of a horseshoe and one of them, turned to the left and crossed, getting on a hill about a mile off, and sat there on his horse until the fight was over and then pulled out for the Fort Sill agency, I suppose. That will be about my ticket if the North and South get to fighting again, and I won't care how high the hill is.

The other six Indians rode straight into the bend and I said to myself, "Now's your chance to get revenge for Josephus' death," so I pushed Old Nance to her top speed, intending to dismount on the bank of the creek, and as they rode up on the other side to give them both barrels of my shotgun and empty my six-shooter at them. To my surprise, however, as soon as they got to the creek they all struck the ground together just like a lot of cow-birds lighting around an old steer, and took shelter under the bank, but popped up like a lot of jumping-jacks and began shooting at me. I dismounted and as soon as they were not over thirty-five yards off I ran back about ten steps, taking a lesson from the Indian the day before. I ran to the left to keep them from killing Old Nance when shooting at me. Luckily for me, five of them got into a small hollow that came out towards me from the creek.

By standing up they could shoot and by dropping on their knees they were out of sight. One of them—he looked awfully big to me—ran to the right, having to pass a place where the bank of the creek was a bluff and he had to expose himself for ten or twelve feet. He made his move, however, whil'st I was dismounting and the other Indians [were] getting into position. The five Indians in front of me kept the air full of arrows, but as I kept aiming at them every time they would raise up to shoot, they did some awful poor shooting. Some of their arrows went ten feet over my head.

I was jumping and dodging and dancing the "can-can" all the time; only one arrow would have struck me. I had to keep my eye on the Indian on the right, and threw my gun on him. He dodged down, and as I turned, one of the Indians in front let an arrow fly and I caught the glint of it in the sun coming straight for my breast. I stepped to one side and it whistled by my ear. Just then I heard brother's voice saying, "Look out, Pat, for that Indian on your right." I answered, "I am looking out for all of them as well as I can." Brother dismounted, and kneeling, kept his gun on the spot, waiting for his fellow and when his head next popped up, he let drive, striking the ground in front of his face. The other Indian evidently thought something must be done as the other boys had come up and were dismounting, so three of them, probably by arrangement, raised up ready to shoot at the same time; but as I had shot jack-snipes on a windy day and taken snapshots at wood chucks in brushy ground, my gun was to my shoulder and I got in the first shot, aiming at the center Indian, and badly wounded all of them. I raised a yell and the Indian on the right, thinking the thing was getting too hot, ran and as he passed over the high bank I spoke of, I let him have the left hand barrel and tumbled him over. He arose, however, and ran to a tremendous big mule they had stolen and as he put his foot in the stirrup brother's Colt rifle cracked again, and throwing up his hands, the Indian staggered backwards and fell off the bank, striking the bed of the creek about forty feet below.

The boys had not gotten a chance to shoot, and brother who still had four shots in his rifle, wanted to charge after the Indians. We could see them making good time up the rocky bed of the creek. But I begged them to let me load my gun before they moved. Tom Stockton and Elias Hale mounted their horses and went full speed up the creek and crossed where the first Indian had. Min Wright guarded our horses and those left by the Indians. Keeping up the south bank, brother and John B. Dawson crossed the creek and going up a little way they got up on a rocky point that commanded the bed of the creek, and hid themselves. As soon as I loaded my gun I ran across the bend of the creek and got behind a liveoak tree at the edge of an awful green brier and bushy thicket taking care to keep the tree on my right so they could not take me unaware. I kept my eye on the bank of the creek opposite. I soon had the satisfaction of seeing ahead and back of the Indian going up the bank on the opposite side and about seventy-five yards off. I had to exert a good deal of self-control to keep from shooting at this one, but I waited and the four followed. As soon as they got strung out I let drive, and I knew from the way they jumped and slapped their hands behind them I had got in my work.

The boys above came in sight at the same moment and the Indians wheeled to the right and ran down under the bank again. Loading quickly, I ran across to where they had stood, and looking to the right, I saw one cautiously peeping over the bank. I drew my six-shooter and fired. The ball cut the brush just over his head and he disappeared. In a minute more I heard two rifle shots almost simultaneously, and thinking that five to three might be too much of a good thing for brother and the boys, I ran full speed for them down the left bank of the creek. I heard another shot and an unearthly yell, followed by still another shot. This made me feel uneasy about my big brother and I made the best time I could and ran down into the bed of the creek and nearly over my brother and John Dawson, who was standing over a dead Indian. I saw the form of another under an old drift pile. After my pistol shot the five Indians started down the bed of the creek and when they got to the point commanded by brother and John Dawson, they both fired. John's rifle was brand new and he had never trained it. He said he fired at the Indian's breast but the bullet hit him just under the eye. We concluded, however, that could pass as a good shot. Brother had wounded his Indian and they both ran down to where the dead Indian lay.

Brother said he looked around carefully, knowing that an arrow might come whizzing at any moment and seeing a pair of moccasins under the drift pile, he got the position of the Indian and fired with his revolver. The unearthly yell I had heard was the result. Knowing from the tone of the voice that it was a squaw, he fired again to put her out of her misery. The Indians on their raids nearly always carried a few squaws and they were more cruel to our women and children, if such a thing were possible, than the men. So we shed no tears over her death.

We now knew there were but three Indians left and the question was how to get them. After a short council of war we decided to wade up the creek [where] the water stood in holes and was from one to three feet deep. We moved cautiously up to where I shot and back again, but saw no Comanches, but I saw where the Indians had crossed the creek and entered the brush, as the water was still dripping from the wet leaves.

Another confab was held and the consensus of opinion (this is a new phrase I have coined for the occasion) was that no one cared to investigate that thicket at the risk of having a feathered dogwood switch stuck in his digester. We concluded that we had done pretty well anyhow—seven Indian scalps, seven good Indians and nobody hurt on the side. The thicket was in the bend of the creek spoken of and a conglomeration of green briers and liveoak and dogwood brush, besides the large liveoaks that gave it a decidedly somber and graveyard look. It was the latter part of June and a long ride to a surgeon if any of us should be wounded seriously. I don't know that any kind of a wound should be taken as a joke. We decided that we might die before we could get help, so brother gave them a "cussing" in Comanche and told them to go back and tell who killed their companions.

Having settled the matter we walked up on the bank and brother turned and said in a positive way, "Boys, if we go back to the settlements and tell that six of us went off and left three Indians wounded and only armed with bows in half an acre of green brier thicket, it won't sound well," "Then we'll have them out," we chorused. Our plan was to get our horses together, let one man guard them, and the balance of us go through the thicket, following their trail.

Before we had decided to go into the thicket, Min Wright said, "I'll just shell the thicket, anyway," so he turned his old cannon loose, shooting through the thicket in every direction, and the sequel proved it was a good plan, as it made them "hide out," so to speak. John Dawson said, "George and I are good wing shots—I'll swap guns with Min Wight. We will go ahead and the rifles can bring up the rear." Now if these Indians had been armed with rifles it would have been sheer madness to have gone into the thicket, for the three could have laid down and concealed themselves, covering our trail, and killed three of us the first fire. The other two would have broken their necks getting out of the wilderness. The one left with the horses would have selected the best one and soon been in the settlements.

John and myself went in on the trail—I on the right. Brother and Elias Hale were behind us and Min Wright brought up the rear. We had hardly got into the thicket before I saw something that looked reddish and slick so I threw my gun on it and fired. Every one stood at present arms and as soon as the smoke cleared away we saw that I had shot a hole in a slick old log that the high water had left in the briars half way up the bank. So the boys began to guy me about my wooden Indian. As soon as I loaded we moved on again. It was no trouble to follow the trail. I stopped and said, "Boys, I was mistaken about that log being an Indian, but I smell one now. So look out." As I spoke John Dawson threw down his gun and fired almost at my feet. I saw a red form and fired one barrel and then a fusillade followed from all hands. This Indian had doubled himself up in a hole cut in the earth by the rain falling over the bank of the creek and hid by the green briers. Min's shelling had made him double himself up in a bowknot.

Loading up again we followed the trail that turned up the creek along the bank. We had not gone ten steps until we saw an Indian start to rise so he could use his bow, but John Dawson and brother fired about the same time and he fell forward shot in the top of the head, and then Min took a shot at him. Loading again we started on, and hearing a terrible racket of some one running through the brush and briars behind us, we turned and saw Tom Stockton and thought maybe a strong band of Indians had gotten our horses while we were in the thicket. However, as soon as he could speak he said, "I counted the shots, boys, and knew there was only one Indian left, and I am determined to get a shot at him. We can beat him to the horses if he leaves the thicket."

Following the trail I came to the open ground and soon found his bow and quiver, and some of his arrows, and could plainly follow his moccasin tracks in the loose dry earth. I said, "Boys there's no danger now; he is badly wounded and in open ground, and here is his bow and quiver of arrows." The trail all at once gave out, to my astonishment, because we were in a perfectly open place and I could have seen his tracks in any direction. So all I could do was to stand still and try and work out the mystery. John Dawson was using his eyes too, and sharp ones. All at once he threw his gun down and fired almost at my feet. It raised a great dust and I thought I would have the laugh on him. "Now," said I, "John, where is your Indian?" "Don't know," said he, "but I saw his eyes a minute ago," and sure enough looking down I saw the blood spurting from the leaves and ashes.

This Indian had gotten into a hole made by an old dead tree burning down into the ground and had managed to pull the ashes, dirt and leaves and grass around him so that nothing was to be seen but his eyes and nose. But to show his determination he had an arrow in one hand and his knife stuck in the ground in front of him where he could grab it and make a last desperate charge. But he was not quick enough and waited rather too long. We had now killed six Indians that we knew of and felt sure we could find the one that brother and I had shot, and two or three of us went down into the bed of the creek to look for him. I spied him in a bunch of tules and gave him a shot as did the others, so now we had seven Indians and about fifteen head of horses, and best of all, none of us wounded.

John Dawson then said to me, "George, I thought you would be killed before we got to you. The way the sun shone on them, it looked to me like the air was full of arrows all the time." I told him he ought to have taken the splendid dodging into account. I told him I had not seen the Indian on my right shoot a single time, but was certain he had. So to satisfy my curiosity I went and found my position and brother Jack went to where the Indian was. The boys got the direction and between six and seven arrows were found. We found quite a number shot by the five in front of me. The squaw only had a lance. Examining the Indians' wounds the boys gave me credit for having drawn first blood from three with the right and one with the left hand barrel in the beginning of the first fight—i.e. four Indians with one volley. It offered me great satisfaction for I felt I was getting even with them for killing and scalping my young friend. Gathering up our trophies and horses, we rode back to our trail. Each one had a good bow and a quiver of arrows, which we knew how to use. We had shot away a lot of ammunition and were glad to have bows to fall back on in case of a pinch. I had my feelings harrowed up by seeing my hard-tack scattered along on the route for our bread was getting low, but we knew the woods were full of game.

We camped on the Clear Fork of the Brazos about ten miles below Phantom Hill. The Indians had burned the houses and left the chimneys standing. I don't know whether it got its name before or after the burning. After we had dismounted and hobbled our horses and began cooking, I noticed brother scratching himself at a terrible rate, and he soon moved off in the brush and commenced, to disrobe. "Hello," says I, "What's the matter?" "Why Pat, the lice are about to get away with me." He had put the scalps during the fight inside the bosom of his gray flannel shirt and the Indian lice were trying to get even with him. The boys had a good laugh at his expense, but we managed to divide our clothes up so he could have all his fumigated over a brush fire. He took a good swim as we all did. We then fumigated the scalps and all the Indian equipment.

It was getting rather late when we got through dinner and we started for our homes feeling quite elated at our success. I rode ahead and the balance drove the horses. We had just gotten on top of a mesa or flat topped hill between two small branches when I looked ahead and saw about thirty-five head of horses coming directly toward us driven by six Indians. I whirled and stopped our horses, and turned them down the hill and told the boys what I had seen. All was excitement. We dismounted, tightened up our cinches, examined our arms and made sure all was right, and then I went to peep over the top of our hill to see if the Indians were in sight, but they were not, having gone down in the valley between our hill and the one they were on. We started in the one they were on.

We waited, it seemed to us, a long time and became afraid that they had passed down by us in one of the branches that were on each side and we would have a race back to the river where they would have a better chance to get away in the brush. So we mounted and rode in the direction of where I had seen them, where we would have a view of them on either side of our mesa. When we got to the south side of the mesa I heard the sound of horses' feet and said, "Here they are, boys." We formed a line facing them and about twenty feet apart. Their horses came right up the steep hill and were so tired that they never swerved to the right or the left, but passed through our line. We sat as still as statues.

The Comanches came on laughing and talking and were astounded at seeing us between them and their horses they had so much trouble stealing. They broke to run to our right and we kept opposite to them on top of the hill, intending to charge down on them. They halted suddenly, and brother, who spoke Comanche fluently, said the chief called to his men, "There's only six of them and six of us, let's get down and whip them and take their horses." If there was anything in this world that an Indian will fight for it is a good bunch of American horses that don't belong to him. The mesa on our right was not broad and the chief came up on top of it, his men behind him, each selecting his Texan to kill and scalp.

Brother was ahead of us, John Dawson, Tom Stockton, Elias Hale, myself, and Min Wright in the order as named. Brother dismounted as we all did, but only three of the Indians did. One was a regular six-footer—another, a small wiry youngster, evidently his brother; the third one, a medium sized Indian. Brother fired first at the young Indian and wounded him. The chief, who had a lance, thinking no doubt, that brother's gun was empty, charged him, but as brother sat perfectly still and kept a bead on him, the Indian must have mistrusted something was behind and suddenly whirled. Brother's rifle cracked, and the chief fell forward, grabbing his horse's neck and yelled to one of his men to come to him, which he did. Springing up behind him and throwing his arms around his body, they started off down the hill. Brother put in another shot in the backs of the pair before they got out of sight. This chief was a very tall, large man, and wore as an ornament a long leather strap ornamented with circular pieces of silver hammered thin and decreasing in size from two and a half inches across to the smallest Mexican coin—a quartilla. Brother put a bullet through the center of one of these silver ornaments and probably through both the Indians as they ran off.

While this was going on the other boys had been shooting too. I selected my partner to swing corners and fired and saw a cloud of dust and lint fly from his shirt. Glancing to my right I saw two Indians on foot coming rather too much in my direction to suit me, and not caring to shoot my second barrel until compelled, I whirled to Min and said in an excited tone, "Give me your gun, quick, Min." Nine times out of ten a fellow will hand you over his gun, but Min, too, had only one barrel loaded, and said dryly, "Oh, you don't come on me like that."

Then I told him, pointing out an Indian to our left, "Take good aim at that fellow, Min," and he did. At the crack of his gun the dust flew out of the Indian's shirt and he pitched off down the trail at a two-forty gait. We had now only the two brothers and it looked an easy going fight, but the hottest part was yet to come. The big Indian ran along our front to draw our fire.

They all began shooting and soon emptied their rifles and began to empty their six-shooters. But the Indian cut so many didoes it seemed impossible to hit him. I followed him with my gun, but as he had his shield between us I knew it was useless to shoot, but watched for my chance, and when he got to one of these little round sinks so common on the plains, where a badger had dug out a hole and the loose rocks were lying around, his foot struck one of them. Just for a moment his shield flew up, my gun fired and down he went. He yelled to the other Indian, who ran to him. They said something to each other and the small Indian, who ran to him and stooped over, pulled a handful of arrows from his quiver and then came straight up the hill for me, seeing no doubt that I had shot down his brother.

In the beginning of the fight, after shooting one barrel of my gun, I had drawn my revolver and shot twice at an Indian stringing his bow, making him duck his head each time and then pointed him out to Min Wright as mentioned before. I then ran a little way to the right and fired only one shot as I thought, and would have sworn I had two loads when I put my pistol back in the scabbard.

I knew in reason that if those Comanches would stop on that bald mesa where there was not a switch between us and them, to fight six cowboys well armed with guns and revolvers, they had grit and meant business, and I intended to keep two or three loads in my pistol, for I just felt it in my bones that I would need them after the fight was over. I trusted principally to my shotgun, but almost as much in my pistol. I had taken a rat tail file and made a buckhorn sight of the hammer and put a silver bead in front, and could kill a jack rabbit at seventy-five yards by squatting down and taking the pistol in both hands. So as soon as this little fellow started for me, I squatted down on my hunkers and felt as sure of killing him as though I had him already down and was sitting on top of him. When he got in about thirty-five steps I concluded that that was near enough. My pistol failed to fire; a hasty glance showed me that I had emptied it. So grabbing my gun I made the best time of old Lexington towards Old Nance. God bless her, she was standing off about twenty yards as unconcerned as though I had dismounted to butcher a deer. The Indian must have shot at me, but I don't think any of his arrows moved as swiftly as I flew. After I got to Old Nance, I put her between me and the Indian and he made for her also. I clubbed my gun, intending if he tried to come on my side or tried to get in my saddle to knock him in the head. The boys seeing my danger, started towards me, and that caused him to break for the brink of the hill, and in one or two bounds he disappeared.

I then began loading as fast as I could and had got down powder (I had a big copper flask such as the U.S. Government used) and got down my wads, when I heard the sound of a horse running and a Comanche war whoop, and looking to my right I saw my little Indian coming again. Elias Hale was the only one who had either gun or pistol loaded and brother called to him, "Elias, shoot that Indian's horse or he will kill some of us." Elias had two loads in his pistol and shot the mare, a beautiful animal, through the heart. She made one or two plunges and went down, but the Indian lit on his feet like a cat and made for me again. It just so happened I was nearest to him. Old Nance had fed off a little way and John Dawson's horse was nearest to me, so I got to him in a few jumps. The Indian made for me, but he must have thought my gun was loaded, for he grabbed the pommel of the saddle and brother yelled out, "Kill him. Kill him, Elias." He shot his last load, but missed. The horse shied from the Indian and gave him a sling toward the brink of the mesa and he went over it like a flying squirrel. If the Indian had known it he had won the battle—his quiver was full of arrows and our guns were empty and he could have shot every one of us.

Things were getting rather serious, so I did not count, but put a handful of six-shooter balls in each barrel of my gun and we moved back a little from the brink of the mesa, and after I got my shotgun loaded, I commenced loading my revolver—in fact all were as busy loading as little girls making mud cakes. John Dawson and brother only loaded their six-shooters, thinking the fight was over, and rode to the brink of the hill to see what had become of our pet. They soon had their curiosity gratified. I heard the sound of horse's feet and the Comanche war whoop again and the boys said, "Look he will kill your brother." I dropped my pistol and ran towards him. The little Indian had mounted himself again on a splendid animal and came right back to attack all of us. Brother and John started back towards us. John had a Spanish bit on his horse, and in trying to jerk him around suddenly, the severe bit had gotten somehow up and down in his mouth and he stood still in his tracks. The Indian shot an arrow that hit the horse in the neck and he took the hint and then did not wait for the word "go." Brother was to the left of John and the Indian took after him. John turned half around and shot at the Indian, who then whirled on John, passing in behind him so as to have him on his left side so he could use his bow and shoot at the same time. They looked to me as though they were not over six feet apart and shot at the same time. The Indian's arrow went through John's hand, split the stock of his pistol and the iron shaft curved around the main spring of the pistol, rendering it useless.

Of course the Indian had him at his mercy, but brother, when he saw John's danger, had checked up and rode up nearly close enough to powder burn the Indian and leaning forward, shot him in the back. The nervy

Comanche though had another arrow ready for John when my old shotgun went off. Brother yelled to me, "Shoot him again, Pat, dam[n] him, I don't believe we can kill him." So I turned loose the other barrel and he was about fifty yards off. He had a Spanish bit and gave a jerk that threw the mare on her haunches. He went over her head as though shot from a catapult, turning a complete somersault as a clown in a circus and fell on his back. When we got to him he was perfectly dead and held his bow with such a firm grip in his hand that we could hardly release it. The mare staggered around and fell, too. I had killed them both. As soon as we could load our guns we went to finish our other Indian. He was protected by the badger hole and would draw his bow back like he would stave an arrow clean through us every time we tried to get near him; but I noticed no arrow ever left his bow. We finally cross-fired on him and killed him. On examining him we saw evidently an older brother of the brave boy who had fought desperately. I don't think during the entire War Between the States or in all my frontier experiences that I ever saw such cool, desperate valor displayed as this young Indian showed. If this should meet the eye of Quanah Parker he can tell this Indian's name. I would like to name a strain of game cock after him. He was Pee Wichee Wah Pah—Peenataikah.

We found out why our Indian in the badger hole did not shoot. One of my buckshot had split his bow from end to end. We gave this bow to Dr. Pugh of Louisiana, and I expect his family have it yet. We all loaded up our guns again and found our ammunition about gone. We gathered up our stock and found, besides the two mares killed, several shot with arrows intended for us. Brother and I rode down to see if any of the Indians were dead under the brow of the hill, for we knew in reason they must be. Just before we got where we went to look, I cast my eyes towards the settlements and the sight made me check my horse suddenly. "Look, brother," I said, "the whole horizon is covered with Indians." We saw what looked like four or five hundred head of horses, some thirty or forty Indians behind them, and twelve or fifteen on each side as flankers. Brother said, "Pat, this is no place for us—we must light out."

Galloping back we told the boys what we had seen and two rode ahead and four behind our *caballado* of horses. We bore in towards Clear Fork at a full gallop and kept it up down the valley four or five miles and then bore in towards the old government road from Phantom Hill, where we arrived during the night and went into camp pretty well worn out, thankful to the God of battles that we were safe.

The news going to Camp Cooper in the morning, Major Thomas ordered out a scout at once. They took our trail back, and beyond where we had had the fight. They found the chief with his shield under his head and his lance stuck down through his heart and a dead warrior on each side of him. This was the owner of the silver ornaments. His shield had a handsome head dress of feathers such as the Comanche warrior carried, inside of a buckskin covering on his shield. It also had a woman's scalp painted and beaded.[8] It was a pretty golden color, plaited nicely and tied with a piece of red flannel. In addition, it was ornamented with a little baby's scalp, with hair not over an inch long. I can't say who have those shields now, but my mark is on the one the Indian boy fought over so, a buckshot in it. I think one was given to Mrs. Bradley of Houston, and all the lances, etc., given to different friends.

Our government troops, instead of taking the trail of the Indians and stolen horses, took our trail back to Paint Creek and west, but finding no further trail, came back to Cooper, under the impression, no doubt, that we were mistaken about seeing so many Indians. But Major Thomas said he knew John R. Baylor, and if he said he saw the Indians they were there, and so he sent them back again and they went where he told them to and found the trail sure enough. It appeared the Indians had seen us and the bunch of horses and magnified us into a big army—they ran one way and we ran the other. Like Hood's *bon mot* [witty saying]—"the man ran with all his might and the lion with all his mane." The soldiers followed the trail until it took them near where they had turned back before. Of course it was then too late to catch them, so they turned back to Camp Cooper.

We had quite an ovation on our arrival in the settlements and felt proud of our success, having in a five days scout killed twelve Indians (a thirteenth died after getting to Fort Sill) and recaptured fifty-five head of horses and the scalp of my young friend.[9] We still had a hard duty to perform to take the scalp of Josephus to his old father and mother and his sisters. Brother handed the scalp to the old man and said, "Uncle Billy, we can't bring your boy back, but there is his scalp and nine of his murderers." The old man threw his arms around Old Belton's neck and burst into tears. We received the tearful thanks of mother, and sisters and turned our horses' heads for home again. I would rather have another round with the Comanches than go thorough that scene again.

A big barbecue was the next thing in order, and the people of Young County turned out en masse; Old Gaddus Miller, Aunt Kit, his wife, the general, his son, Old Uncle Tom Dawson and Aunt Lou, his wife. The latter said God, she knew, had spared her boy when brother aimed at his heart. And Old Joe Curtis, Uncle Joe Matthews—alas, few of them are alive today. Some barely keeping soul and body together, waiting for the United States Court of Claims to pay them for stock stolen thirty years ago. But I am afraid most of them are in their graves or will be before they ever get anything. Witnesses will all be dead soon, and no proof can be made and the government will save money for campaign purposes.

Palo Pinto County said we must eat some of her barbecued meat and pies, and when we got to Weatherford, Dr. Ward said Parker County didn't intend that only those counties could feed us, but we must go to Walnut Creek or Veats Station, and so we did and had a glorious time. Brother made speeches at each place, for he shot off his mouth or pen as well as he could his rifle.

I am afraid that what I have to say in conclusion will greatly shock all those who get their ideas about Indians from Cooper's novels. Weatherford was the home of brother and me and they wanted to show their appreciation of our services and decided to give a grand ball and supper. And as flags and ornaments of that kind were not to be had some of the committee suggested the use of our Indian trophies to adorn the courthouse where the dance was to be given.

No sooner said than done. A rope was stretched from pillar to pillar and the shields of the chiefs and the scalps all strung up above the heads of the dancers.[10] And so we had a regular "scalp dance." A band of music, pretty women, girls, and brave men, all danced till the wee sma' hours. Among these barbarians I can recall, Judge Hood, Jack Ball, Judge Couts, the Hitsons, Pollards, Rushings, Inges, Shannons, Jack Leonard, the Lovings, old Billy Mosely, John Squires, Sisks—in fact, everybody nearly in Parker County.

My brother led the dance with Mrs. J. D. Smith, at present of Pecos City, Texas. I kicked up my heels nearly as high as I did on Paint Creek. The *Philadelphia Times* gave us Hail Columbia—said we were as bad as the Indians, having a regular scalp dance. They gave me an extra dig after this fashion: "They (the Texans) speak of one of the young men noted for his amiability and kind, gentle manner and gave as an evidence of it the statement that he killed and scalped six Indians one morning before breakfast," Vale, Mr. Times I owe you one.

The actors in the fight are scattered as far as I can learn. John B. Dawson is at Colfax, New Mexico; has a stock ranch and orchard.[11] Tom Stockton is a ranchman somewhere in New Mexico or Arizona. Elias Hale was the trusted courier of General Polignac during the Banks campaign from Mansfield to Yellow Bayou, Louisiana. I don't know his address or if he survived the last campaign. Min Wright, I heard, was killed during the war. Gen. John R. Baylor died at his home at Montell, Uvalde County, after serving Texas from 1840 to 1894, in many places, legislator, congressman C.S.A., soldier of the Republic of Texas and private citizen—all with honor to himself and his name. Brave as lion in battle, gentle and tender hearted as a woman at his own fireside, few men had more devoted friends. He has gone across the river to camp with Stonewall Jackson, where I hope to join him.

NOTES

1 The Brownings' ranch was on the Clear Fork of the Brazos, north of present-day Breckenridge in what is today Stephens County. John Henry Brown, *Indian Wars and Pioneers of Texas* (Austin: State House Press, 1988), 121.

2 There does not appear to be such a letter in the Letters Received, in either the Texas or Wichita Agencies, or the Office of the Superintendent of Indian Affairs (Record Group 75, National Archives).

3 Neighbours, *Indian Exodus*, 118-19; James K. Greer, *Buck Barry: Texas Ranger and Frontiersman* (Lincoln: University of Nebraska Press, 1978), 113-17. Also see n. 11, Ch. 1, Sec. II.

4 Major Thomas was in command of a company of the elite 2d Cavalry at Camp Cooper. Neighbours, *Robert Simpson Neighbors*, 229.

5 One version has both boys unarmed and a badly frightened Josephus easily killed when he was unable to unhobble his horse. Another said that Josephus had cut the hobbles in such a way that his horse tripped and he was easily overtaken. J.W. Wilbarger, *Indian Depredations in Texas* (Austin: Hutchings Printing House, 1889), 517-21; W.K. Baylor, "The Killing of Josephus Browning Avenged," *Frontier Times* 16 (October 1933): 1-4.

6 Located between the Elm and Clear forks of the Brazos River, about a mile above their junction and fifteen miles north of present day Abilene, Phantom Hill was referred to as the "Post on the Clear Fork of the Brazos." Constructed in November 1851 by men of the 5th Infantry under Maj. John Joseph Abercrombie, the post was built of upright poles woven with sticks and plastered with mud over which thatched roofs were constructed. The post was abandoned in April 1854. Only the stone commissary, guard house, powder magazine, and several solitary stone chimneys remain today. C.C. Rister, "The Border Post of Phantom Hill," *West Texas Historical Association Yearbook* (October 1938): 5; and M.L. Crimmins, ed., "W.G. Freeman's Report of the Eighth Military Department," *Southwestern Historical Quarterly,* 53 (April 1950): 448-53.

7 Paint Creek rises in southeastern Haskell County and runs northeast to join the Clear Fork of the Brazos in southwestern Throckmorton County. A few of the events Baylor describes may have occurred beneath what is today Lake Stamford.

8 This appears to have been the scalp of a woman named Jackson. Because of the controversy over his extermination policy toward the Apache in New Mexico Territory during the Civil War, and after his dismissal, Baylor sent the scalp to Pres. Jefferson Davis. Gen. John B. Magruder intervened, however, and the scalp never reached Richmond. Baylor to Magruder, 29 December 1862, *OR*, 1, 15:914-15. See n. 38, Ch. 1, Sec. III.

9 Other accounts reported the party was "lionized for their prowess and daring." Wilbager, *Indian Depredations in Texas,* 519.

10 With the scalp of the white woman on display, "exterminate the Indians" was said to have been the watchword. Wilbarger, *Indian Depredations in Texas*, 519; and Rupert Norval Richardson, *The Frontier of Northwest Texas, 1846-1876* (Glendale: Arthur H. Clark Co., 1963), 207.

11 See n. 1, Ch. 4, this section.

CHAPTER FIFTEEN

Famous Buffalo Hunt

I WAS A COMMANDER IN THE FAMOUS BUFFALO HUNT IN 1861 in the Panhandle, when we tried to catch the thieving, murdering Comanches off the Fort Sill Reservation. I can't help but smile when I recall some of the ludicrous scenes of our campaign, in one of which, if I am not mistaken, [W.D.] Vance took a leading part.

The buffalo hunt was the beginning of my services for the grand old State of Texas as a captain, but I had seen some pretty active service in fights with these same Indians, and as Vance says, there were some 250 men in the expedition, and the command was given by brother, Gen. John R. Baylor, and such old Texas heroes as old Ben Brown of Robertson County, Capt. [Henry Wax] Karnes, Col. [Samuel C. A.] Rogers of Waxahachie, and many others who had helped free the Republic of Texas from Santa Anna's vicious and barbarous rule.[1] We camped at the deserted cattle ranch in Jack County, where the [William] Cameron and Mason families were massacred in 1858, but before we got there we had passed the home of Mr. Brown, killed within three miles of Weatherford on the Jacksboro road.[2] So the kids in the Ellis County boys were all the time on the lookout for Indians.

It was a beautiful clear moonlight night such as we often had on the frontier, and one of our old January blue northers was blowing great guns. At midnight there was a sharp crack of a rifle from our south side picket, followed instantly by a boom like a cannon from the sentinel on the east. Instantly all hands were up, and as all slept in their clothes and many in their boots, we were soon out with the pickets. The one on the south side said he was lying down in an old cow trail, skylighting, when he discovered a Comanche crawling in the same trail toward him and gave the command "halt." When the Indian raised up he looked like he was seven feet high, and he fired and the Comanche ran off toward the creek. Several of us ran down to the bank hoping to get a shot, but no Indians were discovered. The other sentinel had discovered the hide of the beef we had killed and hung on the fence waving about on the wind, and was sure it was an Indian, and when the other sentinel fired he turned loose both barrels of an old shotgun loaded with blue whistlers. The joke on him was that he never touched the hide, but spattered three or four panels of the old fence beyond the hide. Next morning I found a coyote's tracks where the other Indian was.

We got together with other companies near where Seymour now is in Baylor County and marched north and camped on the bank of that Epsom salt stream, the main Wichita.[3] Here's where I had the smile at Vance's expense. He was only a kid, and kid-like, [he] had lost the stopper out of the powder horn and luckily for him, most of the powder. A blue norther was blowing and we were all standing around the fire to keep from freezing. Suddenly, there was a flash and a loud report. A spark of fire had gone into Vance's powder horn and he started off like a deer, when a spark of fire got into his coat pocket where he had about a half pound of powder tied up in a paper, and that went off with such force it blew off his coat tail. "Now laugh, gol darn you." Ain't that so, Vance?

You said you would like to hear from some of your old comrades you met in 1895 at Houston, so now let me hear from you. You may not know it, but I lived on the Taylor Plantation, below Pine Bluff, in 1838 or 1839 and never liked that city because Dr. Jack Embree pulled a tooth for me and I gave the rebel yell even at that early date. The Embrees came to Bell County afterward and he and Brother Elias were with me in Louisiana and heard the genuine yell at Caroncrow battle.

To go back to our "mutton." We camped on the main Wichita and though not wishing to hurt the feelings of any of the Wichitans, especially sweet Alice Ben B., I must say the river is not first-class drinking water. Everybody was making a great kick about the taste; it was between rotten eggs and Epsom salts, when it just occurred to me, though I had not been with Sir John Franklin hunting the north pole, the Dame Nature with her marvelous skill had converted salt water into pure sweet icebergs, so I soon had a camp kettle full of ice and soon good drinking water.

An account of our campaign would take a volume, so [I] will only give a few incidents. We went up the Big Wichita, then over to the other branch of same, on the Pease River to the lakes on its head, but found no fresh Indian signs and turned south. When we got to the head waters of the salt prong of the Brazos we rode down into a deep canyon, where there was a beaver dam and quite a lake and grove of cottonwoods, with promise of wood and water and out of the cutting north wind.[4]

We had gone into camp and began to cook our dinner and supper. Brother Jack and a few men of my company rode up on an Indian village. They had discovered us when we came down the trail from the mesa, and being on [the] south side of the creek where there was quite a skirt of timber, we had not seen them, and they had thrown down all their tepees. So we did not see them even after we had crossed the stream and turned down it. As soon as the boys saw the village they guessed what was up and started off on a hot trail up the creek and sent a man back to notify us, who unsaddled his horse, lay down and said not a word. Brother and five or six men overtook the Indians, who sent back warriors to meet them. Only one came near and Sam Fonderen sent a load of buckshot after him and he joined the others in their wild stampede.

The Indians, having fresh horses, were soon out of sight. Our messenger finally mentioned about the Indian village. We all soon mounted and started off in hot haste. This was the only chance we had to make a good killing, for with all their plunder we could easily have brought them to bay somewhere up that canyon. Old Ben Brown wanted to hang the messenger who failed to give Colonel Baylor's message. He always contended he did so and no one thought him in earnest. I'm afraid he was no glutton about fighting Comanches.

We went down the stream we were camped on, it being quite a nice little stream of sweet, clear water but later in the day some wanting a drink, found it as salty as brine and we bore off to [the] southwest. We had only started with about ten or twelve days rations of bread, some coffee and salt, a small herd of beef cattle and stayed out nearly six weeks, but had passed above the buffalo herds that were moving southwest and had sheared the grass off close to the ground, making it very hard on our horses. Our beeves slipped off one night when we thought they were too tired to get up and made as straight a line for old Oliver Loring's ranch as though they had a compass. I followed them the next morning, but soon saw the long horns were too fleet for us. Now having no meat, and having to depend on our arms for grub, it was thought best to divide the command with the hope some of us would strike a camp. Colonel Baylor took the middle route, some going to our right and some to the left. Colonel Baylor made a splendid shot that day and killed a very fat buck antelope that was cutting the wind and was some 300 yards distant. I killed a grouse. This wasn't much, but made us supper, and next day late in the evening we killed an old bull buffalo. On my word, he did not have hair on him, except a tiff between his horns and a bunch on the end of his tail. We camped on what we called Croton Creek. The old bull was tough "for keeps," so we made soup. I won't harrow the feelings of any of the men who are now alive by recalling how the old bull got even with us.

We struck out by daylight and soon saw fresh signs of buffalo, and by evening we came in sight of the immense herds that covered the Texas frontier at that time. As far as the eye could reach great, dark masses, all moving in the same direction, southwest and soon as the wind carried our scent to the nearest ones they stampeded, and the whole herd as far as we could see were affected and went off their feet, making a roar like a train in a canyon. Before we got to camp that evening Colonel Baylor detached a man named Brantly and myself to kill what meat we wanted as he did not care to have all the command running after buffalo, as, if there were many Indians in that section, they would at once suspect what was the matter. He gave me his Colt's six-shooting rifle, and Brantly had a "human rifle," as the muzzle loaders were called. We saw a small herd coming in from the west to water and hid in a thicket on the east bank, the wind being in our favor, and as the herd came snorting down the bank at a gallop we turned loose and soon had fat meat enough for all the command. The boys in camp, hearing the firing, came with the pack mules, and such roasting as we had—buffalo hump, marrow bones and marrow gut, the last, as Mark Twain said of Wagner's music, [it] "is not as bad as it sounds."

Next day we struck a flock of turkeys and unless a man had been on the frontier forty years ago he would not believe the quantity of turkeys there were out there. The Indians did not care for them and they increased faster than the wildcats, panthers and coyotes could destroy them. Every man took after a turkey and I followed a big old gobbler for half a mile. When I saw him come out from a bush where he had squatted, I turned him over. Back in camp every man was roasting turkey, and I learned what the old Dutchman said was true, a turkey is too large for one man, but not large enough for two.

One night the column found the Comanches, or Kiowas, but the Indians on their fat horses just played around the boys. At night orders were given to stake and hobble all horses and double guards were put on, with orders not to hail any one coming in from the outside of the line of sentinels. What old Galvestonian does not remember genial Capt. J. H. Collett, mine host of the old Capitol Hotel? It was his misfortune to be on guard when a hard-headed man went outside without permission and started to come back after Collett had been put on guard. Although the order was not to hail any one, Collett challenged three times, and receiving no answer, fired with a shotgun and was horrified to find he had killed one of our own men.

This was not all the bad luck we had. When we got down where the Elm Fork enters the Clear Fork of the Brazos, in the neighborhood of Thornton, Hill, one of the men, was trying to wipe out his gun that had an iron ramrod. It was the celebrated Mississippi rifle that the great Rebel chief, Jefferson

Davis' regiment was armed with and saved the army of Gen. Zach Taylor from going down in defeat at Buena Vista. The rod got stuck in the barrel and the man picked powder in the tube and in letting down the hammer, it slipped from his thumb and fired the gun, sending the ramrod through the body of a messmate, killing him instantly.

Our campaign, the last made by Texans in any force, was a failure, except it was preparing us for hard times soon to come. As Vance says, we soon entered the Confederate army. I was selected first lieutenant of Hamner's Company A of Second Mounted Rifles, first regiment raised by Texas.

If any of my old soldiers see this I hope they will write to me. I am a stranger in a strange land.

NOTES

[1] The Philadelphia-born Richard Brown was a Perote prisoner and a Robertson County surveyor. Arriving in Texas from Tennessee, Karnes fought in the 1835 Battle of Concepción and Siege of Bexar. In 1836, he organized and commanded a company of cavalry that provided Gen. Sam Houston with much information on the Mexican Army. In 1838, Karnes enlisted eight companies for defense against the Comanches. He contracted yellow fever and died on 16 August 1840. Rogers, a Virginian and a veteran of the Siege of Bexar and the 1840 Battle of Plum Creek, also fought Tonkawas and Lipan Apaches. Webb and Carroll, *Handbook of Texas*, 1:226, 938; 2:499.

[2] In 1859, Comanches killed most of the Cameron and Mason families and carried off a child who was later rescued by a party of travelers on their way to California. Wilbarger, *Indian Depredations in Texas*, 536-38.

[3] Created in 1858, Baylor County was named after George Baylor's older brother, Henry Weidner Baylor, Mexican-American War veteran and Indian fighter.

[4] Probably in Kent or eastern Garza County where the Salt Fork of the Brazos emerges from the Caprock, northeast of present-day Post, Texas.

Civil War

~

We began behind a little

and could never catch up.

George Wythe Baylor, 1906

II

PERHAPS BAYLOR'S MOST VALUABLE WRITINGS are his Civil War recollections. His brief biography of his controversial brother, Col. John Robert Baylor, whom he deeply admired and whom he always referred to as "General Baylor," is rich in historical detail. The version that follows is one of three that he wrote at various times during his life. Published in three installments of the El Paso Herald in November 1901, it varies from that published by the Arizona Historical Society in 1966 in that it devotes more space to the 1861 Confederate occupation of southern New Mexico, especially the skirmish at Mesilla and the surrender of Federal forces at St. Agustín Springs.

Baylor's account of the death of Lt. Reuben E. Mays and fourteen of his men at the hands of Mescalero Apaches deep in the arid expanses of the Big Bend in August 1861 was a sincere effort to investigate the circumstances and location of the massacre. Baylor not only corrects several misconceptions about the massacre, but provides an account of earlier Confederate attempts to make peace with Nicolás, chief of the Davis Mountain band of Mescalero Apaches. His remembrance of the death of other Confederates in the Gallinas Mountains, northwest of Fort Stanton, New Mexico, although chronicled in the Official Records of the War of the Rebellion, is equally significant.

Undeniably, Baylor's best-written article is his account of having served as senior aide to Gen. Albert Sidney Johnston during the bloody battle of Shiloh in Tennessee in 1862. Baylor's characterization of General Johnston's death matches other sketches of the tragic scene. Although there is no collaborating evidence to substantiate that Johnston died in Baylor's arms, there is nothing in the historical record to disprove it, either. With Baylor's affection for Johnston, the scene as Baylor describes it appears plausible, if not probable.

Even more valuable is Baylor's description of his role in the 1864 Red River Campaign in Louisiana. Moreover, Baylor's account of events leading up to his killing of Gen. John A. Wharton in a Houston hotel room in April 1865 is objective and historically significant.

∼

CHAPTER ONE

John Robert Baylor
of Texas

~

GEN. JOHN ROBERT BAYLOR WAS BORN in Paris, Bourbon County, Kentucky, July 27, 1822. On his mother's side, he had German and French blood. His mother, Sophie Mary Weidner, born in Baltimore, Maryland, being the only daughter of Heinrich Weidner, of Hesscassel, and Sophie Marie [Christine] Chastelle, descended from an old Huguenot family.[1] On his father's side he was descended from an old English family, John Baylor—the oldest we have record of, being born at Tiverton, Devonshire, England, in 1650, and was related to the Freres, Tuckers, Hodges, Nortons, Lauries, and Courten[a]ys of Powderham Castle.

General Baylor's grandfather, Walker Baylor, was a captain in the American Army, and served as color bearer at the age of seventeen, in the regiment of horse guards, commanded by his brother, Col. George Baylor.[2] He had been senior aide to General Washington.

The family settled first in Gloucester County, [Virginia], but afterwards settled at New Market, then in King and Queen in 1726, having a large grant of land from the king. The old homestead has been in possession of the Baylors up to the present time.

General Baylor's father having moved to Fort Gibson in the Cherokee Nation, at the early date, 1827, he grew up within the sound of fife, drum and bugle, and as his father was an officer of the Seventh Regiment of Infantry, he naturally took to a soldier's life.[3] When merely a lad he went off with his brother, Henry W[eidner] Baylor, from school [Woodward College] in Cincinnati, in a skiff, intending to go to Texas and join an older brother

Walker in the war between Mexico and Texas.[4] He stopped to get something to eat on the Kentucky side of the river, being about starved out, and a man who heard them talking persuaded them to return to Cincinnati, and paid their fare on the first boat.

They were mere kids and the only punishment they received on their return was that the professor called them up on the platform and introduced them as "General Henry Baylor and his army returned from the conquest of Mexico."

Dr. John Walker Baylor, the general's father, having moved to Second Creek, near Natchez, Mississippi, and died, his mother and a widowed daughter, moved to the Taylor Plantation, near Pine Bluff, Arkansas, and from there to Little Rock. Again he and his brother decided to go to Texas. Santa Anna, in spite of his promises when in the hands of General Houston, had violated his pledges and sent Gen. Adrian Woll, with quite a force, to Texas, and they had captured San Antonio, taking the principal citizens prisoners.[5]

The general and his brother had stopped with an uncle in Fayette County, near La Grange, and with a cousin, Walker Baylor, who belonged to Capt. Nick Dawson's company. As soon as the alarm was given the Texans began to move out to meet the invaders. The brothers and cousins were delayed a day in hunting their ponies, and did not start with the balance of the ill-fated company, and it now seems providential. They were further delayed by a sudden rise in Peach Creek and passed Captain Dawson's company in the night, while off the main route. They reached Col. Clint Caldwell's command on the Salado Creek, near San Antonio and were in the battle of the Salado where 202 Texans defeated 1,450 Mexicans.[6] The Texans having a natural breastwork formed by the river bluff, whil'st the Mexicans were on the open ground. They heard cannon east of them where the Mexicans caught Dawson's company on open ground, and killed forty-one, captured ten, and two escaped by miracle.

General Baylor returned to Fort Gibson where his mother had gone, and later came back to Marshall, Texas, and married a beautiful young girl from Louisiana, Miss Emily Hanna.[7] He settled at Ross Prairie, Fayette County, when there were only two families in that lonely spot—J. Monroe Hill and George Kerr.[8]

In 1851 he was elected to the legislature and afterwards was appointed agent of the Comanche Indians, and moved his family to the Clear Fork of the Brazos.

Not long after he was in charge of the Comanches he began to suspect that the rascals were simply using the agency as headquarters for the stealing expeditions along the Texas border and finally they brought in a lot of horses belonging to a Mr. [Fred] Gentry who lived near Georgetown, Williamson County.[9] The general knew the brand of the stock and the owner, and on asking the Indians where they got the horses from, received the same story they always gave—that they had had a fight with the Kiowas and taken the horses from them.

But as none of the Comanches were wounded he determined to investigate, and sent an old Indian he had to act as a constable, to bring a young squaw, that went out with the party, to his office. When she came in he locked the door and told the constable to string and put an arrow in his bow, and he cocked his revolver and told the squaw if she did not tell the truth about where they got the horses he would kill her. She gave the whole thing away, saying that they had stolen them down in the white settlements.

General Baylor wrote to Gentry who came down and got his stock and some of his neighbor's horses and corroborated all the squaw had told. The general then wrote to the interior department, saying that he had indisputable evidence that the Indians under his control were robbing and murdering our own people, and asked what should be done in the matter. He soon received a stiff, formal letter telling him that his services were no longer needed as Indian agent.

This aroused his fighting blood, for he had been in several campaigns after these same Comanches, under Col. John H[enry] Moore, and on other occasions.[10] So he got in a few cowboys and began to "hive" the Indians every time he caught them off the reservation, and sent runners to the surrounding counties for men.

Soon such men as Capt. [James] Buck[ner] Barry, Peter Garland, Captain Motherell, G.M. Gano, Joe Bledsoe, and others were on hand, with some twelve hundred Texas frontiersmen.[11] General Baylor was elected colonel, and moved at once against the Comanche Reservation and they came out to fight him, but getting badly worsted, retreated to the agency. Several Texans were killed and wounded and quite a number of Indians.

Maj. George H. Thomas was at the time in command of the United States soldiers and had gone to the agency to protect the Indians.[12] When General Baylor advanced to attack them again, Thomas sent him word that if he would withdraw he would see that the Indians were moved out of Texas. The General then sent him word that that was all the Texans wanted, but they must be moved at once, and accordingly they were sent to Fort Sill, across Red River.

They now considered that the United States soldiers were their friends, and the Texans their enemies, so they raided Texas for nearly twenty-five years, carrying death and poverty to many a frontier home, whil'st their squaws and children were comfortably housed and fed by Uncle Sam. Only the narrow escape of Gen. W[illiam] T. Sherman and staff, near Jacksboro, where these government pets attacked a train and massacred all the teamsters, tying many of them to the wagon wheels and setting fire to them—even brought the matter close to the commander of the army and divulged the rottenness of the Interior Department on our border.[13]

General Baylor moved his family from the Clear Fork of the Brazos to Weatherford, knowing full well his ranch would be marked for vengeance by the Comanches, though he had some good friends among them, having gone out with them on their buffalo hunts, and using a bow and arrow as skillfully as their best warriors, and killing several panthers with a big knife he carried. This inspired them with admiration and as he was a splendid shot with a pistol and rifle, they had also a wholesome fear of him as an enemy.

The general's ranch was well stocked with cattle, and in the best stock country in the world, at that time, a country of free grass, abundant water, and no wire fences. He did not care to give up to these savages and so he left his stock on the ranch, taking his chances with his neighbors, when every man on the frontier carried his life in his hands.

On one occasion a band of Comanches came into his neighborhood and killed a young man named Josephus Browning, and the general with a younger brother, Col. George Wythe Baylor, John B. Dawson, Tom Stockton, Elias Hale, and Armenius Wright, followed them and returned on the fifth day, having killed thirteen Indians and recovered fifty-five head of horses which had been stolen, and were being carried to the sutler at Fort Sill, who bought pretty much all the stolen stock at his own price.[14] The Comanches on another occasion were followed and five of them killed, and they gave that neighborhood a wide berth.

The murders and robberies got to be so bold that the old frontiersmen, who had so long borne their depredations, determined to retaliate and an expedition was planned to catch the Comanches off the reservation and make a good killing that they would remember. Among those who came were some of the most noted men in the early struggle of Texas against both the hostile Indians and Mexicans, Capt. [Henry Wax] Karnes, after whom Karnes County is named; old Ben Brown, from Robertson County; Col. [Samuel C.A.] Rogers, from Waxahachie, Ellis County; and several others assembled near what is now Baylor County, and George W. Baylor was elected captain of a company from Palo Pinto, Parker, and Young counties.[15] General Baylor was elected to command the entire force of some three hundred men.

The Indians, however, got notice of the expedition, though it was given out that we were going on a grand buffalo hunt, and they kept out of the way, only one Indian being killed. Only a few were found, as the Texans' horses were poor, it being the winter of '60. The Indians kept out of the way, but the campaign made them move cautious for the time being.

We now come to the time of the Civil War. The buffalo hunters were ready to begin at once and Texas was ablaze of excitement. General Baylor and his brother were in Austin on their return from a visit to their mother and sisters in San Antonio, and on their way to the frontier the sisters had made the Lone Star Flag and put it on the lance taken from the Comanches in the fight spoken of, and this George W. Baylor hoisted in front of the old Capitol Hotel, being the first "secesh" flag raised in Texas. It came near breeding a fight at the time, as there was, and continued to be until the close of the war, a strong Union sentiment in Austin.

General Baylor on reaching home was recalled to Austin, the act of secession having passed, and decided to raise two regiments of mounted rifles. The first regiment was commanded by Col. Henry B. McCullough, one of the bravest and purest of men, the Second Regiment by Col. John S. Ford (Old Rip). General Baylor was appointed lieutenant-colonel, and Edwin Waller major, and the regiment was ordered to assemble at San Antonio, where they were mustered into the service in May, 1861, for three years or the war.

General Baylor with four companies of the regiment was ordered to go to El Paso, Texas, and take the companies of Capt. Ike Stafford of Houston, Capt. Peter Hardeman, Capt. James Walker, of Hallettsville, and Capt. [H.A.] Hamner of Weatherford.[16] These companies were present and took part in the capture of Maj. [Isaac Van Duzer] Reeves's command at San Lucas Springs, near San Antonio.[17]

The Germans having turned out in mass and being well trained soldiers and well equipped with arms taken at the San Antonio arsenal, made a fine display, and Major Reeves, who had demanded that a display of sufficient force should be made to justify his unconditional surrender, must have been gratified when he saw the regiments of McCullough, Baylor, and the German contingent in line of battle.

It was a bloodless battle, but more lager beer was shed than during any subsequent battle of the war. It is a pity all were not as bloodless, even though the American soldier could not have had a chance to prove himself the ideal soldier by his bravery, intelligence, and individuality.

General Baylor started his battalion ahead of him on the old Overland Immigrant Trail for El Paso, and they were stationed, Hamner at Fort Clark, Walker at Fort Davis, and Stafford and Hardeman at El Paso, Maj. Edwin Waller being in command at the latter point. The general remained a short time at San Antonio to arrange for the necessary supplies for his command,

and then took the Overland Stage to El Paso, taking his brother, George, first lieutenant of Hamner's company, with him to act as adjutant of his battalion. Ford with the rest of the regiment was sent to the lower Rio Grande, to watch that border.

On his arrival in El Paso, General Baylor began at once to organize for a campaign against the Federals at Fort Fil[l]more, New Mexico, for with his energetic restless spirit he could not sit idle, with an enemy within fifty miles. Maj. [Issac] Lynde with some five hundred or more men of the Seventh Regiment of Infantry, was known to be there and Lt. [Richard S.C.] Lord and Maj. [Alfred] Gibbs were to join him.[18] So taking Stafford's and Hardeman's companies and Capt. Bethel Coopwood with him, he started for Fil[l]more, leaving behind Maj. Trevanion T. Teel with a battery of six field guns, and Capt. [Samuel Williams] McAllister with a small company of infantry organized at El Paso.[19]

Capt. [Joseph Haydn] Potter with a few men was stationed at a small village [Santo Tomás] on the west side of the Rio Grande, some two miles from the fort, and the Confederates intended to take him in, but he had notice and left hurriedly, so that when the Confederates got near Fil[l]more they heard the long roll beaten and knew it was useless to run up against infantry behind adobe walls, with cavalry.[20] They crossed the Rio Grande again, taking possession of La Mesilla, a small town four miles from the fort.

The next day Major Lynde, having been informed as to our strength by Union men in Mesilla, came out to meet us, and came up to Mesilla. We this time had the old adobe walls, the best protection against artillery or infantry that could be devised.[21]

The enemy made an imposing appearance as they came on in line of battle with their two howitzers in the center. General Baylor had made Coopwood ride up one street and down another to make them think that we were being constantly reinforced, and told his men to keep concealed behind the houses and walls until he gave orders to fire.

Some of the men climbed on top of the houses, and out of curiosity peeped over the parapet to see what the enemy were doing. They soon saw a cloud of smoke and a flash and heard the boom of the first gun fired in the anger of war in the far west and they heard the scream of the shell overhead so familiar in after years. They slid off the house in a hurry, reminding one of turtles tumbling off a log. No reply was given by our forces and the enemy after several shots, that did no further damage than breaking a dog's leg on a hill, moved a little nearer.

General Baylor called to one of his men by name, and said, "Shoot at that officer and see if they are in range of our Mississippi rifles." At the crack of

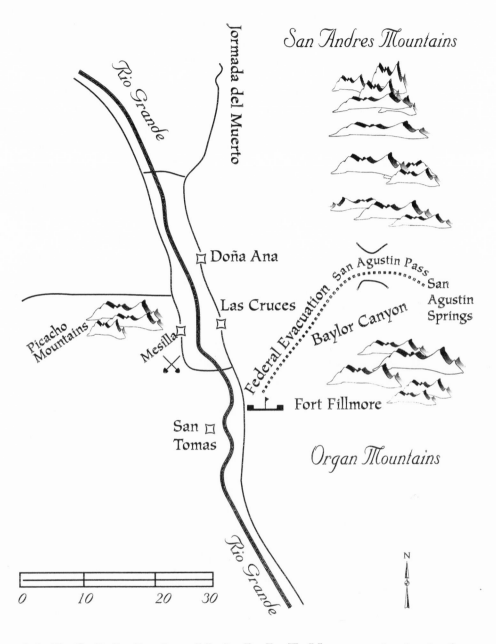

Rio Grande

Jormada del Muerto

San Andres Mountains

☐ Doña Ana

Federal Evacuation San Agustin Pass

San Agustin Springs

Las Cruces

Picacho Mountains

Baylor Canyon

Mesilla

Fort Fillmore

San Tomas

Organ Mountains

0   10   20   30

Rio Grande

N

MESILLA VALLEY · 1861

the gun the officer was seen to be wounded. He proved to be [1st] Lt. [Christopher Hely] McNally.[22] A fire from all along the line was delivered and with the advantage of our side, the enemy being in an open field, they fell back in some confusion, and retreated across the river to the fort. Not a Confederate was hurt, but the Federals had several killed and wounded.[23] First blood for the "Johnny Rebs."

A courier was sent for our artillery and infantry—it sounded big, and a courier that did not tell everybody he met all he knew, would have been a wonder. So Major Lynde, knowing a battery of six and twelve pounders would not be a nice thing to have about his ears, began to make preparations to leave, and before the Confederates knew it he was off.

General Baylor, who with a group of his officers was on [Thomas J.] Bull's store, saw far across the plains towards the Organ Mountains the flash from a stream of bayonets, and knew at once what it meant.[24] Soon there was a mounting in hot haste and the Texans were strung out on the plains in pursuit, and the Rebel yell was heard.

The Regulars of that day in the ranks had a weakness for fire water and we learned that many instead of filling their canteens with water, filled them with whiskey, instead of destroying it as ordered.[25] So, many fell by the wayside, and the adjutant and two men surrounded nineteen, like the Irishmen who had taken a drink at a small spring, set their guns against a rock, and stepped off about forty yards and were lying down under the shade of a liveoak tree. Lieutenant Baylor crawled up and ran between them and their guns. Dr. Bradley and Private Barnes close behind, and the Feds were scooped.

Lieutenant Baylor had been ordered by his brother to go with a company to the right of the line of retreat of the Federals and from the side of the mountains had a fair view of the panorama on the plain below him. Major Gibbs and his squadron of dragoons came across from the Rio Grande and fell in behind Lynde's command, ostensibly to protect the rear and prevent capture of the transportation, supplies, and artillery.[26] They formed in line of battle, and General Baylor, as soon as he came close to them, ordered a charge in column. If Major Gibbs had stood his ground there would have been a head-end collision, but he did not.

Coopwood's company opened fire from above him enfilading his line and using the captured Springfield rifles with good effect.[27] Gibbs' command passed on by all the wagons, guns, grub, and everything, and only stopped at St. Augustine Springs, where W.W. Cox now has a ranch, and where Major Lynde and his command had arrived, pretty well worn out with a long, dirty march in July.[28] Any one who has ever been on the plains of Arizona or New

Mexico knows what that means, for one can get hotter, dryer, and suffer more from thirst than any place except the Mohave or Colorado deserts.

General Baylor pushed on, capturing [the] enemy's transportation, commissary stores, artillery, stragglers, and camp equipage generally. Passing on through what is known today as Baylor's Pass in the Organ Mountains, [he] came down close to the Federal camp on the gallop and halting his men he sent in a flag of truce, Lt. William Lloyd bearing the flag.[29] The demand was made for unconditional surrender. Major Lynde came out with his staff and several officers, Captain Potter among'st them, and negotiations began for a surrender.

General Baylor told Major Lynde that as he had all his supplies and transportation and howitzers, while the major had only a scant supply of water and was encumbered with the wives and children of officers and men, it was only a question of time when he could starve him into a surrender; moreover he believed he had plenty of men to carry his camp by assault, and once the fight began he could not be responsible for what would occur in the heat of the battle.

Major Lynde listened to his statement and evidently saw the dark side of it. Captain Potter spoke up and said "Colonel, how many of your men are constructive." "Enough," was the reply, "constructed so as to take in your camp," and turning to Major Lynde he said, "Who is in command here anyhow?" The major replied, "I am, and I surrender the United States forces under my command."[30]

The general had turned to Lieutenant Baylor after Captain Potter spoke, saying, "Adjutant go back and order up our artillery and infantry." If Major Lynde could have seen the adjutant's face he would have suspected a "ruse de guerre" for as a matter of fact Captain Teel and Captain McAllister were fifty-five miles distant, but on the march.

After the surrender, as water was a vital question, General Baylor sent back all his command including Capt. George M[ilton] Frazer's company of about thirty southern men of Mesilla and Las Cruces, who volunteered, and the captain rendered good service, being a natural frontiersman and familiar with the people and country.[31] He served as major at the close of the war in [Walter P.] Lane's Brigade, Hardeman's Division.

At that time there was none of that bitterness that was shown towards the close of our family quarrel and the general, his brother, and a company left more for form's sake than anything else, felt as safe as though no war had been declared and we were simply guests. To the general and his brother there was no little sentiment behind it all. Was it not our father's old regiment, many of the officers our friends and the flag, the one that floated over us in our youthful days? Had not our kinsmen, Col. George Armistad, by his heroic defense of Fort McHenry, during the War of 1812, inspired Key to write that grand song of liberty, the Star Spangled Banner?

After the surrender, there being only a small supply of water at St. Augustine, most of the command returned to La Mesilla but a few scattered in the mountains to hunt for water. When they came into San Augustine next morning, General Baylor ordered Lt. W.H. Lloyd to take command of them and to escort the prisoners to Fort Fil[l]more. The vexed question of what to do with them came up and General Baylor paroled them and gave them arms, and loaned them twenty-eight wagons and teams and also ambulances for officers and families, to convey them to Fort Craig.

I am sorry to record that Gen. [Edward Richard Sprigg] Canby refused to send any back, and although it is an axiom that all things are fair in love and war, I don't think he acted with that knightly courtesy which should be part of a soldier's religion.[32]

The Federal officers captured warmly appreciated the kindness shown them and gave General Baylor a beautiful memorial expressing their gratitude for kindness to themselves and families.

Among those who volunteered for the fight was Sherard [Sherod] Hunter, who was one of the most gallant men in the Confederate Army; he was major of Col. George Wythe Baylor's regiment and when the dangerous assault was made on the Federal forces at Brashear City, now Morgan City, where three hundred and sixty men passed over in boats, sugar coolers, and any old thing that would carry a soldier, and captured fifteen hundred well equipped federal soldiers, Major Hunter was chosen to command the expedition.

Major Lynde had under his command nine companies of the Seventh Infantry, two companies of Mounted Rifles under Major Gibbs, and a battery of artillery, a total of seven hundred and forty-two men.

The Texas legislature was so well pleased with General Baylor's conduct and success that they sent him a complimentary message, which was communicated to the troops under his command.

Company A: Second Regiment, Texas Cavalry (organized as Second Texas Mounted Rifles); Peter Hardeman, captain, eighty men; John [T.] Aycock, first lieutenant; Marsh[all] Glenn, second lieutenant; [Malcolm] Ken Hunter, third lieutenant.

Company E: Second Regiment Texas Cavalry, I[saac] C. Stafford, captain, eighty men; R[ichard] B. Wilson, first lieutenant; W[illiam] H. Lloyd, second lieutenant; B[enjamin] W. Loveland, third lieutenant.

Teel's Battery: Fifty men armed as mounted infantry; T[revanion] T. Teel, captain; remained with battery: Jordon [W.] Bennett, first lieutenant, commanding; [James] Bradford, second lieutenant; [Bartholomew] McFarland, third lieutenant.

Coopwood's Company: fifty men; Bethel Coopwood, captain; [J.R.] Parsons, first lieutenant; Jess[e H.] Holden, second lieutenant; Lev Sutherland, third lieutenant.

Fraz[i]er's Company: George M[ilton] Fraz[i]er, captain; Frank [H.] Bushick, lieutenant, thirty men. Total 290.

General Baylor now started out to try and intercept Lieutenant Lord's command, coming on the old emigrant route from California, but the Federals had heard of the capture of the Seventh Infantry and Major Gibbs command and turned north.[33]

It was at this time that all Texans were looking eagerly for the arrival on southern soil of Gen. Albert Sidney Johnston. General Baylor had known him as secretary of war during the days of the Republic of Texas, and afterwards, and we knew he had resigned command of the army in California, but didn't know he had started across the plains with a few chosen, bold spirits. Still we were looking as anxiously for him as the Jews are for a temporal king and messiah.

While the general and his men were lying in wait for Lord's men, a man caught trying to steal some of the horses of the Confederates was captured and taken to the general's camp. We asked him quite a number of questions and said: "You do not bear the appearance of a horse thief." "No, Sir," was the answer, "I am no thief. I was trying to get them because I need them."

"You have come across the plains, you say; did you see or hear anything of Gen. Albert Sidney Johnston."

The man hesitated before replying, afraid to talk until he knew whether he was talking to Rebels or Federals; if the latter he would be giving away his commander. But feeling quite sure of his ground he answered boldly; "Yes, sire, I have seen him within the last hour and he is not far from here. I was trying to get horses for him."

The general and a few friends were soon in the saddle galloping over the hill towards General Johnston's camp with the late suspect. As they drew near they could see there was quite a commotion for in those wild mountains and at that time, every man was looked on as an enemy until you tried him.

The steady approach of so small a number soon satisfied them the Rebs were coming and a yell often heard afterwards on many a bloody field proclaimed their joy. General Baylor sprang to the ground and the two brave hearts were soon beating together in heart's warm embrace and not a few tears were shed by those present.

General Johnston was at once offered command of the Confederate forces, but [he] modestly declined and said he was anxious to hurry on to the Confederate capital.[34] After a brief rest he resumed his journey. Before leaving he said to Lieutenant Baylor; "I don't know if I will be given a command, but if I am, I want you to serve on my staff," an honor which he afterwards conferred on the lieutenant by appointing him senior aide-de-camp. Only the general's death on the fatal field of Shiloh terminated the pleasant relationship.

General Baylor did not remain long in Arizona, as all that country was then called. Being appointed military governor by President Davis he might have rested on his laurels, but receiving authority to raise a brigade he returned to Texas.

General Sibley with a brigade of soldiers having arrived and being senior officer, took command in Arizona and made his disastrous campaign.

General Baylor organized what was known as the Arizona Brigade, First Regiment commanded by Col. Peter Hardeman; Second Regiment, Col. George Wythe Baylor; Third Regiment, Col. [Joseph] Phillips, a gallant young Virginian, who was afterwards killed at the storming of Fort Butler on the Mississippi River in Louisiana.[35] A battalion was also raised by Colonel Griffin (an old West Pointer), of four companies of infantry and two of cavalry, was attached to the brigade, which was afterward commanded by Col. A[shley] W. Spaight, now a citizen of Galveston.[36]

The brigade was assembled at Eagle Lake, near Columbus, and was being armed and drilled, when some of General Sibley's command at Mesilla wrote to President Davis, stating that General Baylor, while in command at Mesilla, had issued an order to Capt. [Thomas J.] Masten [Mastin] at Pinos Altos to poison or get them drunk and massacre some Apache Indians who wanted to come in and make peace.[37] The president suspended the general and asked for an explanation. The general had an Indian shield taken from a chief in his fight on the frontier; it was gaudily ornamented with eagle feathers and paint and had as ornaments a woman's scalp (a Mrs. Woods of Erath County), plaited and tied with red flannel and beaded and painted.[38] This shield he sent by a messenger, and a verbal message that he did not consider such brutes entitled to the usages of civilized warfare.

Gen. [John Bankhead] Magruder when he learned of this, persuaded General Baylor to let him send a runner after the shield, which he did, but the general went to the frontier and ran on the ticket that "there was no good Apache except a dead one," and was elected to congress by an overwhelming majority over Malcolm D. Graham, an accomplished lawyer.

On his arrival at Richmond and after he had become personally acquainted with the president, Davis gave him a commission to raise another brigade.

The fact about the Indian matter was that a Mescalero chief named Nicolás had come to El Paso and made a solemn treaty of peace, and on the way back to Fort Davis had stolen two revolvers and jumped from the stage, and the next day killed the herders and took beef and sheep. When Captain Walker sent a scout after them, the Indians got the soldiers into a canyon and massacred a lieutenant, twelve men, and two citizens. When they wanted to make another treaty the general sent word to Captain Masten at Pinos Altos, New Mexico, if those liars, murderers, and thieves came into the camp, to kill them any way he could either by whiskey, poison, or bullets.

They never came in for a peace, but attacked the camp and mortally wounded Masten, and their only object in talking peace was to learn the strength of the whites and get some advantages over them.

The general on his arrival from Richmond with authority to organize a second brigade, found it a different matter from forming the Arizona Brigade. The gallant spirits that sprang to arms in the early days of the struggle were [now] sleeping on the battlefields, and the South, bleeding at its every pore, lay almost helpless before its powerful foe. Only one company commanded by Captain Sorrel of Colorado County could be organized. It was called the Ladies' Rangers as a compliment to the ladies of Houston and Galveston, who had taken great interest in organizing the company. They went to the frontier and were stationed at Weatherford to watch for Comanches as well as stragglers from the army and deserters.

They took with them the first breech loading cannon ever made, which was invented by General Baylor. It was made at the Cushman foundry at Houston, from one of the piston rods or some portion of the *Westfield*, the war vessel that was sunk at Galveston by the Confederates under General Magruder, January 1, 1863. Neither Krupp nor any northern brethren ever gave any token that they appreciated General Baylor's inventive genius. George Clark, of Montel[l], put up this gun.

General Baylor returned to Richmond and remained until the surrender of Lee's army. Then he came back to Texas. He told President Davis if he would go with him and take only a few chosen men, he would guarantee him a safe trip to Texas soil, that an army could be fed from buffalo alone on our frontier, and that the best fighting men would join him and give the worn out soldiers a breathing spell so as to be able to take up the fight with fresh vigor.

Gen. John R. Baylor was what we call a typical American, getting the restless blood and spirit from German and French ancestors besides being "pizened" up with Irish fighting blood, a maternal ancestress being Miss Lucy Todd O'Brien—which evidently is neither French nor Italian. In stature he was almost a Hercules, being six feet three, without being corpulent, and weighing 230 pounds, with the rosy complexion and clear blue eyes of the German, and a military carriage that would have attracted attention in any crowd. He had a keen sense of the ludicrous, and was a natural crafter, a talent probably inherited from old Jesse Bledsoe of Kentucky, who was a near kinsman, in his day the peer of Henry Clay as an orator. The general never forgot anything funny he heard and always had a crowd around him wherever he went. His courage was leonine and bordered too much on rashness. He had that peculiar magnetism that made his soldiers, officers, and privates alike, adore him. He was a friend to every private in his command and held the same opinion as old Col. [William] Fitzhugh of North Texas. When Fitz had been summoned to Gen. [Theophilus Hunter] Holmes's headquarters at Little Rock, Arkansas, General Holmes said, "Colonel, I learn you have a splendid body of men but you do not keep up proper discipline; you do not let your men know that you are an officer and they are privates." The old colonel sprang from his chair and exclaimed, "General Holmes, I would have you understand, sir, one half of my regiment are my friends, my neighbors, my kinsmen; they are just as good as I am, and the other half are a damn sight better."

The general illustrated the quotation, "The bravest are the tenderest," for he had an unusually kind heart, easily moved by the sorrows of others. Being an unusually handsome man, he was always a great favorite among the ladies and numbered many warm friends among the female sex.

He died at the ripe age of seventy-three, at Montel[l], his home in the lovely Nueces Canyon, on February 5, 1894, surrounded by his wife and children and sorrowing neighbors. Near the Episcopal Church a handsome granite monument bears the words that made Theodore O'Hara's name immortal:

> On Fame's eternal camping ground,
> Their silent tents are spread,
> And Honor guards with solemn round.
> The bivouac of the dead.

•••••••••••••••••••••••••••••••••••

General Baylor's father, John Walker Baylor, was born at New Market, Caroline County, Virginia, and like most of the old Virginians, was related by blood or marriage with the Washingtons, Lees, Fitzhughs, Carters, Harrisons, Armisteads, and many of the first settlers of Virginia. Through the Earl of Devon's family, the Courtenays, he could trace his family to Peter de Courtenay, emperor of Constantinople, and no doubt had the general lived in the days of the old Crusaders, he would have been close by the side of England's warrior king, Richard Coeur de Leon, or the old crusader knight, Sir

Jocelyn de Courtenay, or any of the bold Crusaders of their day in their battles with the Saracens; for with his courage he had the strength of a giant, and
his coat of mail and lance would have gleamed in the thickest of the fight.[39]

He passed through some trying scenes in his life, and they well illustrate
his total absence of fear. During his residence at Montel[l] he had a yoke of
fine work oxen stolen; and old friend Jasper Mayberry, who had been "best
man" at his wedding, was in Brackett[ville] and found the hides of them in a
butcher shop. He learned that a neighbor named [E.S.] Gilcrease had sold
them. General Baylor made a complaint and Gilcrease was arrested and a
time set for his trail.[40] He had three sons grown and a following among the
people. The general and his son George and sons-in-law, Will Hardeman and
John Aflock and Honorable A.T. Walton of San Antonio went to attend the
trial, so here was a pretty fine start for a feud.

The justice of the peace was to hold the examining trial at the old Steve
Walker place, an old-fashioned frontier house located in a beautiful pecan
grove, quiet and peaceful looking enough, but soon to resound with the cries
and oaths of angry men.

One of Gilcrease's moles rode up just before the court was called to order,
armed to the teeth. He was supposed to be a desperado from the "head waters
of Bitter Creek," and had threatened loud and long before his friends that he
would "do up George Baylor in short order the very first time he met him."
So George stepped up to him and told him now was a good time to carry his
bragging and threats into execution. But though he probably had never seen
or heard of Sir John Falstaff he thought "discretion the better part of valor"
and began whining denial of the charge.

George pulled him off his horse and cuffed him around a bit. Old
Gilcrease, fearing that his forces might become demoralized, spoke up and
said he thought they had come to settle by law, but if them Baylors wanted a
fight they could get it right then and there. General Baylor, who had said
nothing up to this time, but sat glaring at old Gilcrease like a tiger, sprang to
his feet and drawing a Bowie knife made at Gilcrease, who was armed in a
similar manner.

The challenger to mortal combat took to his heels, and sprinted around
the Temple of Justice twice with the general close after him. Fearing that the
race is not always to the swift, he darted in at the front door among the
crowd, but as his opponent followed, he went out the back door.

The general's son and son-in-law then grabbed the general and put a gun
across the back door so when he struck that he had to stop out of breath. Not
so with Gilcrease; he imitated the "brook" and went on. Pity he had not kept
up his lick, as he might have been alive today. His entire crowd then left and

the grand old "state of Texas" being the only party on the ground, the court adjourned *sine die*, and the case was transferred to Uvalde.

Not long after this the general was visiting a neighbor of his, old Steve Goodman, one of the immortal Mier pioneers. While they were sitting talking in the house, John Gilcrease and one of his brothers were seen by one of Goodman's daughters riding up towards the house, and as they had threatened to kill General Baylor on sight, she went in and told them, saying, "General, yonder comes the Gilcrease boys and they are always armed and say they intend to kill you; you had better go out the back door, and go down in the brush and they won't." "Laura, that ain't my way of settling a difficulty," and [he] walked out to the front gate, where he had left his Winchester rifle setting.

He addressed them with, "Young gents, I understand you are going to kill me on sight and now is your time." Both the boys started to draw their revolvers, but the old general grabbed his Winchester and as soon as they saw that, they whirled their horses and used their spurs on them. John, being behind, leaned forward Comanche Indian style, to hide his body and the general took a snap shot at him. The bullet struck him just at the base of the spine and ploughed the entire length of his body, coming out between his shoulder blades. An inch lower and the back bone would have been split and instant death would have resulted. The general kept up a running fire until the magazine was empty. This ought to have warned them they were tampering with dynamite, that a blow would set off at any time.

The case being ready for trail again, the general and George Baylor went to Uvalde. George and G[eorge] K. Chinn, an ex-Texas Ranger, were sitting at the courthouse chatting when John Arnold, one of Company A, Peter Hardeman's command, and one of General Baylor's warmest friends, went to them and said, "Boys, I see the Gilcrease party here and heavily armed, and gather from what I hear that they mean mischief and threaten to kill the general, so you had better keep your eyes on them and on him for we won't suspicion foul play."[41] Neither of them was armed, so they went to Chinn's room and he gave George his pistol that had only three cartridges in the chambers and borrowed another for himself with five loads.

They were returned to the courthouse, and looking over towards where Piper then had his store on the southwest corner of the plaza, they saw General Baylor who had unsaddled his horse, leading him around to the back of the store, where there was a gate leading into a feed lot and well. The general had put off his pistol and left his Winchester rifle in the front of Piper's store, as there was a kind of tacit understanding that the parties were not to be armed. Luckily for the general he had a common butcher knife in his bosom and forgot to take it off.

George Chinn knew the entire Gilcrease crowd was camped in the lot with their wagon and they realized the general's danger if they saw him come in unarmed. The temptation to get even by killing him was too great to be resisted. So they started at once for the wagon yard.

Gilcrease and his son John, now fully recovered, and another son, Tom, or Bob, were sitting by their wagon on the ground talking, probably planning a campaign, and so engrossed that they did not see the general until he nearly stumbled over them, as much surprised as they were. A glance showed that he was unarmed, and as he passed with his back to them they rose to their feet.

Just at this moment Chinn and George came in at the gate, and as soon as John Gilcrease saw them he drew his pistol and fired, breaking George's right arm, and his pistol fell to the ground, but he picked it up with his left and began firing. John had walked around the wagon, keeping it between him and George. They were in close quarters, and George having emptied his three loads, was shot again just above the pelvis in the front, and the force of the ball knocked him around so his father saw his face, which was the first intimation he had as to who was doing the shooting. Chinn, who had stepped over the tongue of the wagon, fired a shot at John Gilcrease, who fell with a wound in his spine.

Old Gilcrease had been jumping up and down and yelling at the top of his voice, "Kill 'em, kill 'em." He had a large double-edged dagger in his hand ground to a keen point and sharp as a razor.

It was now to be a fight to a finish. Both men were giants in size and armed only with knives. The general had instinctively run his hand in his bosom and felt the friendly handle of his knife and rushed on Gilcrease with the fury of a tiger, not knowing but that his boy was mortally wounded. Gilcrease was no doubt animated by the same sight, as his son lay on the ground before him.

Both were Texans and frontiersmen and they had seen and experienced the dangers of the frontier among hostile Comanches and wild animals, and no less dangerous men. So now everything depended on nerve and skill in a hand to hand fight.

Chinn, as soon as John Gilcrease fell, had rushed toward the general to try and prevent any further bloodshed, and caught him by the left arm, but in speaking of it to me, Chinn said the general shook him off as though he had been a fly, and went straight at his opponent.

Gilcrease threw up his left arm to shield himself. General Baylor grabbed it with his left hand, gave him a jerk towards him, and drove his knife through his heart. He sank down without a word.

The general then ran to John, Chinn still holding to him, and raised his knife to strike him; but what Chinn by main strength could not do, pity did in a moment. John wailed out piteously, "General, don't stab me; I am dying now." This stayed his hand, and looking down on his helpless foe he exclaimed, "And you be sure you do die," and then turned to his son.

Neither of them proved to be mortally wounded and they are alive and well today. John is a steady sober citizen of this state, and so far as the writer could learn when commanding the Rangers, has led a peaceful, blameless life, though still a cripple. The other son neither helped John nor his father, but went over the top of an eight-foot fence and never stopped running while in sight.[42]

The other incident occurred shortly after Major Lynde's command was captured. The editor of the *Mesilla Times* thought his importance had not been sufficiently appreciated by General Baylor and began to fill his paper with abuse of him. He was unfortunate enough to think that the general was afraid of him, as he did not notice him. His officers, however, took the matter greatly to heart and after an unusually abusive article went to the general and said, "If you don't notice this article we will." General Baylor had paid no attention to him because he did not consider it just in good form for him surrounded by his soldiers, to get into a personal difficulty with the editor of the local paper; he had pretty liberal views about the liberty of the press. But he did not want his soldiers to take up the affair, so on meeting [Robert] Kell[e]y, the editor, in Bull's store the next day he said, "Mr. Kell[e]y, if you don't stop your abuse of me in the paper I shall make it a personal matter between us." Kelly answered with an insulting remark and an oath, and drew a large Bowie knife and started toward him.[43]

It so happened that an empty Springfield rifle was standing against the wall and the general picked [it up] and struck Kell[e]y over the head, knocking him down, and then jumped on him. Grabbing his hand that had the knife with his right hand, he held him down. Kell[e]y was a powerful man and as soon as he got over the daze from the blow over his skull he began to struggle to thrown the general off of him, and free his right hand that still gripped the glittering Bowie knife.

General Baylor had just gotten up from an attack of fever, and found [at] each succeeding struggle, he was getting weaker and Kell[e]y was getting stronger, so he said, "Kell[e]y, if you don't drop that knife I'll kill you."

There was no reply but a desperate effort to get his knife arm free. General Baylor then reached around behind with his left hand and drew a pistol and shot Kelly in the jaw, the bullet coming out at the back of his neck. The knife flew out of his hand fast enough then. If Kell[e]y had had any sense he would have dropped the knife and waited for a better break. Neither the civil nor military authorities took any cognizance of the affair and the people justified General Baylor.

NOTES

1 Weidner was a paroled Hessian who was captured at the Battle of Trenton. John R. Baylor's mother, Sophie Marie Weidner Baylor, died at San Antonio in 1862. *Baylor Genealogy*, 15.

2 George Baylor was aide-de-camp to Gen. George Washington. He distinguished himself at the Battle of Trenton and later presented the captured Hessian colors to the Continental Congress. He was promoted colonel and placed in command of the 3d Regiment of Continental Dragoons, one of the first regiments of cavalry authorized by the Continental Congress. He died in Barbados in 1784 of "lung disease" caused by an old bayonet wound received during the war. John Walker Baylor served as a lieutenant in the 3d Continental Dragoons and the headquarters troop that served as Washington's bodyguard. Wounded in the foot by a spent cannon ball at the Battle of Germantown, he moved in 1873 to Lexington, Kentucky, where he operated a flour mill, saloon, and gambling house. Ibid., 8, 10-11.

3 Dr. John Walker Baylor, the oldest son of John Walker Baylor and Jane Bledsoe, and father of John R. and George W. Baylor, was born in 1783. He joined the army as an assistant surgeon during the Blackhawk War. While stationed at Fort Gibson, Indian Territory, he resigned and moved to Second Creek near Natchez, Mississippi, where he died in 1836. Ibid., 15.

4 John Walker Baylor, oldest child of Dr. John W. Baylor and Sophie Weidner, was born in Kentucky around 1812. After studying medicine, he came to Texas, was wounded at San Jacinto, and died shortly thereafter while visiting an uncle in Mobile, Alabama, when the wound became infected. Dr. Henry W. Baylor, fourth child of Dr. John W. Baylor and Sophie Weidner, was born in Paris, Bourbon County, Kentucky, in 1818. Henry moved to Texas where he practiced medicine at La Grange. During the Mexican-American War, he served as a surgeon with Col. Jack Hays's Texas Rangers and in the Battle of Monterrey was in the attack on the Bishop's Palace. Returning to Fayette County, he recruited a company of Rangers and returned to Mexico to join Gen. Zachary Taylor. After the war he went back to La Grange where he married Laura Metcalf. Baylor County in North Texas was named in his honor. Ibid., 19.

5 A French soldier of fortune, Woll had served as a quartermaster under Gen. Antonio López de Santa Anna in 1836 and led the Mexican army that occupied San Antonio in 1842. As governor of Tamaulipas in 1855, he returned to France following the fall of Santa Anna, but later assisted the French in an unsuccessful plot to seize Matamoros.

6 When General Woll invaded Texas in 1842, Nicholas Mosby Dawson assembled fifty-three men from Fayette County and marched toward San Antonio. While the Battle of Salado was in progress, Dawson and his men were attacked a few miles from the battlefield by a detachment of Mexican cavalry supported by artillery. Thirty-five Texans, including Dawson, were killed, some while trying to surrender. Five others were wounded, while fifteen were captured and five escaped. The captives were marched to Mexico and confined in Perote Prison. At Salado Creek, about six miles east of San Antonio, about 200 volunteers from Gonzales under Mathew Caldwell decisively defeated Woll's larger Mexican Army, killing sixty, while losing only one man. Webb and Carroll, *Handbook of Texas*, 1:474; 2:532.

7 Emily Jane Hanna was sixteen at the time. The Baylors were to become the parents of ten

children, seven sons and three daughters. Two sons, John William and Walker Keith, served in the Confederate Army, while one son, Henry Weidner, was in the Rebel Navy. Emily Hanna Baylor, who outlived her husband by twenty-three years, died on 1 August 1917 at the age of ninety. Thompson, *John Robert Baylor*, 5; Tombstone data, Montell Cemetery, Montell, Texas.

8 See n. 3, Ch. 1, Sec. I.

9 See Ch. 14, Sec. I.

10 Following the 1840 "Great Comanche Raid" on Victoria and Linnville and the defeat of the Indians at Plum Creek, John R. Baylor joined with Moore and men from Bastrop and Fayette counties in a punitive expedition that proceeded west as far as the Red Fork of the Colorado River near present-day Colorado City; there the Comanches were decisively defeated. In all, 126 Indians, including women and children, were killed, and their village burned. Donaly E. Brice, *The Great Comanche Raid* (Austin: Eakin Press, 1987), 49-56, 70.

11 Formerly the sheriff of Navarro County, Barry lived at Flag Pond, Bosque County. A victim of at least one Comanche raid that stole a herd of his horses, Barry joined John R. Baylor in an attempt to have Robert S. Neighbors removed as Indian Agent. An ardent secessionist, Barry served as a lieutenant colonel in the Frontier Regiment, Texas Cavalry, during the Civil War. Richardson, *Frontier of Northwest Texas*, 198, 238.

In 1858-1859, Garland, a prominent citizen of Erath County, did much, as did John R. Baylor, to inflame public opinion on the northwestern frontier against the Reservation Indians. With about twenty men from Erath County, Garland attacked a band of Indians near Palo Pinto on 27 December 1858, killing seven, three of whom were women. Neighbors tried, with little success, to have Garland, who bragged of the deed, arrested. Neighbours, *Robert Simpson Neighbors*, 196-97, 219, 224-28.

12 See Ch. 12, Sec. I.

13 Ten freight wagons carrying government corn from Jacksboro to Fort Griffin were attacked on 17 May 1871, on Salt Creek Prairie, about twenty-two miles from Fort Richardson. A large force of Kiowas under Chiefs Satanta, Satank, Eagle Heart, Big Bow, and the medicine man, Mamanti, killed the wagon master and six teamsters. Five others, although wounded, escaped. General Sherman, who was at Fort Richardson when the survivors reported the attack, had passed over the same ground the previous day. The Kiowas were massed at the time and were prepared to attack Sherman, but were restrained by a medicine man, Owl Prophet, who prophesied that the second party to pass could be more easily captured. In response to the attack, Sherman ordered an all-out pursuit of the raiders. The Kiowas who were responsible for the incident were later identified when Satanta boasted of the attack at Fort Sill. In a violent confrontation, in which Sherman was almost killed, the chiefs were arrested. While being transported back to Texas for trial, the aging Satank was killed while attempting to escape. Satanta and Big Tree were convicted at Jacksboro and sentenced to death by hanging. Their sentences, however, were commuted to life in prison by Gov. Edmund J. Davis, and in 1873, they were granted parole. Both chiefs continued to lead raids into Texas and Satanta was arrested again in 1874 and returned to Huntsville where he died as a result of a jump or fall from an upper story window of the prison hospital. Big Tree was arrested in 1875, then was released at the request of Federal officials. William T. Sherman, *Memoirs of General William T. Sherman* (New York: Library of America, 1900), 1111; Robert M. Utley, *The Indian Frontier of the American West, 1846-1890* (Albuquerque: University of New Mexico Press, 1984), 143-48. Also, Benjamin Capp, *The Warren Wagontrain Raid* (Dallas: Southern Methodist University Press, 1974).

14 See Ch. 14, Sec. I.

15 See Ch. 15, Sec. I.

16 Twenty-three year old Stafford, a merchant from Houston, raised a company of men, mostly from Harris County, in March and April 1861. Mustered into Confederate service for twelve months at San Antonio as Company E, 2d Regiment, Texas Mounted Rifles, the men were sent to Fort Bliss where they arrived on 3 July 1861. The company saw action at Mesilla, Cañada Alamosa, and during Sibley's New Mexico Campaign at both Valverde and Glorieta. After Valverde, however, Stafford resigned and left with Col. John R. Baylor for Richmond. He died in Houston on 21 November 1906.

Hardeman, thirty, a farmer from Travis County, recruited his men from Anderson, Cherokee, Houston, and Nacogdoches counties. Mustered as Company A of the 2d Regiment for twelve months at San Antonio, they arrived at Fort Bliss at the same time as Stafford's company. Company A was in the skirmish at Mesilla, but because so many of the men were stricken with smallpox, they remained behind during the New Mexico Campaign. Hardeman was promoted to lieutenant colonel on 16 December 1861. He died in Americana, Brazil, on 18 May 1882.

English-born James Walker, a physician from Hallettsville, recruited Company D of the 2d Texas from Lavaca County. After muster in San Antonio in May 1861, Walker led his men west to Fort Davis. Leaving twenty-three men at the post, he continued to Mesilla, arriving in August 1861, shortly after the capture of the Fort Fillmore garrison. Part of Company D fought at Valverde, Albuquerque, and Peralta. Walker died at Hallettsville on 7 February 1886.

Before the war, Hamner and John R. Baylor published *The White Man,* a racist newspaper that promoted their anti-Indian philosophy and did much to arouse passions on the frontier, first at Jacksboro and then at Weatherford. The office of the *White Man* at Jacksboro was consumed by fire, probably arson, on the evening of 29 July 1860. Only a few copies of *The White Man* are known to exist today. Hall, *Confederate Army of New Mexico*, 303, 305, 309, 327-28, 333, 319-21, 325; Thompson, *John Robert Baylor*, 16, 24-26; Richardson, *Frontier of Northwest Texas*, 235; Jacksboro *White Man*, 8 March 1860; Weatherford *White Man*, 13 September 1860.

17 Both George W. and John R. Baylor were at San Lucas Spring on the west side of Adams Hill, twenty-four miles west of San Antonio, when Major Reeves, who had marched east from Fort Bliss with six companies of the 8th Infantry (270 men), surrendered to 1,370 Texans under McCulloch on 9 May 1861. Many of the Federals were not exchanged until February 1863. During the Civil War, the bespectacled Reeves, an 1835 West Point graduate, rose to become colonel of the 13th Infantry. He died on 31 December 1890. J.J. Bowden, *The Exodus of Federal Forces from Texas, 1861* (Austin: Eakin Press, 1986), 109-15; Thomas W. Cutrer, *Ben McCulloch and the Frontier Military Tradition* (Chapel Hill: University of North Carolina Press, 1993), 184-85; I.V.D. Reeves to L. Thomas, 12 May 1861, *OR*, 1, 1:569-70; and Earl Van Dorn to S. Cooper, 10 May 1861, *OR*, 1, 1:572-73.

18 Lynde was a thirty-four-year veteran of the frontier army. A Vermont native, he had graduated from West Point in 1827. One of the best descriptions of Lynde is by James Cooper McKee, assistant surgeon at Fort Fillmore at the time of the evacuation and surrender: "His hair and beard were gray, giving him a venerable appearance; he was quiet, reticent, and retired, giving the impression of wisdom and a knowledge of his profession." After the skirmish at Mesilla, however, McKee remarked that Lynde's "gray beard and hair . . . were a fitting frame for that pale and cowardly soul." James McKee, *Narrative of the Surrender*, 7, 20.

Lord, an 1856 West Point graduate from Ohio, was in command of Company D of the 1st Dragoons at Fort Breckenridge and then Fort Buchanan in 1861. His conduct during the Battle of Valverde was criticized although a Court of Inquiry at Santa Fe found the allegations to be unjustified. Lord fought at Gettysburg, where he earned a brevet, and at Boonesboro, Maryland, where he was wounded again. He earned a second brevet for gallantry at Five Forts near Petersburg, Virginia. Lord died of tuberculosis at Bellefontaine, Ohio, on 15 October 1866. Constance Wynn Altshuler, *Cavalry Yellow & Infantry Blue: Army Officers in Arizona Between 1851 and 1886* (Tucson: Arizona Historical Society, 1991), 206-36.

The heavy-set Gibbs, from Astoria, Long Island, had attended Dartmouth College before graduating from West Point in 1846. During the Mexican-American War, he was breveted for gallantry at Cerro Gordo, where he was wounded, and again at Garita de Belén at the gates of Mexico City. In the Civil War in the east, Gibbs rose to the rank of brigadier general. In 1866, while serving as a major in the 7th Cavalry, he died suddenly at Fort Leavenworth, Kansas, of "congestion of the brain." Warner, *Generals in Blue,* 172-73; and Heitman, *Historical Register*, 1:452-53.

[19] Teel was born in Pittsburgh, Pennsylvania, in 1824 and moved with his family to Indiana, Illinois, Tennessee, and finally Missouri, where he studied law and opened a law office. In 1843, he joined an expedition of the American Fur Company to the Rocky Mountains, where he was captured and held captive by the Yankton Lakota. Enlisting in an infantry company of Indiana volunteers, Teel fought in the Mexican War and was twice wounded at Buena Vista. After the war, he settled in Lockhart, Texas, but later moved to San Antonio. Teel's Light Company B of the 1st Regiment of Artillery was recruited from Bexar County. The company arrived at Fort Bliss on 10 July 1861. Company B fought at Cañada Alamosa, Valverde (where Teel was slightly wounded), Apache Canyon, and Peralta. As part of Col. William Steele's rear guard, the company was one of the last to abandon the Mesilla Valley and West Texas in the summer of 1862. While practicing law in El Paso in 1889, Teel returned to Albuquerque to locate the six mountain howitzers that had been buried there under his supervision twenty-seven years earlier. He died of heart failure at El Paso on 6 July 1899. Efforts to locate a diary Teel allegedly kept during the Civil War have proven fruitless. Hall, *Confederate Army of New Mexico,* 335-36; William A. Keleher, *Turmoil in New Mexico* (Santa Fe: Rydal Press, 1952), 207-8; Howard Bryan, "The Man Who Buried the Cannons," *New Mexico Magazine* 40 (January 1962):13-15, 32; Conrey Bryson, *Down Went McGinty: El Paso in the Wonderful Nineties* (El Paso: Texas Western Press, 1977), 51-56; El Paso *Times*, 14 March 1937; and Richard K. McMaster and George Ruhlen, "The Guns of Val Verde," *Password* 5 (January 1960).

McAllister, born in Danville, Boyle County, Kentucky, in 1831, came to San Antonio as a teenager in 1847 to enter commercial life. McAllister's Rangers were incorporated into Col. John R. Baylor's command and designated Company A, 1st Regiment of Texas Infantry. On 7 August 1861, upon the expiration of their six-months' service, McAllister and several of his men returned to San Antonio. Merrick, *From Desert to Bayou*, 7-9; and Chabot, *With the Makers of San Antonio,* 404.

[20] Potter, from New Hampshire and an 1843 West Point graduate, was breveted a first lieutenant for gallantry at Monterrey during the Mexican-American War. As colonel of the 12th New Hampshire during the Civil War, Potter fought bravely at Fredericksburg and Chancellorsville. Heitman, *Historical Register*, 1:801.

The adobe village of Santo Tomás, nestled along the west bank of the Rio Grande, had a population of 120 in 1860.

21 After Maj. Edwin Waller had made a reconnaissance of Fort Fillmore, Colonel Baylor concluded that it would be possible to position his command between the post and the Rio Grande. Baylor subsequently captured seven men and a large quantity of provisions at Santo Tomás before triumphantly marching into Mesilla on 25 July 1861. Maj. Isaac Lynde, commanding Fort Fillmore, moved to drive the Rebels out. Leaving one company of infantry and the regimental band of the 7th Infantry at the post, he crossed the river with six companies of 380 men. When Baylor refused an "unconditional and immediate surrender" and vowed that he would "fight first, and surrender afterwards," Lynde decided to attack the town. Following a brief artillery barrage, the Federals launched a half-hearted advance through a cornfield, only to be fired on by the concealed Rebels and driven off. McKee, *Narrative of the Surrender*, 6-39; Mills, *Forty Years at El Paso*, 37-57; John R. Baylor to Sir, 1 August 1861, George Wythe Baylor IV Papers; John R. Baylor to T.A. Washington, 21 September 1861, *OR*, 1, 4:17-20; and I. Lynde to Acting Assistant Adjutant General, 26 July 1861, *OR*, 1, 4:4-5; Hall, "The Skirmish at Mesilla," *Arizona and the West* (Winter 1958): 343-51; and Donald S. Frazer, *Blood and Treasure: Confederate Empire in the Southwest* (College Station: Texas A&M University Press, 1995), 57-58.

22 McNally was seriously wounded in the chest. Assistant Surgeon McKee reported: "Lieutenant McNally pluckily rode up on his gray horse, and said that he was shot. I helped him off his horse when he fainted, and fell on the sand. I opened his coat and shirt, saw the bullet hole, ran my finger into it, detected at once the pulsation of the subclavian artery and saw that he was safe for the present." McKee, *Narrative of the Surrender*, 19-21. The English-born McNally had enlisted as a private in the army in 1848 and in 1855 was commissioned a lieutenant in the Mounted Rifles. McNally recovered from his wound and was breveted a captain. During the Civil War in the east, he rose to command the 3d United States Infantry. He retired in 1866 and died on 14 February 1889. McKee, *Narrative of the Surrender,* 19-21; and Heitman, *Historical Register,* 1:678.

23 Four Federals, Privates Lane, Cyrus Jenkins, Pelig Sherwood, and a Sergeant Callaghan, were killed, while five others were wounded, including NcNally and Lieutenant Brooks, who received a flesh wound in the forearm. Case of Major Isaac Lynde, File no. 107, RG 109, AGO, NA. Also, Regimental Returns, 7th Infantry, July and August, 1861, RG 391, AGO, NA.

24 "On the morning of the 27th, a little after daylight," Colonel Baylor recalled, "my spies reported a column of dust seen in the direction of the Organ Mountains, distance 15 miles, on the Fort Stanton road. I could from the top of a house with a glass see the movements of the enemy. I immediately ordered the command to saddle and mount, for the purpose of intercepting them at San Augustine Pass." Baylor to Washington, 21 September 1861, *OR*, 1, 4:18.

Bull, who had served in the Mexican-American War as a civilian clerk in the Quartermaster's Department, returned to the Mesilla Valley after the war and settled at San Agustín Springs where he obtained the lumber contract with the army. Bull also established a store in Mesilla. A Unionist and native of Ohio, Bull served four times as chief executive of Doña Ana County. At various times, he also held the offices of sheriff, probate judge, school commissioner, and county commissioner. Paxton P. Price, *Pioneers of the Mesilla Valley* (Las Cruces: Yucca Tree Press, 1995), 89-93.

25 In a well-documented study of the Federal evacuation and retreat, John P. Wilson confirms, as it was widely rumored at the time, that many Federals filled their canteens with

whiskey. John P. Wilson, "Whiskey at Fort Fillmore: A Story of the Civil War," *New Mexico Historical Review* 68 (April 1993): 109-32.

26 Gibbs, with Company I of the Mounted Rifles, was driving one hundred head of beef cattle from Fort Craig to Fort Fillmore, where he was to report to Major Lynde. Gibbs proceeded down the Jornada del Muerto without incident until the morning of 26 July, when he met 1st Lt. William Bartlett Lane with a commissary train. Lane expressed fears of being captured by the Confederates who, he said, had occupied Mesilla. Hoping to reach Fort Fillmore from the east, Gibbs struck out toward the Organ Mountains, where at noon on 27 July he met the retreating Federal column. Lynde, who was already at San Agustín Springs, ordered Gibbs to guard the Federal rear. Gibbs hurried back to the western entrance to the pass and attempted to place two twelve-pounder mountain howitzers into place but could not find the ammunition for the guns. Moreover, four Federal wagons, loaded with stores and women and children, were blocking the road. Riding back to San Agustín Springs, Gibbs found Lynde in the process of surrendering to Lieutenant Colonel Baylor. Gibbs claimed he protested the decision but Lynde paid him no attention. Statement of Captain Gibbs, Court of Inquiry, 7 November 1861, *OR,* 1, 4:9-11; John R. Baylor to Sir, 1 August 1861, George Wythe Baylor IV, Papers.

27 Only one soldier, Pvt. John A. Bishop, Co. K, 7th Infantry, was killed in the confrontation. RR, 7th Infantry, July and August, 1861, RG 391, AGO.

28 Los Salteros, or salt traders, had used the San Agustín Springs or El Ojo del Espíritu (Spirit Springs), as early as the Spanish colonial era. After the Mexican-American War, Thomas J. Bull, a civilian clerk from Indiana who had come to New Mexico with the army in 1846, acquired the property and built several adobe structures near the spring and a grove of giant cottonwoods. By 1851, Bull was cutting lumber in the area under contract with the army. Bull later sold the property to Warren T. Shedd, a St. Louis adventurer, who built a small inn and stage station at the location. In 1875, Benjamin B. Davies, a Welshman who had come to the area with the California Column in 1862, purchased the property and ran several large herds of sheep and cattle in the Organ Mountains. In 1893, William W. Cox, a tall Texan from Lavaca County, purchased the property. Cox had come to New Mexico following the death of his father, James W. Cox, a United States marshal who was killed by John Wesley Hardin's gang. Cox had first settled in the San Andrés Mountains where the family lived temporarily in a dugout. Later, the family moved to Fort Defiance where they ran a restaurant. They eventually purchased a ranch seven miles north of Cooke's Peak in Luna County before acquiring the St. Augustine Ranch. Cox died on 31 December 1923. Margaret Rhodes Cox followed her husband in death in 1956. K.D. Stoes, "The Story of San Agustin Ranch," *The New Mexico Stockman* 22 (March 1957): 36, 60-61, and 22 (April 1957): 30-34; and Marshall Hail, "San Augustine Ranch House," *Frontier Times* 43 (August-September 1969): 38-40, 64-65.

29 Lloyd, twenty, was a second lieutenant in Captain Stafford's Company E of the 2d Mounted Rifles.

30 Gibbs's version of the surrender agrees with that of George Baylor. "When we came up, all the officers being present, I think, Major Lynde said: 'Colonel Baylor, to avoid bloodshed, I conditionally surrender this whole force to you, on condition that officers and their families shall be protected from insult and private property respected.' Nearly every officer protested earnestly, and even violently, against this base surrender; but Major Lynde said: 'I am commander of these forces, and I take upon my shoulders the responsibility of my action in the matter.'" Statement of Alfred Gibbs, Court of Inquiry, *OR,* 1, 4:10-11. Lynde

was widely condemned and ridiculed because of his decision to surrender. Following a court of inquiry in St. Louis, he was dropped from the rolls of the army on 25 November 1861. After the war, he was reinstated and assigned to the 18th Infantry. He died on 10 April 1886.

31 During the Mexican-American War, Frazer fought with Capt. Henry Weidner Baylor's company of lancers at Monterrey and was accidentally wounded in August 1847. After the war, Frazer accompanied Col. Joseph E. Johnston's reconnaissance to El Paso where he went on to Mesilla and then Santa Fe, where he became a wagonmaster for the army. He later settled at Mesilla where he operated the "Frazier House" hotel. The Tennessee-born, thirty-three-year-old Frazer mustered his "Arizona Rangers" at Mesilla on 1 August 1861. The company saw action at Valverde, Glorieta, and Peralta. Frazier served as county judge of Pecos County from 1872 to 1884. He died probably at Toyah in Reeves County, Texas, on 11 January 1891. Hall, *Confederate Army of New Mexico*, 353-55, 59.

32 When Col. William Wing Loring, commanding the Department of New Mexico, departed, Canby, a loyal Kentuckian, assumed command at Santa Fe on 11 June 1861. Canby, widely respected in the antebellum army as a man of impeccable integrity and gentle manners, had fought in Mexico and was in the 1857 expedition against the Mormons before being stationed in New Mexico, where he led a punitive and unsuccessful expedition against the Navajo in 1860. He was killed on 11 April 1873 by Captain Jack during the Modoc War in the lava beds of northern California, and thereby became the only general in United States history to be killed by Indians. Odie B. and Laura E. Faulk, *The Modoc* (New York: Chelsea House, 1988), 54-55; and Max L. Heyman, Jr., *Prudent Soldier: A Biography of Major General E.R.S. Canby, 1817-1873* (Glendale: Arthur H. Clark Co., 1959), 375-76.

33 The two companies of dragoons and two companies of infantry from Forts Buchanan and Breckenridge were commanded by Capt. Isaiah N. Moore. At Cooke's Spring on 6 August 1861, Moore learned that Fort Fillmore had been evacuated and that he was likely to be attacked. Well into the night, the Federals went about spiking their artillery and destroying all quartermaster and commissary supplies and considerable personal property. The sick, along with sixteen laundresses, escorted by twenty-five men, were sent northeast toward Fort Craig and the Rio Grande. Captain Moore and the bulk of the command, by using a different route through the mountains, also struck out for Fort Craig. I.N. Moore to E.D. Townsend, 1 September 1861, in *William S. Grant v. United States*, Court of Claims, case no. 1883, RG 123, NA.

34 In an attempt to capture the Federals who had abandoned Forts Breckenridge and Buchanan and were known to be marching east under Captain Moore, Lieutenant Colonel Baylor temporarily turned command of his small army over to Johnston. "Having been placed temporarily in command of the Texas forces of this district by the generous desire of yourself," Johnston wrote Baylor, "the special object being the capture of the only remaining column of the enemy forces in this territory . . . my duty required that I should now proceed on my journey, I therefore respectfully restore to you the authority vested in me . . . I will hold in lasting grateful remembrance your kind courtesy to me and my companions." A.S. Johnston to Baylor, 27 August 1861, letter in private collection.

35 Virginia-born Col. Joseph Phillips rose rapidly through the ranks in the war in the east. He is probably the Joseph Phillips of the "Old Dominion Dragoons," under Maj. John Bell Hood in the fighting around Newport News shortly after First Bull Run. Maj. Gen. John Bankhead Magruder singled Phillips out for commendation in August 1861 in the fighting

near Hampton Roads. During Gen. George B. McClellan's seige of Yorktown, General Magruder made mention of Phillips' "local knowledge" of the area which was "of great advantage" and wrote of Phillips' "intrepidity and enterprise" which was of "the highest degree . . . on every occasion." During the Seven Days, Magruder again made mention of "Lt. Phillips of my staff" for his "meritorious and distinguished manner." At Second Bull Run, Phillips was praised by Brig. Gen. Hood for his "Valuable service . . . in bringing forward and placing in position additonal brigades upon the long to be remembered heights around the Chinn House." At the head of his Texas-Arizona regiment, Phillips was reported missing and assumed killed at the Battle of Donaldsonville on 28 June 1863. John B. Hood to G.B. Cosby, 12 July 1861, *OR,* 1, 2, 2:297-98; Magruder to R.E. Lee, 12 August 1862, *OR,* 1, 11:666-68, 673, 718; and Hood to G. Maxley Sorrel, 27 September 1862, *OR,* 1, 19: 924. Also, CMSR of Joseph Phillips, RG 109, NA.

36 Spaight fought in the Creek War and served one term in the Alabama legislature before coming in 1860 to Texas where he settled in Liberty County. In April 1861, Spaight raised a company of infantry in Liberty County known as the "Moss Bluff Rebels." Promoted to lieutenant colonel, he commanded the 11th Texas Cavalry Battalion which was expanded to become the 21st Texas Infantry Regiment. He died in Galveston on 21 December 1911. Wright, *Texas in the War,* 109.

37 Mastin, twenty-three, was born at Aberdeen, Monroe County, Mississippi, on 13 September 1839. After several years in California with his father, he returned to settle at Gila City (Yuma) in 1858 and later moved to Pinos Altos where he operated a mercantile store and worked the Pacific Mine with a partner, Thomas Jefferson Helm. With Helm, Mastin recruited the Arizona Guards at Pinos Altos, mainly to protect the mines and the Mesilla-Tucson Road. The company was involved in numerous scouts against the Apaches, even pursuing the Indians as far south as Lake Guzmán, Chihuahua. In one fight, the Confederates dealt the Chiricahua under Cochise and Mangas Coloradas a serious defeat in the Florida Mountains. Possibly in retaliation, Cochise and Mangas, with as many as 300 warriors, led an attack on Pinos Altos on 27 September 1861. In the fighting, much of which was hand-to-hand, the Indians tried to burn the village. Ten Apaches and one soldier, J.B. Corwin, along with three civilians, died in the fight. Wounded in the arm, Mastin died on 7 October 1861. Partly as a result of Mastin's death, Lieutenant Colonel Baylor issued his infamous extermination order of 20 March 1862: "You will therefore use all means to persuade the Apaches or any tribe to come in for the purpose of making peace, and when you get them together kill all the grown Indians. Buy whiskey and such other goods as may be necessary for the Indians and I will order vouchers to cover the amount expended. Leave nothing undone to insure success, and have sufficient number of men around to allow no Indians to escape." The graves of Thomas J. "Maston," who "Died of Fatal Wounds Recd in Action As he led the Settlers in Defense and Repulsed 400 Apaches Led by Cochise," and his brother Virgil, who was killed by Indians near Silver Bell Mine on Whiskey Creek about 1870, are in the Pinos Altos Cemetery, Pinos Altos, New Mexico. Hall, *Confederate Army of New Mexico* 367, 369; Sweeney, *Cochise,* 184-88; and Baylor to Helm, 20 March 1862, *OR,* 1, 50:942.

38 This is probably the incident Baylor describes in Chap. 14, Sec. II. A Mrs. Woods had been raped, killed, and scalped by a band of Comanches on the North Bosque River in Erath County during the winter of 1857. Baylor reported in 1862, however, that the shield of an Indian chief he killed in "hand to hand conflict in the month of June 1860," contained the scalp of a Miss Jackson. Wilbarger, *Indian Depredations in Texas,* 440-41; Baylor to Magruder, 29 December 1862, *OR,* 1, 15:914-15.

[39] See *A Baylor Genealogy,* 3-18.

[40] Uvalde County court records contain a number of cases involving the Baylor and Gilcrease families. See: *State of Texas vs. Tom Gilcrease,* Cause no. 510, and *State of Texas vs. John and Tom G. Gilcrease,* Cause no. 518. All in County Clerk's Office, Uvalde, Texas.

[41] Chinn, forty-seven, is listed on the 1900 Uvalde County census with his wife, Ella, forty-one, and their five children. John Gilcrease had previously sued Chinn. "Arnold" is probably J.B. Arnold who served in Company C of the 2d Texas Regiment of Mounted Rifles during the Civil War. *John Gilcrease vs. G.K. Chinn,* Cause no. 296, County Clerk's Office, Uvalde, Texas; 12th Census, Uvalde County, Texas, NA; and Hall, *Confederate Army of New Mexico,* 321.

[42] The Gilcrease-Baylor fight was on 19 April 1881. As a result of the violence, arrest warrants were issued for Tom and John Gilcrease, who were charged with assault with intent to murder. John R. Baylor was charged with second degree murder in that he did "stab, cut, and kill" E.S. Gilcrease. The Gilcrease brothers fled for the border although John Gilcrease was later arrested near Uvalde. Court records indicate that Baylor was acquitted. See: *State of Texas vs. John and Tom Gilcrease,* Cause nos. 505, 518, 519, and 522; and *State of Texas vs. John R. Baylor,* Cause no. 513, County Clerk's Office, Uvalde, Texas. Also, George W. Baylor IV to Jerry Thompson, 17 September 1968, editor's files; *Galveston Weekly News* 24 April 1881; and *Comanche Chief,* 7 May 1881.

[43] Robert P. Kelley, editor of the *Mesilla Times,* had migrated to Texas from Kentucky by way of Palmyra, Missouri, before moving to San Antonio and then Mesilla. A fire-eating secessionist, Kelley was also one of Mesilla's most prominent citizens. Besides his mercantile establishment and a real estate office, he owned a sawmill and gristmill at Pinos Altos. A surveyor by profession, Kelley also produced an elaborate map of Arizona. When Baylor made plans for an evacuation of the Mesilla Valley, Kelley, fearing a sizeable Federal invasion, editorially attacked the colonel. Although Federal forces never advanced, Kelley, who had spirited his press off to Mexico, blamed Baylor for the resulting chaos. The crisis reached a climax when Baylor read one of Kelley's scathing editorials in the *Times* on 12 December 1861. Baylor demanded a retraction and Kelley refused. On the same afternoon, just as the feast of the Virgin of Guadalupe and high mass concluded in Mesilla's San Albino Church, Kelley was accosted by Baylor as he walked down Calle Principal, the town's main thoroughfare. In the ensuing fracas, Baylor mortally wounded Kelley. Although a hastily summoned jury, with four Rebel privates as witnesses, found Baylor innocent, the colonel was indicted in June 1863. He was never brought to trial, however, since the Rebels had been gone from the valley for a year. Martin H. Hall, "The Baylor-Kelley Fight: A Civil War Incident in Old Mesilla," *Password,* 5, (July 1960): 83-90; Nona W. Barrick and Mary Helen Taylor, "Murder in Mesilla," *New Mexico Magazine* (November 1960): 4-5; and Hattie M. Anderson, ed., "With the Confederates in New Mexico During the Civil War: Memoirs of Hank Smith," *Panhandle-Plains Historical Review,* 1, (1929): 89-92. Copies of the 1863 indictment and depositions in the case courtesy of L. Boyd Finch, Tucson, Arizona. For a sketch of the site of the shooting, see: Merrick, *Desert to Bayou,* 29.

CHAPTER TWO

Massacre of Confederates in the Big Bend

~

THE WRITER IS ANXIOUS TO PRESERVE THE NAMES of some of the brave men of the days of 1861 to 1865, and transmit to the generation now coming on some of the stirring events of that time. Histories galore have been written by leading men on both sides, each giving the general course of events, but often so biased by the sympathies of the writer that those who were deadly enemies at the time of the battles, and on opposite sides, would fail to recognize the events were it not for the names and dates given. But the writer does not purpose going into these disputed points, and will try as stated to preserve a few of the affairs that never have become history but still have a local interest, especially to the few old frontiersmen now alive in Texas and the west.

In 1861 the Second Regiment of Texas Mounted Riflemen was organized at San Antonio, Texas, and those companies present were sworn in for three years or for the war. Col. John S[almon] Ford, known as "Old Rip," had part of the regiment down near Brownsville on the Rio Grande.[1] He was appointed colonel; John R. Baylor, lieutenant-colonel; and [Edwin] Waller, major.

The companies with Colonel Baylor were started up the Overland Stage route and stationed as follows: Capt. [H.A.] Hamner at Fort Clark (the writer was first-lieutenant of this company); Capt. [James] Walker at Fort Davis; and Capt. Peter Hardeman and Capt. Ike Stafford went on with Major Waller to El Paso.[2] Colonel Baylor stayed at Fort Clark a short time and then took the Overland Stage for El Paso, and the writer went with him as adjutant of the battalion.

At the time Nicolás was the chief of the Mescalero Apaches, and his home was on the eastern border of the Davis Mountains, on some of the numerous creeks that make their way thorough deep canyons to the open plains.[3] At that time little was known of this country, only an occasional scout being made by army officers after the Apaches. The latter were constantly ambuscading travelers, and killing them and running off their stock. The coming of the war did not make any difference to them, for they would kill Confederates as willingly as Yankees and were not desirable neighbors.

At this time the company of Capt. J.W. Walker was scattered along from Camp Hudson to Fort Davis, most of them being at Fort Davis. The captain had been an old army officer and was living at Hallettsville when the cry "to arms" came. He was elected captain and had nearly a hundred fine young soldiers.

At the post as sutler was Col. [James] McCarthy, a generous big-hearted "old Irish gentlemen" and he conceived the plan of making an ally of the Apache chief, instead of having him as an enemy, on one long line of communication.[4] So he got word to Nicolás to come into the fort, as his pale-faced brothers were anxious to see him and smoke the pipe of peace, with extras. Making treaties of peace and swearing eternal friendship are two of the strong points in the Apache character, as they promised a chance to show off in gaudy Indian toggery and get whiskey, tobacco and a good square meal. They broke the treaty as easily as they did bread. Nicolás came in and Colonel McCarthy was highly elated. He treated him to the best to eat and drink in the camp and told him that the head chief of the soldiers was at El Paso, and that he would welcome him as a brother, make a great feast, have a smoke and make a treaty.

Nicolás did not take to the idea of leaving his people and going in a stage so far, but under the influence of old peach and honey, and the genial smile and blarney of Colonel McCarthy, he agreed to go. They arrived on time and were received with great ceremony. Old Judge Santiago Magoffin, father of Honorable Joseph Magoffin now mayor of El Paso, acted as interpreter and host in a manner to win the heart of the noble red man. Nicolás was wined and dined to his heart's content, and speeches being in order, Colonel Baylor, a good off-hand speaker, greeted the chief in a handsome talk. Colonel McCarthy also had his say, and stuttered a few nice phrases. Then Nicolás, who was a tall fine looking man, arose and made a speech that was as pretty as it was hollow. It was such a talk as old frontiersmen and the Mexicans he had robbed time and again will recognize as the genuine article.

"I am glad I have come. My heart is full of love for my pale-faced brothers. They have not spoken with forked tongues. We have made a treaty of peace and friendship. When I lie down at night the treaty will be in my heart, and when I arise in the morning it will still be there. And I will be glad that I am at peace with my pale-faced brothers. I have spoken." So Judge Magoffin gave as a toast "Nicolás, our friend," and all drank.

We thought we had made a trusty ally, and got the start of Uncle Sam. Colonel McCarthy gave Nicolás a hug "a la Mexicana." Next morning when the chief left, Colonel McCarthy went with him and the usual guards on the stage. That night they reached the Barrel Springs, twenty-two miles west of Fort Davis, being a small seep spring between El Muerto and Fort Davis where the mules were given water.[5] As the coach stopped Nicolás grabbed the colonel's six-shooter and with a bold bound disappeared. As soon as the colonel realized his little game, he turned loose a rapid-fire gun, loaded with good Irish and English curse words, after the friend of the pale-faced brethren. The guards were too much astonished to even fire at the sound of his retreating foot steps, and there was nothing to do but go to Fort Davis. The next day the Apaches attacked the guards and stampeded the herd of beef cattle. An American and a Mexican who were guarding them were killed, proving that Nicolás had overslept himself and forgotten the peace he had so solemnly made. But it was about the same with Old Espejo in 1854, Cuchillo Negro, and then Nicolás.

• • • • • • • • • • • • • • • • • • • •

It is nearly forty-one years since Lieutenant Reuben E. Mays and a squad of his men, with a number of citizens of Fort Davis, were slaughtered by Mescalero Apaches.[6] After a long and persistent search for the facts of this bloody tragedy, the writer through the kindness of old Confederates of that country, has been able to get at the truth as near as can ever be until the sea shall give up its dead. John Buchanan, the worthy clerk of Lavaca County and a member of this company of the Second Texas Rifles, has taken great interest in the matter and written a very interesting account that ought to be in our war records.[7] The company was organized, April 15, 1861, at Hallettsville with one hundred brave young Texans willing to do or die for Dixie's land. Only a remnant came home after close of the war; their bones are scattered from Glorieta to Fordoche. They are certainly unfortunate in their fights with Indians; the Apaches always outnumbered them, and had them at a disadvantage.

The company was stationed at Fort Davis at the time Col. John R. Baylor fought Maj. [Issac] Lynde's command at Mesilla, the old Seventh Regiment of

Infantry, and afterwards captured them at San Agustín Springs in the Organ Mountains. Captain Walker left Lieutenant Mays and a portion of his company at Fort Davis and came on to El Paso and a portion went to Fort Stanton under Lt. [John R.] Pulliam.[8] It was there Pulliam had a spy named Forsythe shot, and captured a wagon train near the fort.[9]

At Gallina[s] Springs the Apaches and Mexicans attacked a scouting party, killing Jo[seph] Emernecker [Emmanacker] and a man named T[homas] G. Pemberton, and wounding J[ames V.] Massey [Mosse], who escaped from them and was killed by one of Kit Carson's men.[10] The Apaches cut out the tongues of Emernecker and Pemberton, stuck arrows down their throats, and scalped them.

Floyd Sanderson [Sanders] of this party escaped on horseback, and killed an Apache that followed him.[11] The horse was afterwards killed at the battle of Valverde under Captain Walker. Walker joined Sibley's expedition, afterwards known to fame as Green's Brigade, or "Mr. Tom Green's Crittur Company," and on reorganization, [Charles Lynn] Pyron's regiment was formed.[12] It would take a good sized book to tell all the hardships these men suffered during the campaign in New Mexico. One of the men, when asked by a lady if they did not have a hard time, said, "Ma'am we stood what killed the mules."

To go back to the massacre of a detachment of the company through the treachery of Nicolás and Old Espejo, war captain and chief of the Mescalero Apaches, readers of the [El Paso] Herald will recall the account given the writer by [Parker] Burnham of Ysleta, who was a driver of one of the overland stages between San Antonio and El Paso.[13] His account was correct as to killing of all the men except the Mexican guide, but wrong as to direction taken by the Indians and in other respects. The Indians went towards the Rio Grande and crossed, taking refuge with their kindred, the San Carlos Indians, in the state of Chihuahua. Burnham's account sent them northeast from Fort Davis to the head waters of Toyah Creek, in what is now Jeff Davis County.[14] John Freed of San Antonio gave the writer a very graphic account of the fight.

In substance, he said that when the Confederates spied out the Indian camp the guide protested against making an attack and said if they did, they would never come out of the canyon where the Indian camp was, alive. Freed said the men dismounted and attacked at daylight and he was left in charge of the horses, and as soon as the firing began, he knew from the sound that the Confederates were retreating to their camp. After firing ceased he saw some Indians coming on foot and began cutting the rawhide hobbles and finished before they got to him. He mounted and gave a yell, and began shooting at the

Indians and began yelling and [they began] sending their arrows after him. The horses stampeded and willingly enough took the back trail and he was soon out of sight of his foes.

His hardships on the return for one or two days and nights, without anything to eat or drink, were something terrible. He got back safe with all the horses and returned with the scouts to the battlefield and helped bring in the bodies of the men killed. This statement dovetails in very nicely, but he stated also [that] the men were buried at the foot of the cliff of rocks northeast of Fort Davis. Subsequent history shows that Freed's account was erroneous; that the horses were never brought in, the bodies never recovered [and] never buried. But this is like a good deal of war history. We seldom got "walloped" unless our entire force was captured with no chance to gain a victory or make a standoff. The historian is yet to be born who will give unprejudiced war history.

Another account of the massacre is given by Frank L. Fritter, a citizen of Bracketville, who was also a driver on an Overland Stage coach, a position that at the time required a man of courage, sobriety, skill in use of fire arms, and endurance. Every trip these hardy men took they were liable to attack from the treacherous, wily Apache Indians. Night and day, rain or shine, they were always at their post. His account is one of great interest. Gathered just after the occurrence from the Mexican who escaped (and of course we have only [what] the Mexican says as to the truth of his statements), the writer has always been strongly of the opinion that the Mexican drew largely on his imagination, but his account agrees in some respects with the true account of the unfortunate fight. Fritter says the Mexican guide, whose name he has forgotten, said that Judge James Magoffin, an old and respected citizen of El Paso, and father of Judge Joseph Magoffin, with three Confederate commissioners, had engaged Chief Espejo, the war captains Nicolás and Antonio as scouts [before] they deserted and made this raid on the beef herd of the post. This Mexican went as trailer and when they overtook the Indians, Jack Woodland, who was with the party, told the lieutenant in command if they went into the canyon against such fearful odds (there was supposed to be some 300 Apaches) they would never come out of the canyon alive.[15] The lieutenant very wisely took the advice of this old frontiersman and gave orders not to attack, but at that time every Confederate private was commander, and they said they were no cowards and did not intend to run away. So he unfortunately yielded to their clamor and ordered an attack. Woodland said, "All right, lieutenant, but mark my words, we will not come out alive; if you want to fight I will lead you in and stay with you."

Most of the men were new hands and knew but little or nothing about Indian fighting, and before they realized their danger, were fired on from ambuscades on all sides. Many were killed outright and nearly every man wounded, and all he saw were fighting as only brave men could, trying to secure shelter among the rocks.

The Mexican assisted Woodland, who was hardly wounded, to a kind of shelf under one of the hills where they lay concealed until after nightfall. Woodland then told the Mexican he wanted him to try and escape and carry the news to Fort Davis, saying, "I am done for and cannot escape. I have two pistols loaded. I will fight them until my last load, then kill myself rather than fall into their hands and be tortured. I will leave my pistol right here."

The Mexican got in safe, and went back with the rescuing party, Capt. Bill Adams and thirty men.[16] They found the battlefield but no bodies. The guide looked for the pistol and found it where Woodland had put it. On the field some buttons, buckles, etc., were found.

They followed the Indian trail to the Rio Grande, lost it and gave up the search. Later, during one of the Indian dances in Mexico, "celebrating their victory," the Mexican guide with others tried to find out all they could, but the Indians were not communicative. They saw John Woodland's sleeve buttons in the possession of one of the Apaches, and there is no doubt but what it was the Mescalero Apaches [who] for years lived in the Davis Mountains, and [who] committed numerous thefts and murders, the last being the killing of Morgan, the old stage driver, and a passenger in Quitman Canyon in January 1881, when the Rangers followed them for three days into Chihuahua and back into Texas, overtaking them in the Devil Mountains north of Van Horn Station on the mountain west of Apache Springs, where Gus Cox has a cow ranch. The writer with fifteen men and Lt. Charlie Nevil[l] with ten men, surprised their camp at daylight, killing 13 and capturing three, thus in a measure evening up the count against us.[17]

John Woodland was a young Englishman and had been at Fort Davis a long while and knew well the Apache character; before the war he was clerk for Maj. James Dawson, who was sutler at the fort, owning a large train, and the comrade of [Henry] Skillman, [William A.] Wallace, and other old brave, hardy frontiersmen, who like nothing better than a set to with the Indians.[18]

The writer was at El Paso when old Nicolás came up to make a treaty with Col. John R. Baylor. He was brought up from Fort Davis in the Over-land Stage. Colonel McCarthy, who later died at Eagle Lake, brought the old scoundrel up in the Overland Stage and Don Santiago Magoffin gave him a splendid dinner and he was wined and dined in the best style. The Confeder-ates were much elated when old Nic swore eternal friendship, for the Mescaleros were bad enemies to have on our long line of communications.

When the stage stopped at Point of Rocks, a spring, west of Fort Davis, to water their horses, Nic grabbed two six-shooters the colonel had lying on a seat and it being night, he was out of the stage and disappeared in the darkness before the surprised colonel or driver could do anything to prevent him.[19] Of course the whole thing had been planned before he left his tribe and his warriors were there to meet him. The next day the Mescaleros stole the beef herd and were followed by Lieutenant Mays with the result as stated.

It is made known now by a letter written at the time by Lt. [William P.] White, in command at Fort Davis, that Woodland's pistol was not found, only Lieutenant Mays' pistol near his horse that was also killed.[20] [Thomas E.] Carrol[l], a brave Irish man, was carried away from his companions by his horse, a fleet one, stampeding with him.[21] He overtook the Mexican who had taken time by the forelock and as soon as he could get control of his horse tried to get the Mexican to go back as he heard the firing and knew the men had stopped to fight. They had commenced a retreat back to their horses, having made the attack on foot; the Mexican thought "discretion the better part of valor" and continued his flight, whil'st [Thomas], the gallant fellow that he was, turned back to die with his comrades. "Greater love hath no man than this, that he giveth his life for his friend."

There was only one body found, that of John Deprose, and that could only be identified by the clothing, for the country was full of coyotes.[22] The chances are that the Apaches threw the bodies into holes and covered them over with rocks or brush, and if a party of Lavaca County people would go with Mr. Turk or Mr. Porton to Brewster County, locate the place where the fight occurred, and make a careful search, the bodies will be found. It is quite certain the bones found in a cave near Alpine are not those of Walker's men, as they followed the Indians several days before they overtook them. Why, when they captured one-hundred head of the Indians' horses, they did not "let well enough alone" and return with the booty, is one of the strangest things imaginable; it would have hurt them nearly as much as killing a lot of them. But getting so many horses without a fight caused them to commit the very grave mistake of underrating an enemy. Doubtless, the Indians had no idea they would be followed and their pursuers thought they were in full flight and they had the contempt for bows and dogwood switches common among those who had not seen any of their work.

A Comanche or Apache warrior with his good bow made of mountain mulberry and quiver full of arrows, twenty-five or thirty, was no foe to meet, especially at that time when we had only muzzle loaders, and once your gun or pistol was emptied there was little chance to load even on foot and none at all in a running fight on horseback. We can imagine that his little squad of men, probably emptying their guns and revolvers rapidly, were soon at the mercy of the swarm of Apaches around them.

Juan Fernández, the name of the Mexican guide, who had lived as a prisoner with these same Indians for so many years, was always suspected by Walker's men of leading the men into an ambuscade, and the fact that he disappeared from Fort Davis and was at the scalp dance given by these Indians at the San Carlos agency and saw one of the Indians with John Woodland's sleeve buttons, would seem to point that way; he could have been there to see about his share of the booty.

The following is a copy of the letter written by Lt. W.R. White, commander of the post at the time, to Dr. W.E. East of Halletsville, Lavaca County, and now in possession of Miss A.D. Lay of that place. Having been written at the time of the occurrence it is the correct account of the unfortunate tragedy:

Fort Davis, Texas, Aug. 24, 1861

Dear Sir: On the 5th inst. Lieutenant R.E. Mays started after a party of Mescalero Apaches and on the 10th inst. overhauled them and captured 100 head of horses after night without a fight. On the 11th inst. he attempted to whip almost 80 or 100 Indians with 14 men, and the whole party was killed except one, a Mexican by the name of Juan, who made good his escape and brought in the news.

I sent out 19 men as a relief scout which found relics enough to satisfy me that the whole party was dead, or worse than dead, taken prisoner; they found hats, boots, parts of pants, and coats of all except a few of the party, the names are as follows. Lt. R.E. Mays, Thos. Carrol of Hallettsville, John H. Brown, Samuel R. Desper, Frederick Perkins, Samuel Shelby, John S. Walker of Lavaca County, belonging to Capt. Walker's company, and John [Fred] Turner, guide of the post, John Deprose, R.H. Spence, Joseph Lambert, Jack Woodland, and two Mexican citizens; and the one Mexican is all that ever returned or been heard of except John Deprose, whose body was found by the relief scout, which was as follows: Dr. Evans S. Weisinger, surgeon of the post; J.C. Allen, Martin Burke, John Cleghorn, Louis Kaufman, Benj. F. Lee, Joel Ponton, Eli Stevens and Felix Tucker of the company. Thos. Chandler, Thos. Baker, Thos. O'Niely, a Frenchman, and five Mexican citizens and the Mexican that escaped of the first party.

The reason that I wrote you, doctor, is that Ruben used to talk more of you than any one else, and I thought you would probably know more about his business than any one else, and as he has some money coming to him from the government, some one must attend to it and let the proper heirs have it. His horse was killed under him I suppose, or near the same time the poor fellow fell. I have his watch in my possession, as he carried mine with him on the scout, and his was not in running order. Lt. Mays had my watch, minie rifle, saddle and Bowie knife, and if you or any of his relative or friends want the watch I will freely give it up. All I want is just pay for watch, etc. I have several letters to answer written to Ruben, so I will close. Hoping to hear from you on this subject, I remain your obedient servant, W.P. White, 2nd Lt. Comd'g Post.

The above letter gives the correct names of all the men killed belonging to the company. Lt. R.E. Mays resided at Hallettsville, was related to Dr. J.E. Lay, Joe Lay and others of that family now of Hallettsville, was also related to W.J. Mays, formerly of Lavaca County. Thos. Carroll was from Lavaca County and had relatives there. John S. Walker was related to the Walkers of Moulton, Perkins to the Livergoods of Lavaca County, Joseph Lambert resided at Fort Davis and [his] relatives live there now.

NOTES

[1] By 1861, Ford was already a legend on the southwestern frontier. Born in South Carolina in 1815, Ford came to Texas in 1836, served in the Texas Army, commanded a spy company in the Mexican-American War, and, along with R.S. Neighbors, explored the area between San Antonio and El Paso. Besides practicing medicine, Ford was a captain in the Rangers on the border in the early 1850s, established a newspaper in Austin, served in the Texas State Senate, and fought in the Cortina War. John Salmon Ford, *Rip Ford's Texas* (Austin: University of Texas Press, 1963), ed. Stephen B. Oates; and W.J. Hughes, *Rebellious Ranger: Rip Ford and the Old Southwest* (Norman: University of Oklahoma Press, 1964).

[2] See n. 16, Ch.. 1, this section.

[3] C.L. Sonnichsen, in his study of the Mescalero Apaches, could find little information on Nicolás other than what Baylor had written. In May 1861, Nicolás attacked the San Antonio-El Paso stage three miles east of Barilla Springs on the eastern rim of the Davis Mountains. Wounding one of the drivers and killing one of the mules, the Apaches chased the stage to the Barilla Springs stage station, where they were repulsed. When the Confederates evacuated the Mesilla Valley and West Texas in the summer of 1862, it was Nicolás who plundered and partly burned Fort Davis. C.L. Sonnichsen, *The Mescalero Apaches* (Norman: University of Oklahoma Press, 1973), 103-4; and Wayne R. Austerman, *Sharps Rifles and Spanish Mules: The San Antonio-El Paso Mail, 1851-1881* (College Station: Texas A&M University Press, 1985), 166-67, 186.

4 McCarthy was the Confederate commissioner at Fort Davis. It is probably McCarthy who is listed on the 1860 census as thirty-one, Alabama-born, and a station-keeper near Wild Rose Pass. Merrick, *Desert to Bayou*, 11, 105; 8th Census, Presidio County, Tex., NA.

5 Barrel Springs, on the southwestern edge of the Davis Mountains, is about eighteen miles west of Fort Davis. El Muerto or Dead Man's Hole, is at the base of El Muerto Mountain on the west side of the Davis Mountains, some thirty-two miles west of Fort Davis. For the exact location of El Muerto, see U.S. Geological Survey topographical map (7.5 Minute Series) El Muerto Peak, Tex. (1978).

6 Mays, twenty-six, enlisted in Capt. James Walker's Company D of the 2d Regiment at Hallettsville on 19 April 1861. Hall, *Confederate Army of New Mexico,* 320-21.

7 Buchanan was only sixteen when he enlisted in Co. D of the 2d Regiment. Ibid., 321.

8 Col. Benjamin S. Roberts had two companies of infantry and two of Mounted Rifles under his command at Fort Stanton. When he learned on 2 August 1861 of the Federal surrender at San Agustín Springs, he set fire to the post and destroyed a considerable amount of supplies. A thunder storm extinguished the fire, however, and the stores were plundered by Mescaleros and local residents, although citizens living near the post tried to restore order. Captain Walker reported capturing fifty-one wagonloads of supplies and thirteen more near San Mateo, less than fifty miles from Albuquerque. The South Carolina-born Pulliam was the son of Wiley Pulliam, a well-to-do Hallettsville farmer. Originally enlisting in Co. D as an orderly sergeant, he was elected first lieutenant on 25 July 1861. When Captain Walker returned to Mesilla, Pulliam, only twenty, was left in command at Fort Stanton. After returning to Mesilla, Pulliam was treated for gonorrhea at the Doña Ana hospital. B.S. Roberts to E.R.S. Canby, 2 August 1861, *OR*, 1, 4:22; Baylor to Earl Van Dorn, 14 August 1861, *OR*, 1, 4:22-23; Pulliam to Baylor, 1 September 1861, *OR*, 1, 4:24; Hall, *Confederate Army of New Mexico,* 321; and 8th Census, Lavaca County, Texas.

9 Official records make no mention of the Forsythe execution. On the evening of the Confederate occupation of Fort Stanton and the Rio Bonito, an anonymous correspondent, evidently someone who was well educated but afraid to sign his name since he was still on the Rio Bonito, wrote that the Rebels, upon occupying the area, were involved in "raping women and children." John P. Wilson, *Merchants, Guns, and Money: The Story of Lincoln County and Its Wars* (Santa Fe: Museum of New Mexico, 1987), 13-15.

10 Pulliam sent the four-man patrol to the Gallinas Springs on the west side of the Gallinas Mountains, some fifty-five miles northwest of Fort Stanton, to watch the Manzano-Fort Stanton Road. On 29 August 1861, contrary to orders, the small party camped in a grove of ponderosa pines one hundred yards above the spring. The next morning they built a fire and were in the process of cooking breakfast when they were attacked. That same evening, Pulliam sent a rescue party of fourteen men and three citizens back to the scene of the attack. Pemberton, twenty-five, and Emmanacker, twenty-five, were found scalped. Both were buried and a cross was cut in a tree to mark the site. Mosse's body could not be found. After Walker returned briefly to the post, Fort Stanton was evacuated and by 21 September 1861 the Rebels were back in the Mesilla Valley. Pulliam to Baylor, 25 August [September] 1861, *OR*, 1, 4:24-25.

It was at the Gallinas Springs in October 1862, that Capt. James "Paddy" Graydon massacred Manuelito and several of his Mescaleros. Jerry Thompson, *Desert Tiger: Capt. Paddy Graydon and the Civil War in the Southwest* (El Paso: Texas Western Press, 1992), 51-54.

[11] Fourth Sergeant Sanders, eighteen, had been reduced to ranks on 23 July 1861. Back in the Mesilla Valley, he died of smallpox on 28 November 1861. Hall, *Confederate Army of New Mexico*, 324.

[12] Pyron, forty-two, migrated to Texas about 1840. He fought with the Texas Rangers at Monterrey during the Mexican-American War. After the war he purchased a ranch on the San Antonio River below Mission San José. On 15 April 1861, Pyron enrolled in what became Company B of the 2d Regiment in San Antonio. The company was at San Lucas Spring when the Federals under Colonel Reeves surrendered. Pyron's men occupied Forts Lancaster and Stockton and some fought at Cañada Alamosa, Valverde, and Glorieta. Pyron died at his ranch near San Antonio on 24 August 1869. Hall, *Confederate Army of New Mexico*, 311-12, 316.

[13] The red-haired Burnham had been a stage driver on the San Antonio-El Paso route prior to the war and was known as "Dandy" among frontiersmen for always wearing a clean white shirt when taking the reins of the stage. In May 1861, Burnham was at the reins when Nicolás attacked the San Antonio-El Paso stage, with George Giddings aboard, near Barrilla Springs. He was shot in the hip and neck with arrows but recovered. After serving in Co. A of the 5th Texas Cavalry during the Civil War, Burnham returned to the El Paso area where he married a young Mexican woman, Cornelia. The couple eventually settled at Ysleta where Cornelia bore thirteen children, only six of whom reached adulthood. In 1903, he joined the El Paso Police Department where he remained for thirteen years. Burnham died in Los Angeles, Calif., on 3 August 1917. Wayne R. Austerman, "Parker Burnham: An Expressman of Old El Paso," *Password* 27 (Spring 1982): 5-13.

[14] Mays and his men were killed on 11 August 1861. In 1963, while preparing a report for an exhibition at Fort Davis National Historical Site, park officials identified three canyons between Bone Springs and Persimmons Gap, deep in the Big Bend, as the possible location of the massacre. Two of the sites, Dog and Devils canyons, were eventually ruled out since they were too far off the trail leading south through Persimmons Gap. Grapevine Canyon, a spring-fed, dead-end canyon with rocky walls, was eventually settled on as the probable site. Gordon Geldard of Las Cruces, N.M., devoted considerable effort in trying to locate the site of the massacre. Geldard concluded the site was west of Persimmons Gap, probably three or four miles west of Small Pox Springs and south of Corazones Peak. Due primarily to the vastness of the region and the lack of artifacts, the exact location where Mays and his men died may never be determined with any certainty. "Mays Massacre, 1861," Background Report for Exhibit 11 (December 1963), Fort Davis National Historical Site; Gordon W. Geldard, "The Lost Patrol," Unpublished ms., Fort Davis National Historical Site.

[15] English-born John Woodland, thirty-three, is listed on the 1860 El Paso census as a "trader" at Fort Quitman. 8th Census, El Paso County, Texas.

[16] See n. 3, Ch. 11, Sec. I.

[17] See Ch. 8, Sec. III.

[18] At six-feet two-inches tall and 240 pounds, William Alexander Anderson "Bigfoot" Wallace was a legendary figure of the Southwest. Wallace arrived in Texas from Virginia, fought during General Woll's invasion, and was captured at Mier. He served in Col. Jack Hays' Ranger regiment during the Mexican-American War and later commanded a Ranger company in the 1850s. He was also a mail driver on the San Antonio-El Paso

Road. He retired to a ranch on the Medina River where he died on 7 January 1899. Shortly thereafter his remains were moved to the State Cemetery in Austin. Several biographies of Wallace exist.

[19] Earlier, Baylor identified the spot where Nicolás left the stage as Barrel Springs. Due to its ruggedness, Point of Rocks, seven miles west of Fort Davis and near a small seepage, would have been ideal for any escape. Jno. R. Baylor to J.B. Magruder, 29 December 1862, *OR*, 1, 15:915-16.

[20] Brevet Second Lieutenant White, twenty-nine, commanded Fort Davis from September to November 1861.

[21] Carroll, from Hallettsville, Lavaca County, is listed on company rolls as twenty-five.

[22] In 1860, Deprose listed his occupation as a teamster. Lambert was a clerk from Ohio. For Woodland, see n. 15, this chapter. Williams, *Texas' Last Frontier,* 25.

CHAPTER THREE

With General Albert Sidney Johnston at Shiloh

~

SO MUCH HAS BEEN SAID BY THE PROMINENT COMMANDERS on both sides of the fierce and bloody struggle at Shiloh that it may seem presumptuous for one who was only a lieutenant at the time to attempt to throw any light on the scene; nor do I pretend to give a full account of what transpired; but as I was senior aide-de-camp to General Johnston, and with him from the time he left Columbus, Kentucky, until his death, and during that time acted as his secretary, even copying his letters to Pres. [Jefferson] Davis, I think what I have to say may be of interest to the numerous Albert Sidney Johnston camps and all others. I write from memory; yet, after a lapse of thirty-five years those events are vividly recalled. The impressions left by this deadly struggle between people of the same name and blood, opposed in internecine strife, each side actuated by love of country and of causes that seemed more dear than life—are not easily forgotten.

After General Johnston reached Corinth we were very busy organizing the commands that came from so many different points into brigades, divisions, and corps. This was Gen. [Braxton] Bragg's forte. On the 4th of April, 1862 (Friday), we rode out from General Johnston's headquarters at Corinth and took the road for Pittsburgh Landing where we knew Gen. [Ulysses S.] Grant's army lay. General Johnston talked little of his intentions, but he had said at the breakfast table that he was "going to hit Grant, and hit him hard." His staff was composed of Gen. [William Whann] McKall, chief adjutant-general; Gen. William Preston, Col. A.P. Brewster, Capt. Nat Wickliffe,

Majors Dudley Haydon and Calhoun Brenham, assistants; Maj. [Jeremy Francis] Gilmer, chief engineer; Majors [E.W.] Munford and [Theodore] O'Hara, voluntary aids; Maj. Albert [J.] Smith, chief quartermaster; Capt. Leigh Wi[c]kham, assistant quartermaster; Lt. Thomas [M.] Jack, junior aid; and myself, senior aid.[1] Colonel Brewster, Lieutenant Jack, and I were [from] Texas. When we rode off General Bragg and staff and Gen. [Pierre Gustave Toutant de] Beauregard and staff joined us, so we formed quite a cavalcade.[2] When we reached the troops we found them lining the sides of the road. They had been cautioned to keep silent, but they knew their commander, and pressed forward. We reined up on the crest of the hill overlooking the field of Shiloh, and General Johnston spoke encouragingly to the men about him, enjoining them to "be cool tomorrow, and take good aim at their belts." We pressed on by a log house on the right, and dismounted in a wood just beyond.

While we were getting the troops in position night came on, and a council of war was held in General Johnston's tent. Among those present were General Bragg, Beauregard, [Leonidas] Polk, [William J.] Hardee, and [John C.] Breckinridge, and quite a number of their respective staffs.[3] I heard each opinion as it was given of the course that should be pursued, and all spoke hopefully of the morrow. Only one, General Beauregard, uttered a doubt—and he the bravest of the brave. His words were strangely impressed upon me, because of their difference from the others. He said: "In the struggle tomorrow we shall be fighting men of our own blood, Western men, who understand the use of firearms. The struggle will be a desperate one, and if we drive them to the brink of the river and they make a last determined stand there, our troops may be repulsed and our victory turned to defeat." I believe these words account for the order to retire on Sunday at nightfall, when we had the victory in our hands. The battle has created a great deal of dispute and much criticism that was unjust to commanders of both armies. Those who did not experience it could hardly arrive at equitable conclusions. The only reason why Grant's army was not destroyed or captured was that the rain on Friday night prevented our getting our army into line of battle and making the attack at daylight, Saturday morning. The impassable condition of the roads prevented General Breckinridge bringing up his artillery. After a battle is over any one who has had any experience can plan an easy victory. All we had to do was to arrange an order of battle, let the artillery stick in the mud—for it was a battle of small arms—and we could soon have had all the artillery we wanted from the foe. As it was, we captured entire batteries.

It has always been a matter of wonder to me how the Federal army lay in camp all Friday evening near enough for us to hear their drums beat and fail to discover our proximity, especially as there were nearly fifty thousand of us (forty-six thousand, I think), and some of our overly zealous men had brought about a skirmish, in which they used a field-piece, and captured some prisoners. The Terry Rangers had fired their guns to load them afresh, greatly to General Johnston's annoyance, and Col. John A. Wharton was put under arrest for it. That brave officer put in an earnest appeal to the general, saying he "would rather be shot than not allowed to go into the fight," and upon being released did gallant service with the Terry Rangers in the battle.

After the meeting at General Johnston's tent Friday evening we had a heavy downpour of rain. Our tent had been stretched so that a path ran diagonally through it, and I was sleeping on the side where it first entered. I had laid down in my clothes, overcoat and all, and being aroused by the rain, I put out my hand and found the water banking up against the tent. I arose, found a spade, and soon had the path filled and a trench dug that turned the water off from the tent. When I returned to the tent I had a vote of thanks from the staff, and the general spoke in his kind way of the small service.

After the rain, which was very heavy, General Johnston called me to him and said: "Lieutenant, I wish you would go to General Beauregard and ask him if we had not better postpone the attack until Sunday, on account of the rain." I started on this errand, and soon found a French sentinel, who knew little English, and the extent of my French was "*Beaugar,*" but it was sufficient to so put me at the general's tent. I found him still up although it was past midnight, and delivered General Johnston's message. He reflected a moment, then said, "Tell General Johnston that time is of such importance, I think we had better commence the attack at daylight." Why we did not has been explained. The condition of the roads, the utter impossibility of getting raw troops into position in a given time (except from the extreme front under a hot fire to the extreme rear, which is generally done with promptness and despatch), and for many reasons the day was so far advanced before order was obtained that the attack was postponed until Sunday morning, April 6.

General Grant said, in his article to the *Century* magazine of February, 1895, "It was a battle of *ifs;*" and I am convinced that *if* we had begun the attack on the 5th, instead of the 6th, of April, *if* General Johnston had not been killed on the afternoon of the 6th, and *if* Don Carlos Buell had not come up at all, why there would have been no "ifs" about it; but the chances are that General Grant would have shared the fate of our own gallant leader and the horrors of the war would probably have been prolonged for several years.[4]

But to return to the incidents of the battle. A young lieutenant was captured on the 5th, and General Johnston turned him over to me. We were both young, and talked freely. I said to him: "You Yankees are very determined in trying to deny us the right to regulate our own state affairs." He flared up at the word "Yankees," and replied: "I want you to understand that, I am no *Yankee*; I am a Western man, and fighting for the Union."

That evening there was an informal meeting of corps commanders, and as the weather had cleared up, it was decided to attack at daylight. While breakfasting at dawn we heard the crack of skirmishers' guns, so hurrying the meal, we mounted, and were soon on our way to the front. When we drew near the reserves under Breckenridge we found the brave Kentuckians pressing forward, almost on the heels of the first line. The front by this time was hard at it, and the rattling fire was a constant roar. General Johnston rode straight to the front, and we were soon where the bullets were singing around us and where we could see the Federal tents. Here I discarded my overcoat, and as I was riding by the general's side he said to me: "Lieutenant, you had better keep that coat; you will need it before the war is over." I replied that if we won this battle I should get another, and if we didn't, I should probably not need it. This spirit animated the young men of the South at the time. It was "death or victory." Later on we would have preferred "badly crippled or victory." I was wearing a dark-blue coat, and Dr. David Yandell, seeing the danger that it subjected me to, insisted that I should exchange with him. Many a poor fellow during the day, seeing the surgeon's stripes, hailed me with, "Doctor, can you do something for me?"

When we struck the line, some hundred yards from the first tents, the Federals were making a fight for their grub and tarpaulins, and there was a slight break in our lines. The general and staff rode right through the gap, and just then Gen. [Thomas Carmichael] Hindman passed in front of us, going to the left.[5] His horse was at full gallop, his long hair streaming out behind him, and he was waving his cap over his head and cheering the men on. I shall never forget what a picture of daring and courage he was. Gen. William Preston turned to the right, and galloping down the line, called the attention of the troops to General Johnston. As they recognized him a cheer went up, and a charge made at double-quick brought us into the Federal camp. I never knew what command it was but they were either surprised or thought we were only joking. There was an old field to the right of the camp, and across it a long row of overcoats and knapsacks, as thought they had been in line for inspection and had to hasten to the rear before it was over. We rode through this old field to the right. There was a creek crossing it in front of the encampment, and we saw the gleam of bayonets and cannon in an old field beyond, where they had rallied. The Second Texas, under Col. [John Creed] Moore, was just west of us, under cover of the creek-bank.[6] Just here the Federals sent a shell over our heads that went into the ground near the line of their own overcoats. I believe all the staff bowed respectfully to this missile, but the general sat as straight as an Indian. Several orders were given by the general, and then we rode toward our right wing, where he gave me the last order that I ever had from him: "Lieutenant, go to Gen. [James Ronald] Chalmers, and tell him to sweep round to the left and drive the enemy into the river."[7] I had seen some severe criticisms of this order from the Northern press, who denominated it "barbarous, inhuman," etc.; but there was no such spirit underlying it. It was just such an order as any general would give to impress his men with his own determination to win the battle.

On my return I found that the general had moved still further to the right, and was on a high hill in the rear of this Second Texas regiment, I think. While sitting there we noticed an officer fall, and riding forward, I found it was Capt. Clark Owens, whom I knew. The general also knew him as a gallant soldier in earlier days in Texas, and was much distressed at his death. Orders were given to the Texas troops to advance, when I asked and received permission to join them in the charge. Colonel Benham, whom I had known in San Francisco, also got permission to go. After the charge we rode back to where we had left the general, and learned that he had ridden toward the left again. We took the same direction, riding at a canter, and soon became separated. I was some time on the way, making inquiries here and there, and finally came to a battalion of soldierly looking men, and inquired for their commander. A captain in gray uniform stepped up and said the commander, Maj. [A.B.] Hardcastle, had gone to the front to get orders, as they had evidently been overlooked.[8] I told him that I was aid of General Johnston, and that they could safely move to the front. I afterward learned that this captain was Robert McNair, once Superintendent of Public Schools of New Orleans.[9]

I began to feel uneasy about being so long absent from my general, and concluding that I should find him, where the firing was the heaviest, I rode in just behind the line of battle. Presently, I saw an officer galloping toward me, and was glad to recognize Major O'Hara, of the general's staff. He seeing my surgeon's uniform, had ridden straight for me. I asked for General Johnston, and he replied, "He is wounded, and I fear seriously. I am now looking for a surgeon, as well as others of the staff," adding that he was just from the general, and had left him in an awful hot place. I went to him at once, and the major, hoping that a surgeon had already been found, rode back with me. After riding some distance beyond it, we found the general and staff in a depression that emptied into the branch.[10] No surgeon had been found, and the group gathered around the dying general was a sad one.

As I dismounted I saw that a stream of blood had run from the general's body some six or eight feet off and ended in a dark pool. Around were gathered, as well as I can now recall them, Gen. William Preston, Gov. Isham G. Harris (who aced as assistant adjutant-general during the battle, and rendered most valuable aid, especially among the Tennessee troops), Maj. Albert Smith, Capt. Leigh Wickham, Major O'Hara, Lieutenant Jack, and myself.[11] General Preston was kneeling and holding General Johnston's head. Becoming cramped with the position, he asked me to relieve him which I did. As I looked upon his noble face, I though of the dauntless warrior who had ridden out of camp that morning so full of life and hope, his face alight with the excitement of approaching battle, whose very presence was an inspiration to those under its magic influence, the personification of Southern chivalry. I also thought of the gentle wife on the golden sands of the Pacific, whose heart would be pierced by the same bullet that brought him death; and learning over him, I asked: "General, do you know me?" My tears were falling in his face, and his frame quivered for a moment, then he opened his eyes, looked me full in the face, seeming to comprehend, and closed them again. He died as a soldier must like to die; at the moment of victory and surrounded by loving comrades in arms. There was not a dry eye in that sad group, and Gen. William Preston sobbed aloud. He said, as though to explain it: "Pardon me, gentlemen; you all know how I loved him."[12]

After a while I was relieved by Lieutenant Jack, and at the request of General Preston, started to look for an ambulance. I rode for some distance, but failing to find one, turned back, thinking some of the others might have been more successful. While returning I met one of General Bragg's staff, who had been sent to tell General Johnston that they had carried everything on the left. This officer's grief on hearing of General Johnston's fate was another tribute of love and admiration that the great man aroused in all who came in contact with him. When I reached the spot where I had left the general's body I found that it had been removed, and followed the tracks of the ambulance back to camp.

Governor Harris and Captain Wickham told me, concerning the death-wound, that the general had led in a charge and received a wound that severed the artery below the right knee and just above the boot-top. The wound seemed to have been inflicted by a navy revolver or buckshot. The sole of the boot also was cut by a minie ball and a spent shot had struck him under the shoulder blade. To an inquiry from Governor Harris after the charge he replied that he had been wounded, but that it was "only a scratch." He then gave an order to Governor Harris, who returned after its execution to find him pale and faint. He asked if the general had been wounded again, and was sure that he had not, but that the wound was more serious than he had first thought, and he would ride to the rear and look for a surgeon. Governor Harris and Captain Wickham rode back with him, but before they had proceeded far the general was reeling in his saddle, and the governor sprang to the ground and caught him in his arms as he fell. He was then carried to the depression in the ravine before mentioned, where he died. I have seen pictures of this spot, but none of them bear the slightest resemblance to it. We were among tall post-oak trees, and, unless these have been cut, I believe I could now find the exact spot.

To return to the condition of our men and the enemy at sunset. In 1863 there was in my brigade a Lt. Col. Alonzo Ridley, of Col. [Joseph] Phillips' Regiment, formerly sheriff of Los Angeles County, California, who had come across the plains with General Johnston.[13] At Bowling Green he received a captain's commission, and was given authority to select from the soldiers a company to act as scouts. He told me that late in the evening at the battle of Shiloh he rode up on the bank of the Tennessee River, opposite one of the gunboats. He concluded that he would give them a round, as his men were armed with Enfield rifles; so he formed them in line and fired a volley. Every man on deck of the gunboat disappeared in a moment, and, to his utter astonishment, a cloud of bluecoats swarmed up from under the river-bank, holding up their hands, and saying: "We surrender." The stream continued to crowd up the hill, until he was afraid they would disarm his company, so he marched off with what he could guard. Colonel Ridley still lives near Phoenix, Arizona.

In El Paso, Texas, a few years ago, I met a Mr. Burton, who belonged to a Tennessee regiment engaged in this battle, and he told me that when his regiment had nearly reached the brink of the river they were halted, but moved by curiosity, he walked forward and looked over at the crowd. He said he had never seen such a sight—officers, men, mules, horses, cannon, all mixed together, no one paying the least attention to orders. He even saw one officer on a stump waving his sword over his head and trying to rally his men, but none of them heeded; and one Federal soldier, who stood near enough for Mr. Burton to hear his words, said: "Wouldn't he make a daisy stump speaker?" This shows how utterly all discipline or thought of resistance was at an end. Now, let us suppose that one Tennessee regiment had advanced and fired a volley into this demoralized crowd. What would have been the result? I am convinced, with Josh Billings, that "there is a great deal of human nature in mankind," and I am sure that a panic started there would soon have spread to the brave men who were making such a desperate resistance on our left. A lot of men stampeded have no more sense than so many Texas "long-horns," and I have seen them stampeded by a cotton-tail rabbit. I am convinced that Generals Grant and Sherman and a good many more who have expressed the same opinion were sadly mistaken in thinking that the battle of the 7th could have been gained without General Buell's army. We knew that he had arrived during the night, and it was believed that he had fifty thousand fresh men. The moral effect of this is not hard to determine: it depressed our men and encouraged the Federals.

General Grant, in his account of the battle of Shiloh, says: "Nothing occurred in his brief command of an army to prove or disprove the high estimate that had been placed upon General Johnston's military abilities." When the order came to the Confederates to fall back they were flushed with victory and ready for a final struggle. Hardly any Federal soldier in that army can seriously doubt what would have been the result of such a charge at sunset, with Buell a day's march away.

That night I lay on the ground by the cot which held General Johnston's body and listened to the beating of the drums as Buell's army arrived. I was born at Fort Gibson, and have lived nearly all my life with the army. The notes of drum, fife, and bugle are as familiar to me as my own voice, and as I noted the tones of the different drums of regiments I knew that it meant a death-struggle for us on the morrow. It was generally believed by our army that if we could not defeat Grant before Buell came up, we would have to fall back to Corinth on the 7th.

On the morning of the 7th I rode to Shiloh church, General Beauregard's headquarters, to ask for permission to accompany the body of General Johnston from the field and for instructions. He told me to say to any Confederate commanders or soldiers that I saw that the enemy were making a stand at only one point, and he expected to capture them that morning; he also asked me to direct them to the point of the heaviest firing. This was about daylight. As I left him he kindly offered me a position on his staff if I returned. I have never been able to determine whether General Beauregard really believed there would only be a slight struggle to gain the victory or whether he only hoped to encourage the men; but no one can say, brilliant as had been their dash of the day before, that it was eclipsed by their dogged determination on the 7th when they believed they were fighting the defeated army of the day before, reenforced by fifty thousand.

Two acts of General Grant have endeared him to the entire South: the one was his conduct at Appomattox when our Lee surrendered his broken-down, half-starved men, and the other was the stand he took when fanatical abolitionists wanted to hang President Davis. These things did more to conquer—or to pacify—the South than all the powder that was wasted from Sumter to the Rio Grande.

And there was one act, in the short career of General Johnston that if more generally known would bring to him the tender regard of the North: At Shiloh after a heavy charge, he passed a group of wounded men wearing both blue and gray, and ordered his own surgeon, Dr. David [W.] Yandell, to "stop and attend to all alike," saying: "They were our enemies, but are fellow sufferers now." This very care for the wounded soldiers cost him his life; for, had Dr. Yandell been with him when he was wounded, a simple tourniquet or a silk handkerchief twisted with a stick would have stopped the hemorrhage and have saved his life. His staff seemed dazed with the great calamity, and there was no surgeon near to apply the simple bandage.

NOTES

1 An 1837 West Point graduate from Maryland, McKall was wounded in the Seminole War while serving in the 1st Artillery. In the Mexican-American War, he fought at Monterrey, Contreras, and Churubusco. Promoted brigadier general, he was responsible for the surrender of Island No. 10 and its 7,000-man garrison and 123 heavy guns in April 1862. Exchanged, he served as chief of staff to Gen. Joseph E. Johnston. When Johnston was relieved at Atlanta, McKall declined to serve under Gen. John B. Hood. After the war, he retired to Fairfax County, Virginia, where he ran several farms. Heitman, *Historical Register*, 1:670; Warner, *Generals in Gray*, 203-4; and Judith Lee Hallock, "William W. McKall," *Encyclopedia of the Confederacy*, 3:937.

William Preston's sister, Henrietta, was Johnston's first wife. Preston was an 1838 graduate of Harvard who practiced law in Louisville, fought in Mexico, served in the Kentucky legislature, and in 1852 was elected to the United States Congress. In 1858, he was appointed minister to Spain but returned to the United States during the secession crisis. After Shiloh, he was promoted brigadier general and fought at Corinth and Stones River. Because of his diplomatic experience, he was appointed minister to the Mexican government of Maximilian, but the war ended before he could assume his duties. After the war, Preston traveled in Mexico, England, and Canada before returning to Kentucky. He died in Lexington on 21 September 1887. Anne J. Bailey, "William Preston," *Encyclopedia of the Confederacy*, 3:1250; and Roland, *Soldier of Three Republics*, 27-28, 51.

After the death of General Johnston, Brewster, Wickliffe, Munford, and Haydon continued as staff officers to General Beauregard. G.T. Beauregard to S. Cooper, 11 April 1862, *OR*, 1, 10:390.

Benham served as volunteer aide-de-camp to General Johnston.

Gilmer, fourth in the West Point class of 1839, was chief engineer in the Army of the West in New Mexico in the Mexican-American War and supervised the building of Fort Marcy at Santa Fe. From 1858 to 1861, he directed the construction of the defenses of San Francisco. At the beginning of the war, Gilmer supervised the construction of the defenses of Forts Henry and Donelson. On the second day at Shiloh, Gilmer was wounded but recovered and went east where in August 1862, Gen. Robert E. Lee made him chief engineer of the Army of Northern Virginia. Later he was appointed chief of the Engineer

Bureau of the War Department and rose to the rank of brigadier general. Gilmer helped design the defenses of Richmond, Petersburg, and Atlanta. He died on 1 December 1883, at Savannah, Georgia. Michael G. Mahon, "J.F. Gilmer," *Encyclopedia of the Confederacy*, 2:686.

Along with Baylor, Wickham, Munford, O'Hara, Smith, and Jack accompanied Gen. Johnston's body from the field to the little church on the Shiloh battlefield whence it was then escorted to New Orleans. Roland, *Soldier of Three Republics*, 337-38, 352-53.

2   A successful sugar planter from Louisiana, Bragg commanded the 2d Corps and acted as chief of staff to General Johnston at Shiloh where he led the forces in the center of the battlefield as well as the attack on the Hornet's Nest. Bragg always thought that had Beauregard pressed the attack following Johnston's death, the Confederates could have won the field. The controversial Bragg became a full general a week after Shiloh and held a number of commands for the remainder of the war. He died in Galveston, Texas, on 27 February 1876. Judith Lee Hallock, "Braxton Bragg," *Encyclopedia of the Confederacy*, 1:203-6.

A French creole from Louisiana, Beauregard rose to become one of eight full generals in the Confederate Army. As commander of Confederate forces at Fort Sumter and First Bull Run, he was already a southern hero by the time of Shiloh. He was severely criticized for his failure to press the attack on 6 April 1862, following Johnston's death. Driven from Corinth, President Davis dismissed him from command. In April 1864, he was placed in charge of the southern approaches to Richmond; after Cold Harbor he was the only Confederate commander to anticipate Grant's move south of the James River and successfully blocked the Union advance on Petersburg. Beauregard died in New Orleans on 21 February 1893. T. Harry Williams, *P.G.T. Beauregard: Napoleon in Gray* (Baton Rouge: Louisiana State University Press, 1954).

3   Polk, an 1827 West Point graduate, was ordained a bishop of the Episcopal church in 1838. Commissioned a major general in 1861, he commanded the 1st Corps at Shiloh which consisted of the brigades of Col. R.M. Russell and Brig. Gen. A.P. Stewart. Although the leader of the anti-Bragg clique in the Army of Tennessee, Polk continued to command his corps at Chickamauga. At Pine Mountain, Georgia, Polk was killed by Union artillery on 14 June 1864. Joseph H. Parks, *General Leonidas Polk, C.S.A.: Fighting Bishop* (Baton Rouge: Louisiana State University Press, 1962).

Hardee, a veteran officer of the 2d Dragoons, was captured in the first engagement of the Mexican-American War. His *Rifle and Light Infantry Tactics* was extensively used in both armies during the Civil War. At Shiloh, Hardee led the 3d Corps, which consisted of the brigades of Generals T.C. Hindman, P.R. Cleburne, and S.A.M. Woods. Hardee fought well at Stones River and Chattanooga and served under Gen. Joseph E. Johnston in the Atlanta campaign, but saw his corps severely battered after Gen. John B. Hood took command. Hardee died in Wytheville, Virginia, on 6 November 1873. Nathan C. Hughes, Jr., *General William J. Hardee, C.S.A.* (Baton Rouge: Louisiana State University Press, 1965). Also, Organization of the Army of the Mississippi, 6-7 April 1863, *OR*, 1, 10, 1:382.

From one of Kentucky's more illustrious families, Breckinridge had been a congressman, vice president under James Buchanan, and presidential candidate of the Southern Democrats in 1860. When compromise failed, Breckinridge organized a Confederate government for Kentucky. One of the better "political" generals, Breckinridge commanded the reserve corps at Shiloh. As a major general, he fought at Vicksburg, Stones River, Chickamauga, and Missionary Ridge. Transferring to the Army of Northern Virginia, he saw action at Cold Harbor and in February 1865 became secretary of war. He died at the age of fifty-four in 1875. Breckinridge to Thomas Jordan, *OR*, 1, 10, 1:613; and Lowell H. Harrison, "John C. Breckinridge," *Encyclopedia of the Confederacy*, 1:213-14.

[4] See Ulysses S. Grant, "The Battle of Shiloh," *Century Magazine* 29 (February 1885): 593-613.

[5] An 1846 graduate of Princeton, the five-feet one-inch tall Hindman fought in Mexico and practiced law in Mississippi. In 1861, he recruited the 2d Arkansas Infantry. At Shiloh, Hindman command the 1st Brigade (mostly Arkansas regiments) of Maj. Gen W.J. Hardee's 3d Corps. After Shiloh be was promoted major general and led the Confederate forces in defeat at Prairie Grove, Arkansas. Wounded at Chickamauga, he returned to action at Chattanooga, but was partially blinded at Kennesaw Mountain. Disabled, he moved to Mexico for three years but returned to Helena, Arkansas, where he was assassinated in 1868. Organization of the Army of Mississippi, *OR*, 1, 10, 1:382-83; and Anne J. Bailey, "Thomas C. Hindman," *Encyclopedia of the Confederacy*, 2:776-77.

[6] Moore graduated from West Point in 1849, but resigned his commission in 1855 to teach school in Tennessee. At the beginning of the Civil War, he was commissioned a captain of artillery and placed in command of the defenses of Galveston. Elected colonel of the 2d Texas Infantry, he was later promoted brigadier general. After Shiloh, he fought at Corinth and Vicksburg. Later assigned to the defenses of Mobile, he resigned in February 1864 and returned to Texas to teach school. Moore died on 31 December 1910. Wright, *Texas in the War*, 88-89.

Twenty-four years later, Baylor recalled: "At that time, Calhoun Benham, also on the general's staff and myself, by the general's permission, went into the charge made by the 2nd Texas Infantry. It was their maiden effort and right well did they sustain the name of Texas. We were pitted again[st] some Western troops and it was diamond cut diamond. Benham and I both got in a pretty large assortment of charging right then and there." Baylor to E.C. Wharton, 21 August 1886, Albert Sidney Johnston Papers, Jenkins Garrett Library, University of Texas at Arlington.

[7] A United States congressman, Chalmers rose from captain to brigadier general and served under Bragg at Shiloh where he led several charges against the final Union line. Chalmers fought at Stones River, became a division commander under Maj. Gen. Nathan Bedford Forrest, and was present at the Fort Pillow Massacre in April 1864. After the war, he practiced law at Memphis, Tennessee, until his death on 9 April 1898. Brian S. Wills, "James Ronald Chalmers," *Encyclopedia of the Confederacy*, 1:275-76.

[8] Hardcastle commanded the 3d Mississippi Infantry Brigade. Hardcastle to S.A.M. Wood, n.d., *OR*, 1, 10, 1:602-4.

[9] McNair, captain of Company H of the 3d Mississippi Battalion, was mortally wounded at Shiloh. Ibid.

[10] From Ysleta, Texas, in 1886, Baylor could still recall the scene: "The Genl. had on a Confed[erate] grey coat with his insignia of rank, a forage cap, a pair of dark pants, not grey, cavalry boots and his sword and belt. Gen. Wm. Preston was dressed in full uniform, grey cloth, as also were Col. Nat[haniel] Wickliffe, Maj. Albert J. Smith, Capt. Leigh Wickham, Major OHarra [O'Hara] and Tom Jack. I wore a grey cap I got in N[ew] O[rleans] such as the L[ouisian]a troops had, grey pants and coat. I had my sword and ivory handled six shooter, and also carried a fine double barreled shot gun given me by citizens of Denton Co[unty] for killing some Indians in 1860. I remember on dismounting, I set my gun against a post oak tree. Governor Harris, as well as I can remember, had on citizens dress of some dark material and black felt hat. Dr. Yandell had my blue coat. . . . I remember so

well when we were getting ready to mount, Dr. Yandell put his hand on my shoulder, and said in his kind way, "George, you will be in some hot places today and blue is not a good color. Take my coat and I will wear yours as I will not be in as much danger." So we swapped coats and I wore a surgeon's uniform. It gave me some heart pangs too as several poor fellows called to me, "Oh, Doctor, for God sake, can't you help me." I can't recall if Major Mumford, [Lt. Col.] Gil[mer] or [Captain] Brewster were present. [Captain] Hayden was, I think, but he can speak for himself. General Johnston had three horses, one a beautiful chestnut Arabian stallion given, I think, by citizens of Baltimore, quite fiery, and I was elected to take the starch out of him generally. His favorite horse was a large dappled grey, but on this day he rode a bay, almost black horse, and I think Major Hayden afterwards owned him. The horse received an ugly wound in the left ham about half way between the hock and tail. I remember noticing the blood ran down to his hoof. I rode a beautiful little black horse, three white feet and a star on his forehead. I got him at Bowling Green, with saddle and rigging made in Texas style." Baylor to W.C. Wharton, 21 August 1886, Johnston Papers, Jenkins Garrett Library, University of Texas at Arlington.

11 As governor of Tennessee, Harris led the secession movement in his state and helped to raise and arm troops for the Confederacy. After the fall of Forts Henry and Donelson, he moved the state capital to Memphis. A member of General Johnston's staff at Shiloh, Harris went on to serve in virtually every campaign of the Army of Tennessee. When he was charged with treason after the war, he fled to Mexico but returned in 1867 to Memphis where he was elected to the United States Senate. He died in Washington, D.C., in June 1897. Charles F. Bryan, Jr., "Isham G. Harris," *Encyclopedia of the Confederacy*, 2:745-46; G.T. Beauregard to S. Cooper, 11 April 1862, *OR*, 1, 10, 1:385-92; and W. Preston to Thomas Jordan, 20 April 1862, *OR*, 1, 10, 1:403-5.

12 Baylor later recalled the setting: "The creek where our line was formed, forked about fifty or sixty yards below where General Johnston fell. He was in a depression of the ground between the forks and probably about 75 yards from our line. The ground being higher between [the lines], we could not see them except when standing up. As well as I could see for the smoke, the Federals were on an elevation beyond the creek, the ground rising from the creek back towards [the] Federal line. . . . If no changes have been made I could go to the very spot. General J[ohnston] rode some distance after being wounded and was caught in Governor Harris['] arms when falling from his horse, the governor and Wickham lifting him down." Baylor to E.C. Wharton, 21 August 1886, Johnston Papers, Jenkins Garrett Library, University of Texas at Arlington.

13 Ridley, who led the march overland from Los Angeles, California, to Mesilla, New Mexico Territory, in July 1861, later served as a major in Col. George T. Madison's 3d Regiment of the Arizona Brigade.

For Phillips, see n. 34, Ch. 1, Sec. II.

CHAPTER FOUR

My Troubles with General John A. Wharton

AFTER GEN. JOHN R. BAYLOR WAS DEPRIVED OF HIS COMMAND by President Davis the brigade was broken up and the 2nd and 3rd Regiments under myself and Col. Joseph Phillips were ordered to Louisiana post haste (as the brigade under General Sibley had been defeated at Camp Bisland) and with Col. [Isham] Chi[su]m's Regiment formed the Brigade known as Major's Brigade and commanded by Gen. James P[atrick] Major, a graduate of West Point, I being senior colonel.[1]

The brigade fought through all the campaigns in Louisiana and at the capture of Brashier City, a good portion of my men and some selected from other regiments of [Gen. Tom] Green's old brigade under Maj. Sherod Hunter of my regiment crossed the Atchafalaya in the night in skiffs, sugar coolers or any old thing that could be rowed and came on the Federals rear whil'st General Green engaging their attention in front and with the Valverde Battery engaged with a Federal tin clad gunboat.[2] I was placed in command of the men on the island formed at [the] mouth of Bayou Teche and could do nothing but stand the shelling from the Yankee battery opposite—but we were first to cross and raise the Confederate's beautiful battle flag on the enemy's work—it had just been made by my young wife of [the] best material and was greeted by the Rebels with their historic yell. Major's Brigade did well in all the fights in Louisiana and were run back and forth between Louisiana and Texas to repel invasion—and when Gen. [Nathaniel P.] Banks commenced his triumphal march to Mansfield, my regiment that was in Texas at the time [and] was ordered at once to join the brigade then under command of that gallant old Texan, Gen. Walter P. Lane (the youngest soldier at San Jacinto), and crossed the Sabine on hearing of the cannon of the Yankee Army that was driving the Confederates before them.[3] In the morning as they passed through Mansfield on the trot the patriotic and beautiful women of that city cheered them on, and the regiment after joining the brigade, was soon engaged in a sharp skirmish at Wilson's Farm.[4]

The next day, the Battle of Mansfield was fought and the complete victory of [Gen. Richard] Taylor over Banks is a matter of history.[5] General Lane who had served all through the war of the Republic and United States against Mexico was wounded and I, being senior colonel, took command of the brigade (then known as Lane's Brigade and was so called to the close of the campaign at Yellow Bayou).[6]

Gen. [Arthur Pendleton] Bagby was in command of the Division at the Battle of Mansfield—Lane's Brigade joined with [the] N[ew] O[rleans] Crescent Infantry Regiment that had been almost decimated by concentrated cross fire of Yankee Infantry lying down behind a fence and resting guns on the rails—most of their officers had been killed and the regiment was lying down protected by formation of the ground to some extent.[7] Our division— Lane's and Green's brigades under those brave old Texans—were dismounted in line of battle completely covered from the enemy's fire though they knew our location and kept the air humming with minie balls raising such a dust in the open field two or three hundred yards wide, we could hardly see through it. General Bagby could not be located at this moment, but these two brave old soldiers knew that victory depended on our immediate action—General Green, I was told, ordered the charge to be made. My regiment was on the side of the brigade and orders came for me to take the lead—I never expected to get across the field but did make the longest speech of the war—"Boys, there are the Yankees, the sooner we get to the fence the better for us and worse for the Yanks, forward, double quick" and so we did—it was a grand sight to see our men as they swept forward yelling like demons. We turned the enemy's right and I claim the honor for Baylor's Regiment of leading the charge that gained the Battle of Mansfield. We took 800 or 1,000 prisoners but most of these further West escaped, their last volley killed Gen. [Jean Jacques Alfred Alexander] Mouton, one of the bravest of the brave; General Lane was wounded in this charge.[8]

The Battle of Pleasant Hill was fought and might be called in slang parlance, a "dog fall," both sides fighting with great bravery but Banks continued his retreat, the Confederates following, and harassing him to his gunboats at Grand Ecore, where, if one of the greatest blunders of the war had not occurred—Gen. [Andrew Jackson] Smith our main force to meet Gen.

[William] Steel[e] who would have retreated as soon as he had heard of General Banks defeat—General Banks army and the Federal Navy would have been captured at that point, but only to prolong the war and cause more precious blood to be shed.[9] General Green having been killed while rashly exposed to [the] fire of a gunboat at Blair['s] Landing, Gen. H[amilton] P[rioleau] Bee, senior officer, took command and after Gen. Tom Green's vigorous style of fighting, his old command passed some very severe criticisms of General Bee's conduct of the campaign, but there never was a purer or braver man than Ham. P. Bee—he only lacked experience.[10]

After the Yankee army reached Alexandria and got their gunboats out of Chancery they began to move down the river. General Major, who now commanded a corps, ordered me with Lane's brigade to Red River below Alexandria to stop any supplies going to Banks or news getting below and in this the Brigade did good service capturing the *City Bell* with troops and afterwards the destruction of the gunboats *Covington, Signal No. 8,* and *[John] Warner,* a steamboat.[11] Green's command came in to the river and were engaged also. On learning that Gen. W[illiam] P[olk] Hardeman (Old Gotch) was on the field, I reported to him at once, but that grand old Texan with his usual modesty only said, "Oh you go ahead, you are doing very well."[12]

It was now that Gen. John A. Wharton appeared on the scene. Banks with his overwhelming army left Red River and began to move by way of Marksville and Mansura towards the mouth of Yellow Bayou where the Federal gunboats, their haven of rest, would stop the pursuit of their enemies. Lane's Brigade had been engaged with the enemy until dark and opened the fight next morning at daylight; [Col. Augustus C.] Buchel's Regiment under command of Lt. Col. [William O.] Yager, having been ordered to report to me, was placed on my right in the advance across Marksville's Prairie.[13] The Federals moved forward steadily using artillery almost exclusively, the Confederate batteries replying—there was probably more noise and less execution done than at any time during the campaign. Lane's Brigade had by hard work gotten two 32 pd. Parrot Rifles and plenty [of] ammunition off of one of the gunboats captured and they out classed the Yankees as to calibre and range, but numbers prevailed. During the move across the prairie, General Wharton and staff rode up to me and the general said in rather a brusque manner, "Colonel Baylor, why are you falling back, why don't you strengthen your skirmishers?" I replied, "General, my whole brigade as well as Buchel['s] Regiment are now on the skirmish line." General Wharton rode off and in less than fifteen minutes afterwards our entire force had to get out of the road in a hurry and the Yankee army passed in review, but we closed in behind them and it was a continuous fight and a foot race to Yellow Bayou where their gunboats and transportation [were] waiting for them.

The Confederates were crowding close on their heels and they turned at bay, savage as an Andalusian bull, with our constant prodding. Hardeman's Brigade was on their left, a bayou on their left, Lane's Brigade on their right and fortunately in thick timber. After the first charge, in which we met double our numbers with artillery, Hardeman's command fell back exposed to heavy artillery and rifle fire, and Lane's in consequence, being flanked, also retreated but preserving line of battle and making a charge, drove the enemy back. After they had reformed in an open sugar field and were expected to make another attack, General Major naturally came up to see his old brigade and speak encouragement and hope to them and came to where I was with his staff. I said to him, "General, I don't like the looks of this thing just now, Gen. [Camille Armand Jules Marie Prince de] Polignac with our infantry is, I learn, three miles to the rear and the Yanks are getting away as fast as they can and I am glad of it for Banks could turn around now and march back to Texas if he only knew it."[14] Major replied, "Colonel, I want you to understand that this is not my fight but General Wharton's." I answered, "That may do for you, general, but it is my fight; my men are going in and I am going with them. I don't want to see them uselessly butchered." The command was given to move forward and we again struck the enemy who had greatly enforced their line and were again driven back and more men were killed and captured than had been during the retreat from Pleasant Hill.

The next day, myself and my colonels were asked to report at General Wharton's headquarters. We were expecting compliments for gallantry, but instead the general reprimanded us for criticizing the campaign and saying it was ended, for he intended to water his horse in the Mississippi in front of New Orleans. As these officers had tried that once but failed, the reprimand was not appreciated and subsequent events showed that the brigade fell back to Bayou Bouef and ate up all the black berries in a mile of camp and several tons of farmer's sugar.

At this time I received a telegram from my mother-in-law, Mrs. J.S. Sydnor, at Houston saying, "If you wish to see your wife alive again you must hurry home." General Major gave me permission to leave at once and an application for thirty days furlough was sent to Gen. [Edmund] Kirby Smith.[15] On my arrival in Houston, I found my young wife better but very low and asked for an extension of twenty days. This was approved by Generals Kirby Smith, Magruder, Walker, and Lane, but General Wharton wrote across the back of the application, "I know nothing of the condition of Mrs. Baylor's health, Colonel Baylor is needed with his regiment." Here was a pretty broad hint that I had lied to get an extension of my furlough! So I returned to my regiment after a short stay and found instead of having been needed I was not needed; several ambitious officers wanted to command the brigade since General Lane had not fully recovered. When my regiment was organized at Eagle Lake, I had eight companies in camp and two ordered to report, but as they were western men and were ordered east they went west to some other command. Two cavalry companies raised for [William H.] Griffin's Battery had been ordered and did report to the regiment in Louisiana, Captains Marsh and Duncan, but as soon as I learned that Col. [Ashley W.] Spaight, a gallant officer then in command of the battery, would be reduced from lieutenant colonel to major, I made a personal request that these two companies be returned to Texas and their battalion.

There was so much friction that I decided to lay the matter before President Davis, and bidding farewell to my regiment, returned to Texas. General Magruder gave me a most flattering letter to the president recommending that I be promoted to brigadier general. This was endorsed by Gen. John G. Walker, and at Shreveport by Gen. Kirby Smith, and I started for Richmond. President Davis had appointed me colonel and I wanted to have the matter of rank settled. As a miserable train of circumstances would have it, General Wharton met me just as I came out of General Smith's office and after mutual greetings, asked me where I was going and being told, said, "Colonel Baylor we have learned that Texas is to be invaded this winter by a formidable army. Gen. [Winfield Scott] Hancock is to land at the mouth of the Brazos and will enlist all the Negroes in his army and Banks or other will attack our coast cities, you can do more than anyone else with your regiment. I wish you would return to Texas with us." I replied, "General, I have been greatly worried about the question of my rank and I am willing to return, but as I have been fighting as a colonel and commanding a brigade, I won't report to any officer who is my junior and especially Col. David S. Terry, and Col. A[lexander] W[atkins] Terrell for I have reason to believe they have taken advantage of my being in the field to take companies raised for me to make regiments for themselves and would have gall enough to dispute my rank on the field of battle so I won't report to either of them."[16] General Wharton's reply was, "You can go back to your regiment, colonel, and *I promise you no more trouble on account of your rank.*"[17] With this assurance I rejoined my regiment. After the regiment reached Texas and was stationed near Bryan two more companies, Captain Sorrell and Capt. Ben McCullough, Jr., being commanders, were added to my regiment. A short time afterwards the regiment was dismounted, much to the disgust of officers and men as it was one of the oldest cavalry regiments—it seemed there must be some favoritism shown in other quarters. The regiment was then ordered to Millican, that being the terminus of the Texas Central Railway at that time, and about one third of the men limped into camp with bruised heels and skinned ankles the second day's march.

A short time afterwards, Lieutenant Bell of General Wharton's staff came to the regiment and brought a verbal order for me to report to Col. David S. Terry with my regiment and on asking what that meant, said, "Terry is to be made a brigadier general and your regiment, Terry's, and another are to form the brigade." My answer to this order was "Lieutenant Bell, you go back to General Wharton and tell him I'll see him in Hell first." Bell then said, "I would not send such a message as that, you will be court martialed and probably dismissed from the army." "All right," I said, "then I will be dismissed but won't be imposed on any longer. General Wharton and I have an agreement on this very point and he will understand just what I mean."

I and Bell left on the same train, the latter stopped off at Hempstead and General Wharton never received the message or he would have been justified in being mad enough at such a message from a colonel to the major general commanding, unless he should have recalled the conversation at Shreveport.

On my arrival in Houston, I went straight to General Magruder's office but he was not in. Gen. Walter P. Lane was at the Central Depot ready to leave on the train, [and] hearing that I had come down on the Central, sent one of his staff after me and asked me to come at once to the train as he was anxious to see me. I went at once and was very warmly received by my old commander for whom I felt the warmest attachment—he and an older brother Walker Baylor or Doc. Baylor on the muster rolls of troops at San Jacinto, had served with him in the same company, Patterson's, at the Battle of San Jacinto. He told me he had come down to see Magruder and was going to organize his old brigade and hearing I had had trouble about my rank, asked that my regiment be remounted and assigned to his command. I told him I was glad to hear it and would be only too glad to serve under him again. I then started to go to the Fannin House where my wife was with her father and family and, as my evil star destined, I met General Wharton just after crossing the bridge over Buffalo Bayou, driven in a buggy by Gen. [James Edward] Harrison of Waco.[18]

I did not notice who it was until opposite them when General Wharton addressed me about as one would at the time on seeing a strange Negro about the house with the query, "What are you doing here, sir?" My answer was, "I came down on business to see General Magruder." He said, "Your place, sir, is with your regiment." I answered, "I think, General Wharton, I know something about army regulations and army etiquette. I am commanding officer at Millican [and have] a right to come down in the interest of my regiment and especially in regard to my rank, for I want to say to you, I have stood about as much of that as I intend to." This led to a heated reply from him and a rejoinder from me. I told him he was trying to foist his political friends over my head into positions and I regarded him as "an infernal demagogue." He rose from his seat and yelled, "you are a damned liar." I sprang at him as soon as the words were uttered and we exchanged blows. I then stepped back and drew my revolver half way out of the scabbard. General Harrison struck the horse moving a little away but General Wharton grabbed the reins and stopped him; I had expected him to draw a pistol and only waited to see and then said, "General Wharton, it does seem to me, sir, that we certainly have enough Yankees to fight without fighting each other, and if you will wait until the war is over we could settle our difficulty in five minutes." He replied, "I will meet you, sir, anyway you choose to name." I then said, "We will drop the matter then, until after the war," [and] turned and walked away.

General Harrison told me afterwards that General Wharton was furious and after he got to the depot, the longer he talked the more furious he became. I didn't blame him, for when we both got mad, the compliments that passed between us were none of the mildest, and had he received my message sent in a moment of intense indignation he would have been justified in breaking a fence rail over my head. General [Harrison] said, "I tried to persuade him to get on the train and go on to Hempstead where his friends and kindred had prepared an ovation for him, but he would not listen to me and said, 'Did you see Baylor start to draw his pistol.' 'Yes, I did and that's why I struck the horse to move on.' It is sad to think now he did not heed the danger signal and go on to his loving wife, mother and sweet little daughter and kindred for he was a man that loved his friends and hated his enemies.

I went at once to see General Magruder and found him in his private room and on being admitted, found him alone and at once I related what had occurred and said, "General, you by authority of the president appointed me a colonel and I want you to define my status." He answered at once, "You are a colonel and I intend to support you, but you are excited colonel, sit down. I am going out for a minute and when I return we will talk the matter over. As there was only one chair in the room, I sat down on the foot of his bed in no very amiable frame of mind. I heard the tramp of two men coming down the hall and when one of them knocked on the door, said, come in, and General Wharton opened the door and walked in, apparently as much astonished as I was as I thought him on the way to Hempstead and he had expected to see General Magruder. His first question was, "Where is Magruder?" "He has gone out but will return in a moment," I answered. He resumed our quarrel, saying, "Colonel Baylor you insulted me this morning." "General Wharton," I answered, "you must remember, sir, we were both angry and I leave to this gentleman (turning to General Harrison who had stepped in also) to say who was right or wrong. You insulted me and called me a damn liar." "Yes," he almost shrieked, "you are a damned liar" and sprang at me with the fierceness of a tiger. It was so sudden and unexpected to me after our agreement to drop the matter. He struck me a glancing blow on my cheek, throwing me on my back on the bed. I drew up both feet and kicking him in the stomach, sent him across the narrow room—his head and shoulders striking the wall. I then straightened up and drew my revolver and cocked it—General Harrison then sprang between us and grabbed my pistol by the barrel and tried to take it from me. Wharton advanced on me still and feeling that my own life was in danger, I jerked my pistol from Harrison's hand and fired under his arm. General Harrison had pushed me back until I just could distinguish Wharton as he advanced and knew he was a hot headed impervious man, totally unconscious of fear, and supposed he came back armed to seek me—he should have been armed. General Harrison spoke as soon as General Wharton fell, saying, "Colonel, he was totally unarmed." I answered, "General, I had no right or reason to know it or I should have never used my pistol."

In speaking of this afterwards General Harrison said General Wharton had seemed so worried over my language that General Harrison thought if he could get my pistol away and let us have a round with our fists it might satisfy him. "That was a good idea," I said, "provided you had let me know before hand, but General Wharton ought to have known that to resume the quarrel and use the same offensive epithet meant a fight and probably death to one or both of us."

I trust everyone who knows me personally will believe me when I say the whole thing was a matter of sorrow and regret to me. I had known his wife, a lovely woman, and little girl, who were once placed under my escort on a trip from Hempstead to Houston—and his old mother was of the type only to be described as a Roman matron. In her early struggle for liberty, Texas had been well represented at San Jacinto by the Whartons.[19] I had a nephew, Maj. E.C. Wharton, a distant connection, so there was really no reason why we should not have been the best of friends. An evil destiny willed otherwise.

Gen. John R. Baylor did not present my recommendations for promotion to President Davis as he afterwards told me, as the president was greatly worried as he saw the days of the Confederacy numbered. I told him I would have been proud to have been known as a brigadier general, C.S.A., if only for a day. On what straw does the destiny of men and nations sometimes rest?

Had I been promoted there would have been no order to report to Col. David S. Terry and no quarrel with General Wharton. Gen. Walter P. Lane could have claimed his brigade with me and the regiments intended for Terry, or had Wharton gone to Hempstead, we would have heard of the surrender of Lee. I am sure I would have felt more like embracing him in tears for both our hearts were in the cause.

There was a great deal of feeling in the army among'st mutual friends and a clash seemed eminent at that time. Col. Peter Hardeman and his regiment were stationed near Houston and after I was arrested and put into the courthouse, he sent me a note.[20] I burned it for fear of getting him into trouble, but I will never forget its wording: "Dear George, I hear Wharton's friends talk of mobbing you tonight. I want you and your wife to sleep soundly and fear no evil, I have issued ammunition to my men, we will be in Houston tonight and if a shot is fired, we will close in around the courthouse and kill everyone we find outside of it. Peter Hardeman."

I felt no uneasiness for the captain of the company acting as guards had said to me, "Colonel, I understand there is some talk of a mob, and although I am a friend of Wharton's, I want you to know I will defend you as long as I have a man or a cartridge left and will give you your pistol to defend yourself." I received numerous messages and telegrams from my own and other regiments of Green's old brigade. One was "The best shot ever fired in the Trans Mississippi Department," another—"If you don't want to be confined, say so, and we will take you out and destroy the courthouse."

I was turned loose on surrender of the C.S.A. by General Taylor and placed under bond and after a tedious trial acquitted. Col. George Mason, who was one of my attorneys, came to me before the trial and said, "Colonel, you can get rid of a trial, as it has been hinted strongly to me by the prosecuting attorney that the court holds if you put in a plea that you killed a public enemy of the United States, you will be released." I was very much angered that such a proposition should be made and answered with considerable wrath, "No, Sir! General Wharton was a brave Confederate soldier and we were both Rebels—I will be hung as high as Haemin before I will enter any such plea!" In conclusion, I can say I was acquitted by my countrymen and my own conscience; and as much as I regret and deplore the sad tragedy, under the same circumstances, I would do the same thing again.

NOTES

1 For Phillips, see n. 34, Ch. 1, Sec. II. As a prelude to moving up the Red River for an advance against East Texas, Banks sent Federal gunboats into the Atchafalaya River and Grand Lake. Driving the Confederates back in the Battle of Bisland and Irish Bend on 13 April 1863, Banks occupied Franklin and captured the temporary state capital at Opelousas, thereby forcing the Louisiana state government to retreat to Shreveport. As a result of his drunken demeanor at Fort Bisland, Gen. Henry H. Sibley was court-martialed, and although acquitted, he was replaced by Col. Tom Green, who was promoted to brigadier general. Green, who was widely respected in the brigade, had commanded the 5th Texas Mounted Rifles during the New Mexico Campaign and at Galveston. Thompson, *Henry Hopkins Sibley,* 324-31.

Chisum commanded the 2d Regiment of Partisan Rangers, which fought at Mansfield and Pleasant Hill. In early 1865, the regiment was dismounted and assigned to Gen. John G. Walker's division.

Major, an 1856 West Point graduate from Missouri, served in the elite 2d Cavalry in Texas before the war. Major joined Gen. Earl Van Dorn's staff as acting chief of artillery early in the war and remained in that position until Van Dorn's death. In July 1863, following the Bayou Teche campaign, he was promoted brigadier general. Major saw action at Mansfield and Pleasant Hill. After the war, he moved to France but returned to Texas where he died in Austin on 7 May 1877. Anne J. Bailey, "James Patrick Major," *Encyclopedia of the Confederacy*, 3:990.

2 Using sugar coolers for boats and with muffled oars, Major Hunter, with 325 volunteers, paddled down Bayou Teche and the Atchafalaya River to strike the rear of Brashear City at sunrise, 23 June 1863. As the Valverde battery from Green's Brigade (formerly Sibley's) opened fire from across the bay, Hunter's force advanced in two columns, overrunning the Federal garrison. More than 1,200 Federal prisoners, many of them convalescents, were captured. Forty-six Federals were killed and forty wounded. Eleven guns were taken as well as 2,500 rifles and over 200 wagons. Rebel losses were placed at three killed and eighteen wounded. L. Boyd Finch, "Sunrise at Brashear City: Sherod Hunter's Sugar Cooler Cavalry," *Louisiana History* 25 (Fall 1984): 403-34. Also, Hunter to General Mouton, 26 June 1863, *OR*, 1, 26, 1:223-24.

After studying law in Tennessee, Green came to Texas in 1835 and helped to man the famous "Twin Sisters" as a private at the Battle of San Jacinto. He fought Comanches, served as a lieutenant colonel in the Texas army during Gen. Rafael Vásquez's invasion of Texas in March 1842, was in the ill-fated Somervell Expedition that followed, and fought under Col. John Coffee Hays at the Battle of Monterrey during the Mexican-American War. After leading the Sibley Brigade in the recapture of Galveston on 1 January 1863, he was promoted to brigadier general and led the brigade at Mansfield and Pleasant Hill. He was decapitated while leading a drunken and suicidal attack on Federal gunboats at Blair's Landing on the Red River on 12 April 1864. Tom Green is often confused with Thomas Jefferson Green, second in command of the Somervell Expedition, who surrendered to Gen. Pedro Ampudia at Mier in 1842 and was imprisoned at Perote. Odie B. Faulk, *General Tom Green: Fightin' Texan* (Waco: Texian Press, 1963); Alwyn Barr, "Tom Green: The Forrest of the Trans Mississippi," *Lincoln Herald,* 88:2, 39-42; Johnson, *Red River Campaign,* 132-50; Winters, *Civil War in Louisiana*, 358-59; Hall, *Confederate Army of New Mexico,* 132-38; and Thompson, *Henry Hopkins Sibley*, 334-35.

The Valverde Battery, commanded by Capt. Joseph Draper Sayers, future governor of Texas, was organized after the capture of Capt. Alexander McRae's Battery at the Battle of Valverde. Originally equipped with "six brass pieces, two twelve pound[er] field pieces, three six pound[er] guns, and one pound[er] howitzer," the battery fought in Texas and Louisiana. Two of the guns are at Mejia and Fairfield, Texas, today. Hall, *Confederate Army of New Mexico*, 289-90; San Antonio *Herald*, 12 July 1862; P.N. Broune, "Captain T.D. Neddles and the Valverde Battery," *Texana* 2 (no. 1).

3 One-time Republican governor of Massachusetts, Banks commanded the Department of the Gulf. After driving the Confederates back in the Battle of Bisland and Irish Bend in April 1863, he began a push up the Red River toward the new Louisiana capital of Shreveport.

Lane, from County Cork, Ireland, was a veteran of San Jacinto and the battles of Monterrey and Buena Vista during the Mexican-American War. On a scouting expedition south of Saltillo, Lane captured and held the mayor of Salado until he yielded up the bones of the men of the Mier Expedition who had been executed in the notorious black bean incident. On 2 July 1861, Lane was commissioned a lieutenant colonel in the 3d Texas Cavalry and fought at Wilson's Creek, Chustenallah, and Pea Ridge. Although severely wounded at Mansfield, he was promoted brigadier general. Lane died at Marshall, Texas, on 28 January 1892. "No braver man than Gen. Lane ever lived," Baylor wrote on p. 98 of his copy of H.S. Thrall's *A History of Texas*. Wright, *Texas in the War*, 85-86; and Warner, *Generals in Gray,* 173-74.

4 On the afternoon of 7 April 1864, at Wilson's Farm, some three miles north of Pleasant Hill, Union cavalry under Gen. A.L. Lee ran into four regiments of Green's Brigade. The Confederates charged the Federals with a yell and it was not until Union reinforcements were rushed forward that the Rebels were finally repulsed. Johnson, *Red River Campaign*, 124-25. Baylor reported: "On the 7th instant . . . my regiment was placed on the left wing, and was strongly posted on the crest of a hill, being dismounted . . . The enemy charged boldly up to within 50 yards of our position, but the men stood their ground firmly, loading and firing with great coolness. This close work soon became too hot for the enemy and when we charged them with a yell they broke in confusion. . . . We drove them back nearly a mile when we found them in greatly superior force, and were obliged in turn to fall back to prevent being flanked." Geo. Wythe Baylor to Captain Ogden, 18 April 1864, *OR*, 1, 34, 1:616-17.

5 On 8 April 1864, General Taylor decisively turned back General Banks's advance on Shreveport. Union soldiers were soundly routed, losing twenty cannon, scores of wagons, and hundreds of prisoners. Of the 12,000 Federals who were engaged, 2,235 were killed, wounded, or captured. Confederate losses were half those of the Federals. Baylor reported: "We were moved forward and found the enemy in force strongly posted behind a fence in the woods. We had to cross an open field half a mile in face of their artillery and infantry; drove them from their position, captured one piece of artillery and a number of prisoners. . . . The loss in my regiment was quite severe in killed and wounded." Baylor to Ogden, 18 April 1864, *OR*, 1, 34, 1:616-17

Kentucky-born Yale graduate Taylor was the son of Pres. Zachary Taylor and brother of Jefferson Davis's first wife. Widely acclaimed for his intelligence and wit, Taylor proved during the 1862 Shenandoah campaign and the Seven Days before Richmond, to be one of Maj. Gen. Thomas J. "Stonewall" Jackson's most effective brigadiers. Promoted to major general in July 1862, he was assigned to command the District of West Louisiana. In the spring of 1864 he was responsible for the repulse of Banks's Red River expedition at Mansfield and Pleasant Hill. Shortly before his death in New York City on 12 April 1879, Taylor finished his *Destruction and Reconstruction,* thought by many historians to be the finest memoir of the Civil War era. Taylor was later entombed in Metairie Cemetery, New Orleans. T. Michael Parrish, *Richard Taylor: Soldier Prince of Dixie* (Chapel Hill: University of North Carolina Press, 1992).

6 For two hours in terrible heat on 18 May 1864 at Norwood's Plantation (or Yellow Bayou), south of Mansura, Union and Confederate forces clashed as Taylor attempted to prevent General Banks's Federals from crossing the Atchafalaya River. Gen. Andrew J. Smith's Federal Division held off General Major's dismounted cavalry division and Polignac's brigade of Texans, as the Union forces slipped away. Union losses were placed at 350, while Confederate casualties were 608. Yellow Bayou, the final action of the Red River Campaign, allowed the Union forces to escape downriver. Anne J. Bailey, "Chasing Banks out of Louisiana: Parson's Texas Cavalry in the Red River Campaign," *Civil War Regiments,* 2 (no. 3): 223-35. In the margin on page forty-nine of his copy of *Bull Run to Bull Run,* George Baylor wrote: "My horse was shot thro[ugh] the neck at Yellow Bayou & began going around backward like a crawfish. I yelled to my men just behind me, 'Look out boys, you have shot my horse.' They answered, 'Look over there, Col., you'll see who wounded your horse,' & to my left some 60 yds in the woods, I saw a group of officers & escort & opened fire with my revolver & soon scattered them."

7 Bagby, an 1852 West Point graduate from Alabama, resigned from the army in 1855 to study law. Three years later he moved to Gonzales, Texas. Early in the war, Bagby served in Sibley's New Mexico Campaign as a major in the 7th Texas Cavalry. In the summer of 1862, following the Confederate retreat from northern New Mexico, he was court-martialed for drunkenness and drawing a pistol on a fellow officer. Acquitted, he was promoted to colonel of the 7th Texas and fought well at Galveston on 1 January 1863 and at Mansfield and Pleasant Hill, and was promoted to major general in May 1865. After the war, Bagby returned to his law practice and died at Hallettsville, Texas, on 21 February 1921. Roy R. Stephenson, "Arthur P. Bagby," *Encyclopedia of the Confederacy,* 1:121; and Martin H. Hall, "The Court-Martial of Arthur Pendleton Bagby, C.S.A.," *East Texas Historical Journal* 49 (April 1974).

The Crescent Regiment under Col. James Beard sustained two hundred casualties at Mansfield. Winters, *Civil War in Louisiana,* 342.

8 Mouton, son of Alexander Mouton, governor of Louisiana and United States senator, graduated from West Point in 1850. At the beginning of the Civil War, he was elected colonel of the 18th Louisiana Infantry and was severely wounded on the second day at Shiloh. Promoted brigadier general, he commanded a brigade in the Bayou Teche campaign. He was killed at the head of his division at Mansfield in the charge that routed the Federal right. Thomas J. Legg, "Alfred Mouton," *Encyclopedia of the Confederacy,* 3:1092; Winters, *Civil War in Louisiana,* 342.

9 At Pleasant Hill, early on the morning of 9 April 1864, General Banks's 18,000 demoralized Federals rallied to turn back General Taylor's 13,000 advancing Confederates. On the verge of victory, Taylor suffered a resounding defeat, losing 1,621 men to Banks's 1,369. Despite his tactical victory, however, Banks continued his retreat the following day while Taylor regrouped and then pursued. Baylor reported: "On the morning of the 9th, we were ordered forward in pursuit, Colonel Madison in the advance. We found every evidence of a disorderly retreat—burned wagons, the dead and wounded scattered along the

road. We captured many prisoners who were left in the retreat. We overtook the enemy's rear guard about 3 miles from Pleasant Hill, and soon came on the main body drawn up in line of battle. Were ordered to dismount and skirmish, which we did, drawing the fire of their artillery. . . . Late in the evening our infantry and artillery came up, when we were ordered to charge. We immediately mounted and moved forward. . . . General Major then ordered our brigade to the left wing, where we were dismounted and attacked the enemy in flank and drove them rapidly back to their breast-works, which had been hastily made of pine saplings and rails. The fighting was close and hot. . . . The enemy had a very strong position. The pine logs and rails, of which I have spoken, were piled up at a right angle with the main road. Behind this the enemy were lying and could only be shot when in the act of firing. Across a small inclosure and in rear of this temporary work was an abrupt hollow running parallel with it, where the enemy were securely posted in heavy numbers. We were not strong enough to dislodge them or flank them. Our position was such that we received a good portion of Buchel's fire, which we returned. It was now becoming dark and difficult to distinguish friend from foe. . . . A little more daylight would have enabled us, with Polignac's division, to flank the enemy, but General Polignac not knowing the enemy's position did not wish to risk his men under so many cross-fires from friend and foe." Baylor to Ogden, 18 April 1864, *OR*, 1, 34, 1:617-18. Also, Winters, *Civil War in Louisiana*, 349-57.

Smith, an 1838 West Point graduate, served in the 1st Dragoons before the war. Smith rose steadily to become a major general in May 1864 and command elements of the 16th and 17th Corps under General Banks in the Red River Campaign. He served for four years in the Regular Army after the war and died in St. Louis on 30 January 1897. Warner, *Generals in Blue*, 454; and Winters, *Civil War in Louisiana*, 349-56.

Steel, West Point class of 1840, commanded a portion of the 7th Texas Cavalry during Sibley's New Mexico Campaign. Promoted to brigadier general in September 1862, he took command of Confederate forces in Indian Territory but was ordered to Louisiana to reinforce General Taylor during the Red River campaign. Steele commanded a brigade in General Green's division at Mansfield and Pleasant Hill and took command of the division after Green's death at Blair's Landing, but was replaced by Gen. John A. Wharton. Steele died in San Antonio in 1885.

10 Bee was the older brother of Brig. Gen. Barnard E. Bee who was killed at First Bull Run. Bee commanded Confederate forces on the Rio Grande frontier until he was chased from Brownsville in December 1863. Baylor's assessment of Bee is probably correct. Bee, who had two horses shot from under him at Pleasant Hill, fought bravely. At Monett's Ferry, however, he was easily pushed aside by Banks's much larger army. As a consequence, Taylor blamed Bee for allowing Banks's army to escape downriver and said Bee showed "no generalship." After a lengthy, poverty-plagued exile in Mexico, Bee returned to Texas and died in San Antonio in 1897. Thomas J. Legg, "Hamilton P. Bee," *Encyclopedia of the Confederacy,* 151.

11 On 4 May 1864, the *City Belle*, with 700 men of the 120th Ohio on board, was attacked. Three hundred men were taken prisoner and many others were either killed or wounded. The same day, the *John Warner*, with the 56th Ohio on board and accompanied by the gunboat *Covington*, proceeded downriver to be joined by the gunboat *Signal*. The next morning the ships were attacked by Colonel Baylor with 1,000 dismounted cavalry fielding two howitzers and two ten-pounder Parrots. The *Warner's* rudders were disabled and she ran aground and the men of the 56th Ohio were slaughtered by Confederate artillery and cav-

alrymen. Both the *Signal*, which had been disabled, and the *Covington* were captured, although both crews were able to escape to the opposite bank of the river. Johnson, *Red River Campaign*, 255-57; and Baylor to Ogden, 18 April 1864, *OR*, 1, 34, 1:622-23. Also, margin notes on p. 60 of Baylor's *Bull Run to Bull Run*.

12 At age nineteen, Hardeman moved to Texas from Tennessee. A veteran of the Mexican-American War, he was commissioned a captain in the 4th Texas Cavalry of the Sibley Brigade and fought bravely at Valverde. Promoted to colonel, he was at Mansfield and Pleasant Hill and in October 1864 was promoted brigadier general. After the war, Hardeman returned to Texas where he inspected railroads and supervised the Texas Confederate Soldiers' Home. He died at his home in Austin on 8 April 1898. Fred L. Schultz, "William Polk Hardeman," *Historical Times Illustrated Encyclopedia of the Civil War* (New York: Harper and Row, 1986), 339.

13 From Mainz, Germany, Buchel was a graduate of the Ecole Militaire in Paris. Buchel was a military instructor to the Turkish army of Ali Pasha and fought in the Carlist Wars in Spain. Buchel came to Texas in 1845, raised a company in the Mexican-American War, and served as aide-de-camp to Gen. Zachary Taylor. In 1861, he joined the 3d Texas Infantry and later organized the 1st Texas Cavalry Regiment. He was fatally wounded at Pleasant Hill and died in Mansfield on 15 April 1864. Yager assumed command of the 1st Texas upon Buchel's death. Wright, *Texas in the War*, 101; and Johnson, *Red River Campaign*, 157.

14 Camille J. Polignac, affectionately called "General Polecat" by the Texans he commanded, was the only noncitizen to achieve the rank of major general in the Civil War. A veteran of the Crimean War, Polignac was made a lieutenant colonel on the staff of General Beauregard. Promoted brigadier general, he fought bravely at Shiloh and Corinth and was transferred to the Trans-Mississippi Department in March 1863. At Mansfield, he commanded a brigade in Mouton's division and took command when Mouton was killed. After Pleasant Hill, Polignac pursued Banks for more than a month. He was made major general and in January 1865 was sent to France to elicit support from Napoleon III for the Confederacy. After the Civil War, he was decorated for bravery in the Franco-Prussian War. He died in Paris on 15 November 1913, the last surviving Confederate major general. Thomas J. Legg, "Camille J. Polignac," *Encyclopedia of the Confederacy*, 3:1,222-3; and Warner, *Generals in Gray*, 242.

15 Smith, an 1845 West Point graduate, fought in Mexico, and served in the 2d Cavalry in Texas before the war. He was slightly wounded at First Bull Run. Promoted to major general, he took command of the Department of East Tennessee at Knoxville. Promoted to lieutenant general and placed in charge of the Trans-Mississippi Department, with a wide range of powers, Smith frequently disagreed with General Taylor during the Red River Campaign and eventually had Taylor transferred. On 2 June 1865, Smith surrendered the Trans-Mississippi Department aboard a Federal steamer in Galveston Harbor and went to Mexico. The last survivor of eight full Confederate generals, he died at Sewanee, Tennessee, on 28 March 1893. Anne J. Bailey, "E. Kirby Smith," *Encyclopedia of the Confederacy*, 4:1,472-4; and Joseph Howard Parks, *General Edmund Kirby Smith, C.S.A.* (Baton Rouge: Louisiana State University Press, 1954).

16 Baylor's dislike of Terry seems to have originated from the time Baylor was with the San Francisco Vigilance Committee and Terry was arrested and almost hanged. See n. 5, Ch. 5, Sec. I.

Terrell moved to Austin, Texas, in 1852 from Missouri where he practiced law. In 1861, he was appointed a major in the 1st Texas Cavalry Regiment. Later, as a colonel in Terrell's Texas Cavalry Regiment, he fought at Mansfield and Pleasant Hill and was promoted to brigadier general on 16 May 1865. After the war, Terrell fled to Mexico where he served with the forces of Emperor Maximilian as "Chief de Battalion." Returning to Texas, he practiced law, served in both houses of the Texas legislature and was made minister plenipotentiary to Turkey by Pres. Grover Cleveland. He died at Mineral Springs, Texas, on 8 September 1912. Wright, *Texas in the War,* 93-94; and Alexander Watkins Terrell, *From Texas to Mexico and the Court of Maximilian in 1865* (Dallas, 1933).

[17] Emphasis is Baylor's.

[18] James Edward Harrison was the older brother of another Confederate general, Thomas Harrison. Harrison came to Texas from Mississippi and was a member of the Texas secession convention. He entered service as a lieutenant colonel in the 15th Texas Infantry. He fought in the Bayou Teche campaign, and in 1864 tried to establish a military alliance with the southern Plains Indians, especially the Comanches. Harrison had been promoted to brigadier general in November 1864. A trustee of Baylor University, he died in 1875. Thomas J. Legg, "James Edward Harrison," *Encyclopedia of the Confederacy,* 2; 748-49.

[19] John Austin Wharton, adjutant general on Houston's staff at San Jacinto and secretary of war in the early days of the Republic of Texas, should not be confused with Gen. John Austin Wharton of Civil War fame. Wharton was born on 3 July 1828 in Nashville, Tennessee, the son of Sarah Ann Groce and William Harris Wharton. He was married in 1848 to Penelope Johnson, the daughter of the governor of South Carolina. Margaret Swett Henson to Jerry Thompson, 10 November 1995, editor's files.

[20] For Peter Hardeman, see n. 16, Ch. 1, this section.

West of the Pecos

~

I want you to remember out in that
far, wild country you represent
the honor and dignity of
the great state of Texas.

Gov. Oran M. Roberts to
George W. Baylor, July 1879

III

ALTHOUGH OTHER PRIMARY SOURCES DESCRIBE the 1861 Apache attacks on travelers at Stein's Peak and Cooke's Canyon, Baylor's account is rich in detail as are his recollections of his fights with Victorio's Warm Springs Apaches in the Trans-Pecos and Northern Mexico in the late 1870s and early 1880s. And his description of Victorio's massacre of two small parties of Mexicans in the Candelaria Mountains in Northeastern Chihuahua in November 1879 is especially valuable in reconstructing the event. The same is true of his description of the fight with Apaches in the Sierra Ventana a month earlier.

Baylor's sketch of Cochise's raid on a ranch in Arizona's San Simeon Valley in October 1871, which he gleaned from a survivor, matches other accounts, civilian and military, of the attack. His recalling of the rescue of two wayward travelers at barren Crow Flats stage station west of the Guadalupe Mountains in Texas, as well as the destruction of Price Cooper's wagon trains on the Pecos River in 1871, which Baylor heard about from Cooper at Ysleta, provides a rare glimpse into the dangers of life on the Texas frontier.

But no doubt the most dramatic of Baylor's recollections is his detailed account of the massacre of a small band of Victorio's Apaches high in the Sierra Diablo of the Trans-Pecos in January 1881. Although the Apaches were surprised and helplessly shot down, the attack brought acclaim throughout the state and is still recorded today in textbooks as the "last Indian fight in Texas." One of the few available sources of the massacre, as well as Baylor's excursions into Mexico, has traditionally been James B. Gillett's Six Years with the Texas Rangers, *first published in 1921. Unnoticed by editors of future editions of the book, however, was the fact that Gillett, Baylor's son-in-law for a time, clearly plagiarized a large part of six chapters, often word-for-word, from Baylor's articles in the* El Paso Herald.

Baylor's account of the deadly El Paso gun battle in April 1881, in which four men died in four seconds, as well as the deaths of Dallas Stoudenmire in the Manning Saloon in September 1882, and Samuel M. "Doc" Cummings at the Coliseum Saloon in February 1882, are all illustrative of the rough frontier violence that was common in El Paso at the time.

~

CHAPTER ONE

Apache Raids on the Overland Trail

~

AMONG THE MANY BLOODY DEEDS THAT OCCURRED on the old Overland Stage Line, none was more tragic perhaps than the death of [John] James Giddings, a brother of Col. George H. Giddings, which occurred some time in April 1861.[1] The guards to the Overland Stage that made the discovery of the massacre of Giddings and the men at the station were under that veteran old frontiersman, Capt. [Henry] Skillman, whose tragic death afterwards will be remembered by old citizens of West Texas.[2] The party consisted of the following men, some of whom not long afterwards met with a tragic death near Cook[e]'s Springs: Bob [L.] Swope, Bob Avaline, William Wright, Freeman Thomas, John Wilson, Mat[thew] Champi[o]n, Charley Lowry, and William Ramsey.[3]

The Indians had ambuscaded the road by building blinds on each side, about a quarter of a mile east of Stein's Peak Station. They fired into the stage with bullets and arrows. Probably the first intimation Giddings and his men had that hostile Indians were around was the volley of bullets and arrows from the Indians behind these blinds. The Indians followed and cut him off from the station, but the men at the station had probably all been killed before the stage coach was attacked, as the stage ran near the station and turned east again and was upset about a hundred yards from the road. There was a great deal of blood on the dashboard and the bottom of the stage was covered with blood, showing the first volley at close range must have killed or wounded most of the party.

Nothing was seen of Giddings or his party. The Indians had built a fire within 200 yards of the station and eaten two of the stage mules, their bones showing that they had been roasted for the marrow, and the ribs giving evidence of being barbecued. There is no meat the Indians fancy more than that of a fat mule. They would rather kill and scalp a white man and eat his mule than have the best rations the government could issue. At this fire a pair of gloves was found, and the chips as though some one had been whittling. Some poor devil of the party reserved for torture could not resist this pleasure from force of habit. As none of the bodies were found at the stage station or Indian camp, Captain Skillman concluded they had been carried off and tortured, affording a scalp dance and general merry making to the savages.

Several small fires were found about thirty yards west of the station under some small liveoak trees and the signs indicated that they had been used to torture the men of the station. A big trail left going south towards Old Mexico. Some of the watches and jewelry that the Indians sold in Mexico were recognized by Bob Swope and Snap Mitchell as belonging to the Giddings Party. The body of one of them was subsequently found about three hundred yards east of the station, but the coyotes had picked the bones and there was no way of identifying whose it was. The Overland Stage and its guard seemed to offer a constant temptation to the Apaches to rob and murder, but as there was hardly ever a brush in which the Indians did not lose some of their warriors, they got to be shy about making attacks and never unless the men at the station got careless, and it was hard for them to keep strung up to concert pitch all the time.

The following account of a fight at the Eighteen Mile Water Hole was given to me by J[ames] Eli Terry, a well known contractor of El Paso, and a brave and faithful Confederate soldier in Baylor's regiment during the War Between the States.[4]

Terry was in the employ of the Overland Stage Company. The party left with the stage and consisted of Jack Sullivan, who was wounded in a fight in San Elizario between the Rangers and a Mexican mob when Judge Howard Ellis and [John] Atkinson were killed; Vining, who was afterwards a member of Capt. (now Governor) Joe Sayers' battery; Will Lampert, who long afterwards served Presidio County faithfully as clerk, and Gus Stewart, who afterwards was killed by a man named Curry who shot him with a double-barreled shotgun.[5] Ordinarily a knife or colt's revolver was used to settle arguments, but a shotgun with fifteen blue whistlers was considered "dead medicine" and much the safest for the shooters.

At San Elizario, they left the stage, there being no passengers, as was the custom. The Apaches, being bold and plentiful, men with pack mules, stood a better chance either to fight or run. They passed old Fort Quitman and the canyon of that name, which was a noted place for the Mescaleros to ambush the stage or travelers, and were congratulating themselves when they emerged from the canyon and struck the plain where they could see for miles and anticipated no danger between there and Eagle Springs, where the next station was. Mr. Lo, though, is fond of a joke, and knew naturally that the guard would keep a sharp lookout at the dangerous places and become careless on open ground, so when the men got to Eighteen Mile Water Hole, where water could be had for some time after a rain, a party of fifteen mounted Apaches suddenly appeared from a dry arroyo.

There was a shallow hole in the rocks where the stock usually watered at the foot of a regular sugarloaf shaped hill. The hole is on the south of the hill, and the Indians waited for the small party to get there, no doubt expecting conquest if they could get them hived on the hill. The road runs just on the west of the hill and the long range of hills between the stage road and Sierra Blanca. The boys at first decided to make a stand-off fight from where they were, but just then twenty-five more Apaches on foot showed up, and they beat a retreat for the hill.

Before they reached the hill Lampert was shot, but the Indian had used a minie rifle, and to make sure of "a palpable hit" had cut a minie ball into slugs. Two of these struck Lampert, one in the back and one in the knee. If the ball had been used Presidio County would have been without the services of a splendid citizen in after years.

The Indians had crowded them so close that they had left all their mules except Terry, who had managed to lead his halfway up the hill, but when Lampert was wounded he turned his mule loose to help his wounded friend. Vining, who had a big old shotgun, turned loose both barrels loaded with buck into the Apaches, knocking one over and wounding several. The crest of the hill was gained. Eli pulled the slug out of Lampert's back, and he was good and full of fight, and as he and Stewart both had Sharps rifles, the only breech-loader at that time, they kept up a hot fire on the retreating savages, who also had a few guns, made the rock and gravel fly, but their bows and arrows were of no avail except in close quarters. In the lull they had thrown up a circle of rock on the top of the hill, and felt pretty safe. After the Indians drew off they had the gall to raise a white flag and doubtless would have liked to have had the men surrender and receive "kind treatment," but Stewart and Lampert sent a couple of bullets at the flag, and Mr. Lo, with yells of rage raised the black flag, which also got a volley.

Terry had not fired a shot, but kept his double-barrel gun loaded, expecting a charge, knowing the villains were liable to even count the shot and charge when the white men's guns were empty. The guard had taken refuge on the hill about 2 p.m. and did not get off until sunrise next morning, when they struck the road for Eagle Springs and "hoofed it" back to that place of refuge, keeping an eye on all suspicious shadows, for naturally they would expect to have some new trick sprung on them, but the scarcity of water which compelled them to leave and risk their lives also forced the Apaches to leave, well satisfied, as they had all the mules, grub and latest news by mail, and knew perfectly well that the crowd they had left were just in the right humor to make a wicked fight, and many a warrior would have been laid out before the stage guard would have been destroyed.

This was not the only fight on this hill—that seemed put there to defend the weak against the strong. When old Victorio, the chief of the Mescalero Apaches, made his last raid into Texas, Gen. [Benjamin H.] Grierson, who was at Fort Quitman on the Rio Grande, learning that the Apaches had crossed from Mexico into Texas at Hot Springs, some thirty miles below, started on the Overland Road to meet the troops that had started from Eagle Springs toward Quitman.[6] The general had reason to believe the Indians were making for the Sierra Diablos, intending to reach the Guadalupe Mountains, which they would have done, but he made a forced march from the stage road between Van Horn's Wells and El Muerto (Dead Man's Hole) in the Davis Mountains, to Rattlesnake Springs on the east side of the Sierra Diablos, some sixty odd miles, and turned the Indians back toward Mexico.

I believe there were only eight persons left. Capt. [Nicholas] Nolan and his company of the Ninth Cavalry at Quitman had pushed on ahead to meet the companies coming.[7] I can't recall the names of the officers, but remember Major Courtney, Capt. [Thomas Coverly] Lebo and Dr. Kingly, who were with the general.[8] When the general and his staff had nearly reached this hill, which might be given the Russian name Standemoffski, they discovered a big dust down the valley toward Bosque Bonito, and on mounting the hill with their glasses made out old Vic's band, supposed to number 150 warriors.[9] As neither Nolan nor the troops from Eagle Springs were in sight, there was nothing to do but to prepare for a desperate struggle. After securing their horses as best they could to bushes at the foot of the hill, they began to strengthen the Rebel works that Capt. Eli Terry had found so useful twenty-one years before.

Some of the Indians ahead of the main body had discovered the general's party and were coming full speed, but as the staff had Springfield rifles and began to open on them, they scattered out and opened fire, also having the same arms and ammunition furnished by a benevolent Quaker policy. The bullets began to whistle around the crown of Stand[e]moffski and the little band returned the fire, and one Indian was seen to fall and his companions took him off.[10] The main body of Indians were now nearing the Americans, and it would have been all up with the general and staff, but eagerly scanning the road to the west, they saw the dust of Nolan's column, and they probably had discovered the dust down the valley and interpreted its meaning, which soldiers on the plains soon learn, and came forward on the run. They were the same colored troops that marched bravely up San Juan Hill with Teddy Roosevelt's Rough Riders. Their timely arrival saved the staff, who had made a gallant fight. The combined force now moved on to meet the other troops, and the Indians followed and there was pretty much of a continuous fire until the two commands met. Here quite a hot fight occurred, and the Indians were driven off, going south and around the Eagle Mountains to some spring.[11] Old Victorio had intended to cross the road here and make for the Sierra Diablo to Victorio tanks, named for him, this being the most direct route to the Guadalupe Mountains, where the old thief would have been in a very rough county, with plenty of grass, game, water, and near the [Fort] Stanton Reservation, where he would have had recruits and ammunition.

The writer had left Ysleta with Company A, Texas Rangers, and reported for duty to General Grierson at Quitman by telegraph, the general having his operator with him at Eagle Springs, and was ordered to come on and keep a sharp lookout for Victorio and his band. The general and troops had moved on toward Van Horn and were uncertain whether the wily old chief was ahead of or behind him. There were twenty-seven Pueblo Indians with me and thirteen of my own men.[12] When we struck the fresh sign of Indians and empty shells, it showed a fight had occurred. We pushed on, and where the stage road passed around the Sierra Blanca plains a ledge of rock juts up out of the ground, and here we saw plenty of empty shells and a dark splotch of blood where one of the soldiers had been killed. Beyond Bass Canyon, where the same Indians had committed so many murders, we struck the Indian trail going toward where Van Horn Station now is.

Old Vic had been smart enough to pull down the telegraph poles for a quarter of a mile, cut the wire at both ends of the break, and then with rocks or axes broke all the insulators and packed off the wire to make sure we could not repair the damage. He hoped then to get such a start that General Grierson could not overtake him until safe in the Guadalupes, but as stated, the general had made a forced march to the east of the Baylor Mountains and confronted old Vic at Rattlesnake Springs, where there was quite a skirmish, and turned him back into the Sierra Diablos and the tanks named after him.[13] Victorio then kept spies out, and when he saw a force of cavalry start around the north side of the Sierra and Captain Nolan's company and the

Rangers start south toward Carrizo Springs, he understood he was in no safe place, as the general still had force enough to prevent him crossing the plains to the Guadalupe Mountains, and he pulled out once more for Mexico.[14]

We had camped at Carrizo Springs and as soon as we heard of Victorio's move we put out at sunset after him, and at daylight next morning struck the Overland Road where the fight had occurred when the soldier was killed, and found the trail took the road for the Rio Grande. We followed on down to Standemoffski, and there the Indians left the road towards Bosque Bonito. As at that time there was no treaty allowing United States troops to cross the border and the Indians had twelve hours start on us, we kept the road, as both men and horses were suffering for water. To our surprise, the Indian trail came back into the road about where the Sierra Blanca and Bosque Bonito crosses the old stage road. No doubt they saw they could beat us to the Rio Grande and across it [and] would be safe. When they got to General Grierson hill they perpetrated a small joke at his expense. They had managed to get a woman's bonnet and dress, probably in the murder of Mrs. [Margaret] Graham and old man [James] Grant at Bass Canyon, and they placed it on top of Standemoffski, making a scarecrow of dagger stalks, intending as much to say, "why didn't you come out and fight on open ground and not hide behind rocks, like an old woman?"[15]

When we had passed through the worst part of Quitman Canyon and beyond what was known as the Apache postoffice, where the Indians had some hieroglyphics on the rocks, we came on to signs where the Overland Stage the day before had been ambuscaded and we saw where it had turned back and the ground and gravel [were] covered with blood. We examined the signs and found moccasin tracks beside a Spanish dagger, and two empty .45 government cartridges. At Quitman we saw Gen. [James J.] Byrne's corpse.[16] One bullet entered his thigh from the front and another his back, showing the Indian had made good use of the army supplies. A detachment of Rangers and the Ninth Cavalry buried him with usual military honors. I could not but 9809feel sad as I had known him at Galveston as a revenue officer, and pondered on the strange death of a brave soldier who, surviving the many battles of the Civil War, should be buried by a former foe in this desolate spot.

The Indians crossed the Rio Grande at the ranch of Don Jesús Cobos, and here perpetrated another practical joke.[17] Don Jesús and the herder who was frying out tallow from a beef was killed and his head stuck in the tallow, making him a greaser, but General Terrazas and his men turned the joke on them at Tres Castillos and fed the coyotes and buzzards with eighty-eight of their carcasses.

But to return to our hill: It saw a cold-blooded murder committed by one Brown on a one-legged man who was seen with him near Alpine. The cripple's body was found near the hill with a bullet hole in his head. The writer arrested Brown at a ranch below Fort Hancock, his last arrest made as a Texas Ranger.

NOTES

[1] On 29 April 1861, at the foot of Stein's Peak, near the mouth of Doubtful Canyon, Cochise and Mangas Coloradas attacked the westbound stage, killing John James Giddings, brother of George Giddings. The stage was alleged to be carrying $28,000 in gold. Other victims included Edward Briggs, Samuel Neely, W. McNess, and Anthony Elder. Berndt Kuhn, an authority on the Apache attacks along the San Antonio-El Paso and Mesilla-Tucson roads, thoroughly scouted the Stein's Peak massacre site in the summer of 1994. Kuhn found a site southwest of the stage station that corresponds with what Baylor describes. Edward Donnelly and Patrick Donaghue, who were returning from San Simon Station to Barney's Station with a provision wagon, were killed on or about 24 April 1861 and were found hanging head down near the Stein's Peak Station by a government wagon train on 5 May 1861. Austerman, *Sharps Rifles and Spanish Mules*, 167-69; John P. Wilson, *Islands in the Desert: A History of the Uplands of Southeastern Arizona* (Albuquerque: University of New Mexico Press, 1995), 83-85; and Dan L. Thrapp, "Stein's Pass: Gateway to Adventure," *New Mexico Magazine* (June, 1981): 8-9; Berndt Kuhn to Jerry Thompson, 25 May 1995, editor's files. For a sketch of the massacre, see: Merrick, *From Desert to Bayou*, 77.

George H. Giddings was born in Susquehanna County, Pennsylvania, on 8 October 1814. He came to Texas in 1846 and in 1857 obtained the Santa Fe to San Diego mail contract. While in Washington during the secession crisis, Pres. Abraham Lincoln allegedly gave Giddings a letter for Gov. Sam Houston promising 70,000 troops to keep the Lone Star State in the Union. During the Civil War, Giddings commanded Giddings' Texas Cavalry Battalion along the lower Rio Grande. Colonel Giddings fought with Col. John S. Ford in the last land battle of the war at Palmito Hill on 13 May 1865. Giddings died in Mexico City in 1903. Another brother, Dr. Francis Marion Giddings, was killed in Ben Dowell's billiard saloon in El Paso by Tom Smith, a gambler, on 23 or 24 March 1858. Giddings' memoirs were published in the *San Antonio Express* on 4, 11, 18, 15 May, and 1 June 1902. Also, Mills, *Forty Years at El Paso,* 180-81; and Nancy Hamilton, *Ben Dowell: El Paso's First Mayor* (El Paso: Texas Western Press, 1976), 21-22.

[2] See n. 22, Ch. 2, Sec. I.

[3] On Sunday morning, 21 July 1861, Cochise and Mangas Coloradas attacked the westbound stage near the mouth of Cooke's Canyon about a mile beyond Cooke's Springs. Freeman Thomas, Joseph Roeser, John Wilson, John Portell, Robert S. Avaline, Matthew Champion, and Emmett Mills (younger brother of William W. and Anson Mills), were all killed. The bodies, which were discovered by the Pinos Altos mail rider on 26 July, were all stripped and three were scalped. Lt. Col. John R. Baylor sent a patrol from Mesilla that examined the scene and buried the victims. Robert L. Swope enlisted as a first lieutenant in Capt. Sherod Hunter's Co. A, Arizona Rangers, at Doña Ana on 25 January 1862 and

helped occupy Tucson the following month. For a crude sketch of the massacre, see: Merrick, *From Desert to Bayou*, 78. Keith Humphries, "Seven Brave Men," *Old West* 14 (Winter 1877): 26-27; *Mesilla Times,* 27 July, 3 August 1861; *New Orleans Delta*, 25 August 1861; *Houston Tri-Weekly Telegraph*, 17 August 1861; *Sacramento Daily Union*, n.d., Bancroft Clippings, Huntington Library, San Marino, California; and Mills, *Forty Years at El Paso*, 185, 195-96; Douglas J. Hamilton to Jerry Thompson, 27 July 1992, editor's files; Berndt Kuhn to Jerry Thompson, 25 May 1995, editor's files.

4 The *Mesilla Times*, 19 September 1861, as quoted in the *Memphis Daily Appeal*, 30 October 1861, states that the fight at Eighteen Mile Water Hole or Tinaja de las Palmas, took place on 13 September and that it lasted from 3 p.m. until midnight. The following morning the party returned safely to Fort Quitman. Terry was born in Autauga County, Alabama, in 1834. He was a stage driver on the San Antonio-El Paso Road in the later 1850s and fought with Col. George W. Baylor in Louisiana during the Civil War. He returned to El Paso with the railroads in 1881 and died there on 24 January 1910. Wayne R. Austerman, "Tinaja de las Palmas: A Landmark on the El Paso Road," *Password*, 28 (Spring 1983): 7-15; Mills, *Forty Years at El Paso,* 191. Also, U.S. Geological Survey topographical map (7.5 minute series) Devil Ridge, Tex.

5 For the death of Ellis and Atkinson at San Elizario during the El Paso Salt War, see C.L. Sonnichsen, *El Paso Salt War*, 55-57.

6 By the time he was commissioned colonel of the 10th Cavalry in July 1866, Grierson, a former music teacher and unsuccessful merchant from Illinois, was already well known for one of the most spectacular cavalry raids of the Civil War. For sixteen days in April and May 1863, Grierson tore up railroad tracks, and telegraph lines, confiscated horses and mules, and destroyed arms and supplies as he swept some six hundred miles from La Grange, Tennessee, through Mississippi to the Federal lines near Baton Rouge, Louisiana. Bruce J. Dinges, "Benjamin H. Grierson," *Soldiers West: Biographies From the Military Frontier*, ed. Paul Andrew Hutton (Lincoln: University of Nebraska Press, 1987), 157-76. Also, Baylor to Jones, 26 August 1880, Letters Received, Adjutant General's Office, Record Group 401, Texas State Archives, Austin.

7 Irish-born Nolan had enlisted in the 4th Artillery as a private in 1852. He became a second lieutenant in the 6th Cavalry during the Civil War. After his tour in the Trans-Pecos, Nolan was promoted major in the 3d Cavalry in 1882 and died one year later on 25 October 1883. Heitman, *Historical Register, 1:750.*

8 From Pennsylvania, Lebo had fought with Pennsylvania infantry and cavalry regiments during the Civil War, and in June 1867 was commissioned a first lieutenant in the 10th Cavalry. Heitman, *Historical Register*, 1:622.

   Baylor has his facts of the fight at Tinaja de las Palmas slightly misconstrued. The headquarters detachment that took refuge on Rocky Ridge on Devil Ridge consisted of 1st Lt. William H. Beck; Grierson's nineteen-year-old son, Robert; a non-commissioned officer; and five privates, besides the colonel. Shortly before the Apache attack, they were joined by 2d Lt. Leighton Finley and fifteen men of Company C of the 10th Cavalry from the substation at Eagle Springs. After considerable skirmishing, mostly in the desert below the hill, Captain Nolan and Company A arrived from Fort Quitman. As a result Victorio broke off the battle, and retreated toward the Quitman Mountains. Seven Apaches and one Buffalo Soldier died in the fighting. Baylor apparently has Lieutenant Finley confused with "Dr. Kingly." Moreover, he may have "Major Courtney" confused with Lieutenant Beck. For the best account of the fight see: Douglas C. McChristian, "Grierson's Fight at

Tinaja de las Palmas: An Episode in the Victorio Campaign," *Red River Valley Historical Review* (Winter 1982): 45-63. Also, Thrapp, *Victorio and the Mimbres Apaches*, 286-88; Frank M. Temple, "Colonel B.H. Grierson's Administration of the District of the Pecos," *West Texas Historical Association Yearbook* 38 (October 1962): 85-94; Frank M. Temple, "Colonel B.H. Grierson's Victorio Campaign," *West Texas History Association Yearbook* 35 (October 1959): 99-111; and William H. Leckie, *The Buffalo Soldiers: A Narrative of the Negro Cavalry in the West* (Norman: University of Oklahoma Press, 1967), 223-25.

9 At the time, Baylor and his Tigua scouts estimated the number of Apaches as not more than sixty or seventy.

10 At Tinaja de las Palmas, Baylor reported seeing "the usual dead horses that are strewed over every cavalry battle field, bullet marks on the rocks and the blood of a soldier still fresh and crying to heaven for vengeance." General Grierson "and his escort of seven men were fortified in certainly the strongest place imaginable, being on the top of a rocky ridge where from a small rocky parapet a soldier could fire on either side of the hill," Baylor reported. "Alexander and his army could not have ousted them without loss of half [their] troops." Baylor to Jones, 26 August 1880, AGO, RG 401, TSA.

11 Beyond Tinaja de las Palmas, Baylor also reported finding where Victorio's warriors had "waylaid the stage & killed the two men, the driver, [Frank Wyant], [and E.C.] Baker from Georgia, his real name not known but supposed to be the man who killed the Deputy Sheriff of Las Vegas." The Apaches "had cut the mail sacks open, cut canvass off of the buck board & tore the mail matter into shreds—the men were mutilated and papers stuffed in their wounds. Capt. Coldwell escaped by a miracle." Baylor to Jones, 26 August 1880, AGO, RG 401, TSA.

12 The Ysleta scouts were commanded by Mariano Colmenaro. *Galveston Daily News,* 29 November 1905. At least fifteen Tiguas are listed on the 1880 El Paso County census as "army scouts." 10th Census, El Paso County, Texas.

13 When Baylor arrived at Rattlesnake Springs after the Buffalo Soldiers had turned the Apaches back into the Sierra Diablos, Grierson suggested that the Rangers be sent around the mountains to see if Victorio had escaped to the south or west. Baylor declined, asserting that his horses were "about broken down" and a ride of seventy miles would further render his small command ineffective. Instead Baylor suggested that he rendezvous with a small force of cavalry on the west side of the Sierra Diablos, and if Victorio was still in the mountains, along with Grierson, "go in on foot from both sides." Baylor to Jones, 26 August 1880, AGO, RG 401, TSA.

14 Carrizo Springs, now dry, is about seven miles northwest of present-day Van Horn. Brune, *Springs of Texas*, 1:149.

15 In a lengthy letter to the *Galveston Daily News*, 29 November 1905, Baylor recalled the incident and was sure the "scarecrow" was to show Victorio's contempt for Grierson's "not coming on the plain to fight him." Baylor had written in response to a letter by a woman named Pauline Periwinkle saying that Victorio's "band was fought to the finish . . . by Gen. Grierson." It was "that gallant old Mexican soldier, Col. Jo[a]quín Terrazas, cousin of Gov. Luis Terrazas, who finished Old Vic up at Tres Castillos, Chihuahua, Oct. 14 and 15, 1880," Baylor wrote. Recalling his attack on the remnants of Victorio's band in the Sierra Diablo at daylight on 27 January 1881, he assured the newspaper that "it was the Texas Rangers who 'fought Victorio's band to the finish.'" *Galveston Daily News*, 29 November 1905.

16 From Ireland, Byrne commanded the 18th New York Cavalry during the Civil War and was in the Red River Campaign in 1864. He was breveted a brigadier general for gallantry

at the battles of Moore's Plantation and Yellow Bayou. Byrne had been mustered out of the army in May 1866. The two men, as Baylor indicates, had evidently shared their war experiences when Byrne was United States deputy marshal in Galveston during Reconstruction. In his official report, Baylor described the exact circumstances of Byrne's death: "He received all his wounds after they had whirled back. One shattered his thigh and strangely enough was within an inch of a wound he received at Gettysburg—another passed through the back of the seat and entered the body low down ranging up into his bowels, without coming out. He must have suffered 10,000 deaths. We buried him (a mixed crowd of Confederates and citizens and U.S. soldiers), and fired a couple of volleys over his grave." After the attack, the driver, Ed Walde, quit the stage company and enlisted in Baylor's Rangers. Heitman, *Historical Register*, 1:271; Austerman, *Sharps Rifles and Spanish Mules*, 303; and Baylor to Jones, 26 August 1880, AGO, RG 401, TSA.

[17] Cobos was a large landholder and a leading citizen of San Elizario. The Apaches, Baylor reported, made off with 160 head of Cobos's cattle. The expedition after Victorio had lasted for twenty days and the Rangers had ridden 500 miles. Baylor to Jones, 26 August 1880, AGO, RG 401, TSA.

CHAPTER TWO

Destruction of Price Cooper's Wagon Trains on the Pecos River

~

THE WRITER OBTAINED THE STATEMENT OF THE FOLLOWING FACTS from Price Cooper who was for many years his near neighbor, and a kind and hospitable one, and who now lives in the quiet little town of Ysleta.[1] The writer will tell the tale just as it was told to him. It needs no coloring to make it tragic enough, for at the time the frontier was inhabited by a bold and hardy set of men who knew no such word as fear. They embarked in enterprises that promised large returns of death with apparent indifference to the final result.

Old Uncle Price, as we always called him, was born in New York and drifted west when a mere boy.[2] When he reached the western plains and slept out of doors a while, drank alkali water and filled up on fat buffalo meat, he come to look upon a scrap with Indians, or a shooting bee with some desperado, as a matter of course. It came as natural as for a bronco to go to bucking, as soon as he had a day's rest and his paunch full of mesquite for bunch grass.

Uncle Price left Ysleta for the purpose of hauling salt from the lakes near Horsehead Crossing on the Pecos River, down to the settlers on the Conchos River.[3] It seemed almost like flying in the face of providence to make such a trip at that time, for during the war the Comanches and Apaches had robbed and scalped both sides with the most charming indifference. Emboldened by comparative safety from punishment from either the John Rebs or the Yanks, they had become unusually bold, and for six or seven men to make such trips, when the Indians could muster fifty or one hundred warriors, looked like tempting fate.

Old Price had bought from old John [Simpson] Chisum, on Brady Creek, thirty-five yoke of oxen.[4] Having seven wagons, he had loaded these up with salt at the Horsehead Salt Laguna, and made one successful trip down on Brady Creek and the Conchos, selling the salt at good prices. For, although dame nature had put unlimited quantities at the laguna, manufactured by her own simple process of evaporation, yet the men who went to gather it took their lives in their hands in the venture.

Uncle Price immediately started back for a second trip and had camped at an old deserted Overland Stage station, with which he was familiar, having worked for the Overland Mail company, usually known as the Butterfield Company. Here he left no alarm. It is a strange fact, but quite true, that the sight of even an old deserted stage stand was a pleasant and reassuring sight on these desert plains. Although experience had demonstrated that it was at these places that the murderous and thieving Indians most frequently made their attacks, yet the sight of human habitations robbed the place of some of its gloom.

The little band, consisting of seven Mexican drivers and Cooper, struck camp, turned out their oxen, cooked their supper and passed the evening with songs and stories, of which they accumulated a wonderful supply in their wild life. Bringing in their teams close to camp, the tired oxen were soon lying down chewing their cuds and blowing long breaths of content.

By daylight the morning watch had taken the oxen off to graze while the men cooked breakfast, and old Price went out, taking his revolver and rifle, to help drive them back to camp. He had started with them for camp when he heard a terrible noise at the camp, the shouting of the men and the shrill war-whoop of Indians. Hurrying towards camp they suddenly found themselves surrounded by hideously painted warriors. Cooper leveled his rifle at them and they sheered off from him, for although they looked as peaceful as lambs, yet he had seen too much of them, having been a prisoner among them a long while, to put any confidence in them. The herder, a young Mexican, who was mounted on Cooper's riding horse, a very fine animal he had bought from Gabe Valdez, seemed to have lost his head, for though Cooper yelled at him to come to him, he bore off farther, intending no doubt to make a break for liberty.[5] But an Indian rode up to his side and pushed him off of the horse, for the beautiful animal, with a fine silver mounted Chihuahua saddle and silver mounted bridle, was more than an Indian could consistently pass by, and especially as a few Mexicans lived [who] stood between them and ownership. The Mexican took to his heels, but between the Indians followed, filling him full of arrows and lancing him. This momentary diversion in Uncle Price's favor gave him time to think. So he made a break for the thick brush on the Conchos and as he was one of the fastest sprinters in the country and best jumpers, he was putting distance between himself and his enemies at a marvelous rate. But they had no idea of letting him get off so easily and raising a yell, took after him.

As good luck would have it there was a ravine ten or twelve feet deep and quite wide between him and the river bottom, and when he saw it he determined to try and clear it, for if he should fall the Indians could run above and below him, and he would be like a rat in a trap where they could kill him with arrows at their leisure. "How wide was it, Uncle Price?" I asked. "Lord, colonel, don't ask me. I just knowed it had to be jumped, and I went at it with all my strength and riz and sailed over it like a flying squirrel." When the Indians saw the ravine they were afraid to try it, even on their horses, and broke to the right and left to find a crossing. Before they got over the old man was in the thicket, and luck again favored him, for where he struck the river there was a large drift pile of logs, trash and trees left by a flood. Under this Uncle Price crawled and squirmed along until he got under the thickest portion where he was perfectly concealed. He heard them galloping and shouting and they were evidently dubious about poking around under the drift looking for a white man well armed. But one adventurous warrior came in on the drift and he felt the trash dropping down on him, but the Indian's sharp eyes could not detect him. He then began to think of the possibility of their setting fire to the drift. This kept him in a painful state of anxiety. But they evidently were satisfied with the haul they had made, and being unwilling to risk losing any of their braves further they drove off the stock.

As soon as night came he began to consider what he should do to be saved. He was afraid some of them would be concealed waiting for him to make his appearance. Still he could not stay under the drift long. It was a long way to the settlements, so waiting and listening patiently, and everything getting quiet, he carefully made his way to the bank and crawled along until well out in the bottom. Here he struck off down the bottom towards the settlements and by daylight was a long way on his road.

Cooper traveled all day and into the night, traveling in the woods during the day for fear of the Indians, and in the road at night. He passed any amount of game. Deer and turkeys would hardly get out of his way, seeming to know he could or would not shoot. He was afraid the report of his rifle would bring the Indians down on him. So he preferred to go hungry until he reached the settlements. It was quite seventy-five miles and he was nearly starved before he got to the first settler. After a short rest he got three young men to go back with him, Jim Comprary, John Ketcham, and another whose name is forgotten. They found the bodies of four of the Mexican drivers in the camp, lanced and shot full of arrows. The young Mexican's body, who was on herd, was also found. One of the Mexicans, named Francisco Torres, could not be found, but the men followed his trail and that of a large fierce bulldog that Cooper had for a camp guard, for some distance. They probably happened not to be right in camp when the attack was made, as the dog had never been known to leave the camp before. But the wild yells of the Apaches were too much for even his nerves. Neither man or dog was ever heard of again. It is likely they died a horrid death from hunger and thirst between the Conchos and Pecos rivers. The arms, clothing, grub and wagon sheets were all taken away. The Mexicans had not fired a shot. The Indians, some fifty or sixty from the signs, played the Filipino amigo game until they got all around the men.

Both Jim Comprary and John Ketcham were afterwards killed by Indians, showing what a very shadowy tenure of life these old frontiersmen held in those days. Uncle Price, nothing daunted, went back to the settlements, and the people generously aided him in getting another outfit. Among'st those who contributed was that gallant old Confederate soldier, Judge [George] M. Frazer, of Reeves [County], a typical big-hearted, brave old frontiersman.[6]

Uncle Price got six wagons and thirty yoke of oxen, and started for the Salt Laguna on the Pecos River again, with all the persistence of Robert Bruce's spider, but not with its final success. The train got to the Laguna again and went into camp. Two Mexicans mounted on mules went to guard the oxen, and four others went to work to fill the wagons with salt. When dinner came the herders failed to put in an appearance, and when a camper fails to come to dinner, Uncle Price's suspicions were at once aroused, but what to do was the question. There were five of them, but if three went to look for the herders and oxen, when Indians were about, they would kill the two men in camp and follow and kill the others. So they concluded to stay together, and taking their canteens full of water and some cooked grub, they took the trail. They had not gone a mile until they found the bodies of the men, lanced and shot full of arrows. All the oxen and mules were gone and the signs indicated that quite a body of Indians had done the work. A hurried retreat for camp was in order for fear the Indians would be ahead of them.

They were now in a sad plight, being all afoot, while it was fully ninety miles back to the Conchos River settlements and much farther to Presidio del Norte. Besides there were plenty of Indians on either route, and long, dry stretches without water, but they decided to go to Presidio.

Taking such grub as they could best carry, salt, coffee and flour, they pulled out at night for Leon Holes, on the old emigrant road near [Fort] Stockton.[7] They hoped to catch some soldiers or emigrants on the route, but in this they were disappointed. They took the old road towards Fort Davis, but fearing to go though Limpia Canyon on account of the Mescalero Apaches, who infested the country from Barilla Springs to Wild Rose Pass, they turned off and took the old route to Presidio.[8] After many hardships they reached the Mexican settlements.

Here Uncle Price found friends who assisted him, and he made his way back to Ysleta, contented to let some one else make a fortune hauling salt among the Apache Indians.

NOTES

[1] Cooper was born in Pennsylvania around 1811 and went to Missouri at an early age with his family. He came to El Paso with a brother, Richard, as early as 1824 and for ten years was a trader on the Santa Fe to Chihuahua to Durango Trail. He settled at Ysleta around 1835 and drove the stage for George Giddings on both the El Paso-Santa Fe and San Antonio-El Paso routes. Rex Strickland found evidence that Cooper also worked as a wagon boss, farmer, and contractor. In October 1897, Cooper and Baylor completed an agreement in which Baylor promised to assist Cooper in filing a claim against the government for the loss of his wagon trains. Cooper's son, Santiago, who was a Ranger during the Salt War, also became one of Baylor's close friends and confidants. The names of Santiago and Santos Cooper can still be seen carved in stone at Hueco Tanks and other watering holes west of the Pecos. Price Cooper died at Ysleta on 11 November 1900. Wayne Austerman describes him as "tall, gaunt, ham-fisted, and crowned with a shock of fiery red hair." Josiah Crosby, an early settler at El Paso, remembered Cooper as "a brave man, but in no sense an adventurer . . . quiet, [a] good citizen, [and] always honest." Cooper, sixty-four and a farmer, is listed on the 1880 census at Ysleta along with his wife, Antonia, forty, and three sons, James, Tomás, and José, and two daughters, Mariana and Antonia. Mills, *Forty Years at El Paso*, 176; Agreement, George W. Baylor and Price Cooper, 21 October 1897, Baylor-Carrington Papers; and Austerman, *Sharps Rifles and Spanish Mules*, 60-61, 84; 10th Census, El Paso County, Texas, NA.

[2] Cooper was actually born in Pennsylvania.

[3] Known today as Juan Cordona Lake, the salt deposits had attracted travelers since prehistoric times. Two miles north of the Pecos River, fifteen miles west of Castle Gap, and fifty miles southwest of present-day Midland, the lake consists of two basins, the largest of which is two and a half miles by three miles by three quarters of a mile in size. Surrounded by sand dunes, it is connected to a second lake one half as large. Patrick Dearen, *Castle Gap and the Pecos Frontier* (Fort Worth: Texas Christian University Press, 1988), 64.

4 Chisum came to Paris, Texas, from Tennessee at the age of thirteen. By the time of the Civil War he had established a ranch headquarters at Denton and was one of the largest cattle ranchers in the state. During the war he served as beef contractor for the Confederacy, delivering herds of cattle to Rebel armies in Louisiana, Arkansas, and Indian Territory. At the same time he established a ranch in Concho County near the Colorado River. He later moved his headquarters to Bosque Grande on the Pecos River in New Mexico, and in 1873 settled at South Spring near present-day Roswell. Chisum died at Eureka Springs, Arkansas, on 22 December 1884. Webb and Carroll, *Handbook of Texas*, 1:342-43.

The main branch of Brady Creek heads in southwestern Concho County and runs east for a hundred miles through Concho and McCulloch counties into San Saba County and past the town of Brady where it joins the San Saba River.

5 Along with William T. Smith, Benjamin Coons, Marciano Varela, August Santiesteban, and James and John Edgar, Valdez was a leading freighter in the El Paso area. Mills, *Forty Years at El Paso*, 180.

6 George Frazer, who owned a 1,900-acre farm at Leon Springs, served as Pecos County judge from 1872 to 1884. Reeves County was carved from Pecos County in 1883. Marsha Lea Daggett, ed., *Pecos County History* (Canyon: Staked Plains Press, 1984), 107-10, 127.

7 A green oasis, nine miles west of Fort Stockton, in a vast greasewood-studded desert, Leon Springs or Leon Holes was a welcome site to weary travelers on the San Antonio-El Paso Road. The springs consisted of three watering holes that averaged thirty feet in diameter and twenty feet deep. In the decade before the Civil War and in the era that followed, the springs were the scene of numerous confrontations with hostile Kiowas, Comanches, and Mescalero Apaches. Austerman, *Sharps Rifles and Spanish Mules*, 39; and Williams, *Texas' Last Frontier*, 132-33.

8 Barrilla or Varela Spring is near the junction of Reeves, Pecos, and Jeff Davis counties, just south of the Barrilla Mountains and east of Wild Rose Pass, about eight miles from State Highway 17. Only a seepage and a few trees are found at the site today. Roscoe P. and Margaret B. Conkling, *The Butterfield Overland Mail, 1857-1869* (Glendale: Arthur H. Clark Co., 1947), 2:23; Williams, *Texas' Last Frontier*, 263; and Thompson, ed. *Westward the Texans*, 142.

CHAPTER THREE

Fight with Apaches, San Simón Valley, Arizona, 1871

~

THE FOLLOWING ACCOUNT OF A DESPERATE ENCOUNTER with a murderous band of Apaches Indians was given the writer by Mr. Gilbert, an old time frontiersman and at present the owner of a beautiful home on Seven Rivers in Eddy County, New Mexico, where he has a fine orchard of choice fruit trees, enjoying a quiet life after many hair-breadth escapes in encounters with Indians.

Gilbert was born in Jackson County, Tennessee, November 7th, 1828, and came to Texas in 1837, too late to be a hero of San Jacinto, but in plenty of time to see much of the stirring events after that. The family numbered just an even dozen, the father, mother, seven sons and three daughters, and settled near Bonham in Fannin County, at that time a comparative wilderness, filled with buffalo, deer, turkeys and many "varmints," besides too many Indians to agree with the idea of safety among even the hardy pioneers of that day. Although those who came from Tennessee and the dark and bloody ground had heard of the struggles of their fathers with the Indians, still they were willing to risk all dangers in order to have ample elbow room and enjoy the pleasure of a wild life in a new country teeming with game and literally flowing with milk and honey.

Gilbert remained in Texas until 1849, when the discovery of glittering gold in the mill race of Sutter caused a general stampede for California. He got the fever and joined an emigrant train bound for the new El Dorado, but he found, as many a poor devil did, that it was "all work and no play—or pay," and the broad beautiful prairies of Texas seemed good. So he returned in 1852, but like all men who have ever humped themselves up over a rocker, or watched the water run through leaving a small nugget now and then in the riffle box, he could not be content and again pulled out for California to again woo the fickle goddess, Fortune. It was the same old story, however, and the writer can deeply sympathize with him as he is one of the originals [of] Greenhorn Gulch, on Kern River. Very few people at that time who passed over the hills and dales of Arizona, looking forward eagerly to the golden sands of California being under their feet, ever thought of looking for the precious metal there, and young Gilbert was seized with an irresistible impulse to go back and take a look. As all his former trips back and forth had been in wagons, he decided to try it on horseback and, buying a good animal at Bakersfield, on April 3, 1871, he started for Arizona.

Arriving in due course of time at Prescott he found a large party of miners gathered there, who believed as he did, that gold in abundance could be found by prospecting. There were two hundred and nine men who organized, armed and provisioned themselves, and felt no uneasiness about holding their own with the entire Apache nation. In fact they would have enjoyed a brush with them. Gov. [Anson P.K.] Safford was appointed as leader of the expedition, and they set out full of hope and prospected the country north of the Gila River, and then turning up Salt River, went to its head waters, but found nothing worthy of note.[1] Not even the settlement of disappointed office seekers, whose headquarters are supposed to be "thar abouts," were to be found.

Gilbert now thought he would try New Mexico, for a rumor was in the air that a party of returning Californians had discovered rich placer diggings in the Guadalupe Mountains, but the Indians were so bad they could not work them. This rumor caused "Old Gotch," alias Gen. William Hardeman of Texas, to head an expedition up there, but the placers are still quietly sleeping, waiting for some cowboy or tenderfoot to stumble [on] them, as at Leadville or Cripple Creek.[2]

Gilbert and a young man named R[ichard] Barnes then started out for Seven Rivers, New Mexico. You will observe these two men started out with no more hesitation than an old farmer would feel in Kentucky in visiting his nearest neighbor. Gilbert had been over the road so often that he was quite familiar with it, and also with danger, as one will become who lives long on the frontier, constant exposure to death robbing it of its horrors, or rather dread.

They reached San Simón Valley, now a noted and prosperous cattle ranch, where they found an Irishman had settled, without asking permission of the Apaches who were the original owners of the country, and had several intimations that he had better move if he valued his scalp.[3] But with the well known lack of fear and delight in scrapping, he had determined to stop there and make a fortune raising "spuds" and other truck for the soldiers at Camp Bowie, and for the traveling public.

The San Simón Valley was such a beautiful valley lying like an emerald in the waste, and the grass and game and everything suiting Gilbert's fancy, he determined to buy the place and give up roving and mining. After a good deal of talk the Irishman, whose name was Hugh O'Neal, agreed to sell to Gilbert, giving a quit claim to his little improvements, consisting of about ten acres of irrigable land, an adobe house thatched with tule, and incidentally the prospect of being scalped.[4] Gilbert took Barnes in as a partner. Poor fellow. It fell to his lot to furnish the scalp.

The partners worked on for about a month, when Gilbert suggested that the tule swamp was a good place in which to raise all their meat and some to sell. Venison, antelope and small game were abundant, but spare ribs, sausage and lard, fresh and sweet, were better, so Barnes went to Camp Bowie and got a few hogs for "seed" and no doubt the poor fellow counted his pigs before they were hatched.

On his way back Barnes saw Indian signs and although he made the trip safely he felt uneasy about the Apaches and they both remained close about the house. One day Barnes went a short distance from the house to get some wood to cook with and have a little fire at night. It was in October and Gilbert was working about the house. Barnes, with the heedlessness that has lost many a man on the frontier his life, had gone without his gun or pistol. Suddenly the usual silence of the place was broken by six shots fired in rapid succession, followed by an ominous silence.[5]

Gilbert, hearing the reports of the gun, knew what they meant at once and ran into the house for his rifle to aid his partner, if possible, but soon a band of thirty or forty Apaches came on a charge from the direction Barnes had gone and Gilbert knew that the poor fellow's fate was sealed and ran into the house, closing the door and determined to avenge his death and make it hot for the murderers.[6] He opened fire at once, using the rifles principally and reserving one pistol for an emergency.

The old Irishman had cut port holes on all four sides of the house, just large enough to shoot through, and flared outwardly so as to pretty well command all the ground. Gilbert, being a cool brave man such as you might expect from the land of Davy Crockett, and a quick shot, soon had seven of the Indians laid on the ground and others wounded.

The Indians, battled in their attempt to carry the house by assault, retired out of range in the brush, but not without having wounded Gilbert. A stray bullet had struck the door knob, glanced and struck him in the side, but as the ball was flattened and its force somewhat spent, it did not penetrate to any depth. It carried into the wound a wad of his clothes, and finally dropped out while he was running from one port hole to the other during the fight.

Having time, Gilbert hastily reloaded the empty pistols and determined to make a break for the tule swamp. The spring was about one hundred yards from the house and the water flowing from it caused quite a large body of land to be densely covered by tules or cat-tails as we call them. These cat-tails have been used a great deal for that purpose all over the west. They were hard to set on fire, but once started, would burn fiercely, and he knew the Indians would resort to fire and roast him. Peeping through one of the port holes he saw smoke, felt that they would soon charge again, and set fire to the roof, and there was no time to be lost, so he cautiously opened the door and looked out. All was clear between him and "the haven where he would be," but glancing to the right his eye caught the shadow of a big Indian on the ground at the corner of the house standing with his gun ready to shoot. This, in the language of old Texas Rangers, was "a dead give away," and settled the fate of the Apache. With his rifle over his left arm and revolver in his hand, he tiptoed along and sprang with the shrill scream of a panther to the corner. The Indian was so astonished and unnerved, he did not shoot, but fell backward with a ball through his heart.

Gilbert then sprang away with the speed of an old black-tail buck going down a mountain. The Indians saw their little scheme defeated, and made the welkin ring with hideous yells. They opened fire on him and soon bullets were knocking up the dust all around him, and whizzing about his ears, but that only made him run the faster. He fired back at them as he ran four shots from Barnes's pistol and then plunged into the thick tules ahead of them and disappeared from "hound and hunter's ken" as suddenly as the stag from Fitz James.

The Indians dared not follow him, nor could they remain on the open ground. The tules were green, so they could not burn him out. He moved in towards the center of the patch, which was three hundred yards wide, and soon found he had to face a danger almost as great as that from the Apache bullets, arrows and lances. The soft, black mud was giving way under him, and unless he could find some way to prevent it, he would probably be smothered—a death, however, that he preferred to being roasted.

Gilbert's genius for making the most of adverse circumstances did not fail in this new danger and he bent down some of the largest clusters of the cattails and managed to pull up and lay across these enough to keep him from sinking. He had trouble to keep "his powder dry," but after making a regular alligator's nest he got on top of it and reloaded Barnes's pistol.

It was 10 o'clock in the morning when he entered the tules, and the Indians, after robbing the house of everything in it, had given up the fight, pretty badly worsted, for they got only one scalp and lost eight of their warriors. The little plunder in the house was very poor pay for their losses. They did not care to poke around in the tules for a man that could put up such a fight as Gilbert, and accordingly left for their stronghold in the Chiricahua Mountains, knowing that the troops from Bowie would be after them as soon as they got the news.

Gilbert stayed in the tules until dark. Then he managed to wade through the bog to the edge and crawled for some distance for fear some of the Apaches had remained to watch him. He got away safely, however, on the Camp Bowie side of the tules, and by daylight next morning was fifteen miles from his ranch, on the road to Camp Bowie.

As soon as the sun rose the heat became quite oppressive, and being faint from loss of blood and the pain from his wound he left the road to seek water, shade, and rest. Knowing from long experience that the cliff and rocks generally afforded these luxuries, he turned towards them. Finding a dim trail on the mountain side that showed it had been freshly used by the coyotes and other "varmints" he followed it into a deep rough, rocky canyon, and was delighted to see swarms of butterflies and wasps—a sure indication that water could be found near the surface.

Looking around Gilbert found where the coyotes had dug quite a deep hole in a crevice in the rocks. He saw it showed moisture in the bottom and began to clean out the black mud and leaves and insects, that did not smell at all like Lubin's extract. Digging down as far as he could reach, he had the satisfaction of feeling the cool water fill into the bottom of the hole and felt the joy of anticipation that only a man who has been nearly dead on the plains for need of water can appreciate. But while impatiently waiting for the water to run in and become somewhat clear, a new difficulty presented itself. The water was three feet down in a hole or crevice and he had no cup or canteen, and not being a coyote or a crane, it would be hard to get a drink. His talent for making the best of a bad bargain then came into play again and he hauled off his boot and putting it down got this impromptu "old oaken bucket" full of water. Although he had drank water from the coldest springs of the mountains of Tennessee out of an old gourd, from the rivulets in the Sierra Nevada from melted snow, and from wells of pure sweet water, Gilbert said that was the sweetest drink of water he had ever taken in his life, but he had to acknowledge it tasted a little of bucket and curbing.

He now felt the real comfort that the wayfarer of old had in being "in the shadow of a great rock in the desert" and sought "nature's sweet restorer, balmy sleep," though he began to feel the need of something to eat, having been thirty hours without food. He slept soundly for several hours, and being greatly refreshed started on his journey again with renewed vigor and visions of Uncle Sam's ham and eggs, hot coffee, baker's bread, and other substantials that would be a very pleasant change from water out of a boot.

When he had gone about eight miles he began to feel very faint and had to lie down and rest every two or three hundred yards. His wound was very painful and still bleeding when he came suddenly on the herd of horses and mules of the men at a hay camp.[7] The Mexican in charge took him to be an Indian, and hastily mounting his horse, began to round up his stock.

Gilbert yelled at the Mexican and finally threatened to kill him if he did not come to him. He finally got him to understand his condition and then the Mexican was all kindness as Mexicans always are to those in distress. He put Gilbert on his horse and took him to the hay camp, where he was kindly received, and had his vision of good United States grub realized. The soldiers sent him to Camp Bowie and there he received every attention and care that a skillful surgeon could give.

As soon as Post Commander Capt. [Harry M.] Smith, of the Twenty-first Infantry, heard of the murder he started Capt. G[erald] Russell of the Third Cavalry out after the Apaches with a force of thirty men.[8] They found poor Barnes's body full of bullet holes, arrow and lance wounds, and scalped and horribly mutilated. The Indians had gotten what little satisfaction they could for their defeat by mutilating his dead body. Captain Russell buried him and then took the trail of the Indians that led direct to their stronghold in the Chiricahua Mountains. The captain found them in Horseshoe Canyon and a hot fight began at once with all the advantages in favor of the Indians.[9]

It often happened that very unjust reflections on our army officers and men were indulged in by civilians, but if they had followed the Apaches a few times they would have seen the difficulty attending campaigning in the mountain vastness. The Indians always made for some deep narrow canyon and after getting in a few miles could get on the cliff and go back and ambuscade their trail. When the troop reached the mouth of a canyon they knew perfectly well if they entered the canyon the Indians could kill their horses from the cliffs; if they left the horses, unless there was a strong guard, the Indians could ride back, kill the guards and stampede their horses and set them afoot. So really to make a fair thing of it the officers should have had three times as many men as the Indians, and also a strong guard for their horses, and a flanking form to prevent the Indians from ambuscading them in the cliffs, while the force that marched up the canyon should be equal in strength to the enemy. Of course the Indians then would have nothing to do, unless they chose to fight, but mount their ponies and leave the troops to walk back to their horses.

Captain Russell had ridden in on the trail and the Indians opened fire on him, killing two men and three horses.[10] He was compelled to retreat, but kept his men well in hand. The Indians followed him, it being a clear moonlight night, until he reached the valley, keeping however, at a respectful distance and afraid to come into the open where a charge could be made by the cavalry.

Gilbert remained at Camp Bowie and was in the hospital for two months under the care of United States Surgeon Dr. Atchell, for whom he entertained always afterwards the kindest feeling.[11]

Satisfied with enough mining and farming among'st the noble Redmen, he turned his face towards Seven Rivers, although he did not get rid of the Apaches, for they were at Fort Stanton Reservation, near the present town of Tularosa, and, although their habit was not to steal and murder near the home Uncle Sam generously provided for them, yet they could not resist stealing and murdering when a good opportunity offered, so the early settlers on the Pecos River suffered for years from their depredations.

Let us hope the old frontiersman in his declining years may have the quiet and peace denied him in his younger days.

NOTES

[1] Known as the little governor because of his diminutive size, Safford promoted mines and schools. He was also governor at the time of the infamous Camp Grant Massacre. Poor health kept him from accepting a second appointment as governor in 1877. Thomas E. Sheridan, *Arizona: A History* (Tucson: University of Arizona Press, 1995), 81, 86, 109.

[2] See n. 16, Ch. 1, Sec. II.

[3] In the heart of Apachería, the rich grasses of the San Simón Valley were noted by the Mormon Battalion in 1847. The San Simón River was known to early settlers as the Rio de Suaz (River of Willows). Maps prepared in the 1850s note a "Ciénaga de Suaz" or Willow Springs. In 1859, the Butterfield Stage Line built a relay station in the valley, half way between Stein's Peak and Apache Pass. The Gilbert-Barnes Ranch at Ciénaga de Sauz or Ciénaga de San Simón, which consisted of two adobe houses about two hundred yards apart, was fifteen miles from the San Simón Station and twenty-five miles from Fort Bowie. Marshall Trimble, *Roadside History of Arizona* (Missoula: Mountain Press Publish-

ing Co., 1986), 34-35; James M. Barney, *Tales of Apache Warfare: True Stories of Massacres, Fights and Raids in Arizona and New Mexico* (By the author, 1933), 22-23.

4 North of the Chiricahua Mountains and northeast of Apache Pass, the site was at what is today the village of San Simón.

5 The attack was on Saturday, 21 October 1871, at about six in the morning. Barnes' body was later found and buried by Capt. Harry M. Smith of the 21st Infantry from Fort Bowie. Barney, *Tales of Apache Warfare*, 21.

6 For the best account of Gilbert and Barnes's fight with the Chiricahua Apaches, see: Sweeney, *Cochise*, 326. The Apaches were reported to number as many as sixty.

7 This was the camp of David Wood, nine miles from Fort Bowie.

8 Born at Washington, Pennsylvania, about 1832, Smith fought with the Ohio Volunteers during the Civil War. Although discharged in 1865, he was commissioned in the 19th Infantry but transferred to the 28th Infantry in 1869 and later to the 21st Infantry. In command of Co. G, he was stationed at Camp Bowie at the time of the attack. In investigating the Apache raid and the death of Barnes, Smith found Gilbert's "statements to be correct." Smith died in Idaho on 23 April 1877. Altshuler, *Cavalry Yellow & Infantry Blue*, 309; Barney, *Tales of Apache Warfare*, 22.

Born at Tipperrary, Ireland, 1 May 1832, Russell enlisted in the Mounted Rifles in Philadelphia in 1851. During the Civil War he was commissioned a 2d lieutenant in the 3d Cavalry. In command of Co. K of the 3d Cavalry, he arrived at Camp Bowie in May 1870. He retired from the army in 1890 and died in New York City on 2 April 1905. Altshuler, *Cavalry Yellow & Infantry Blue*, 290-91.

9 After the fight at San Simón, Captain Russell and twenty-five men followed the Chiricahuas' trail south along the eastern slopes of the Chiricahua Mountains and then west into Horseshoe Canyon. Here Col. Reuben Bernard had fought Cochise two years earlier. As Russell's Bluecoats halted to water their mounts, the Indians opened fire on the patrol from several directions. Sweeney, *Cochise*, 326-27.

10 Russell's guide, Bob Whitney, was killed in the fight and two other troopers were wounded. Since the soldiers had fired two thousand rounds in the four-hour encounter, Russell was sure the Apaches had been severely punished. Ibid.

11 Atchell, or possibly Mitchell, cannot be identified with any certainty.

CHAPTER FOUR

Fight in the Sierra Ventana

~

IN AUGUST 1879, the writer with a detachment of Company C (Capt. [George W.] Arrington), left San Antonio, Texas, for Ysleta in El Paso County.[1]

I had been farming in a small way, raising mostly game chickens, and being in bad health, I found that I was no match for the big-fisted, broad-backed Germans gardening. So I wrote to Adjt. Gen. John B. Jones and told him that if he had any Indians out west that he wanted killed and scalped, I thought I was better muscled for that than for raising cabbages and onions.[2]

I soon had an answer saying that the only vacancy at the time was a lieutenancy out at El Paso where I would have ten men and the pay was $75 per month with my rations, forage and quarters. As I had been about two years on scant rations and no pay, I told him I would accept the offer.

He then telegraphed me to come to Austin, and on my arrival in the capital, he explained to me the situation. A mob of Mexicans had killed Judge [Charles W.] Howard, [Charles] Ellis, [John] Atkinson and [John] McBride of the Rangers, and there was still a bitter feeling between the Mexicans and the Americans.[3] There were two parties, and I would have to use a great deal of discretion in order to avoid further trouble. As I had lived in San Antonio since 1846, off and on, and spoke Spanish fairly well, while some of my most intimate friends were Mexicans, I had no fear about getting along very well, especially as I had formed acquaintances there in 1861. Furthermore, my brother, Gen. John R. Baylor, had a great many warm friends among the Mexicans.

NEW MEXICO

Cornudas
Mountains

Guadalupe Mountains

EL PASO DEL NORTE
(Juarez)

EL PASO

Crow Flats ×

Sierra Diablo

Davis Mountains

Laguna
de Guzman

Ysleta

Eagle Mountains

Janos

Rio Casas Grandes

Candelaria

Mountains

Zaragoza

Guadalupe

Fort Quitman

Quitman Mountains

Fort Davis

Corralitos

Carrizal

Rancheria
Mountains

TEXAS

Casas Grandes

Rio Santa Maria

Sierra
Ventanas

×

Tres
Castillos ×

MEXICO

Cuidad
Chihuahua

0   25   50   75

VICTORIO WAR   •   1879–1881

The adjutant general went with me to call on Gov. O[ran] M[ilo] Roberts, the old alcalde of blessed memory, who gave me instructions as to my duties under the circumstances.[4] When I arose to leave, he said: "Lieutenant Baylor, I want you to remember out in that far, wild country that you represent the honor and dignity of the great state of Texas." So I straightened up and replied: "Governor, as far as an army of ten men can do it, you may rest assured I will."

As a nucleus for a company, Adjutant General Jones said he would give me two well tried Rangers, Sgt. James B. Gillett and Henry Mortimer. Three more men were willing to go with me and take chances of getting in my company, namely, Dick Hedges, Gus Kraukauer [Krimpkau], who was after killed by Johnnie Hale in El Paso, and George Hoerld, one of your very best detective and police officers.[5] He is of German extraction and hence his name is not Harold. Several others joined me, so we were quite-a-little party. My ambulance, with my wife and two girls and sister-in-law, and two of my own wagons with a company wagon made quite a train.[6]

We came through without seeing any Indians, though they passed just behind us at Howard's Wells, and just ahead of us between El Muerto, in the Davis Mountains, and Van Horn's Wells.[7] They were likely the same Indians who had been on a raid down the settlements, and were returning to the Mescalero Reservation near Tularosa. At Howard's Wells we saw the evidence of Apache work, where they had captured a train of government supplies. Quite a number of wagons had been burned, and the empty cans all left in great piles just where the wagons stood. The Indians cared little for canned goods. Naturally we were on the alert and the guards extra vigilant, and becoming suspicious of danger from the action of some of the mules, our herd was brought in and tied up to the wagons. There I issued my first special order, No. 1, and to my wife: "If a row comes off tonight, don't scream. Put Mary (the youngest girl) in the oven of the cooking stove. Lie down with Kate and Helen, and remain quiet."

Happily the Indians, seeing we were ready for them and held the water, passed on to the west of Howards's Wells. These wells were dug by Maj. Tom Howard, of San Antonio, who commanded the Texas troops when the fight occurred in San Antonio with the Comanches.[8]

We arrived at [Fort] Quitman and traveled slowly up the Rio Grande, which at that time was not navigable for even mud turtles, as the water holes were far apart. We could scarcely get enough to water ourselves and stock. On the 12th of September, 1879, we landed in the plaza of Ysleta, after six weeks of hard travel, and were kindly received by the citizens. It was then the county seat.

On October 4, we received by a runner from my old friend Capt. Gregorio N. García, a letter stating that the Indians had attacked a camp of *grameros* (hay cutters), in front of La Cuadrilla on the mesa, and all but one, who escaped and brought the alarm, were killed.[9] There were some eight or nine in the party. It was near midnight, but the Rangers were soon up and as anxious to get off as though it was a picnic they were invited to. Sgt. James B. Gillett soon had our grub out, and calling off each article of the grub, the only way to keep from leaving something. It was soon on our two pack mules. Roll being called, we were ready to ride. Detailing one man to keep camp, we silently filed out at midnight, and by daylight were at Hawkin's Station near where Fabens' Station is now.[10] There we were told we would find the sole survivor of the terrible massacre.

Riding to the door, we had to thump some time before we had any evidence that any one was alive on the premises. Finally the door opened about an inch, very cautiously, and I saw the eye of a Mexican. Asking him if he had been one of the *grameros*, he answered "Si, Señor." I then asked for the account of the affair. He said it was nearly dark when the Apaches, anywhere from twenty-five to fifty, charged their camp, and uttered such horrid yells that everybody took to his heels and was soon in the chaparral. He said he saw his "*pobrecito papá*" running with Apaches about to lance him, and he knew that he and all the balance of the party were killed. He only escaped. As he mentioned the tragic death of his beloved parent the tears rolled down his cheeks. I comforted him as well as I could, and asked if he could guide us out to their camp. But he declined with thanks, saying he must stay to help the station keeper take care of the stage mules. But if I would go down below a mile I would see the ranch where some of the dead men's families lived, where I could no doubt get a guide. We had come by San Elizario, and I found that grand, brave old Mexican, Capt. Gregorio García, waiting for us, his horse saddled and blankets and grub ready. It was nothing new to him, as he was always ready to go after the Apaches. He served under Col. John R. Baylor in the campaign against the Federal troops at Fort Fil[l]more, when Maj. [Isaac] Lynde was captured at San Agustín Springs in 1861. Captain García, with some of the citizens of San Elizario, prevented the massacre of the United States troops in Dog Canyon by his skill and courage. Martín Alarcón, a brother of Mrs. Ellis, also joined us.

When we arrived at the ranch below Hawkins' Station, it was sunrise and we halted for breakfast. The people of the ranch were very uneasy when we rode up, but were rejoiced when they saw we were Texas Rangers and learned our mission. They showed us every attention. Among the first to come out was an old Mexican who was in the hay camp when it was attacked.

He gave a lurid account of the onset. His son was of the party, and when he mentioned it the tears began to flow. "*Ah, hijo de mi corazón!*[11] I shall never see him again. All were killed and I alone escaped." I could hardly keep my face straight, when I told him I had just left his son, who was very much alive and mourned him as dead. It turned out that all the dead men turned up alive. They had scattered each man for himself, and the Apaches were too busy looting the camp to follow them. Moreover, those ranchers would fight, and the Indians did not care to follow them in the brush.

A bright young Mexican went with us to the hay camp, which was on the mesa about six miles towards the Comales, where Don Juan Armendáriz now has a cow ranch. The Apaches had made a mess of it sure enough. They had broken all the cups and plates, poured salt into the sugar, this combination into the flour and beans, and the conglomeration of the whole onto the ground, as the sacks were all they wanted. They then took an ax and smashed the coffee pot, frying pan and skillet. They took all the blankets and started out east as though they intended to go to the Sierra Prieta. But after going a mile the trail turned south. Our guide went back to give the alarm below to the ranches, and we followed the trail down the mesa until opposite Guadalupe. There we crossed the Overland Stage Road near the present Rio Grande Station, where we found our guide waiting for us on the trail. He had discovered the trail, and not knowing but that the Indians might ambuscade the road below, he waited for us. The trail made straight for the Rio Grande crossing, just above the town of Guadalupe on the Mexican side.

We had some trouble in following the sign after we got in the river bottom, where loose horses and cattle ran, but a few of us dismounted, worked it across the river and struck camp for dinner. Captain García was sent down to Guadalupe to ask permission of the alcalde to follow the trail into Mexico. The Rangers had never crossed the river since the death of Howard and others, and we were not sure whether we would be welcome. The alcalde sent me word he would gladly give me permission, and they would organize and go with us after the Indians. This suited us first-rate, as there were eighteen warriors from the sign, and we knew they were as well armed as we were. Just after we crossed the river we came across a Mexican herder with a flock of goats. As soon as he heard we were trailing Apaches he began yelling at the top of his voice, and soon had his goats on the jump for town, though the Apaches had passed the night before. We were soon in the saddle, and as we rode into the pueblo we were kindly greeted by the people. There was great excitement. A man had found a mare killed just on the edge of town, having been lanced, and some of the choice steaks taken by the Indians. A runner, too, had just ridden into town sent by that brave old ranchero, Don Ramón

Ar[r]anda, from Contar Resio, or Tanks, saying a band of eighteen Apaches had killed his herder and run off all the stage mules. His ranch [San Marcos de Cantarricia] was on the stage road to Chihuahua, and about twenty miles southwest from Guadalupe.

We only halted a few minutes and pushed on for Ar[r]anda's ranch, where we arrived in time to see the old warrior sallying out to recover the body of the herder. At first we could hardly make out who or what they were, as old Ramón was mounted bareback on a fiery horse, his Winchester in hand, while another man was riding behind, also armed, and two or three of the ranchmen were clattering at his heels. They came down the road to meet us, raising a cloud of dust, and could easily have been mistaken for Apaches. We dismounted at his ranch and went into camp, pretty well tired out, having made quite sixty miles since we left Ysleta. As I had not been on horseback at that time for nearly eight years, my feelings can be imagined.[12]

As soon as Don Ramón returned with the body of the herder, he came out and insisted on our coming into the house. But we told him we had rather too large a family, and besides preferred to be near our horses. I went over to see the old Don. The body of the herder lay on a table, with candles at his head and feet. His face was rigid in death and made a weird picture. Combined with the fact that we had brought along a pick and shovel it made me feel a little "melancholy" anticipating what might be the close of our scout. But the soldier does not dwell long on the sad side of war, and, as the volunteers from Guadalupe and San Ignacio came riding in, all was bustle and excitement. The thought of a brush with Apaches and the avenging of the herder's death dispelled all gloomy forebodings.

By daylight we were off on the trail, going south towards the Cañada de los Mar[r]anos in the Sierra Ventana, our Mexican allies, twenty-three men, good and true, taking the lead.[13] After riding briskly for about twenty-five miles on the trail, it turned into the mouth of the canyon, a rough dark forbidding looking place, the cliffs of rock suggesting lurking Apaches and death. The Mexicans who were a little way ahead turned to the left at the foot of the mountain and waited for us, and when we came up we held a council of war. They suggested that I should take my nine men and they would select ten and follow the trail into the canyon. I told them that would never do, as the Apaches had no doubt anticipated just such a move and were hidden in the cliffs where they could kill us without exposing themselves in the least. But we would have an even break by going up the side of the mountain and following right down on top of the ridge in their rear. No sooner was this said than done. The Mexicans left four or five men and I left Dick Hedges, an old frontiersman, and Gus Small of San Antonio, with our horses; for the

Indians, in case our guard had been too small, could have come out of the canyon on horseback, killed our guard, got our grub and blankets and set us afoot. So I asked Captain García and Alarcón to stay with the guard.

The Mexicans got off ahead of me, so I took the near shoot to reach the crest of the mountain, which was about six or eight hundred yards off, and between them and the canyon, where I knew the Apaches were laying for us. It was a pretty steep pull, and as we went along I pulled a lot of bunch grass and stuck it all around under my hat band, so my head would look like a big bunch of grass. It would also conceal my head and body in a measure if I should have to flatten myself out on the ground, which I always did when necessary, although in no disgrace, and cautioning my boys to do the same. The loss of Gen. Albert Sidney Johnston at Shiloh, the loss of English officers in the Transvaal, and more as common horse-sense. It demoralizes the men more to see a beloved commander shot down before them, than to see him safely under cover until the command to charge is given, when it would be proper for him to be in front or close behind the firing line.

The Apaches, seeing we would not "walk into their parlor," and having the nearest cut, got on the crest of the mountain first. There they met the Mexicans, who fired the first shot and killed an Indian. Hurrying up to their right, we had almost reached the crest where there was a mass of rough boulders, when a big Apache arose and fired. The bullet whizzed so close to my nose that I could almost smell it, and it cut the rim of Sergeant Gillett's hat, who was just behind me.[14] The sergeant, who was one of the quickest and best shots with a Winchester that I ever saw, threw up his carbine and fired at the Indian, who was not over fifteen yards distant, and bored him through the ribs. I looked back to give the order to take cover, but the first bullet had acted better than the command of the major general of militia. Every man was behind a rock. I sprawled out behind a big *palma* or Spanish dagger, and would have been glad to have had even a ladies' pasteboard hat-box between me and the ugly looking boulder. Bang and a bullet went through my *palma*, just over my head. I heard the noise a Winchester makes when another cartridge is thrown into the barrel, and bang! whiz! another bullet followed, showing the Indian had me pretty well located. The last shot filled my face with the trash and bark of the *palma*.[15] As there was a rock close and I could crawfish down the hill easily, I wriggled back behind the friendly solid stone, slipping my rifle forward and keeping my eye on the rocks that I saw the smoke issue from. I hoped the Apache would peep over the top to see if I was dead, when I could easily have shot his eye out.

The Mexicans on our left were keeping up a lively fire, and the Apaches to our right had opened fire on our guard and the horses. Sgt. [Tom] Swilling's horse, a large white one, was shot through the heart. We could see the bullets knocking up the dust all around and the guard shooting back, and when Swilling's horse was hit he staggered around and tumbled over. The sergeant began to mourn, having the horror all western men have of walking. John Thomas got the laugh on him in time by saying: "Sergeant, you better wait and see if you are going back to camp." I heard the Indians in front chattering. It sounded like the Guinea hen's "pot-racks, pot-racks." But Pablo Mejía, who had been a guide from the United States cavalry and knew some of their lingo, said the leader's order was—that they must "get together and shoot fast." This was good advice. So, as George Hoerld told me, the Mexicans had a good place to fight from, and the Indians had quit us in front and quit shooting at our guard and horses, [so] we joined the Mexicans. They were on a high bluff, overlooking the valley where the water tanks were, and there were some of the stage stock in full view, about 500 yards distant but way below us. From this bluff we began shooting at the smoke of the Indians and occasionally a black bushy head would appear. The only damage I did individually was to shoot a mule, and when an Indian came out to try to get him under cover I took a pop at him. This made him hunt his cover in a hurry. Some of the Apaches had gotten up on the same ridge we were on, and opened fire on us. But we could see only the smoke of their guns. We sent one bullet back at them. One Indian was across the canyon on the top of a high peak. He must have been nearly a mile off. He had an old 50-caliber United States Minie rifle. He would occasionally hit the cliff below us and knock off a chunk as big as a washtub. We kept up our fire until nearly dark. By that time the Indians had posted themselves so as to command the water. We did not care to take any chance of being set afoot, by making a charge, for they could easily have mounted their horses, and by running out of the canyon could have beaten us to our horse guard. So we deemed it best to return to the guard. We might have taken the tanks where the water was, but it would have made the "drinks" too high.

Sergeant Swilling did not walk. Each one of the men took his blankets, and one pack mule could carry all the grub. Old Beck took the sergeant to Ar[r]anda's ranch, where we all arrived after midnight pretty well tired out. The next night we spent with the hospitable *ciudadaños* of Guadalupe, who treated us royally.[16] The 8th act saw us back at our quarters, glad we had had no occasion to use our pick and shovel.

The following is a list of our Rangers: Some are dead, and others are scattered over the West. First Sgt. James B. Gillett, Second Sergeant Swilling, Privates George Lloyd, Henry Mortimer, John Thomas, George Hoerld, Gus Small, Richard Head, and Pablo Mejía. The last named was a citizen of San

Elizario, and a regular little game cock. He was killed in the massacre of the Mexicans between Galeana and Casas Grandes, by old Juh and Geronimo's band. It was at the same time that Juan Mata Ortiz and many of the leading Mexicans of Galeana were killed.[17] The Apaches knew and hated Pablo Mejía, and they had placed his head on a stone and pounded it flat.

I send New Year's greetings to my old Rangers, wherever they may be.

NOTES

[1] Arrington was born at Greensboro, Alabama, on 23 December 1844. He fought with John S. Mosby's guerrillas during the Civil War and later with the French Imperialists in Mexico. He joined the Rangers about 1875 and served in the Lower Rio Grande Valley after which he was made captain of Company C of the Frontier Battalion. Stationed in the Panhandle to investigate depredations on Charles Goodnight's ranch, he became the first Ranger captain in the area and in Walter Prescott Webb's words, "the iron-handed man of the Panhandle." In 1882 Arrington resigned to manage a ranch and pursue his own ranching interests. He was later elected sheriff of Wheeler County. Arrington died in 1923. Webb, *Texas Rangers*, 411-20.

[2] In 1838, Jones came to Texas from South Carolina with his father. During the Civil War he became a captain in Terry's Texas Rangers. In 1865, he fled to Mexico and then Brazil. After the war, he was commissioned a major in the Frontier Battalion and with six companies was ordered to stop the frontier violence in the state. Jones went to El Paso in 1877 to quell the Salt War and was temporarily successful but after he left, the violence was renewed. In January 1879, Jones became adjutant general of Texas and continued in that capacity until his death on 19 July 1881. W.P. Webb, "John B. Jones," *Handbook of Texas*, 1:924-25; and Webb, *Texas Rangers*, 309-57.

[3] The best study of the Salt War remains Sonnichsen's *The El Paso Salt War*.

[4] Roberts, the "Old Alcalde," was born in South Carolina in 1815 and studied law at the University of Alabama. In 1841, he moved to Texas and set up a law office at San Augustine. He rose to become associate justice of the Supreme Court of Texas, and in 1861 was instrumental in calling the Secession Convention of which he was elected president. In 1862, he helped recruit a regiment of the 11th Texas Infantry and served as its colonel until 1864. After the war, he was elected to the United States Senate but was refused admission by the Radical Republican Congress. Roberts returned to the Texas Supreme Court and in 1878 was elected governor. He retired in 1883 to become professor of law at the University of Texas and died in Austin on 19 May 1898. Claude Elliott, "Oran Milo Roberts," *Handbook of Texas*, 2:484-85.

[5] None of the men Baylor listed were still with the Rangers by the summer of 1880. 10th Census, El Paso County, Tex. For the shooting of Krimpkau, see Ch. 10, Sec. III. For an excellent overview of the Rangers in far West Texas, see James M. Day, "El Paso's Texas Rangers," *Password* 24 (Winter 1979): 153-72.

[6] Baylor's lengthy trip to El Paso is poignantly depicted by Tom Lea in his "Ranger Escort West of the Pecos." This painting, which was donated to the state of Texas, was used by the University of Texas Press for the dust jacket of Walter Prescott Webb's *Texas Rangers*.

7 Forty-four miles northwest of Beaver Lake, Howard Spring or Well was a primary water-
  ing stop on the San Antonio-El Paso Road. Since the water level was twelve feet from the
  surface, the precious liquid had to be brought up in buckets. The spring is located on
  Howard Creek near Ozona in southern Crockett County. Austerman, *Sharps Rifles and
  Spanish Mules*, 41; and James Collette, "Bloody Legacy of Howard's Well," *Old West* 21
  (Spring 1985): 55-59.

  For El Muerto, see n. 14, Ch. 2, Sec. I.

  Van Horn's Wells, some twelve miles south of modern-day Van Horn, was a small spring
  on the east side of the Van Horn Mountains. The spring and a roughly finished rock and
  adobe relay post on the San Antonio-El Paso Road were named for Maj. Jefferson Van
  Horne who began his military career in West Texas in 1849.

8 Howard Well was named after Richard A. Howard, an ex-Texas Ranger from San Antonio who came upon the water in 1848 as part of the expedition of Col. John Coffee Hays.

9 Gregorio Nacianceno García I, was born in San Elizario in 1820. He was married to María
  de los Santos Albillar at an early age and served in the Mexican Army during the Mexican-
  American War. García served as justice of the peace in San Elizario from 1851 to 1860 and
  county commissioner from 1852 to 1855. In 1861, he assisted the Baylor brothers in the
  occupation of the El Paso area and the Mesilla Valley. In 1869-70, when Indians raided the
  area killing several citizens, García organized a sixty-man defense force. In one engagement with hostile Apaches, he received an arrow wound which left one arm paralyzed for
  the rest of his life. On 7 October 1898, García died at the age of seventy-seven and was
  buried in the San Elizario Cemetery. His son, Gregorio Nacianceno García II, became
  mayor of San Elizario, county commissioner, United States Customs inspector, postmaster,
  and deputy sheriff. Neither father nor son should be confused with Gregorio N. García
  who was one of the most influential citizens of San Elizario and county judge at the time
  of the Salt War. During the Salt War Judge García was closely allied with Judge Charles
  W. Howard. Bill Lockhart, "Gregorio Nacianceno García, 1st," *Password* 40 (Fall 1995):
  119-25; Mills, *Forty Years at El Paso*, 153-54; and Gillett, *Six Years with the Texas Rangers*,
  151.

10 Fabens was named for George Fabens, an official of the Southern Pacific Railroad. As part
   of the San Elizario Grant, the site was owned by Sabas Grijalva and Diego Loya prior to
   1887.

11 Gillett changed the quotation to: *"Ah, hijo de mi cara Juan."* Gillett, *Six Years With the Texas
   Rangers*, 152.

12 At Arranda's ranch the Rangers were joined by twenty-three men from Guadalupe commanded by Capt. Francisco Escajeda and Lieutenants José María Escajeda, Vicente
   Bustillo, and Antonio Varela. The Rangers, Baylor reported, had "traveled seventy-eight
   miles since 11 o'clock the night before." Baylor's official report, which was dated at Ysleta,
   10 October 1879, was published in the *San Antonio Daily Express* on 24 October 1879 and
   the *Galveston Weekly News,* 30 October 1879.

13 The Sierra Ventana are northeast of the Sierra de la Ranchería and southeast of
   Samalayuca on the El Paso del Norte-Chihuahua Road and form the southern end of the
   Sierra del Presidio. Baylor also refers to the Sierra Ventana in his official report as the
   Sierra Armagora. *San Antonio Daily Express*, 24 October 1879; *Galveston Weekly News,* 30
   October 1879.

14 Baylor was sure the Apaches were equipped with Sharps and Winchester rifles. Gillett
   recalled: "We came to a rock ledge three or four feet high. I quickly scaled this, but before

I could straighten up an Indian rose from behind a rock about fifteen to twenty yards ahead and fired point-blank at me. The bullet struck a small soap-weed three feet in front of me and knocked the leaves into my mouth and face. I felt as if I had been hit, but it was leaves and not blood that I wiped out of my mouth with my left hand. I turned my head and called to the boys to look out, but the warning was unnecessary—they had already taken shelter under the ledge of rock. Just as I turned my head a second shot from the Apache carried away the entire front part of my hat brim." Gillett, *Six Years With the Texas Rangers*, 157. The fight in the Sierra Ventanas is briefly mentioned in Joseph A. Stout, Jr., *Apache Lightning: The Last Battles of the Ojo Calientes* (New York: Oxford University Press, 1974), 116-17.

15 "Had the bullet been six inches lower it would have struck him full in the face," Gillett wrote. "'Darn that old Indian,' exclaimed Baylor, ducking his head. 'If I had a shotgun I would run up and jump right on top of him.' The lieutenant was mad now, and ordered a charge. The boys hesitated, and George H[oe]rld, an old scout, said, 'Lieutenant, if we leave this shelter and start up the mountain the Indians hidden behind those rocks seventy-five yards above will kill us all.' 'Yes, I suppose you are right; they would be hard to dislodge,' replied Baylor." Gillett, *Six Years with the Texas Rangers,* 158.

16 Reaching Guadalupe, the Rangers were entertained by Máximo Arranda, custom-house official at San Elizario, and brother of Ramón Arranda. Baylor reported to Adj. Gen. John B. Jones that he made a "treaty of amity" with the alcalde of Guadalupe, Don Matías Uretega, whereby the alcalde agreed to join the Rangers "in pursuit of Indians [and] I generously extended to him the privilege of coming over on our side and killing all the reservation Indians he could find, and agreed to join him in the good work." *San Antonio Daily Express*, 24, 25 October, 4 November 1879.

17 Ortiz was a veteran Indian fighter and notorious scalp hunter who was several times political chief of the canton of Galeana. On 13 November 1882, Ortiz with twenty-one men chased a band of Apaches under Juh and Geronimo to a divide separating the Casas Grandes and Galeana watersheds some fourteen miles north of Galeana where the Indians turned on Ortiz. In the fight that followed on what is known today as Cerrito Mata Ortiz, all of the Mexicans except one (who was probably allowed to escape with the news), were killed. Thrapp, *Victorio and the Mimbres Apaches*, 312, 373; Dan Thrapp, *Juh: An Incredible Indian* (El Paso: Texas Western Press, 1973), 33-35.

CHAPTER FIVE

Massacre in the Candelaria Mountains

~

IN NOVEMBER 1879, Victorio, the chief of the Mescalero Apaches, finding that New Mexico was getting to be too warm on account of the United States soldiers and cowboys, came down to Mexico to rest.[1] At that time the United States had no agreement with Mexico allowing troops to cross the boundary between the two republics in pursuit of hostile Indians. Thus, all the blood-thirsty, thieving Apaches had to do when the United States soldiers got after them was to cross into Mexico, and when the Mexicans got after them, they would go back into Texas, New Mexico or Arizona. This was a most unfortunate state of affairs, for many of the best and bravest men of each country lost their lives before an agreement was reached allowing the troops of each country to cross the boundary at will. This agreement finally resulted in the destruction of Victorio's band by Col. Joaquín Terrazas at Tres Castillos, in southeastern Chihuahua, and in the capture of Geronimo afterwards in Arizona by the United States troops.

Victorio knew every foot of the country and where to find wood, water, grass and abundance of game. So he took his time and came from New Mexico down into Chihuahua, stopping first at the Santa María, a good sized stream furnishing plenty of water and grass, where he could take refuge in case of an attack from the Mexicans.[2] Of this, however, there was not much danger at that time, the country being thinly settled, and farming and stock ranching being confined to the neighborhood of the small towns. Gradually Victorio moved down to the Candelaria Mountains to get new range and to be nearer to the settlement of San José owned by Don Mariano Samaniego, and also to watch the public road between the city of Chihuahua and El Paso del Norte, present Juárez.[3]

One of the saddest and most heartrending tragedies resulted from this move. Victorio was at the large tank on the north side of the Candelaria Mountains, where he had fine range for his stock, plenty of wood and game, and could see every movement made by travelers or bodies of men. He could see from these almost inaccessible mountains for twenty or thirty miles in any direction everything being in plain view. Reports coming in of Indian signs having been [seen] south of the Candelarias, a company of the principal Mexicans of Carrizal, fifteen in number, under the command of Don José Rodriguez, left to locate the Indians.[4] The following is the list of brave men who took their lives in their hands and went on a perilous expedition, giving up their lives in the performance of duty: José Rodriguez, commander; Antonio Hernández, Mauricio Solís, Inéz Ortega, Blas Villanueva, Florencio Villanueva, Rosalio Villanueva, Hermenejildo Ruiz, Santos Contreras, Serapio Trujillo, Braulio Perea, and Cayetano García.

The little band of brave men went to the north side of Candelaria Mountain and struck the trial of Victorio's band, on an old beaten route used by the Indians passing from the Santa María River to the big tank on the northern slope of the Candelaria.[5] The trail led up a canyon by a large hill north of Candelaria Mountain, and passed between two rocky peaks, and then down the side of the hills to the plain between this hill, or rather series of hills, and the Candelaria, making for the big tank. Old Victorio, who was a natural soldier, knew that the Mexicans would never come up on the Candelaria after seeing the size of this trail. From his position on the tall peaks he had seen the little body of Mexicans long before they struck his trail, and had sent forty or fifty of his warriors down to form an ambuscade where the trail crossed the crest between the two peaks. He must have been with the men himself, for the thing was most skillfully planned and executed. On the north side of the trail there were only a few boulders, but on the south side it was rough rising in rough tiers of boulders. The Apaches hid in these rocks, and when the Mexicans got between them, those on the north fired a volley, and naturally the Mexicans made for the cover of the rocks on the south. Only a few tied their horses, and these were shot and killed. Those that were turned loose must have stampeded.

The Indians on the south side were in the cliffs above the devoted little band and opened fire on them. It was a real death trap, with no hope of escape or rescue. I saw where one Mexican had got into a crevice, and from his position could have shot anyone coming at him from east or west. He was hidden also from the Indians in the cliffs above him, but his legs were exposed to the fire of the warriors on the north side, and they had literally shot them off up to the knees.[6] The horses, only a few that had been tied, in their struggles after being shot, had rolled down the deep canyon on the east, breaking their lariats and not stopping until they had reached the bottom of what we named Cañada del Muerte (Canyon of Death). This massacre occurred on the 7th of November [1879].

When the company did not return, there was great sorrow and alarm in Carrizal, for it was supposed that only a small band of Apaches, bent on horse stealing, was in the Candelarias. So another company of fourteen men volunteered to go and see what had become of their friends and kindred.

Don José María Rodríguez was appointed commander, and the little band with sad forebodings took the trail of their comrades and kinsmen. Old Victorio from his mountain peak saw this body of Mexicans and prepared the plan for their destruction. The signs showed that they had walked into the same death trap, except that they had scattered more in fighting and a good many of the Mexicans were killed on the southern slope of the hills. Two had attempted to escape on horseback but were followed and killed.

When neither party returned, there was indeed sorrow in the little town of Carrizal. For twenty-nine of her principal citizens had left, never to return again. The last company was composed of José M. Rodríguez, captain, and Jesús Domínguez, Jesús Baca, Ynés Nuñez, Guadalupe Ruiz, Juan Alarcón, Tiburcio Contreras, Desiderio Sanchez, Julio Hernández, Francisco Cervantes, Santa Cruz Herrera, Jesús José Noristia, Panfilo Frejo and Manuel Aguirre, the last two being the ones who attempted to escape on horseback.

It was several days before the people could get over the horrid reality, and wives, mothers and sweethearts mourned the loss of their dear ones. A runner was sent to El Paso del Norte and they began to organize at once, calling on Zaragoza, Tres Jacales, Guadalupe and San Ignacio for their quota. They responded quickly and soon a hundred Mexicans were ready to take the field.

A note was sent to me asking if the Rangers would go with the command, to which I readily agreed, for I knew it was only a question of time when old Victorio would be on our side again murdering and robbing. A detachment of Company C had been in one fight, as already related, and the Mexicans had a very kind feeling for us. We crossed the river at Zaragoza, a little town opposite Ysleta, and joined the Mexicans under Señor Ramos. We marched to the ranch of Don Ynocente Ochoa, to wait until the volunteers from the other towns came in to Samalayuca Springs.[7] Then the Rangers moved down, and our combined command amounted to one hundred and ten men, the ten being Texas Rangers.

Here the Mexicans, after organizing, sent Señor Ramos to inform me that on account of my experience as a soldier and as a compliment to the Rangers, they had selected me to command the entire force.[8] I thanked him, but told him as the campaign was on Mexican soil, and to rescue or bury Mexicans, it would be proper to appoint one of their own men, and I would cheerfully serve under him. Señor Ramos returned after a short time and told me they had selected Don Francisco Escajeda of Guadalupe as commander in chief, and myself as second in command. This suited me, because there was an element that might have caused some friction. Old Chico Barela, the *pueblo cacique*, and principal commander of the mob that killed Judge Charlie Howard, Elias Atkinson, and [John] McBride at San Elizario, was with us and we had at our headquarters writs for the arrest of himself and many others.[9] So I gave the old fellow to understand we were now fighting a common enemy and should act in harmony together. I did this the more willingly because I learned that after Judge Howard and the others were killed, the mob wanted to kill all the Rangers barricaded in an adobe house. But Old Chico said it could not be done unless they killed him first. Leaving one wagon at the Ochoa Ranch, and taking three days' rations cooked, and more in case of a siege, we went out in the night to avoid Victorio's spies seeing us. Don Francisco Escajeda and the writer were at the head of the column. Sgt. James B. Gillett and my eight Rangers followed in Indian file, each Ranger with a Mexican by his side, showing they looked on us as volunteers in the Mexican service.

We rode out on the horrid sand road beyond Samalayuca, and sent spies ahead to locate the Apaches, if possible. Before we reached the Candelarias, we halted behind some mountains to await the report of the spies, but they could learn nothing certain. It was a bitterly cold night and a few of us made fires in the deep arroyos. We moved on towards the mountains north of the Candelarias, and reached there early next morning to find a large fresh trail about two days old, going in the direction of Lake Santa María. But for fear of some trick, we divided our men and some took the crest south of the trail, where the massacre took place, so as to have an even break, and the others went to the right. It was soon evident that the entire Apache band had left, and nothing remained for us to do, but the sad duty of collecting the bodies for burial.

They were scattered around, none very far from where the attack had commenced. It was evident that the last party had found the bodies of their kinsmen and collected and put them in a big crevice in the rocks and had begun to cover them with loose stones, the Indians watching them all the time, just as a cat plays with a mouse before killing it. They then opened fire on them when all probably had set their guns against the rocks and were busy in the last sad rites of burying their loved ones, little dreaming it was soon to be their own grave.

The saddest scene that I ever witnessed was that presented as we gathered the bodies of the murdered men. As each fresh discovery of a loved friend, bother or father was made, and the last hope fled that any had escaped, a wail of sorrow went up, and I doubt if there was a dry eye either of Texan or Mexican. It has been well said "a touch of human nature makes all men akin."

While the immediate relatives were hunting for those who had scattered in attempting to escape, we moved south to the main tank in the Candelarias. The ascent was up a winding path on the steep mountain side to the bench where the tank was situated, one of the largest in the west. The water coming down from quite a height and big boulders falling into the tank, had cut a deep hole in the solid rock. Although Victorio's band of some 200 animals and 150 Indians, and our command, had been using the water it could scarcely be missed. We sent scouts to the right and left to make sure no game was put up on us, for the cunning old chief could have sent his women and children on and hid his warriors completely in the cliffs that towered high above the tank of water, completely commanding it and slaughtering those below.

We remained all day at the tank and the Mexicans in looking around found nearly all the saddles and many of the hats of the Carrizaleños hidden in the cliffs. All the hats that I noticed had bullet holes in them.[10]

The bodies having all been recovered, except two, they were buried in the crevice of the mountain where they were killed. All were in a perfect state of preservation owing to the pure cold air of the mountains. It is a strange fact, but beyond question, that no wild animal or bird of prey will touch the body of a Mexican. These men laid there on the ground nearly two weeks. If they had been Indians, Negroes or Americans, the coyotes, buzzards and crows would have eaten them the first day and night.

It is a grim satisfaction to know that these same Apaches were afterwards annihilated by the Mexicans at Tres Castillos, and old Victorio and eighty-nine of his warriors were left on the plains by the command under Col. Joaquín Terrazas, and some eighty-eight women and children captured and sent down into the interior of Mexico.[11]

Nothing of interest occurred on our return. We got out of bread, and our Mexican allies divided with us. The men as usual always ate up their three days' rations the first camp they made. Don Ynocente Ochoa's *mayordomo* gave us all the fresh beef we could eat and *carne seca* to take on the campaign.

Quite a company had come out to meet us from Carrizal, and we returned sad to the widows of the brave men who fell in this, probably the most wholesale slaughter ever made by Victorio's band. The citizens of Galeana were nearly as unfortunate, but it was old Juh and Geronimo who massacred them.[12]

We arrived safely in our old adobe quarters, and appreciated them after sleeping out of doors. All the Saragoza men made for their church to offer up thanks for a safe return. Men, women and children uttered their *"gracias, señores,"* as the Texas Rangers rode through their town.

NOTES

[1] Born in southwestern New Mexico about 1825, Victorio (Bidu-ya or Beduiat) was a Mimbres, not Mescalero, chief who is thought by historians of the Apaches to have been America's greatest guerrilla leader. He may have fought the California Column in the 1862 Battle of Apache Pass. Victorio later settled with his people at Cañada Alamosa, south of the San Mateo Mountains, in New Mexico, but in 1872 was moved a reservation at Tularosa (Aragon), in the rugged and cold mountains of what is now Catron County. After two years, he returned to the Ojo Caliente Reservation west of Cañada Alamosa. In 1877, Victorio was again moved to the arid San Carlos Reservation on the Gila River in Arizona. On 2 September 1878, about 300 Mimbres led by Victorio and Loco broke out and fled into the mountains of western New Mexico. Persuaded to come into Fort Wingate, they were returned to the barren San Carlos Reservation from which Victorio again broke out and went to the Mescalero Reservation in the Sacramento Mountains of southern New Mexico. On 21 August 1879, fearing that he would be arrested, Victorio fled with his followers into the rugged Black Range where he fought a number of successful engagements with the army before turning south into Mexico to the Candelaria Range. Again, however, he returned to New Mexico to the Black Range and the San Andrés Mountains, and eventually recrossing the Rio Grande, he again sought refuge in the Black Range. Defeated, he fled into Mexico and met his death at Tres Castillos. Dan Thrapp, "Victorio," *Encyclopedia of Frontier Biography*, ed. Dan Thrapp (Spokane: Arthur H. Clark Company, 1990), 3:1483-84; Thrapp, *Victorio and the Mimbres Apaches* (Norman; University of Oklahoma Press, 1974).

[2] With its headwaters eighty miles west of Ciudad Chihuahua, the Santa María River cuts through the mountains and arid plains of central Chihuahua for some 190 miles before emptying into Laguna de Santa María, northwest of Carrizal.

[3] Rex Strickland provides an excellent biographical sketch of Samaniego in Mills, *Forty Years at El Paso*, 188. Samaniego was born at Bavispe, Sonora, in June or July 1831, where his father, Florentino Samaniego, was commander of the presidio. When his father died in an Apache raid in 1838, his mother, María Josefa Delgado, brought the family to El Paso del Norte to live in the household of Padre Ramón Ortiz. Samaniego was educated in the seminary at Durango and in the School of Medicine at the University of Paris where one of his teachers was Louis Pasteur. During the period of the Empire, Samaniego served in the Republican Army of the North under Luis Terrazas as a surgeon. A leading freighter

and rancher, he was twice selected as the *ad interim* governor of Chihuahua. Following the massacre in the Candelaria Mountains, Samaniego urged a Mexican retaliatory raid on the Mescalero Reservation in the Sacramento Mountains. The father of six sons and two daughters, he died on 2 October 1905. In August 1880, Baylor reported that "Emperor Victorio" had run off 200 head of horses belonging to Samaniego within nine miles of El Paso. Ironically, Samaniego had brought the horses from Carrizal, fearing the Apaches would steal them. In April 1883, when several border criminals took refuge in central Chihuahua, Baylor went by rail to see Samaniego, who was acting governor at the time. Since Saminego was "a personal friend of mine & my brother Genl. Baylor, [I] feel pretty confident I can get some of the many bad characters down there," Baylor wrote. Thrapp, *Victorio and the Mimbres Apaches*, 255-56; *Diccionario Porrua*, 1374; Baylor to Neal Coldwell, 31 August 1880, AGO, RG 401, TSA; Baylor to W.H. King, 5 April 1883, AGO, RG 401, TSA.

4   Described as a cluster of sun-baked adobe dwellings around "a gravelly plaza of indeterminate shape," Carrizal was on a tributary of the Rio Carmel in northern Chihuahua, eighty-five miles south of El Paso. The small community is perhaps best remembered as the site of a clash between Brig. Gen. John J. Pershing's Punitive Expedition and the forces of Venustiano Carranza on 21 June 1916. In his *Six Years with the Texas Rangers*, Gillett mistakenly refers to Carrizal as Carbajal. Thrapp, *Victorio and the Mimbres Apaches*, 252-56, 366. Also, Baylor to Jones, 3 December 1879, AGO, RG 401, TSA.

5   The rugged Candelaria Mountains, some fifty-five miles south of El Paso and thirty-five miles north of Carrizal, rise out of the arid plain to an elevation of 7,060 feet. Baylor described them as "a group of peaks surrounded by open plains." Baylor to Jones, 3 December 1879, AGO, RG 401, TSA. Adjutant General Jones sent a copy of Baylor's report to Brig. Gen. E.O.C. Ord in San Antonio who forwarded it to army headquarters in Chicago. E.D. Townsend then passed it on to the secretary of war, the Department of State, and the Interior Department. Various endorsements on Baylor to Jones, 3 December 1879, LR, AGO, RG 393, NA.

6   "The scene of the conflict was perfectly horrible," Baylor wrote. "I saw in one little narrow parapet, which the beleaguered Mexicans had hastily thrown up, seven men piled up in a space 6 x 7 feet." Baylor also said that "a letter written by them asking for help was found outside their breastwork and near the body of two men who had evidently attempted to escape but were riddled by balls." Baylor to Jones, 3 December 1879, AGO, RG 401, TSA.

7   Ochoa, the merchant prince of El Paso del Norte, was born in Aldama, Chihuahua, on 27 December 1832 and came to El Paso del Norte after the Mexican-American War in 1849. In 1865 and 1866, Benito Juárez was said to have stayed at Ochoa's home on Calle de Dies y Seis de Septiembre. In 1867 he was head of the stage company that operated between El Paso del Norte and Chihuahua. When Ochoa died on 19 May 1909, he was said to have been the wealthiest man in El Paso del Norte with a fortune of a million dollars. Mills, *Forty Years at El Paso*, 21, 186.

   Just north of the extensive sand dunes, some thirty miles south of El Paso, Samalayuca Spring is today a station on the Ciudad Juárez-Ciudad Chihuahua Railroad.

8   The entire force of 179 men, armed mostly with breech loading rifles, was comprised of forty-two men under Jesús Vargas from El Paso del Norte, twenty-five from Guadalupe under Francisco Escageda, eighteen from San Ignacio, and thirteen from Zaragoza. They were later joined by eleven men from Carrizal, fifteen from Lucereo, and forty-one from Carmel. Baylor to Jones, 3 December 1879, AGO, RG 401, TSA.

9 Varela (Barela), principal leader of the San Elizario citizens in the Salt War, allegedly asserted that enough blood had been shed and only if they "killed him could any more Americans be killed." Mills, *Forty Years at the Pass*, 156; and Sonnichsen, *El Paso Salt War*, 57.

10 Baylor estimated that the Apaches remained on the scene of the massacre for two days before striking out north across the desert for the border. Besides several saddles that were discovered hidden in a crevasse, a number of muzzle loading rifles and swords, all broken, were found. This showed, Baylor thought, "that Victorio is well supplied with arms." Baylor to Jones, 3 December 1879, AGO, RG 401, TSA.

11 Joaquín Terrazas was said to have collected $17,250 for the scalps taken at Tres Castillos and another $10,200 from the captives he sold into peonage. Thrapp, *Victorio and the Mimbres Apaches*, 373.

12 A reference to the death of Ortiz and sixteen men north of Galeana on 13 November 1882. Thrapp, *Juh*, 33-35. See n. 17, Ch. 4, this section.

CHAPTER SIX

Rescue at Crow Flats

IN THE SPRING OF 1880, two young men named [J.P.] Andrew[s] and [W.P.] Wiswald, of Denver, Colorado, came west to grow up with the country. After looking over the valley of the Rio Grande, and an insignificant little dirt daubed place called El Paso, Franklin, or Magoffinsville, according to one's taste, they concluded to try Black River, or Seven Rivers in the Pecos Valley. Getting an ambulance with a good pair of horses, plenty of grub and an outfit for camping, they started on the old Butterfield Overland Stage road.[1]

At Crow Flat they stopped for dinner at the old deserted station.[2] They had hobbled their horses and were soon busy with baking bread, frying meat and boiling coffee, not dreaming there was an Indian in the area, though they had been warned to look out for them. It is an open country with some few trees and tules around the water holes and sand hills. When they had commenced eating—like all men traveling in that country, they had the appetites of coyotes and became deeply absorbed in stowing away rations—the horses had grazed off about a hundred yards and the first thing they knew they heard a yelling and trampling of horses' feet, and looking up they saw four or five Indians driving off their horses. Grabbing their guns they started after the Indians at top speed, both being western men and good shots. They hoped to get near enough to the Indians to prevent them from taking the hobbles off the horses by opening fire on them, with their Winchesters. But the Apaches can't be taught anything about stealing horses. So some of the Indians stopped and began shooting at the boys, who returned their fire. But the horses made about as good time as though they were foot loose. This fact was well known to the Texas Rangers, who hobbled and side-lined also, and even then their horses when stampeded would run as fast as the guards could run on foot for a considerable distance. The boys kept advancing and firing, but it was no use. The danger was that the Apaches might make a circuit and beat them back to the ambulance, thus setting them afoot without grub or blankets which would be a bad fix to be in during January in that country. So they could only return to their camp feeling very blue indeed.

A council of war was held and they were determined as to the best course to pursue. To walk back 100 miles to El Paso, packing grub and blankets, was no picnic. On the other hand it was at least forty or fifty miles to the first ranch on Black River. But they finally decided to take the shortest way to assistance, which proved the traditional longest way. They determined to stay within the friendly adobe walls of the old stage stand until night. To keep up appearances they made two dummy sentinels and put them on guard, and got their ambulance inside. They had no fear of an attack at night, especially as they had a splendid Mexican shepherd dog to keep watch. As usual after going to sleep they overslept and did not get away until after midnight. Shep, the dog, wanted to go too, but they put a sack of corn and a muddle of bacon under the ambulance and give him to understand he was to guard it.

By daybreak they were well on their way to San Martin Springs at the foot of Guadalupe Peak.[3] The road is a horrible one, mostly deep sand, and when they arrived at San Martin they were pretty well worn out. But after a cup, or rather two or three cups of strong coffee, some Old Ned and camp bread they were ready for the road again.

The old stage road here turns to the right, and gradually winds around the mountains to get on the mesa land. It makes quite a circuit before getting to the next water, Pine Springs, but there is an old Indian trail that leads up a canyon and straight through.[4] As they were afoot, and taking all short cuts, they took this trail. It was nearly sunset when in a sudden bend of the trail they came in full view of an entire village of Indians coming towards them, taking the near cut also. The Indians were three or four hundred yards off, and had discovered them also. Under such circumstances, the frontiersman has to think quick and act accordingly. They determined there was only one chance for their lives. There was no use running. The Indians, most of them, were mounted, and they themselves were pretty well worn out. Fortunately to the south of the trail there was a sharp sugar loaf peak, and for this they made with all their speed.[5] Getting on top, they hastily threw up a breast works with the loose rocks, and as soon as the Indians came in sight they opened fire on them. The Indians began firing too, but soon discovered it was a waste of ammunition and ceased firing. The boys were suspicious of some trick and kept a sharp lookout. They soon discovered that the Indians were crawling and pushing boulders ahead of them large enough to shelter their bodies, and were gradually nearing the top of the hill. The boys then decided to keep perfectly still, one on each side, and watch for a chance to kill an Indian, run over him and dash down the hill, trusting to their heels.

The one on the west side, where the fading light still enabled him to see, saw a black mop of hair rise cautiously over the rock he was rolling, and fired. The head disappeared and the boulder went thundering down the hill, with the two men after it running over the Indian who was kicking around on the ground like a chicken with its head cut off. As good luck would have it, most of the Apaches were on the east side, taking it for granted the men would try and escape in that direction. Before the astonished Indians could make out just what was occurring the boys were running like old black-tail bucks and were soon out of hearing, while night spread her dark mantle over them in kindness. Keeping clear of the road and being good woodsmen, they had no trouble in shaping their course for Crow Flat again. Worn out and weary they made the old stage stand, and found their dummy sentinels still on guard, with the faithful shepherd dog at his post and overjoyed at their return.

At the old adobe they were in a measure safe, having grub and water, while the walls of the old house were about five feet high and would shelter them. The fact that no attempt had been made to kill the dog, or rob the ambulance, satisfied them that the Apaches, after getting their horses, had kept on their way to the Mescalero Agency near Tularosa. This was the highway of these murderous, thieving rascals, who were constantly raiding Texas and Chihuahua. In the raids they had made a great deep trail leading north from the Crow Flat Springs towards the Sacramento Mountains. After they had cooked and rested, the two boys decided they would pull out after dark, and hoof it for El Paso. Again giving Shep his orders, with heavy hearts and sore feet they turned their faces to the Cornudas Mountains, the next stage station, and made it through safely.[6] Among'st its shady nooks they found sweet, cold water and rest. After several days they dragged their weary bodies into El Paso, and went to the commanding officer at Fort Bliss. But as he had only infantry he refused to go after their ambulance. They then went to the Ranger camp at Ysleta, and asked me if we would go. As I had promised the old alcalde to "represent the honor and dignity of grand old Texas" we began preparations at once. Leaving two men in camp, I took eight Rangers and one Pueblo Indian, and with Andrews and Wiswall we had a dozen in our crowd. We started out, not to find the North Pole, but to see if the pole of the ambulance left by Wiswall was safe.

The first day we made the Hueco Tanks, so called. But "hueco" in Spanish means tank, and in early days travelers spelled it Waco Tanks. Señor Juan Armendáriz has now utilized the immense pile of granite rock, which is

equal to a tiled rock, in filling reservoirs of water for his stock. And a splendid ranch it is too, while Don Juan is one of the most progressive men of the
Rio Grande Valley.

Many wild adventures have occurred at these tanks—fights between the
Mexicans and Comanche Indians. During the gold excitement it was the
main emigrant route to California. Here, too, the old Overland Stage Company had a stand. The names of [Randolph B.] Marcy, Gen. [Robert E.] Lee,
and [a] thousand of others could be seen cut or written on the rocks.[7] The
Indians had made many crude pictures, one of which was quite artistic, being
a huge rattlesnake on the rock under the cave, near the old stage stand, on the
eastern side of Hueco. Old man Hart was the vandal who destroyed it, and
hundreds of names, by camping under the cave and building a fire against
the wall. He was punished for it by the hand of fate. Once going on a scout to
the Sacramentos to look after the Indians with my Rangers, and being anxious to know about water at the Jarillas, in a tank made by Hart, we met an
old dusty, tired prospector driving his burros.[8] I asked him if he knew
whether we could get water at the Jarillas. "Not unless you got plenty scads,"
he replied. "Do you know old Hart?" I asked. He looked at me without
cracking a smile. "Yes, I licked him this morning."

Our next halt was at the Alamos across the beautiful plains [which] at
that time [was] covered with antelope that could be seen scudding away with
their swift change of direction, looking like a flock of white birds. At the
Alamos we found some Indian sign on the flat above the springs. But it was
old. At the Cornudas we again saw old sign of the Apaches. This was a
favorite watering place with the Tularosa Agency Indians on their raids into
Texas. The Rangers under Lt. [John B.] Tays had quite a battle with them
here.[9] One Ranger, said to be a Russian nobleman and nihilist who had
joined the Rangers, was killed in the fight, and for many years a head board
was placed where he was buried. But the Indians had defaced it. He stood up
straight, though he could have had splendid cover, according to the etiquette
prevailing amongst British officers in the Transvaal, and was shot through
the brain, but not until he had killed an Indian. We saw the Indian's blood on
the rocks long afterwards.

From Cornudas to Crow Flat is a long, monotonous tramp of some
thirty-six miles, and we arrived in the night and were challenged by the faithful sentinel, old Shep. But when he heard his master's voice he went wild
with joy, barked, rolled over, stood on his head, and came as near talking as
any African monkey or gorilla could, and we gave him a cheer. He had been
there alone for fifteen days. His side of bacon was eaten, and the sack of corn
getting very low. The Rangers were as much delighted as if it had been a

human being they had rescued. He had worn the top of the wall of the old stage stand perfectly smooth, standing off the sneaking coyotes. Tracks of the latter were thick all around the place, but Shep had held the fort with the assistance of the dummy sentinels.

We found everything just as the boys had left it. The Indians probably were on their way to the reservation, and never came back. This was on their main trail when they raided Texas and Chihuahua, and the broad deep trail showed thousands of head of cattle and horses had been driven over it by these government pets.

We arrived safely in camp, having made the two hundred miles in a week. Andrews and Wiseall wanted to [charge the] post commander at Fort Bliss, Maj. [Nathan Ward] Osborne, with cowardice, but I told them I knew him personally and he was both a gentleman and soldier.[10] He could hardly be expected to tramp infantry two hundred miles for an ambulance and dog, with the probability that neither would be found. We found that news had beaten us back to Ysleta, and that according to the "reliable gentleman or intelligent contraband" our entire party had been massacred. This was quite a probability, as three hundred Apaches were reported by Wiswall, and our little band would have had a tight old squeeze to get through. I don't know if Wiswall and Andrews are alive, but that Mexican shepherd dog is entitled to a monument in the El Paso plaza instead of those eagles and rabbits.

NOTES

[1] Relying on Gillett's *Six Years With the Texas Rangers*, Walter Prescott Webb recalls this incident in his *The Texas Rangers*, 398-99, and in an article, "Last War Trail of Victorio," *True West* 4 (March-April 1957): 20-21, 43. See also: Baylor to Jones, 18 January 1880, AGO, RG 401, TSA.

[2] Crow Flats is the northern portion of the extensive Salt Flats northwest of El Capitan and Guadalupe Peak. Named for the birds that flocked around the springs in abundance, Crow Springs (Ojos del Cuervo) was eight miles east of present-day Dell City and one mile south of the New Mexico border. Indians had used the small oasis for centuries and it was here that the Butterfield Overland Mail built a rock, adobe and gypsum block station in 1858. In 1851, Capt. Randolph B. Marcy said the spring contained "a large supply of water at all seasons; and although it [is] sulphurous, yet animals are very fond of it." In 1854, John Pope reported the springs fed two small lakes covering four or five acres. Waterman L. Ormsby, the only through passenger on the first westbound stage in 1858, said the spring was "of sulphur but palatable enough when one is thirsty. It is situated on a level plain some distance from the road, and would be passed unnoticed were it not known to the traveler." Today the springs are dry because the water table has dropped due to irrigation, the rocks and adobe blocks have been carried off by local ranchers, and the crows have disappeared.

It was at the western entrance to Guadalupe Pass, across the Salt Flats from Crow Station, that the first eastbound Butterfield coach, which had left San Francisco on 15 September 1858 with five through passengers, and the westbound stage with Ormsby aboard, which had left St. Louis on 16 September 1858, met. Gunner Brune, *Springs of Texas* (Fort Worth: Branch Smith, 1981), 1:239. Waterman L. Ormsby, *The Butterfield Overland Mail*, ed. Lyle H. Wright and Josephine M. Bynum (San Marino: Huntington Library, 1988), 82; A.C. Greene, *900 Miles on the Butterfield Trail* (Denton: University of North Texas Press, 1994), 72-74; J.W. Williams, "The Butterfield Overland Mail Road Across Texas," *Southwestern Historical Quarterly,* 61 (July 1957):17; Conkling, *Butterfield Overland Mail*, 1:396.

3 San Martin Springs is Delaware Springs, some twenty-one miles east of Pine Springs. Capt. Francisco Armangual reported the location of the springs as early as 1808. In 1851, Captain Marcy said the spring burst "out of a solid limestone rock in a volume of sufficient magnitude to drive an ordinary saw-mill at the fountain head, and is as pure, sweet water as I ever drank." Brune, *Springs of Texas*, 1:147

4 Pine Springs is two miles east of Guadalupe Peak and El Capitan. The ruins of the Pinery Station, which was operated as a stage station for the Butterfield Overland Stage for eleven months in 1858 and 1859, are visible today and preserved by the National Park Service. W.C. Jameson, *The Guadalupe Mountains: Islands in the Desert* (El Paso: Texas Western Press, 1994), 23.

5 This was probably Lone Cone Peak near where State Highway 54 and U.S. Highway 62 and 180 intersect, south of El Capitan, on the western approach to Guadalupe Pass. The Apaches, Wiswald and Andrews told Baylor, numbered approximately 100 and were driving a large herd of horses. Baylor to Jones, 18 January 1880, AGO, RG 401, TSA.

6 The barren Cornudas, on the Texas-New Mexico border, rise to a height of 7,280 feet and consist of several peaks including Deer, Wind, Black, Callfield, Washburn, and San Antonio. Herbert E. Ungnade, *Guide to the New Mexico Mountains* (Albuquerque: University of New Mexico Press, 1973), 159.

7 Archaeologists believe that man visited the Hueco Tanks as early as 10,000 years ago. It is very possible that Marcy may have carved his name at the site. Robert Neighbors certainly stopped there on 6 May 1849 with his exploring party, after leaving San Elizario on his return to central Texas. Lt. Francis T. Bryan of the Topographical Engineers and Col. Joseph E. Johnston also stopped at the site in 1849 as did John Bartlett of the United States Boundary Survey in 1854. Lee, of course, never got west of the Pecos during the time he commanded the Department of Texas. The California Gold Rush and westward migration sent thousands of travelers past the tanks. The Butterfield Overland Mail later built a stone and adobe station at the site and for almost a year, stagecoaches made regular stops for quick meals and fresh mule teams. In 1859, however, the route was changed to follow the lower road because of better water supplies. Kay Sutherland, *Rock Paintings at Hueco Tanks State Historical Park* (Austin: Texas Parks and Wildlife, 1991); Dixie L. Dominguez, "Hueco Tanks—A Vital Resource in Southwestern History," *Password* 31 (Fall 1986): 123-36.

8 The Jarilla Mountains, on the eastern edge of the parched Tularosa Basin just north of present-day Orogrande, New Mexico, rise to a height of some 4,851 feet. Ungnade, *New Mexico Mountains*, 159-60.

9 From Nova Scotia and a British subject, Tays commanded a detachment of Company C of the Frontier Battalion at San Elizario during the Salt War and holds the indistinction of being the only Texas Ranger to have ever surrendered. In 1880, Tays became the El Paso

town marshal but was removed after three months whereupon he took the job as deputy collector of customs. Sonnichsen, *El Paso Salt War*, 37-40, 48-53, 57-60.

[10] Osborne served in the 13th Infantry during the Civil War and was breveted a major for gallantry at Vicksburg. He was promoted to major in the 11th Infantry in December 1873 and commanded Fort Bliss from 1878 to 1880. He died on 30 January 1895. Heitman, *Historical Register*, 1:761; and Leon C. Metz, *Desert Army: Fort Bliss on the Texas Border* (El Paso: Mangan Books, 1988), 187.

CHAPTER SEVEN

Victorio Raids Northern Chihuahua

~

IN 1881 OCCURRED ONE OF THOSE BLOODY SCENES that were so common twenty-five or thirty years ago on the frontiers of Arizona, Texas and Mexico, now happily among the things that were. One may lie down in peace and have no fear of hearing the war whoop of the Apaches at dawn and the fast retreating sound of his horses and mules in stampede.

In 1881 a son of Sen. [George E.] Pugh of Ohio, who had been down to the city of Chihuahua on a mining deal, a passenger named Chambers or Chalmers, and the *cochere* [stage driver] and his assistant were on the stage going to El Paso.[1] When near the Ranchería Mountain they were fired on by Apache Indians from an ambuscade on the north side of the road.[2] The driver was killed and the passengers and assistant ran into the brush on the south side. It being dark they escaped notice of the Indians, who had shot down one of the stage mules to keep the stage from making a race—for these little Mexican mules when frightened could run like jack rabbits.

After they had got off and were perfectly safe, Pugh returned to try to get some important papers in regard to the mining deal he had made—a piece of insanity that could only be accounted for by supposing he had his ideas of the "noble Redman" from reading Cooper's delightful novels.

But these were quite a different breed. His companions tried to persuade him not to trust the Indians, but he thought that after killing one man and getting the mules and plunder they would not molest him. His companions watched him go to the stage, which the Indians had driven off on the north side some little distance, where they had built a fire. The moment they saw him they seized him and tied him to the stage wheels.

The two men then started for San José, Dr. Mariano Samaniego's hacienda, and gave the alarm.[3] A party of Upham's surveyors went out and took the trail of the Indians. They found Pugh's body; the Indians had shot him in the eye, the bullet going through his brain. They buried him very hurriedly, but a party afterwards finding the coyotes had nearly dug down to his body, reinterred it and covered the grave with rocks.

The Ranchería Mountain is a single peak out on the plains. Passengers going from El Paso to Chihuahua can see it by looking southeast before they get to the Candelaria Mountains. It was a noted place for old Victorio's band. There is a canyon and spring on the east side of the mountain and good grass, and from the south side the stage road from Don Ramón Arranda's ranch, Canteresio, or San José, could be seen as well as the road to Samalayuca Springs. So they could plan their murders long before travelers would arrive opposite the Ranchería.

The same day Pugh was killed a Mexican ox train was attacked and some of the party killed. About same time a surveying party that was at San José, becoming alarmed at the Indian depredations, concluded to leave the country and return to Texas.[4] They took the road to Samalayuca, and no doubt were seen by these same Indians, who roamed the country at their own sweet will. The party was composed of Guy Leavitt, surveyor, Fordham, Wallace and Charles Haynes, the teamster. Before they got to the sand hill, or Medanos, they were attacked by the Apaches, who had concealed themselves in an arroyo.

The men left the wagon and endeavored to reach a hill east of the road, but the entire party of four men were all killed within seventy-five yards of their wagon. Probably the first volley fired by Apaches wounded some of them and those able to fight would not desert a wounded comrade. This was apparent from the number of empty shells found between where the wagon was left and where the bodies of Leavitt, Fordham and Wallace were found. Haynes managed to get to a big cactus plant some 200 yards from the road and must have made a desperate struggle for his life. All the frontiersmen, both Mexicans and Americans, knew they carried their lives in their hands and therefore were made of that stuff that would fight to the bitter end, knowing they would receive no quarter.

Haynes must have fought for some time, for the ground all around the cactus was trampled down and a great many empty shells were lying around on the ground. Another incident of his bravery was that his right arm had been cut off. The Apaches believed that if they took the arm of a brave man, they would inherit his skill and bravery. They did the same with a Mexican, who was among the citizens of Carrizal massacred by Victorio's band in the Candelaria Mountains. He had managed to get some distance before he was overtaken. He had only the protection of a large Spanish dagger and the empty shells showed he had given his life after a desperate struggle.

H. Snyder, one of the engineers of the Mexican Central, was sent out from Samalayuca by Maj. G.W. Vaughn, whose headquarters at that time were at Paso del Norte, with a party to put up crosses over the graves of the murdered men and inter them decently. Another party had buried them hastily, and Richard Haynes' body had been only covered with rocks, as it was lying on a rocky point. Snyder, who is now a well-known citizen of Guadalajara, had all the men buried, where they fell. Their wagon had been burned and the bones of a faithful watch dog, that probably resented the attempt of the Indians to loot the wagon, were found in the ashes of the wagon.

Strange are the decrees of fate. These were probably the same men who had buried young Pugh and the *cochero* only a few days before and the sight of their mangled bodies decided them to give up such a dangerous job. Had they gone towards Chihuahua or remained at San José a few days they would have been safe, but now their own bodies were returned to mother earth in one of its most desolate, forbidden spots.

The Apaches of Victorio's band at this time were encamped in the Candelaria Mountains, north of the track of the Mexican Central. On the top of the mountains on the north side, there is an immense tank in solid rock, capable of supplying a large force for several months. Victorio was encamped here when he massacred some thirty of the principal citizens of Carrizal and only left, going back into New Mexico, when he knew in reason a large force would be sent to dislodge him.

Before he left he added another bloody chapter to his long list. I send you a letter of J. Leslie Phillips, who was prominent mining engineer in the state of Michoacán. The letter will doubtless be read with pleasure by his many friends in El Paso and Ysleta, who knew him in those stirring times.

The Mexicans who followed the trail of the victims of the Samalayuca massacre, from where they were attacked by the Apaches, said they left the road going south. All being mounted, they hoped to escape by flight, but as they were near the end of a hard day's ride and their merciless pursuers were on fresh horses, there was no hope of escape. Realizing this, they coolly prepared for a death struggle, killed their animals and prepared to sell their lives as dearly as possible. Behind the insufficient breast work their bodies were found, empty cartridges strewn around, showing they had made a gallant defense. It is a pity we have only the names of Cunningham and Black to preserve. Roundy, evidently, was not made of the same stuff as the old Overland Stage drivers, or may have been of Sir John Falstaff's opinion, that "discretion is the better part of valor."

It occurs to the writer that the Mexican Central Railroad, the great commercial artery that is carrying life into Mexico and stretching out its steel arms over all the republic from Saltillo to San Marcos, from the Rio Grande to the Balsas, could do a gracious act of gratitude to the relatives of these men and in memory of their services, by gathering their bones and erecting a monument, not in some city, but where Haynes fell. Thus, the people who glide by in the Pullman cars with every luxury may recall the hardships and heroic deaths of these pioneers.

****

Colonel G. Wythe Baylor
Guadalajara:

My Dear Colonel: On the 30th of May last I wrote promising to give you some of my recollections about the early times on the northern division of the Mexican Central Railway, but I have been so busy and have been so troubled with insomnia that I have had to neglect a great deal of my correspondence. As you suggested, I have put on my thinking cap, but I find it difficult to call up vividly the scenes to which you refer.

It was in the fall of 1881 when I reached Samalayuca with my camp. We pulled in there early one bright morning and found that a band of Indians, probably twenty, and Apaches, had just left there. The embers of their camp fires were still alive and the tracks made by their moccasins and the trails of their tepee poles were still perfectly fresh.

We heard nothing more of the Indians until the massacre of the contractors to which you refer. Those contractors passed their last night at my camp. There were four of them and a driver of a small buckboard. I remember only the names of two of the contractors, Black and Cunningham, and that of the driver, Roundy.

The contractors, who were rather indifferently mounted, left my camp about sunrise. Roundy, with the buckboard carrying the bedding, provisions and a small keg of water, pulled out a little later. When I returned to camp with my party at sunset, having spent the day surveying in the sand hills toward Chihuahua, we found Roundy in camp. He stated that when he reached the pass between the hills at the edge of the sand hills, on the old Chihuahua Stage Road, the scene that spread out before him was so wild and desolate that his courage failed him and he turned back. He remained in camp a day or two and returned to El Paso.

As there was more or less travel every day through the sand hills we naturally supposed that the contractors had passed on to San José, where they were to inspect the ground with the view of taking a contact for grading the road. As they did not return on the third day, we started out to hunt for them and met some Mexicans coming from the south, who reported that they had followed the trail of the Indians from a point near Ojo Lucero and had found the bodies of the four contractors. We sent out a party who buried the bodies. Their horses and mules were not found as well as I remember. Indians had driven off stock belonging to the Mexicans who were following their trail.

Within a few days after the massacre of these four contractors, the main body of engineers and contractors came pouring in from the north, and soon there were more than a thousand men engaged in grading between San José and Samalayuca and we had no further trouble with the Indians.

In all probability the Indians who murdered the contractors and the members of the surveying party were a remnant of Victorio's notoriously murderous band that was rounded up by Colonel Terrazas at Tres Castillos.

It may be that I am wrong in some of the above details, but I give them to you according to my remembrance.

J.L. Phillips

NOTES

[1] Pugh is best remembered as a Peace Democrat during the Civil War and a close supporter of the controversial Clement Vallandigham.

[2] Some twelve miles west of the Sierra de la Nariz and ten miles northeast of the Candelaria Mountains, Ranchería Mountain rises from the arid plain to a height of 7,244 feet.

[3] See n. 3, Ch. 5, this section.

[4] For the arrival of the different railroads at El Paso, see: Edward A. Leonard, *Rails at the Pass of the North* (El Paso: Texas Western Press, 1981); and J. Morgan Broaddus, Jr., *The Legal Heritage of El Paso* (El Paso: Texas Western Press, 1983), 134.

CHAPTER EIGHT

The Last Indian Fight in Texas

~

THE WRITER HAVING BEEN PROMOTED CAPTAIN OF COMPANY A, Frontier Battalion, in October 1880, the strength of the company was increased to twenty men, stationed at Ysleta. The Overland Stage, then carrying United States mail and passengers between San Antonio and El Paso, was attacked in Quitman Canyon, between Eagle Springs and the Rio Grande. It was bumping along the rocky, ugly looking canyon, and had arrived at the roughest place, known as the Apache postoffice on account of the hieroglyphics cut in the rocks by the Indians. It was an ideal place for an ambuscade, the cliffs and boulders enabling the wily savages to conceal themselves perfectly until the stage was almost under them and the driver and passengers at their mercy.

An old time stage driver named Morgan was handling the reins and there was one passenger in the coach.[1] Morgan had driven hundreds of times by himself and felt like one passenger made him almost secure from attack, and probably was looking at the mules and rocks in the road when the Indians fired on them. Both the passenger, a sporting man of those days and handy with shooting irons, and Morgan were armed, and one of the mules being killed, both of the men jumped from the coach and ran up among the boulders on the north side of the road. The chances are both may have been wounded.[2] Their bones were found long afterward by John Ford, an ex-ranger living at that time at old Fort Quitman.

Ford at the time, with a few of the ranchmen and Overland employees, went out to look for the stage when it failed to show up at the proper time, feeling pretty sure the Apaches had either captured or killed the driver and passengers. The searchers found the stage, one mule killed, and the canvas curtains cut off, the mailbags cut open and mail scattered over the ground, a leather boot cut up and carried off, but did not find the bodies of the men. Examining the signs, Ford believed there were only four Indians, and they had left the road and gone off southwest toward the river. The party took it for granted the driver and passenger had been taken prisoners and carried off to be tortured, and followed five or six miles, expecting to find their bodies.

Ford wrote to me, and Rangers were soon on the road. I had twelve of my men and three Pueblo Indians, making our force sixteen, quite small enough, but I had telegraphed Lt. Charley Nevill who was camped near Fort Davis, in Mosquite [Musquiz] Canyon, to meet me at Quitman, and he started with nine men and his wagon and a driver, a half-breed Digger Indian named Potter, who was afterwards with the men who tried to hold up the stage near San Angelo, but Lt. Kirk Trimbo [Turnbo] of my company happened to be on the stage and wounded Potter.[3]

Fitzgerald, a brother-in-law of Jim White, the present collector of El Paso, was killed in the fight. The Rangers afterward caught Potter and his corporation showed the mark of Kirk's bullet, but at the time I speak of Potter was good Injun heap. Our first night out, January 17, 1881, it began to snow, and in the morning when I poked my head out from under my blanket I saw nothing but white mounds where the boys lay snoring peacefully, but the guards had orders to wake us at daylight and had a big fire, so we were soon all up and cooking and shaking the snow from our blankets.

It was cold for keeps. One of the men, although the water was not over fifty yards, had to jump on his horse and gallop to the water, and when the horse put his head down to drink both Ranger and horse went down in the ice water. He got no sympathy. I never knew a Ranger that did unless he was half killed.

Our next camp was between Rife Station—named after the old Tom Rife, who kept the station then, afterward in charge of the Alamo at San Antonio.[4] It was one of the bitterly cold winds from the west, but the snow had melted off and we were in the bottom, with plenty of wood, and got along first rate.

The next morning we got to Quitman and John Ford told us it was not worthwhile to go out to the canyon, but keep on down the river and he was sure we would strike the trail of the Indians. We pushed on down the Rio Grande and camped. The weather had cleared up. The snow, except in shady places, had vanished, and one of the warm, bright, lovely days for which our west is celebrated had followed the bitter cold winds and snow. Even an old rattler had crawled out to enjoy the last rays of the sun and some of the younger members of the company, anxious to get his rattles, got after him, but he wriggled under a pile of driftwood and the greenies set fire to the pile, making a huge bonfire that lasted all night, and had the Indians been anywhere near and been on the watch for us, they would have seen us. Subsequent events, however, proved they were in a deep canyon, fully thirty miles south of us.

By sunrise we were off and took a trail that left the river and wound through some rough hills. Coming in below again, we struck the trail where the Indians had come from the southeast, and picked up a small, handsome fur-tipped [red] glove, and our conjecture was it had been dropped by the passenger for the benefit of pursuers, and gave us hopes that both the men were alive. The trail showed one fresh shod mule, which had been taken by the Apaches from a colored soldier who was repairing the telegraph wire in Quitman Canyon. I once overheard him relating the affair to an admiring crowd on a San Antonio street. He was up the telegraph pole and did not see the Indians until they had him treed and were getting ready to shoot him like a 'coon, when the Rangers charged and saved his life, but he lost his mule. This evidently did not happen as we had not left Ysleta at that time.

On reaching the river pretty well supplied with water, we followed a ledge of rocks crossing diagonally and making a splendid ford, and followed the trail down the river, they taking the old trail used by the Mexican customhouse guards. Where this leaves and strikes the rough hills we found the first camp of the Apaches after the murder in the canyon.[5]

We were puzzled by the signs at the camp, for there were no moccasin tracks around the fire at all, and only a small shoe track of Mexican make, also a box of Mexican wax matches, partly used, some scattered around on the ground. This was a puzzler but the next camp made by them for a noon rest, showed the Apaches too plain to be mistaken. They had killed a mule and roasted the ribs, cut off a lot of the meat, and their moccasin tracks were thick.

The explanation of this I learned years afterward. They had a Mexican prisoner, and the Indians—there were only three of them—sat on their blankets at their first camp and made the Mexican do all the work around the camp, and left the matches to throw suspicion on the Mexicans. The Mexican managed to make his escape that night, and they showed the cloven foot afterward.

Following the trail, we came to a wide gravely stream that came from the mountains to our right, and the trail led to the west, but when we struck the creek bed we found a fresh trail going east of some fourteen unshod ponies and knew in reason they were the game we were after, and we followed the fresh sign. We had with us old Bernardo Olguín, Domingo Olguín, his son, and Aniceto Durán, a nephew of the old Pueblo chief.[6]

Bernardo, [who] had for a long while been acting as scout and trailer for the United States troops, was familiar with the whole county, brave, sober and reliable, and could read wood signs like a book. The old fellow is dead, and it is only a question of time when the Tiguas who settled Ysleta will be a name only, as the Sinecus, their one time powerful neighbors are. Domingo, his son, a bright, intelligent young fellow, is also dead. Aniceto was alive a year ago.

The three Pueblos had a score to settle with these same Apaches, as Simón Olguín, a brother of Bernardo and noted guide for the United States Army, was killed at Ojo Viejo when a company of Pueblos under a Lieutenant Bell was ambushed, or rather surprised, in a camp that Simón begged the Lieutenant not to stop at.[7] But to go back to our trail.

The Apaches rode northeast, and late in the evening we came to a high bluff, and below half a mile was spread out a picture quite inviting to us—a ciénega, with a fine pool of water, tules and green grass. Taking my field glass, I carefully scanned the valley, hoping to find our game resting at their ease. But nothing but the omnipresent raven and barking coyotes could be seen. There had been at some prehistoric time an earthquake that made a deep rent in the cliff, and down this the Apaches, after dismounting, had slid their ponies, and the Rangers followed suit. We had our dinner and gave our stock a good rest, and resumed the chase. The signs were getting quite fresh and the boys were eager for a scrap.

Sunset found us in the open land between the hills and the Rio Grande. We struck camp, not caring to run into the Indians at nightfall, and we expected to find them on the river. Orders were given not to make any fires. It was bitterly cold, but the danger of our being seen was too great to take any chances.

At daylight we were off, and the trail crossed the river and went down it, putting us on Texas soil again and on our own dunghill. Following on until we came to the Indians' old camp, we stopped for dinner, and in pirouetting around the men found where a cache had been made on the bank of the river and dug down some four or five feet, but as we had all we could pack anyhow, [we] concluded to let it rest until some future day, which it has done to the present time.

Here the hills came in to the river and there was an exceedingly ugly place to pass, for the rocks sloped toward the cliff, and if a horse, pack mule or man should happen to slip he would have gone hundreds of feet below to certain death, rider and all. So we dismounted and moved very slowly and carefully until we gained level ground, and after following the river a short distance, the trail turned among the low hills on the river and made a bee line for the southern end of [the] Eagle Mountains.

We crossed the big valley, where a road now runs between Sierra Blanca Station and Capt. Charlie Davis' Ranch, and sunset found us in the rough hills about three miles from the foot of the Eagle Mountains canyon, with a few scattered cedars around us. The sign was so fresh we felt pretty sure we would find the Apaches in some of the numerous little canyons in the morning.

Orders were again given for no fires to be built after night except by the sentinel, and that must be a very small one and completely hidden from the mountains. About midnight, being awake, I was very much astounded to see a bright blaze that shot up into the air at least fifty feet. Frank Beaumont, who was the sentinel on guard at the time, had found a secluded little nook completely hidden from the mountains, and built a fire under a green cedar tree, harboring the delusion that green cedar would not burn. Frank was about as green as the cedar, for no sooner did the green boughs get thoroughly heated than the blaze ran up like it was a barrel of kerosene oil. There was no use calling out the fire brigade, and we could only hope the Indians were all asleep. Frank got the green rubbed off afterward and made a good Ranger.

We were off bright and early, and within a mile found another mule the Apaches had butchered to eat. Keeping a sharp lookout, we rode up to the base of a high cliff, where there was a small spring, and there we found a moccasin track so fresh that it looked as though the Indians had just left. All was eagerness and excitement, and all wanted to go, but Cpl. Nat Harrison made a detail to watch our horses, and we followed the path to the right of the cliff up a steep hill, and after following the moccasin track about 250 yards we came to the crest of a ridge that ran to our right, and from the tops of cedars and oaks in view we had every reason to believe we would find our game.

Cautiously in line we crept up and peeped over. Just across a little valley a hundred yards away stood a tepee of old canvas fluttering in the breeze, and we saw hides and some articles lying around, so, in Ranger parlance, we made sure we "had 'em grabbed," but as we straightened up and had a full view we saw only empty tepees. The birds had flown. The one Indian whose track we saw had been drunk, probably, and went to get a drink about the time Frank Beaumont made his accidental bonfire. The anti[prohibitionist]s can use that as an argument in favor of getting drunk and sitting up till midnight, as it saved his life and the village.

Everything denoted a hasty flight, quirts lying around, old blankets, deer and elk hides showing the thieving rascals were from the Tularosa Agency, as the Sacramento Mountains at that time were full of elk, as well as bear, deer and turkeys. Among other things in the camp was a silver urn, evidently used in some church, which I still have.

The Indians had dug a hole in the ground and put the green horse hide in it, and had been sitting all around, chewing mescal and spitting into the hide.[8] This was to be allowed to ferment so it would "make drunk come" and no doubt if the Rangers had not spoiled the fun they would have had a scalp dance over poor old Morgan's scalp and a big celebration.

We began to look for a trail off from camp, and although we cut for signs all around the camp, we never saw a pony track. These Apaches were a remnant of Victorio's band that escaped at Tres Castillos when Gen. Joaquín Terrazas made such a killing, and they had no idea of being caught again. They probably grabbed up their saddles and such things as they could pack and went afoot to their ponies. The ground was frozen so hard they made no sign.

It was useless to try to overtake them with the start they had, so I determined to try a little strategy. Nearly all my boys had Mexican hats, and as we had come out of Mexico I determined to take the back track as though we had given up the chase and were going back to Chihuahua. After doing about six miles we scattered out so as not to make any more dust than possible and started north to go around the Eagle Mountains and strike the old Overland Stage Road, and perhaps meet Lieutenant Nevill and his detachment.

By sundown we had ridden within some five miles of Eagle Springs, and found plenty of water for ourselves and horses from the melted snow. It was a bitterly cold night and all the canteens that had been filled with water froze and burst.

By 10 o'clock next morning we reached Eagle Springs, and learned that Lieutenant Nevill had left that morning for Fort Quitman to meet us. Len Peveler was sent after him and overtook him camped for dinner at Eighteen Mile Waterhole and they came back that night.[9] Lieutenant Nevill told us he had seen where quite a bunch of barefoot ponies had crossed the road six or eight miles east of our camp and we told him that was our band of Apaches.

Early in the morning we took the road back, leaving Lieutenant Nevill's wagon, and the aforesaid Digger at the stage stand, and struck the trail again. They made straight for Victorio's tank, named after the old Apache chief, who, with his band, camped there when General Grierson and the United States troop and my company of Rangers had followed him on his last raid in Texas.[10]

The valley between the Eagle and Devil's mountains, or in the sweet

Castillian tongue, Sierra Aguila and Sierra Diablos, is quite broad. The Galveston, Harrisburg and San Antonio Railroad and Texas and Pacific now run through it, and from the car windows looking northeast one can see a tall, flat-top mountain called by the Mexican El Nariz—the Nose.[11] Our Apaches rode just at the southern foot of it, on this, their last raid in Texas.

Midway of the plains we came to where another horse had been killed and the meat taken had probably given out. They ride until an animal gives out and then use him as commissary stores. No wonder they were hard to catch where they could then steal a fresh horse. We stopped for dinner where they did, and learned a lesson from them in border warfare. There was no water, but plenty of snow, and they had built a mud dam across a narrow ravine and heated boulders and rolled them into it, melting the snow until all their animals and themselves had water.

Passing along the foot of El Nariz the trail turned toward an ugly looking canyon to our right, but as I knew the country we went ahead to Victorio's tank. At the mouth of the canyon that leads to it, we came across their trail again, looking quite fresh, as they had camped the night before in the rough canyon. The next morning bright and early we were off and made such good time by noon we had come to where they had camped for the night. It showed they were a little suspicious that they might be followed, as their camp was in a thicket near the head of a rough canyon that ran east toward Rattlesnake Springs, where they could not be followed on horseback easily, and could have been safe from anyone on foot unless they were trained sprinters.[12]

We now had to be extra careful, as we found an enormous head of deer horns in this camp, and knew the Indians were hunting and had a good chance for them to see us before we did them. Sunset found us at their camp, where they killed another horse for the commissary department, and as there was plenty of water and good grass, we stopped also. Here they must have given up the idea of danger and roasted a big lot of mescal plants.[13] The pit where it had been roasted was still warm and the odor as sweet as June apples. I told the boys I hoped we would catch them before they ate it all up, as it was a might good substitute for old sweet yams.

These Apaches got their name from relying much on this plant as a food, hence, their name, Mescaleros, and it may interest hunters and woodsmen to know how the Indians prepare it. They dig a pit three or four feet deep and about five in diameter and built a fire in this, collecting the mescal heads, not too old or tough. When the fire burns down they pile in the mescal in pyramid forms, cover with trash and earth, hot coals and ashes that had been all raked out, hot rocks also being used. This done at night, they have in the morning as nice an article of food as one could wish. There are many kinds of yucca, but the kind they cook has thick leaves at the base and sharp black points. One is apt to remember if he rams his foot against it. It grows all over the mountains.

The chase was now becoming very exciting. The signs showed the Mescaleros had left that morning and were traveling slowly and carelessly, having come to the conclusion their last murders would be unavenged. We passed plenty of deer and antelope, but orders not to shoot anything but an Indian were positive. The Pueblos rode ahead a quarter of a mile, and often were strung up to the highest pitch. Every coyote, antelope or moving thing seen was eagerly scanned.

In the evening we came to their camp, and an examination of the ashes showed that live coals of fire were still burning. In hunting large game, as the pleasure of the chase is in proportion to the danger, so we felt all the eagerness of tiger or lion hunter, but I doubt much if either comes up to the Apache warrior with his Winchester and fierceness and cunning.

Rushing ahead, by sunset we had covered a good deal of ground, and nearing the high bluff on the east side of the Sierra Diablos, and striking a deep arroyo, the trail went up over a high ridge, but I stopped in the arroyo. There was too much risk in crossing the ridge. The Indians might be in full view, or a hunter, lagging behind, spy us. At nightfall, too, was no time to jump their camp.

Taking Old Bernardo and a couple of men with me we went up to where the trail crossed the crest of the mountains and with our glass scanned the hills in front of us, but no head of ponies, smoke, nor Indian could be seen. Whil'st we were standing there a flock of doves came sweeping by our heads and I said: "Boys, where those are going to water we will find the Indians in the morning." No fire could be seen from our front, so we cooked and were soon asleep, the sentinel instructed to waken us before day-break.

We were good tired and it seemed I had hardly been asleep an hour until we were awakened and had a hasty breakfast and were off on the trail. It was bitterly cold, so we walked and led our horses, and had to stoop down in places to work out the trail. Old Bernardo was ahead and I and Lieutenant Nevill just behind, and just as day began to dawn, the Old Pueblo squatted down and said: "*Hay, están los Indios,* captain," and looking in the direction he pointed we distinguished two camp fires burning up brightly.

Luckily we were just on the crest of a hill and turning back, were soon out of sight, and by taking advantage of the ground, we got within four hundred yards of them and Sergeant Carruthers of Nevill's Company and Cpl. Nat Harrison, Company A, made a detail to guard our horses, the usual kick coming, as all the Rangers wanted to take a hand, and five had to sit quietly and hear their comrades cheering and Winchesters popping.

We were able to get within two hundred yards of their camp.[14] Sergeant Carruthers with nine or ten men was sent to the left and instructed to get as near as he could to the Indians without being discovered and when we opened fire to do the same and charge their camp. My squad by following in Indian file and stooping as low as possible got within a hundred yards of the eastern camp. Here we came to a swag or low place between us and the Indians, who were huddled up around their fires cooking breakfast and not conscious of a Ranger being within a hundred miles. One was just coming to the fire with some wood and looked as big as a skinned horse, having an army cape on taken from some Negro soldiers killed at Hot Springs on the Rio Grande.[15] It proved to be a little girl not over five years old, and goes to show how easily one can let his imagination run away with him. I was afraid if we passed down this swag some of the Apaches would see us and being just on the crest of the hill with a deep canyon beyond a few jumps would take them out of sight. So I kneeled down and motioned to the men to fall into line on my right and passed the word down the line when I fired to turn loose.

Old Bernardo's eyes were glistening like a panther's at the chance of getting even with the murderers of his brothers, his son and nephew by his side. Lieutenant Nevill was at my side and the muzzle of his gun within an inch of old Bernardo's ear, and when Nevill fired I saw the old fellow dodge like a mule with a tick in his ear. It was a complete surprise to the Indians, and there was plenty of blood all around their camp fire, showing some of us had good aim. Sergeant Carruthers got three at the other fire. Nearly all the men had Winchester carbines and rifles, but I used a Springfield rifle with hair trigger such as the United States officers used and I doubt if a better army gun was ever made for reliability.

We only had a few shots when the Apaches broke over the hill like a herd of deer and we charged the camp, as did the other squad, and when we got where we could see, the Indians were making two-forty time down the steep canyon. Only one tried to mount a horse and every Ranger in sight began pumping lead at him. He tumbled off the horse, as we supposed dead, but after playing possum until we ceased firing, he jumped up and made better time than he did on horseback. The Apaches ran, some to the west and some east down the deep canyon and one warrior went up the opposite side of the canyon.

He bore along the hill in full view and drew the fire of every one and occasionally would turn around and shoot back at us. All we could do was to hold our breath until he shot, not knowing which one was his target. I took five pops at him myself.[16] Frank De Jarnette and another Ranger followed his trail for over a mile and said he was bleeding like a beef, but still making big jumps toward the Tularosa Agency. Four or five Indians ran down the arroyo and I called to Frank De Jarnette and told him the arroyo was so crooked that if we would leave it and run along the side of the canyon I believed we could get ahead of the Indians and kill some of them. So away we went at full speed, Frank ahead.

Suddenly I saw him sit down and start to slide, and I reached down and grabbed him back, when he sat still panting like a lizard chased by a chaparral cock without being able to speak. We had come square on the brink of a cliff that must have been four or five hundred feet perpendicular. If he had gone over I could not have stopped and we would both have been killed by the fall and no one been the wiser except Old Bernardo would have followed our trail. It was one of the times I humbly thanked God he had spared my life.

Finding we could make no further progress in that direction, and the firing in the canyon ceasing, we turned back to the arroyo, and soon saw Sergeant Carruthers and a squad of Rangers coming up the bed of the arroyo with two squaws and a child, prisoners. They had run down the bed of the arroyo until they came to the same cliff that stopped us, and hid in a cave where the men found them. This explained why one of the warriors had taken the chance on the side of the mountain instead of running down the arroyo with the squaws. After the squaws hid, some of the bucks ran up the side of the mountain and got into a clump of rocks and opened fire on us.

I saw the smoke of their guns, and the bullet went just above my knees, striking the ground at De Jarnette's feet. I was mystified for a moment, as the wind from the bullet was quite as hard as though a blow had come from a stick.[17] The Indian squaws were both wounded, and at this moment young [Sam] Graham came up, and he was perfectly wild with rage at the sight of them, for this same band had, not a great while before this, ambushed an emigrant train in Bass Canyon, on the old Overland Stage Road between Van Horn's Well and Eagle Springs; had shot his brother, making him a cripple and killing his sister-in-law, a daughter of Mr. Little of Bexar County, and killed an old man named [James] Grant.[18] Another man, named Murphy, saved the life of his family by hiding them.

Of course, young Graham, a hot headed boy, wanted to kill the women. The prisoners soon took in the situation and cowered behind me as they saw his angry face and hostile attitude, but I told him I could never agree to killing women, crying and begging for their lives, but would go with him after the warriors willingly. This appeal quieted him and leaving Ed Fitch, one of my company in charge of them, we started up the arroyo, and soon heard such a roar of Winchesters we thought the Apaches must have rallied and returned to their camp. We were pretty badly scattered, for the Indians went in every direction and the Rangers after them, but as we were afoot we were not in it in a race with fleet-footed Apaches, especially as they were running for dear life, assisted by a lively fusillade of Winchester bullets.

We all started off at a double-quick, some up the bed of the creek, but Lieutenant Nevill and myself took the near shoot up the side of the mountain. By the time we had run a hundred yards, Nevill sung out: "Colonel, I can't run another foot." He was fat and heavy, but being thin, I made the top of the hill and was mad enough. Some of the boys were shooting the dead Indians, to make sure they did not rob and murder anymore. Louis Peveler, one of my boys, who had quite a race after an Indian, said: "Colonel, I passed a little Indian girl, about five years old and did not want to kill her. She pointed the way the other Indians had gone and was smiling as though it was quite a joke." "Bring her in, and I'll take her home to Mary," I said. My little girl had always asked me to bring her ferns, flowers, pretty rocks or something every time I went on a scout, and as we rode off she said; "papa, please bring me a little Indian." So my promise was out, and here was a chance to make it good. When he brought her to camp she was all smiles, but when she saw the dead Indians lying around and the squaws spoke to her, her eyes flashed fire and she looked like some wild animal. I made a mental note of it for future reference.

We then went to work getting dinner and as there was a big pile of meat in camp, I was put on the smelling committee to separate the venison from horse meat.[19] Venison has a smell no one can mistake after drying it, and I selected it easily, but did not eat any myself, preferring old Ranger chuck, coffee, bread and bacon. One of the boys brought me a bundle of the roasted mescal put up in [a] plaited sotol basket and ready to hang on the pommel of my saddle, thanks to Mr. Lo.

There was only one hole of water in the arroyo, and the Apaches in their flight had passed through it and left a broad streak of blood easily seen through the clear water lying on the rock bottom, and though the Texas Ranger was looked on as a savage animal, none of us cared to drink the blood of our enemies, and so we decided to make a straight shoot for Victorio's tank, instead of following our crooked trail back. When we got through dinner, we began to take stock so as to administer on the estate of the late, but not lamented to any great extent, Apaches.

We found in their camp women and children's clothing, showing we had struck the band that murdered Mrs. [Margaret] Graham and robbed their wagons. We found five United States cavalry saddles, showing that they had killed the six colored soldiers at the Hot Springs below Fort Quitman. We found the tops of old Morgan's boots which, no doubt, would have been used to make moccasins, and the pants of the passenger who was on the stage. They had cut them off at the body and above the knees and made them into sacks filled with tobacco and such little trinkets as delight the Indians. We had got the identical Indians that had killed ten people we knew of within a few months.

We found a very pretty double action 41-Colt revolver, two Winchester carbines and [a] Remington carbine; the pistol we sent the adjutant general, John B. Jones, dearly loved by all Rangers—the Remington that was decorated with pinhead cut off and driven in the stock, we sent our very efficient quartermaster, Captain Coldwell. A buckskin *talma* I sent the old alcalde, Gov. O.M. Roberts (God bless his dear memory), and we got all their horses, thirteen, and three mules, all their saddles, ropes, buckskin, etc. Among the many things in camp, we found several bolts of calico prints that had not been cut open, showing that these Indians had been trading with those cold blooded scoundrels who furnished them ammunition and clothing—when they knew they were raiding on our people.[20] They no doubt had left a pile in their cache on the banks of the Rio Grande. We always intended to go back there but never did.

Having plenty of saddles and pack animals, we hurriedly gathered up everything worth carrying, and got ready to move. The next thing to consider was our prisoners. One of the squaws was severely, but not mortally wounded, so we left her and her child, and piled up the meat near her and filled the Indian jars with water, believing that some of the Indians would come back as soon as we left, at least after nightfall. The other, one of the prettiest squaws I ever saw, had three bullets through her right hand, and her little boy, a two-year-old, had one of his toes shot off. She was about sixteen and the little fellow evidently her first child.

I was the bold warrior that shot his toe off as we charged through the camp. I spied a black bushy head that looked as big as a pack measure, and he had on a big white sheet, probably the passenger's killed in the stage. I threw up my rifle and took a quick snapshot and having neglected to set the hair trigger, I pulled, taking a toe off instead of his head, as I intended.

We put the squaw on her horse and the little girl produced her saddle, quirt and army cape and selected her pony, and appeared as contented as if with her own people.[21] We strung out and by 11 o'clock that night were back at Victorio's tank, pretty well tired out, thankful that none of the men were hurt, and satisfied we had given the Apaches a lesson that they would remember; in fact, they never committed another murder in Texas.

We did not leave Victorio tank until noon the next day, and Cpl. Nat Harrison and some of the other Rangers organized a temporary medical corps, tied up the little papoose's toe after washing it, and made splints to fix the squaw's hand. It was doubled up, and they tried to open it, using as gentle care as they could, but as soon as she saw what they wanted she grabbed her wounded hand and straightened it out without a murmur or change of countenance, showing the traditional pride the Indian has in ignoring pain.

Strung out after dinner we made quite a cavalcade; and passing by the base of El Nariz, we made a bee line for Ojo de Aguila. Well out in the plain, we found a good place with plenty of grass and made a dry camp. We were still not "out of the woods," for one Indian could stampede our stock and set us afoot. So strict orders were given to hobble or tie securely every horse and mule in camp. Just before day one of the Pueblo Indians on guard had untied his horse to give him a better chance to fill up—a big mistake—for if a horse is tied up he will eat every blade of grass within his reach, and if loose will wander around looking for better grass and likely run off.

The Pueblo Indian pony fed off and probably was scared by a sneaking coyote and broke for the herd. In an instant there was snorting, trampling of horses' feet and the Rangers had grabbed their guns and were on their feet running to the herd, expecting the Apaches were trying to set us afoot. A sentinel was near the little squaw to keep her from escaping, and when the alarm began she knew at once what the trouble was, and feared the sentinel would kill her to prevent her escaping, as is the Indian custom, so she sprang up and made about two jumps and lit on the top of Cpl. Nat Harrison with a squall like an old hen when an owl rushes her off of her roost.

Nat, who was one of the bravest, best, most sleepy-headed Rangers that ever went on a scout, was sure an Indian was trying to scalp him, and the little squaw got her one good arm around his neck and held on to him like grim death, and by the time he could loose her the whole camp was awake and had gotten on the ridiculous side of the tragedy. Nat went after the sentinel and we heard him turn loose what he supposed was pure Castillian; "Hey, hombre! Por que you no hobble your mule or tie him with a rope."

All being now awaken, we began cooking and soon the Rangers began in stage whispers to talk of the event. The truth was the poor little squaw was frightened nearly to death and he had been kind, as was his nature, to her, and she knew if she got hold of him the sentinel would not try to shoot for fear of hitting the corporal. It was a long time before Nat heard the last of it.

We arrived safely at Eagle Springs in the evening and were received with rejoicing by the stage employees who had been so long annoyed by this band of Apaches, and the writer took advantage of the Overland Stage being on hand to sent a message to Mayor [Joseph] Magoffin and his own family to get ahead of the Kaffirgrams, that always reported all the Rangers killed, in spite of the obvious fact that no news could possibly get back unless we brought it.[22] Arrived at the springs we took a much needed rest, and to help pass away the time all plunder taken in camp, consisting of buckskins, lariats, saddles, calicos and Apache gew gaws, were by a committee, made into twenty-six piles, and old Bernardo, standing with his back to the piles, was asked who is to have No. 1, and so on to the end and then swapping articles afforded amusement to the men.

Early next morning we got ready to go each to his appointed station, and Nevill said; "How about the little girl, colonel? Will you take her home to Mary?"

"Not if I know myself. She will get mad some day, playing, brain Mary, and take to the woods. You can turn them over to the commanding officer at Fort Davis with my compliments," I replied. Soon the Rangers strung out on the plains, Lieutenant Nevill and his squad headed toward Musqu[iz] Canyon and Company A toward Ysleta, which place we reached February 5, having been out twenty-two days and marched 502 miles.

This was the last fight on Texas soil between the Indians and Texas Rangers—as poor Louis Napoleon expressed it, "the battle between civilization and barbarism." We never knew exactly how many Indians were in the party, but Mr. Bingham, a stock raiser, found a skull and bones near Escondido Springs, near Guadalupe Peak, and the direction probably taken by one of the wounded Indians making for the Tularosa Agency via the Guadalupe Springs. Baker and Osmer, who were prospecting afterward near where we had the fight, found two Indian skeletons in a cave, their hair and portion of dress still intact.

Gen. George W. Russ of San Antonio also found two fresh graves on an old Indian trail between Carrizo Springs and what is now Allamoore Station, on the Texas and Pacific Railroad, and unless they were some of our lame ducks, and buried by their friends, they must have crawled into their holes and pulled them in after them.[23] Shortly after we returned to our station I received a letter from a lieutenant of the United States army at Fort [Stanton], New Mexico, saying that a band of the Mescalero Apaches had represented to him that some of their people were in trouble down in Texas and that they wanted to go after them and bring them back, and seeing they were determined to go anyhow, he had "made a virtue of necessity and given them a pass."

In reply I called his attention to the fact that an account of the numerous murders and outrages committed by the reservation Indians from Fort Sill,

Indian Territory, to San Carlos, New Mexico, Sen. Richard Coke of Texas had gotten an order from the Secretary of War forbidding officers or agents giving Indians passes into Texas. A courteous letter came in reply, saying he was not aware of such [an] order or he should not have given them a pass. Luckily for this band, we had our own little troubles, in the war between law and order and rowdyism in the then very wild and wooly village of El Paso, Franklin, Magoffinsville or Ponce (for it had all these names at that time), or the Rangers would certainly have followed the Apaches and "made good Indians of them."

Jake Owens, the very efficient county clerk of Eddy County, told me he was at the Mescalero or Fort Stanton Reservation when a lone Apache Indian came in and told a tale of woe that the Rangers had attacked them and killed every one of the party except himself; that there were thirteen of them; but if that was the number then there would have been no necessity for a band of the Apaches to bring any one in, for we left six, on the ground, three were taken prisoners, one was found by Bingham, and graves were found by Gen. George W. Russ, and Baker and Osmer found two. The Apache evidently lied as to the number, unless they had separated and part of the band gone into the Davis Mountains, a favorite haunt of theirs after we jumped them in the Eagle Mountains.

We had a congratulatory letter from Adj. Gen. John B. Jones and also one from Captain [Neal] Coldwell, who regarded in a cold, strictly business manner, our victory as he had had to pay for various Ranger horses that had been killed in the service and were rated at as full value as though they were full blood Herefords or Jerseys, and killed by the locomotives.[24] "Hurrah!" said the captain, "for Company A we are ahead on the horse account."

Soon the name of Texas Rangers will be an echo of the past and let us hope the Daughters of the Republic, before they, too, shall have passed over the silent river, will interest themselves and see that a monument is erected on the capitol grounds in Austin in memory of the Texas Rangers.

P.S.—I enclose your letter from L.B. Carruthers, the treasurer of Brewster Country, giving names of the men that should be preserved; some are dead, others scattered to the four corners of the earth.

Alpine, Texas

Colonel George W. Baylor
Cuernavaca, Mexico

Dear Colonel: Your favor came duly to hand and would have been answered earlier if I had not been so crippled with the rheumatism.

On looking ever my old papers, I found my guard list for one scout to the Sierra Diablo Mountains in January 1881. We left camp in Monja [Musquiz] Canyon on January 21, under command of Lieutenant C.L. Nevill, namely, Sergeant L.B. Carruthers, Corporal Sam Graham and Privates L.B. [De] Jarnette, F.W. De Jarnette, W.H. Guyse, Ike Lee, R.L. Nevill, W.H. Roberts, and Shape Rogers, making ten men, rank and file. Besides these there were Rangers as follows: Captain G.W. Baylor, Corporal Nat Harrison, Privates Brown, Beaumont, Connely, Palmer, Peveler, L. Wells, Tandy, Walde, Johnson, Hardin and the three Pueblo Indians, namely, Bernardo Olguín, Domingo Olguín, and Ameneseto Durán, making fifteen men, rank and file.

We struck the Indians in camp on the summit of the Diablos, overlooked the Salt Lakes at sunrise on the morning of the 29th and to the best of my recollection we killed twelve and captured a squaw and two children, out of the band of twenty; the squaw and child were captured by me and the child by Peveler. I trust the foregoing may be of use to you and that you will pardon my delay in the premises. With kindest regards to Mr. Lee and self, I remain your friend.

L.B. Carruthers

NOTES

[1] Gillett identified the passenger as a gambler named Crenshaw. Gillett, *Six Years with the Texas Rangers*, 232.

[2] The attack on the stagecoach was on 8 January 1881. Baylor initially speculated that the driver and passenger had robbed the stage. Austerman, *Sharps Rifles and Spanish Mules*, 305; Kenneth A. Goldblatt, "Ambush in Quitman Canyon," *Password* 14 (Winter 1969): 109-16; Baylor to John B. Jones, 9 February 1881, AGO, RG 401, TSA. Baylor's report was ably edited and published by Kenneth A. Goldblatt as "Scout to Quitman Canyon: Report of Captain Geo. W. Baylor of the Frontier Battalion," *West Texas Historical Association Yearbook* 44 (October 1968): 149-59.

[3] In November 1881, Nevill accompanied the Gano surveying expedition by boat down the Rio Grande, thereby becoming, in Walter Prescott Webb's words, the only Texas Ranger to operate on water. Nevill barely escaped drowning when the boat he was in capsized. Well into 1882, he continued to scout the Big Bend region for hostiles. He finally resigned to become sheriff of Presidio County and a ranching partner with James B. Gillett. Webb, *The Texas Rangers*, 409-10. For the Gano Expedition, see: Nevill to W.R. King, 4 February 1882 and Neville to Coldwell, 8 February 1882, both in AGO, RG 401, TSA.

[4] The 1850 Bexar County census lists Rife as single, twenty-five, born in Mississippi, and a "Ranger." He was one of the first stage drivers for Henry Skillman on the San Antonio-El

Paso Mail. Rife later drove for George Giddings and was with Henry Skillman when Capt. Albert H. French, Company A, 1st California Cavalry (California Column), attacked Skillman's camp at Spencer's Ranch near Presidio del Norte in the early morning hours of 14 April 1864. For a sketch of Rife during the Civil War, see: Merrick, *From Desert to Bayou*, 75; Austerman, *Sharps Rifles and Spanish Mules*, 34, 45, 117, 142; 7th Census, Bexar County, Texas; Roy L. Smith, *Three Roads to Chihuahua* (Austin: Eakin Press, 1988), 200-201; Jack C. Scannell, "Henry Skillman, Texas Frontiersman," *Permian Historical Annual* 18 (December 1978): 29; and Jerry D. Thompson, "Drama in the Desert: The Hunt for Henry Skillman in the Trans-Pecos, 1862-1864," *Password* 37 (Fall 1992): 107-26.

5 It was in the "foot-hills of the Los Pinos Mountains" the previous year that Baylor parted from Gen. Joaquín Terrazas prior to the massacre of Victorio and his band at Tres Castillos. Baylor to Jones, 9 February 1881, AGO, RG 401, TSA.

6 Bernardo, sixty, "scout, U.S.A.," and Domingo, twenty-nine, "Indian scout, U.S.A.," are both listed on the 1880 El Paso Census at Ysleta. During the Civil War, Simón and Bernardo Olguín were employed by Ben Dowell to spy on Union forces in the area. 10th Census, El Paso County, Texas; and Hamilton, *Ben Dowell*, 32-33.

7 In mid-June 1880 a party of Tigua scouts on their way to Fort Davis were attacked in Viejo Pass in the Sierra Vieja, northwest of Presidio. As Baylor indicates, Simón Olguín, the chief scout, was killed. Leckie, *The Buffalo Soldiers*, 230.

8 "They had just killed, and had piled up in camp, two horses and one mule, and had the blood in tin vessels, had mule tongue stewing, and everything indicated they were on the eve of having a jolly war dance—a five gallon mescal wine they made, and a horse-skin sunk in the ground and some fifteen or twenty gallons in it. We got there the mate of Morgan's boot-top, and a bag made from the leg of the passenger's pantaloons, and some express receipts, postal cards and other mail matter taken from the stage," Baylor wrote in his official report. Baylor to Jones, 8 February 1881, AGO, RG 401, TSA.

9 Baylor probably means Len Peterson.

10 In his official report, Baylor refers to Victorio Tank as Apache Tank.

11 Baylor reported passing by Chili Peak, which is not to be confused with Chilicotal Mountain in southern Brewster County.

12 Rattlesnake Springs is some twenty-two miles north of Van Horn on the east side of the Sierra Diablos at the mouth of Victorio Canyon. The spring had been popular with the prehistoric people of the area but is dry today. R.F. Joyce's 1880 "Map of the Military District of the Pecos, Dept. of Texas" indicates both Rattlesnake and Little Rattlesnake springs. The desert around Rattlesnake Springs was the site of Grierson's running fight with Victorio on 6 August 1880. Dan L. Thrapp, *The Conquest of Apacheria* (Norman: University of Oklahoma, 1967), 204-5.

13 The mescal or agave plant was a staple of the Mescaleros. It was gathered in such quantities by the Mescalero women that it became the name of the tribe. Yearly treks were made to the gathering grounds where the crowns of the plant were dug up and baked in large underground ovens. Men usually accompanied the women on the journeys, providing protection, helping to dig the pits, and using the excursions to hunt. Verne F. Ray, *Ethnohistorical Analysis of Documents Relating to the Apache Indians* (New York: Garland, 1974), 205-6.

14 The men approached the Apache camp by using several large Yucca plants as cover. Baylor to Jones, 9 February 1881, AGO, RG 401, TSA. Also, Webb, "Last War Trail of Victorio," 20-21, 43.

[15] On 28 October 1880, Apaches ambushed one of Grierson's patrols on the Rio Grande below Ojo Caliente, some twenty-nine miles downriver from Fort Quitman, killing Cpl. William Backus and Pvts. Jeremiah Griffin, James Stanley, Carter Burns, and George Mill. Leckie, *Buffalo Soldiers,* 230.

[16] "One Indian, whom we had named Big-Foot, from his enormous track, ran up a mountain in front of us some 400 yards, in full view, and not less than 200 shots were fired [at] him, most of them with good results, but he passed over the hill, only stopping long enough to fire two shots," Baylor reported. Baylor to Jones, 9 February 1881, AGO, RG 401, TSA.

[17] In his official report, Baylor was far more graphic in describing the attack on the Apache camp. "One warrior stood his ground principally because he got the gable end of his head shot off early in the action. On examination a .45 cartridge was found hung in his Winchester." In reference to the Rangers' inability to distinguish men from women and children, Baylor proclaimed that "the law under which the Frontier Battalion was organized don't require it." In letters written from the Ranger camp in Musquiz Canyon near Fort Davis on 8 and 9 February 1881, Nevill was highly critical of Baylor's lack of discipline during the expedition and stated frankly that he did not care to serve under Baylor again, unless more stringent discipline was maintained. Nevill to Jones, 8 and 9 February 1881, AGO, RG 401, TSA.

[18] On 12 May 1880, Apaches attacked a wagon train in Bass Canyon, killing Margaret Graham and James Grant. Harry Graham, husband of the victim, had his thigh broken and a man named Murphy was wounded. Sam Graham and four German immigrants, along with Mrs. Murphy and her four children, survived by hiding in the desert vegetation. The grave of Margaret Graham can be seen at Van Horn Wells today. The party had been repeatedly warned at Fort Stockton and Fort Davis that Apaches had been seen in the area west of the Davis Mountains. Leckie, *Buffalo Soldiers*, 223; and Gillett, *Six Years with the Texas Rangers*, 202.

[19] Baylor also reported that he and his men "took our breakfast on the ground occupied by the Indians, which all enjoyed, as we had eaten nothing since dinner the day before. Some of the men found horse meat good enough. We had almost a boundless view from our breakfast table—toward the north the grand old Cathedral Peak [El Capitan] of the Guadalupe Mountains; further west the San Antonio Mountains, the Cornudas, Los Alamos; Sierra Alto at the Hueco Tanks, only twenty-four miles from our headquarters; to the [south]east El Muerto, and south, the Eagle Mountains, the beauty of the scenery only marred by 'man's inhumanity to man'—the ghastly forms of the dead lying around." Baylor to Jones, 9 February 1881, AGO, RG 401, TSA.

[20] Baylor speculated at the time, however, that the items had been taken in a raid south of the border. Baylor to Jones, 9 February 1881, AGO, RG 401, TSA.

[21] Baylor was told by the girl's mother that the child was Victorio's daughter. Neville said in his report that the "baby" had previously been wounded in the leg and the wound had almost healed. At Fort Davis, Nevill wrote that the younger girl would begin to scream every time she heard a gunshot. In October 1881, when it was reported that a band of Apache were moving north out of the Davis Mountains, Baylor, not knowing that the Indian woman captured in the attack had been killed at Fort Davis, was sure the "track of a small squaw" proved the Indians had with them "the prisoner we turned over to the Govt. last spring." Neville reported that the Indian woman had been "bound by the hands

and outraged then had her skull above the forehead laid open with an ax." *Galveston Daily News*, 29 November 1905; and Neville to Jones, 6 February 1881; Neville to Jones, 9 February 1881; Baylor to King, 5 October 1881; Neville to Coldwell, 10 January 1882; all in AGO, RG 401, TSA.

22 Baylor wired Adjutant General Jones from Eagle Springs: "I and Lt. Nevill surprised Indians in Sierra Diablo on twenty ninth . . . killed six captured three and sixteen head stock several of their trails very bloody where they ran off no dangers but are same Indians that massacred Mrs. Graham in Bass Canyon Soldiers at Hot Springs and Driver & passengers in Quitman Canyon Particulars in Mail." Baylor to Jones, 2 February 1881, AGO, RG 401, TSA. The massacre was joyously reported in the *San Antonio Daily Express,* 6 February 1881, and the *Galveston Weekly News*, 10 February 1881.

23 Allamoore Station is about ten miles west of present-day Van Horn and twenty-two miles east of Sierra Blanca. Since those who escaped the Sierra Diablo Massacre were certain to have fled toward the Guadalupe Mountains, it is doubtful that the graves were those of Indians wounded in the attack.

24 Coldwell, born in Dade County, Missouri, in May 1844, served in the 32d Texas Cavalry during the Civil War. In 1874, he was commissioned captain of Company F of the Rangers and sent to scout the region around the headwaters of the Guadalupe, Nueces, Llano, and Devils rivers. In 1876-1877, Coldwell's Rangers broke up a band of thieves operating in northwestern Atascosa County near San Antonio. Gillett, *Six Years with the Texas Rangers*, 67-69.

CHAPTER NINE

An El Paso Street Duel

I SEE COLONEL MOORE HAS BEEN GIVING his experience in the early days at El Paso and an account of the bloody fight at the old Ben Dowell place on El Paso Street. Though correct in the main, yet he has the actual facts of the killing of Johnny Hale, Gus Krempkau, George Campbell, and a Mexican, "pretty much mixed."

Gus Krempkau had been one of my Rangers, coming up from San Antonio with my detachment of Company C, but at the time of his death he was not in the service of the state.[1] Moore has given the facts leading up to the shooting, but there was something behind the statement. We had frequently followed trails up to Johnny Hale's place and lost them.[2] Long afterwards I was scouting in the winter there and found an explanation of the mysterious disappearance of persons that had evidently gone to the house. Up in some big cottonwood trees beyond the house on an old road leading up the river I saw, up among the thick branches and leaves, platforms where a thief could take a comfortable snooze up in a tree, whil'st the Rangers were looking for his trail on the ground.

Gus Krempkau was with us; Johnny did not fancy our visiting him and knowing it would not do to buck up against the Rangers, picked a quarrel with Gus, or took up Campbell's quarrel.

There had been bitter feeling between Dallas Stoudemeyer [Stoudenmire] and George [Washington] Campbell, both being candidates for city marshal, and talks and threats between the parties and their friends had been frequent, so a quarrel between Hale and Krempkau soon drew a crowd.[3] Johnny no doubt thought, now here's my chance to get even; this fellow is not in the Ranger Company and I'll do him up.

Without a moment's warning he drew his pistol and put a .45 Colt's bullet near Krempkau's heart. Stoudemeyer, who was near the men and had just been appointed marshall, had to prove that he was equal to any occasion. He drew his pistol, and by the time Hale's pistol cracked, Stoudemeyer shot him in the side of the head, just above the ear.

Krempkau was pure game and drew, and though shot near the heart, he emptied his revolver and probably killed the Mexican, who while running to get out of the way, was shot in the back. Krempkau's shooting was wild, as he was in death agonies; it is not certain whether he or Stoudemeyer killed Campbell, but the latter only had one wound.[4]

This was not the end of this bloody feud. Before you could say "scat" four men had been killed. The next week some one fired at Stoudemeyer, who was walking where Fassett & Kelly have a hardware store now, from under the portal at old Ben Dowell's where the Mannings had a saloon. There were a number of shots fired, one going through the head of little Mary Blacker's bed, just missing her head. Mary Blacker then lived where Phil Young afterwards had a saloon.

The Rangers went under whip and spur from Ysleta and went into camp at the one-story adobe, where the Lesinsky block now stands. Stoudemeyer stayed with us a week or ten days.

The Rangers were instructed if any more shooting occurred on the streets at night, to open fire on both parties. The *Herald* had an old picture showing some men cooking on the north side of this old "dobe" that was probably intended for the Rangers at that time.

Still there was no peace. Dallas Stoudemeyer was reckless enough to go into the Manning's saloon and engage in a quarrel with Dr. [George Felix] Manning, who had served on Gen. Joe Wheeler's staff during the war.[5] The doctor was a very small man, but game as they make them. Stoudemeyer was six feet two or three inches and large in proportion. During the struggle between the two men when they clinched, either Jim or Frank Manning shot Stoudemeyer through the head, just as he had Johnny Hale.

There was only temporary peace, for Dr. [Samuel M.] Cummin[g]s, a brother-in-law of Stoudemeyer, vowed vengeance, and as he was a brave man and dangerous when under the influence of drink, the Mannings were still in danger.[6] They went to see him at his saloon and asked for drinks. They were watching each other like cats, and in a moment, before Cummings could get his pistol the Mannings fired on him. One shot hit him on the right side above the nipple and the other on the left; the bullets crossed in the center of his body.

We then had that peace that Josh Billings says will come at the last day, when the lion and the lamb will lie down in peace together, the lamb being on the inside of the lion.

The wild and wooly days are past, the Rangers are forgotten; even the governor of Chihuahua says he can find no one to testify that they ever served in campaigns in Chihuahua against the Apaches. *Sic transit gloria mundi.* [So goes the glory of the world.]

NOTES

[1] Krempkau was serving as a constable at the time he was killed in the gun battle on 14 April 1881. For Mills' version of the shooting, see Mills, *Forty Years at El Paso*, 161-62. For Gillett's version, see: Gillett, *Six Years with the Texas Rangers*, 325-26. Also, El Paso *Lone Star*, 20 April 1881.

[2] Hale, a husky, thirty-six-year-old Iowan, owned a small, eighty-acre ranch about ten miles upriver from El Paso in the bosque near Canutillo. The ranch adjoined that of the Manning Brothers which Hale managed. The ranches were conveniently located for smuggling and rustling, and Hale's ranch had the reputation of being a haven for local desperadoes. Generally considered a rustler and a man of unsavory reputation, Hale had gone to California at an early age but came to El Paso with the California Column in 1862. "His career is little known," Leon Metz has written. Metz, *Dallas Stoudenmire: El Paso Marshal* (Norman: University of Oklahoma Press, 1993), 22, 38, 42. Also, Mills, *Forty Years at El Paso*, 161.

[3] Stoudenmire was born on 11 December 1845 in Aberfoil, Macon County, Alabama, a descendant of German colonists who had settled the Orangeburg district of South Carolina a decade earlier. At sixteen, Stoudenmire enlisted as a private in the 45th Alabama Infantry but was dismissed for being under age, whereupon he enlisted in the 6th Alabama Cavalry but was discharged after six months. He then joined the 17th Alabama Volunteers and was wounded several times while fighting with Gen. Joseph E. Johnston in the Carolinas. After the war, he settled near Columbus in Colorado County, Texas, and in 1874 enlisted in the Texas Rangers but resigned and drifted to the Texas Panhandle where he operated a sheep ranch with Cummings, his brother-in-law. Stoudenmire next appeared in Llano County where he was engaged in the mercantile business. In April 1881, he was made El Paso town marshal. After his death on 18 September 1882, his body was viewed at the Freemason Lodge and then sent to Colorado County where it lay in state at Alleyton where he was buried. Metz, *Stoudenmire*, 1-33, 125-26; and El Paso *Lone Star*, 18 September 1882.

Born on 23 December 1850 in Greenup County, Kentucky, Campbell came to Henrietta, Clay County, Texas, in late 1875 or early 1876 and he became a deputy sheriff. In 1880 he resigned and went to Las Vegas, New Mexico, but wound up in Silver City where he staked an unsuccessful mining claim before moving on to El Paso. Recommended by George Baylor, he became town marshal on 1 December 1880 and a close associate of the Manning Brothers. Campbell was initially buried in El Paso but the family later had the body shipped to Ashland, Kentucky, for burial in the family plot. Fred R. Egloff, *El Paso Lawman, G.W. Campbell* (College Station: Creative Publishing Co., 1982), 17-36, 134.

[4] Newspapers from as far away as San Francisco, Kansas City, and Chicago headlined the deaths of the four men.

5   The Manning Brothers, James, Frank, and George Felix, headed what Metz has called a "rustling empire." George Felix "Doc" Manning, the oldest, was born in 1837 on a plantation near Huntsville, Alabama. He studied medicine at the University of Alabama and in Paris, France. Like his brothers, George was a die-hard southerner and vowed never to shave until the lost cause was avenged. Probably serving with Maximilian and the French in Mexico, "Doc" later moved to Belton, Texas, and then to Giddings in Lee County where he opened an office. Manning remained in Giddings from 1874 to 1878 during which time he fought a duel with a rival physician in a woods with Bowie knives. After his brothers had drifted west to El Paso in 1880, "Doc" followed in June 1881, and opened an office in the Palace Drug Store. Shortly after the 18 September 1882 killing of Stoudenmire in the Manning Saloon, in which "Doc" was wounded in the right arm and charged with murder, but acquitted, he moved to Flagstaff, Arizona Territory, where it was said he led a respectable life. He died on 9 March 1925. Metz, *Stoudenmire*, 95-97, 115-17, 123.

6   Cummings, heavy drinking, quick to fight, stout, loud, and arrogant, was married to Stoudenmire's sister, Virginia. He had previously served as justice of peace in Oldham County in the Texas Panhandle where he ran a sheep ranch with his brother-in-law. With his wife and small daughter, Cummings moved to San Marcial, New Mexico Territory, where he ran a hotel and became known as a "dangerous man." He drifted downriver to El Paso to open several restaurants, only one of which, the elegant Globe on El Paso Street, was successful. Cummings had enlisted as a private in the Rangers with George Baylor on 1 June 1881, but only lasted for six weeks before he asked for and was granted a discharge. Cummings was with his brother-in-law during the gun battle on 14 April 1881, and the shooting of Bill Johnson, a drunken Manning ally, three days later, after which he helped organize the "Law and Order League." Cummings was killed by Jim Manning and bartender David King at the Coliseum Saloon on 15 February 1882. He was buried the next day in a small cemetery north of El Paso. Metz, *Stoudenmire*, 82-91.

CHAPTER TEN

Notorious Murders
Near Old El Paso

~

I HAVE SEEN A GOOD DEAL SAID ABOUT THE BRUTAL MURDER of Merrill and his young wife, and wish to contribute to the *Herald* such knowledge as I have of the sad event. A friend of the murdered man has already given a sketch of his life and romantic marriage to an accomplished young girl, and I can only give from memory some of the incidents connected with the horrid crime.

Company "A," Frontier Battalion, or more familiarly known as the Texas Rangers, was stationed at Murphyville (now Alpine). Lt. Kirk Turnbo of the company, with a detachment of five men, went at once to the scene of the murder, and I had from him the details of the fiendish outrage which has already been described.

Lieutenant Turnbo, who was an old Ranger, made as careful a search as possible of the premises in hopes of getting some clue as to the murderers, but there was no trail leaving the ranch going in any direction, but the place had been thoroughly looted, and everything valuable taken off. If the plunder had been taken off on a pack animal of course the trail could have been followed, but the murderers had put everything in a skiff kept at the place, and gone down the river. Satisfied of this, Lieutenant Turnbo followed down the Rio Grande, making a close search for the boat or any evidence of any landing on either side, but no trail was ever found.

Among the things taken was a beautiful crazy quilt, made by the young bride or a present from loving friends, and it was hoped that some day it might prove the means of bringing the murderers to justice.

Lieutenant Turnbo was of the opinion that the murderers went down near Presidio del Norte and landed on the Mexican side and sank or destroyed the skiff, and took their ill gotten booty to some of the ranches in the interior. From all he could learn, the two Mexicans sent down to work for Merrill committed the murder, and one of them was a one-eyed man and they were missing.

This reminds me of a similar murder committed at Terlingua. When a man named Petty, wife and child, were murdered under almost similar circumstances an ax was used. The murderer had robbed the house and the trail went straight to San Vicente and again Lieutenant Turnbo followed it to the Rio Grande, and waited for the Seminole scouts to come down and decide as to following the trail into Mexico.[1] It was decided not to cross but I don't think Pres. [Porforio] Díaz or Gov. Luis Terrazas would have cared if they had followed and killed the murderers, for such stock is not wanted any more in Mexico than here. Here again, according to all we could learn, a one-eyed Mexican figured, and there is scarcely a doubt in my mind but what the sheriff has the murderer of both the Pettys and the Merrills, and it is to be hoped that enough evidence will be found to hang him.

These two recall to my mind another murder near [Fort] Hancock. Two miners stopping at Rife's Station on their way from New Mexico to some of the southern states had stopped to camp, and a Mexican told them he could take them on a new and nearer route and cut off several miles, and as they were afoot and had a pack animal, they were glad of any change to save a little distance, especially as they were promised water on the route—quite an important item.

He led them off between the old stage road and the river, and after getting down in some high sunflowers he dropped behind and shot one of the men in the back, killing him instantly, and opened fire on the other one, and slightly wounded him; but he proved a first class sprinter and out ran his kind guide that wanted to show him the shortest road to the next world.

My recollection now is, that Sgt. James B. Gillett went down and followed the trail of the murderer to a ranch on the Mexican side of the Rio Grande, between San Ignacio and Guadalupe, and my impression is he found the stolen goods and the pistol of the murdered man, and that afterwards the Rangers caught the murderer—a shepherd. But the miner who was wounded never stopped running and no evidence could be had without him. Readers of the *Herald* will recall the murder of Pat Curack's partner in this same neighborhood, probably by some shepherd emboldened by former immunity.

Another murder that went unpunished was that of a Mexican killed near the Reyes Ranch below Canutillo. The Mexican, Encarnación, and two Negro soldiers, his sons-in-law, had camped near Reyes' and Reyes rode out east of his ranch to look after his milk cows and found two Mexicans skinning one. They had roped it in a gully. Reyes galloped back to get help and Encarnación went back with him. It was nearly dark and they rode right up over the cow thieves before being discovered, and the thieves had no idea of giving up the beef after all the trouble they had to rope and kill it. They showed fight, and fired one shot, I think to frighten Reyes, intending to shoot over his head, but in the dusk his aim was too low and the ball struck Encarnación square in the forehead. Reyes took to his heels and sent for the Rangers. The thieves went the other way.

I went up as soon as I could and found Encarnación and buried him, putting a rude cross at the head of his grave, and then took the trail of his murderers. There were two of them. They went first toward the Franklin Mountains, leaving a white burro where they had killed the cow and [the] man. We followed the trail until it came into the main road near the old White Ranch, and we were satisfied they would go to Juárez.

The next day I crossed the river and made inquiries as to the owner of a certain white burro, and soon found the burro and her owner were well known, and that he had loaned or rented her to two men who were in the habit of supplying the soldiers with beef once and a while, but neither of these thrifty butchers nor the owner of the burro could be found.

Once again a man's body was found near where the smelter is, and a runner was sent to Ysleta for the Rangers. We went and found the man, evidently an American miner, who had a burro packed and was walking. He camped near a hole of water, the Rio Grande not being running and the bed being dry. The man had evidently camped, cooked and lain down to peaceful dreams of home. The assassin's tracks were perfectly plain in the sandy bed of the river, and he had walked up within three feet of the sleeping man and shot his brains out. All he got was the camp traps and an old brass-mounted Winchester, which we learned he had when he passed through Canutillo. We never knew his name or home.

Probably the most brutal murder of that early day was two young Mexicans from Juárez; I don't remember their names; think one was Domínguez. They had followed the trail of some cattle stolen from Don Ynocente Ochoa's ranch at Samalayuca, over near Judge [Allen] Blacker's ranch, where Johnny Hale, a first class thief, held forth.[2] Old citizens of El Paso will remember that Johnny started the row in El Paso when he shot Gus Krempkau through the heart. Gus emptied his six-shooter before he died. Studemeyer [Stoudenmire], who had just been appointed city marshal to hold the wild Pass City down, shot Johnny through the head, and there was a general fusillade, and when the smoke cleared away, Krempkau, Hale, and a Mexican were dead, and Campbell, a young Kentuckian, was mortally wounded.[3]

The two young Mexicans had followed the trail very close to the old Phillips' Ranch, where Tom Mode was staying, and had dismounted to eat a lunch there. Tom Peveler, and another ex-Ranger whose name I cannot recall [Jack Bond], came up on them. They had evidently stolen the cattle and expected to be followed, and when they rode up these young men murdered them in cold blood. Peveler's chum was afterwards killed by Dan Tucker, deputy sheriff at Deming.[4] The pair had been painting the town red, and the one Tucker killed had knocked some old man in the head for amusement, with his six-shooter. So Dan took a double-barreled shotgun and went after them. His first shot killed one, and Peveler just barely did save his bacon by throwing up his hands, and the load of buckshot intended for him went in the wall, just missing him.

The cattle stolen were driven into the bosque above Tom Mode's ranch, and he was paid $7 a head to kill and butcher them, and to deliver them to Jack—a butcher in El Paso. I got on the this by following some horse tracks to Tom's house, not the first time, either. Tom said, "Colonel, I know you think it strange that trails you follow come here, but I can't help it, and my life would not be worth ten cents if I made a kick about those fellows coming here. They would be sure to murder me." "Well, Tom," I said, "you have been an old Ranger yourself, and know the duty of a Ranger, and if any more trails of thieves come to your place we will have to take you into camp." Tom then quit and moved into El Paso and was appointed on the police force, and was afterwards killed by Howard Dougherty.

A book could be filled with similar scenes in the early days of El Paso. Few of its present citizens can realize what the quiet city, held so well in hand by Jim White and Sheriff [James H.] Boone, was in its early days, and what the Rangers of that day did and the present small force under Capt. [John R.] Hughes is doing to maintain the peace and dignity of the grand old state of Texas.

NOTES

[1] San Vicente, Chihuahua, is a small village near the mouth of Santa Elena Canyon in the Big Bend.

[2] Blacker was district judge for the Trans-Pecos at the time of the Salt War and while Baylor commanded the Rangers in the area. When Blacker held court at Fort Davis and Fort Stockton, he frequently asked Baylor for an escort.

[3] See Ch. 9, this section, especially notes 1-3.

[4] See Gillett, *Six Years with the Texas Rangers*, 198. Gillett identified the other Ranger as Len Peterson.

CHAPTER ELEVEN

Murder Most Foul

IN THE EARLY PART OF LAST APRIL [1899], when the Nineteenth Century was clothing itself for the last time in the beautiful blue bonnets and the oceans of wild flowers, such as we had not seen since early days in Texas, a bloody tragedy was enacted in the lovely picturesque Nueces Canyon that has been a mystery to the officers of the law until a few days ago when the old adage, "Tis an ill wind that blows no good," was exemplified in a peculiar manner, also bringing to mind another saying that "Murder will out."

Near the grand old cliff called Chalk Bluff, that for centuries has looked down on the blue lake at its foot, and heard the cry of the wild fowl and the splash of eight-pound bass as they chased their prey, the yells of the savage tribes that contended for the mastery in this cool retreat, or witnessed the cavalcade of Spanish knights in armor and old San Franciscan monks in a cowl, as they moved up the valley to establish the old mission of San Bruno—this grand old cliff looked down and saw carried out a cold-blooded and premeditated murder.

Señora Bruno Córdova, a woman who had arrived at the stage of life known as "fat, fair and forty," of very pleasing exterior and the soft captivating manner inherent in the race, was living in a little box house (now owned by a Mr. Henigan, who has given up work on the "Sunset" to try out at farming in the arid west); a good rich piece of land afforded a good garden and with the generous rains of last spring, there was an abundance of corn, calabazas, sandias, melons, and a yard full of poultry, and bleating lambs and large fat hogs added to the general tone of peace and plenty.[1]

With the very loose ideas of holy sacrament of marriage she was living with Don Juan Rodríguez, a pastor, who was herding angoras for Mr. Higly, a German ranchman who lived on the Nueces River some two miles below.[2]

331

His business kept him away from home a great deal as he camped in the mountains with the angora goat herd, and [he] was considered a splendid goat herder.

For several years things went along smoothly until Juan was taken quite ill and had to visit San Antonio for medical treatment. But the "absence that conquers love" had a boom so to speak, for at this time Don Ramón Muñoz Ramos appeared on the scene, and as the link that bound her to Don Juan had not been tied securely by Squire [William] Gibbens, our worthy Justice of the Peace, nor blessed by the priest, it did not require much of a strain to break it.[3] Don Juan found himself in danger of being supplanted in the affections of the lady Dulcinea del Toboso, and this Cavalleria Rusticana decided to settle the matter according to his own ideas of justice. He sent for his son, Jinero Rodríguez, who was in Mexico. This worthy, who had served a term in a Mexican prison for some crime, came, and a villainous looking fellow he was—his looks would hang him before any jury. Jinero and his father, Don Juan, had a quarrel with Ramos in which the lady took part, and even all animated nature seemed to sympathize; dogs, goats, hogs, and fowls felt the contagion.

Juan and Jinero went to the goat camp and there planned about as cunning a plot as could be devised by even De Wet to circumvent his rival. He sent Jinero to Ramos, possibly with the olive branch of peace, and asked him to come and see him so that the trouble could be settled.

The rough mountain was between them and in order to keep the appointment Ramón had to go by a circular path on horseback, the distance being some six miles, whil'st a "berada" (mountain path) of two miles could be followed by Jinero on foot. Jinero had been for some time staying at a house using of the rooms. Ramos saddled his horse and taking his trusty Winchester rifle and a big knife, bid Señora Bruno "adios amigo." It was the last time she was to see him. Jinero was left, and likely went straight to the angora goat herd and the plan to meet and murder Ramón was decided upon.

We can only imagine what occurred. Ramón was met on the lonely trail and as both the father and the son were armed—Juan with a Remington .45 revolver and the son with a .38 Colt—he had little show for his life. Old Juan brought his angoras to the camp earlier than usual, but said he had lost his knife and went back to look for it. As it was nearly nightfall and misting rain, this would seem to be a poor excuse for his absence during the greater part of the night.

Señora Bruno had her misgivings about Ramón's fate, and when night came she was afraid to go to bed for fear Juan and Jinero would kill her. So she sat up all night, and listened for any suspicious noise. But all was quiet; no one came to her house.

A day or so afterwards, John Roy Baylor, son of the sheriff, was looking for his horse on the east side of the river—the Mexicans lived on the west side—and met Jinero leading Ramón's horse that was saddled and bridled, and hailed him to inquire about his horses. As he heard of Ramón's mysterious disappearance, his suspicions were aroused and he asked, "How comes it that you have Ramón's horse?" "I found him out in the pasture," answered he, "and as no one had come for him I thought it best to take him to the house and unsaddle him." John Baylor then asked him, "Where is Ramón?" "Why he went to Uvalde for some coffee." "How do you know he did?" "Well, maybe he didn't. I don't know whether he went or not, but you see, he was not murdered, for look there's no blood on the saddle." "A guilty conscience needs no accuser." Jinero was denying murder before a charge was made.

Henry Baylor, the Sheriff of Uvalde [County], as soon as he heard of the [murder], went at once and arrested both father and son, and they were put in jail and held for some time.[4] In the meantime he and other citizens of the neighborhood scoured the whole country looking for the body, for the reason (and it's very poor law) that no conviction could be had unless the body of Ramón could be found. They were both released and an error made in not having a preliminary trial to preserve evidence. The pair of murderers put out for Mexico and the woman has gone—no one knows where.

Now comes the hand of evidence. Higly's herder was out with the angoras and had a kid under each arm staggering along during the cyclone the other day. It was an exposed place, and he was tumbled over, falling sprawled near a clump of guajilla (wah-hee-yah) the great honey plant of the bees. On straightening up he saw to his dismay that a foot farther he would have tumbled into a cave, the mouth being not much larger than a hog's head. As he had never seen this hole before, nor even been told of it, his curiosity was excited and he began to examine it. He saw just on the edge, the point of the blade over the hole, a long bladed butcher knife, and the portion of a hat the mice had nibbled, but showing that it had been slashed with a keen knife.

The herder brought the knife to the camp and told of his discovery and Higly at once saw that this was a clue to the mysterious disappearance of Ramón. Manor Ramos, an uncle of Ramon and a friend, then went to the cave with the herder, Camilio Cruz, making a 40-foot rope, and one of them descended and saw the bones of Ramón. They got one of his shoes—the bones on the foot still in it, and came and reported to the sheriff.

A party was at once made up and the next morning Justice of the Peace W.A. Gibbens, County Attorney Tom Baker, Sheriff Baylor, Deputy [Sheriff]

Sid[ney] J. Baylor, County Clerk H.J. Bowles, L[ouis] Schwartz, a merchant of our town, and the writer, started out and found Don Manuel Canales, who owns a large herd of angoras, nearby the cave and some of the Mexican citizens ready to go and explore the cave.[5]

Arrived at the cave, which was some two miles from the river and near the crest of the hill on a shallow draw, we found this curious freak, that is, however, quite common in limestone formations, but strange as it may appear, although Higly who has lived near there some fifteen years and who with quite a number of others came out also, told that he had killed two deer there, butchered one not more than fifty yards distant, neither he nor any of his family or neighbors had ever discovered it. Juan and Jinero had exhibited a great cunning in hiding the mouth of the cave—a little brush was put over it, and a number of Spanish dagger stalks that will keep green a long time, were put in with the tops showing—any one would have thought, well, that's a shallow hole and Spanish daggers growing out of it.

Sid Baylor, the deputy sheriff, stripped for the exploration and a strong rope forty feet long was tied securely to a mesquite bush and he went down with a lantern. The hole is straight down for fifteen feet and then makes a turn so that nothing can be seen from the top.

Sid soon called out to send down another man and another lantern. One of the Mexicans, Cartlunos, went down and in a short time we were told to haul up and a gunny sack with skull and bones was brought to view. The flesh was all gone, but the pants held the thigh and pelvis intact. The next sack brought up more bones and a sack with the head and hide of an angora kid, Higly's mark in its ears. No doubt these two murderers had killed the kid and made Ramón a present of it to disarm suspicion, and when they killed him tumbled him in this hole, the sack with the head and hide being found on top of him.

Sid then called out, "I've found his Winchester," and that was sent up and looked very much as I suppose Rip Van Winkle's gun did. The lever was thrown half open. His belt was around his body, but empty, the assassins in their hurry and it being a pitch black night did not notice it had dropped out, and was thus the means of attracting Camilo Cruz's attention and we hope will lead to their conviction. His flint steel and pocket knife were in his pocket and part of the clothes he wore were well enough preserved to show the material and color.

Dr. Watts put the skeleton together and several bones are missing, which a further search will bring to light. These cold blooded assassins are citizens of Mexico and formerly could not be extradited but we feel pretty sure that neither President [Porforio] Díaz nor [the] governor [of] Coahuila want such citizens and we trust to see them hung in Uvalde, but "catch your hare first."

I have not seen Dr. Watts, our country physician yet, but learn from our county attorney that he took the gunny sack of bones and soon had the skeleton of a man laid out as deftly as a young girl could string beads and then pronounced him legally dead. I was of that opinion before, but there's nothing like expert testimony, to clinch a matter (or before a jury).

NOTES

1   Córdova cannot be identified from the 1900 Uvalde County census.

2   Neither Rodríguez or Higly, perhaps Wigly, can be identified from the 1900 Uvalde County census.

3   Ramos cannot be identified with certainty. Gibbens, sixty-five and born in Missouri, was justice of the peace at the time.

4   Born in November 1850, Henry Baylor, forty-nine and the son of John R. Baylor, is listed on the 1900 Uvalde County census, along with his thirty-three-year-old wife, Florence.

5   Baker, forty-nine, is listed on the census as a lawyer. Sidney Baylor, born in February 1866 and thirty-four in 1900, was the son of John R. Baylor and Emily Hanna. He is listed on the 1900 Uvalde County census along with his wife Lola, four children, and his seventy-two-year-old mother, Emily. Bowles, thirty-four and district clerk, along with his wife, Sallie, twenty-nine, is also listed. Schwartz, fifty-seven, was a German-born merchant. Canales, forty-four and born in Texas in December 1865, is enumerated as a "goat breeder," along with his Mexican-born wife and seven children.

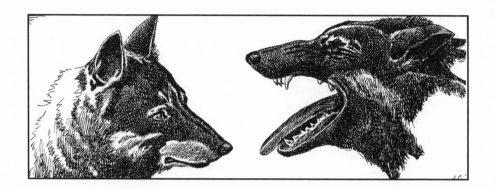

Cito the Wolf-dog

and Other Stories

~

Have you seen my story in [the] El Paso Herald,

Cito the Wolf Dog[?] It came on 13 Jan & is used every Saturday,

the kids have been doing the illustrations & get prizes

& seem to have a lot of fun — Old Gregorio Maltos is hero.

He told me of his capture by Indians & I made

a story of it — get it for your scrap book.

George W. Baylor, March 1906

IV

A FEW OF BAYLOR'S ARTICLES CLEARLY REFLECT the lighter side of life on the Texas frontier in the nineteenth century. His light-hearted portrayal of Perk, a resident of El Paso and the mining town of White Oaks, New Mexico, is more folklore than history, for instance. Even more humorous is Baylor's Pecos Bill-like story of a rabbit hunter who loses an eye to a Spanish dagger plant and is persuaded by an overly zealous surgeon to replace it with the eye of a jack rabbit. All goes well until the hunter goes for a short walk and is approached by his hunting hound, whom the hunter sees through the eye of a rabbit. The third chapter in this section is a travelogue of Baylor's visit with his daughter, Helen, and his grandson, Frank, to Lake Chapala, Mexico.

"Cito, the Wolf Dog," is certainly Baylor's most ambitious undertaking as a writer. The story, clearly written for children and young adults, appeared in twenty-seven chapters in ten consecutive Sunday issues of the El Paso Daily Herald *in 1906. Reader response, especially from El Paso school children, was immediate and positive. H.D. Slater, the aggressive editor of the* Herald, *went as far as to offer prizes for the best illustrations of the articles and then published the winners in the newspaper. The story itself is based on the harrowing childhood recollections of Gregorio Maltos, who was captured when the "Indios bárbaros" swept down on the small village of Santa Rosa, Coahuila, sometime in the 1830s. In telling Maltos' story, Baylor used what he called "the poet's privilege, interweaving my own knowledge of woodcraft into the story."*

The Eleventh Census (1890) enumerating Union veterans for Zavala County, Texas, lists Maltos as sixty-five and a farmer. Born in September 1824 in Mexico, Gregorio never learned to read and write but spoke English well. In 1900, he was living on the Leona River below Uvalde with his English-born wife, Leonore, and an adopted son, Melchor. When Baylor first met Maltos, the Union veteran had a small herd of cattle and a dairy. Maltos told Baylor of how he had enlisted in the Union Army and how he was seriously wounded, probably in Louisiana. In fact, Maltos was one of the few Tejanos to remain in the Federal Army throughout the war. Baylor also related how Leonore, the well-educated daughter of an English officer and a Spanish lady, told a story of how during a cattle round-up she was approached by an Anglo cowboy who expressed astonishment at seeing a "white woman . . . married to a Mexican."

Leonore "turned toward him, her eyes blazing and then replied, 'why I had a sister who did heap worse than that.'"

"What did she do?" the cowboy inquired.

"Why, she married a cowboy," Leonore calmly responded.

~

CHAPTER ONE

Perk the Wolfer

THE OLD TIMERS OF EL PASO AND WHITE OAKS, a little hunch back man going under the name of Perk, the Wolfer, will be recognized.[1] Though dame nature with her canny hand had denied him a huge stature, she lavishly gave him a big heart that seems to grow best amid'st the wild mountains and plains of the arid west, and added to a bright intellect and keen sense of the ludicrous, a good use of his tongue.

I first met Perk in El Paso about 1880 or 1881. He introduced himself in quite the original way, saying; "Colonel, I've heard of you ever since I came to Texas more than twenty years ago, as a man always ready to go wherever the Indians made a raid, spending your own time and money in defense of the frontier people, risking your life in giving peace and protection, to helping women and children, and I never heard of anyone giving you anything and I want to give you a good interest in a good prospect in the Jarilla Mountains. I came down to have an assay made and it runs to 430 silver with a trace of gold and copper."

I grasped his horny hand with a firm grip and with a voice choked with emotion answered, "You are eminently correct, Perk, and the man I've been looking for. We will adjourn to my Ysleta home and kill the fatted calf, as the old Negro preacher said, I've been keeping lo, these many years. I want to make a scout in the Sacramento Mountains for I know in reason those infernal Reservation Indians are the ones robbing our people and murdering emigrants on the Overland Route and I am anxious to get a whack at them off of the reservation."

My claim turned out as thousands have. I got the other half—called it the "Little Mary" after my little girl and spent $200 in assessment work and probably [Charles B.] Eddy now stands with his thumbs in his vest button holes admiring his claim.

As soon as we could get permission from the Governor of New Mexico—I think it Governor [William Henry Harrison] Llewellyn—we started out.[2] I had asked if I could kill any Indians found off the reservation, and asked for permission to cross the New Mexican line. The answer came promptly, that it would afford him the greatest pleasure to give me the desired permission and he hoped I would be successful in reducing the population of the reservation.

We got our twenty days rations and went and camped the first night on the acequia below the Marsh Ranch where a road leads off to Mundy's Springs, called then Sierra Colorado. Here we were joined by Gen. Isaac Harrison, that big hearted, brave old Confed[erate], a true friend and uncompromising enemy, and Charlie Davis, who is so well and favorably known in El Paso. Our second camp was Mundy Springs, where every one filled up canteens with water and braced himself for the long dry ride to Soledad Springs, some 40 miles distant in the San Augustín [Organ] Mountains.[3]

There were in the citizen contingent several brown jugs, not the "little one" spoke of in song and story, but such as old farmers used in the early settlement of Kentucky and Tennessee; and also demijohns and full grown Johns. The drought was severe and plains hot, so that by the time our party reached the Soledad, between the Rangers (a favored few) and the citizens contingent, several of the jugs and Johns had fallen by the wayside and when we reached Soledad we were tired and had to rest a day before starting for nearly a fifty mile tramp to the Sacramento Mountains without water.

This don't seem much to men behind a good pair of high stepping Kentucky geldings in a buggy, a man on a wheel, or on the cars, but on horse back the way is long and weary.

During the rest at Soledad the jugs began to dwindle in contents and it was clear to me, being an impartial judge, as I never drink but on Christmas or Fourth of July, or some convivial occasion, but Charlie Davis believed that General Harrison was responsible for the leakage while the general was quite as positive Charlie was conspiring to end the campaign by cutting off the supply of snake medicine. The result was that Charlie struck out for San Augustine Springs but the general stayed with us.

It has been my observation after many years' experience that it required that steadfast friendship that existed between Tom O'Shanter and Johnnie to stand the strain when the whiskey runs low. On one notable occasion, I went with Dr. Irvin and Charlie Davis and [William J.] Bill Fewel, on a hunt in the Sacramento Mountains. The doctor turned blue and got sick and quit us, but when Fewel was measuring a drink, Charlie always turned his back and closed his eyes, and when Charlie's turn came Fewel turned his back and knelt as though in silent prayer. But whether he prayed or counted the good-good-good's as they came from the jug, deponent saith not.

At daylight we took out across the dry plains for the Jarillas and nooned there 25 miles distant. The turquoise mines that caused poor [Amos J.] De Meules to lose his life could have been mine but the impression then was that the stones were worthless and the color a vegetable stain.[4] I might have made a fortune, then again I might have taken De Meules's place in the grave-yard—and under the circumstances would prefer being a poor live man, than a rich dead one.

It was a long stretch to the foot of the Sacramentos, and the mountains and cliffs that appeared only a few miles distant were only reached in the night. We got some water at a small spring called Agua Chiquita, and next morning Perk led us around to the south up to a log house he had built on a small branch.

We then went to his fort on the Sacramento and his place looked very much like Robinson Crusoe had just left there. This was the first house built and I built the next on the west bank of the Sacramento at the only prairies on the stream.[5] He wanted a place to go to in case a snow storm caught us, or the Indians proved too strong. The Ranger force, Company A, had fifteen men, and five left for duty in camp.

But I am going around about to get Perk's story, and he had many. He was one of the buffalo hunters that thinned out the immense herds on the Texas frontier. They used almost exclusively the old Sharp's reliable .50 cal-iber and with rest sticks, getting to the windward of a herd of buffalos, they could drop one nearly every shot, and the animals scarcely heard the report of the rifles. A ground would soon be covered with their big, black carcasses. All they got was a dollar a piece for the hides, the meat of the bulls was rarely saved, only tongue and hide, but fat cows and calves were cut into chunks, dipped in boiling brine, and hung up to dry. The hot brine formed a crust, but inside the meat was moist and very fine eating.

Many exclaimed against the ruthless destruction of the noble bison but I shed no tears for I knew that as long as the Kiowas and Comanches and other Plains Indians could go out and in a week kill meat enough to do them six months, they would harass, rob and murder only frontier people, but as soon as the buffalo were destroyed, then they would be compelled in a great mea-sure to go on the reservations and live on Uncle Sam.

Perk said after hunting hard all one winter killing buffalo and skinning coyotes, wild cats, lobos, skunks, until he smelt like one, on making a settlement with his merchant he found he was in debt. The merchant seeing what a long face he put on, cheered him up by saying, "Never mind the balance, you can pay me in fur next winter." Perk said, "I did, I got off just as fast and fur as I could."

During one summer he was walking along through a green briar thicket on the edge of a very deep gully, and an old tree had fallen down across the path. He had five or six cur dogs trailing along at his heels and when they came to the log they began sniffing, growling and scratching at the log and he came back and saw the log was cracked open and a mere shell. He saw too that it was an old she coon and lots of young ones.

It was summer, and the fur useless, but he wanted to see a little fun, so he raised his foot and came down with the heel of his shoe with all his strength and the log split wide open.

Old Zip coon is a fighter from away back, and in common with most wild animals will make fight for their young. So no sooner did Perk's heel enter the hollow log than she grabbed him by the heel. Any one who has hunted coons in his boyhood days will remember that whenever a coon got a hound by the lip or ear he held on until the hold broke or cut out, although the other dogs all had hold of him and were dragging him around; he would holler "nuff" all the time but never quit fighting.

So as soon as the coon grabbed Perk's heel, the dogs grabbed the old she coon and started down the hill, jerking Perk's heels from under him, and away they went down the steep side of the gully. Some times Perk was on top and again the dog and coon were piled on him, and high above the yells of the man and barking of dogs, was heard the shrill slogan of the coon and the Booers—"Death or victory."

Perk had dropped his Winchester and could not use knife or pistol for fear of killing some of the dogs or himself. When the pile reached the bottom of the gully he was minus hat, his shirt in shreds and the green briars had made a map of the Philippine Islands on his back, "and would you believe it, colonel, the blankety blank coon held on to my heel until she was plum dead and her eyes green. Why I had to pry her infernal mouth open with my six shooter before I got shet of her."

Another of Perk's stories is worthy of being preserved. Some young tender foot from the east hearing of him and his dogs wanted to carry home the hide of a cinnamon or silver tip [bear] as a trophy. There were plenty of the kind there then, but Perk had a kind heart and did not care to lead these innocent lambs to slaughter, so he went to where he knew a black bear used to be and the dogs were soon in full cry. In the race in the chaparral the bear was wounded and made for the nearest cave. Perk took his time getting there knowing exactly where the cave was and bent on having some fun out of the chase.

The excited hunters had all assembled at the mouth of the cave and were gesticulating excitedly as to the next move. When Perk came up they at once clamored to know what was to be done to get the bear out of his hole. He put on a matter of fact expression of face and answered, "Oh, that's the simplest thing in the world. You have only to take my big knife and make a torch of some of this old fat pine log and light it and crawl in the hole with your six-shooter and you can crawl up almost to the bear and shine his eyes. Shoot him between them. Put a rope around his neck and we will haul him out. Now I'd go in a minute, but that hole is small, crooked and pretty deep, and I've got such a hump on my back I can't squeeze it."

Perk said they were all standing around him as erect as the Emperor Wilhelm's body guard, but when he said this and looked up at the crowd there wasn't a man that didn't have a bigger hump on his back than he did.

NOTES

[1] White Oaks was a mining community eleven miles northeast of what is today Carrizozo, New Mexico. Founded in 1879, the community was named for the trees that surrounded two large springs. By the early 1890s White Oaks had a population of 2,500 and was the largest town in southeast New Mexico. In twenty-five years, three million dollars in gold and silver was taken from the nearby mines.

[2] Llewellyn was born in Minnesota and came west where he served as Indian agent to the Mescalero in the late 1870s and early 1880s. Efficient and optimistic, Llewellyn gained the friendship of the Mescaleros, who called him "Tata Crooked Nose." In 1885 he moved to Las Cruces to practice law. During the Spanish-American War, he helped recruit Troop G of the Rough Riders and fought at San Juan Hill with Col. Theodore Roosevelt. Llewellyn and Roosevelt became close friends during Roosevelt's presidency and afterwards. Llewellyn later served as United States district attorney and was repeatedly elected to the legislature. He became speaker of the House, and a member of the Constitutional Convention of 1912. Having led a stormy political life, he died at El Paso on 11 June 1927. William A. Keleher, *The Fabulous Frontier: Twelve New Mexico Items* (Albuquerque: University of New Mexico Press, 1962), 47; and Sonnichsen, *Mescalero Apaches*, 211, 231-33.

[3] Soledad Springs in Soledad Canyon, twelve miles east of Las Cruces, New Mexico, on the eastern slopes of the Organ Mountains, is thought to commemorate Nuestra Señora de la Soledad or perhaps to describe the loneliness of the location.

[4] De Mules, "the Turquoise King of the Jarillas," was murdered by an employee, Jacobo Flores, in November 1898. In the two years prior to his death, De Mules had mined considerable amounts of quality turquoise from shafts as deep as seventy feet. David L. Carmichael, "Archeological Settlement Patterns in the Southern Tularosa Basin, New Mexico: Alternative Models of Prehistoric Adaptations" (Ph.D. diss., University of Illinois, 1983); Francis Joan Mathien, "Evidence of Prehistoric Turquoise Mining at Orogrande, Jarilla Mountains, New Mexico," *Of Pots and Rocks* (Archaeological Society of New Mexico, 1995), 77-91. Also, *El Paso Weekly Herald,* 5 November 1898; *El Paso Daily Herald*, 28, 29, November 1898. All courtesy of John P. Wilson, Las Cruces, New Mexico.

[5] Sacramento Creek has its source near the summit of Sacramento Peak near what is today the solar observatory at Sunspot, New Mexico. The stream drains a large part of the southern part of the Sacramento Mountains.

CHAPTER TWO

The Man with the Jack Rabbit Eye

~

KNOWING WHAT GREAT INTEREST the *Herald* takes in scientific experiments, especially those of local interest, the writer [offers] a most remarkable cure effected by the aid and science of a doctor now living in Barclay, Edwards County, a modest man and his name is therefore withheld—but he enjoys a large and lucrative practice and keeps up with the strides made in his profession in this age of progress.[1]

We saw in the papers how a man's stomach was taken out, washed, scraped and put back again, and a woman's stomach taken and left out, evidently a mistake—so we are prepared for most any miracle that the "medicos" bring about. But to our story.

Two wealthy young Englishmen were sent out here to learn the cattle business, branding mavericks, dogies and other means by which large fortunes are made. These young men brought with them in addition to their verdancy, the finest guns, fishing rods and outfits in way of high boots and bob tail coats that could be bought; in fact, they came more to frolic and hunt and fish, than acquire any useful information. They brought letters to our doctor—we'll call him Ratworth, he being also from the same kingdom, and the first thing they did was to get out their guns and go out for small game. They had setters, pointers and a large beautiful shaggy yellow deer hound, of royal pedigree.

Anyone who has been hunting in the west can't fail to have observed that when a jack rabbit pops up suddenly under your nose, almost where you hardly supposed a lizard could be concealed, it startles you; and when he goes off twisting his hind legs as though his spine was dislocated, he is a fine mark and appears as large as a deer. So the amateurs both turned loose number six at him, and a stray shot struck him in the head. He bounded into the air like a clown on a spring board and kept up his gymnastics, until the setters got to him and the hunters got him by his hind legs. All Jack's strength seems concentrated in his hind legs and they can kick nearly as hard as a mule, so after a few struggles he got loose, and having partially recovered from the shock, started off at the rate that would have soon put him beyond reach of dog and man. But he ran around in short circles and this afforded great fun for all concerned except Jack—as the hunters and dogs chased him tumbling over each other in their eagerness and when they finally got hold of him again— but here one of those sad accidents occurred that seem to be on tap for hunters. One of the young men ran into a Spanish dagger and the sharp point from one of the leaves penetrated his eye. With a cry of anguish he sunk down, throwing his gun away. His friend ran to him to see the cause of his outcry and learned the painful truth. Still holding on to the cause of the mishap with a firmer grip, for the Jack was their first prize and not to be lost to the collection to be sent home, after being stuffed.

They went back as soon as they could and were met by the doctor, who seeing that something was wrong and guessing from the bombarding he had heard, that one or both were wounded, was quite alarmed. Asking what was the matter the young man said, "Great heavens, doctor, I have lost my sight, and will have to go through life maimed and disfigured."

The rabbit was still kicking and squalling and a brilliant thought passed through [the doctor's] mind. Here was a chance to distinguish himself and bring him prominently before the scientific world. So he answered, "Not so, my young friend. You may lose your eye, but if you are willing to submit to a painful operation I can restore your sight." "Anything doctor rather than to be disfigured for life." "Then come into my room. I will soon take out your eye and replace it with the Jack's eye. It is a very difficult operation, but I feel quite confident I can succeed." The young man was soon on a table and the doctor, with the assistance of his companion, gave chloroform, and successfully performed the operation, taking out the man's eye and putting in the jack rabbit's, connecting lens, nerves, etc., and leaving much to dame nature, who often assists at these experiments.

In time, after being closely confined in a dark room, a perfect cure was effected, and soon the invalid was able to go out on the front porch late [in the] evening. It was noticed, however, that every time one of those large yellow hawks that kill and eat jack rabbits came sailing over the house the invalid would jump up hastily and run into his room and turn his head to one side as if afraid of some danger. Nothing, however, was thought of it and it was attributed to his nervous condition after the painful illness.

In due course of time, however, he became quite strong, and concluded to take a short walk. His favorite deer hound, even in repose, was of a most fierce aspect, but when a smile of genuine joy spread over his dog's countenance it was enough to try the nerves of a well person. So you can imagine what would be the effect on this nervous young invalid when the dog delighted to see his young master out, galloped up behind him, his red tongue lolling out, his great white fangs glistening, ears set up and the hair around his mouth bristling. All would have been well, but the young man happened to turn around and got a view of him with his jack rabbit eye. In an instant he was off with something of a rabbit's movements and the deer hound thinking it was for a romp bounded after him, filling his soul with terror. On he sped, but the race could not last long for his only object seemed to be to get away from the terrible beast following him, and he saw nothing in front of him. Running full speed into a barbed wire fence, he was instantly killed.

It is a great pity that he could not have lived and a commission have been appointed by Congress to get his ideas and sensations when being chased by coyotes, shot with number six, in melon patches, caught by hawks, trapped, [and] poisoned. As Congress don't seem disposed to give us an international dam, they might have gotten some useful scientific pointers from a jack rabbit point of view.

NOTES

1 Barclay is a small community on Little Pond Creek in Falls County, Texas. Baylor is probably referring to the village of Barksdale on the upper Nueces, a few miles north of Camp Wood.

CHAPTER THREE

Lovely Lake Chapala

~

ON THE EIGHTH [OF OCTOBER 1902], the writer, with Mrs. Sam H. Lee and Panchito, her little son, left Guadalajara for the lovely lake of Chapala, the immediate cause of the move being the mandate of the doctor—the city ordinance commanding all property owners to have connection with the city sewers.[1] The tearing up of old pipes and the placing of new modern ones was accused of turning loose a whole lot of malaria, in shape of microbes, chills and fever among'st our neighbors, and as Mrs. Lee had just recovered from a two years' siege of malaria, and the writer was, in the language of the piney woods, "powerful puny," we left with the understanding that the plumbing would be completed in eight days.

A few hours' run on the Mexican Central carried us to the station called Atequiza, after the magnificent hacienda nearby of that name. This hacienda is carried on according to Mexican modes and is an immense affair with a town for its workmen, a church, and palatial residence for the owner. Over five-hundred laborers are required, as they have extensive coffee plantations —though wheat, corn, beans and all the produce known to this region are grown. A street car runs to the depot.

A young orange grove we noticed, looking in thrifty condition, as the lands can be irrigated. Why American fruits, such as peaches, apples, plums, pears and our luscious cantaloupes and watermelons are not grown in this state is a mystery, for the soil is unusually rich and climate suitable. Year old trees should soon be in fruit with this genial climate.

Young, sentimental ladies may look out of the Pullman windows and sigh as they pass Atequiza, for tradition says this was the location of Mira Flores Christian Reid's beautiful romance, "A Cast of Fortune."

347

We had taken the precaution to get our transportation to Chapala in the stage office at Guadalajara, and when we went to the stage found all the choice seats filled comfortably, but seeing they were ladies, we soon got settled down and started off with the driver cracking his whip, and *mozos* [servants] running by the side of the little mules and nearly lifting them off the ground every lick with their *"chicotes."* Why is it that all the stages in all the nations of the earth start off from the stations with such a grand flourish, taming down before they get out of sight, and "come under the wire" under whip and spur?

Once on the way there was much to see to interest one, the scenery being very beautiful, and when we reached the crest of the mountain pass and the beautiful lake lay before us, there was an exclamation of delight from all the passengers.

An amusing incident of the trip was after we were on the way we learned that three of the ladies were from Mexico, and began to inquire if they knew such and such a person, and the question was put to a very pretty, rosy young lady. "Do you know Tom Weston, formerly of El Paso?" "Why, I'm Tom Weston's wife." It was rather funny that we did not know they spoke English, and at first they did not know we spoke Spanish.

Arriving at the quaint little pueblo of Chapala about one o'clock, we had a "down hill pull" over the cobble stone paved street to the large *"zaguán"* of the Arzapalo Hotel, at a full gallop, a dozen small boys running alongside and grabbing at all *valises* as they came in sight; the writer stood them off when they made a lunge for his old violin case and Bristol rod.[2]

Mine host, a genial gentleman, proprietor of the Arzopala Hotel, received us with the courtesy so pronounced in the hotel fraternity, but as Mrs. Lee had been here on two former occasions, we crossed the street to a very unpretentious house, kept by Señora Trinidad Flores, who owned the premises and gave it its name, the Flores Hotel, and we were soon in comfortable rooms.

The fare is Mexican and cooking ditto but as we like the Mexicans and their style of cooking, we were *"muy contento."* We had sure enough spring chickens every night for supper—not those that had been spring chickens once; the best chocolate in Mexico made by madame herself, and unless one saw the process from toasting the cocoa beans to molding the cakes he would not believe it such a delicate operation as it is to put the proper proportion of the various condiments in, so as to give the flavor that makes the Mexican chocolate so celebrated and delicious. They use a wooden utensil, somewhat like our patent egg beater, to make it foam, and make a cup at a time, as ordered; it is "food fit for the gods." The eggs are fresh, though no contract such as the United States government is to make is required. Fruit that we needed we had to buy, though at a price next to nothing. Vegetables were scarce, as it was the dry season, but later on they are in the greatest abundance.

Why it has never occurred to anyone to put up a windmill and use the never failing water of the beautiful lake, is one of those things Dundreary could not find out. To one satisfied with simple Mexican to put on style, just step across the street and you can be accommodated, as the hotel owns the "*diligencia*," and old-fashioned stage coach such as was used in the early days in "Kaintuck" when the only sign over a noted inn was "squirrels and buttermilk." The per diem is scalded to suit the customer—just as the wind is tempered to the fare we say, go to Hotel Flores. If you have "money to burn" and want shorn lamb—anywhere from $2.50 to $1.50 per day, and hotel Arzopala has your room. The *diligencia* brings over the daily mail, vegetables and ice, so you can have pretty much anything you need, but all extras are charged for separately. Hotel Flores charges $1.50 per day, and hotel Arzopala as above stated.

Well, you will ask, what can one see at Lake Chapala? A most beautiful body of water, surrounded by mountains, that in many places come down so close to the water's edge as to leave only room for a road. A fringe of ever-green trees and mango groves add beauty to the scenery. There is no Matterhorn for foolish people to climb, and fall down smashing themselves among glaciers, but anyone wanting exercise can find mountains covered with flowers all the way to the top, and hunters can find deer; small game, such as quail, cottontails and doves are quite plentiful, whil'st in season there never was a resort for duck, geese, and many water fowls we never see in the United States. Two hunters last winter went from this city and in a day's hunt killed 190 geese and ducks, so, you see, there are no sporting journals here to cry out against such slaughter, nor game laws. The high price of shot guns and ammunition is the only protection game has at present.

The lake is studded with little islands that seem just formed for picnickers, and there are plenty of Mexican boats to take your crowd any place you may choose to go. There are quite a number of little pueblos around the lake, of mixed Mexican and Indian population and valleys where quite extensive farming is done—and very many farms sticking on the sides of the mountains, like Bill Nye's slippery Elmhurst in "North Carliny, God bless you."

When the Spaniards first visited this lovely lake, some three hundred years ago, they "estimated" that there were at least three million Indians inhabiting its shores, but the estimate taken at that time must be taken with salt in carload lots. There are not many more thousands now.

The baths are of both iron and sulphur water and just warm enough to be pleasant, but the arrangement is quite old-fashioned, as the water runs into a cement tank, some four feet wide and deep and six feet long, the water entering on one side and out on the other at the same height, and as you can't be sure what kind of ailment or skin disease the person just ahead of you may have had, it is not at all pleasant. The baths ought to be so conducted that all the water could be turned off and the bath tub be washed before [being] used again. This can be easily done, as there is plenty of fall between where the spring comes out of the side of the mountain and the lake. One of the baths is more of a swimming pool, some 12 feet wide, five or six feet deep and 40 or 50 feet long, but same objection as to entrance and exit of water. The price is reasonable enough—15 cents if you are supplied with soap and towels, and 10 cents if you bring your own.

Fastidious persons will demand a change. These are not all, however, for you have the mimic Galveston beach in front of Hotel Arzapalo, with frame bathhouses. They keep bathing suits for rent, but the pretty señoritas bring their own costumes and look very charming, for be it known, this is the Newport of Jalisco and the Jentavine or 400 of not only Guadalajara, but the City of Mexico and other places, come here to enjoy themselves, to see and to be seen, and the wealthy citizens of Guadalajara have elegant residences furnished in latest style, without regard to cost. They spend only a short time at these beautiful homes, and their housekeeper and gang of *criadas* enjoy the beautiful tropical flowers, well kept lawns and boats. It's enough to make one exclaim with Alec Sweet of Siftings, "Confound these bloated bond-holders, I wish I was one myself."

The fashionable summer months here are March, April and May, for as soon as the rainy season sets in the atmosphere is cooled and the climate perfectly entrancing.

Chapala has quite a navy—all kinds of boats, from handsome rowboats from the states to steam launches, the great Mexican *"canovas"* being greatest in number. They sail all over the lake and carry large cargoes. Chapala has a commodore also, bearing same name but no relation to Jim Crow. That he is capable and quick to grasp the situation in an emergency may be gathered from the following incident: "Once, in a sudden squall, his boat turned somersault and the *mozo* made for him with a loud squall, but he met them with a louder squall,"—"you, never mind me, save my wig;" known to all Confed[erate]s as "Xariffa" (who wrote some fine poems and recited one at the unveiling of the Confederate monument at Winchester, Virginia,) was improved by the commodore. She has passed over the river. We were told the lovely place was a present from her son-in-law. Now he and his daughter have passed away, and only a little girl is left.

The commodore's strongest hold is building and beautifying homes, his present home being a gem. Monte Carlo is the home of Mrs. Townsend, as strong and beautiful woman as ever graced the Old South. Monte Carlo, besides the mansion, has quite a body of land, and was sold while we were at Chapala to Señor Aurelio Hermosillo, a wealthy Mexican gentleman of Guadalajara, and doubtless it will soon be as lovely as money and taste can make it.

Among other attractions we must mention fishing.[3] I think I see Judge [Wyndham] Kemp, Capt. [T.J.] Beall, Judge Brack and Charlie Davis prick up their ears. Well there are millions of fish in the lake, but they are of the *mañana* kind and do not afford the sport they should in such an immense body of fresh water, with several good sized rivers emptying into it. The only ones disposed to bite are the catfish *(bargeri)*, and the largest caught are twelve pounds. We got several of five or six pounds, but they do not bite freely. But what they lack in activity is made up for by the turtles, that worry the fishermen out of patience. Luckily, there are no gars. The turtles are worthless as food. They have a small clam, about the size of those around Galveston, that formed the main food supply of the Carancahua [Karankawa] Indians, and the mounds of shells made by these people are all that are left of what was a powerful race fifty years ago.

Before I ever saw Lake Chapala I had inquired diligently about the chance of getting a bite, and was told that the fish called the Blanco would not bite at all, and were only taken in nets, and at Chapala they all confirmed this statement. Every Mexican or Indian stated positively that no one had even been known to catch one with hook and line. So the writer thought if the people who had been living there for four-hundred years, and maybe for four-thousand, had never had a bite it was useless for him to try. Any one looking at a *blanco* would size him up as a game fish—great big yellow eyes, trim form, and mouth not large, but filled with small teeth, evidently intended to hold on to their prey—so I cut one open and found a minnow. This was a starter, so I took some live minnows and tried them, letting them swim around, but never had even a "glorious nibble." I said to myself, I'll try to troll as they won't take a minnow staked out—may be suspicious like an old six or eight pound bass. My first cast I lost a minnow; the second, a tug at my line, and I landed a pretty *blanco*. The mystery of how to catch *blanco* was solved—troll.

No doubt at the proper season, which must be learned, they can be caught with artificial minnows or spoon bait. The writer hopes to use some of Abbey and Imbrie's finest tackle, the smallest line, and such hooks as could be used for brook trout, and believes sportsmen have in store some rare sport with this game fish. Their flavor is excellent and they are just a nice sized pan fish, from one-half to a pound weight. When first caught they are almost transparent, with a band like a white satin ribbon down the side. During the Lenten season they are caught in immense seines and shipped in car loads to different cities but are always for sale in the Guadalajara market on Friday— also the biggest frogs this side of Yank-a-Tank.

It is to be hoped that the Republic of Mexico or State of Jalisco will take steps to have Chapala stocked with game fish from the United States. The Pecos River has catfish that weigh from fifty to seventy-five pounds, and soft shelled turtles that will run from twenty-five to forty pounds, and the latter are splendid to eat. Our old darkies used to say you could find chicken, pork, beef, ram, lamb, sheep and mutton inside of the soft-shell turtle. There are thousands in the Pecos and Rio Grande, and being amphibious they can be shipped in crates easier than ducks. One acre of water is said to be worth more than ten acres of land, if properly stocked with fish. But don't ever get German carp; they would eat all the eggs of other fish and fill the lake with their worthless bones. Bass would do fine, as there are myriads of minnows all around the edges of the lake. A little Chapala fisherman with one or two throws from a cast net got more minnows than we could use in a day. There are several varieties; a small one called *pintado*, one like a chub, and a quick motioned, greenish, tough fellow, splendid for bait, and the kind *blanco* feed on.

In addition to the sandy, gravely clean beach in front of the Hotel Arzopala, to the east for quite half a mile you will find the same, and numberless little and big people bathing. Tourists all take this walk, examining the water's edge closely for ollitas and various kinds of toys which are washed up every night from the lake. Some represent bake ovens, chairs, ducks or geese, volcanoes, and after a storm they are quite plentiful, and an early rise and race is made to get them. They can be bought quite cheap but most every visitor wants to say, "I found this on the beach at Lake Chapala." One is that there was at one time an island in front of Chapala on which there was quite a populous city, and say that this is more than likely, as innumerable pieces of porous burnt rock keep washing ashore.

Another probable explanation is that those three million people that have lived on the borders of the lake since the year 1, threw those toys into the water to propitiate their god of water and rain, Tlalos, and from the quantities that are carried off by tourists and others annually, each of the three millions of ancients must have put in a bushel apiece. They are made of yellow and blue clay, and burned, and occasionally of stone.

Horrible figures of idols come from the foothills, where in ages past were probably pueblas swarming with Indians. Others are dug from the banks of arroyos in a white cement. Others well, they are manufactured up to date and are sold to innocent parties as contemporaneous with Adam and Eve—nothing later than Montezuma. They are ugly "for keeps"—Mr. Punch is an Adonis compared with them.

We found at Chapala an old friend, and the boys and girls of El Paso will remember him, Will Alston; he and his sister, Mrs. Helen Hasey, living in "a cot by the sea." Will was raised on the lakes in New York and is a fine sailor, and having his own boat (made by a native), the *Elena*, made our time pass most delightfully, as we went to the pretty little island, Alacran, that lies some eight miles out in the lake, and had a basket lunch. Rev. Mr. Gray and wife, of the Methodist mission, Guadalajara, were of our party. Mrs. Gray was the only one to find any curios in form of arrow heads of Itzla, so much in evidence. "Noche Triste" to Cortés and his wearied soldiers.

Some Mexican fishermen were on the island and had a fine garden coming on, principally tomatoes and watermelons. I gave them some of our American melon seed, such as grow to sixty-five pounds at Ysleta. Theirs weigh from one to ten pounds, of inferior flavor, and their musk melons are also small and equally insipid.

As soon as I could get my rod and reel ready I went for a fish and got a turtle. On asking them about it, they showed some of their parties out in a boat and told me they set out lines at night, marked by Spanish gourds, and caught only catfish. "Do you ever catch *blanco?*" "No, señor, they won't bite at a hook; we set seines for them."

Among those we found at Chapala was W. Townly Benson, a noted artist, being well known in the City of Mexico and Cuernavaca. He is a Canadian by birth and has been some time at the lake, making numerous oil paintings of lake scenery. He certainly has mastered the art of picking up a dainty piece of nature and placing it on canvas with exquisite blending of colors, as the little gems in his studio will verify. They are mostly done on orders from the City of Mexico, but the lover of art can find something to carry away as a souvenir of this romantic locality.

Our intended week visit had spun out to a month and the plumbers were still hammering away. We received such genuine hospitality as could only spring from kind hearts, and here the writer would enter a solemn protest to an interview spoken of in a later issue of your paper, in which a gentleman just returned from a tour in Mexico, says, "the Mexicans are polite, if you have the price." Such courtesy as we have enjoyed in Mexico during the past six years was such as only ladies and gentlemen of gentle breeding, accustomed to the amenities of social life could bestow, and done with charming grace. If your informant had the wealth of Morgan he could not purchase it, for it is above price.

The genial host of Hotel Arzapala, Don Antonio Simonte, has a dance on tap at all times, and a good Mexican string band furnishes sweet music, and there is a piano for those who wish to sing or play.

The yachting fever did not die out because one of the crews came out behind in the recent regatta, but since that time Mr. Pomeroy has brought in a car boat eighteen feet long and a sloop twenty-five feet long, made by the Yacht and Motor Company of St. Louis, Missouri, and defies all creation. And although he is no sailor himself, he has Mr. Valparaiso, a contractor from Louisiana, who can beat anybody on Lake Chapala. Of course this statement might have to be changed a little after the race, for Mr. Pomeroy is quite sure his boat can't be beat, and then he has Don Julio Lewel and Commodore Crew to be consulted. The talk is for a regatta. So far, wealthy Mexicans have not entered into the spirit of the thing, but yachting is like the hen fever, when you get it, it is bad, and we look for a club to be formal and as good boats as money can buy to be on Lake Chapala before many years, and certainly there is not a more lovely body of water for the purpose in America.

NOTES

[1] Hail, *Knight in the Sun*, 4, 23, 27, 36. El Lago Chapala, sometimes called El Mar Chapalico, is the largest lake in Mexico. Located on the boundary between the states of Jalisco and Michoacán, the lake is some seventy miles long and twenty miles wide with an area of 1400 square miles. The climate of the region around the lake is one of perpetual Indian summer. "I thoroughly enjoyed my trip to Lake Chapala, a beautiful spot, nature has done everything for it," Baylor wrote in 1904. "I don't think I ever saw anything more exquisite than the scenery around Lake Chapala," he wrote three years later. Baylor to Florence, 27 July 1904 and Baylor to Susie, 25 December 1907, Baylor-Carrington Papers.

[2] The village of Chapala, on the north shore of the lake, was ten miles south of Atequiza. Early travelogues mention only the Arzapaloabave Hotel in the village.

[3] Baylor's letters to relatives in Texas during the years spent in Mexico relate different attempts to stock Lake Chapala with American "game fish." With the assistance of his grandsons, he was eventually able to stock the lake with three dozen bass and crappie imported from San Antonio. Baylor to John, 26 July 1904; Baylor to Susie, 26 August 1906; Baylor to Susie, 28 August 1907; Baylor to Susie, 25 December 1907; all in Baylor-Carrington Papers. Also, Hail, *Knight in the Sun*, 36.

CHAPTER FOUR

Cito, The Wolf Dog

I
THE INDIANS CAPTURE GREGORIO

LONG, LONG AGO, AT LEAST HALF A CENTURY, four little Mexican boys were out in the woods near Santa Rosa, a little Mexican town in the state of Coahuila, Mexico, gathering pecan nuts.

At that time the Mexicans could claim ownership only to the land covered by the range of their guns or within the adobe walls of their pueblos; and as their guns at that time were of a very primitive kind, known as *escopetas*— flint locks and bell muzzles—their right to rule the country was on a very uncertain basis.

Once out of sight of their towns, those on either business or pleasure, had to rely on their arms and courage; for the Comanche, Apache, and Lipan Indians looked on the Mexicans as their legitimate prey, and robbed and murdered them whenever they had the advantage.

It was in the fall of the year, after the first "blue norther," or heavy frost, and the ground, they knew by experience, would be covered with rich pecan nuts. Although the boys knew the danger from prowling Indians, they could not resist the temptation of going nutting, so dear to the hearts of all children.

Now had they asked permission of their parents, they would have been forbidden to leave the protection of the friendly adobe walls, as they were the best kind of breastworks in a fight, and the savage never knew what moment a gun would be poked up over the walls at him.

The boys would have been told not to go on such an expedition, unless an armed party went out, and placed sentinels to guard against attack, and to make a circuit and see if there were any fresh pony or moccasin tracks made

355

during the night. The boys thought they would chance it and get a sack full of the rich nuts before any one else got out on the creek where the pecan trees grew.

They slipped out of town by early dawn and when they reached the pecan trees, sure enough, the norther had shaken the nuts down, and the ground was red with the rich pecans. They had seen nothing to alarm them. A few sneaking, cowardly coyotes were seen trotting off, looking back furtively over their shoulders at them, but as they had their faithful shepherd dogs with them—a courageous breed of animals, probably brought from Spain at the same time the horses were—the boys felt no uneasiness, for coyotes were a common sight, and no match for the shepherd dogs.

The boys were soon busy picking up the pecans, and their sacks were getting full, when they heard a terrible uproar among the dogs that had been looking around for rabbits or any kind of sport. They thought the dogs had perhaps jumped a bunch of javelinas, which are great fighters, and often very dangerous. They are commonly called Mexican hogs, and are natives of the American continent.

Aroused by the loud, angry barking of the dogs, the boys looked up and were horrified to see a party of Indians, painted in their hideous manner, mounted on their swift ponies, not over a hundred yards distant, coming towards them at full speed, and yelling at the top of their voices.

As a flock of quail scatters when the hawk swoops, so these little fellows took to their heels, scattering in the brush, every one for himself—and a badly scared boy can run nearly as fast as a cottontail rabbit for a little while.

As each one took a separate route, they were scudding away and soon lost sight of in the brush. The shepherd dogs, being courageous and faithful to a trust, made a good fight for their young masters, snapping at the Indians' feet, but a few arrows soon laid them out dead.

By fast running and good luck, three of the little fellows escaped, and told the sad news in the pueblo. One little boy, nine years old, was overtaken, and an Indian, riding up by his side, grabbed him and put him up in front of him. As soon as they got the sacks of pecans the boys had risked so much for, the Indians were off like a flock of pigeons.

They did not tarry long on the way, but made off for their village, that was about a hundred miles distant in the rugged mountains northeast of Santa Rosa.

All was excitement in the little town. The church bell rang out the signal always given when the Indians made a raid; it was a notice to all who might be out of the place to hurry back. Those who knew that some member of the family was out after wood or with stock, mounted their horses in haste, and arming themselves, went at top speed to assist them. Others were preparing to go out and look for the missing boy.

At first it was hard to get at the truth, as the boys that escaped said all the others were killed or carried off. But, as one failed to show up it was learned that little Gregorio Maltos was missing.

You can imagine the sorrow and grief of his father, mother, little brothers and sisters, when the other boys returned and Gregorio was not with them. The Indians nearly always killed and scalped the men, but if a woman or child was captured, they carried them off. A little baby that cried or worried them, they would dash to death against a tree or rock. Sometimes a shepherd would be carried off and made to do drudgery around the Indian camp, packing in wood or herding horses. But as the herders generally ran off with their best horses, they often did not care to take chances, and killed them. The children carried off, in a short time became used to Indian life and could not be distinguished from the Indian children, and often got to be chiefs among their captors.

II
GREGORIO IN THE INDIAN CAMP

It took some time to get together a party strong enough to follow the Indians, and it was quite late before they got off. Those who went out first, had found Gregorio's hat, but not his body; so they naturally concluded that he had been carried off and only followed the trail a little ways to make sure which direction the Indians had gone. They did this so that no time would be lost hunting for the trail when the others came out to follow it.

As food had to be prepared, ammunition provided, and guns cleaned up or reloaded, it was quite late before they took up the trail. As they knew an ambuscade would probably be formed on the trail, they moved cautiously, and when they came to a canyon or rough brushy place they would send a man on each side to see if it was clear.

Very slow progress was made but their precaution was very necessary, for they found where the Indians had formed an ambuscade at a place where the Indians would be above the Mexicans and among the rocks, with every advantage on the inside. But these old frontier pioneers were too smart to be caught in any such trap.

It was found that only ten or twelve Indians had made the raid on the boys, and had gone back at once, hoping that some of the impetuous young men would follow them, and that they could massacre their pursuers and get some horses and scalps to take back to their village to brag about and dance over.

As it was nearly night, it was decided to give up the pursuit, though the father of little Gregorio, and two brothers, wanted to follow on. But as the Indians had gone on, it was evident that they could not be overtaken before dark, and then the trail could not be seen. Besides, if the Indians got the worst of the fight, they would be apt to kill Gregorio.

Now the Mexicans knew that if the little fellow could not manage to make his escape, there was always a chance to ransom him, by paying the Indians a good sum of money, horses or goods—the Indians preferred a gun and ammunition, but that was too precious to bargain, and putting a club in the hands of the Indians to break Mexican heads with.

Little Gregorio was, as you may well imagine, terribly frightened when the painted warrior reached down and roughly grabbed him. It was as natural for him to yell with terror and kick and struggle to get away, as for a fawn to bleat and struggle when seized by an eagle or wild cat. But the warrior cuffed and boxed his ears, and threatened to kill him if he did not keep quiet. So he had to content himself with sobbing, his little heart filled with grief at the idea of being carried away from a dear mother and loved ones.

The Indians, after finding they were not followed by a small party at once, and not caring to face a strong force from the town, moved on rapidly until sundown. Then they went into camp leaving sentinels behind on their trail to avoid surprise.

As they had ridden along, Gregorio had noticed a deep gap in the tall range of mountains, which they passed through, and said to himself, "If I can escape from the Indians, I can easily remember the gap, for it is the only one in sight in these mountains," and so the first thought came to him to look out for some object that would be a guide to him in returning. He was riding behind one of his captors then and occasionally cast a furtive glance back to keep the gap in view.

Gregorio was so tired by night that once asleep he did not awake until the Indians were getting up to cook breakfast. One of them offered him some of the pecans, and grinned when the little fellow refused them; they had been the cause of all his trouble and brought to mind too vividly, his home and loved ones.

The Indians made him bring up wood to build a fire to cook with, and then gave him a piece of dried meat; but whether it was mule, beef, bear, deer, donkey, or horse meat, he could not tell. However, it was something to eat and smelled very nice, as he broiled it on the coals, and he ate it with relish.

The next day at sunset the warriors reached their village. The village was located in a beautiful valley in the mountains, where a clear stream of water ran, and there was plenty of wood, water, and grass, and an abundance of game near by. They were received with shouts of joy by the women and children.

But a messenger had been sent ahead and had not been able to announce that they had killed any Mexicans, so they could not have a scalp dance, and they had not even stolen any horses or cattle, so the warriors thought it beneath their dignity to join in the demonstration.

Gregorio felt sad enough when he saw the village, and the women and children running to meet them. He thought of how different the evening was to loved ones at his own home. He felt very uncertain, too, as to how he would be treated, for he had heard the stories of cruelty to prisoners—how they were beaten, made to work hard, and half-starved. So he was very agreeably disappointed when the Indian children received him kindly—which they would not have been allowed to do had any of their warriors been killed during the raid.

Two or three months passed by and Gregorio was still with the Indians. In order to disarm them of any suspicions that he had the least idea of trying to make his escape, and to bring about confidence in his pretended content-ment, he joined the children cheerfully in any work they had to do, and joined them in their play, making himself as useful and agreeable as possible.

But all this time he was thinking of his mother and the little adobe house at Santa Rosa, and of the gap in the mountains he must pass through, for if he should miss that, he might perish for want of water or from hunger, or per-haps be killed by a mountain lion or cinnamon bear.

III
GREGORIO PREPARES TO ESCAPE

Little Mexican boys at that time did not have the opportunities which they have now, under President Díaz, to acquire an education. They had no free schools where a good education could be had, and a trade or profession acquired to fit them for a useful life; but they nevertheless learned many things quite useful to them in the life they led on the wild frontier. They learned that the "Carro Grande" and "Carro Chiquito," corresponding to our constellations known as Ursa Major and Ursa Minor, or commonly known as the great dipper and little dipper, are in the north, and that the two lower stars in the bowl of the Carro Grande always point to the north or polar star, and that when one stands with his face to the north, the right hand is east, the left hand west, and the back is south.

This was very valuable information to them, as they often must travel by night where there were no roads, and only the stars to guide them; having no compass as the sailor has to guide them, they had to depend on their wits to direct them and keep them from being lost.

Then they knew that when they were in the woods and needed water they must not go down the dry beds of the streams to look for it, but up stream towards the mountains, and among the rocks where tanks of water could be found; for in the west nearly all the streams sink in the ground when they reach the plains, and you must dig down in the body of the stream to find water.

Gregorio had often listened to his father and friends as they talked of this woodcraft, in their scouts after the thieving Indians, and was, therefore, better prepared to make his escape from the Indians than a boy fifteen years old, reared in a city, or perhaps many grown people, who are lost as soon as they got out of sight of a road.

To steal out of an Indian village where there were numberless dogs—not to mention the cautious Indians always on the lookout for enemies—without giving alarm, he well knew was no easy matter, so Gregorio made the dogs his friends by petting them and dividing his rations with them when he could.

Food was necessary on the tramp through the woods, he knew, but water more so. One can stand hunger much longer than thirst, especially on the western plains, and to be without water a few days even in the fall of the year, is almost certain death.

So Gregorio kept all these things in his mind, and got possession of a Mexican water gourd. The gourd seems to have been given by a kind Providence to the people of the west, to use in the place of canteens. The gourds used as canteens are large at each end, and small in the middle, and of various sizes, from a pint to a gallon. They have a neck just long enough for a stopper. Sometimes they were covered with deer hide to make them strong. They could be cleaned after picking either by putting water in them and setting them aside until the seed and soft part could be shaken out, or by pouring sweetened water in them. After the inside was well soaked and sweetened, the water was drained off and the gourd put on one of the big red-ant beds, where the ants would cut out and carry away all of the soft part. A strange thing about these gourds is that if taken to a northern clime where nature has provided an abundance of water, in a short time the seed will produce only an ordinary round gourd.

In addition to his water gourd, Gregorio had a small cord used in tying wood in a bundle when the squaws and children went out to bring it into camp. The rope was long enough so a noose could be made in one end and thrown over a dead limb on a tree; two or three pulls and the rope would break off the limb. This is also a common trick among cowboys. The warriors never did such drudgery, and would have thought themselves disgraced by such menial squaw-like work.

The Indians, at first suspicious of the little fellow, were at last deceived by his apparent cheerful manner, and gave him a little bow and half a dozen arrows. As all little Mexican boys were in the habit of carrying and using such bows, when herding goats, sheep or other stock around the town, they became quite skillful in the use of them and rarely came home at night without rabbits, quail, or even jack rabbits.

So Gregorio was now pretty well equipped to make a break for liberty. The only question was, which was best; to try to leave late at night and take the chance of being discovered, or to slip away some evening when they brought in the Indian ponies they had been herding, and have all night to put as much distance as possible between himself and the Indians by morning.

He though once of getting a pony—one of the swiftest, for the boys raced them enough to know the best—and making a break for liberty. But he knew pursuit would be immediate, and the Indians could easily follow his trail. And a horse could be seen so easily at a great distance, he decided it was best to slip off on foot. In such a rough country a horseman could not follow him, and he could conceal his route by keeping in a rocky country.

It was not unusual for the Indians to carry off little children in the raids which they often made on the little Mexican towns, and the children often escaped. Of course they would tell all the smart things they did to throw the Indians off their trail and fool them. Those topics always fascinated the children, and were listened to with great interest, and the consequence was that each one was pretty familiar with those stories, and felt quite sure he could escape too, if ever he should be carried off by Indians.

Gregorio had his plan of escape decided upon at last. He began to make a pet of a poor little dog, that was half coyote, and on account of his looks got many a kick from the old squaws. For Cito had the coyote talent for helping himself to anything capable when hungry, and as he was seldom fed, he was hungry all the time, and had to steal to keep even with the village.

Gregorio soon won Cito's unbounded affection by dividing his rations with him and petting him—something the pup never experienced before. The dog proved to be quick, courageous and unusually intelligent, and the little captive and his dog Cito soon became fast friends.

IV
Gregorio Runs Away

The day Gregorio fixed for leaving, he took his water gourd, rope, and bow and arrows. He had been going out regularly with the other boys with the horses of the village, and they were brought into camp every evening about sunset. The boys took their dinner with them, cooking the dried meat, and often killing rabbits, squirrels, or other small game to give a change from "jerked" or dried meat.

Luckily for Gregorio, he had to carry the jerked beef and venison; for he was looked on still as a slave, and all extra work was put on him, such as rounding up the horses every time they got scattered, and bringing water to drink when they ate their dinner. Those things he always did willingly, having an object in view.

When the boys got ready for dinner, he brought the wood and ate with the others quite heartily and as the dried meat made them all thirsty, he was sent with his gourd to the creek to get some more water.

He took all the meat left after they had eaten, and hid it in a crevice in the rocks above the reach of a sneaking coyote. Then he went back with his gourd of water.

When it was time to drive the horses back to camp, Gregorio as usual was sent to round them up. His little dog went with him, for Cito had shown great intelligence. Cito had learned to run after the horses that refused to keep with the herd; he would run up behind and snap one by the heels, and when the pony kicked at him, Cito would lie flat on the ground. Of course, the horse would kick over him, and by the time his feet struck the ground the little dog would nip him again. So all Gregorio had to do to round up the stock was to swing his rope over his head and shout, when the dog would dart off and the horses would start for the village.

This evening Gregorio went around the stock, and purposely let some of them stay out. When the boys got to camp, several ponies were missed and Gregorio was ordered to go back and look for them.

He pretended to be afraid and asked one of the boys to go back with him; but none cared to take the walk and he started back, taking the dog by their permission, and was told that he could have or kill him if he wanted to.

You may rest assured Gregorio made quick time back to the meat he had hid; filling his gourd with water and making a coil of his rope, he hung it over his shoulder, and was off for home and liberty. The thought filled his little heart with joy, for already he pictured the happiness of his mother when she should see him once more and he stepped off as lightly as a deer.

The herd had been out north of the village and Gregorio very wisely concluded to go in that direction, as the Indians, he knew, would be sure to look for him in the direction of Santa Rosa and guard carefully the route by which they came after making the raid. The Indians would suppose he did not know the way back home, and that he would either be starved out and have to come back to the village, or be killed by some wild beast.

Gregorio continued traveling toward the north star, which Carro Grande located for him, as it was shining so beautifully in the northern sky.

Midnight found Gregorio ten or twelve miles further from home, but he argued, nearer to liberty.

The Indians had not watched him very closely during his captivity among them, but had promised him that they would kill and scalp him and use his hide to cover a saddle, if he ever attempted to escape, thinking such a threat would be enough to keep him from making any attempt to get away.

As soon as he struck one of those dry arroyos or creeks that rise in the mountains and run toward the Sabinas River, he changed his direction and turned to the west towards the mountains. The bed of these streams is nearly always of flat rocks, and during the flood season the rocks and gravel carried down make them very smooth; it is seldom that any deep holes are made in them that will hold water for any length of time, except where there is a fall, and there the boulders and gravel twisting and turning from the water falling on them, wear great deep holes that hold water for a long time after the rainy season is over.

Gregorio remembering the instructions of his father, took the center of the creek bed, and as it was quite flat and smooth, he got over a good deal of ground, and finally came to one of the falls where there was a deep hole of water.

Here he filled up his gourd and took a good drink also. The little dog was quite rejoiced to find water, as they had been traveling at a pretty brisk rate. Gregorio had named him Pobrecito, which in the Spanish tongue means "poor little thing," but as that was too long a name for such a short dog, he nicknamed him Cito. Cito had soon learned his new name, as it was always accompanied by a caress, and sometimes something to eat, whereas his Indian name was accompanied by a kick or a rock.

Cito had become very fond of his young master, and trotted along at his heels, quite contented; but several times he whined as much as to say he thought it was about time to camp and have supper. Gregorio began to think so, too, but he had heard his father say that it was at such places game collected, and bears, panthers, and other animals came to drink at night, and he did not care to meet them.

It had required all his courage to brace up enough to run off in the night time. For not only children but grown up people feel much braver when in the glorious sunshine, with the birds singing around them, than in the night; especially if they must now and then pass under some great tall trees, that even in the day time give a heavy shade, and at night make darkness visible, and cause a cold streak to run down one's backbone.

Gregorio saw a well beaten trail leading from the water hole up the steep bank of the creek, but he was afraid to take it for fear of leaving tracks that would enable the Indians to follow his trail. So he scrambled up through the brush and rocks until he reached the creek bed above the fall and continue on up it until he came to a dry branch that entered the arroyo which he had been following.

As was about to enter this little branch, a rock came tumbling down the bank. Cito gave a sharp, angry bark.

Gregorio, catching sight of three great dark shapes, coming down into the bed of the creek, gave a cry of terror and surprise and darted off up the creek, followed closely by Cito, who did not exactly understand what was the matter.

The three black objects started off down the creek as badly scared as the boy. They were an old black she bear and two cubs. It was a lucky thing for Gregorio that it was not a cinnamon or a silver tip, for they are both very savage, especially when they have cubs, and will not hesitate to attack a person if he comes suddenly on them. But the black bears are quite timid, and will not attack a person unless worried by dogs or wounded when they are dangerous. This old one snorted and started off.

Gregorio, seeing how badly scared the bears were, regained his courage and watched them until they disappeared in the gloom.

V

SUPPER IN A CAVE

Little Gregorio was too wide awake to think of camping so near such unwelcome company, and he decided to get off a little farther from the water hole, before stopping.

He found another little branch and turned into it. The moon, though only half full, was well overhead and gave a good light; a person, however, who has been out all night, can see quite well, but on stepping out of a well lighted room would say, what a dark night!

Gregorio was soon out of sight of the main arroyo (in case any of the Indians should come that way). He found a bluff and quite a number of caves. So he made up his mind to camp there and rest until daylight.

He was real hungry, too, after his long tramp. He soon gathered a few sticks and made a small fire after the Indian style—for they economize, where all the wood has to be carried on their backs. It is quite necessary to do so. The Indians break the wood into thin short pieces, and after a little blaze is started they lay their pieces around it in a circle. You can always tell an

Indian fire by there being a circle of ashes left. We would set fire to a big log, or dead tree (at the risk of burning it down and killing or crippling some one), and pile on big logs to burn in two, and be piled on again.

The Indian says, "White men heap big fool, make big fire have to sit far off, Indian make little fire, sit up close."

Gregorio had been thoughtful enough to get hold of a flint and steel, and had some "punk," a soft yellow substance found in the knots of trees, and very easy to catch fire from a spark from the flint and steel. He soon started a small fire, and began to broil some of the dried meat.

Cito looked on with a great deal of interest, and the smell of the meat made his mouth water. He gave a little deprecating whine which called his young master's attention to him; and when Gregorio saw his mouth water and he licked out his tongue in pleasing anticipation, it just occurred to him that Cito would take his share cold, and with as little ceremony as possible. So Gregorio made a fair "divy" and gave him a long piece, which Cito took to one side and began to tear to pieces.

Gregorio soon had his meat broiled and with no other sauce than the best brand of the frontier, hunger, his simple meat tasted very sweet.

After a good drink of water from his gourd, he began to make a bed of leaves in the back part of one of the caves. He had a piece of cotton cloth the Indians had given him which was his only covering at night. So he took his cloth and began packing the dead leaves that had accumulated in piles, and soon had a very comfortable bed.

He was putting some more wood on the fire, and about to go to bed, when he saw Cito looking very earnestly at the water gourd, twisting his head first one side and then the other, as much as to say, "That beef was pretty dry eating—what's the matter with my having a drink?"

Gregorio took the hint and poured some water in a hole in the rocks; Cito drank eagerly, wagging his tail all the time to express his appreciation of the courtesy.

The friends then crawled into the cave and doubled up as close together as possible to get the benefit of the warmth from each other's body, and were soon asleep, two little midgets in the heart of the mountains.

Towards morning it became quite cool and Gregorio felt the change. So he got up and put some more wood on the live coals among the ashes and soon had a blaze that felt very comfortable indeed, shedding warmth around. So he concluded not to go to sleep again but gave Cito his breakfast and began to broil a piece of meat for himself.

By the time he had finished his early meal, the faint light began to appear, and then "Dame nature began to try her canny hand" in painting the east in all the prismatic colors. Then he heard the concert that always greets the moon; the soft note of the red bird, Bob White, calling his family to get up, the mournful note of whippoorwill, the gobble of turkeys and sharp call of hens. Off in the distance he heard the dismal howl of the lobo or buffalo wolf as he is called on the plains of the west—they are as large as a Newfoundland dog, and able to pull down a yearling steer. Far down toward the mesa he heard the ki-yi of the sneaking, thieving coyote or prairie wolf; they are afraid to venture up in the rough mountains, as panthers catch and eat them, so they confine themselves to little valleys, open woods or plains. A fox's rough grating bark was heard on the mountain side, and the cat owl gave his unearthly scream, followed by a haw-hawing. The solemn old chicken thief, the horned owl, filled the echoes with his dismal note.

Gregorio had heard all these noises before, and knew it was the reveille of the morning dawn, by nature's choir. The howls of wild beasts lose their terror when one is in a house and the sounds are borne from the distance; but to little Gregorio and Cito, they were too near and horrible to be at all agreeable.

The red bird's sweet note was the signal for Gregorio to be off, for he wanted to get up the canyon to where it would be too rough for the Indians to follow him on horseback, and he thought he could travel nearly as fast on foot as they could.

His plan of escape was to travel up the arroyo westward until he passed the crest of mountains, and when he reached the foothills on that side, to turn south again.

VI
THE INDIANS IN PURSUIT

Back in the Indian village, when the boys brought in the herd of horses and the evening grew to darkness and no Gregorio turned up, they thought at once that he had taken one of the animals, and would try to make his escape.

So several of the warriors and one of the boys who had been out with the herd, mounted their ponies and went out to see if they could find him.

Another party mounted and rode swiftly towards Santa Rosa, on the trail over which they had brought him into their camp. Their plan was to go on and guard the gap in the mountains at the only place where a horse could pass through.

They felt pretty sure that they would catch the boy, and so three Indians pushed on rapidly towards the gap Gregorio had remembered so carefully, and the others camped on the trail after riding rapidly until midnight. They knew that if any one passed them, their horses would snort and wake them up.

The Indians examined the trail after the moon got up, and found neither pony nor boy tracks, so they reasoned that they were ahead of the little fugitive, and felt pretty sure of catching him; and they intended to give him such a beating that he would never attempt to escape again.

They were off by daylight and rode on swiftly towards the gap, keeping a sharp lookout for any fresh signs.

A young warrior ahead uttered an exclamation of surprise, and as the others rode up, he pointed to fresh bare foot tracks in the path, and wondered how it could be possible for the little Mexican to get so far on foot. But after following the trail a little distance, they saw a large track and two small ones, and recognized that it was an old she bear and her cubs, and the first sign seen dimly in the early dawn that they took to be a boy's footprint, was that of one of the cubs. The human and bear tracks are so much alike that it is hard to tell one from the other at first glance.

They pushed on towards the gap. Late in the evening they found where the three warriors, who had gone ahead, had turned out of the trail. The three horses were staked out in a little valley, half a mile off the trail where there was plenty of grass, but no water. The party now dismounted and went on to the gap on foot, leaving one warrior to watch their horses, in case little Gregorio should blunder on them and perform an old Indian trick and set his pursuers all afoot.

Arrived at the gap, one of the warriors howled like a wolf, and hearing no answer, he gobbled like a turkey, and was answered by a yelping, like turkey hens, from the cliff at the gap, and by the hooting of an owl. So from these sounds they soon located the advance spies, and learned that nothing had passed during the day.

They remained all next day on the lookout, and again at night, but no Gregorio came in sight. So they knew he had not stolen a horse, but was on foot, and would probably be found near the village, having been lost looking for the missing horses. As their gourds had no water, they decided to return to the village, keeping a good lookout on their way back.

The Indians back in the village had gone out by daylight to see if they could find Gregorio, and the boys took them to where they had eaten dinner the day before. After a search the missing horses were found, and then they knew Gregorio had either become lost the evening before, or had run off.

So they began with the cunning that comes from a life in the woods, and went to the place where they had eaten dinner, and then took his trail to the creek.

There they found where he had filled his gourd after getting the dried beef, and had started off north.

The tracks of the boy and dog were followed easily by the pursuers, and although they were puzzled to understand why he was going away instead of towards Santa Rosa, it was evident to them that he was not looking for the missing horses, but trying to escape.

Realizing this, they were put on their mettle to see that he did not get away; for a little boy to outwit a village of Indian braves was something that must not be allowed.

It was plain sailing until they got to the broad arroyo, and here they met the first illustration of Gregorio's cuteness. The flat, dry, rocky bed of the creek gave no sign they could read, and whether the boy had gone up or down the creek was the point to be solved.

They searched the bank of the creek on the north side, and up and down on each side, but no sign of the boy or dog could be seen. So they concluded that he had turned down towards the Rio Sabinas.

The Indians therefore decided to return to the village, get some provisions, and make a scout in the direction of the river to hunt for his trail. Getting their blankets and a quantity of dried meat, they started for the Rio Sabinas, examining the ground carefully as they went.

A runner was also sent to the party that had gone to the gap, telling them the little Mexican was afoot and had gone towards the Rio Sabinas, commanding them also to make a count in that direction. They further sent word that in case they caught him they should raise signal smokes, and promised to do the same.

The runner met the returning party and gave them provisions and orders, and they turned east to look for the fugitive.

In order to make a white signal smoke, the Indians would gather a large armful of dry grass, and after putting fire in the center of the bundle they waved it around until sure it was burning. Then they put it on the ground, throwing a damp blanket over it, and holding the edge of the blanket down on the ground, so the grass would not burn too quickly.

As soon as they saw it was about to break out, they threw the blanket off, and the smoke being heated, and so much lighter than the surrounding atmosphere, shot up in the air like a balloon, getting slower and slower in its ascent as it became cooler, until it hung finally like a great ball in the air. In our clear western atmosphere this curious signal could be seen for seventy-five or one-hundred miles.

A black smoke was made in the same way, except that cedar or some sappy substance was used, with only enough dry, dead grass to start the blaze.

Gregorio made good headway until he got up some distance, where the canyon was narrow and the sides of the mountains very steep. Here during the annual floods the great boulders, detached from the cliffs, were rolled along by the torrents and piled up on each other in endless confusion, and the nearer he got to the crest of the mountains, the rougher became the bed of the arroyo.

But Gregorio managed to squeeze under or climb over the great boulders and Cito followed. Gregorio often had to help him get over some boulder or cliff too high for the little dog to climb.

Patiently the pair clambered upward, stopping occasionally to rest awhile in the shade of some great rock or cave, for it gets to be quite hot in the middle of the day, even in the winter months. These boulders piled together are a great resort for foxes, wild cats, panthers, and other animals during the dry season, being cool in the middle of the day and warm at night. Gregorio frequently startled these animals from their slumbers, but they scampered away. Luckily they did not disturb any cinnamon or silvertip bears, for then the little travelers would have had to do the running.

VII

A JOKE ON CITO

Gregorio was very anxious to get over the divide and go down to the low hills on the west side, where he knew it would be warmer at night. For a fire is not a good thing to have around a camp, when you are "on the dodge," and the altitude he knew made a great difference in the temperature.

Therefore he did not want to spend the night on the crest of the mountain, or at the head of the arroyo. He would see the tall pines on the ridges showing plainly against the clear blue sky, and hoped to reach them by the middle of the day when he would seek a roosting place down near the plains on the other side.

In a sudden bend of the arroyo, Gregorio came suddenly on a large flock of turkeys, but as he had never killed anything larger than a cottontail, quail, or dove, he did not dare to risk losing an arrow by shooting such a large bird. For, unless the turkey was killed, it would fly away with the arrow.

He was sorely tempted, however, for the turkeys, after trotting along ahead of him in the bed of the creek, turned out to go up the steep bank, and one lazy, fat old gobbler would hardly get out of the way.

Gregorio could not resist the temptation, and let drive with an arrow. But it only served to put some life into the old gobbler, which went sailing off with the arrow sticking in him. This was a serious loss to Gregorio, as he had so few, and he decided he would better keep his arrows for the small game.

Continuing on up the creek, he finally came to a bluff, at the foot of which was a deep hole made during floods by the action of the falling water and boulders grinding in the solid rocks. Here a herd of deer were drinking, and Gregorio, being barefooted, made no noise and was right over them before they saw him or he saw them.

Both were frightened, but the deer snorted and trotted off down the arroyo, their white tails in the air. Cito was for making a dash at them, having an eye of business; but Gregorio wanted no barking there, as the echo would soon repeat itself and perhaps take the sound to his pursuers. So he called Cito off; but the dog had already learned that it was a waste of time to run after a well deer, and came back very willingly.

After getting a drink and filling his gourd (Cito filling his tank also), Gregorio looked around to see how he could get up above the fall, for it was fifty or sixty feet high, and the cliff extended around on each side for some distance.

He concluded to follow the deer, for he knew they had some way to get out to their feeding grounds. So he went back down the arroyo in the direction they had disappeared, and soon found a trail leading up on the north side of the arroyo. As before, he did not care to walk in it, but took a little gully to the right of it and began to follow it, sometimes having to crawl through brush.

After going up a quarter of a mile, the deer path crossed his gully, but he concluded to follow the rocky gully and thus leave no signs for the Indians. After another quarter mile he again came across the deer path, and their fresh track told him they were making for the open ground above the fall.

As they were going in the right direction to suit him, and as he did not fear the Indians would come so far, he followed the trail that zigzagged up the mountain side among crevices in the rocks.

Gregorio came up quite close to the herd of deer, and they again bounded off, making a clatter among the loose rocks and giving their shrill snort.

The little fugitives finally got up on the slope above the fall, and saw a bluff ahead of them, but as it did not appear very high, Gregorio made straight for it.

After going a mile, they reached the foot of the cliff, but instead of being only a few feet high, as the boy thought, it was about twenty feet high, and extended around for several miles on each side.

Gregorio's heart went up in his throat when he looked at this wall right between himself and liberty.

Glancing to the right and left he saw no break in it. If he should go to the left, it would take him, probably, too near the Indian village and some of the searching parties might find him. He turned north along the foot of the cliff, watching closely for some crevice or break in the rocks that would enable him to reach the top of the cliff.

The little fellow passed over more than a mile in this search and had almost despaired of success, when he found a pine tree growing close to the foot of the cliff, and a friendly branch leaped out over the top of it. Now all his fears were gone, and he soon climbed up and left his bow, arrows and water gourd on top of the cliff.

All this time Cito had been dancing around on his hind legs, and whining a protest to what looked like desertion by his young master, but Gregorio had no idea of leaving him to the tender mercies of the Indians, who would likely consider him as an accomplice and take his hide to cover the saddle.

He uncoiled his rope, dropped the end down to see how near it would come to reaching the ground and saw that it lacked about six feet. He could easily lengthen it by tying it to a pole but could not tie the pole to the top of the cliff or to the dog below. So he very carefully tore off several narrow strips from his piece of cloth, tied the end of the rope to a brush on the brink of the precipice, and climbed down the tree to the ground.

Gregorio was received with great demonstrations of joy by Cito. The boy tied the cloth rope around Cito behind his fore legs, and again scaled up the ladder that nature had made for him. But when he got up and looked down, he saw that the little dog, again thinking he was to be left, had wound the rope around the tree, so there was nothing to do but go down again.

After unwinding the rope he put it a little further from the tree and placed a rock on it to make Cito believe he was tied and stay still—all Indian dogs are accustomed to this.

When Gregorio got up on top of the cliff again, he peeped over at the dog. That startled Cito again, and the rock was moved. But before the little dog could entangle himself Gregorio yanked him up off the ground, and could hardly pull him up for laughing; for Cito, as soon as he left the ground, began to kick and paw, working his tail like a rudder, and the rope began to twist, with the funny little dog spinning like a top.

Gregorio had taken the precaution to lie down flat on his stomach, so that no struggle of the dog would make him lose his balance and fall over the cliff. But he was very glad indeed when he landed his little companion safe above.

Cito was too dizzy to stand up at first, but as soon as he could straightened up he began to caper around and express his joy that they were together once more.

VIII
OVER THE DIVIDE

Gregorio was overjoyed to find that it was only a short distance to the top of the ridge, and hastily gathering up his traps, started off at a brisk walk towards the crest. There a beautiful scene awaited him. As far as eye could reach toward the west stretched a series of gentle valleys and blue mountains. Turning to the southwest he saw the dark peaks against the blue sky—and what was more beautiful to his eyes, he saw the gap, which he felt was the door to his freedom. Gregorio had all this time been going away from his home, and from the gap that was his guide for direction. He was in the heart of the high mountains now, and would have to traverse many valleys and weary mountains before he could reach the gap and from there start on the final stretch of his journey home.

His heart was filled with grateful joy and tears dimmed his sight. Fervently the little fellow prayed to the Virgin Mary, and promised without mental reservation that, if she would only guide him safely to his home again, he would never, never go pecan gathering again, without permission of his mother, and then only with a strong armed party, and sentinels stationed around them.

Gregorio did not care to remain long in such an open place, and had the feeling common to man and beast when being hunted, that he was safer in the thick brush. A backbone, or ridge, ran down from where he stood towards the plains. On each side of it there was a deep canyon, one leading to the northwest, and the other to the southwest.

He hardly knew which one to take, but as the one tending southeast led towards home, his heart strings pulled him in that direction and he started off at once for the canyon.

It was not as steep as the one on the other side had been, for if one side of a range of mountains is very rough and abrupt, the other side is very apt to slope gently towards the plains.

Gregorio did not feel comfortable until he got away from the open ground where he could be seen, and where the Indians could ride. He made for the deep canyon, so that his tracks could not be seen in the rocky bed of the arroyo.

In the bed of the canyon he found a nice spring of cool water, coming out from under a cliff of rocks, with ferns growing all around and grateful shade from overhanging oaks.

Stooping down to drink, little Gregorio was startled to see an Indian face peering up at him hideously painted.

He had forgotten that the boys, for amusement, had painted white circles around his eyes, then black and red, and lines from these across his cheeks, forehead, and chin; these with the hawk feathers tied in the top of his head made him look like a savage warrior.

Gregorio refilled his canteen, and felt like taking a rest, but he knew it was not a safe place for him to stop. Such watering places were all known to the Indians, and he might fall asleep, and be in danger, not only of Indians, but of wild beasts. The leopard or jaguar usually stayed around such springs, to kill the deer that came to quench their thirst. They would get up in the limbs of trees overhanging the trails made by the different kinds of game, and as the unsuspecting animals came beneath them, the big cats would pounce down on them. Bears like to be convenient to water, and Gregorio did not care to meet one, for he had heard too many horrible stories of hunters being torn to pieces by these savage animals.

Seeing some bees watering and flying down the creek, Gregorio started down in the same direction and presently came to a bluff on the side of the creek. Here he began to keep a sharp lookout for something to eat, for his long tramp had given him a keen appetite.

At last he saw the little busy bees flying in and out of a hole in the cliff, but alas! It was far above the reach of Gregorio, and even had he been able to reach it, the hole where the bees went into the cave was too small for him to get out any honey.

Continuing on down the creek he finally found another swarm in an open mouthed cave, where the tempting honey was displayed in full view, making the boy's mouth water just to look at it. The busy little workers generally show a great deal of skill in selecting a home where bears and men cannot easily reach their treasures, and as they seem to know exactly to a foot where high water mark is on the cliff, their home is apt to be secure from robbery. Occasionally, however, they become wearied by a long flight and alight almost any place and set to work—under a big oak limb, or in a crevice in the rocks.

Gregorio was determined to have some of that nice sealed comb, that hung so temptingly in view, so laying aside his bow, arrows, rope, and water gourd, he began to bombard the bees with rocks.

Cito had been on many a squirrel hunt, and concluded Gregorio was after a squirrel, so every time a rock fell he would run to it and smell it.

The bees at first hardly knew what to make of this rude attack, but it did not take them long to find out, and a dozen or more made a charge on Gregorio. He had to beat a temporary retreat, but selected a lot of flat rocks that had scaled off from the cliff and came back to the attack.

By this time the honey comb had been broken and the bees began to eat it and quit fighting, as is their habit. Gregorio kept pounding away, and finally a big piece of sealed comb fell down.

Gregorio knew what to expect and took to his heels and hid behind a rock. Cito thought of course the squirrel must have been knocked down, and he charged the comb. But around fifty bees had clung to the honey, and made a counter charge, and all on poor Cito's nose, ears, and head, putting him to flight.

Gregorio waited until the bees that were not daubed in honey rose to their home again, and then, selecting a piece of flat, thin rock, he put the comb on it as well as he could, and went on down the arroyo to get his dinner.

IX
DREAMING OF HOME

Leaving the main creek, he turned up a little branch, to be out of sight in case the Indians should come along.

In order to make as little smoke as possible, he gathered a few dry sticks, and with flint and steel soon had a fire. Cooking dried beef is a small affair, and while the meat was on the coals he enjoyed the honey, giving the most of it to Cito, who looked very comical with his swollen nose and closed eye, and declined to be under further obligations to the bees for food or sport.

Gregorio enjoyed the honey immensely and also the jerked beef. The fact that it was the last piece he had added to the favor. He ended his meal by storing away all the honey where it would do the most good, and then took a big drink of water—not a wise thing to do. All old bee hunters will tell you to eat some bee bread with the honey and not to drink any water for half an hour afterwards, or you are sure to be sick at the stomach. Given a hungry boy and plenty of nice honey, and the usual result follows in due course of time. Gregorio was pretty sick and stretched himself under a cedar tree, the accumulation of its fallen foliage for years making a nice bed, and soon fell asleep.

Gregorio would probably have slept until far into the night, but a sweet dream of home and loved ones in the family circle, was rudely broken by an angry growl and sharp bark from his sentinel, Cito. Cito must have slept with one eye open—the other being closed by the bees, but his nose, that was his sentinel, had detected an intruder.

Gregorio sprang to his feet, and found Cito standing stiff, bristles up, and his corkscrew tail rigid. He was having a growling match with a large lynx, just across the branch, in front of him, her three little kittens just behind her, peeping around timidly at this strange animal. Neither seemed to have the advantage, but when that horrid, painted face popped up suddenly, mother cat whirled and darted off, followed by the kittens, spitting and tumbling over each other in their fright.

This incident warned Gregorio that he would better move on farther from the spring; it was late in the evening and the wild cat was out for a drink at the spring and a supper for herself and family. It was the hour when game, if not disturbed, usually visited the springs.

If, instead of a wild cat, it had been a leopard or mountain lion, Gregorio and Cito would have furnished the supper, though these beasts seldom attack a man unless driven by great hunger. Where game is abundant, there is no danger, as they catch and destroy more than they can eat.

It was sunset when Gregorio was so rudely disturbed in his dream, so he started off at once briskly to try and find a safe place to sleep, the cat incident having its natural effect on his nerves. Just at dusk he found just what he needed, a cave in a bluff on the east side of the creek, that had been warmed by the evening sun shining in it.

It was at least 12 feet above the bed of the creek, but that was just what Gregorio wanted, and he had been in the woods often enough to know just what to do. A drift pile of logs and brush, washed down from the head of the arroyo during the rainy season, furnished him a ladder and he was soon at the mouth of the cave.

It opened into quite a nice room and there was enough loose sand and dirt in the back of it to make a soft bed. The next move was to get Cito up. Leaving his pack, he started down, but his ladder turned and came near landing him on the hard rocks. So he found another ladder that had wide spreading roots and would not turn.

He knew he could not climb the pole and carry Cito, so he had brought down his rope. He put a noose around Cito again and after getting up he pulled the little dog up easily for Cito now had an idea what was to be done.

It would not do to leave his ladder standing in front of his temporary lodging room, for a leopard could use it, too, and if an Indian should happen along and see it, he would investigate at once, and have the pair hived. Panthers make their dens in such caves, and bear also, but they are smart enough to get at the foot of some cliff, above high water mark.

Gregorio threw his ladder down and felt very comfortable, knowing how safe he was and securely hid, and that he could easily rope his ladder again in the morning—for he had learned the trick common among cowboys and campers of throwing a lasso over the dead limb of a tree and breaking it off for firewood.

The boy and dog cuddled up close together, and by the time Gregorio had said his prayers to Our Lady of Guadalupe he was asleep.

X
BREAKFAST UNDER DIFFICULTIES

Daybreak brought its usual serenade of beast and bird. Gregorio aroused from a deep sleep, had to rub his eyes and look around before he realized where he was. He crawled out of his cave and began to fish for his ladder, and soon had it in place.

He put the rope around Cito and let him down safely, then followed, and pulled down his ladder. The ladder he put again on the drift pile, so that if the Indians should pass that way, they would see nothing to excite suspicion—for a rock turned over, or a broken weed or brush, meant something had passed that way, and they would begin to look for the cause.

Once more the little waifs started off down the bed of the creek, that was now flat, smooth rock, and much easier to travel. But they still had some falls and rough boulders to get over, and catclaw and other thorny bushes to scratch and bruise them.

Gregorio had improvised a garment from his piece of cotton cloth, or "*manta*," as the Mexicans called it, by cutting a hole in the center large enough to slip over his head; and using the strips he had torn off, he made a belt to tie around his waist. With his buckskin leggings, painted face, and top knot of eagle feathers, he looked very warlike, especially as he carried his bow and arrows. His own mother would scarcely have known him had she seen him in her own yard.

Walking before breakfast to get an appetite, when you know your breakfast is being prepared by the cook at home, and walking when you have a large, fine appetite along with you, and no breakfast in sight, are two entirely different things. Gregorio stepped along briskly, the cool, bracing air of early dawn requiring quick movement to keep warm. Both eyes were wide open and searched the brush and rocks to the right and left for something to furnish a "short order breakfast" for two.

But with the luck usual under such circumstances, all the birds and other game seemed to see him first. There were hundreds of the blue speckled breast quail, with white topknots, but they always flew before the boy got near them. The cottontails ran like the wind, and even the stupid jackrabbit started off as if a yellow jacket had stung him, twisting his body first one side and then the other as if a hind leg were broken. They never stopped running as far as the boy could see them.

This is a very common state of things on the western plains, and comes to every hunter who has camped in the woods; when the food gives out, none of the hunters seem to have any luck; and they come straggling into camp, tired and hungry, with cock and bull stories about how they shot a big buck, and the ground was covered with blood, and his back was broken, and finally, after trailing him a mile or so, he quit bleeding and they lost his trail among so many fresh tracks; and how they had got within fifty yards of a deer with horns like a rocking chair, and were so excited they forgot they had hair triggers and shot before they had drawn a bead; the shotgun man had come suddenly on an immense flock of turkeys, and shot a load of blue whistlers at them instead of number twos, and so on through the whole shooting match; but let one bring in a fawn and hang it up in camp, and luck returns and the poorest hunter in camp can kill game.

It was getting late for fashionable people, and no breakfast in sight. Cito had made several very handsome spurts for cottontails, but they always managed to get to their holes in the rocks; in rocky country they do not run into hollow trees or logs, where they can be chopped out, or twisted out with a stick, as all country boys well understand.

After a while an inquisitive squirrel spied the two little wanderers, and began chattering; while ones unhunted always chatter. When they are hunted they learn by sad experience, it is best to keep quiet, but this one not only chattered long and loud, but kept wagging his bushy tail, as if he were pumping the barks out.

Gregorio crept cautiously towards him, keeping bushes and trees between himself and his prospective breakfast. When he got up quite close, he located him on a small tree, and made a rush. The squirrel skipped around on the other side of the tree for though he had never seen a man, instinct told him it was an enemy.

Gregorio had laid aside his rope and gourd when he made his charge, and now walked around to the side of the tree the squirrel was on. But by this time the squirrel was on the other side, and skillfully managed to keep a tree between himself and Gregorio.

It began to look as though breakfast would be postponed. At last the boy played a trick on the squirrel. He picked up a rock and threw it up through the limbs so it would fall on the opposite side of the tree from him. Cito, having had experience from squirrel hunts with the Indian boys, thinking it was the squirrel making a break for liberty, ran to it, but made a cautious approach to see if there were any bees on it, for a dog has a very retentive memory and does not forget who gives him a kick or a caress.

The ruse proved a good one, and having had his bow ready, as soon as the squirrel came around on his side, Gregorio sent an arrow through him. The poor little bundle of fur gave a squeak and tumbled out of the tree. Cito made a rush for the squirrel, as did the boy, for Gregorio knew that unless the squirrel was dead when he struck the ground, there would be a lively scrap, and his arrow broken in the fight. A squirrel has grit, and as soon as Cito made a grab for him, he fastened his long, sharp teeth in his nose, and the little dog had to stand on his hind legs and shake his head to get rid of him. Then, grabbing him by the back, he gave him a vicious shake that finished him. The arrow was broken, but not so badly but what it could be mended again; it would be shorter than the others, and would be held in reserve.

XI
An Amateur Cook

This was only part of a breakfast. The pair trampled on down the arroyo, and had gone only a little way, when Gregorio spied a half grown rabbit. Instead of scampering off, it sat up on its hind feet, still chewing, its mouth full of green weed, and pricked up its ears staring with wonder at this strange painted animal.

Gregorio dropped his squirrel and kneeling down sent an arrow through the little fellow. Although a rabbit is a small animal, like the bullfrog, his voice is out of proportion to his size, and the terrific squall that the rabbit gave made the little archer's hair stand on end; he made a rush though and grabbed his arrow, and Cito made a grab for the cottontail's head and soon put an end to him.

Gregorio thought it was about time for breakfast, but he had no knife, and how to dress the game was the next thing to be considered. Here the boy's woodcraft came into play. As soon as he came to a place where there were plenty of flint rocks, he laid all his traps down, and picking up a good size rock, threw it with all his might against another one. It broke into a number of pieces, and after trying this a number of times, a thin piece was at last broken off, as sharp edged as a razor.

With this he was provided with as good a knife as he could want for dressing small game.

Gregorio had taken several drinks during the morning tramp and had given some to Cito, so he did not care to use any more out of his gourd until he saw some way to refill it. But of this he felt pretty sure for several flocks of doves had passed close over his head going down the branch, and he was woodman enough to know that meant either a spring or tank of water in the rocks not far away. He trudged on, and sure enough he came to a fall, and below it, a deep hole of clear water.

Gregorio did not care to leave any sign near the water that could be read by the Indians and after filling up his canteen and getting a drink, he went off to one side in a thicket to prepare his game for breakfast.

He began with the squirrel, as the squirrel's hide is the toughest and hard to get off. He first cut the skin across its back, and gradually got it loose enough to put his fingers under it, and by pulling with both hands with all his strength, he soon had it stripped off. The skinning of the cottontail was an easy matter as the hide comes off very easily.

He washed the meat nice and clean, and as the game was very fat, it looked quite tempting. Building a small fire, and placing some flat rocks in front of it, he soon enjoyed the pleasant odor of roasting meat.

Cito had disposed of the head and skin of the squirrel and also the head of the rabbit, and took up a position on the opposite side of the fire from his young master, where he watched with great interest the cooking of the game. Cito twisted his head first on one side and then the other every time Gregorio turned the roast over, as much as to say, "I think I am entitled to a share of that, for my nose is sore yet where that squirrel bit it."

Gregorio was not sure which he would prefer, and so was cooking both, to have a choice. After both were brown and well done, he tried the squirrel, and as it was so fat, tender, and juicy, he never left a bit, giving Cito only the bones.

The boy then began on the rabbit but it was very dry meat. The old dark-eys say, "Brer rabbit good any way you take him," but old hunters and pioneers will tell you that eating rabbit for a change, and eating rabbit because you can't get any other meat, are entirely different matters. So most of the rabbit was passed over to Cito, greatly to his satisfaction.

Breakfast over and no dishes to wash, Gregorio went back to the bank and filled up his gourd. Both he and the dog took a drink. He decided now to make as straight a line as possible for the gap in the mountains. He could not see the gap on account of the many spurs that run down from the main mountain to the plains, but knew the direction and struck out boldly for home and liberty.

XII
SOME STIRRING ADVENTURES

Gregorio still took the precaution to keep on the rocky ground, so as to leave no tracks for the lynx eyed warriors, and stepped off briskly, animated by the hope that within three or four days at most, if no evil luck befell him, he would see his dear mother again.

He intended to travel as fast as he could safely, keeping his eyes open for Indians. For he thought he must be getting nearly opposite to the Indian village, and scouting parties most likely would be out on foot looking for him, and would cross over the crest as he had, on foot and search for him or his tracks. He would stand a poor chance for his liberty or even his life, if they once got on his trail and found the direction in which he was traveling.

The warriors who had gone out on horseback to find the little fellow had returned, and reported that no sign of him was found to the east, and he must either be to the west, or had gone off to the north and would be starved, die of thirst, or be killed by a wild beast. They were greatly comforted in their chagrin, by these pleasant anticipations of what was in store for the brave little boy.

Patiently he trudged along until late in the evening, and again the question of something for a late dinner or early supper became uppermost in his mind, and more apparent in his stomach's lusty call, like Oliver Twist, for "more."

He came suddenly on an immense flock of blue quail. These beautiful birds, common all over the Southwest, are marked as pretty on the breast as a prize Plymouth Rock cock, the breast of the male being tinged with a yellowish chrome color. The female is of paler color. When they turn to run from you, the back of their topknot that is shaped like that of the cardinal or red bird and is blue in front, is white as snow. They are plump and round, a trifle heavier than Bob White, but so fleet of foot that it takes a man running at full speed to catch one even with its wing broken; chances even then are that the wounded bird will run into a wood rat's hole and escape.

The quail have a world of curiosity, a fact well known to Gregorio; so as soon as he spied them, he dropped down on his knees behind a bush and dropped his gourd and rope. Then he peered over the top of the bush and ducked down his head quickly.

The birds had started off at full speed at first, uttering their cry of danger, quee-che, quee-che, quee-che. But as they were not followed they stopped and faced the boy; when his strange painted face now appeared, now disappeared, the curious quail began to come back towards him, crowding up in a bunch. At each move made by the little hunter they came nearer to him, until at last he sent an arrow with unerring skill in the center of the bunch and pinned two of the birds together.

Before they recovered from surprise he sent another arrow through one, and might have killed several more, but the fluttering of the wounded birds was too much for Cito's nerves, and he bounded in among the covey, sending them to the right and left.

This was a pretty good starter for supper, and the fugitives pushed on. Gregorio's face being now turned towards home, he felt no fatigue, and did not follow the covey, but trusted to adding to their store by finding some other kind of game. He felt too, that the time was better spent hurrying away from such a dangerous locality.

Along towards sundown Cito made a dash into a thicket and Gregorio heard a noise like some one dancing and using castanets, or rather more like "Bones" in the Negro minstrels keeping up his end.

Cito came dashing out again in a bigger hurry than he had gone in, and close behind him came six or seven animals of dark bluish color and with a brown band on the shoulder.

Gregorio knew at once what they were, and dropping all his load he took to his heels with all speed, heading towards the nearest tree, knowing that the dog would run straight to him.

He just had time to climb up out of reach, when Cito passed just under him, with a drove of javelinas at his heels. As they caught sight of Gregorio, they stopped and looked up in the tree, popping their teeth.

The javelinas or wild hogs are very dangerous, being quick in their movements, and until they have been hunted a great deal, [they are] absolutely without fear of man or beast. They do not strike sideways as the common boar does, for their tusks are set straight up and down, but the tusks are sharp as a razor. The javelina grabs hold as a dog would, and soon cuts a dog to pieces.

Cito had been sampled by them once and he had no idea of letting them get hold of him again.

If Gregorio had been armed as was Peter Parley's Indian with a blow gun and a lot of poisoned arrows, he could have laid in enough meat to do him all winter; but with his bow he could only have stuck an arrow in one's back, enough to make it real fighting mad.

Cito had no idea of deserting his young master; as soon as the javelinas stopped following him he turned and made a dash at them, when the whole herd took after him again.

This was Gregorio's chance, and jumping down, he gathered up his things and started off at top speed, and was soon out of sight. After Cito had led the herd off after him he gave them the dodge, and being much swifter afoot, was soon back at the tree. Finding his master gone, he took his trail and tore off after him, and soon overtook him to the joy of both.

They were now down in the prickly pear region, which abounded in cottontail, quail, and a small squirrel not unlike the chipmunk in size, but lacking its pretty bars, being yellowish colored, with numerous white spots on it.

Kangaroo rats there were, too, with their short fore-legs and long hind-legs which gives them their name. The wood rat, blue in color with white stomach, also lives in the cactus plains; he is an architect, building a house and using every loose thing he can carry until a round mound is built two or three feet high. This is to turn the rain off from the house and the ground. The house has several doors around it, showing the architect's cuteness, as rattlesnakes follow him and if there were only one way of getting out the rattlesnake would have him penned up.

The sun was getting low and Gregorio thought it best to be on the lookout for a place where he could get his supper and a safe place to sleep, for at that time of the year the prickly pears were still very abundant, and all kinds of game had collected to feed on them. Bears, deer, coyotes, quail, and mountain lions are fond of them, but the wildcats and lions come to feed on the deer, turkeys, and small game, rather than on the pears. Here, too, the rattlesnake lies coiled up in some well beaten trail, perfectly motionless, and being the color of the ground, rats, rabbits, and quail fall an easy prey to him.

XIII
A Foraging Expedition

Gregorio found a deep arroyo running in the direction he wanted to go, and followed on down it. He knew he would come to a cliff after awhile, where he would find a cave. He found a cliff on the south side of the arroyo, and warmed by the sun, made a little fire. Cleaning his three quail, he cooked them—not a very large meal for a hungry boy and dog.

Gregorio got the meat and Cito the bones, as he could grind them up into meal. Neither felt at all satisfied, and Gregorio concluded as it was only sunset, to look around for something more.

There was no water hole where he could hide and watch for game, but nevertheless there were plenty of quail and cottontails. Nature makes provision for her creatures, and if water were absolutely necessary to sustain life, million of acres of arid lands in the west would be entirely without animal life. Black-tail deer, antelope, blue quail, coyotes, panthers, rats, and squirrels, live and grow fat without being in thirty miles of water or twice that. They always find some young and tender plant, or eat the young and thornless leaves of the prickly pear, that answer for both food and water. During the heat of the day they find shade and remain quiet until towards the cool of evening.

Doves must have water, and there is no better evidence of water being near than to see doves late in the evening flying in a given direction. Many a thirsty hunter has found water by watching their evening flight, so they are useful even when there is no food.

Gregorio did not have to go very far before he found a cottontail, as sunset is their favorite time for promenading. He sent an arrow through him, and returned to camp. As the water in his gourd was getting quite low, he cut off the hind quarters of the rabbit after skinning them, and washed them, giving Cito the other portion. Gregorio put his on a stick and stuck it up before the fire until it was nice and brown. But he could not eat it in peace for Cito, having finished his share, took up a convenient position to watch his young master finish his.

Every time the boy took a bite, Cito's eyes followed the meat, and when it was lowered, Cito cocked his head on one side and licked his chops. This got Gregorio so badly hypnotized that he felt like throwing the hind quarters at his head, but he thought of a better plan. So he tore them in two, and gave Cito one half. This broke the spell. The dog never knows when he has enough, but as some Yale graduates do not do any better, Cito was not to be blamed.

Gregorio then began to climb up and examine the cave to see what sort of accommodation it would afford. Although it was not as safe as the other cave, because a bear or panther could have climbed up as easily as he did, he found plenty of room, and saw that he could use some loose pieces of rock, and build up a wall at the only place where any animal could reach them.

He then went down and gathered up some leaves, pulling up his cloth full with his rope. Cito had to be hoisted up over places too high and steep for him to jump or climb, and after they got in the cave, Gregorio gathered up enough loose rocks to build a small Chinese wall to keep out all enemies.

Gregorio crossed himself, and prayed to the Virgin to protect him and make him a good boy, and was soon asleep. Nothing like solitude, danger, and a dark night to bring out a boy's piety.

He was awakened at daylight by the howling of a pack of the grey wool wolves. The grey wolf is in size between the buffalo wolf and the coyote, or prairie wolf, and his is a most dismal melancholy howl.

The wolves were so close that the boy was startled and Cito jumped up and tumbled over his master, not so sure about the Chinese wall.

Gregorio could hardly believe it was daylight, so soundly had he slept; but making his toilet was a brief affair, and removing all the rocks again, so the cave would look natural, he scrambled down hastily to the bed of the creek, and was soon stepping off at a good gait towards home. Not counting station stops for quail or cottontail sandwiches, Gregorio intended to make his greatest day's travel.

XIV
INDIANS

The little arroyo led down into a larger one, that he crossed and climbed to the top of the next hill. Here he was cautious enough to stop behind some rocks and take a careful survey of the next ridge for he knew he would be exposed to view in case any of the Indians should be on the hill.

He had about concluded it was safe to go over the brow of the hill, when his keen eyes caught a flash of light made by the sun on a moving lance blade, off to the east towards the Indian village.

At first he could not see anything but an occasional bright flash of the lance. But after a little he could see it was a party of warriors following down the ridge towards the plains.

Gregorio squatted down, hardly daring to show his nose. It was surely a lucky thing for him that he had not passed over the crest of the hill or ahead of them, for when they got opposite to where he was, he saw they were examining closely every foot of ground they passed over, and it would have been a miracle if some of them had not seen his tracks.

Being so close he would have suffered the fate of the "early worm" had he been a little farther on his way. It made his heart almost jump out his mouth to think how near he came to being lost.

The Indians passed on toward the west and the little fugitive kept his eye on them not daring to move.

Much depended on which direction the party took after reaching the valley. If they turned to the south, it would be nearly impossible for him to escape, as they would be zigzagging looking for him or his trail, and he would be liable to run upon them at any moment watching for him.

So he was delighted to see them after reaching the valley, turn towards the northwest across the plains, evidently satisfied that he had not passed back south, and that they would find him towards the north of their village, for they argued as he had not passed along on the foot hills, his trail must be in the valley.

It was a good thing for Gregorio that he had turned up into the hills to find a safe place to sleep or he would have been camping near where the warriors passed, and the place where he built a fire would have been found, as the smell of smoke can be detected at a good distance.

When he saw them going away from the direction of his trail and camp, he fell on his knees and fervently thanked the Virgin for protecting him.

He now followed a gulch that ran down towards the main arroyo, and then turned up towards the mountains knowing that was the safest place for him.

He turned into the first little brush that came from the south, and almost trotted, so anxious was he to put as much distance between himself and the dreaded warriors as possible, and in the least possible time.

It was with feelings of intense relief that he passed the trail of the Indians on top of the hill—knowing they were going in an opposite direction.

He saw several rabbits and a good many mountain quail and blue quail, but the sight of the warriors had taken away his appetite. The mountain quail or fool quail, as the cowboy call them, because they are so stupid they kill them with cow whips or rocks, would hardly get out of the way. Gregorio had no other thought but to get away from that part of the country as fast as possible, and made no attempt to kill any game.

Thus, the little boy and dog dredged along, and every time they got to the top of the hill they were cheered by a sight of the gap in the distant mountains but it did not seem much nearer than it did when he saw it from the top of the main mountain.

Towards evening, Gregorio found he was not only very tired, but also very hungry. Both dinner and breakfast hours had passed without a halt, and the more he thought about how nice broiled quail, or fat tender, barbecued squirrel would be, the hungrier he became.

But as usual the cottontails sped away like the old Nick was after them and got into their holes in the rocks, Cito making a good second in the race. The blue quail flew long before he got close to them, and kept on the wing as far as he could see them.

At last the tired, hungry little hunter came onto a large covey of mountain quail, and those beautiful little birds sustained their reputation for being fool quail. He did not see them until they were at his feet, and not then until he heard a soft, flute like note, and they began to move in front of him. To drop his traps and place an arrow on his bow was the work of a moment, and he sent it through one.

But Cito put a sudden end to the hunt by making a rush for the fluttering bird, and flushed the covey. They did not fly very far, however, and giving Cito a tap on the head with his bow to let him know he was to wait for orders in hunting birds, though quite right in hunting squirrels or rabbits, the boy followed in the direction taken by the birds.

He soon found them again and shot two more, which made a good beginning for a meal. The boy had a pretty good idea of his own capacity to stow away birds, but no limit could be fixed for the dog's, and he continued on the march hoping to get something more, for it would take as much time to cook three birds as a dozen.

He was rewarded for his patience when a young jackrabbit started up before him, and after making a few jumps stopped, and looked back over his shoulders.

Cito's appetite got the best of his judgement, and he made a break for Jack, but the rabbit found his legs and flew. Cito put up a good quarter race, keeping close to his heels.

Gregorio knew the habit of the jackrabbit of returning to his form, and sat down to wait for him. Cito had the keen scent of his ancestor, the coyote, and also his speed, and followed the trail after losing sight of the quarry.

Pretty soon Gregorio saw Jack coming, his long ears laid on his neck; running up close to his bed Jack stopped, lying so close [to] the ground one could scarcely see him. The boy sent an arrow through him, and he gave a squall that made Gregorio's hair stand on end for he feared some lurking warrior might be in hearing and would investigate at once. He ran to the little beast and grabbed his arrow, intending to knock him in the head; but freed from the arrow, Jack started off as if nothing was the matter with him, and would have got away from Gregorio. But Cito had been following and knew what the squall meant so he took the trail, now easily followed as it had blood on it, and soon found the rabbit, dead.

Now there was a plenty for a good square meal; for a young jackrabbit is fat and tender, and is pretty good eating, especially with a good appetite as sauce, and nothing better in sight.

Gregorio soon got to one of those deep arroyos and followed down it, but as it was getting quite late, and seeing no cliff where a cave might be found, he stopped at the edge of a thicket. After making a small fire in the thicket, he cut the jack in two, and gave Cito the fore quarters, skinning the hind quarters for himself. Washing them he put them on a stick before the fire, and began picking the quail for his next morning's breakfast.

Both the little travelers made a good meal, and after a drop of water apiece from the almost empty gourd, they started once more in the direction of the gap.

Towards sunset they came to a deep arroyo, and Gregorio decided to follow it up towards the mountains, but remembering how cold it was, concluded to stop at the first cave he could find in the cliffs. He soon found one, crawled in, scraped away a smooth place, and dropped off in sleep.

XV
The Wolves' Concert

Gregorio was roused from a sound sleep by the howling of a pack of big buffalo wolves, or lobos as the Mexicans call them. It startled him from a pleasant dream of home, for he had been thinking of his mother all day, and our dreams are often echoes of daily events.

As the pack was just in front of him in the bed of the arroyo, their blood curdling howls made the cold chills run up and down his back, and Cito, as on a former occasion, put his master between himself and danger.

As soon as the boy got his ideas collected, curiosity prompted him to take a look, and he had a good view of what one seldom has an opportunity of seeing, a pack of wolves in the act of howling.

The old leader of the band begins by sticking his nose straight up in the air, and giving a long mournful note, as an introduction to the sonata; the others join in, gathering quickly in a circle around him and jumping in a circle around him and jumping up and down. The females sing soprano, the young males taking the alto part, and the old wolves howl bass.

The yells of the pack had scarcely died away before he heard far in the distance the cry of other lobos; and then the coyotes took up the refrain, and with their ki-yi-yi put in several frills and trills high above concert pitch.

As soon as the concert was over the pack of lobos trotted off down the arroyo, while Gregorio and Cito climbed down from "Sprawls hotel," and started up the creek. For the boy felt pretty sure that the wolves had come from a tank or spring of water, and were making for where the prickly pears were, and game more abundant.

As Gregorio and his little dog moved swiftly up the bed of the arroyo, several flocks of doves flew swiftly by them, almost touching Gregorio's head, and going up the creek. So he knew that he would soon find water. Deer were seen, and a flock of turkeys were calling to each other, scattered no doubt by wild cats, that always lie in wait for them at the springs.

Gregorio also, whenever there was any sand in the bed of the creek, saw bear, deer, and jaguar tracks. He was afraid to approach this watering place by traveling up the bed of the stream where he could be easily seen, and he was not so sure but what some horrid, painted warrior might be hid in a thicket on the lookout for a certain little runaway prisoner and a little dog. He believed that if caught, he would be killed and scalped, and the dog skinned; so he left the bed of the creek, and took to the brush keeping parallel with it. It was much harder work, and slower progress was made, but it was safer.

XVI
The Leopard's Prey

Gregorio worked his way along until he struck a trail running down the mountain side towards the water. He had a plain view of the tank of water, below a fall in the bed of the creek. A herd of deer was standing around drinking, and he knew from that, that no Indians were near the watering place, for these intelligent animals have a wonderfully delicate sense of smell, and would have detected the odor of their foes, had they been there any time during the previous night.

Gregorio was afraid to walk in this path, for although bears or other game might obscure his tracks, yet, if one of his tracks, or even a portion of one, should be seen by the Indians, they would be able to tell how long it had been made, and follow it. The Indians and old frontiersmen, too, read these signs as other people do books. Knowing this, he kept the path in view and moved slowly and cautiously down towards the tank, until he got where he had a good view of it, and made sure that no warriors, bears, leopards, or panthers were around.

While closely watching the herd of deer, his attention was riveted on an object that at first he took to be a snake that had climbed up a tree, as snakes frequently do in search of birds' eggs or young birds. The object was moving up and down with a nervous kind of twitching as though swallowing a young bird.

At first he saw only about a foot of it, but his keen eye following it, detected a large yellow object and soon outlined the body of an immense leopard; it was the tail he had seen, kept moving in the same nervous way pussy waves her tail when she is watching a bird feeding near her. It was fortunate for him he had not gone down the path at once. The leopard had been so intent watching the deer that he had not seen or heard the boy and dog though within seventy-five yards.

The deer, having quenched their thirst, finally started back up the trail towards the tree where the leopard lay stretched out on a large limb directly over the path. Instinct guiding him, the big cat had watched the deer from one side of the trail until they passed this tree and then climbed up in it. The advantage of the wind being in his favor, the deer could not smell him.

The herd came on very leisurely, stopping to look and listen now and then, the fawns, now nearly grown, running and skipping ahead. A stately old buck with immense horns brought up the rear, keeping pretty well back, for age and former experience had made him crafty, and he may have thought, if a leopard is watching for us, he will take a doe or fawn, and I will escape.

But the leopard with greedy eyes had selected the buck for his meal; the other deer passed the tree safely, but as the wary old buck got to it there was a flash of yellow, the leopard landed on the back of the poor fellow and bore him to the ground. After a brief struggle the leopard had him by the throat, and put an end to his pitiful bleat of agony and fear.

The rest of the herd scattered, tearing through the brush, and sending rocks and gravel in showers down the steep hillside. One of the animals came near running over Gregorio, and Cito, not knowing of the dangerous brute so near, could not lose sight of the main chance for breakfast, and made a grab for him. But Gregorio was seized with the general panic, and ran as fast as his legs would take him in the direction taken by the frightened deer, anxious to get away from such a dangerous neighborhood.

Water, however, he must have, and after traveling along parallel with the arroyo for a mile he turned toward it again and followed up the bed for a mile or more. At last he found a place where the water barely seeped up to the top of the ground, and from the turkey tracks around, he had hopes of getting one.

He laid aside his load and began digging in the damp earth with both hands. Soon he had quite a deep hole. As it was not quite clear or deep enough to fill his gourd he sat down at the foot of a tree to wait and rest. A squirrel, which was there for water too, and as long as the boy kept working had kept mute, now had his curiosity excited and began to chatter a little at first, but finally broke into a loud angry tone, and began to come slowly down the tree.

Gregorio sat motionless, and Cito never showed that he heard the squirrel at all, except by working his little ears. Ages had developed in his wolf ancestors the necessity for cunning in securing daily food, and this cunning had descended to Cito. To have gone rushing around and barking like an ordinary dog, would have meant to go hungry. So he remained motionless and his master sat ready with an arrow on his bow.

The squirrel came down the tree, stopping at convenient limbs to bark and wag his tail. When he was right over the young archer, Gregorio sent an arrow through his heart and he dropped into Cito's jaws, too far gone to offer a fight.

Gregorio kept grabbing at his arrow to keep the dog from whipping it to pieces, for Cito's nose was still sore from the bite given him in the last squirrel hunt, and he was taking revenge out on this one—two legged dogs do the same thing sometimes.

XVII
A Turkey Dinner

The water in the hole was not yet quite clear enough to fill the gourd, so Gregorio concluded to wait awhile. The seep spring seemed to be a favorite place for small game to water, the large tank below being too closely watched by wild rats, foxes, and bobcats, as well as leopards and panthers, that did not object to a fat turkey now and then as a change of diet.

He had not waited very long until he heard the yelping of a turkey. Quickly he hid in a thicket close to the spring, making Cito lie down behind him, but that was not hard to do, as the little dog crept along as carefully as a coyote trying to crawl close to a fat hen.

The yelping continued, and occasionally the gobblers would turn loose, as they often do in places where they are not hunted. Spring is the time when they do their best, and they afford great sport to hunters, though none but an expert can yelp so as to fool an old gobbler that has been shot around a few times.

Gregorio determined to risk losing another arrow, in the effort to kill a turkey, for being hungry, visions of a fat roast turkey were very inspiring. He would almost smell it.

But having doubts about being able to kill one by using his bow in the ordinary way he decided to adopt the squaw plan—to lie on his back, put his feet against the bow, and use both hands on the string.

The turkeys were coming towards the spring yelping and jumping in the air with spread wings and seemed quite delighted to find the spring in so much better condition than usual; the older ones, however, eyed with suspicion the pile of dirt the boy had thrown out.

A tremendous old gobbler came waddling along, so fat he could hardly walk, and pushed aside the younger turkeys in a most pompous manner. After getting his drink, he stepped out of the circle around the water, and began attitudinizing. With his head nearly reaching the ground, and his brilliant feathers shining in the sun, he was indeed a beautiful bird; he had his bill stuck up in the air in a supercilious way, and his wings dropped a little, the feathers standing out.

All this suddenly changed when he saw something move only a little in the thicket; his feather dropped at once, and his lordly air changed, as he gave the turkey signal of danger—"put, put, put"—and turned to run.

But Gregorio had taken good aim, and sent an arrow squarely in his back, reaching his vitals. He ran with cropping wings, and the ever alert Cito dashed after him. Overtaking him in the bed of the arroyo, he grabbed him by the neck.

For awhile it was hard to tell which was on top or which was dog and which turkey, for a large old wild gobbler, even in his dying struggles, is very strong and uses his wings like a drummer does his sticks.

Cito knew his dinner depended on hanging on, so he never turned loose his grip until Gregorio came up. Then the gobbler quit flopping his wings, and used his long legs, armed with a pair of spurs like a game cock.

Cito was a comical sight then, his mouth full of feathers, and a grin that seemed to say, Didn't we do that old gobbler up in style?

The arrow was broken beyond repair, but Gregorio was only too glad to make the exchange, for now he had a good supply of meat of the best kind, and still had four arrows left.

With a knife he could have made some arrows, for those the boys around the Indians and Mexican villages used were made of a species of cane, called carrizo—not so tough as our cane. A piece of hard wood was put in the hollow at the point, fastened with wet sinew, and after being hardened in the fire it was made very sharp. For killing small birds in the trees, an arrow with a knob on the end was used so as not to stick in the tree limbs or tear the bird to pieces.

An arrow used by the warriors was a different affair, being made of dogwood switches or wild china. The bark was stripped off and the arrow shaft was run through a groove made in two pieces of sand stone until it was the same size from end to end, then a spike of iron, brass, or copper, made as keen as possible, was inserted. The Indians in early days used to pick up old pieces of hoop around the forts, for making pikes, but after they got to be "in amity with Uncle Sam," steel and iron spikes were made by the keg full, and distributed at Fort Sill, and other Indian reservations—and many were left sticking in butchered men, women, children, and cattle along the frontier. These arrow heads were fastened on with sinew from deer or buffalo. This sinew as soon as it was shot into a person, got wet and soft, and came off, leaving the spike in the wound. Indians rarely used poisoned arrows; they were too dangerous, as in handling them a warrior might cut himself.

There was now plenty of food in camp, and Gregorio did not try to kill any more turkeys, though a number were sitting around in trees, scared up by Cito's rushing through them. Gregorio felt a little uneasy about the fresh feathers in the bed of the creek—a common enough thing around where wild cats are, but it might show the Indians his work on the spring; so he moved the mound of dirt and after filling his water gourd, he scattered leaves around the spring to conceal his tracks, trusting the turkeys would soon obliterate his tracks entirely.

It would not do to cook near the water. So he went back into a thicket, and found a cave in a cliff entirely out of sight, should any warriors pass down the arroyo. The old gobbler made quite a load, but Gregorio took along the squirrel too. A person who has once suffered from hunger in the woods, is not apt to throw away anything good to eat.

A fire was built up against the back of the cave, and the squirrel was dressed and propped up before the blaze. Then as soon as he picked away some of the feathers from the breast of the old gobbler it, too, was cut and several slices were set before the fire on clear rocks. The turkey then was picked and cleaned nicely and after the meat was cut off it did not seem so very large; the legs and back were put before the fire, and Cito got the carcass and never stopped cracking bones until he had stowed away the long neck clean to the bill.

XVIII
GREGORIO TRAPPED AT LAST

As soon as the squirrel was done, Gregorio began his meal, and being free from Cito's inquisitive looks, he enjoyed both squirrel and turkey. After a drink of water he was ready to travel again. But all the turkey was not cooked quite enough. So he went to a Spanish dagger and managed with his flint knife to cut several of the long leaves; heating them before the fire he tore them into stirps, and made a very good basket to carry his barbecued meat in.

Cito was so full he was in misery—for once both had a full meal. The little dog coiled up before the fire, as much as to say, this is a good camp; the best thing I've struck and I would like to stay here a week or so. But not so the boy; the mother's face was before him, and shouldering his load he left his pleasant camp with some regret.

Cito raised his head and looked in astonishment, the idea of leaving a place where they had water, wood, game, and a nice dry cave—that, according to his experience among the Indians, was all that was necessary to happiness. But as soon as Gregorio spoke to him he got up, shook himself all the way out to the end of his tail, and trotted off after him.

Gregorio filled his water gourd at the spring, taking a good drink himself, and Cito followed his example. Then once more they struck out for home.

Towards noon Cito spied what he thought was a jackrabbit, darting through the brush. He gave immediate chase, but had not gone far until Gregorio heard him returning. It sounded like a pony race—Cito ran straight to his master's feet and whirled around brave enough. A pack of coyotes was just behind him, and came near running over both boy and dog; but the coyotes were as badly scared as either, when they saw a painted warrior, and took the back track. Cito made a bluff by rushing after them at prudent distance— every dog that has been interviewed by four or five coyotes, has his bump of caution enlarged a bit. Gregorio and Cito were both glad enough to play quits with such ugly looking customers.

Dinner came around again, and as a long tramp had been made, the hungry boy concluded to stop and warm over his barbecued turkey. So he turned into a deep gulch and soon had a little fire kindled of dry wood. Placing the meat on some clean rocks he soon had it warmed and almost envied Cito the large pieces of turkey white meat he had to give him. For although they had seen plenty of game, and almost walked over fool quail and cottontails, Gregorio had not thought to kill any for Cito, but had put all his energies into his feet to get over as much ground as possible.

Dinner over, he felt like taking a nap, but as the water in his gourd was getting quite low, he was afraid he might oversleep himself. So he started off again. As he mounted the crest of each one of the "hogbacks" that ran from the mountains to the plains, he saw the beautiful gap in the mountains, and it seemed only a little way off. The rays of the setting sun shining against the cliffs made it appear as only a matter of a few miles until he would reach the little adobe house and its grape-vine arbor, his mother at the door watching with longing heart, and tearful eyes for her little boy.

His pleasant reverie was rudely broken, for he heard a loud savage snort. Looking ahead not over seventy-five yards, he saw a cinnamon bear and two cubs feeding on prickly pear fruit. The old she bear had heard the noise, as a bear has a wonderfully acute sense of hearing, and rearing on her hind legs, she caught sight of the boy and made straight for him.

Cito had heard the noise and ran forward to see what it meant. This attracted attention of the bear, and saved the life of his young master, for the cinnamon bear is the crossest, most ill natured beast in the woods, and the she bear is especially savage when she had cubs and thinks her young are in the least danger.

So when she met Cito coming full speed toward her cubs, she gave a savage growl and took after him; he had been in many a scrap with bears when with the Indians, and was on his guard. Running to a bunch of thick chaparral and prickly pear, he disappeared under the thorny brush, knowing full well the big beast could not follow him.

This changed her course a little but she now started after Gregorio, popping her teeth and giving a horrid snort. Run, run, little boy! For your life depends on your heels; once she overtakes you, you will be no more than a mouse in pussy's claws.

Gregorio knew the danger, and knew too that his only chance for life was to get to a small tree with few limbs and climb up out of reach, before the old bear got to him. Gregorio selected a tree only some fifty yards distant, and dropping all his baggage, he ran for it.

But the infuriated old monster, swift though seeming so clumsy, beat him to it.

Poor little Gregorio glanced around and saw the terrible shape looming up. Now he felt the beast's hot breath, as the bear reared to strike him down.

Instinct told him that there was no escape from an awful death. Agonized with fear, the poor little boy gave one piercing shriek, and there was no one to hear his cry.

XIX
BRAVE LITTLE CITO

Poor little Gregorio covered his face with his arms and sank to his knees in terror, before the dreadful shape that threatened instant death.

But Cito, the wolf dog, had been watching the bear from his safe retreat in the low growing thicket, where the prickly pear, the agave, and the interlacing spikes of the "wolf's candle" protected him from the savage beast's attack. He saw the bear pass him and saw her rush upon his little master. That was too much for the faithful dog to endure, and he broke from cover and made for the bear as fast as his half civilized four legs and bristly tail could drive him.

It certainly did look as it were all up with Gregorio, and Cito darted like the wind, his instinct telling him that his master was in awful peril.

Now the bear was rearing on her hind legs, preparing to strike Gregorio down with her mighty paw. The bear intent on her natural enemy, now her prey, expected no attack from the rear.

But Cito, rushing up being the bear, has seized a hind leg in his jaws like a steel trap, and has given it a crunch and a jerk that almost upsets Mrs. Cinnamon.

Cito is taking no foolish chances, and letting go he makes for the nearest clump of thorny brush.

The old she bear, more surprised than hurt, turns quickly and takes out after the little raider. Cito darts out and in, and leads Mrs. Bear a merry chase, now snapping at a leg and now disappearing behind a hedge of cactus.

Now the bear turns toward Gregorio again, where he is trying to climb a tree, but Cito rushes at her and worries her into another savage charge.

At last Cito executed a movement that entitled him clearly to every bit of the breast meat of the next fat turkey. Instead of turning after the old mother bear, Cito ran straight for one of the scared little cubs and gave the cub such a shake up that it roared with fright and pain.

This so infuriated the old bear that she gave up all thought of the boy, now safely in his tree, and went after Cito to annihilate him for his imprudence. Cito skillfully led the old bear from thicket to thicket, always away from Gregorio's tree, and finally made a long circuit and was well out of reach of the thoroughly outwitted old murderer.

Gregorio had witnessed the whole performance from his safe perch up in the tree, and now he slipped down, gathered up his bow, arrows, and other traps, and started off with all speed. Cito, having given the bear the dodge, as on former occasions, when javelinas followed him, returned to the tree. Gregorio was not there, but taking his master's trail, Cito went bounding after him.

Soon he joined his master, and capering around Gregorio in the greatest glee, he wagged his tail, and looked up with a grin, as much as to say, didn't we do up the old bear in fine style! I bet the cub won't forget the shaking I gave him as long as he lives.

Gregorio took the little dog up in his arms and kissed him and petted him and cried over him all the endearing terms he could think of. If a sack of gold had been offered him at that moment for Cito it would have been declined.

XX
The Warfare of Nature

After such hard excitement, Cito and Gregorio were sure enough hungry. Seeking shade, they finished the last of the barbecued turkey meat, and taking a hearty drink, after a little rest, they started off again.

As they must now depend on the bow and arrow for food, Gregorio turned again towards the valley, where small game was more abundant.

Gregorio came near stepping on an immense rattlesnake coiled up in a path. It was also looking out for supper. He hardly knew which way to jump; when he first heard the rattler give his chay-r-r-r-r, it was difficult to locate him, as the sound seemed to be all around him. Gregorio was frightened, but dropping everything, he gathered up some rocks and began to throw at him. The snake uncoiled, keeping up his music, and crawled as fast as he could toward a rat nest near by, and would have gone down in the rat's hole in the ground.

Gregorio began to think he never would hit him, but at last a lucky lick struck his back and stopped him. Gregorio, after pounding him until he was dead, pulled off his rattles to take home and show his mother and father so they could see what a brave boy they had, and also what danger he had passed through.

Tramping along, Gregorio came in sight of two chaparral cocks, "road-runners," or as the Mexicans call them *paisanos*, (countrymen or peasants); at first he was greatly puzzled to know what they were up to, for they were moving back and forth towards each other like two little girls dancing, and they held out their wings pretty much as the little maidens would have held out their dresses. They were circling around some object on the ground, and when one would spring back or into the air, the other would spring forward and strike at something. Gregorio walked up quite close, as the birds were so intent on what they were doing, that they never paid any attention to him; so led by curiosity, he stopped to see what they were doing.

The birds feed almost entirely on lizards and small snakes, and do not hesitate to attack quite large ones. These two birds were fighting a rattlesnake, and using as much skill as a prize fighter trying for an opening. One would advance as close as he could, keeping his wing thrown out and approaching sideways, he would make a feint with his wing. When the snake struck at him, he would spring quickly back, and the other bird, taking advantage of the snake's being stretched out, would jump and give a blow with his long sharp bill. Finally, one bird gave the snake a blow on the head that addled him so they quickly made a finish of him.

Whether they had attacked for the purpose of making a meal off of him or for sport, Gregorio did not know. But although he had eaten a good many "*paisanos*," and was fond of them, as they are nearly always very fat, he decided he would not harm either of those brave birds, and so went on his way. Many things are told of this bird that have no foundation in truth. It is gravely stated that if they find a rattlesnake asleep, they will pile cactus and prickly pear thorns around him, and he cannot crawl over them, and so dies a miserable death. This is not likely, as the rattlesnake has a tough skin, and is not heavy enough to cause the thorns to enter his body—crawling among cactus thorns is one of his daily occupations. The chaparral cock is a born robber, and will eat every hen or bird egg he can find; he also eats young birds, and frequently kills young chickens. But the main supply of food comes from lizards, and the bird is so swift that even the green striped lizard that runs so swiftly is no match for him, and unless the lizard dodges into some brush or runs into a hole, he will be picked up after a very short race.

Gregorio and Cito kept up a steady gait until near sunset, and had no trouble in killing all the quail and cottontails needed for supper and breakfast. So far, except on the first night, Gregorio had been lucky enough to find a cave and so roost high, as chickens prefer to do. But as the shades of evening now began to lengthen, and no friendly cave could be found he stopped in a deep canyon and cooked his birds, giving his brave little dog all the rabbit meat he wanted.

After supper he selected a thorny thicket and began to make a temporary house and fort; for the fact that he had been chased by a bear that day, and barely escaped a horrible death, was too fresh in his mind to be forgotten. He took a load of leaves and fixed his bed, and then by using dead trees made a frame. This he covered over with quite a coat of green weeds, and the worst thorns he could find, mixing in different kinds of cactus, leaving only a hole that he and Cito could crawl through to get to his bedroom; next, he gathered quite a lot of species of cactus that grows in links like sausages, and easily breaks off if stepped on, and these he scattered plentifully all round his little home, only a narrow path for himself and Cito being left.

After he got inside, with a stick he filled the path, and it would have taken a bold animal to attack this hastily made citadel. All animals avoid this species of cactus, as its thorns are bearded like a fish hook and can only be pulled out by tearing the skin and flesh. The little Indian dog has a time of it when he accidentally steps on one, for he tries to pull it out, with his teeth, and the points that set in every direction stick in his mouth and fasten mouth and foot together, and he rolls over and gets full of them, howling with pain, joined in his lamentations by the old squaw and children. The squaw has to pull the thorns all out, and put him on her pack if afoot, or on her horse behind her, where he sits up very contentedly. (This may be a scheme for doggie to fool his mistress, and get a ride. I know some little girls who after running all evening and starting home late, suddenly get "so lame" that papa or mama has to carry them.)

After a prayer to the Virgin Mary, Gregorio was soon fast asleep, and knew no more until daylight. He was awakened by the usual serenade, the ever present coyote taking the leading part, quail, scattered by some marauding civet cat or skunk, calling to one another, and numerous birds filling the woods with sweetest melody; an impudent squirrel had noticed him, too, and began chattering. Gregorio took a stick and pulled all of the joint cactus from his path, he crawled out, followed by Cito stepping very carefully.

A fire being made, breakfast was soon cooked, Cito taking his rabbit raw, though he enjoyed chewing up the bird bones thrown to him. Both took a good drink, and they again started out briskly for home, Gregorio hoping to reach the pass by noon. As he had a view of it on the first ridge he climbed, it seemed so very near his heart leaped with joy, and he increased his gait. Alas, it was much farther away than he dreamed, and new dangers were to be braved before he could reach it.

XXI
GREGORIO LOSES HIS WAY

Gregorio kept up a brisk walk, but as he reached the top of a ridge a great white cloud came between him and the sun. It appeared to drag along the ground, and almost before he knew it, it was so dark he could not see things distinctly a hundred yards off. He did not feel at all sure now about the course he was going, but not wishing to stop he kept moving. After a two hour tramp he descended quite a steep bank, and found himself in the bed of a creek. He started down it feeling pretty sure that he was making good headway, and that this gulch was sure to run to one of the main arroyos coming from the mountains.

All at once he came on a fresh fire. Some of the pieces of wood were still smoking, and Gregorio was panic stricken for he naturally thought it must be the Indians on the watch for him.

He turned to run, but what was his confusion to see a rude brush hut, and the joint cactus all around it—it was his own camp of the night before!

He remembered now how he had heard his father and friends in talking say that persons when they lost their way, were almost sure to travel in a circle, and that the best thing to do, when it was cloudy and they could not see the sun, was to stop and wait until the sun came out and they could get their bearings.

Poor Gregorio was tired and disappointed, and as it was quite chilly he built up the fire a little and sat before it warming himself. Cito hugged the fire pretty close, too; when it got too hot he would move quickly back, and stare at the blaze as though he thought it would jump at him.

The clouds that had been dragging along on the ground now arose in the air and disappeared as suddenly as they came; the blue sky never looked so beautiful to the boy.

Again he started on his journey, and on top of the next ridge he again saw the pass. The sun was shining full on the cliffs, and it appeared to be not more than an hour's travel away. Onward the little fellow pushed, almost at a trot, his heart full of hope, but the sun gradually rose above the distant mountain peaks, higher and higher, and ridge after ridge was crossed, and still the pass appeared to be about the same distance off.

Gregorio was getting thoroughly tired out, and it was quite hot again since the sun had come out. The water in the gourd, too, was getting quite low, and that worried him as much as the thought of Indians, for they, if they caught him, might show him some mercy, but thirst, the insatiable fiend of the desert, he knew would not.

He thought of a great, cold, clear spring near Santa Rosa that burst from under a cliff, and of the cool water in the *olla* hanging up in the shade at home, and of all the cool water he had ever seen. He saw himself kneeling down and drinking at the great spring, and thought how, running quickly into town, he would surprise his mother and all the family at the supper table. So full was he of such sweet pictures that he naturally increased his gait.

XXII
AN ADVENTURE WITH A PANTHER

But all his bright hopes were suddenly dashed to the ground, when not over thirty yards ahead of him he saw an immense panther lying under the shade of a tree.

There was no chance to run, for the panther had seen him about the same time, and had dropped his head between his paws as a cat does when ready to spring on a mouse or bird. The panther began switching his tail from side to side, in a nervous way that boded no good to the boy.

Gregorio sank on his knees, crossed himself, and uttered a silent prayer to the Virgin Mary, asking her protection from the terrible beast. He hardly had time to think, but in danger the mind works fast. He thought of all he had heard his father say about no wild animal being able to stand the steady gaze of a man's eye, but the gaze was not to be thought of, especially at long range, and the panther looked too terrible to the little fellow for him to think of a staring match.

He could not depend on his little bow and arrow, for if an arrow should even strike an eye it could do no more than dangerously wound the beast and make him the more savage. Little Cito could stop a bear from catching him when up a tree, but the panther would climb any tree and one blow would settle Cito.

All at once it flashed through his mind that he had heard his father say that the largest, fiercest dog could be frightened by the sight of something he did not understand.

Gregorio lowered his body in the grass and began to crawl straight toward the panther, carrying one of his arrows in his hand ready to use it if things came to the worst.

The panther lay like a bronze statue, and motionless, except for the nervous movement of the tip of his tail. The boy moved toward him, and every few feet he raised his head and uttered a loud growl, first showing his painted face, and then dropped down and began to crawl again.

The panther had his ears laid back in an angry way, but soon they stood up straight, and his head, that had been down between his paws, was raised. Fear was now evidently taking the place of anger.

Finally, when the boy had covered about half the distance, the panther sprung up and made off with tremendous bounds.

Cito had been creeping along behind Gregorio, peeping out from behind him now and then; Cito was evidently under the impression that it was either turkey, squirrel or cottontail, and as it was getting along towards dinner he was ready for anything that meant food.

Gregorio, seeing the panther turn, sprang to his feet, rattled his bow and gourd, and gave a yell, hissing on the dog; Cito sprang off like he was made of steel springs, and was soon at the panther's heels. He gave such a fierce bark that the huge beast rushed up a tree to think it over.

Gregorio did not care to scare the beast any more, and as soon as the panther ran in one direction, he ran in the other. Cito knew when he had done enough, and after dancing around on his hind legs under the tree, barking fiercely at the panther, he suddenly darted off, for the panther had been looking down at him with ears back, and a show of the teeth that did not invite much of a stay on the part of the little dog. When Cito joined his master he could not help his usual grin of delight, and described a circle or two around the fleeing Gregorio. Gregorio was badly scared, but Cito would not have feared to attack a Bengal tiger.

XXIII
THE MIRAGE

Gregorio did not stop until he had put a good long mile between himself and the panther. Then he took a good big drink of water and gave Cito some, as he was panting with his tongue out. After sitting under the shade of a tree a few moments, Gregorio started off again and as the sun was coming down quite hot, he decided to go towards the mountains and hunt for water, as the supply in the gourd was very low. But he did not change his direction at once, for he did not want to lose so much time, but gradually bore to the left, hoping to find water either in a spring or a hole in the rock; for he would thus be gaining on the pass at the same time.

On reaching the crest of a high divide, or spur from the mountains, he was delighted to see down in the valley to his right a beautiful lake, surrounded by some tall bushy trees that were reflected in the bosom of the lake, and seemed to invite the boy to a rest in the shade with abundance of water.

A few white cranes were around the lake, and that, Gregorio argues, was a sure sign of fresh water, as the cranes were after frogs or fish.

He immediately changed his direction towards the lake, as it was also some distance in his front and would bring him nearer home. He increased his speed now that water was in sight, and in imagination was stooping down to drink of the cool water and resting under the shade of the trees; he even saw animals moving under the trees and thought possibly they were deer and turkey.

It was much further to the lake than he had supposed, and consequently he had used the last water in the gourd, dividing with the little dog. At last, tired and thirsty, he reached the plain near the lake and almost trotted, so eager was he to get to the water. Cito was hot, too, and made quick little trips from one shade tree to another, and would begin to scratch off the hot surface earth to make a cool place to lie down in, but by the time the hole was fixed to suit him and he had turned around four or five times before lying down, Gregorio would pass him. Finally, Cito was sure he saw the lake and rushed off, but came to a sudden halt when the animals under the trees began to move, for it was a lot of sneaking coyotes.

Alas, when Gregorio got quite close, his beautiful lake vanished in a moment, and all he saw was a bare place where water stood after a rain, and a lot of bleached bones around it, those of some poor horse, also lured by the mirage so common on western plains.

When the dismal fact was plain that he had been deceived, Gregorio dropped down under the shade of one of the trees, sobbing bitterly for in addition to the now distressing pangs of thirst, was the thought that he might not see his dear ones again. Cito took a position in front of him, looking as sorrowful as he knew how, for a dog knows well enough if his master is sad or glad, and Cito knew something was wrong and licked Gregorio's hands.

This loss of both time and distance was serious, even not taking into consideration the question of water, which they must have before many hours, or suffer greatly. It was almost as near, apparently to the pass as it was to the head of the arroyo east of him, where he might hope to find water and even that was doubtful for only now and then could living springs be found that gave water during the entire season.

He knew it was some distance beyond the pass to the big, beautiful spring that came out from under the cliff of rocks, where he had so often quenched his thirst. The question for him to decide was whether to go in a direct line for the pass, knowing pretty well there would be no water except the kind in the lake before him or turn square to the left away from home, hunt for water, and lose a day in the search.

The sun that was coming down straight and hot decided him, and he took a course between the two plains, bearing towards the mountains again. His rest in the shade made him feel more like traveling, and gathering up his load, he started off again.

XXIV
A Miraculous Cave

Gregorio saw ahead of him a streak of dust, and for a moment could not make out what it could be, but as it was coming towards him, he stopped; he soon saw that it was a chaparral cock in close pursuit of a lizard, and both were doing their best, the bird to get a dinner, and the lizard hunting his hole. The lizard was one of the brown kind, with little black spots; they lie flat on the ground when still, but when they start to run, they look as tall as a mouse. During the heat of the day, when running from one shade to another, they curve their tails up, and you can just see a streak. The chaparral cock is built with care by dame nature for just such spurts and was running close to the ground, his neck and bill stretched out, and Gregorio could see that the lizard stood a poor show for his life. They had not run far until the bird stopped suddenly, and his tail flew up until it nearly struck the back of his head; he had the lizard in his bill and trotting to the shade of a bush shook him pretty much as an English black and tan terrier would a rat; after slamming the lizard against the ground a few times, he swallowed him.

Gregorio was glad to get out of the prickly pear and thick brush, for in addition to danger from snake bites he would occasionally get a thorn in his foot, and that meant a few minutes, delay of precious time. Once more up on the high ground he saw several beautiful lakes, but had no desire to bathe or drink of the waters. He kept steadily on bearing towards the mountains on his left, for his thirst was now telling on him, and poor little Cito's tongue was hanging out and tears running from his eyes that shone like glass.

Gregorio knew it would not do to stop, perhaps when he got nearer to the crest of the mountains he would find either a spring, or a tank in the shade of some cave where the evaporation was so little that water would remain long after a rain. As he made the top of the successive ridges, he saw the gap in the mountains more distinctly, the cliff began to show the breaks and crevices in it and the pine trees showed up plainly against the blue sky; so he knew he was getting pretty close and it kept up his spirits.

Coming at last to one unusually deep, rough canyon, he decided to travel up it until he could find water. After following up it for a few miles, he saw that the walls on each side were becoming perpendicular and increasing in height and he knew if he did not find water at the head of the canyon or climb out on the crest, he must come all the way back before he could continue on his course towards the gap, and this meant another day in the hot sun, and maybe worse. Casting a lingering look up the canyon, he turned aside to a cave to rest in the shade before retracing his steps and starting for the pass.

Sadly he turned into the cave and sank down weeping bitterly for he thought that he would never see his mother again, and that his bones would some day be the only evidence that he had died alone in the woods was too much for the little fellow, now tired, thirsty and hungry. But still he did not forget what the good padre had told him, to ask God to protect him when in danger, and putting up his hands, he lifted his eyes and prayed earnestly that he might be spared to reach his dear mother, and then asked the Virgin Mary to pity him.

As he prayed he saw a dim circle of light on the roof of smooth rock above him in the cave and to his distorted imagination it was the holy circle of light he had seen around the head of the Virgin in all pictures of her, and the sweet face of the Virgin seemed to look down on him.

At each puff of wind he saw the same strange light that would spread and disappear; as he gazed in astonishment, mixed with fear, a flock of pigeons swooped down and fluttering around settled on a bench of rocks and the circle of light again appeared.

The mystery was explained. It was one of the tanks of seep water on a shelf of rock in the shade and every time there was a ripple on its surface, it was reflected on the smooth rocks in the roof of the cave; still he firmly believed that it was the work of the Virgin Mary—had he not seen the strange crown of light just as he prayed, and did she not show him the water in the rocks?

XXV
Both Food and Drink

Gregorio did not wait long in turning his attention to temporal affairs, and fixing an arrow on his bow, he brought down a fat pigeon; the flock took flight, but as none of them had seen the boy, and were thirsty, they settled back again, and another fell to the little archer's skill, but the suspicions of the flock were by this time aroused and they sailed away.

This was a starter for dinner, but just at that time thirst was calling on him louder than hunger, and he ran to a drift pile and soon had a pole up against the shelving rock. He climbed up, and to his delight, found quite a large tank of sweet, clear, cold water.

He took a drink at once, but remembering the stories of his father and friends, he drank only a little at first. Cito was dancing around on his hind legs, whining piteously, and making a dash, would run up the pole, and fall off again. Gregorio had thought of his little friend, and had his rope and gourd. Filling it he let it down, it fell over and the water began to run out on the rocks, the little dog lapping it up eagerly.

Refilling the gourd, Gregorio slid down, and going behind some big boulders near the cave, he soon started a little fire and began to pick his pigeons. He soon had the pigeons roasting before his fire, and Cito got the heads and feet, and had hopes of a share when the birds were cooked.

As soon as the pigeons were done, Gregorio began to eat one, but the painful anxiety of Cito's comical little face, as the birds disappeared, was too much for the boy, and after eating the meat all off the breast he threw the rest to the hungry dog.

As good luck would have it, he heard the chattering of some squirrels, that were fighting. They came near running over the boy, and stopped on top of the boulder looking down in amazement at these intruders on their home. Gregorio had grabbed his bow, and sent an arrow through one that tumbled him over. Cito soon had hold of him, but forgetful of his former experience, he put his nose in the squirrel's mouth. If there is anything a squirrel does understand it is how to use his long yellow curved teeth, and this was one of the large black variety that make their homes in cliffs and rocks.

Cito gave the squirrel such a savage shake that it went in one direction and the arrow in another, the squirrel in his dying struggles managed to run into a crevice in the rocks and Cito stood on his hind legs peeping in where he could hear it scratching and struggling. Cito was whining piteously at the loss of his dinner, after getting such a bite; but Gregorio soon got a stick, twisted it into the squirrel's hide and pulled him out—a trick known to every boy who has ever hunted rabbits with dogs.

The squirrel was very fat, and was soon made ready for the fire. By this time the other squirrel having had only a hasty view of his visitors, after a few preliminary barks that put the boy on his guard, poked his head over the top of a boulder and got an arrow in his throat. Cito ran around the rock but the recollection of the last fight was too fresh in his memory and his nose to be forgotten, so he grabbed the part that doesn't bite, and shook the squirrel to his heart's content, breaking the arrow.

Gregorio soon had the other squirrel dressed and up before a good bed of coals. He hated to see the grease going to waste on the rocks, but waited patiently until the squirrels were perfectly brown before beginning to eat, and gave the bones not entirely stripped of meat, to the dog. Both were quite satisfied, and Gregorio, after taking a drink and giving Cito all he wanted, went to refill his water gourd, scaling up his ladder quickly. Soon he had it full, but instead of letting the gourd down with his rope, he tried to climb down with it in his hand. When halfway down the ladder turned and to save himself from a fall that might have crippled him, he let the gourd fall; he felt like crying, but lost no time in weeping over spilt water, and started off briskly down the bed of the arroyo, left at the first branch coming from the south side, and was soon climbing, with fresh strength, the hill side.

XXVI
THE CREAKING WHEELS

His meal had been very much relished, the water was pure and cool, and the squirrels very fat and juicy.

The though of the dear, sad mother, and the happiness his return would give her, nerved him for the final effort, for he determined to make his home by nightfall, if possible; he knew he could make the big springs, so the thought of water did not worry him, and he stepped along like a race horse.

He saw any number of cottontails, and they would hardly get out of his way. Several times he came near tramping on the beautiful mountain or fool quail, but he felt no hunger and did not care to waste any of the previous minutes, between him and the little mother.

He bore down towards the valley, as the hills were steep and rough and the climbing was very trying. Once he was nearly scared out of his wits. He was slipping along making so little noise, that he came right on a herd of old blacktail bucks before they saw him. With shrill snorts they bounded off down the side of the mountain, stiff legged, like a bucking pony; they do not run as red deer do, but spring into the air and strike the ground with all four feet at once, a wise provision of nature for they are essentially a mountain deer and rarely go far from them, and in the rough, steep places, if they lit on their fore feet only in making their tremendous jumps, they certainly would break their legs.

Our little hero kept on as well as he could, but he had to rest often. Once his attention was attracted to the loud chattering of a squirrel, close by, but he did not care to harm it, as he had had such a hearty dinner. Nevertheless, curiosity led him to watch it. The squirrel was in the lower branches of the tree, moving about excitedly, evidently watching something on the ground. It kept coming a little lower down, chattering all the time until it reached a limb not more than four feet from the ground, and sat with the end of its tail in the form of a shepherd's crook, giving it a vigorous shake every time it barked. Gradually its movements became slower, its barking became a low squeak, and it had let its body down until it hung on only by its hind claws. Weaker and weaker became its voice, and finally it dropped, and Gregorio saw it was into the wide extended jaws of an immense rattlesnake. He had literally been charmed. Gregorio did not have any time to waste, but he hated a rattlesnake, and never passed one without giving battle; it was too late to save the squirrel, but he gathered up a lot of rocks and bombarded the snake until he had crushed its head.

Gregorio was now at the gulch that led up to the pass, and followed the bed so as to be concealed from view, if the Indians were still watching the pass for him.

Cautiously he worked his way up to the trail he knew ran through the pass. As he scanned the rough rocks and cliff, all seemed quiet, and there were not tracks in the trail except foxes, armadillos, and small animals.

Gregorio was soon at the highest part of the gap where he could see the valley beyond. His eyes filled with tears of joy, and he almost flew down the mountains, scarcely daring to look around for fear he would see a hideous painted face peering from behind a rock or bush. No halt was made, and fear lent wings to his feet.

Soon he had reached the bench lands and came to a road.

The boy felt like kneeling down and kissing the broad tracks made by the old Mexican carros. For a moment he was bewildered as to which end of the road to take, but took the right hand and hurried along rapidly.

It was a good thing for him, that he met no one on the road, for had they seen him first they would have ambushed him and killed him. The boys had made an Indian of him, by painting his face, tying hawks' feathers in his hair, and taking his Mexican shirt and trousers, giving him leggings.

He had become very thirsty from his rapid trip down the mountain side, and was made happy by coming to the beautiful spring of cold, clear water, that gushed out from the foot of the cliff. Gregorio stopped to rest a bit before pushing on, intending to take another drink before leaving, but he remembered that he was a fugitive, and still some distance from home, so he hid in the brush close by, keeping a close watch for foe or friend.

About the time he decided to make another start, he heard a familiar noise that had never sounded so sweet before; it was the creaking of the wheels of a Mexican cart, and he soon heard the sound of the Mexican drivers urging on their teams.

Gregorio was so delighted, that he forgot his appearance. The joy of hearing his mother tongue spoken by his own people, completely upset him, and he dashed up the road to meet them. Gregorio's heart was full of meeting his people, and his astonishment was complete at the reception they gave him.

On turning a bend in the road he came in full view of the front wagon not over seventy-five yards distant; the driver ran to the front oxen and turned them around, easily done as their carts have only two wheels, and at the same time he yelled as loud as he could, "Indios! Indios!" The front carts turned back and those behind drove up rapidly and formed a corral, with the oxen all on the inside of the circle. Amidst much confusion and shouting they soon all had their guns in their hands, ready for a fight.

Gregorio had by this time taken in the situation. He threw down his bow, and his shrill, boyish voice rang out far above all others. Throwing up both hands he yelled, "I am an Indian captive and have escaped, a Mexican boy named Gregorio!"

This was as pleasant news to the Mexican carters, as their language had been to the little boy. The information came none too soon, for some of the men had covered him with their guns, and could hardly be kept from firing on him; for the Indians were so treacherous that the Mexicans placed but little confidence in them, and suspected some stratagem. So while some went forward to see Gregorio, the others kept their guns aimed at him, ready to fire on the least evidence of treachery.

XXVII
HOME AT LAST!

The news had gone to other towns, that a little boy had been carried off by the Indians, and the people of Santa Rosa were willing to pay a good sum to ransom him. When the Mexicans saw what a little fellow he was, they picked him up in their arms, and kissed [him], and all were soon around him, asking many questions. But as the big spring was near by, where they intended to stop, cook, and rest awhile, the train moved on to the spring.

Cito at first had not quite understood these demonstrations, and was dancing around waiting for an opening to sample some one's leg; at a word from his master, he would have sailed into a fight, as quickly as he had with the bear.

As soon as the train reached the spring they again formed the "corral," and turning out the oxen hobbled, they put out sentinels. As soon as they had put on the dinner to cook, they gathered around Gregorio to hear of his capture and escape. But first they told him to wash and gave him Mexican clothes, which changed him so much that Cito was not sure of him until he spoke.

Gregorio received much sympathy and praise; Cito came in for his share of glory and petting, and had all he could eat.

Dinner over, the teams hitched up quickly, as they knew how anxious the boy was to get home. Gregorio and Cito had a seat in the front wagon.

As the train approached Santa Rosa and Gregorio recognized familiar places, it was all he could do to keep from jumping out and running ahead. When at last the gray walls of the adobe houses and dome and cross of the church came in view, he could restrain himself no longer, and springing to the ground, he ran as fast as his feet would take him.

Gregorio turned neither to the right nor left, but made straight for his own home. He had not gone far until some of his little playmates recognized him, and a shout went up from a dozen throats, "Gregorio, Gregorio!" and was taken up and carried on ahead of him, as the people ran to their doors and saw him.

The cry soon reached the mother, and she was soon in the street. Her mother's heart told her the boy running with outstretched arms was her own little one. With a cry of joy she sprang forward to meet him, and clasped him in her arms.

The father, his brothers, and sisters and neighbors soon followed, and just then the little church bell tolled for vespers, and with one impulse, all uncovered their heads and turned towards the church, and the good padre offered up thanks for the safe return of the little captive.

For many days Gregorio was the hero of Santa Rosa de Muzquiz, and among his own family and the children of the pueblo, Cito stood next; the little dog never lacked for food or kind treatment again.

Gregorio is now an old man, and lives in Uvalde County, Texas, where he has his little flock of goats, his cattle, and apiary. He served through the war in the Federal army and was severely wounded. He has never received a pension, but hopes to before he dies of old age. He stands well as a brave, honest man, among Mexicans and Americans alike.

I do not know where Cito is.

Bibliography

BOOKS

Agnew, Brad. *Fort Gibson, Terminal on the Trail of Tears*. Norman: University of Oklahoma Press, 1980.

Alberts, Don E., ed. *Rebels on the Rio Grande: The Civil War Journal of A.B. Peticolas*. Albuquerque: University of New Mexico Press, 1984.

Allardice, Bruce S. *More Generals in Gray*. Baton Rouge: Louisiana State University Press, 1995.

Altshuler, Constance Lynn. *Cavalry Yellow & Infantry Blue: Army Officers in Arizona Between 1851 and 1886*. Tucson: Arizona Historical Society, 1991.

Askins, Charles. *Texans, Guns & History*. New York: Bonanza Books, 1970.

Austerman, Wayne R. *Sharps Rifles and Spanish Mules: The San Antonio-El Paso Mail, 1851-1881*. College Station: Texas A&M University Press, 1985.

Bailey, Anne J. *Between the Enemy and Texas: Parson's Texas Cavalry in the Civil War*. Fort Worth: Texas Christian University Press, 1989.

Baldridge, Michael. *A Reminiscence of the Parker H. French Expedition through Texas and Mexico to California in the Spring of 1850*. Los Angeles: Westernlore Press, 1959.

Ball, Eve. *In the Days of Victorio: Recollections of a Warm Springs Apache*. Tucson: University of Arizona Press, 1986.

Barney, James M. *Tales of Apache Warfare: True Stories of Massacres, Fights and Raids in Arizona and New Mexico*. By the author, 1933.

Barr, Alwyn, ed. *Charles Porter's Account of the Confederate Attempt to Seize Arizona and New Mexico*. Austin: Pemberton Press, 1964.

Bartlett, John Russell. *Personal Narrative of Explorations and Incidents in Texas, Mexico, California, Sonora, and Chihuahua Connected with the United States Boundary Commission during the Years 1850-1853*. New York: D. Appleton Co., 1854.

Baylor, Frances Courtney. *Juan and Juanita*. Cambridge: Houghton Mifflin Co., 1886.

Baylor, George Wythe. *John Robert Baylor: Confederate Governor of Arizona*. Edited by Odie B. Faulk. Tucson: Arizona Pioneers' Historical Society, 1966.

Baylor, Orval Walker, and Henry Bedinger Baylor, eds. *Baylor's History of the Baylors: A Collection of Records and Important Family Data*. Le Roy, Indiana: Le Roy Journal Printing Co., 1914.

Bowden, J.J. *The Exodus of Federal Forces From Texas, 1861*. Austin: Eakin Press, 1986.

Brice, Donaly E. *The Great Comanche Raid*. Austin: Eakin Press, 1987.

Broaddus, J. Morgan Jr. *The Legal Heritage of El Paso*. Edited by Samuel D. Myres. El Paso: Texas Western Press, 1963.

Brown, John Henry. *Indian Wars and Pioneers of Texas*. Austin: State House Press, 1988.

Bryson, Conrey. *Down Went McGinty: El Paso in the Wonderful Nineties*. El Paso: Texas Western Press, 1977.

Brune, Gunner. *Springs of Texas*. 2 vols. Fort Worth: Branch Smith, 1981.

Buchanan, A. Russell. *David S. Terry of California: Dueling Judge*. San Marino: Huntington Library, 1956.

Carr, Albert A. *The World and William Walker*. New York: Harper and Row, 1963.

Cartwright, Gary. *Galveston: A History of the Island*. New York: Atheneum, 1991.

Chabot, Frederick C. *With the Makers of San Antonio*. San Antonio: Artes Gráficas, 1987.

Colton, Ray C. *The Civil War in the Western Territories*. Norman: University of Oklahoma Press, 1959.

Conkling, Roscoe P. and Margaret B. *The Butterfield Overland Mail, 1857-1869*. 3 vols. Glendale: Arthur H. Clark Co., 1947

Cutrer, Thomas W. *Ben McCulloch and the Frontier Military Tradition*. Chapel Hill: University of North Carolina Press, 1993.

Daggett, Marsha Lea, ed. *Pecos County History*. Canyon: Staked Plains Press, 1984.

Daniell, L.E. *Personnel of the Texas State Government*. Austin: City Printing Co., 1887.

D'Hamel, Enrique B. *The Adventures of a Tenderfoot*. Waco: W.M. Morrison Books, n.d.

Diccionario Porrua de Historía, Biografía y Geografía de Mexico. Mexico City: Editorial Porrua, 1970.

Dobie, J. Frank, and Mody C. Boatright, eds. *Straight Texas*. Austin: Steck Co., 1937.

Dobie, J. Frank. *Tales of Old-Time Texas*. Boston: Little, Brown, and Co., 1955.

Egan, Ferol. *The El Dorado Trail: The Story of the Gold Rush Routes Across Mexico*. Lincoln: University of Nebraska Press, 1970.

Egloff, Fred R. *El Paso Lawman: G.W. Campbell*. College Station: Creative Publishing Co., 1982.

Ellis, Olin O. *Life in Uvalde, Texas, 1882-1903*. Baltimore: Press of Harry S. Scott, 1963.

Emory, William H. *Report on the United States and Mexican Boundary Survey Made Under the Direction of the Secretary of the Interior*. Washington: Cornelius Wendell, 1857.

Farr, Warner D. *Resting Rebels: A Historical and Medical Study of the San Antonio Confederate Cemetery*. San Antonio, 1990.

Faulk, Odie. *General Tom Green, Fightin' Texan*. Waco: Texian Press, 1963.

_____. *Land of Many Frontiers*. New York: Oxford University Press, 1968.

Ford, John Salmon. *Rip Ford's Texas*. Edited by Stephen B. Oates. Austin: University of Texas Press, 1963.

Frazer, Donald S. *Blood & Treasure: Confederate Empire in the Southwest*. College Station: Texas A&M University Press, 1995.

Frazer, Robert. *Forts of the West*. Norman: University of Oklahoma Press, 1965.

Gardner, Mark L., ed. *Brothers on the Santa Fe Trails: Edward Glasgow and William Henry Glasgow*. Niwot: University of Colorado Press, 1993.

Gibson, A.M. *The Life and Death of Colonel Albert Jennings Fountain*. Norman: University of Oklahoma Press, 1986.

Gillett, James B. *Six Years with the Texas Rangers*. New Haven: Yale University Press, 1963.

_____. *Fugitives From Justice: The Notebook of Texas Ranger Sergeant James B. Billett*. Austin: State House Press, 1996.

Green, A.C. *900 Miles on the Butterfield Trail*. Denton: University of North Texas Press, 1994.

Greer, James K. *Buck Barry: Texas Ranger and Frontiersman*. Lincoln: University of Nebraska Press, 1978.

Hail, Marshall. *Knight in the Sun: Harper B. Lee, First Yankee Matador*. Boston: Little, Brown, and Co., 1962.

Haley, J. Evetts. *Charles Goodnight: Cowman and Plainsman*. Norman: University of Oklahoma Press, 1949.

Hall, Martin Hardwick. *Sibley's New Mexico Campaign*. Austin: University of Texas Press, 1960.

_____. *The Confederate Army of New Mexico*. Austin: Presidial Press, 1978.

Hamilton, Nancy. *Ben Dowell: El Paso's First Mayor*. El Paso: Texas Western Press, 1976.

Harris, Benjamin Butler. *The Gila Trail: The Texas Argonauts and the California Gold Rush*. Edited by Richard H. Dillon. Norman: University of Oklahoma Press, 1960.

Hayes, Claude W. *Galveston: History of the Island and the City*. Austin: Jenkins Garrett Press, 1974.

Heartsill, W.W. *Fourteen Hundred and 91 Days in the Confederate Army*. Marshall: W.W. Heartsill, 1876.

Heitman, Francis B. *Historical Register and Dictionary of the United States Army from Its Organization, September 19, 1789, to March 2, 1903*. 2 vols. Urbana: University of Illinois Press, 1969.

Heyman, Max. *Prudent Soldier: A Biography of Major General E.R.S. Canby, 1817-1873*. Glendale: Arthur H. Clark Co., 1959.

Hughes, Nathan C., Jr. *General William J. Hardee, C.S.A.* Baton Rouge: Louisiana State University Press, 1965.

Hughes, W.H. *Rebellious Ranger: Rip Ford and the Old Southwest*. Norman: University of Oklahoma Press, 1964.

Jackson, Donald Dale. *Gold Dust: The Saga of the Forty-Niners—Their Adventures and Ordeals, Their Courage and Greed, Their Ingenuities, Delusions, Bonanzas and Catastrophes—in California and on the Way There*. New York: Alfred A. Knopf, 1980.

Jameson, W.C. *The Guadalupe Mountains: Islands in the Desert*. El Paso: Texas Western Press, 1994.

Jenkins, John Holland. *Recollections of Early Texas*. Austin: University of Texas Press, 1958.

Johnson, Ludwell H. *Red River Campaign: Politics and Cotton in the Civil War*. Baltimore: Johns Hopkins University Press, 1979.

Keleher, William A. *Turmoil in New Mexico*. Santa Fe: Rydal Press, 1952.

_____. *The Fabulous Frontier: Twelve New Mexico Items*. Albuquerque: University of New Mexico Press, 1962.

Kerby, Robert Lee. *The Confederate Invasion of New Mexico and Arizona, 1861-1862*. Los Angeles: Westernlore Press, 1958.

_____. *Kirby Smith's Confederacy: The Trans-Mississippi South, 1863-1865*. New York: Columbia University Press, 1972.

Kemp, Ben W. *Cow Dust and Saddle Leather*. Norman: University of Oklahoma Press, 1968.

Leckie, William H. *The Buffalo Soldiers: A Narrative of the Negro Cavalry in the West*. Norman: University of Oklahoma Press, 1967.

Leonard, Edward A. *Rails at the Pass of the North*. El Paso: Texas Western Press, 1981.

Lewis, Oscar. *The War in the Far West*. Garden City: Doubleday and Co., 1961.

Loftin, Jack. *Trails Through Archer: A Centennial History—1880-1980*. Burnet: Eakin Press, 1979.

McKee, James Cooper. *Narrative of the Surrender of U.S. Forces at Fort Fillmore, New Mexico in July A.D. 1861*. Houston: Stagecoach Press, 1961.

McCaslin, Richard B. *The Great Hanging at Gainesville, Texas, 1862*. Baton Rouge: Louisiana State University Press, 1994.

McGowan, Edward. *The Strange Eventful History of Parker H. French.* Los Angeles: Glen Dawson, 1959.

Maffly-Kipp, Laurie F. *Religion and Society in Frontier California.* New Haven: Yale University Press, 1994.

Magoffin, Susan Shelby. *Down the Santa Fe Trail and into Mexico.* Edited by Stella M. Drumm. Lincoln: University of Nebraska Press, 1982.

Mayhall, Mildred P. *Indian Wars of Texas.* Waco: Texian Press, 1965.

Metz, Leon Claire. *Dallas Stoudenmire: El Paso Marshal.* Austin: Pemberton Press, 1969.

_____. *Desert Army: Fort Bliss on the Texas Border.* El Paso: Mangan Books, 1988.

_____. *Fort Bliss: An Illustrated History.* El Paso: Mangan Books, 1981.

_____. *Turning Points in El Paso, Texas.* El Paso: Mangan Books, 1985.

Middagh, John J. *Frontier Newspaper: El Paso Times.* El Paso: Texas Western Press, 1958.

Miles, William. *Journal of the Sufferings and Hardships of Captain Parker H. French's Overland Expedition to California.* Fairfield, Washington: Ye Galleon Press, 1970.

Mills, W.W. *Forty Years at El Paso, 1858-1898.* Edited by Rex Strickland. El Paso: Carl Hertzog, 1962.

Nance, Joseph Milton. *Attack and Counter-Attack: The Texas Mexican Frontier, 1842.* Austin: University of Texas Press, 1964.

_____, ed. *Mier Expedition Diary: A Texas Prisoner's Account.* Austin: University of Texas Press, 1978.

Neighbours, Kenneth Franklin. *Indian Exodus: Texas Indian Affairs, 1835-1859.* Nortex, 1973.

_____. *Robert Simpson Neighbors and the Texas Frontier, 1836-1859.* Waco: Texian Press, 1975.

Noel, Theophilus. *A Campaign From Santa Fe to the Mississippi, Being a History of the Old Sibley Brigade.* Edited by Martin Hardwick Hall and Edwin Adams Davis. Houston: Stagecoach Press, 1961.

Ormsby, Waterman L. *The Butterfield Overland Mail.* Edited by Lyle H. Wright and Josephine M. Bynum. San Marino: Huntington Library, 1988.

Parks, Joseph H. *General Edmund Kirby Smith, C.S.A.* Baton Rouge: Louisiana State University Press, 1982.

_____. *General Leonidas Polk, C.S.A.* Baton Rouge: Louisiana State University Press, 1962.

Parrish, T. Michael. *Richard Taylor: Soldier Prince of Dixie.* Chapel Hill: University of North Carolina Press, 1992.

Pierce, Michael D. *The Most Promising Young Officer: A Life of Ranald Slidell Mackenzie.* Norman: University of Oklahoma Press, 1993.

Pike, James. *Scout and Ranger: Being the Personal Adventures of James Pike of the Texas Rangers in 1859-60.* Princeton: Princeton University Press, 1932.

Porter, Eugene O. *San Elizario, A History.* Austin: Pemberton Press, 1973.

Raht, Carlysle Graham. *Romance of the Davis Mountains and Big Bend Country.* El Paso: Rath Books, 1918.

Ray, Verne F. *Ethnohistorical Analysis of Documents Relating to the Apache Indians.* New York: Garland, 1974.

Richardson, Rupert Norval. *The Frontier of Northwest Texas, 1846-1876.* Glendale: Arthur H. Clark Co., 1963.

Rister, Carl Coke. *Fort Griffin on the Texas Frontier.* Norman: University of Oklahoma Press, 1956.

Robinson, Charles M. III. *Bad Hand: A Biography of General Ranald Mackenzie.* Austin: State House Press, 1993.

Roland, Charles P. *Albert Sidney Johnston: Soldier of Three Republics.* Austin: University of Texas Press, 1964.

Senkewicz, Robert M. *Vigilantes in Gold Rush California.* Palo Alto: Stanford University Press, 1985.

Sherman, William T. *Memoirs of General William T. Sherman.* New York: Library of America, 1900.

Smith, Roy L. *Three Roads to Chihuahua.* Austin: Eakin Press, 1988.

Smith, Thomas Tyres. *Fort Inge: Sharps, Spurs, and Sabers on the Texas Frontier, 1849-1869.* Austin: Eakin Press, 1993.

Smith, Toby. *Coal Town: The Life and Times of Dawson, New Mexico.* Santa Fe: Ancient City Press, 1994.

Sonnichsen, C.L. *The El Paso Salt War of 1877.* El Paso: Texas Western Press, 1961.

_____. *Pass of the North: Four Centuries on the Rio Grande.* El Paso: Texas Western Press, 1968.

_____. *The Mescalero Apache.* Norman: University of Oklahoma Press, 1958.

Stewart, George R. *Committee of Vigilance: Revolution in San Francisco, 1851.* Boston: Houghton Mifflin, 1964.

Storey, Tracy I., and Tevis, Lloyd P., Jr. *California Grizzly.* Lincoln: University of Nebraska Press, 1988.

Stout, Joseph A., Jr. *Apache Lightning: The Last Battles of the Ojo Calientes.* New York: Oxford University Press, 1974.

Strickland, Rex W. *Six Who Came to El Paso, Pioneers of the 1840's.* El Paso: Texas Western Press, 1963.

Sutherland, Kay. *Rock Paintings at Hueco Tanks State Historical Park.* Austin: Texas Parks and Wildlife, 1991.

Sweeny, Edwin R. *Cochise: Chiricahua Apache Chief.* Norman: University of Oklahoma Press, 1991.

Swift, Roy L. *Three Roads to Chihuahua: The Great Wagon Roads that Opened the Southwest, 1823-1883.* Austin: Eakin Press, 1988.

Thompson, Jerry. *Colonel John Robert Baylor: Texas Indian Fighter and Confederate Soldier.* Hillsboro: Hill College Press, 1971.

_____. *Desert Tiger: Captain Paddy Graydon and the Civil War in the Far Southwest.* El Paso: Texas Western Press, 1992.

_____. *Henry Hopkins Sibley: Confederate General of the West.* Natchitoches: Northwestern State University Press, 1987.

_____, ed. *From Desert to Bayou: The Civil War Journal and Sketches of Morgan Wolfe Merrick.* El Paso: Texas Western Press, 1991.

_____, ed. *Westward the Texans: The Civil War Journal of Private William Randolph Howell.* El Paso: Texas Western Press, 1990.

Thrapp, Dan. *Conquest of Apacheria*. Norman: University of Oklahoma Press, 1967.

_____. *Juh: An Incredible Indian*. El Paso: Texas Western Press, 1973.

_____. *Victorio and the Mimbres Apaches*. Norman: University of Oklahoma Press, 1974.

_____, ed. *Encyclopedia of Frontier Biography*. 3 vols. Spokane: Arthur H. Clark Co., 1990.

Timmons, W.H. *El Paso: A Borderlands History*. El Paso: Texas Western Press, 1990.

Trimble, Marshall. *Roadside History of Arizona*. Missoula: Mountain Press Publishing Co., 1986.

Ungnade, Herbert E. *Guide to the New Mexico Mountains*. University of New Mexico Press, 1973.

Utley, Robert M. *The Indian Frontiers of the American West, 1846-1890*. Albuquerque: University of New Mexico Press, 1984.

Warner, Ezra J. *Generals in Gray*. Baton Rouge: Louisiana State University Press, 1959.

Webb, Walter Prescott. *The Texas Rangers*. Austin: University of Texas Press, 1965.

Wilbarger, J.W. *Indian Depredations in Texas: Reliable Accounts of Battles, Wars, Adventures, Forays, Murders, Massacres, etc., etc., Together with Biographical Sketches of Many of the Most Noted Indian Fighters and Frontiersmen of Texas*. Austin: Hutchings Printing House, 1889.

Williams, Clayton W. *Texas' Last Frontier: Fort Stockton and the Trans Pecos, 1861-1865*. Edited by Ernest Wallace. College Station: Texas A&M University Press, 1982.

Williams, R.H. *With the Border Ruffians: Memories of the Far West, 1852-1868*. Lincoln: University of Nebraska Press, 1982.

Williams, T. Harry. *P.G.T. Beauregard: Napoleon in Gray*. Baton Rouge: Louisiana State University Press, 1954.

Winfrey, Dorman H., and James M. Day. *The Indian Papers of Texas and the Southwest, 1825-1916*. Vols. 3, 4, and 5. Austin: Pemberton Press, 1966.

Winters, John D. *Civil War in Louisiana*. Baton Rouge: Louisiana State University Press, 1963.

Wise, Jennings Cooper, comp. *Old Ministers and Families of Virginia* by Bishop William Meade. Baltimore: Genealogical Publishing Co., 1966.

Wooster, Robert. *Soldiers, Sutlers, and Settlers: Garrison Life on the Texas Frontier.* College Station: Texas A&M University Press, 1987.

Wright, J. Leitch, Jr. *Creeks and Seminoles: The Destruction and Regeneration of the Muscogulge People.* Lincoln: University of Nebraska Press, 1986.

Wright, Marcus J., comp. *Texas in the War, 1861-1865.* Edited by Harold B. Simpson. Hillsboro: Hill College Press, 1965.

Yeary, Mamie, ed. *Reminiscences of the Boys in Gray, 1861-1865.* Dayton: Morningside Press, 1986.

ARTICLES

Anderson, Hattie M., ed. "With the Confederates in New Mexico During the Civil War—Memoirs of Hank Smith." *Panhandle-Plains Historical Review* 2 (1929).

Archambeau, Ernest R., Jr. "The New Mexico Campaign of 1861-1862." *Panhandle-Plains Historical Review* 37 (1964).

Armstrong, A.F.H. "The Case of Major Isaac Lynde." *New Mexico Historical Review* 36 (January, 1961).

Austerman, Wayne. "Old Nighthawk and the Pass of the North." *Password* 27 (Fall 1982).

_____. "Tinaja de las Palmas: A Landmark on the El Paso Road." *Password* 28 (Spring 1983).

Barr, Alwyn. "Texan Losses in the Red River Campaign, 1864." *Texas Military History* 3 (Summer 1963).

_____. "Tom Green: The Forest of the Trans Mississippi." *Lincoln Herald* 88 (No. 2).

Barrick, Nona W., and Taylor, Mary Helen. "Murder in Mesilla." *New Mexico Magazine* (November 1960).

Baylor, George Wythe. "Duel Between Gens. Johnston and Huston." *Confederate Veteran* 17 (May 1909).

_____. "Mister, Here's Your Mule." *Confederate Veteran* 14 (October 1906).

_____. "Plea for a Brave Confederate Woman." *Confederate Veteran* 21 (February 1913).

_____. "Sentiment, By a Confederate." *Confederate Veteran* 6 (November 1889).

_____. "Tragedies on the Old Overland Stage." *Frontier Times* 26 (March 1949).

Baylor, W.K. "Killing of Josephus Browning Avenged." *Frontier Times* 16 (October 1933).

_____. "The Old Frontier: Events of Long Ago," in J. Marvin Hunter, ed. *The Bloody Trail in Texas: Sketches and Narratives of Indian Raids and Atrocities on Our Frontier*. Bandera: J. Marvin Hunter, 1931.

_____. "Pioneer Vengeance." *Vanishing Texas* 1 (July 1981).

Brooksher, William R. "Desert Passage Contested." *America's Civil War* 1 (May 1988).

Broune, P.N. "Captain T.D. Nettles and the Valverde Battery." *Texana* 2 (No. 1).

Browder, Shirley, "General John Robert Baylor." *Junior Historian* 14 (November 1953).

_____. "Rough, Wild, and Rowdy!" *Frontier Times* 33 (Summer 1959).

Bryan, Howard. "The Man Who Buried the Cannons." *New Mexico Magazine* 40 (January 1962).

Bugbee, Lester G. "The Old Three Hundred." *Quarterly of the Texas State Historical Association* 1 (October 1897).

Clendenen, Clarence C. "Dan Showalter—California Secessionist." *California Historical Society Quarterly* 40 (1961).

Crimmins, M.L. "Fort Fillmore." *New Mexico Historical Review* 6 (October 1931).

_____, ed. "W.G. Freeman's Report of the Eighth Military Department." *Southwestern Historical Quarterly* 53 (April 1950).

Day, James M. "El Paso's Texas Rangers." *Password* 24 (Winter 1979).

Dinges, Bruce J. "Benjamin H. Grierson." In *Soldiers West: Biographies from the Military Frontier*. Edited by Paul Andrew Hutton. Lincoln: University of Nebraska Press, 1987.

Dominguez, Dixie L. "Hueco Tanks: A Vital Resource in Southwestern History ." *Password* 31 (Fall 1986).

Donnell, F.S. "The Confederate Territory of Arizona from Official Sources." *New Mexico Historical Review* 17 (April 1942).

Estep, Raymond, ed. "Lieutenant Wm. E. Burnet: Notes on Removal of Indians from Texas to Indian Territory." *Chronicles of Oklahoma* 38 (Autumn 1960).

Faulkner, Walter A., comp. "With Sibley in New Mexico: The Journal of William Henry Smith." *West Texas Historical Association Year Book* 27 (October 1951).

Finch, L. Boyd. "Arizona's Governors Without Portfolio: A Wonderfully Diverse Lot." *Journal of Arizona History* 26 (Spring 1985).

_____. "Arizona in Exile: Confederate Schemes to Recapture the Far Southwest." *Journal of Arizona History* 33 (Spring 1992).

_____. "Sherod Hunter—Confederate Frontiersman." *Corral Dust* 7 (February 1963).

_____. "Surprise at Brashear City: Sherod Hunter's Sugar Cooler Cavalry." *Louisiana History* 25 (Fall 1984).

_____. "Sherod Hunter and the Confederates in Arizona." *Journal of Arizona History* 10 (Fall 1982).

_____. "The Civil War in Arizona: The Confederates Occupy Tucson," *Arizona Highways* 65 (January 1989).

Gardner, James Henry. "The Lost Captain: J.L. Dawson of Old Fort Gibson." *Chronicles of Oklahoma* 21 (1943).

Goldblatt, Kenneth A. "George Wythe Baylor in West Texas, 1848-1865." *West Texas Historical Association Yearbook* 44 (October 1968).

_____. "Scout to Quitman Canyon: Report of Captain Geo. W. Baylor of the Frontier Battalion." *West Texas Historical Association Yearbook* 44 (October 1968).

Graham, Stanley S. "Campaign for New Mexico." *Military History of Texas and the Southwest* 10 (1972).

Haas, Oscar, trans. "The Diary of Julius Giesecke, 1861-1862." *Military History of Texas* 3 (Winter 1963).

Hail, Marshall. "San Agustine Ranch House." *Frontier Times* (August-September 1969).

Haley, J. Evetts. "John R. Baylor . . . Irrepressible Rebel." *Shamrock* (Fall 1961).

Hall, Martin H. "Albert Sidney Johnston's First Confederate Command." *McNeese Review* 13 (1962).

_____. "Captain Thomas J. Mastin's Arizona Guards, C.S.A." *New Mexico Historical Review* 49 (April 1974).

_____. "Colonel James Reily's Diplomatic Mission to Chihuahua and Sonora." *New Mexico Historical Review* 31 (July 1956).

_____. "Court-Martial of Arthur Pendleton Bagby, C.S.A." *East Texas Historical Journal.* 49 (April 1974).

_____. "Native Mexican Relations in Confederate Arizona, 1861-1862." *Journal of Arizona History* 13 (Autumn 1967).

_____. "Planter vs. Frontiersman: Conflict in Confederate Indian Policy," in *Essays on the American Civil War* (Austin: University of Texas Press, 1968).

_____. "The Skirmish at Picacho." *Civil War History* 4 (March 1959).

_____. "The Skirmish at Mesilla." *Arizona and the West* 1 (Winter 1959).

_____. "The Baylor-Kelly Fight: A Civil War Incident in Old Mesilla." *Password* 5 (July 1960).

_____. " The *Mesilla Times*: A Journal of Confederate Arizona." *Arizona and the West* 5 (Winter, 1963).

_____. ed. "The Taylor Letters: Correspondence from Fort Bliss, 1861." *Military History of Texas* 15 (No. 2).

"How General Baylor was Poisoned." *Texas Siftings* (July 1882).

Humphries, Keith. "Seven Brave Men." *Old West* 14 (Winter 1977).

Hunsaker, William J. "Lansford W. Hastings' Project for the Invasion and Conquest of Arizona and New Mexico for the Southern Confederacy." *Arizona Historical Review* 4 (1931-1932).

Klos, George. "'Our People Could Not Distinguish One Tribe from Another:' The 1859 Expulsion of the Reserve Indians from Texas." *Southwestern Historical Quarterly* 97 (April 1994).

Lockhart, Bill. "Gregorio Naciaceno Garcia, 1st: Indian Fighter and Politician." *Password* (Fall 1995).

McChristian, Douglas C. "Grierson's Fight at Tinaja de las Palmas: An Episode in the Victorio Campaign." *Red River Valley Historical Review* (Winter 1982).

McGowen, Stanley S. "Augustus Buchel: A Forgotten Texas Patriot." *Military History of the West* 25 (Spring 1995).

Merrill, C.E. "Some Singular Fatalities." *Confederate Veteran* 7 (July 1899).

Miller, Darlis A. "Hispanos and the Civil War in New Mexico: A Reconsideration." *New Mexico Historical Review* 54 (April 1979).

Milton, Keith. "Whistlin' Extradition." *True West* 39 (May 1992).

"Of a Noted Military Family." *Confederate Veteran* 6 (April 1898).

Pingenot, Ben E. "The Great Wagon Train Expedition of 1850." *Southwestern Historical Quarterly* 98 (October 1994).

_____. "Journal of a Wagon Train Expedition from Fort Inge to El Paso del Norte in 1850." *Military History of the West* 25 (Spring 1995).

Rister, C.C. "The Border Post of Phantom Hill." *West Texas Historical Association Yearbook* (October 1938).

Robinson, Charles M., III. "Life and Death of an Indian Lover." *True West* (October 1991).

Rodgers, Robert L. "The Confederate States Organize Arizona in 1862." *Southern Historical Papers* 28 (1900).

Ruhlen, George. "The Guns of ValVerde." *Password* 5 (January 1960).

Scannell, Jack C. "Henry Skillman, Texas Frontiersman." *Permian Historical Annual* 18 (December 1978).

Stoes, K.D. "The Story of San Agustin Ranch." *The New Mexico Stockman* 22 (March 1957).

Tate, Michael L. "A Johnny Reb in Sibley's New Mexico Campaign: Reminiscences of Pvt. Henry C. Wright, 1861-1862." *East Texas Historical Journal* 25 and 26 (1988-1989).

Teel, T.T. "Sibley's New Mexico Campaign: Its Objects and the Causes of its Failure." *Battles and Leaders of the Civil War.* Vol. 2. New York: Yoseloff and Co., 1956.

Temple, Frank M. "Colonel B.H. Grierson's Victorio Campaign." *West Texas Historical Association Yearbook* 35 (October 1959).

Thompson, Jerry. "Drama in the Desert: The Hunt for Henry Skillman in the Trans-Pecos, 1862-1864." *Password* 38 (1992).

Thrapp, Dan. "Stein's Pass: Gateway to Adventure." *New Mexico Magazine* (June 1981).

Timmons, W.H. "American El Paso: The Formative Years, 1848-1854." *Southwestern Historical Quarterly* 87 (July 1983).

Townsend, E.E. "The Mays Massacre." *West Texas Historical and Scientific Society Bulletin* 5 (1933).

Walker, Charles S., Jr. "Confederate Government in Doña Ana County." *New Mexico Historical Review* 6 (July 1931).

_____. "Causes of the Confederate Invasion of New Mexico." *New Mexico Historical Quarterly* 44 (October 1944).

Waller, John L. "The Civil War in the El Paso Area." *West Texas Historical Association Yearbook* 22 (October 1946).

_____. "Colonel George Wythe Baylor." *Southwestern Social Science Quarterly*, 24 (1943).

Watford, W.H. "Confederate Western Ambitions." *Southwestern Historical Quarterly* 44 (October 1940).

_____. "The Far Western Wing of the Rebellion." *California Historical Society Quarterly* 34 (June 1955).

Weaver, Ralph J. "The Nine Lives of Captain Frank Jones." *Frontier Times* 34 (Spring 1960).

Webb, Walter Prescott. "Last War Trail of Victorio." *True West* 4 (March-April 1957).

"Wife of Col. G.W. Baylor." *Confederate Veteran* 13 (April 1905).

Williams, J.W. "The Butterfield Overland Mail Road Across Texas." *Southwestern Historical Quarterly* 61 (July 1957).

Wilson, John P. "Whiskey at Fort Fillmore: A Story of the Civil War." *New Mexico Historical Review* 68 (April 1993).

GOVERNMENT PUBLICATIONS

State of Texas. "Journal of the House of Representatives of the Twentieth Legislature." Austin: Triplett and Hutchins, 1887.

U.S. Congress. House. "Report of Regimental Quartermaster, Capt. A.W. Bowman, 3d Infantry." 32nd Cong., 1st sess.

U.S. Congress. Senate. "Report of the Secretary of the Interior." 34th Cong., 3d sess. 1856.

War of the Rebellion: A Compilation of the Official Records of the Union and Confederate Armies. 128 vols. Washington: Government Printing Office, 1889.

Unpublished Material

Geldard, Gordon W. "The Lost Patrol." Fort Davis National Historical Site, Fort Davis, Texas.

Goldblatt, Kenneth A. "The Shooting of John A. Wharton." Editor's files.

_____. "George Wythe Baylor, Frontier Warrior." M.A. thesis, University of Texas at El Paso, 1969.

Hastings, Virginia M. "A History of Arizona During the Civil War, 1861-1865." M.A. thesis, University of Arizona, 1943.

Middagh, John J. "Frontier Journalism in El Paso, 1872-1900." M.A. thesis, Texas Western College.

Rogan, Francis Edward. "Military History of New Mexico Territory During the Civil War." Ph.D. diss., University of Utah, 1961.

NEWSPAPER ARTICLES BY GEORGE WYTHE BAYLOR

El Paso, Texas
El Paso Daily Herald, 18 November, 9, 23 December 1899; 6, 13, 20, 27 January, 10, 17 February, 10, 11, 13, 14, 15 August, 1, 15, 22 December 1900; 23 February, 2, 23, 30 March, 6, 13, 20, 27 April, 4, 25 May, 7, 29 June, 17 July, 3, 10 August, 14, 21 September, 9, 16, 23 November 1901; 15 February, 1, 8 November 1902; 6, 13, 10, 20, 27 January, 3, 10, 17 February, 3, 10, 17, 24 March, 12 May 1906.

Galveston, Texas
Galveston Daily News, 14 February 1881; 19 February 1898; 29 November 1905; 10 January 1906.

NEWSPAPERS

Austin, Texas

Austin Daily Statesman, 9 February 1894.

Texas State Gazette, 6 July, 21, 29 December 1850; 7 May, 13, 20 August, 29 November 1853; 26 October 1861.

Charleston, South Carolina

Daily Courier, 16 June 1859.

Comanche, Texas

Comanche Chief, 7 May 1881.

Dallas, Texas

Dallas Herald, 14 August 1861; 13 April 1865.

Dallas Morning News, 9 February 1894.

Dallas Weekly Herald, 24 November, 8, 15 December 1858; 9 February, 15 June, 13 July 1859; 30 March, 14 December 1872; 25 July, 1 August, 10 October 1874; 16 January 1875.

El Paso, Texas

El Paso Herald, 15 February, 8 March 1882; 25 June 1888; 22 May 1889; 23 April 1890; 7 October 1892; 15 May 1893.

El Paso Daily Herald, 9 November 1901; 8 November 1902; 1 April 1916; 18 October 1935.

El Paso Evening Tribune, 9 November 1901.

El Paso Lone Star, 12, 15, 19, 29 October, 16 November, 17, 21, 24, 28 December 1881; 7, 25 January, 1, 8, 11, 15 February, 8, 11 March, 26 July, 19, 23 August, 6, 9, 13 September, 20, 21, 27 October, 1, 11, 14, 18 November, 6 December 1882; 10, 31 March, 19, 22, 26 September, 14, 17 November 1883; 9, 13 February, 5, 12 March, 5, 17 June, 1884.

El Paso Weekly Herald, 28, 29 November 1898.

El Paso Times, 29 April 1888; 14 July, 8 September, 1, 31 October 1888.

Galveston, Texas

Galveston Daily News, 7, 8, 14, April, 8 December 1865; 25 May 1882, 30 May 1885; 8 December 1895.

Galveston Tri-Weekly News, 14 August 1860; 5 February, 16, 19 March, 3 September, 17 October, 17, 19 November 1861.

Galveston Weekly News, 12 January, 16 March, 15, 20, 31 August 1861; 12 April 1865; 20 January, 30 October, 13 November 1879; 8 April 1880; 13 January, 10 February, 24 April, 4, 18 August 1881.

Houston, Texas

Houston Chronicle, 3 October 1913.

Telegraph and Texas Register, 23 October 1844.

Tri-Weekly Telegraph, 23 March 1861; 17 August, 15 June 1863; 15 January 1864; 7, 10, 12, 15, 19, 25 April, 29 May, 7 September 1865.

Jacksboro, Texas
White Man, 8 March 1860.

Memphis, Tennessee
Memphis Daily Appeal, 30 October 1861.

Mesilla, New Mexico
Mesilla Times, 27 July, 3, 17 August, 19 September 1861.

New Orleans, Louisiana
New Orleans Delta, 25 August 1861.

San Antonio, Texas
Daily Herald, 14, 19, 20, 21 May, 2, 7, 8, 17 June 1859; 12 July 1862.
San Antonio Daily Express, 24, 25 October, 4 November 1879; 6 February 1881; 12 February, 19 April 1884; 7 August 1910; 9 November 1913; 28 March 1916.
San Antonio Express, 8 July 1868.
San Antonio Express-News, 17 March 1990.
San Antonio Free Press, 9 July 1868; 9, 30 March 1875; 4 February, 22 July 1876; 8 July 1878.

Solomonville, Arizona
Graham County Bulletin, 10 November 1893.

Waco, Texas
Waco Tribune-Herald, 26 May 1935; 23 November 1975.

Weatherford, Texas
White Man, September 13, 1860.

ARCHIVAL COLLECTIONS

Adams, William C. Papers. Fort Davis Historical Site, Fort Davis, Texas.

Ballinger, William P. Diary. Center for American History, University of Texas at Austin.

Baylor-Carrington Papers. Texas Collection, Baylor University Library, Waco, Texas.

Baylor Family Papers. Hill Memorial Library, Louisiana State University, Baton Rouge, Louisiana.

Baylor, George Wythe. Compiled Service Record. Confederate War Department, Record Group 109, National Archives, Washington, D.C.

Baylor, George Wythe IV. Papers. Tucson, Arizona.

Baylor, John Robert. Compiled Service Record. Confederate War Department, Record Group 109, National Archives, Washington, D.C.

Baylor, John Robert. Papers. Center for American History, University of Texas at Austin.

Baylor, John Robert. Papers. Texas State Archives, Austin, Texas.

Baylor-Sturges Papers. Private Collection.

Census. National Archives, Washington, D.C.
    Bexar County, Texas, 1860, 1870.
    Colfax County, New Mexico, 1900.
    El Paso County, Texas, 1850, 1860, 1880, 1900.
    Fayette County, Texas, 1850.
    Lavaca County, Texas, 1860.
    Parker County, Texas, 1860.
    Uvalde County Texas, 1870, 1880, 1900.

Carothers, William N. Diary. Texas State Archives, Austin, Texas.

Chilton Papers. Texas State Archives, Austin, Texas.

Clark, Edward. Papers. Texas State Archives, Austin, Texas.

Court of Claims, *William S. Grant v. United States,* Case no. 1883, Record Group 123, National Archives, Washington, D.C.

District Court Records. *State of Texas v. John R. Baylor*, Cause nos. 3506 and 3507, Bexar County, Texas.

District Court Records. *State of Texas v. George W. Baylor*, Cause no. 4271, Harris County, Texas.

District Court Records. *State of Texas v. John and Tom Gilcrease*, Cause nos. 505, 510, 513, 518, 519 and 522, Uvalde County, Texas.

District Court Records. *State of Texas v. John Robert Baylor,* Cause no. 667, Uvalde County, Texas.

Houston, Sam. Papers. Texas State Archives. Austin, Texas.

Johnston, Albert Sidney. Papers. Jenkins Garrett Library. University of Texas at Arlington.

Johnston, Albert Sidney, and William Preston Johnston. Papers. Mrs. Mason Barret Collection, Manuscript Division, Howard-Tilton Memorial Library, Tulane University, New Orleans, Louisiana.

Letters Received. Adjutant General's Office. Record Group 401. Texas State Archives, Austin, Texas.

Letters Received. Confederate Adjutant and Inspector General, Confederate War Department. Record Group 109, National Archives, Washington, D.C.

Letters Received. Office of Indian Affairs, Texas Agency, 1855-1857. Record Group 75, National Archives, Washington, D.C.

Marriage Records. Book D. 22 April 1863, Harris County, Texas.

Post Returns. Record Group 94, National Archives, Washington, D.C.
  El Paso, Texas.
  Fort Bliss, Texas.
  Fort Fillmore, New Mexico.

Wharton, Edward Clifton. Papers. Special Collections, Hill Memorial Library, Louisiana State University, Baton Rouge, Louisiana.

INTERVIEWS

George W. Baylor IV, numerous, 1967-1970.

Roxa Gillette, 10 October 1967.

Virginia Sturges, 10 August 1994.

Index